Linux® Database Bible

Linux® Database Bible

Michele Petrovsky, Stephen Wysham, and Mojo Nichols

Hungry Minds™

Best-Selling Books • Digital Downloads • e-Books • Answer Networks • e-Newsletters • Branded Web Sites • e-Learning
New York, NY ✦ Cleveland, OH ✦ Indianapolis, IN

Linux® Database Bible

Published by
Hungry Minds, Inc.
909 Third Avenue
New York, NY 10022
www.hungryminds.com

Library of Congress Control Number: 2001092731

ISBN: 0-7645-4641-4

Printed in the United States of America

10 9 8 7 6 5 4 3 2 1

IB/RU/QY/QR/IN

Distributed in the United States by Hungry Minds, Inc.

Distributed by CDG Books Canada Inc. for Canada; by Transworld Publishers Limited in the United Kingdom; by IDG Norge Books for Norway; by IDG Sweden Books for Sweden; by IDG Books Australia Publishing Corporation Pty. Ltd. for Australia and New Zealand; by TransQuest Publishers Pte Ltd. for Singapore, Malaysia, Thailand, Indonesia, and Hong Kong; by Gotop Information Inc. for Taiwan; by ICG Muse, Inc. for Japan; by Intersoft for South Africa; by Eyrolles for France; by International Thomson Publishing for Germany, Austria, and Switzerland; by Distribuidora Cuspide for Argentina; by LR International for Brazil; by Galileo Libros for Chile; by Ediciones ZETA S.C.R. Ltda. for Peru; by WS Computer Publishing Corporation, Inc., for the Philippines; by Contemporanea de Ediciones for Venezuela; by Express Computer Distributors for the Caribbean and West Indies; by Micronesia Media Distributor, Inc. for Micronesia; by Chips Computadoras S.A. de C.V. for Mexico; by Editorial Norma de Panama S.A. for Panama; by American Bookshops for Finland.

For general information on Hungry Minds' products and services please contact our Customer Care department within the U.S. at 800-762-2974, outside the U.S. at 317-572-3993 or fax 317-572-4002.

For sales inquiries and reseller information, including discounts, premium and bulk quantity sales, and foreign-language translations, please contact our Customer Care department at 800-434-3422, fax 317-572-4002 or write to Hungry Minds, Inc., Attn: Customer Care Department, 10475 Crosspoint Boulevard, Indianapolis, IN 46256.

For information on licensing foreign or domestic rights, please contact our Sub-Rights Customer Care department at 212-884-5000.

For information on using Hungry Minds' products and services in the classroom or for ordering examination copies, please contact our Educational Sales department at 800-434-2086 or fax 317-572-4005.

For press review copies, author interviews, or other publicity information, please contact our Public Relations department at 317-572-3168 or fax 317-572-4168.

For authorization to photocopy items for corporate, personal, or educational use, please contact Copyright Clearance Center, 222 Rosewood Drive, Danvers, MA 01923, or fax 978-750-4470.

Credits

Contributing Author
Fred Butzen

Acquisitions Editors
Debra Williams Cauley
Terri Varveris

Project Editors
Barbra Guerra
Amanda Munz
Eric Newman

Technical Editor
Kurt Wall

Copy Editor
Richard Adin

Editorial Managers
Ami Sullivan
Colleen Totz

Project Coordinator
Dale White

Graphics and Production Specialists
Joyce Haughey
Jacque Schneider
Brian Torwelle
Erin Zeltner

Quality Control Technician
John Greenough
Susan Moritz

Proofreading and Indexing
TECHBOOKS Production Services

About the Authors

Michele Petrovsky holds a Master of Science in Computer and Information Science from the University of Pittsburgh. Michele has administered UNIX and Linux systems and networks and has programmed at the application level in everything from C to 4GLs. She has worked as a technical editor and writer, published several books on a variety of computing topics, and has taught at the community college and university levels, most recently at Mount Saint Vincent University in Halifax, Nova Scotia, and at Gwynedd-Mercy College in southeast Pennsylvania.

Stephen Wysham has been working in the electronics and software industries since 1973. Until 1990, he worked in both commercial and government electronic hardware development and manufacturing. Since 1990, he has worked strictly in the software field, primarily in database systems. Steve holds a Master of Science in Computer Engineering from Pennsylvania State University.

Mojo Nichols began working on UNIX systems at Los Alamos National Laboratory in 1992. At Los Alamos, Mojo helped develop large image archives using primarily free software. In 1998, Mojo moved into the private sector to work for a small data warehousing company. He uses his Linux box as the primary development tool for very large database applications.

Preface

Welcome to the *Linux Database Bible*. If your job involves developing database applications or administering databases, or you have an interest in the applications that are possible on Linux, then this is the book for you. Experience shows that early adopters of a new paradigm tend to be already technically proficient or driven to become the first expert in their circle of influence. By reading and applying what this book contains, you will become familiar and productive with the databases that run on Linux.

The growth of Linux has been due in no small part to the applications that were readily available or easily ported to it in the Web application space. This would not have been possible without the availability on Linux of capable relational database management systems (RBDMS) that made it easier to support surprisingly robust database applications.

The Importance of This Book

Through the past several years, Linux use and acceptance has been growing rapidly. During this same period several dedicated groups have been porting existing RDBMS to Linux, with more than a few of them available under Open Source licensing. The number of Linux databases is somewhat astounding when you consider them all. Some have already fallen by the wayside; others are gaining features regularly. Those that are thriving are serious contenders for many applications that have had to suffer through the shortcomings of the Microsoft Windows architecture and application paradigm.

Linux lends itself to database development and deployment without the overhead of the proprietary UNIX ports and is a prime way to get much of the same flexibility without the same magnitude of cost.

Quite a few advanced Linux books are available, but this book deals with Linux database application development from a broader perspective. Linux database development is a deep and fertile area of development. Now is definitely an exciting — and potentially rewarding — time to be working with and deploying Linux database solutions.

Getting Started

To get the most out of this book, you should have successfully installed Linux. Most of the Open Source databases and database-integrated applications are installed in a more or less similar way. In some cases, you'll have to make choices in the installation that have some effect further down the road — for example installing the Apache Web Server and having to choose which CGI program to load or installing MySQL with or without built-in PHP support, to name two examples.

To make the best use of this book, you will need:

+ A copy of one of the Open Source databases for Linux, such as MySQL. These are freely downloadable from the Web. A database that includes PHP or has Perl DBI support is desirable.

+ A copy of Linux that is compatible with the version of data that you have chosen. There are numerous Internet sites from which you can download Linux.

+ A programming language that is compatible with both Linux and the database that you've chosen, such as C/C++ or Perl.

Any system that can run Linux will suffice, but you'll be much better off with a fast Pentium-based machine with loads of memory (even though Linux can run in small memory spaces, you should be using at least 32MB of RAM). Also, the plentiful Linux support applications can take up a significant amount of disk space, and don't forget the size of the database that you plan on creating. At any rate, you should be using at least a 1-GB disk to begin with. And a mouse . . . please don't forget the mouse.

How about video board and display? Many of the Linux databases use a command line (that is, text) interface (CLI). In these cases, the display resolution is pretty much moot. Even the application programming will be done in text mode windows. However, for the typical Linux desktop you should have at least a 600×800 pixel resolution video board and display.

Icons in This Book

Take a minute to skim this section and learn what the icons mean that are used throughout this book.

Caution   We want you to be ready for potential pitfalls and hazards that we've experienced firsthand. This icon alerts you to those.

Cross-Reference   You'll find additional information — either elsewhere in this book or in another source — noted with this icon.

A point of interest or piece of information that gives you more understanding about the topic at hand is found next to this icon.

 Here's our opportunity to give you pointers. You'll find suggestions and the best of our good ideas next to this icon.

How This Book Is Organized

This book is organized into five parts: introduction to Linux database with some background on relational databases; installation of a Linux database; interacting with and using an database; programming applications; and general database administration.

Part I — Linux and Databases

Part I introduces you to Linux and provides background about development and history. In addition to a brief history of Linux, you'll find background on databases in general and databases as they pertain to Linux. In this Part we introduce relational databases along with some relational database theory and discuss object databases briefly. We also provide a detailed background on the development and importance of SQL and help you understand the process of building a database system. We wrap up Part I with chapters on determining your own database requirements and choosing the right product to meet your needs.

Part II — Installation and Configuration

Installation and configuration of database products are covered indepth in Part II, referring specifically to Oracle8*i*, MySQL, and PostgreSQL. You'll find detailed discussions of specific products and steps to follow in the process.

Part III — Interaction and Usage

The two chapters that make up Part III of this book delve into ways the Linux database administrator interacts with the database and provide detailed information about tools available to the DBA. In addition to basic operation and navigation, this Part shows you what vendor-supplied tools can help you accomplish.

Part IV — Programming Applications

Part IV reviews and introduces several database Applications Programming Interfaces (API): the ODBC API with C/C++; the Perl DBI API; the Java JDBC API; PHP (and MySQL). Command line client tools and some performance issues are also included. We also present standalone database applications and illustrate how one such application might be specified and implemented. We walk you through the process of building a database application using PHP and MySQL and updating a database from a Web page.

Part V — Administrivia

Part V has an odd-sounding title that simply means administration details that a Linux DBA would need to know. We discuss backing up your system, managing various processes, and dealing with intermittent tasks. We've included important information about security and creating a security policy surrounding your database, as well as telling you how to prevent disastrous breaches. And lastly, we wrap up with a discussion of modern database deployments and a look at the future.

How to Use This Book

You can use this book any way you please. If you choose to read it cover to cover, you are more than welcome to. Often the chapter order is immaterial. We suspect that most readers will skip around, picking up useful tidbits here and there. If you're faced with a challenging task, you may try the index first to see which section in the book specifically addresses your problem.

Additional Information

In addition to the URLs presented throughout this book, we recommend that you consult any of the following for further information on the Linux DBMSs we discuss:

+ `http://postgresql.readysetnet.com/devel-corner/index.html` (the PostgreSQL Developer's Corner)

+ `http://www.mysql.com/documentation/index.html` (the entry-point to all online MySQL documentation)

+ `http://www.mysql.com/development/index.html` (information about, as the site puts it, "the geeks behind MySQL" and "what's planned for future releases")

+ `http://otn.oracle.com` (access to a wealth of Oracle documentation)

Acknowledgments

Both the quality of the work of the Open Source community, as exemplified in this book in the discussions of MySQL and PostgreSQL, and the dedication of the members of that community to their work and the sustaining ideals deserve to be acknowledged. Congratulations, folks, for a job well done.

— Michele Petrovsky

I would like to thank Mary Kay Wysham for her patience while I typed "just a few more things." I would also like to thank Mojo B. Nichols, but I'm not sure just for what.

— Steve Wysham

I would like to acknowledge Deborah Kline for her help in editing and writing and Tim Thomas for his reasonable and invaluable advice on how to proceed.

— Mojo Nichols

Contents at a Glance

Contents

· ·

Linux and Databases

◆ ◆ ◆ ◆

◆ ◆ ◆ ◆

Introduction and Background

Linux is an open source operating system modeled on UNIX. Technically, *Linux* refers to the kernel of the operating system, which manages system resources and running programs. Informally, people often refer to *Linux* as the combination of the Linux kernel and a large collection of software that has been written or rewritten to operate with the Linux kernel. Many of these tools are part of the GNU project, a collection of free software ranging from compilers to text editors. Many companies, either commercial or volunteer, gather the Linux kernel and some selection of Linux software into distributions that can be downloaded over the Internet, in many cases, or purchased by CD-ROM.

Origins of Linux

Linus Torvalds wrote the Linux kernel. In 1991, Torvalds, then a student at Helsinki University, grew dissatisfied with Minix, a UNIX clone for Intel processors that was popular in universities. Torvalds posted a now famous message to the Usenet newsgroup comp.os.minix asking for help and asking about interest in a UNIX-like operating system he planned to write for Intel 386 and higher processors.

Caution

> *Open source* is a term that has been knocked about the press quite a bit lately, but it is important to note that it is a trademark of Software in the Public Interest (SPI), a not-for-profit organization. Both Open Source Initiative (OSI) and SPI have specific definitions of open source, as well as a process for validating software licenses as open source. If you desire to designate your product as Open Source, you need to comply with the requirements of SPI and/or OSI. Please see www.opensource.org for more information.

Linux immediately attracted several key contributors in all areas, ranging from improving Linux's hard-drive compatibility and performance to support for IBM PC sound cards. The project grew steadily in interest among hard-core UNIX hackers and operating systems enthusiasts; version 1.0 of the Linux kernel was released in 1994, reaching approximately a half million Linux users. Throughout the 1990s, Linux gained in popularity. It emerged as a hobbyist favorite over such similar efforts as FreeBSD, and very soon began to attract attention from businesses. It was ported to many platforms, including Alpha, ARM, 68000, PA-RISC, PowerPC, and SPARC. There is no single reason why so many contributors were drawn to the Linux project. Some contributors were drawn to the project because all contributors were given the right to copyright their contribution. A second reason was Torvalds' knowledge, leadership skills, and personality. Regardless of the reason, Linux was gaining a great deal of momentum.

Whirlwind adolescence

In 1997, Eric Raymond presented his paper, *The Cathedral and the Bazaar*, which was instrumental in publicizing and providing the background for open source software in general, including many developments in the Linux community. It also marked a key turning point in the perception of such "free" software by admitting the validity of commercial interests in open source. As such, this paper influenced Netscape's 1998 decision to initiate an open source effort to develop the next major version of Netscape, version 5.0, which was nicknamed Mozilla. While many in the press and big business had little need to think about operating-system kernels, the opening of a well-known product such as Netscape brought a lot of attention to the open source community and to Linux, which was shaping up to be its key success story. In 1997, it had been considered a momentous event when Digital Equipment Corp. officially sanctioned the Alpha port of Linux, but after the frenzy of excitement over Mozilla, big-business interest in Linux became routine.

Many other events shaped Linux's spectacular growth in 1998. In no particular order:

✦ It became publicly known that some scenes from the blockbuster movie Titanic were rendered with groups of Alpha-based machines running Linux.

✦ In an extraordinary gesture, Ralph Nader, erstwhile presidential candidate and perennial libertarian gadfly petitioned PC hardware vendors to preinstall non-Microsoft operating systems on their machines, particularly Linux.

✦ Red Hat, SuSE, and Caldera, as well as a few smaller players began to put increased effort in promoting their existing commercial support for Linux, which removed one of its greatest weakness in the eyes of businesses — the perceived lack of formal technical support.

✦ Several supercomputers based on Beowulf clusters went online, and immediately showed impressive performance, proving Linux's extraordinary strength in distributed computing. Beowulf clusters were developed by Linux users at NASA and elsewhere. They are groups of low-cost Linux machines, up to 140 in the case of the Avalon cluster at Los Alamos National Laboratory, that are connected with Ethernet networks, enabling operations to be distributed to multiple machines for faster processing.

✦ Several organizations launched efforts to standardize aspects of Linux distributions, leading to much publicity in the trade press.

✦ In yet another sign of the internal strife that fame and fortune can bring, OSI and SPI, two prominent organizations in the Linux and open source community, fought over trademark of the term *open source*.

✦ GIMP 1.0, a high-quality open source application that is similar to Photoshop and that was developed on Linux, was released. The quality and popularity of GIMP proved that open source desktop applications on Linux are as viable as Linux servers have proven to be.

✦ The major market research companies began to report on Linux usage and quality. Linus Torvalds appeared in prominent interviews and features in mainstream newspapers and magazines, including an appearance on the cover of Forbes.

✦ IBM, besides making very positive noises about support for Linux, announced that it would incorporate the popular open source Web server Apache into its WebSphere application server, and announced software projects aimed at contributing back to the open source community.

✦ Internal documents from Microsoft were leaked to Eric Raymond, becoming, along with some not-so-internal responses after the fact, the infamous "Halloween Papers," which seemingly signaled Microsoft's war cry against the upstart Linux.

✦ A venture capitalist actually encouraged one of its interests, Digital Creations LLC, to release its flagship application server Zope as an open source product.

✦ Most relevant for this book, commercial database vendors, including IBM, Informix, Oracle, and Sybase, but excluding Microsoft, announced ports of their main database management systems to Linux.

Even with all the media and business attention paid to Linux in 1998, 1999 was the year of Linux. The marketplace's perception of Linux matured as smoothly as did Linux's technical component. The current version, 2.4, of the Linux kernel was developed and released under intense media scrutiny, and many arguments on whether it spelled the end of proprietary operating systems such as Microsoft Windows NT occurred. The 2.4 kernel provides improved multiprocessor support, removes (prior) PCI bus limits, supports up to 64GB of physical RAM and unlimited virtual memory, a larger number of users and groups, an improved scheduler to handle more processes, and improved device support, among other features and improvements.

Microsoft has begun its inevitable counterattack, including hiring Mindcraft Inc. to compare Linux and Windows NT. The study showed NT at a definite advantage, but controversy erupted when it became known that Mindcraft had obtained extensive tuning data for NT, but had done no more than post an obscure newsgroup message on the Linux end. Also, it was alleged that Mindcraft had conducted unfair comparisons against Novell's Netware to discredit that operating system, and that

Microsoft had the authority to forbid the publication of sponsored results. On the positive front, Red Hat, Inc. went public, after offering IPO shares to various open source contributors. Red Hat defied many observers' expectations, gaining dramatic value in a market that appeared to have soured on many recent stock offerings. Additionally, 1999 was the year in which many application-server and middleware companies followed the major databases into the Linux market.

The future

Linux's continued growth appears unstoppable. The biggest question is what transformations this growth will impose on the community and technology. As its pioneers become "netrepreneurs" and celebrities, and as political battles take attention from the software, one wonders whether the circus will impede the tremendous productivity that has been displayed by the open source community. There are open legal questions. The General Public License (GPL), the most pervasive license in Linux distributions, has never been tested in court, and has enough unorthodox provisions to make such a test a lively one. In the "Halloween Papers," Microsoft raised the potential of attacking the open source community with software patents, a danger that cannot be discounted and that has prompted much consideration in Linux discussion groups.

Free software purists also question the result of Linux's increasing commercialization. Will large corporations merely harvest the hard work of open source developers without contributing anything? Will all the open source projects going corporate (Apache, sendmail, TCL, and so on) divert or divide the effort that is currently going into free software? Will slick Linux products from companies with large research and development and user-interface design budgets kill the interest in open source alternatives? Considering that Linux and its sibling projects flourished so well in a software industry in which openness had long appeared to be a distant dream, a fruitful symbiosis is possible between the suits and the hackers.

On a technical level, there is much on the way for Linux. One major expected move in the next several years is to 64-bit architectures. The vast majority of Linux systems are 32-bit, usually on the Intel platform. There is a 64-bit Linux for Ultra-Sparc and DEC, and glibc, a key library that underlies the vast majority of Linux products, has been updated to ensure a smooth transition to 64-bit. Nevertheless, the real test of Linux's 64-bit prowess will come as Intel's next-generation IA-64 microprocessor, a.k.a. Merced, is released and becomes popular in servers and among power users. The 64-bit move will have many benefits, several of which are pertinent to database users. Ext2, the most common file system for Linux has a file-size limit of 2GB on 32-bit systems, which will be vastly raised by the move to 64-bit. Also, the amount of memory that Linux can address will be increased, and the Y2038 bug, should be headed off. The Y2038 bug is caused by the way 32-bit UNIX libraries store time values, which would make affected systems think that January 19, 2038, is December 13, 1901. Note that this bug will also affect other 32-bit non-UNIX systems.

There is little question that Linux will be out of the gate early for IA-64. A group of commercial interests known as the Trillian project is committed to porting Linux to Intel's upcoming IA-64, which could well ensure that Linux is the first OS ported to this long-awaited platform. Intel has also pledged to provide early samples of IA-64 servers to key companies to bootstrap the porting of open source projects to the platform.

Most of the obstacles to Linux's success in the world of enterprise information systems and terabyte databases are being addressed. Whatever happens, it's unlikely to be dull watching Linux march into the next century.

Note Licenses are not the same as copyright. Many software users are accustomed to blindly accepting software licensing terms as encountered on software packaging, or on pages downloaded from the Web. In the Linux community, and the open software community in general, licenses have an extraordinary amount of political and philosophical bearing. Most Linux users are advocates of open source licenses, which emphasize providing the source code of software, whether free or paid for, and allowing the end user to make their own modifications to such source code as needed. The Linux kernel is distributed under the Free Software Foundation's General Public License (GPL), but many of the software additions added by distributors have different licenses. Some distributors, such as Red Hat, make an effort to set standards for licenses of included software, so that end users do not need to worry about such issues as much, and are free to modify and redistribute code as needed.

Some Established Linux Distributions

Founded in 1994, Red Hat is the leader in development, deployment, and management of Linux and open source solutions for Internet infrastructure ranging from small embedded devices to high-availability clusters and secure Web servers. In addition to the award-winning Red Hat Linux server operating system, Red Hat is the principle provider of GNU-based developer tools and support solutions for a variety of embedded processors. Red Hat provides runtime solutions, developer tools, and Linux kernel expertise, and offers support and engineering services to organizations in all embedded and Linux markets.

Caldera, Inc. was founded in 1994 by Ransom Love and Bryan Sparks. In 1998, Caldera Systems, Inc. (Nasdaq-CALD), was created to develop Linux-based business solutions. The shareholders of SCO (nee Santa Cruz Operation) have approved the purchase by Caldera Systems, Inc. of the both the Server Software Division and the Professional Services Division of SCO. A new company, Caldera International, Inc., is planned combining the assets of Caldera Systems with the assets acquired from SCO.

Based in Orem, Utah, Caldera Systems, Inc. is a leader in providing Linux-based business solutions through its award-winning OpenLinux line of products and services. Founded in 1992, SuSE Linux is the international technology leader and solutions provider in open source operating system (OS) software, setting new standards for quality and ease of use. Its award-winning SuSE Linux 6.4 and the newly released 7.0 include thousands of third-party Linux applications supported by extensive professional consulting and support services, excellent documentation, comprehensive hardware support, and an encyclopedic set of Linux tools. Designed for Web and enterprise server environments and efficient as a home and office platform, SuSE's distribution, surrounding features, effective configuration and intelligent design result in the most complete Linux solution available today. SuSE Linux AG, headquartered in Germany, and SuSE Inc., based in Oakland, California, are privately held companies focused entirely on supporting the Linux community, Open Source development, and the GNU General Public License. Additional information about SuSE can be found at `www.suse.com`.

MandrakeSoft, a software company, is the official producer and publisher of the Linux-Mandrake distribution. MandrakeSoft provides small office, home office, and smaller and medium sized organizations a set of GNU Linux and other Open Source software and related services. MandrakeSoft provides a way for (Open Source) developers and technologists a way to offer their services via the MandrakeCampus.com site and the MandrakeExpert.com site. MandrakeSoft has facilities in the United States, the U.K., France, Germany, and Canada.

Slackware Linux

Slackware (a trademark of Walnut Creek CD-ROM Collections) is itself a part of BSDi. BSDi (nee Berkeley Software Design, Inc. and soon to be iXsystems) sells BSD Internet Server systems, operating systems, networking, and Internet technologies that are based on pioneering work done at the Computer Systems Research Group (CSRG) at the University of California at Berkeley. Leading CSRG computer scientists founded BSDi in 1991. BSD technology is known for its powerful, flexible, and portable architecture, and for its advanced development environments. Today, BSDi is recognized for its strength and reliability in demanding network-computing environments. BSDi offers strong products, rich technology, and the knowledge of its computer scientists to its customers.

Debian GNU/Linux

Debian was begun in August 1993 by Ian Murdock, as a new distribution that would be made openly, in the spirit of Linux and GNU. Debian was meant to be carefully and conscientiously put together, and to be maintained and supported with similar care. It started as a small, tightly knit group of free software hackers and gradually grew to become a large, well-organized community of developers and users. Roughly 500 volunteer developers from around the world produce debian in their spare time. Few of the developers have actually met in person. Communication is done primarily through e-mail (mailing lists at `lists.debian.org`) and IRC (#debian channel at `irc.debian.org`).

Introduction to Databases

A database is merely a collection of data organized in some manner in a computer system. Some people use the term strictly to refer such collections hosted in non-volatile storage, for instance, on hard disk or tape, but some people consider organized data within memory a database. A database could be as simple as a list of employee names in your department, or in more complex form it might incorporate all the organizational, payroll and demographic information for such employees. Originally, most databases were just lists of such data in an ASCII file, but in the 1970s much academic and industry research showed that if you organized the data in certain ways, you could speed up applications and improve the value you can get from your databases. In particular, one theory that has remained dominant is that of relational databases; two that have not are network databases and hierarchical databases. E. F. Codd developed the seminal work on the theory of relational databases in the late 1960s. Codd's theoretical work was expounded on by C. J. Date. As a side note, Codd is also known for his twelve criteria for an On-Line Transaction Processing (OLTP)-compliant database, published in the early 1980s.

In practice, relational databases organize data into groups known as tables, in which the columns set formal boundaries of the type and some rules for the different bits of information that combine to form a coherent entity. For example, consider the following representation of the information in Table 1-1 (Employee Table):

Table 1-1 Employee Table			
Employee ID	**Name**	**Age**	**Department**
101	Manny Vegas	42	12
102	Carla Wong	36	15
103	Arnold Page	38	15

Each row of data describes a distinct abstract entity, but the columns make sure that the set of information in each row is consistent. For instance, a relational database would prevent a user from trying to set Carla Wong's age to a string value.

This much could be achieved using flat-file databases. The strength of relational databases lies in providing a methodology for expressing relationships between tables. For instance, we could have another data representation, as shown in Table 1-2:

Table 1-2 Department Table		
Department ID	Department Name	Location
12	Accounting	Miami, FL
15	Human Resources	Gainesville, FL

You could establish a formal relationship between the "Department" field of the first table to an entire row in the second. So, for instance, you would have an orderly way of determining where Carla Wong was located by reading her Department value from the first table, and following the relationship to the second table where her location is specified.

Relational database theory provides rules for keeping such relationships consistent, and for speedy analysis of data even when there are many complex relationships. At its most abstract level, a formal relational calculus details the strict deterministic behavior of relational databases.

A database management system (DBMS) is software to access, manage, and maintain databases. An RDBMS is a DBMS specialized for relational data.

A relatively recent development — in terms of commercial availability — is the Object-Oriented database (or Object Relational DBMS). These differ from traditional relational databases in that the relation between tables is replaced by using inheritance; that is, "embedding" the referenced table in the referencing table. For example, in a RDBMS, one might have an order table related by a foreign key to a customer table, but in an ORDBMS, one would instead have the customer object as an attribute of the order object. This kind of construct obviates the need to explicitly join the two tables in any query.

History of databases on Linux

Soon after Linux started showing its strengths in portability and stability, a few pioneer businesses, especially those that had always used UNIX, began experimenting with Linux in departmental systems. Unsurprisingly, a few vendors in the ferociously competitive database market looked to gain a small competitive advantage by porting to the budding operating system.

Perhaps the first into the breach, in October 1993, was /rdb, by the appropriately named Revolutionary Software. /rdb is a decidedly odd fish among commercial DBMSs. It took the approach, very popular among UNIX users, of dividing all the DBMS management functions into small command-line commands. This is somewhat analogous to the approach of MH among UNIX e-mail user agent software as opposed to such integrated executables as Pine. /rdb consisted of over 120 such commands, so that the UNIX-savvy could write entire RDBMS applications in shell script, rather than using C/C++ call-level interfaces (CLI) or 4GL.

Several companies introduced DBMS programs in 1994. YARD Software GmbH released YARD SQL, an SQL RDBMS with a Motif query interface. Just Logic Technologies Inc. released Just Logic/SQL for Linux, a full-featured client/server SQL DBMS with cross-platform compatibility with other UNIX systems, DOS, Windows, and OS/2.

Multisoft Datentechnik GmbH released Flagship for Linux, a DBMS and applications development system from the xBASE/Clipper/FoxPro mold, which were dominant before SQL took over. Flagship at first even supported the 0.99 version of the Linux kernel. The interesting thing about Flagship is how prolific it is, supporting platforms from MacOS to Mainframes.

Vectorsoft Gesellschaft fuer Datentechnik mbH released CONZEPT 16, a complete application tool-kit with a proprietary RDBMS at its core. Vectorsoft, however, provided no technical support for the Linux version.

POET Software GmbH, a pioneer of object-oriented DBMSs, ported the Personal edition of POET 2.1 to Linux. The Linux version omitted the graphical database interfaces that were provided on Windows and OS/2 platforms. POET software did not port future versions of their DBMS to Linux until 1999.

Postgres, a product of research at the University of California at Berkeley, was becoming a useful product, an RDBMS based on Ingres. Postgres used a proprietary query language, PostQUEL as its interface. PostQUEL is based on QUEL, which was used in earlier versions of Ingres. David Hughes of Bond University in Australia wrote a SQL to PostQUEL translator as a front-end for Postgres. He then decided to also add a back-end to the translator creating a full-blown RDBMS. The RDBMS was free for academic use, called mSQL, which could be compiled on Linux, subject to its copyright restrictions.

The year 1995 was another active Linux year. Pick Systems Inc., ported its multidimensional database engine to Linux. It was one of the first major database companies to notice and support Linux. Pick eventually dropped its Linux version, but revived it in 1999.

Ingres, an experimental academic database from the University of California at Berkeley, was independently ported to Linux. Ingres used the proprietary QUEL query language rather than SQL, a simple fact that led to the development of several of the better-known open source databases for Linux today.

Postgres95 was released as a first milestone in a journey to turn the formerly experimental, academic Postgres DBMS into a full-blown, free, commercial-quality server with SQL support. Mostly the work of Andrew Yu and Jolly Chen, Postgres95 provided Linux support. It was soon renamed PostgreSQL, and it can be argued that the maintainers have done a good job of meeting their goals, especially with the recent release of PostgreSQL 7.1.2.

Michael Widenius created a SQL RDBMS engine based on mSQL and called MySQL. The database was almost immediately ported to Linux and grew tremendously because of its speed, flexibility, and a more liberal copyright than most other free databases had.

OpenLink Software introduced Universal Database Connectivity (UDBC), a software development kit for the popular Open Database Connectivity (ODBC) standard. UDBC supported many platforms, including Linux, and guaranteed portable connectivity across all supported platforms.

Support of SCO UNIX binaries using the iBCS2 emulator in the Linux kernel led to many reports of intrepid users successfully running SCO versions of Oracle (version 7), Sybase, Informix, Dataflex, and Unify/Accell on Linux. Some vendors, particularly Unify, took note of the general satisfaction enjoyed by such experimenters even though their efforts were not officially supported. Eventually a series of HOWTO documents emerged for installing Oracle and other such databases under Linux with the iBCS emulator.

In fact, Sybase, sensing the excitement of its customers who were running its DBMS on Linux under the emulator, soon released its libraries for client application development, ported to Linux. The libraries were available for free on Sybase's Web site, but were unsupported.

Conetic Software Systems, Inc. released C/BASE 4GL for Linux, which provided an xBASE database engine with a 4GL interface.

Infoflex Inc. released ESQLFlex and Infoflex for Linux, which provided low-level, embedded SQL and 4GL interfaces to query and maintain third-party databases. They licensed source code to customers, supporting UNIX, DOS, and VMS platforms.

Empress Software released Empress RDBMS in personal and network (full-function) packages for Linux. Empress was one of several commercial databases sold and supported through the ACC Bookstore, an early outlet for Linux merchandise. (Just Logic/SQL was also sold through ACC).

The following year, 1996, saw two additional advances in the world of Linux. Solid Information Technology Ltd. released a Linux version of its SOLID Server RDBMS. It's probably more than mere coincidence that such an early Linux booster among DBMS vendors is a Finnish company. In 1997, Solid announced a promotion giving away free copies of the SOLID Server for Linux users in order to galvanize the development of apps based on SOLID by Linux developers.

KE Software Inc. released KE Texpress for Linux, a specialized client/server database engine geared towards storing and manipulating relationships between text objects. As such, it had facilities for presenting data sets as HTML and a specialized query language. KE Express was also released for most UNIX varieties as well as Windows and Macintosh.

Then, in 1997, Coromandel Software released Integra4 SQL RDBMS for Linux and promoted it with discounted pricing for Linux users. Coromandel, from India, built a lot of high-end features into Integra4, from ANSI-SQL 92 support to stored procedures, triggers, and 4GL tools: features typical in high end SQL RDBMSes.

Empress updated its Linux RDBMS, adding such features as binary large object (BLOB), HTML application interface support, and several indexing methods for data.

Lastly, Raima Corporation offered Linux versions of Raima Database Manager++, Raima Object Manager and the Velocis Database Server. This ambitious set of products sought to tackle data needs from C/C++ object persistence to full SQL-based relational data stores.

Of course, as we've already discussed, 1998 was the year that the major Database vendors took serious notice of the operating system. For proof of just how the porting frenzy of 1988 surprised even the vendors themselves, see the July 6, 1998, *Infoworld* article (`www.infoworld.com/cgi-bin/displayStory.pl?98076.ehlinux.htm`) reporting that the major DB vendors, Oracle, IBM, Informix, and Sybase had no plans for releasing Linux ports of their DBMSes. Of course, it later became known that some of the quoted vendors were actively beta testing their Linux products at the time, but it did reveal the prevailing expectations in the industry.

But 1998 was also a year of advances. Inprise Corporation (formerly Borland International) released its Interbase SQL RDBMS for Linux, and followed up the release by posting to its Web site a white paper making startling advocacy for InterBase on UNIX and Linux. To quote from the paper: "UNIX and Linux are better as server platforms than Windows NT. In scalability, security, stability, and especially performance, UNIX and Linux contain more mature and proven technology. In all these areas, UNIX and Linux are demonstrating their superiority over Microsoft's resource-hungry server operating system." And this even though there is a Windows NT version of InterBase available!

Computer Associates announced that it would be porting their commercial Ingres II RDBMS.

Informix officially committed itself to Linux, announcing ports of Informix-SE, a well-known SQL RDBMS (but not its enterprise-level Dynamic Server), ESQL/C, and other Informix components, and offering development versions of these tools for a free registration to the Informix Developer Network.

At about the same time as Informix, Oracle announced a Linux porting effort, which became Oracle8.0.5 for Linux. At one point Oracle even declared its intention to begin distributing Linux as a bundle with its DBMS. Oracle, which had always been looking for a way to sell "raw-iron" (the practice of selling the computer without an installed operating system) database servers, bypassing the need for clients to buy Microsoft and other expensive operating systems, saw Linux as a marketable platform for such systems, which approximated the raw-iron goals. Oracle's follow-up release to 8.0.5, 8*i*, made a step towards the raw-iron ambitions by bundling an "Internet" filesystem to the database, so that it could do its own filesystem management rather than relying on the OS. Nevertheless, Oracle8*i*, which also featured other improvements such as XML support, was ported to Linux in 1999.

> **Note**   As of this writing Oracle9*i* is about to be released.

Soon after the major vendors announced their DBMS ports, serious concerns emerged in the Linux community about the dominance of Red Hat software. Most of the vendors struck a partnership with Red Hat, and several released their software only in RPM form. Some, like Oracle, saw a PR problem and pledged support for multiple distributions (four in Oracle's case, including versions of Linux for the Alpha processor).

In 1998, Sybase announced a port of its enterprise-level adaptive server enterprise (ASE) to Linux, and almost immediately struck agreements with Caldera and Red Hat, from which Web sites users could download trial versions of the software for free registration. Bundling on the distributions' application sampler CDs would follow, as well as bundling with SuSE. At about the same time, DB2 announced that it would be porting version 5.2 of its high-end Universal Database Server. Interestingly enough, the DB2 port was performed by a few Linux enthusiasts within IBM without official approval. Luckily, by the time they were nearing completion of the port, the announcements for commercial Linux software were coming along thickly and the developers were able to make a business case for the port and get it sanctioned. Informix released Informix Dynamic Server, Linux Edition Suite. Informix supports the common (generic) Linux component versions, such as Red Hat, SuSE, and Caldera on Intel platforms.

One small problem that emerged after all this activity was that most of the major DBMSs that had been ported to Linux had lower or more expensive support costs. Many of the vendors seemed to be relying on Linux users' extraordinary ability for self-support on online forums and knowledge bases, but this flexibility is probably not characteristic of the large organizations on which Linux DBMSs were poised to make a debut. Many of the vendors involved have since normalized their Linux technical support policies.

In 1998, David E. Storey began developing dbMetrix, an open source SQL query tool for multiple databases, including MySQL, mSQL, PostgreSQL, Solid, and Oracle. dbMetrix has a GTK interface.

In August 2000, Informix Corporation announced the availability of its Informix Dynamic Server.2000 database engine running with SuSE Linux on Compaq Computer Corporation's 64-bit Alpha processor for customer shipments.

In Fall 2000, Informix Corporation simultaneously introduced a developer's edition of its Informix Extended Parallel Server (XPS) Version 8.31 for the Linux platform; and announced Red Brick Decision Server version 6.1, for data warehousing in Web or conventional decision-support environments. Both products are the first for Linux designed expressly for data warehousing and decision support.

Introduction to Linux databases

A variety of databases run on Linux, from in-memory DBMSs such as Gadfly (open source) to full-fledged enterprise systems such as Oracle8*i*.

There are several open source databases that support a subset of ANSI SQL-92, notably PostgreSQL and MySQL, which are discussed throughout this book. mSQL is a similar product to MySQL.

The major commercial databases tend to have support for full ANSI SQL-92; transaction management; stored procedures in C, Java, or a variety of proprietary languages; SQL embedded in C/C++ and Java; sophisticated network interfaces; layered and comprehensive security; and heavy third-party support. These include Oracle8*i*, Informix, Sybase ASE 11, DB2 Universal Database 6.1, ADABAS D, and Inprise Interbase 5.0.

Enterprise databases were traditionally licensed by the number of connected users, but with the advent of the Web, such pricing became unfeasible because there was no practical limit to the number of users that could connect. Nowadays, most enterprise DBMS vendors offer per-CPU pricing, but such software is still very expensive and usually a significant corporate commitment.

Many of the vendors offer special free or deeply discounted development or "personal" versions to encourage third parties to develop tools and applications for their DBMS. This has especially been the case in Linux where vendors have tried to seed excitement in the Linux community with the lure of free downloads. It is important to note that the license for these giveaways usually only extends to noncommercial use. Any deployment in commercial uses, which could be as unassuming as a hobbyist Web site with banner ads, is subject to the full licensing fees.

There are many specialized databases for Linux, such as Empress RDBMS, which is now mainly an Embedded systems database, and Zserver, part of Digital Creations' Zope application server, which is specialized for organizing bits of object-oriented data for Web publishing.

Commercial OODBMS will be available once POET ports its Object Server to Linux. POET will support ODMG OQL and the Java binding for ODMG, but not other aspects of the standard.

There are usually many options for connecting to DBMSs under Linux, although many of them are immature. There are Web-based, Tcl/Tk-based, GTK, and KDE SQL query interfaces for most open source and some commercial databases. There are libraries for Database connectivity from Java, Python, Perl, and, in the case of commercial databases, C and C++. Database connectivity is available through several Web servers, and more than one CGI program has native connectivity to a database; for example, PHP and MySQL.

New Feature   There is now a new version of ANSI SQL available, SQL 99. It remains to be seen how this will affect the development of the many SQL databases that do not meet the ANSI SQL-92 requirements.

Summary

This chapter provided some general background about the use of databases in Linux. As you can see, the field is constantly evolving and drastic changes can occur almost without warning, such as the great Linux migration of enterprise databases in 1998. Linux news outlets such as `www.linux.com`, `www.linux.org`, and `www.linuxgazette.com` are a good way to keep abreast of all that is happening in these areas.

In this chapter, you learned that:

✦ DBMSs have evolved greatly as the types of data being managed have grown more complex.

✦ Linux has grown phenomenally, from its creator's dream of a modern hobbyists' OS in 1991 to the fastest-growing platform for enterprise computer systems in 2000.

✦ Linux DBMSs have similarly evolved from the spate of xBASE-class systems available from medium-sized vendors in 1994 and 1995 to the recent porting of all the major enterprise DBMSs to Linux beginning in 1998.

✦ There is currently a wide variety of RDBMS, query and connectivity tools, and specialty DBMS, with OODBMSs and other advancements close around the corner.

In the next chapter, we shall start the process of sifting through all these possibilities. We shall discuss how to determine if Linux database tools are suitable for your needs, and how to select the best options if so.

✦   ✦   ✦

The Relational Model

This chapter discusses what a database is, and how a database manages data. The relational model for databases, in particular, is introduced, although other types of databases are also discussed.

This chapter is theoretical rather than practical. Some of it may seem arcane to you — after all, theory is fine, but you have work to do and problems to solve. However, you should take the time to read through this chapter and become famil-iar with the theory it describes. The theory is not difficult, and much of it simply codifies common sense. Most impor-tantly, if you grasp the theory, you will find it easier to think coherently about databases — and therefore find it easier to solve your data-related problems.

What Is a Database?

In a book about databases, it is reasonable to ask, "What is a database?"

Our answer is simple: *A database is an orderly body of data, and the software that maintains it.* This answer, however, raises two further questions:

- ✦ What are data?
- ✦ What does it mean to "maintain a body of data"?

Each question is answered in turn.

What are data?

Despite the fact that we use data every hour of every day, "data" is difficult to define exactly. We offer this definition: *A datum (or data item) is a symbol that describes an aspect of an entity or event in the real world.* By "real world," we mean the everyday world that we experience through our senses and speak of in common language.

For example, the book in your hand — an entity in the real world — can be described by data: its title, its ISBN number, the names of its authors, the name of its publisher, the year of its publication and the city from which it was published are all data that describe this book.

Or consider how a baseball game — an event in the real world — is described by data: the date on which the game was played, where it was played, the names of the teams, the score, the names of the winning and losing pitchers, are part of the wealth of data with which an observer can reconstruct practically every pitch.

We use data to portray practically every entity and event in our world. Each data element is a tile in the mosaic used to portray an entity or event.

Types of data

Although data are derived from entities and events in the real world, data have properties of their own. If you wish to become a mosaicist, you must first learn the properties of the tiles from which you will assemble your pictures — their weight, the proper materials for gluing them into place, how best to glaze them for color, and so on. In the same way, if you want to work with databases, you should learn the properties of data so you can assemble them into data-portraits of entities and events in the real world.

To begin, a data item has a *type*. The type can range from the simple to the very complex. An image, a number, your name, a histogram, a DNA sequence, a code, and a software object can each be regarded as a type of data.

Statistical data types

Amongst the most commonly used types of data are the statistical types. These data are used to perform the classic statistical tests. Because many of the questions that you will want to ask of your database will be statistical — for example, what was the average amount of money that your company received each month last year, or what was Wade Boggs' batting average in 1985 — these data types will be most useful to you.

There are four statistical data types:

Nominal   A nominal datum names an entity or event. For example, a man's name is a nominal datum; so is his sex. An address is nominal, and so is a telephone number.

Ordinal   An ordinal datum identifies an entity or event's order within a hierarchy whose intervals are not exactly defined. For example, a soldier's military rank is an ordinal datum: a captain is higher than a lieutenant and lower than a major, but the interval between them is not defined precisely. Another example is a teacher's evaluation of a student's effort: "good" is above "poor" and below "excellent," but again the intervals between them are not defined precisely.

Interval   An interval datum identifies a point on a scale whose intervals are defined exactly, but whose scale does not have a clearly defined zero point. You can say exactly what the interval is from one point on the scale to another, but you cannot compute a ratio between two measurements. For example, the calendar year is not a number of absolute scale, but simply a count of years from some selected historical event — from the foundation of the state or the birth of a noteworthy person. The year 2000 is exactly 1,000 years of time later than the year 1000, but it is not twice as far removed from the beginning of time.

Ratio   A ratio datum identifies a point on a scale whose intervals are defined exactly, and whose scale has a clearly defined zero point. For example, temperature measured as degrees Kelvin (that is, degrees above absolute zero) is a ratio datum — for 12 degrees Kelvin is both 8 degrees hotter than 4 degrees Kelvin, and three times as hot in absolute terms.

As you can see, these four data types give increasingly complex ways to describe entities or events. Ordinal data can hold more information than nominal, interval more than ordinal, and ratio more than interval.

As we mentioned at the beginning of this section, the statistical types are among the most common that you will use in a database. If you can grasp what these data types are, and what properties each possesses, you will be better prepared to work with the data in a database.

Complex data types

Beyond the simple statistical data types that are the bread and butter of databases lies an entire range of complex data types.

We cannot cover the range of complex data types here — these types usually are tailored for a particular task. However, there is one complex data type that you will use continually: *dates*. The type date combines information about the year, month, day; information about hour, minute, and second; time zone; and information about daylight savings time. Dates are among the most common data items that you work with, and because of their complexity, among the most vexing.

Operations upon data

It is worth remembering that we record data in order to perform operations upon them. After all, why would we record how many runs a baseball team scored in a game, except to compare that data item with the number of runs that the other team scored?

A data item's type dictates what operations you can perform upon that data item. The following subsections discuss this in a little more depth.

Statistical data types

The data operations that are usually performed upon the statistical data types fall into two categories: *comparison operations* and *mathematical operations*.

Comparison operations compare two data to determine whether they are identical, or whether one is superior or inferior to the other.

Mathematical operations perform a mathematical transformation upon data. The transformation can be arithmetic — addition, subtraction, multiplication, or division — or a more complicated transformation (for example, computing a statistic).

The following briefly summarizes the operations that usually can be performed upon each type of data:

Nominal   Data are compared only for equality. They usually are not compared for inferiority or superiority, nor are mathematical operations performed upon them. For example, a person's name is a nominal datum; and usually you will compare two names to determine whether they are the same. If the data are text (as is usually the case), they often are compared lexically — that is, compared to determine which comes earlier in alphabetical order.

Ordinal   Data usually are compared for equality, superiority, or inferiority. For example, one will compare two soldiers' ranks to determine whether one is superior to the other. It is not common to perform mathematical operations upon ordinal data.

Interval Data usually are compared for equality, superiority, and inferiority. Interval data often are subtracted from one another to discover the difference between them; for example, to discover how many years lie between 1895 and 1987, you can subtract one from the other to discover the interval between them.

Ratio   These data are compared for equality, superiority, and inferiority. Because they rest upon an absolute scale, they are ideal for an entire range of mathematical operations.

Complex data

Usually, each complex data type supports a handful of specialized operations. For example, a DNA sequence can be regarded as a type of complex data. The following comparison operations can be performed on DNA sequences:

✦ Compare length of sequences

✦ Compare length for equality

✦ Compare homology at percent x

The following transformations, analogous to mathematical operations, can be performed upon DNA sequences:

✦ Determine coding frame

✦ Determine coded amino-acid sequence

✦ Compute percent purine

✦ Compare percent pyrimidine

✦ Determine location of hairpins or palindromes

✦ Determine complementary sequences

As you can see, the transformation operations are strictly tied to the special nature of the data, although the comparison operations are not.

To summarize: We gather data to interpret them, and operations help us to interpret data. A data item's type sets the operations that you can perform upon that data item.

Domains

In addition to type, a data item has a *domain*. The domain states what the data item describes, and therefore defines what values that the data item can hold:

✦ The domain determines what the data item describes. For example, a data item that has type ratio can have the domain *temperature*. Or a data item that has type nominal can have the domain *name*.

✦ The domain also determines the values the data item can hold. For example, the data item with domain *name* will not have a value of "32.6," and the data item with domain *temperature* will not have a value of "Catherine."

A data item can be compared only with another data item in the same domain. For example, comparing the name of an automobile with the name of a human being will not yield a meaningful result, although both are nominal data; nor will comparing a military rank with the grades on a report card yield a meaningful result, even though both are ordinal. Likewise, it is not meaningful to subtract the number of runs scored in a baseball game from the number of points scored in a basketball game, even though both have type ratio.

Before leaving domains for the moment, however, here are two additional thoughts:

✦ First, by definition, a domain is well defined. Here, "well defined" means that we can test precisely whether a given data element belongs to the domain.

✦ Second, an entity or event in the real world has many aspects, and therefore is described by a combination of many domains. For example, a soldier has a name (a nominal domain), a rank (an ordinal domain), a body temperature (an interval domain), and an age (a ratio domain). When a group of domains each describe a different aspect of the same entity or event, they are said to be *related to each other*.

We will return to the subject of domains and their relations shortly. But first, we must discuss another fundamental issue: what it means to maintain a body of data.

What does it mean to "maintain a body of data"?

At the beginning of this chapter, database was defined as "an orderly body of data and the software that maintains it." We have offered a definition of "data"; now we will describe what it means to maintain a body of data.

In brief, maintaining means that we must perform these tasks:

✦ Organize the data

✦ Insert data

✦ Retrieve data

✦ Delete data

✦ Update data

✦ Maintain the data's integrity

Each task is discussed in turn.

Organize data

The first task that must be performed when maintaining a body of data is to *organize* the data. To organize data involves these tasks:

✦ Establish a "bin" for each category of data to be gathered.

✦ Build "slots" within each bin to hold the data, one slot for each datum.

✦ Give each bin and each slot a label, to tell us what it holds.

✦ Write a catalogue of the bins and their slots, so that we do not have to search the entire database to see what the database holds.

✦ When necessary, add new bins and slots, and update the catalogue to describe them.

If it sounds as if we're describing a warehouse instead of a software system, which is not a coincidence: after all, both a warehouse and database are designed to organize things. There's nothing more useless than a pile of screws, washers, and nuts that are jumbled together. However, if the screws, washers, and nuts are well organized—each type in its own bin, each size in its own slot—then each item becomes much more useful, because we can quickly find the exact item that we need for a given task. And so it is with data: without firm organization, data are worthless.

Inserting data

After our software has helped us to build a "warehouse" for our data—regardless of whether or not we have any data—the next step is to insert data into the database.

Put simply, the software should help us to put each datum into its appropriate bin and slot.

Retrieve data

If we cannot read our data after we have stored them, we might as well not have bothered to store them in the first place. Our next task then is to retrieve the data.

The database software should let us retrieve data by naming the bins and slots that hold them—that is, it should let us address the data. It should also give us an orderly way to examine the data that we have retrieved.

Delete data

Sometimes we need to delete data from our database. The database software should let us do so by address. It should remove only the data we address—nothing less, nothing more.

Update data

The last task is to update data within the database.

Strictly speaking, the update task is not a necessary part of our database-maintenance system. After all, we could simply retrieve the data from our database, modify them, then delete the old data, and insert the modified data into the database. Doing this by hand, however, can cause problems—we can easily make a mistake and wreck our data rather than modify them. It is best that our software handle this tricky task for us.

Maintaining integrity

Maintaining a database involves these five tasks—organization, inserting, retrieving, deleting, and updating. There is a difference, however, between simply performing these tasks, and performing them well.

A database-maintenance system not only performs these tasks, but it does so in such a way as to maintain the integrity of the data. In brief, this means that you must protect the data from errors that dilute the meaning of the data.

As you can imagine, maintaining the integrity of your data is extremely important. We discuss throughout the rest of this chapter just what you must do to maintain data integrity.

To this point, we have presented our definitions: what data are and what it means to maintain data. One more concept must be introduced: *relationality,* or how data can be joined together to form a portrait of an entity or event in the real world.

Relationality

So far, we have spoken of the data within a database as if each datum were something unto itself and bore no relation to the other data within the database — as if a database were comprised of randomly collected observations that had nothing to do with each other. This, of course, is not the case: we go to the trouble of building a database because we wish to maintain a body of data for a well-defined purpose. There is a logic to the data that we collect, which logic is dictated by the nature of the entity or event that we are studying. In other words, the data that we collect are *related* to each other.

The relations among data are themselves an important part of the database. Consider, for example, a database that records information about books. Each book has a title, an author, a publisher, a city of publication, a year of publication, and an ISBN number. Each data item has its own type and its own domain; but each has meaning only when it is coupled with the other data that describe a book.

Much of the work of the database software will be to maintain integrity not just among data and within data, but among these related groups of data. The rest of this chapter examines the theory behind maintaining these groups of related data, or *relations*.

The Relational Model

A database management system (DBMS) is a tool that is devised to maintain data: to perform the tasks of reading data from the database, updating the data within the database, and inserting data into the database, while preserving the integrity of the data.

A number of designs for database management systems have been proposed over the years, and several have found favor. This book concentrates on one design — the relational database — for three reasons:

✦ The relational database is by far the most important commercially.

✦ The relational database is the only database that is built upon a model that has been proved mathematically to be complete and consistent. It is difficult to overestimate the importance of this fact.

✦ The relational database is robust; you can use it to solve a great variety of problems.

This is not to say that the relational database is the only one that should be used, or that the competing designs should be discarded. We do say, however, that if you can grasp the relational model, you will have acquired a tool that will help you work with every design for a database.

What is the relational model?

The "relational model" was first proposed by Edgar F. Codd, a mathematician with IBM, in a paper published on August 19, 1969. To put that date into its historical context, Armstrong and Aldrin had walked on the moon just weeks earlier, and Thompson and Ritchie would soon boot the UNIX operating system for the first time.

The subsequent history of the relational database was one of gradual development leading to widespread acceptance. In the early 1970s, two groups, one at IBM and the other at the University of California, Berkeley, took up Codd's ideas. The Berkeley group, led by Michael Stonebraker, led to the development of Ingres and the QUEL inquiry language. IBM's effort in the early 1970s, led to IBM's System/R and Structured Query Language (SQL).

In the late 1970s, commercial products began to appear, in particular Oracle, Informix, and Sybase. Today, the major relational-database manufacturers sell billions of dollars worth of products and services every year.

Beneath all this activity, however, lies Codd's original work. Codd's insights into the design of databases will continue to be built upon and extended, but it is unlikely that they will be superseded for years to come.

The relational model is a model

The rest of this chapter presents the relational model. Before we go further, however, we ask that you remember that the relational model is precisely that — a model, that is, a construct that exists only in thought.

You may well ask why we study the model when we can lay our hands on an implementation and work with it. There are two reasons:

 ✦ First, *the relational model gives us a tool for thinking about databases*. When you begin to grapple with difficult problems in data modeling and data management, you will be glad to have such a tool available.

 ✦ Second, *the model gives us a yardstick against which we can measure implementations*. If we know the rules of the relational model, we can judge how well a given package implements the model.

As you can see, the relational model is well worth learning.

Structure of the relational model

The relational model, as its name implies, is built around relations.

The term *relation* has a precise definition; to help you grasp the definition, we will first review what we said earlier about data.

✦ A *datum* describes an aspect of an entity or event in the real world. A datum has three aspects: its type, its domain, and its value.

✦ A datum has a *type*. The type may be one of the statistical types (nominal, ordinal, interval, or ratio), or it can be a complex type (for example, a date).

✦ A datum's *domain* is the set of values that that datum can contain. A domain can be anywhere from small and finite to infinite, but it must be well defined.

✦ Finally, a datum's *value* is the member of the domain set that applies to the entity or event being described. For example, if the domain is the set of all major league baseball teams, then the value for the datum that describes the team that plays its home games in Chicago's Wrigley Field is "Cubs."

Our purpose in collecting data is to describe an entity or event in the real world. Except in rare instances, a data element cannot describe an entity or event by itself; rather, an entity or event must be described with multiple data elements that are related to each other by the nature of the entity or event we are describing. A data element is one tile in a mosaic with which we portray the entity or event.

For example, consider a baseball game. The game's score is worth knowing; but only if we know the names of the teams playing the game and the date upon which the game was played. If we know the teams without knowing the score, our knowledge is incomplete; likewise, if we know the score and the date, but do not know the teams, we do not really know anything about the game.

So now we are zeroing in on our definition: *A relation is a set of domains that together describe a given entity or event in the real world.* For example, the team, date, and score each is a domain; and together, these domains form a relation that describes a baseball game.

In practice, a relation has two parts:

✦ The first part, called the *heading,* names the domains that comprise the relation. For example, the heading for a relation that described a baseball game would name three domains: *teams, date,* and *score.*

✦ The second part, called the *body,* gives the data that describe instances of the entity or event that the relation describes. For example, the body of a relation that describes a baseball game would hold data that described individual games.

The next two subsections discuss the heading of a relation, and then the body. Then we rejoin the head to the body, so that you can see the relation as a whole.

The heading of a relation

Again, let's consider the example of the score for a baseball game. When we record information for a baseball game, we want to record the following information:

✦ The name of the home team.

✦ The name of the visiting team.

✦ The number of runs scored by the home team.

✦ The number of runs scored by the visiting team.

These are four data. However, as you can see, these four data use only two domains: the name of the home team and the name of the visiting team each use the domain of "names of major league baseball teams"; and the runs scored by the home team and the runs scored by the visiting team both use the domain of "baseball game runs."

As you can imagine, it is important that we ensure that these domains are used unambiguously. We humans do not always grasp how important it is to abolish ambiguity, because we bring information to our reading of a score that helps us to disambiguate the data it presents. For example, when we read "Atlanta Braves," we know that that string names a baseball team — in other words, that that datum belongs to the domain of "names of major league baseball teams." Likewise, we know that the information on the same row of print as that of the team name applies to that team. A computer database, however, has no such body of knowledge upon which to draw: it knows only what you tell it. Therefore, it is vital that what you tell it is clear, complete, and free of ambiguity.

To help remove ambiguity from our relation, we introduce one last element to our definition of a domain: the attribute. An *attribute* identifies a data element in a relation. It has two parts: the name of its domain and an attribute-name. The attribute-name must be unique within the relation.

Attributes: baseball game example

To see how this works, let's translate our baseball game into the heading of a relation. For the sake of simplicity, we will abbreviate the names of our domains: "baseball runs" becomes BR, and "major league baseball team" becomes MLBT. Likewise, we will abbreviate the names of the attributes: "home team" becomes HT and "visiting team" becomes VT. When we do so, our relation becomes as follows:

```
<HT:MLBT>   <VT:MLBT>   <HT-RUNS:BR>   <VT-RUNS:BR>
```

The name of the attribute appears to the left of the colon, the domain name to the right. We've enclosed each domain's name in angle brackets (that is, < and >) to make it a little more readable.

These data tell us the outcome of the game. We add two other data so that we can identify each game unambiguously:

✦ Date the game was played (DG). The attribute has a domain of "game date" (GDAT), which has the type of date. The domain limits the value of this attribute to dates that have had major league baseball games played on them; for example, major league baseball was not played before 1876, nor is it played during the winter.

✦ Number of the game on that date (GNUM). We need this in case the teams played a double-header — that is, played two games on the same day. This attribute has domain NUM; this domain can only have values 1 or 2.

Together, these six attributes let us identify the outcome of any major league baseball game ever played.

Our relation's heading now appears as follows:

```
<HT:MLBT> <VT:MLBT> <HT-RUNS:BR> <VT-RUNS:BR> <DG:GDAT> <GNUM:NUM>
```

Attributes: baseball team example

For another example, consider a relation that describes major league teams in detail. Such a relation will have at least two attributes:

✦ Name of the team (TEAM). This attribute has domain MLBT, which we described in the previous example.

✦ Home stadium (HS). This attribute has domain stadium (STAD), which consists of the names of all stadiums in North America.

These two attributes let us identify major league baseball teams. We could add more attributes to this relation, such as the team's league or its division; but for now, what we have here is sufficient.

The relation's heading appears as follows:

```
<TEAM:MLBT> <HS:STAD>
```

The body of a relation

Now that we have defined the heading of a relation, which is the relation's abstract portion, the next step is to define its body — the relation's "concrete" portion. The body of a relation consists of *rows* of data. Each row consists of one data item from each of the relation's attributes.

The literature on relational databases uses the word tuple for a set of values within a relation. For a number of reasons, this word is more precise than "row" is; however, to help make the following discussion a little more accessible, we will use the more familiar word "row" instead of "tuple."

Consider, for example, the baseball game relation we described earlier. The following shows the relation's heading and some possible rows:

Header:

```
<HT:MLBT>   <VT:MLBT>   <HT-RUNS:BR> <VT-RUNS:BR> <DG:GDAT> <GNUM:NUM>
```

Body:

```
Braves      Cubs        3            5            05/05/95  1
White Sox   Brewers     2            8            05/05/95  1
Angels      Mariners    2            1            05/05/95  1
Angels      Mariners    6            7            05/05/95  2
```

In this example, the header identifies the six attributes that comprise the relation: home team, visiting team, runs scored by the home team, runs scored by the visiting team, date the game was played, and number of the game (that is, first or second game on that date). Each of the four rows gives the score of a game — one in which the Braves at home are beaten by the Cubs, the White Sox at home are beaten by the Brewers, and a double-header in which the Angels beat the Mariners in the first game but lose to them in the second game.

Or consider the relation that describes major league baseball teams. The following shows some rows for it:

Header:

```
<TEAM:MLBT> <HS:STAD>
```

Body:

```
Braves      Turner Field
White Sox   Comiskey Park
Angels      Anaheim Stadium
Mariners    Safeco Field
Cubs        Wrigley Field
```

These rows identify the team that played in the games described in baseball game relation.

Naming relations

For the sake of convenience, we will give names to our relations. Relational theory does not demand that a relation have a name. However, it is useful to be able to refer to a relation by a name, so we will give a name to each of our relations.

So, for our exercise, we will name our first relation (the one that gives the scores of games) GAMES; and we will name our second relation (the one that identifies team) BBTEAMS.

When we speak of an attribute, we will prefix the attribute with the name of the relation that contains it, using a period to separate the names of the relation and the attribute. For example, we can refer to attribute HT in relation GAMES as GAMES.HT. With this notation, we can use the same domain in more than one relation, yet make it perfectly clear just which instance of domain we are referring to.

Properties of a relation

So far, we have seen that a relation has two parts: the heading, which identifies the attributes that comprise the relation; and the body, which consists of rows that give instances of the attributes that are named in the heading. For a collection of attributes to be a true relation, however, it must have three specific properties.

No ordering

Neither the attributes in a relation nor its rows come in any particular order. By convention, we display a relation in the form of a table. However, this is just a convention.

The absence of ordering means that two relations that are comprised of the same set of attributes are identical, regardless of the order in which those attributes appear.

Atomic values

Every attribute within a relation is atomic. This is an important aspect of the relational model.

Atomic means that an attribute cannot be broken down further. This means that a datum within a relation cannot be a structure or a formula (such as can be written into a cell of a spreadsheet); and, most importantly, it cannot be another relation. If you wish to define a domain whose members are themselves relations, you must first break down, or *decompose*, each relation into the atomic data that comprises it, and then insert those data into the relation. This process of breaking down a complex attribute into a simpler one is part of the process called *normalization*. The process of normalization is an important aspect of designing a database. We discuss it in some detail in Chapter 4, when we discuss database design.

We use the term *semantic normalization* to describe the process by which a database designer ensures that each datum in each of his relations contains one, and only one, item of information. Semantic normalization is not a part of the relational model, but it is an important part of database design.

 Cross-Reference   We discuss semantic normalization further in Chapter 4.

No duplicate rows

This is an important point that is often overlooked: *a relation cannot contain duplicate rows*.

Each row within a relation is unique. This is an important property, because it lets us identify (or *address*) each row individually. Because rows come in no particular order, we cannot address a row by its position within the relation. The only way we can address a row is by finding some value within the row that identifies it uniquely within its relation. Therefore, the rule of no duplicate rows ensures that we can address each row individually.

This property has important implications for database design, and in particular for the writing of a database application. It is also an important point upon which the relational model and SQL diverge: the relational model forbids a relation to hold duplicate rows, but SQL allows its tables to hold duplicate rows.

Keys

Arguably, the most important task that we can perform with a database is that of *retrieval*: that is, to recover from the database the information that we have put into it. After all, what use is a filing cabinet if we cannot retrieve the papers that we put into it?

As we noted above, the "uniqueness" property of a relation is especially important to the task of retrieval: that each row within the body of a relation is unique guarantees that we can retrieve that row, and that row alone.

The property of uniqueness guarantees that we can address a row by using all of the attributes of the row within the query that we ask of the relation. However, this may not be very useful to us, because we may know some aspects of the entity or event that the rows describes, but not others. After all, we usually query a database to find some item of information that we do not know.

Consider, for example, our relation for baseball scores. If we already know all six attributes of the row (that is, we know the teams, the date, the game number, and the number of runs that each team scored), then there's no reason for us to query the database for that row. Most often, however, we know the teams involved in the game, the date, and the number of the game — but we do not know the number of runs that each team scored.

When we're examining the data about a baseball game, it would be most useful if we could use the information that we do know to find the information that we do not know. And there is such a method — what the relational model calls *keys*.

Keys come in two "flavors": *primary keys* and *foreign keys*. The following subsections introduce each.

Primary keys

A *primary key* is a set of attributes whose values uniquely identify a row within its relation.

For example, in relation BBTEAMS, attribute TEAM uniquely identifies each row within the relation: the relation can have only one row for the Red Sox, or one row for the Orioles. Thus, attribute TEAM is the primary key for relation BBTEAMS.

A primary key can also combine the values of several attributes. For example, in relation GAMES, the attributes HT, DG, and GNUM (that is, home team, date of game, and game number) identify a game uniquely.

The only restriction that the relational model places upon a primary key is that it cannot itself contain a primary key — that is, a primary key cannot contain attributes that are extraneous to its task of identifying a row uniquely. For example, if we added attribute HT-RUNS to the primary key for attribute GAMES, the primary key would still identify the row uniquely; but the number of runs scored by the home team is extraneous to the task of identifying each row uniquely.

Foreign keys

A *foreign key* is a set of attributes whose value equals that of a primary key in another relation. Thus, a foreign key refers to one row in the other relation.

For example, the attribute TEAM in relation BBTEAMS names a baseball team, and is the primary key for that relation. Attributes HT and VT in relation GAMES also name baseball teams; therefore, each can serve as a foreign key to relation BBTEAMS.

The linking of two relations through a foreign key is called a *join*. Please make note of this term, because you will see it frequently throughout the rest of this book.

Foreign keys have several important properties:

✦ The attributes that comprise a foreign key must have the same domains as the attributes to which they are joined.

✦ A foreign key must match all of the attributes in the primary key to which it is joined, not just some of them.

✦ The relation to which the foreign key is joined must contain a row that contains the data that comprise the foreign key. In other words, a foreign key cannot "point to nowhere." For example, attribute GAMES.HT is joined to attribute BBTEAMS.TEAM; thus, if a row in GAMES sets the value of attribute GAMES.HT to the value of "Orioles," then relation BBTEAMS must have a row that sets the value of attribute BBTEAMS.TEAM to "Orioles," or an error has occurred. This issue is discussed in more detail later, when we discuss the issue of database integrity.

A relation must have at least one primary key; however, a relation does not have to have a foreign key.

Relational algebra and relational calculus

The subject of foreign keys introduces the idea of how relations are "hooked together," or *joined*. In fact, we can use foreign keys to build new relations, by joining together all or part of the relations that a foreign key joins.

One of the most important parts of the relational model is the language with which we examine and compare relations, and build new relations. The relational model offers two such languages: relational algebra and relational calculus.

Please note that the terms *relational algebra* and *relational calculus* have little to do with the algebra and calculus that you attempted to learn in high school. These are conventional terms that describe how we work with relations. You do not need to know either algebra or calculus to grasp the principles of relational algebra and relational calculus. (And there will not be a quiz at the end of this section!)

Relational algebra

Relational algebra performs operations upon relations. Each operation builds a new relation that holds its output.

The core of the relational algebra is eight basic operations. These were first described by E. F. Codd, who invented the relational database. The product of each operation can itself be used as the input to yet another operation. Thus, from these eight elementary operations, we can build elaborate expressions.

The eight operations come in two groups of four. The first four are standard operations for manipulating sets; the other four operations are designed to manipulate relations. We first discuss the four standard operations, and then the four special ones.

Union

The *union* operation compares two relations, and builds a new relation that contains every row that appears in either relation. The relation that the union operation builds, of course, does not contain duplicate rows. Therefore, if a row appears in both parent relations, it appears only once in the product relation.

For a union operation to yield a meaningful result, the relations that are being compared must have identical structures. By "identical structures," we mean that the relations be comprised of the same set of attributes (although the attributes may have different names).

For example, consider two relations, MYGAMES and YOURGAMES.

MYGAMES is our familiar baseball-game relation:

```
<HT:MLBT>    <VT:MLBT>    <HT-RUNS:BR> <VT-RUNS:BR> <DG:GDAT> <GNUM:NUM>
Braves       Cubs         3            5            05/05/95  1
White Sox    Brewers      2            8            05/05/95  1
Angels       Mariners     2            1            05/05/95  1
Angels       Mariners     6            7            05/05/95  2
```

YOURGAMES has the same structure as MYGAMES, but its body is different:

```
<HT:MLBT>    <VT:MLBT>    <HT-RUNS:BR> <VT-RUNS:BR> <DG:GDAT> <GNUM:NUM>
Reds         Marlins      7            6            05/05/95  1
White Sox    Brewers      2            8            05/05/95  1
Red Sox      Yankees      3            4            05/05/95  1
```

The two relations have one row in common — the one that describes the game in which the Brewers played the White Sox in Chicago.

The union of these two relations produces the following:

```
<HT:MLBT>    <VT:MLBT>    <HT-RUNS:BR> <VT-RUNS:BR> <DG:GDAT> <GNUM:NUM>
Braves       Cubs         3            5            05/05/95  1
White Sox    Brewers      2            8            05/05/95  1
Angels       Mariners     2            1            05/05/95  1
Angels       Mariners     6            7            05/05/95  2
Reds         Marlins      7            6            05/05/95  1
Red Sox      Yankees      3            4            05/05/95  1
```

As you can see, the product of the union operation holds all rows that appears in either parent relation.

Intersection

The *intersection* operation compares two relations, and builds a relation that contains an instance of every row that appears in both of the relations it compares.

As with the union operation, the two relations that the intersection operation compares must have identical structures.

For example, consider the relations MYGAMES and YOURGAMES described above. When we perform the intersection operation upon those two relations, it builds this relation:

```
<HT:MLBT>    <VT:MLBT>    <HT-RUNS:BR> <VT-RUNS:BR> <DG:GDAT> <GNUM:NUM>
White Sox    Brewers      2            8            05/05/95  1
```

As you can see, the intersection operation produces a new relation that contains the one row common to both relations that we compared.

Difference

The *difference* operation, as its name implies, determines how two relations differ. It compares two relations and builds a new relation that contains every row that is in the first relation and not in the second. As with the union and intersection operations, the two relations that the difference operation compares must have identical structures.

For example, if we perform a difference operation upon relations MYGAMES and YOURGAMES, we receive the following relation as its product:

```
<HT:MLBT>   <VT:MLBT>   <HT-RUNS:BR> <VT-RUNS:BR> <DG:GDAT> <GNUM:NUM>
 Braves      Cubs        3            5            05/05/95  1
 Angels      Mariners    2            1            05/05/95  1
 Angels      Mariners    6            7            05/05/95  2
```

As you can see, the difference operation produces a relation whose body contains every row that is in MYGAMES and is not in YOURGAMES.

Thus, the row that gives the score for the White Sox-Brewers game is eliminated, because it appears in both parent relations.

Because this operation determines which rows in the first relation are not in the second, it matters which relation comes first. Thus, the operation

```
difference MYGAMES YOURGAMES
```

will not give the same result as operation:

```
difference YOURGAMES MYGAMES
```

Cartesian product

The *Cartesian-product* operation builds a new relation by joining every row in one relation with every row in a second relation. (The "Cartesian product" is named after the French mathematician René Descartes, who first described this operation.) Unlike the union, intersection, and restriction operations, the Cartesian-product operation does not require that the relations being compared be identically structured.

To give a simple example of this operation, consider two relations — named, respectively, FIRST and SECOND — that are each comprised of a single attribute.

Relation FIRST contains the follow attribute and rows:

```
<NUMBER:INT>
1
2
3
```

SECOND contains the following attribute and rows:

```
<LETTER:ALPHA>
A
B
C
```

The Cartesian-product operation creates the following relation:

```
<NUMBER:INT>  <LETTER:ALPHA>
1             A
2             A
3             A
1             B
2             B
3             B
1             C
2             C
3             C
```

As you can see, this operation in effect pasted each row from SECOND onto the end of each row in FIRST, to create every possible unique row from bodies of the two relations.

Naturally, the question arises, What good is this? The answer is that although the Cartesian product of two relations is not much use by itself can be very useful when combined with other operations. In particular, it is useful with the restrict and project operations. We will see this demonstrated in a moment.

Restrict

The first four operations — union, intersection, difference, and Cartesian product — are used to manipulate sets of all types, not just relations. The next four operations are tailored for use with relations.

The *restrict* operation examines a single relation. It builds a new relation whose body consists of rows selected from the original row using specified criteria.

A programmer must give to this operation the criteria with which it selects rows from a relation. For example, we can perform the restrict operation upon the relation MYGAMES to select the rows in which HT equals "Angels." Doing so produces the following relation:

```
<HT:MLBT>   <VT:MLBT>   <HT-RUNS:BR> <VT-RUNS:BR> <DG:GDAT> <GNUM:NUM>
Angels      Mariners    2            1            05/05/95  1
Angels      Mariners    6            7            05/05/95  2
```

The new relation that it builds has the same structure as its parent relation, but its body is restricted to the rows that meet the requested criteria.

Project

The *project* operation examines a single relation. It builds a new relation whose body consists of attributes selected from the original relation. In effect, it does for attributes what the restrict operation performs for rows.

For example, suppose that we were just interested in the number of runs scored by the home team. We could use the project operation on relation MYGAME to eliminate all attributes except HT and HT-RUNS, thus producing the following relation:

```
<HT:MLBT>    <HT-RUNS:BR>
Braves       3
White Sox    2
Angels       2
Angels       6
```

Join

The *join* operation builds a new relation by fusing two existing relations. It resembles the Cartesian-product operation, except that it uses common values from one or more attributes in the two relations to build the new relation selectively.

The join operation lets us refine the Cartesian product by selectively joining the rows based on the contents of one or more attributes that are shared by the two parent relations — that is, based on a foreign key.

For example, if we use the join operation to fuse relation GAMES with relation STADIUMS based on a shared value in attribute HT, we get the following:

```
<HT>       <VT>      <HT-RUNS> <VT-RUNS> <DG>       <GNUM> <HTS>
Braves     Cubs      3         5         05/05/95   1      Fulton County Stadium
White Sox  Brewers   2         8         05/05/95   1      Comiskey Park
Angels     Mariners  2         1         05/05/95   1      Anaheim Stadium
Angels     Mariners  6         7         05/05/95   2      Anaheim Stadium
```

As you can see, this example in effect adds the attribute of home stadium to each row in MYGAMES. The join also eliminated one instance of the shared attribute, because it is redundant.

The join operation is one of the most useful of all operations in the relational algebra. We use it again and again throughout this book. It is not, however, an atomic operation: in fact, it is a combination of the Cartesian product, restrict, and project operations. Because it is so useful, however, we will treat it as if it were an atomic operation.

One last point should be made: the joining we described here is only one of many ways in which two relations can be joined. This type of join is called the *natural join*. The natural join is the most commonly used of the join operations; and usually the one meant when one speaks of joining two relations.

Divide

The *divide* operation is a specialized operation that combines the restrict and project operations to divide one relation by another.

A foreign key must join the relation to be divided and the relation that does the dividing. The divide operation finds every value in the dividend relation's nonkey attributes in which those nonkey attributes share a row with every value in the divisor relation's foreign key.

If this seems obscure, don't worry — the divide operation is more easily explained by example than by definition. Consider one relation, named FRUITS:

```
<FN:NAME>     <DESC:ADJ>
apple         red
apple         crisp
apple         tart
cherry        red
cherry        sweet
cherry        stone
orange        orange
orange        juicy
orange        sweet
peach         fuzzy
peach         juicy
peach         sweet
```

Now, consider the relation SOMEATTS:

```
<DESC:ADJ>
red
sweet
```

A foreign key on the attribute DESC joins FRUITS and SOMEATTS.

When we divide FRUITS by SOMEATTS, we find every value in the nonkeyed attribute of FRUITS that shares a row with every value in the foreign key of SOMEATTS.

In this example, the divide operation will find every value of attribute FRUITS:FN that shares a row with each of the values given in attribute SOMEATTS:DESC — that is, it will find every fruit that is both red and sweet.

In our example, the divide operation produces the following relation as its output:

```
<FN:NAME>
cherry
```

This is because only cherry is both red and sweet.

As we noted above, the divide operation is a hybrid operation—that is, it actually combines the restrict and project operations to perform a special task. As you will see later, this operation can be quite helpful in manipulating relations.

Comparison operations

Each of Codd's eight basic operations manipulates one or two relations, and builds a relation as its output. His suite of operations, however, does not include comparison operations—that is, operations that compare two relations for similarity or dissimilarity and return a simple value that indicates whether they meet the test. Anyone who has programmed knows how important these are to any programming language.

To meet this need, Codd proposed a further set of *comparison operations*. These operations are sometimes called *theta operations,* because in Codd's notation each operation in this set was represented by the Greek letter theta.

The theta operations have the following syntax:

```
expression theta expression
```

where *theta* is one of the following:

=	Equals
!=	Not equals
<=	Subset
<	Proper subset
>=	Superset
>	Proper superset

Please note that the above notation uses C-language operators rather than the mathematical symbols that Codd originally used for the same operations. For example, we use != *for not equals* rather than an equal sign with a slash through it.

As some commentators have noted, the above notation is a little misleading. In particular, the operations >= and < do not necessarily yield inversions of each other. However, the theta operations on the whole are well selected and useful.

Cross-Reference   Examples of their use are given in Chapter 3, when we discuss SQL.

Relational calculus

Relational calculus, unlike the relational algebra, does not describe operations upon relations. Rather, it lets you formulate the relation that you wish to build. Relational calculus does not bother with the details of how to build the relation. In other words, relational algebra is *prescriptive*, whereas relational calculus is *descriptive*.

You probably have noticed that we speak of "relational calculus" instead of "*the* relational calculus.*"* In fact, there are two commonly used systems of relational calculus: *row-oriented calculus* and *domain-oriented calculus*. The two systems are logically equivalent: whatever you can say in one, you can also say in the other.

Each form of calculus is a model for commonly used relational query languages. The domain-oriented calculus is the basis for the Query-by-Example (QBE) language; the row-oriented relational calculus is the basis for IBM's Structured Query Language (SQL). For the sake of brevity, we discuss only the row-oriented relational calculus.

Syntax

The row-oriented calculus has this syntax:

```
target-relation selection-expression
```

`target-relation` defines the relation that is to be built. It consists of one or more attributes. By convention, the names of the attributes are separated by commas. Each attribute must already reside in an existing relation, but you can rename one or more of them if you wish. These attributes will be populated with data that are copied from existing relations.

`selection-expression` describes how to select rows from existing relations. This expression uses a comparison operator (=, !=, <, <=, >, or >=) to couple an attribute with either another attribute or with a constant. Expressions can be coupled with the logical operators AND and OR. By convention, the selection-expression is introduced by the keyword WHERE.

For example, consider the relation MYGAMES, which we described in the previous section. The following creates a new relation that consists of the attribute HT, and populates that attribute with the name of the winning team in games where the game was played on May 5, 1995, and the home team won:

```
MYGAMES.HT
WHERE MYGAMES.DG =  05/05/95
AND MYGAMES.HT-RUNS > MYGAMES.VT-RUNS
```

As you can see, the `selection-expression` sets the conditions under which a row can populate the newly defined relation.

EXISTS and FORALL

The keyword EXISTS can be used to refine a selection. EXISTS states that a row exists that fulfills a given condition. In effect, this keyword lets you select rows based on one or more values in a row that is not itself a candidate for selection.

For example, consider the relations MYGAMES and STADIUMS, described above.

The following code also selects the names of each team that won at home on May 5, 1995 — but only if that team played in Wrigley Field:

```
MYGAMES.HT
WHERE MYGAMES.DG =  05/05/95
AND MYGAMES.HT-RUNS > MYGAMES.VT-RUNS
AND (EXISTS STADIUMS (MYGAMES.HT = STADIUMS.HT
AND STADIUMS.HTS = Wrigley Field))
```

Finally, the keyword FORALL executes selection-expression for each row that meets the given condition.

For example, consider again the relations MYGAMES and STADIUMS.

The following builds a row that holds the name of the stadium in which the home team won a game on May 5, 1995:

```
HTS:STAD
WHERE FORALL MYGAMES (MYGAMES.HT = STADIUMS.HT
AND MYGAMES.DG =  05/05/95
AND MYGAMES.HT-RUNS > MYGAMES.VT-RUNS)
```

The two conditional keywords differ subtly but significantly. EXISTS declares that selection-expression should be executed if at least one row fulfills the condition set in the EXISTS clause.

FOREACH, on the other hand, declares that selection-expression must be executed for every row that fulfills the condition set in the FOREACH clause.

As a rule of thumb, think of EXISTS as resembling an if clause, which turns on or off the execution of an entire expression; whereas FOREACH is more like a loop operator, such as for or while in the C language, which executes an expression for every value that meets its condition.

Relational algebra versus relational calculus

Codd's reduction algorithm proves that the calculus and the algebra are equivalent: every statement within a relational calculus can be reduced to a set of expressions in the relational algebra; and each set of operations within the relational algebra can be summed up by a statement in a relational calculus.

So, how does the relational algebra compare with relational calculus? As we noted earlier, the algebra is prescriptive, whereas the calculus is descriptive: the algebra says what to do, whereas the calculus describes the result that is to be obtained.

This difference is important, because these approaches — algebra or calculus — are used as the models for designing relational query languages. You won't be too far off the mark if you think of relational algebra as being a kind of relational third-generation language, in which you describe the operations, step by step, in order to obtain the result that you have in mind, and think of the relational calculus as being more like a fourth-generation language, in which you describe the outcome that you want but let the system determine the algebraic steps required to bring that end about.

Relational completeness

Most relational query languages are calculus-based, because such languages are easier to grasp, but they include some algebra-like features that let users tune the language's behavior. As discussed in Chapter 3, SQL is such a hybrid.

Because relational calculus and relational algebra are models for relational query languages, they also give us a way to test the robustness of those languages. A language is said to be *relationally complete* if everything that can be expressed in the relational calculus can be expressed in that language without having to use a loop. Because the relational calculus and the relational algebra are equivalent, a language is relationally complete if it implements Codd's eight basic algebraic operators, described above.

To our knowledge, no relational query language is relationally complete. Some come closer than others. You should keep the rule of relational completeness in mind whenever you evaluate a new language or tool for interrogating relational databases.

NULL

To this point in our discussion of the relational model, we have assumed that every attribute of every row is populated with a member of the domain that that attribute represents. Sometimes, however, we run into situations where, for whatever reason, the value of an attribute is not known.

Sometimes, the data are missing due to error or human failing: a person did not type the information into the system, or could not remember it. In other cases, the given item of information does not apply to the entity that the row describes.

To handle these situations, the relational model introduces the notion of NULL. NULL is not a value. Rather, it is a symbol that marks that a given datum is not known.

Three-tiered logic

By design, NULL does not equal any other value, nor does it equal the outcome of any expression, regardless of whether the expression evaluates to TRUE or FALSE. Logically, its value is neither TRUE nor FALSE.

That NULL's logical value is neither TRUE nor FALSE creates some special problems when you evaluate the result of an expression: you must provide for the fact that an expression yields three logical outcomes, not just two.

That a relational expression can yield any of three possible logical outcomes means that the relational model uses a three-tiered logic. The truth tables for the relational model's three-tiered logic follow. Note that T indicates true; F indicates false; and ? indicates NULL.

The AND truth table:

	T	F	?
T	T	F	?
F	F	F	F
?	?	F	?

The OR truth table:

	T	F	?
T	T	T	T
F	T	F	?
?	T	?	?

The NOT truth table:

T	F	?
F	T	?

As you can see, the three-tiered logic creates certain problems for programmers. In particular, it gives you a third value for which you must explicitly check when you examine the logical value returned by an expression.

Although it may not be clear from the truth tables, NULL does not equate with any value, nor can it be greater or lesser than any value: any comparison with a variable that is NULL always yields NULL — including comparing NULL with NULL. As normal coding procedures usually assume that an expression is either TRUE or FALSE, this can create difficulties. For example, if X is TRUE and Y is NULL, then neither expression

```
if (X == Y)
```

nor expression

```
if (X != Y)
```

is TRUE; rather, each returns NULL.

To handle this situation, SQL has a special operation for performing logical comparison (see Chapter 3).

Keys and NULL

As we noted earlier, relations use primary and foreign keys. A primary key is any combination of attributes that uniquely identifies each row within the relation. A foreign key is a combination of one or more attributes that uniquely identifies one or more rows within another relation.

The definition of key requires that we compare attributes to determine whether they are the same. However, when we compare NULL with any value, including NULL, we do not receive a meaningful value — such a comparison always yields NULL. For this reason, NULL cannot be inserted into any attribute that comprises part of any primary or secondary key.

Using NULL in a key will violate database integrity. We discuss database integrity at greater length later in this chapter.

The great NULL controversy

The NULL has both costs and benefits associated with it.

✦ The cost of NULL is mainly that programmers must write code to cope with the fact that an expression can have three logical results, not just two.

✦ On the plus side, NULL offers the benefit of a standard way to handle missing values. Furthermore, NULL gives the relational model a way to permit an attribute to have missing values or forbid it from having them.

C. J. Date and E. F. Codd, who are the two most important expositors of the relational database, have exactly opposite views on the NULL.

Date states unequivocally that NULL is wrong, and that NULLs wreck the relational model. He also suggests that the need for nullity indicates poor database design. Date suggests that to indicate nullity, a database should use a special value that lies within the domain — although the tone of his writing suggests that he is uncomfortable with this suggestion.

On the other hand, Codd, who invented the relational model, states that the NULL is an inherent part of the relational model. Codd's most recent writings describe two types of NULL — one, the *appropriate NULL*, for information that we can know about a subject but just don't know; and the other, *inappropriate NULL*, for data that cannot be known because they describe nonexistent entities.

When faced with such strongly differing opinions from such respected authorities, it is unclear what our position should be. NULLs are a fact of life; however, no law says that a database you write must use them. Our opinion is that NULLs are useful, and for many tasks there simply is no practical substitution. However, you should handle them carefully, and realize that they will complicate your work. This will become clearer as we begin to program databases.

Relational integrity

At this point, we have seen what data are; how data comprise relations; and how relations can be compared and modified to form new relations.

To this point, we have been working with relations that are static — although we have extracted data from relations, we have not inserted rows into them, nor have we removed rows from them or modified rows within them.

After we begin to do so, however, we encounter what is perhaps the most important problem in programming a relational database: maintaining the integrity of the database.

Integrity has three aspects: *database integrity, domain integrity,* and *transaction integrity.* Each is discussed in turn.

Database integrity

In a nutshell, database integrity means that every foreign key points to at least one existing row.

This restriction is easy to understand, but not so easy to enforce. It especially comes into play when we are adding rows to a database or deleting rows from it.

Additions

When a row is added to a relation, one must confirm that each foreign key within that row references a row that exists.

For example, consider again our relations BBTEAMS

```
<TEAM:MLBT>    <HS:STAD>
Braves         Fulton County Stadium
Cubs           Wrigley Field
White Sox      Comiskey Park
Brewers        Milwaukee County Stadium
Mariners       Kingdome
Angels         Anaheim Stadium
```

and GAMES:

```
<HT:MLBT>   <VT:MLBT>   <HT-RUNS:BR>   <VT-RUNS:BR>   <DG:GDAT>   <GNUM:NUM>
Braves      Cubs        3              5              05/05/95    1
White Sox   Brewers     2              8              05/05/95    1
Angels      Mariners    2              1              05/05/95    1
Angels      Mariners    6              7              05/05/95    2
```

It is reasonable to make attribute GAMES:HT a foreign key for attribute BBTEAMS:TEAM. After all, that would let us build, if we wished, a relation that included the name of the stadium in which the game was played.

After we have done so, then we must ensure that for every row that we insert into GAMES, there must be a value for attribute BBTEAMS:TEAM that exactly matches the value for attribute GAMES:HT.

Please note that the relational model dictates that database integrity must be maintained, but it does not indicate how it is to be maintained.

Now, the question arises: what to do if inserting a given row were to violate database integrity? In most instances, the correct response is to throw the row away and return an error message.

Deletions

Database integrity can be a major issue when you attempt to delete rows from a relation. The problem is to ensure that when you remove a row, you do not orphan other rows whose foreign keys reference the row being removed.

There are three strategies for handling this situation:

✦ The first strategy is to refuse to delete a row if another row references it through a foreign key.

✦ The second strategy is to remove all rows that reference the original row. This strategy has obvious problems, especially if the rows that reference the row being deleted themselves are referenced by still more rows. If you are not careful, this strategy will blow a huge hole into your database, with the greatest of ease. This strategy also presents some interesting problems if two rows reference each other and you attempt to delete one of them.

✦ The third strategy is to modify the keys that reference the row being deleted, so that they point to another row — perhaps one that holds a default value. This is safer than the second strategy, but it must be done carefully, or you can wind up with rows whose foreign keys are meaningless.

The relational model does not dictate the strategy to use. As you can see, each of these strategies has its problems. It just goes to show that in a tightly designed relational database, the deletion of rows is, at best, a problematic action.

Updates

When you update a row, you must ensure that the modification:

✦ Does not change a foreign key so that it references a nonexistent row. This is always an error.

✦ Does not change a value that is referenced by a foreign key. This may be an error or it may simply be part of a wave of changes that you make to your database. Thus, in some instances the proper response is to refuse to make the change; in others, the proper response is to cascade the change through the database.

In either case, you must determine whether the change is an error, and do so based in part on domain-level considerations, which leads us to our next topic — domain integrity.

Domain integrity

Domain integrity refers to the fact that although some attributes are not bound to each other logically, they are bound to each other in the real world. That is, the attributes may not necessarily reference each other as keys, or even be part of the same relation, but they are bound to each other by the nature of the entity or event that each describes in part.

Another term for domain integrity is *semantic integrity* (from the Greek word for "meaning").

The word *semantic* pops up in the academic literature in many different combinations — for example, *semantic restrictions* or *semantic-level integrity* — but all refer to restrictions derived from the meaning of the entity or event being described. *Rule* is also used for a semantic-level restriction; thus, a *rule-based system* is one that is based in part upon a programmer's articulation of semantic-level restrictions.

The following gives some of the commoner types of rules:

✦ If A occurs, B cannot occur.

✦ If A occurs, B must also occur.

✦ The value of A limits the possible values of B.

A well-designed database system articulates such rules, and does its best to enforce them. However, the relational model does not address the issue of semantic-level integrity.

Some relational database management systems implement *triggers,* which you can use to enforce some rules. However, for the most part the enforcement of rules is up to you. You will find that much of the work of designing and implementing a database involves articulating and coding the rules with which you will enforce the semantic integrity of your database.

Methods of enforcing integrity

Relational database management systems have implemented a number of methods to help enforce integrity. These methods are not part of the relational model *per se*; however, we introduce them here because you will encounter them throughout your work with relational databases.

Transactions

A *transaction* treats a series of modifications to the database as though it were one modification: either all of the modifications to the database succeed, or none are applied to the database; and if the modifications happen, they all are applied to the database simultaneously.

With transactions, either all modifications are made to the database, or none are. For example, if an order-entry system writes multiple records into the database for each order, a transaction guarantees that a partial order will not be entered: either all the records in an order will be written into the database, or none of them will be. The transaction either all of an order will be written into the database, or none of it will be.

If you discover an error, you can roll back the modifications made since the beginning of the transaction: it will be as if they never occurred. If a modification has side effects — for example, if deletion of a row causes a cascade of deletions of other rows that reference it — those side effects are undone as well.

The transaction mechanism is helpful; however, it is up to you, as the database's implementer, to determine what comprises a transaction. You must, by hand, begin the transaction; then, after an appropriate number of modifications have taken place, you must test whether the result is correct or not, and then either commit the modifications to the database, or roll them back.

Cross-Reference   We will discuss transactions at greater length in Chapter 3, when we introduce SQL.

Indexing

A database index, like the index of a book, gives you an orderly, quick way to find the physical location of a given piece of information.

For example, in our GAMES relation described above, you may wish to build an index for attribute HT. This would let you quickly look up all the rows for which a given team was at home.

We mention indexing here because SQL uses indexes to enforce some integrity rules. In particular, it uses the index to enforce the rule that forbids duplicate rows within a relation.

Indexes are very useful, but they can also consume a great deal of processing time and disk space. Thus, the devising of a set of indexes for your database is something of a black art, based in large part upon a profile of how your database is used, and the bottlenecks therein.

Cross-Reference   We discuss the art of indexing at greater length in Chapter 4.

Query language

One last aspect of the relational model remains to be discussed: the query language.

The relational model mandates the existence of a query language with which a person can establish and manipulate relations and rows. Such a language, to be relationally complete, must be able to implement the eight basic relational operations that we described earlier, in the section on relational algebra.

Many relational-database languages have been created; the most popular is Structured Query Language (SQL), which is introduced in Chapter 3.

A *relational* query language does not have to implement many of the features commonly associated with a programming language. Most query languages implement some features of a true programming language; for example, most query languages let you perform arithmetic and declare variables. However, many query languages depend upon a wrapper language (such as C, Java, or Perl) to implement such features as input/output (I/O) or loops.

Codd's 12 rules of relational databases

The relational model gives us a proven, complete model for our databases. However, translating this model into bits that you can install and run on your Linux system is challenging.

Some complications arise from the fact that aspects of the relational model are difficult to implement. Other complications arise from the fact that some early implementations of the relational model cut corners in some ways. These have affected the development of relational databases, and may well have stunted them. Some persons argue that SQL itself falls into this category; certainly, some features of SQL (such as the fact that it permits a table to hold duplicate rows) are definitely nonrelational.

Other complications arise from the fact that people have an enormous investment in existing technology, and that they simply cannot throw it away, regardless of how good the alternative is — if you have bought a lemon and can't afford to junk it, you just have to drive it.

Given that there is a gap between the ideal of the relational model and the reality of the implemented database, how can we judge whether a database that claims to be relational is, in fact, a relational database? In 1985, E. F. Codd published 12 criteria with which you can judge whether a given database system is truly relational. No database management system fulfills all 12 criteria; but the criteria do give us a rule of thumb with which we can judge the degree to which a database management system fulfills the relational model. The following paraphrases Codd's 12 criteria, and comments upon them:

1. *The database stores all data within rows.* This is the first commandment of relational databases, the rule from which all others flow.

2. *Every datum can be accessed through the combination of the name of its relation, the name of its attribute, and the value of its row's primary key.* This is self-explanatory.

3. *NULL values are implemented systematically.* The NULL must be implemented as described above—that is, as a value that differs from every other value within the attribute's domain, and using three-tiered logic.

4. *The database's catalogue is itself stored within one or more relations that can be read by authorized users.* The catalogue names the relations, attributes, and keys that comprise the database. Its contents can be read by users who have appropriate permission, in order to interrogate the database and manipulate its contents. This rule of Codd's introduces the notion of *permissions*, which is not, strictly speaking, a part of the relational model. In brief, permissions means that certain database tasks are restricted to selected users. These tasks can include creating a database, creating or destroying relations, and granting permissions to other users. We will describe permissions in more detail in the next chapter.

5. *The system implements a query language.* This language lets a user:

   • Define a relation.

   • Define views.

   • Manipulate data.

   • Set constraints to enforce database integrity.

   • Grant and remove permission to view or manipulate a relation.

   • Bundle manipulations of the database as a transaction.

   Codd does not mandate a specific query language. Given his well-articulated distaste for SQL, Codd certainly does not mandate that a relational database management system must implement SQL—even though SQL is supported by most commercial packages that claim to be relational.

6. *The system must be able to update through a view.* A *view* is a temporary relation that exists only to make data available for viewing. Views can be quite convenient, because they permit a user to assemble data for viewing, without having to go through the overhead of defining, creating, and populating a fully featured relation. Many database management systems also can hold views—or rather, the code with which a view is generated—within the database itself, thus permitting users to select and build views as they work.

7. *The system must be able to insert, update, and delete sets of rows—not just one row at a time.* This rule mandates that rows be viewed as elements of a set. This is one feature of the relational database that sets it apart from other types of databases; we discuss this further later in this chapter.

8. *The programs with which the database is manipulated are independent of how the database is physically stored or accessed.* In other words, a relational database should appear the same and behave the same across all computer platforms. Most database management systems strive to fulfill this mandate, although usually there are some differences from platform to platform — some minor, some major.

9. *The programs with which the database is manipulated are independent of how the database is logically organized internally.* This does not apply to the definition of the database's relations, but it does apply to how the database management system implements those relations. Among other things, this rule mandates that code should survive upgrades to DBMS software. Again, most database management systems strive to fulfill this mandate, but not all succeed completely.

10. *Rules that articulate semantic-level integrity should be describable within the database management system's query language, be storable within the database system's catalogues, and be enforceable by the database management system itself.* In other words, a programmer should be able to code semantic integrity directly into the database itself, instead of having to write customized code to enforce semantic rules. To our knowledge, no commercial relational database management system implements this rule, except in a rudimentary way.

11. *A relational database should operate exactly the same whether housed on a single machine or distributed over a network.* This rule is becoming ever more important, as it becomes common to distribute a single database over a network of machines.

12. *No one can use a low-level language to subvert the database's integrity rules.* In other words, everyone must use the high-level language — with its built-in rules and integrity measures — to manipulate the database. This is in part a security measure, and in part a way of slowing down the corruption of the database through shortcuts implemented by well-intentioned programmers. This rule is a key to slowing the effects that the law of entropy inevitably will wreak upon your database.

Codd's rules comprise a scorecard for relational databases: the more a package fulfills the letter of these rules, the closer it adheres to the relational model, and therefore the more robust it is.

Hierarchic and Network Databases

Today, the relational model is the principal database tool, but other database designs are also in use: some preceded the relational model, whereas others claim to be successors.

In this section, we discuss two older designs for databases: hierarchic databases and network databases. In the following section, we discuss two designs that claim to be successors to the relational database: the object database and the object-relational database.

The hierarchic database

Modern machines often are built not out of simple parts, but from other, simpler machines; and these component machines are themselves built out of other machines. For example, your personal computer is built out of a motherboard, memory assemblies, disk drives, a keyboard, a monitor, and various peripheral cards. Each of those machines is built out of smaller machines; for example, the motherboard has a microprocessor, glue chips, sockets, cache chips, and other parts; while a hard-disk drive consists of platters, heads, motor, controller board, firmware, and other parts.

To manage the building of a machine as complex as a computer, manufacturers use a form called a *bill of materials*. The bill of materials lists all of the components that comprise the machine to be shipped. Each of those parts, in turn, has its own bill of materials that list its own parts; and each of those parts can have its own bill of materials, until the components cannot be broken down (or *decomposed*) any further.

In the bill of materials, a machine can be comprised of many parts, but a given part can be installed only into one machine. When taken together, the bills of materials form a hierarchy that describe the machine, from the fully assembled computer down to the smallest nut and screw within it.

The *hierarchic database* models the bill of materials in software. It was the first commercially successful electronic database, appearing in the early 1960s, and is still widely used today in mainframe shops. The hierarchic database is so named because relations are arranged hierarchically. In a hierarchic database, a relation points to exactly one parent relation, which owns the relation, and to an indefinite number of child relations that it owns in turn. Such a system is quite useful in specialized situations, such as manufacturing, in which the bill of materials exactly describes the entity that the database models.

A hierarchic database has many advantages: it is easy to implement; has a simple, easily understood structure; and usually has a very fast access time. However, the hierarchic database also has a number of significant limitations. Its chief limitation is that few of the entities that people wish to model in a database decompose neatly into a hierarchic structure. More often than not, the hierarchic design proves to be a limitation rather than a help.

The term "relation," as we defined it earlier, is alien to the vocabulary of hierarchic systems. Often, the entire hierarchy of data is crowded into a single huge record, with static space allocated for a finite number of child records. A child is addressed as an offset in bytes within the record, rather than being a key to another record.

For example, a hierarchic record that describes a computer may allocate space for exactly two hard disk drives. If a machine has only one hard disk drive, the space for the second is allocated but is left empty; if the machine has more than two hard disk drives, some data are lost.

As you see, such a system can be designed and implemented easily, but is inflexible.

The network database

In 1971, another type of database entered the marketplace: the *network database*. This design came about, in part, to solve some of the limitations of the hierarchic database.

In brief, the network database permits a relation to have multiple parents as well as multiple children.

Consider, for example, a sales system. A record for a salesperson is linked to multiple child records, each of which records an order that that salesperson took. Each order record, in turn, can be linked to other parents — say, one for the person who purchased the item, and another for the item purchased. A network database can traverse the database by moving from salesperson to order, then from order either to the next order that that salesperson took or up to the person who placed the order, and so on — much as a datagram bounces through a network.

The network database lets a programmer build a more data structure that is more complex than what can be built with a hierarchic database. It is also fast and is easy to work with. However, it also shares the limitations of the hierarchic system. In particular, it is inflexible: once a database is established, modifying it is extremely difficult.

It is also worth noting that both the hierarchic and network systems were written for programmers rather than for users. Interrogating either database in most instances requires writing a custom program in a middle-level language. The notion of an ad hoc query through an interpreted query language often is alien to these systems.

Object Databases

To this point, we have discussed relational databases and relational theory, and we have briefly discussed hierarchic and network databases. In this section, we introduce another type of database: the object database.

In the early 1990s, object-oriented technology took over from the procedural model as the industry's preferred model for new software development. This change brought major modifications to the very idea of data storage. Early object-oriented practice often tended to ignore formal database methodology by focusing instead on the persistence of individual, small-scale program objects to files. Object-oriented technology actually allowed some great advances in database integration. For instance, *polymorphism*, which enables objects of different properties to respond in an intelligent way to the same message, enables programmers to completely hide the details of database storage in novel ways, using object stubs that automatically update themselves from databases when their data is described.

But problems were introduced by the object revolution. Relational technology had invested many years of research into scalability and simple object persistence did not benefit from such knowledge. In addition, as object-oriented technology became a greater part of an organization's software infrastructure, the need to integrate into legacy data became more urgent. The first approaches to integrating object programming with relational databases involved encapsulating relational queries into object methods and messages, but this exposed difficulties that have come to be known as an impedance mismatch.

The impedance mismatch problem

An *impedance mismatch* is a fundamental difference in the modeling of the same data in different parts of a system. For instance, object-oriented design tends to access data by direct traversal of relationships between objects, taking advantage of capabilities such as polymorphism, which are almost entirely alien to relational databases. This means that programmers must master the two approaches, and must often make translations between the two in order to perform basic tasks. This reduces performance to some extent, and complicates the programming. In addition, optimizations and algorithms that are simple or effective in one model, often show very different behavior in another, complicating the tuning and development of applications.

In the case of object-oriented code connecting to RDBMS, a key component of the impedance mismatch is that the more highly normalized the database, the less readily it corresponds to an object model. We will discuss normalization in a later chapter; in brief, normalization makes databases conform more closely to relational theory, and thus makes them more efficient and easy to manage. When designers develop RDBMS and object-oriented systems in parallel, they tend to reduce the normalization of the database in order to better match the object design, which can sometimes work against the strengths of relational databases.

Storing objects as they are programmed

The solution was to develop a database theory and practice that corresponds to the object-oriented model. This is not as simple as it might appear because just as object-oriented design introduced complexities to programming, it added a new dimension to databases. In OODBMSs (object-oriented database management systems), direct traversal of object relationships is a common form of query, along with the combinatorial queries at the heart of RDBMSs.

The state of the art had been developing independently in the industry until the Object Database Management Group (ODMG) emerged with standards for data definition and querying. The current version of the standards, ODMG 2.0, offers an object definition language (ODL) and an object query language (OQL), providing bindings for Java, C++, and Smalltalk.

Here is an example of ODL for an object that describes employees:

```
class Employee
{
attribute int id;
attribute string name;
attribute date birthday;
attribute Department dept;
boolean paySalary();
}
```

A `class` is the object database representation of an entity. An `attribute` is the equivalent of a column of data, and the types are similar until we get to the `dept` attribute. You will immediately see one difference in object-oriented databases. The relationship with a different class, `Department`, is clearly and directly expressed in the relevant attribute. Traversing this relationship directly produces a reference to the `Department` instance. We discuss `paySalary()` in a moment, but first let us look at the ODL definition of `Department`.

```
class Department
{
attribute int id;
attribute string name;
attribute string city;
relationship Employee heads
inverse Employee::is_head_of;
}
```

Interestingly, OODBMS does not provide a universal mechanism for adding in instances to these classes. This comes from the keen desire for integration into object-oriented programming. The programmer is expected to just create objects as usual in the language of choice, and the OODBMS engine will take care of storing and manipulating certain objects in the database. Objects that are meant to be kept in the database are called *persistent*, and all other objects are called *transient*. The mechanism by which objects are determined to be persistent or transient differs from language to language. In some languages, all objects in a particular class are persistent, but in most cases, an object is treated as persistent if it is created or handled within a database transaction.

So, let us assume that we have created Employee and Department objects in our favorite language. We could determine Carla Wong's location by the following OQL:

```
select dept.city from Employee where name = "Carla Wong"
```

This OQL query might at first seem similar to the equivalent SQL query, but the subtle difference is key. The `from` clause only includes the Employee *extent,* which is the term for all object instances that are members of the `Employee` class. This eliminates the combinatorial problem we ran into in SQL, in which all tables involved in the query had to be analyzed. In this case, the query engine can evaluate the predicate `where name = "Carla Wong"` by only examining the Employee extent, isolating the matching instances (one in this case). Then the query is completed by following a "path" from the instance to the instance referred to by its `department` attribute, to the `city` attribute of that department instance. Listing 2-1 illustrates a conceptual view of this process. Accordingly, such expressions in OQL queries are known as "path" expressions, because they follow a logical path from object attribute to attribute. OODBMSs are optimized so that evaluating path expressions is very efficient, which enables many types of queries to avoid combinatorial complexity.

Listing 2-1: **Object Query Language Path Expressions**

```
Given:
class Order_Line {
    // . . .
String item_description;
Decimal Unit_Price;
Order_Item Item;
    // . . .
};
which contains the object
class Order_Item {
    // . . .
String SKU;
Employee Buyer;
Decimal Unit_Cost;
    // . . .
};
which contains the object
class Employee{
    //...
String Name;
    //...
};

and an instance of a single order line
Order_Line Line;
The path expression for the name of the buyer for a given item
is given by:
Line.Order_Item.Buyer.Name
```

Unfortunately, there are very few OODBMSs, especially when compared to the huge number of relational DBMSs. This is mainly because OODBMSs are difficult to implement, and have not gained a great deal of market acceptance. Under Linux, the choices are even fewer. There are several object-persistence engines that don't provide full-blown OODBMS capabilities, such as Zope for Python. Python even has an advanced nonpersistent object store in Gadfly. There is also 4ODS, an OODBMS wrapper for relational databases, developed by FourThought LLC, where one author works. We hope that there will be more OODBMS options soon to match the variety of object-oriented tools available for Linux users.

The object-relational compromise

Many RDBMSs, recognizing the great advantages of OODBMSs, have developed a compromise between the two models: object-relational database management system (ORDBMS). The details of ORDBMS differ from product to product, but in general, it involves providing features such as classes as a specialization of tables, inheritance of classes, and more powerful relationships between classes.

ORDBMS enables organizations to migrate gradually to object systems, while protecting their investment in legacy systems. ORDBMS has proven very popular in the marketplace.

Choosing a Type of Database

When you choose the type of database to work with, you should match the database with the requirements of your task.

The hierarchic and network databases can be a good choice when your data have a hierarchic structure, you expect a high volume of processing, and you expect the structure of your data to change infrequently. For example, payroll systems, sales systems, and manufacturing systems all are well suited to hierarchic or network databases. When properly implemented, these systems are fast, robust, and easily developed.

The object-oriented database is a good choice when you will be handling very complex types of data, such as graphics or sound bites, especially when the queries that users will perform on the database are well defined. The object-oriented database shines when users use these data interactively over a network.

The chief advantage of the relational database is its flexibility. The relational database lets you build complex models out of small relations that you hooked together through foreign keys. Because there is no practical limit on the number of relations you can add to a database, or to the number of ways that you can hook those relations together, you can use the relational model to model an extremely complex entity or event.

The relational model lets you graft new relations onto a database without disturbing the relations that are already within the database (except for considerations of relational integrity). Thus, the flexibility of the relational database means that it can withstand change more easily than can the other designs of database.

Finally, the relational model does not limit a user's queries to predefined paths. The user can use all of the database's attributes to build queries — the user is not limited to the queries that the database programmer built into the database. Users can ask questions of the database that were never imagined when the database was designed. This feature alone makes the relational database extremely valuable to business and science.

The bottom line is that the more complex the entity is that you are modeling, and the more that you expect your model to change over time — either as the entity itself grows and changes, or as you learn more about the entity — the more you should consider using a relational database.

Application Architectures

Databases can be so complex and resource-intensive that they appear almost an end in themselves. But it's important to remember that databases are only part of an application. The structure, design, and usage patterns of databases are all dependent on the application architecture that is employed. We have already seen how connecting a relational database to object-oriented code can cause impedance mismatch. By aligning the database design more closely to the immediate needs of other parts of the application, the effect on the database can also be positive.

The software industry has moved through several phases in which various architectures were prevalent. Originally, most database applications were on mainframes and the database and the application sat together, communicating through message protocols, and the user machine was a dumb terminal that displayed a basic form generated by the application on the remote mainframe.

Client-server

For a variety of reasons, personal computer workstations gained great popularity in business, and with it came a major new approach to databases: client-server. Until quite recently, most databases were designed for the client-server model. The server is typically a very high-performance computer hosting the data store, query engine, and perhaps administration tools. There are then multiple clients, each a PC on a user's desk, which host full-blown application code that connects to the server over the network. Figure 2-1 illustrates the client-server architecture.

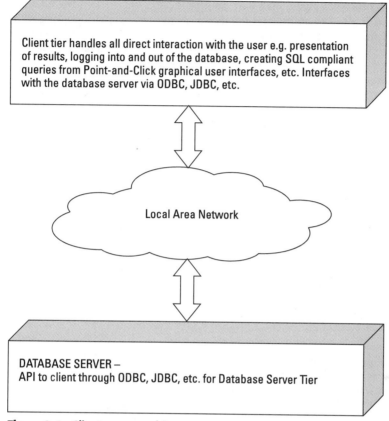

Figure 2-1: Client-server architecture

The client always has the code to display the application interface to the user. Beyond that, the division of labor is fuzzy. A typical approach is that the client code involves much of the logic of the application, processing the raw data according to the user's requests and the business rules. The client manages data coming in from other sources such as real-time data, and collaborates with code libraries and third-party modules. The database server handles the raw data storage. As stored procedures become more prevalent and more mature, developers often migrate routine, low-level processing tasks to the server, especially when they are highly coupled to the persistent data.

Three-tier architecture

Developers discovered that having the display code tightly coupled to the application logic was problematic. When the display layout needed to be changed, a great deal of application logic code would often be affected, and vice versa, causing excessive maintenance costs. This was no new theoretical insight: the basic computer science goals of coupling and cohesion should have forbidden display and logic from being too tightly interwoven. As object-oriented technology emerged and, coincidentally, developers began to attend more to design issues, many business applications separated the display routines from the core logic, bringing about the three-tier architecture (see Figure 2-2).

The user-interface layer contains the display and user input routines. The middle tier contains core application logic. In modern practice, the middle tier is often subdivided according to the needs of the particular application, and so this model is sometimes called the *N-tier model*.

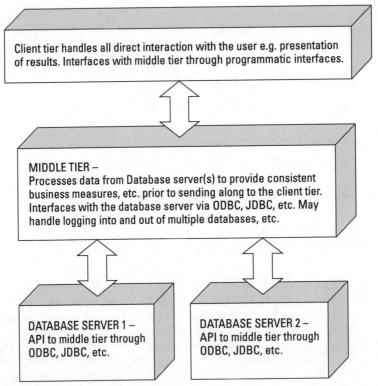

Client tier handles all direct interaction with the user e.g. presentation of results. Interfaces with middle tier through programmatic interfaces.

MIDDLE TIER –
Processes data from Database server(s) to provide consistent business measures, etc. prior to sending along to the client tier. Interfaces with the database server via ODBC, JDBC, etc. May handle logging into and out of multiple databases, etc.

DATABASE SERVER 1 –
API to middle tier through ODBC, JDBC, etc.

DATABASE SERVER 2 –
API to middle tier through ODBC, JDBC, etc.

Figure 2-2: Three-tier architecture

To illustrate the components of a multitier application using a database as the source of the information, we use the three-tier model. The back end is where we conceptually place the database server(s). These servers are the source of the raw data that is eventually presented to the user. If, for example, the user wishes to view sales revenue information along with product description information, the data will most likely come from two databases, one having the sales data, and one having the product and inventory data. However, both sources are part of the back end. If the user is performing order-entry tasks, then the back end includes at least the Sales database and the Product and Inventory database. The actual databases that make up the back end are dependent on the application that is running on the front end.

So, what happens in the middle tier? There are numerous tasks that occur, but the important processes basically fall into one of two classes: applying business rules to the data coming from the back-end databases as the data is passed to the front end; and creating database queries (SQL statements) as a result of the user actions on the front end and sending those queries to the back-end database(s). These processes usually work cooperatively in the middle tier.

For example, it is common to have a specific business rule for determining what profitability actually is. In this case, it is beneficial to have a processing component (often called an object) in the middle tier that takes as its inputs a product identifier (SKU), date, and sales region. From this data, it creates and sends queries to the back-end databases to get values for Gross Revenue, Cost of Sales, Manufacturing Cost, Overhead Expense, and the like. It then manipulates this data according to predefined rules in order to provide a consistent value for profitability as its output, which, in turn, may be sent to the front end.

As another example, for an order-entry application, a middle-tier object (or combination of objects) could take as its inputs a product identifier (SKU), order quantity, and a customer number. It could then create queries to send to the back-end databases to record the sales amount in the Sales database, make an entry for the customer order in the Order Entry database, deduct the available stock from the Inventory Database, and so on.

In theory, one could replace one or more of the back-end databases with those of another vendor and not have to change anything whatsoever in either the front end or in any of the middle-tier objects. The same can be said (in theory!) for the front end and middle-tier objects.

The emergence of Web technologies has brought about a variation of the three-tier model, which variation is suited to the browser/Web server combination. We discuss this increasingly common configuration in-depth in Chapter 12. However, it's worthwhile to point out the similarities of the browser/Web server combination to the three-tier model discussed by way of an example of a Web portal.

Beginning with the three-tier model, we have a presentation layer (the user interface or front end) that is implemented using a Web browser inherently browsing HTML files. At the back end are our information sources, in this case, a number of databases. The purpose of the middle layer then is to format the information coming from the data source(s) as HTML documents and present them to your Web browser. The data that is stored in the back-end databases is the *content* that interests us, the end user. So, to a great extent the back end of our model should consist of generic data sources. Because this book is about Linux and databases, we'll just pretend that these data sources are implemented as databases. So, to successfully view and use the data stored on the back-end database servers, the middle-tier components need to:

1. Present a log-in page (it could be a couple of edit boxes on a *public* HTML page) so that your access privileges can be verified and security can be maintained. This is suggested as the preferred method over cookies in which the data to be accessed has any combination of privacy requirements, is proprietary, or the data is sold.

2. Verify the log-in username and password in a portal security database.

3. After verification of the username and password, retrieve the customizations that were previously created. This implies that the middle tier has a database to store your customizations of the default home page (a customized home page is no more than a custom configuration of a set of standard page features).

4. Processing each parameterized custom URL in turn, the server sends each parameterized URL to the appropriate database server, which returns the results of one or more SQL queries. Each result set is formatted for presentation and inserted into the HTML document (your custom home page). After all of the configurable components of your home page are processed, the resulting HTML document is presented to you as your custom home page.

5. If no personalization exits, a default Web page is created and presented.

Modern Advancements

Recent developments in database and application technology have brought about many fundamental changes in databases, many of which are especially relevant to open-source databases.

The era of open standards

It used to be in the software industry that every meaningful standard was a de facto market triumph for a particular vendor. This was especially so in the database world, in which vendors tried to lock-in customers to their own proprietary features to ensure a predictable market base. The emergence of open database standards such as SQL was a long, fractious, and very political process, and it is only recently that DBMS vendors have dedicated themselves to SQL compliance. Organizations that used different database products in different departments or for different applications often found themselves with serious maintenance and interoperability problems.

Fortunately, developer and end-user demand has produced an atmosphere in which vendors are under pressure to create and follow industrywide standards. SQL continues to develop, and standards have emerged for object databases. Technologies such as XML (eXtensible Markup Language) and Java have been driven by standards bodies from the beginning (although not without a great deal of politics, especially in the Java arena), and are now transforming database technology and practice.

Open standards have also been good for that other recent phenomenon of openness: open source. In the days of proprietary standards, open-source solutions (OSS) developers often had to guess or reverse-engineer protocols for interoperability with commercial tools, greatly slowing down the development process. With open standards, OSS developers have a well-documented programming target, and they can concentrate on more interesting problems. Almost every successful OSS project has enjoyed the benefits of a core industry standard.

✦ Linux follows the POSIX standard for operating systems, which is administered by ANSI.

✦ Apache implements HTTP (hypertext transfer protocol), which is standardized by the IETF.

✦ Mozilla implements HTML and CSS (cascading style sheets), which is recommended specifications of the World Wide Web Consortium (W3C).

✦ XFree86 implements the X11 display standard, which is maintained by The Open Group.

✦ GNOME and KDE both use distributed programming tools, based on CORBA (Common Object Request Broker Architecture), which is a standard of the OMG.

✦ Of course, PostgreSQL and MySQL implement ANSI SQL, as well as Java Database Connectivity (JDBC).

Open standards benefit everyone, including vendors, by improving productivity and speeding up the development cycle. Without the standards in use in most Linux databases, it would be impossible to provide in-depth coverage of seven products in a single book.

eXtensible markup language

XML, a standard format for general documents and data, has gained a lot of media attention as an HTML replacement, because it enables better searching, categorization, and linking on the Internet, but it is far more than that, especially to database users.

XML's importance is in the fact that so many vendors and developers have embraced it as a data format. This provides a great boost to interoperability between software components, and allows a lot of work that formerly needed custom, specialized software to be performed by off-the-shelf utilities.

Many databases are moving to support XML, both to enable users to store documents in a rich format within the database, and to provide a means of transmitting structured data between software components. This latter application is known as *serialization*. A possible XML serialization of the relational database we have been using in our examples is as follows:

```
<?xml version="1.0"?>
<Database>
    <Table name="Employee">
        <Row>
            <Column name="id" type="int4">101</Column>
            <Column name="name" type="string">Manny Vegas</Column>
            <Column name="birthday" type="datetime"> 1950-05-10</Column>
            <Column name="dept" type="int4">12</Column>
        </Row>
        <Row>
            <Column name="id" type="int4">102</Column>
            <Column name="name" type="string">Carla Wong</Column>
            <Column name="birthday" type="datetime">1961-12-02</Column>
            <Column name="dept" type="int4">15</Column>
        </Row>
        <Row>
            <Column name="id" type="int4">103</Column>
            <Column name="name" type="string">Arnold Page</Column>
            <Column name="birthday" type="datetime"> 1965-08-21</Column>
            <Column name="dept" type="int4">15</Column>
        </Row>
    </Table>
    <Table name="Department">
        <Row>
            <Column name="id" type="int4">12</Column>
            <Column name="name" type="string">Accounting</Column>
            <Column name="city" type="string">Miami</Column>
        </Row>
        <Row>
            <Column name="id" type="int4">12</Column>
            <Column name="name" type="string">Human Resources</Column>
            <Column name="city" type="string">Gainesville</Column>
        </Row>
    </Table>
</Database>
```

A more natural view of the data that might be generated by advanced relational or object databases might look like this:

```xml
<?xml version="1.0"?>
<company name="Penguin Gifts, Inc.">
    <employee id="101" >
        <name>Manny Vegas</name>
        <birthday format="ISO8601">1950-05-10</birthday>
        <dept>12</dept>
    </employee>
    <employee id="102" >
        <name>Carla Wong</name>
        <birthday format="ISO8601"> 1961-12-02</birthday>
        <dept>12</dept>
    </employee>
    <employee id="103" >
        <name>Arnold Page</name>
        <birthday format="ISO8601"> 1965-08-21</birthday>
        <dept>12</dept>
    </employee>
    <department id="12">
        <name>Accounting</name>
        <location>Miami</location>
    </department>
    <department id="15">
        <name>Human Resources</name>
        <location>Gainesville</location>
    </department>
</company>
```

A lot of the development of XML capabilities in databases has emerged from broader work in storing and managing different data types than the standard integers, strings, and dates. Models to accommodate a rich variety of data types are often known as Universal Database Systems.

Universal databases

SQL-92, the most implemented version, does not support the storage of arbitrary data types such as image files or word-processor documents. This omission has long plagued database users, and DBMS vendors have devised many methods to get around it. The general approach was to provide a new data type known as the Binary Large Object (BLOB). The user would store a BLOB ID in the regular SQL server, and the database would provide a filelike interface to the object.

This approach has several problems. For instance, the developer must use a very different mechanism to manipulate native SQL data and BLOBs — SQL queries in the former case; file calls in the latter case. It is also impossible to make intelligent queries of objects; for instance, to select all images that are photographs taken against a white background.

Stored procedures help a bit. One can then write database procedures that can intelligently query and manipulate BLOBs. By using ORDBMS techniques, extended data types can be organized into classes with specialized operations. Universal databases combine these various capabilities in order to allow a richer variety of data to be stored in databases. Other extensions involve Character Large Objects (CLOBS), which are similar to BLOBS but consist of text data that makes searching and indexing easier.

Most of the Linux databases we discuss offer universal features in one form or another.

Caution   Don't confuse our use of *universal* with the use of the same term by several database vendors to mean "same features on all supported platforms."

Summary

In this chapter, we discussed what a database is.

A database is an orderly body of data and the software that maintains it. A datum is a symbol that describes an entity or event in the real world. A datum has a type, of which the most common are nominal, ordinal, interval, and ratio. A datum also belongs to a domain, which gives all possible values for the aspect of the entity or event that that datum describes. The meaning of a datum depends in large part upon the domain of which it is a member.

Maintaining data means performing four tasks with our body of data: inserting, retrieving, deleting, and updating data. It also means preserving the integrity of the data.

A database is not just a collection of random data. Rather, it consists of relations — that is, of groups of data that are related to one another, and that together describe an entity or event more or less completely.

When we work with a database, we manipulate relations, or groups of related data, not individual data.

The relational model gives a theoretical model for databases. The relational model manipulates relations; a relation is a set of domains that together describe a given entity or event in the real world. A relation is comprised of attributes; an attribute defines a domain's role within the relation. Each attribute has a name that is unique within the relation. An attribute is to a relation what a column is to a table.

Data within the relation are stored in the form of rows. A row is to a relation what a row is to a table. Each row holds exactly one value drawn from each attribute that comprises the relation. Each row can be identified as unique by one or more primary keys, each of which is composed of one or more attributes. A row can also contain one or more foreign keys, each of which identifies one or more rows in another relation.

The relational model has developed two systems for manipulating relations: relational algebra and relational calculus. The algebra is prescriptive — that is, it describes operations that you can perform upon relations. Relational calculus is descriptive — that is, it defines a view, without going into details as to how it is to be built.

The calculus and the algebra are equivalent — any statement in one can be transformed into an equivalent statement in the other. Both the calculus and the algebra are the basis for query languages; a language is relationally complete if it can express, without loops, any expression that can be expressed in the relational algebra.

The relational model uses NULL to handle situations in which a value for an attribute is not known. NULL is guaranteed to be not equivalent to any value in any domain; thus, comparing any value with NULL will always be false. Logically, NULL is neither TRUE nor FALSE; thus, statements in a relational language must be evaluated with a three-tier logic.

Databases must guard the integrity of their structures, and of the data they contain. Structural integrity ensures that every foreign key points to an existing row. Data integrity means ensuring that data do not contain impossible values, with impossible being determined in part by other data within the relation.

There is a gap between the relational model in the abstract, and its implementation as software. E. F. Codd defined 12 rules for gauging just how relational a relational database management system is.

We compared the relational database with hierarchic, network, and object-oriented databases. There are many variations on these technologies in Linux databases, which we discuss in coming chapters, but most fall into the ORDBMS category.

New technologies and developments are constantly changing the database world, and Linux users are definitely a beneficiary of industry advancements.

Next, we discuss the classifications of data that you might need to manage with Linux DBMS and try to suggest a strategy based on your particular needs.

✦　　✦　　✦

SQL

Chapter 2 discussed the theory of the relational database. This chapter introduces structured query language (SQL). SQL is by far the most popular query language for relational databases, and it is supported by all of the major manufacturers of relational database management systems, including Informix, Sybase, and Oracle.

In this chapter, we begin to write code to implement databases. Doing so prepares you for Chapter 4, which discusses the art and science of designing a database.

Origins of SQL

When E. F. Codd published his initial work on relational databases in 1969, it attracted the interest of a number of database researchers, including a group at IBM.

In 1974, about five years after Codd's initial publication, IBM formed its System/R project, which was given the task of designing and building a prototype relational database system. As you recall, Codd's specification for a relational database mandated that a query language be created, and that this query language must be the only avenue by which data can be manipulated within the database. Thus, as part of its design of a relational database, the System/R project designed a query language that they named SEQUEL, later renamed SQL, or Structured Query Language. (By the way, it is common for the string SQL to be pronounced "sequel" — thus preserving a phonetic ghost of the language's original name.)

System/R began its first customer tests in 1978. The following year, a commercial venture was founded to create a commercial relational database that was modeled after IBM's relational database and SQL. This product was named Oracle; to this day, Oracle remains the largest selling relational database product on the market.

In 1983, IBM introduced DB2, its relational product for mainframe computers. IBM in effect declared the relational database — and in particular SQL — to be its standard for databases. IBM's power in the marketplace, which was much greater in the 1980s than it is today, ensured that SQL became the de facto standard for relational databases throughout the computer market.

Other groups besides IBM were also exploring the relational database. One group led by Professor Michael Stonebraker of the University of California, Berkeley, designed a relational database named Ingres that was built around a query language named QUEL. A commercial version of Ingres was built in 1981 and is still sold, although the SQL-based relational database products dwarf its popularity. To confuse matters, the original Ingres project was continued by UC Berkeley through the 1980s, under the name University Ingres. (Although this group's version of Ingres is no longer being supported or enhanced, University Ingres is widely available for Linux for free.) Ingres' QUEL language is well regarded among cognoscenti of relational databases, but it has never enjoyed the acceptance that the market has bestowed upon SQL.

SQL standards

In 1982, the American National Standards Institute (ANSI) formed a committee to work on a standard for relational database query languages. Through the early years of the 1980s, the committee grappled with the question of just which relational query language should be used as the model for its standard; at the same time, IBM worked to make SQL the standard query language in the marketplace. In 1986, ANSI bowed to reality and adopted SQL as its standard query language for relational databases. Soon thereafter, the International Organization for Standardization (ISO) adopted the ANSI standard as its standard for relational query languages; since then, ANSI and ISO have combined their efforts in this area.

A revised edition of the ANSI/ISO standard was published in 1989; the language described in this standard is known as SQL1 or SQL-89.

In 1992, ANSI/ISO published a new standard for SQL. This standard fixed a number of holes in the original standard, but also extended the language greatly. This standard, called SQL2 or SQL-92, is the standard used today.

Work is proceeding on a third standard for SQL, called (not surprisingly) SQL3. This new standard will again extend the language; in particular, it will define how objects are to be handled within a relational database. (Object databases and object-relational databases were discussed in Chapter 2.) SQL3 is beyond the scope of this book; however, PostgreSQL offers many of the features of an object-relational database, and it is a good place to start an exploration of the object-relational database.

Dialects of SQL

SQL, like any standard language, is meant to be uniform across all products, on all platforms. Unfortunately, implementations of SQL have features that make them mutually exclusive. How an implementation of SQL behaves depends on a number of factors. These include the ANSI/ISO standard supported — SQL1 (1989 standard), SQL2 (1992 standard), or SQL2 plus extensions drawn from the draft SQL3 standard and the package — and vendor-specific extensions to the language. Also, the standards mark some details as being implementor-specific.

Unfortunately, portability of SQL is largely a myth: only rarely will you be able to take a file of SQL code written for one relational database package and run it without modification under another relational database package.

In fairness, we must emphasize that in most instances, these differences are slight, and porting a file of SQL code from one package to another usually is a straightforward job. Also, the advent of Microsoft's Open Database Connectivity (ODBC) and similar protocols help to smooth over the differences between different implementations of SQL.

 Cross-Reference   We discuss ODBC and its relatives JDBC and Perl DBI in Chapters 12 and 13.

Disadvantages and advantages of SQL

SQL does offer a number of advantages and disadvantages. We'll give you the bad news first, then the good news.

Disadvantages

The first problem, obviously, is that SQL is not one language, but a family of languages — albeit closely related languages — as shown in the preceding section.

Another problem is that SQL does not adhere strictly to the relational model. In Chapter 2, we pointed out a number of ways in which SQL and the relational model differ; in particular, SQL permits duplicate rows within a relation. We point out other places in this chapter where SQL departs from the relational model.

Finally, as a programming language, SQL can be quite clumsy, and it can also be ambiguous.

Advantages

SQL, although it has problems, is a standard.

SQL as a language is relatively straightforward and easy to learn. Even nonprogrammers can learn to write their own queries and reports in it. This helps to give ordinary users access to their own data within a database — in effect, it helps to unlock the "data jail," which, to a business, is an advantage that cannot be underestimated.

Although SQL does depart from the relational model on a number of points, by and large it implements the relational model faithfully. SQL places the power of the relational database into the hands of programmers and users — and we can think of no greater recommendation than that.

Implementation of the language

SQL is a language designed to work with a database. It does not contain many of the features offered by a general-purpose programming language, like C or Java; these include instructions for redirecting input or output flow-control statements.

These omissions are not an error. Rather, SQL was designed to work with a host language that provides facilities such as input/output and flow control.

Most database packages use an SQL engine to interpret SQL instructions. The engine is a program that, in effect, acts as the gatekeeper to the database: it executes instructions to set up a database, inserts data into it, selects or deletes data from it, or updates data within it. Most relational database packages also include utilities that let you create a copy of a database's design, or "schema," as well as dump a copy of a database's contents into a text file, and load a file of data directly into a database. For the most part, however, database activity goes through the SQL engine.

For most packages, SQL instructions can be passed to the engine in any of three ways:

SQL interpreter   Such an interpreter receives input directly from the user, interprets it, and returns the output to the user. Earlier interpreters received code typed by the user; nowadays, an interpreter is likelier to receive input from a graphical user interface, which protects the user from having to write code.

Embedded SQL   Here, SQL statements are embedded within a program written in another language, such as C or COBOL. Such a program must first be filtered through a preprocessor, which transforms the embedded SQL into a series of function calls. The preprocessor's output is then compiled and run like any other program. This method of programming SQL is largely outdated and is not explored in this book; but it is available and can be quite useful.

SQL call-level interface (CLI)	In this interface, the programmer writes a series of calls to execute SQL statements. In C, the calls are to functions within a library; in Java, the calls are to the methods within a package of objects. In effect, the programmer writes by hand the code that the embedded-SQL preprocessor generates mechanically.

The ANSI/ISO standards for SQL define both interpreted and embedded SQL; however, they do not define an SQL call-level interface for any other computer language. Thus, each database manufacturer has invented its own CLI, and these are mutually incompatible. Some manufacturers have designed CLIs that can be used with nearly all relational databases; in particular, Microsoft's ODBC protocol and Sun's Java Database Connectivity (JDBC) protocol have attracted support in the marketplace. We explore ODBC and JDBC in Chapters 12 and 13.

SQL Structure

The rest of this chapter introduces SQL. Our discussion is limited to the core features of the SQL2 standard. We do not go into the more esoteric features of the language; however, the information we present enables you to perform all of the tasks ordinarily required when you create and work with a relational database. Each section presents examples written in SQL.

Terminology

In our discussion of relational databases so far, we have used the terms *relation*, *attribute*, and *tuple*. SQL, however, gives different names to each:

✦ Instead of relations, SQL speaks of *tables*.

✦ Instead of attributes, SQL speaks of *columns*.

✦ Instead of tuples, SQL speaks of *rows*.

Because SQL does not adhere perfectly to the relational model, there are some differences between the relational entities *relation*, *attribute*, and *tuple*, and their analogs in SQL. We use the SQL terminology throughout the rest of this chapter. Where the differences between relational entities and the SQL analogs affect our discussion, we identify those differences. For the most part, however, it is correct to regard relation, attribute, and tuple as equivalent to table, column, and row, respectively.

Note Please note that the term "field" often is used as a synonym for "column"; and the term "record" is used as a synonym for "row." However, for the sake of simplicity, we will use "column" and "row" exclusively.

Structure of the language

As we noted earlier, SQL does not implement some of the features of a general-purpose programming language, such as C. The statements within a SQL program are executed in isolation from each other: that is, a statement cannot invoke another statement, nor can it pass information to another statement, nor can it store data in variables for use by another statement. Such features can be provided by the host language within which SQL statements are embedded, but such features are not part of SQL itself.

Thus, learning SQL means learning the syntax of each SQL statement, and what it does. That is one reason why SQL is so easy for nonprogrammers to learn — a person can learn SQL statement by statement, without worrying about the logic of the program as a whole, or about the side effects statements can have on each other.

We must emphasize that SQL is a powerful language. A carefully constructed SQL statement can perform an enormous amount of work very quickly. However, a carelessly constructed SQL statement can destroy a database. You should treat SQL with the care you give to any power tool: with respect for what it can do *for* you, and with fear of what it can do *to* you.

Before we begin exploring statements, we look at the structure of SQL — the scaffolding that holds our statements together.

Keywords

SQL reserves words for its own use — as keywords. You cannot use a keyword to name a database, a table, or a column, or any other namable element in your SQL program.

SQL2 (that is, SQL-92) reserves more than 300 keywords (as compared to 33 in ANSI C). Of this vast number of keywords, you will need only a handful in your day-to-day work with SQL. The following gives the most commonly used SQL keywords:

ALL	BY	CURSOR	END
AND	CHAR	DEFAULT	ESCAPE
ANY	CHARACTER	DATE	EXEC
AS	CHECK	DEC	EXISTS
ASC	CLOSE	DECIMAL	FETCH
AUTHORIZATION	COMMIT	DECLARE	FLOAT
AVG	CONTINUE	DELETE	FOR
BEGIN	COUNT	DESC	FOREIGN
BETWEEN	CREATE	DISTINCT	FOUND
BIT	CURRENT	DOUBLE	FROM

GO	MIN	PRIVILEGES	UNIQUE
GOTO	MODULE	PROCEDURE	UPDATE
GRANT	MONEY	PUBLIC	USER
GROUP	NCHAR	SCHEMA	REAL
HAVING	NOT	SECTION	REFERENCES
INSERT	NULL	SELECT	REVOKE
IN	NUMERIC	SET	ROLLBACK
INTO	OF	SMALLINT	VALUES
INDICATOR	ON	SOME	VARCHAR
INTEGER	OPEN	SUM	VARYING
INTERVAL	OPTION	TABLE	VIEW
IS	OR	TIME	WHENEVER
KEY	ORDER	TIMESTAMP	WHERE
LANGUAGE	PRECISION	TO	WITH
LIKE	PRIMARY	UNION	WORK
MAX			

SQL code is case-insensitive: that is, CHARACTER, character, and chArActEr are all equivalent as far as SQL is concerned. It is customary to type SQL keywords in uppercase letters and to type table names and column names in lowercase; but this is not required.

The following sections introduce each keyword in its proper context.

Data Types

SQL, like all languages, defines types of data. Each data type allocates a defined amount of memory, and can (as its name implies) hold a defined type of datum. SQL's data types dictate not only the varieties of data that a SQL program can manipulate, but the varieties that can be stored in a SQL database.

The following are the simple data types that are recognized by all implementations of SQL:

CHAR(*length*)	Fixed-length array of characters
INTEGER	Four-byte (long) integer
SMALLINT	Two-byte (short) integer
FLOAT	Single-precision floating-point number

These data types should be familiar to anyone who has programmed. Programmers may wish to note that SQL does not support unsigned data types.

The following data types are more complex than the simple types described above. Not every implementation of SQL recognizes all of these data types, but most implementations recognize at least some of them:

VARCHAR(*length*)	Variable-length array of characters
NUMERIC(*precision, scale*)	Decimal number
DECIMAL(*precision, scale*)	Synonym for NUMERIC
DEC(*precision, scale*)	Synonym for NUMERIC
DOUBLE PRECISION	Double-precision floating-point number
DATE	A date
TIME(*precision*)	The time
TIMESTAMP(*precision*)	The current date and time
INTERVAL	The interval between two timestamps

The complex data types extend the simple types in the following ways:

✦ A variable-length array of characters is one whose length is not fixed. If you declare a column to be CHAR(100), SQL allocates space for 100 characters, regardless of whether you insert text into the column. However, if you declare the column to be VARCHAR(100), the database will store only the number of characters that you insert into the column, up to a maximum of 100. The maximum length of a VARCHAR varies from one database package to another; for many, the maximum length is 255 characters.

✦ The NUMERIC data type does not encode numbers in the usual binary manner. Rather, it stores numbers as text, using 1 byte for each digit in the number, to a maximum of *scale* digits. *precision* gives the position of the decimal point within the number. Such numbers are used to store numbers that are too large to fit into a 32-bit integer, that require more precision than is allowed by an ordinary floating-point number, or for which you wish to avoid rounding errors.

✦ A double-precision number is an 8-byte floating-point number that offers twice the precision of a single-precision FLOAT. A double-precision number is used for tasks that require extremely fine precision.

✦ The DATE and TIME types offer a convenient way to record dates and times.

✦ The TIMESTAMP type records both date and time in one column; it's usually used to timestamp an event that occurs right now. The precision of the timestamp can be set down to nanoseconds.

✦ The INTERVAL type records the interval between two timestamps. This is needed because a TIMESTAMP is not an integer type, and so cannot easily be subtracted from another TIMESTAMP.

Other, more exotic data types also are available. You will not use these types often, but some database management systems offer them should you need them:

BLOB	Binary large object
BIT(*length*)	Fixed-length array of bits
BIT VARYING(*length*)	Variable-length array of bits
NCHAR(*length*)	Fixed-length array of national characters
NCHAR VARYING(*length*)	Variable-length array of national characters
SERIAL	Automatically generated serial number
MONEY(*precision, size*)	Money
MONEY	Money
BOOLEAN	A Boolean value

A binary large object is a binary object of indefinite size, for example, a picture or a sound bite. Unlike a true software object, a BLOB does not contain any methods for manipulating the object; all a BLOB contains is the data that comprise the object.

The bit types define an array of individual bits. Such an array can be used for a variety of specialized tasks. Bit arrays can either be fixed length or variable length, just like arrays of characters.

The NCHAR types hold arrays of national characters. A national character is a character that does not appear in the U.S. ASCII set; usually, this is a character with a value from 128 to 255.

The SERIAL type is used by the Informix database management system. This type holds a serial number that is generated by the database engine — that is, the database engine automatically sets the value of this column to the next highest possible integer value. (MySQL uses the keyword AUTO_INCREMENT to do the same thing.)

The MONEY type, as you would expect, holds a sum of money. It is analogous to the NUMERIC data type, in that it is designed to avoid rounding errors when you divide one sum of money by another. Note that not every implementation of this data type uses the arguments in parentheses.

The BOOLEAN holds a Boolean value — TRUE or FALSE — and nothing else.

Many other vendor-specific data types are available. The proliferation of such customized data types is one reason why it is difficult to port SQL code from one database package to another.

Creating a Database

Now that we have discussed the data types that most SQL packages support, we can begin working with SQL. The first step is to create a database. This involves creating the database itself, granting permissions to users, and creating tables and indices.

In this section, and throughout the rest of this chapter, we present examples that run under MySQL. This is not the place to go into the details of running MySQL — we cover that in Chapter 10 — but the example scripts here do work with most popular database packages. When MySQL does something unorthodox, or has a serious limitation, we discuss it.

In the rest of this chapter, we will work with a simple, two-table database that we call "baseball," because it holds data about baseball games. You will learn all about this database as we proceed through this chapter.

CREATE: Create a database

Much of this book to this point has been concerned with defining just what a database is. Therefore, it may strike you as odd that SQL does not have an instruction for creating a database. That is because relational database packages differ in their definition of just what a database is. Some packages let users define any number of databases, each with its own complement of tables and indices, whereas other packages define the entire package as one large database, and still other packages let the system administrator define databases when the system is installed, but not thereafter.

Most database packages that let users define their own databases use a statement of the form:

```
CREATE DATABASE database_name
```

You should check the documentation that comes with the package you are using to determine what the package permits you to do in the way of setting up databases, and how to go about it.

The script in Listing 3-1, creates the baseball database under MySQL:

Listing 3-1: **Creating a Baseball Database**

```
CREATE DATABASE baseball;
```

Please note that under MySQL, a database can be created only by the root user, or by a user to whom the root user has assigned database-creation privileges.

Note, too, that the statement ends with a semicolon, to signal the interpreter `mysql` that the statement is ended and should be executed. Other RDBMS packages use different characters to end a statement; for example, the mini-SQL package mSQL uses the escape sequence \g, whereas Sybase uses the command `go`.

MySQL also implements the statement `DROP DATABASE`, which lets you throw away an existing database.

GRANT: Grant permissions

After the database is created, permissions on the database need to be granted so that users can access and work with the database.

The SQL instruction `GRANT` lets you grant permissions. Database packages vary wildly in how they manage permissions; and the permission scheme used by MySQL is particularly convoluted. The script in Listing 3-2, grants global permissions on the database `baseball` to user `bballfan`:

Listing 3-2: **Granting Permission**

```
GRANT ALL
ON    baseball.*
TO    bballfan@localhost
IDENTIFIED BY 'password';
```

We discuss the MySQL system of permissions at length in Chapter 10. In brief, however, this `GRANT` statement tells MySQL to give all possible permissions on every table in the `baseball` database to user `bballfan`, who accesses the database on the local host (rather than from another host on your network), and whose database password is *password*.

The types of permission that you can set vary from one database package to another. Most packages recognize these types of permission:

CONNECT   The user can connect to the database.

INSERT   The user can insert new rows into the specified table.

DELETE   The user can delete rows from the specified table.

UPDATE   The user can modify rows within the specified table.

Note that for MySQL, `bballfan` does not have to be a Linux login — any user who knows the password can use that login to access database `baseball`. Other database packages, however, require that a login used to access the database must also be a login used by the operating system. For example, these packages would require that `bballfan` be a Linux login as well as a database login.

The SQL instruction `REVOKE` removes a permission that had been granted previously.

Now that we have created the database, the next step is to build the tables that will actually hold data.

CREATE TABLE: Create a table

The statement `CREATE TABLE` creates a table within a given database. This statement has the following syntax:

```
CREATE TABLE table_name(
    column_name column_type[,] [NULL|NOT NULL] ...
    [PRIMARY KEY (column_name [ , column_name, ... ] ) ]
    [FOREIGN KEY [ key_name ] (column_name [ , column_name, ... ] )
        REFERENCES table_name
        [ ON DELETE action ] ]
)
```

table_name names the table. This name must be unique within the database.

Clauses within the `CREATE TABLE` statement must be separated by a comma.

column_name names a column. This name must be unique within the table.

column_type assigns a data type to the column. Earlier in this chapter, we described the data types that are used most commonly; we discuss data types at greater length below.

Optional clause `NULL` states that the column can hold NULL values. Likewise, optional clause `NOT NULL` states that the column cannot hold NULL values. If you do not explicitly state whether a column can hold a NULL value, the database package uses a default, which varies from one package to another. For example, MySQL assumes that a column cannot hold a NULL value unless you explicitly use the `NULL` clause, whereas Sybase assumes that a column can hold a NULL value unless you explicitly use the `NOT NULL` clause.

The optional `PRIMARY KEY` clause names the columns that comprise the table's primary key. SQL lets a table have only one primary key. This is an important point upon which SQL is not quite in sync with relational theory. As you would expect, every row in the table must have a unique value for its primary key; declaring a primary key lets the database engine enforce this rule. Also, when you declare a primary key for a table, SQL lets you declare foreign keys that point to it from other tables.

The optional FOREIGN KEY clause defines a foreign key. It is a little more complex than the PRIMARY KEY clause:

+ The keywords FOREIGN KEY are followed by an optional name for the key. The name is not necessary, but you should name each key in case you later decide to drop it. The optional name is followed by the names of the column or columns that comprise the foreign key. The name or names are enclosed between parentheses.

+ These are followed by the keyword REFERENCES and the name of the table to which this foreign key points. As you can see, a foreign key does not name the columns in the foreign table to which the foreign key points: this is because a foreign key, under SQL, can reference only a primary key.

Obviously, the data types and domains of the columns that comprise the foreign key must exactly match those of the other table's primary key.

This is optionally followed by the keywords ON DELETE, which defines the action to take should the row that the foreign key references be deleted.

ON DELETE accepts the following options:

CASCADE   Automatically deletes every row that references the row that has just been deleted from the foreign table.

SET NULL   Sets the foreign-key column or columns to NULL.

NO ACTION   That is, forbids the references row to be deleted.

You may recall that we discussed these options in Chapter 2, when we discussed the concept of database integrity.

To be declarable as a FOREIGN KEY, the key must point to the declared primary key of the table that that foreign key references. In Chapter 2, when we designed the relations upon which these tables are based, we defined some foreign keys that refer to columns other than a primary key. This is perfectly legal under relational theory, but cannot be done under SQL.

The script in Listing 3-3 shows how to create the tables for the baseball database under MySQL.

Listing 3-3: **Creating Tables for the Baseball Database**

```
CREATE TABLE team (
    team_name CHAR(15) NOT NULL,
    city      CHAR(15) NOT NULL,
    stadium   CHAR(30) NOT NULL,
    league    CHAR(1)  NOT NULL,
    division  CHAR(1)  NOT NULL,
    PRIMARY KEY (team_name)
);

CREATE TABLE game (
    home_team          CHAR(15) NOT NULL,
    visiting_team      CHAR(15) NOT NULL,
    home_team_runs     SMALLINT NOT NULL,
    visiting_team_runs SMALLINT NOT NULL,
    game_date          CHAR(10) NOT NULL,
    game_number        SMALLINT NOT NULL,
    PRIMARY KEY (home_team, visiting_team, game_date, game_number),
    FOREIGN KEY (home_team) REFERENCES team
);
```

The following points should be noted:

✦ The size of an array is enclosed between parentheses. This may be a little confusing to C programmers, who use brackets to enclose the size of an array.

✦ The names of the tables are given in lowercase letters rather than in uppercase letters. Although SQL is not case sensitive, some databases (for example, Sybase) are case sensitive as regards table names and column names. It is customary to type SQL keywords in uppercase letters, and to type the names of all columns and tables in lowercase letters.

✦ Finally, MySQL does not recognize the FOREIGN KEY clause; however, it lets you insert one into a table definition both to document foreign keys and to maintain compatibility with standard SQL. Also, note that MySQL does not let you name a FOREIGN KEY: if you do, it complains of a syntax error.

Assigning data types

Earlier in this chapter, we discussed the SQL data types that are most commonly used. As you can see from the above example, each column in each table must have a data type assigned to it. The assigning of the data type to a column is an important issue that requires more than a little thought. Although we discuss this topic at length in Chapter 4, to help keep you from becoming utterly confused, we briefly discuss why we assigned these data types to the columns in the baseball database.

Table team

In this table, we made columns `team_name` and `city` each a 15-byte character array. (The data type `CHAR` is a synonym for `CHARACTER`.) This enables these columns to hold the longest team name (Metropolitans — aka Mets) and the longest city name (actually, the name of a state — California), plus a couple of extra just for luck.

Column stadium is a 30-character column, to hold such lengthy names as Hubert H. Humphrey Stadium, plus a couple of extra.

We used fixed-length arrays for the string columns, instead of `VARCHAR` types, mainly for the sake of simplicity.

This table will have only 30 rows in it — one for each major-league team. Basically, unless you are intent on wringing every last superfluous byte out of your database, there's little point in using a `VARCHAR` type with a small, static table like this one.

Our counting the number in the names of baseball teams is a mundane example of one of the cardinal principles for assigning a data type: The data type you assign to a column must be physically able to hold every value of that column's domain. Or, to put it another way: You can't jam a ten-pound domain into a five-pound data type. You will see this principle expressed repeatedly throughout this section.

Columns league and division are each one-character columns, because this information can be represented as one character: the league can be flagged by the characters A and N (for American and National, respectively); and the division by the characters E, C, and W (for East, Central, and West, respectively).

Our decision to use one-character codes to identify league and division raises an important question about how information should be stored within a column. In this instance, we can store the names of leagues and divisions as codes because they lend themselves to unique abbreviations that are universally understood by American baseball fans. If we intended our database to be extended to minor leagues or to foreign leagues, then we would write out the names of leagues and divisions in full. After all, there's no guarantee that an American baseball fan would recognize a P as representing the Japanese Pacific League; he might think it meant the Pacific Coast League, an American minor league.

We could use abstract codes (for example, 1 to represent the American League, 2 for the National League — through 99 for the Northern League), with those codes interpreted by a key that we embed in the software, or within another table. But why bother? If we're going to use a code, it should be one that is easily and accurately interpreted by most users.

Table game

Columns `home_team` and `visiting_team` are 15-character text columns to match the type of column `team_name` in table `team`. That we assigned columns `home_team` and `visiting_team` the same data type as column `team_name` is an instance of another of the cardinal rules of assigning data types: When a column is a foreign key, it must have the same data type as the column it is referencing. Most SQL packages have robust methods for comparing columns of different types, but you are simply creating trouble for yourself and for your program if you assign to a foreign key a data type other than that of the column it is referencing.

Columns `home_team_runs` and `visiting_team_runs` are both assigned type `SMALLINT`. Under most implementations, a `SMALLINT` is two signed bytes, which means that it can hold a maximum value of 32,767 — which should be enough for any baseball game.

Column `game_date` is a `DATE`, for obvious reasons.

Column `game_number` is of type `SMALLINT`. This column holds the number of a game played between two teams on a given date, so that we can distinguish the two games of a double-header. As this column will always hold 1 or 2, a small integer will be more than adequate. We could make this field a one-character array; however, that would make this field unlike the other fields in this database that hold numeric information. It's a judgment call, but we believe it is best to put all numeric information into a numeric type, even if it does waste a byte occasionally, as in this instance. If we had decided in Chapter 2 to record the game's number as the time the game started, we might wish to give column `game_number` type `TIME` (if our database package supported such a type — some do not) or combine it with column `game_date` in the form of a `TIMESTAMP` data type (again, if our database package supported such a type).

As you can see, you must keep any number of considerations in mind when you design even a trivial database. In Chapter 4, we will go into database design in much greater detail, and discuss these issues more explicitly.

CREATE INDEX: Create an index

The tables that comprise our baseball database are created, and the next step is to build some indexes for these tables. As we noted in Chapter 2, an index helps to speed the searching of data on an index. Because building an index consumes system resources — both disk resources and CPU cycles — a key part of designing a database is devising the right combination of indexes: enough indexes so that your commonly executed queries are smooth and fast, yet not so many that they hog your system's resources.

The SQL statement `CREATE INDEX` creates an index. It has the following syntax:

```
CREATE INDEX [ UNIQUE ] index_name ON table_name ( column_name [ , ... ] )
```

The keywords CREATE INDEX can optionally be followed by the keyword UNIQUE. This keyword tells SQL that you want this index to be unique—that is, no two rows can contain the same value for the column or columns for which you build the index. This kind of index gives you a rough-and-ready sort of primary key—with the exception that it cannot be referenced by a FOREIGN KEY clause in another table.

The following subsections build indices for our example database.

The script in Listing 3-4 creates the indices for our baseball database:

Listing 3-4: **Creating Indices**

```
CREATE UNIQUE INDEX index1 ON team (team_name);
CREATE UNIQUE INDEX index2 ON game (home_team, game_date, game_number);
CREATE        INDEX index3 ON game (home_team);
CREATE        INDEX index4 ON game (visiting_team);
```

As you can see, the names of the columns that comprise the index are enclosed in parentheses.

The keyword UNIQUE indicates that the index must not allow duplicate values for this column or combination of columns.

DROP: Remove a table or index

SQL enables you to add tables and indices to your database; likewise, it enables you to remove, or drop, tables and indices from a database.

DROP TABLE

The statement DROP TABLE drops a table from your database. It has the following syntax:

```
DROP TABLE table_name [ CASCADE | RESTRICT ]
```

The keywords DROP TABLE are followed by the name of the table you wish to drop. The name of the table can optionally be followed by the keyword CASCADE or the keyword RESTRICT.

In our syntax diagrams, the vertical-bar character | means *exclusive or*: in this instance, you can use either the keyword CASCADE or the keyword RESTRICT, but not both. CASCADE tells the engine to cascade through the database and remove every table that has a foreign key that references the table being dropped. `RESTRICT` tells the engine not to drop the table if it discovers that any other table references `table_name` through a foreign key.

Thus, to drop the table `bad_table` from the database example, you would use the following SQL statement:

```
DROP TABLE bad_table;
```

Naturally, when you drop a table, you also throw away all data that the table contains, and all indexes that had been built on that table.

DROP INDEX

The statement `DROP INDEX`, as you can probably guess, drops an index. It has the following syntax:

```
DROP INDEX index_name
```

To drop index `index1` from database example, you would execute the following SQL statement:

```
DROP INDEX index1;
```

MySQL does not support this statement. Instead, MySQL uses its own nonstandard version of the `ALTER TABLE` instruction to drop an index. For example, to drop index `index1` under MySQL, you would use the SQL statement:

```
ALTER TABLE team DROP INDEX index1;
```

The instruction `ALTER TABLE`, as its name implies, lets you alter the structure of a table. You can add columns to a table, change the type of a column, or (in some implementations) delete columns from a table—while preserving the data that are already loaded into the table. `ALTER TABLE` is rather advanced, and its implementation varies quite a bit from one database package to another; if you want more information, see the documentation that comes with your database package.

INSERT: Insert a row into a table

The SQL statement `INSERT`, as its name implies, inserts data into a table. Its syntax takes several forms. We describe each in turn.

Inserting literal values

The first form of the `INSERT` statement enables you to insert values directly into a table:

```
INSERT INTO table_name
    [ ( column_name [, ... ] ) ]
    VALUES ( value [, ... ] )
```

This form enables you to insert one row into a table, with the values being a set of literal values that you name.

Variable `table_name` names the table into which the values will be inserted.

The optional `column_name` clause names the columns within table `table_name` into which you will be inserting values. All columns that you do not name in this clause will have NULL inserted into them. If you do not use this clause, the default is to insert a value into every column of the table.

The `VALUES` clause gives the values that you are inserting into table `table_name`. There must be one value for each column that is named in the `column_name` clause; if the statement does not have a `column_name` clause, there must be one value for each column in the table. The data type of each value must match that of the column into which it is being inserted; for example, you cannot insert a text string into a column with the data type of `INTEGER`. Character data must be enclosed in quotation marks. For example, the following script inserts three records into table team of our `baseball` database:

```
INSERT INTO team (team_name, city, stadium, league, division)
        VALUES ('Cubs', 'Chicago', 'Wrigley Field', 'N', 'C');
INSERT INTO team (city, stadium, team_name, division, league)
        VALUES ('Atlanta', 'Fulton County Stadium', 'Braves', 'E', 'N');
INSERT INTO team
        VALUES ('White Sox', 'Chicago', 'Comiskey Park', 'A', 'C');
```

Each of the three `INSERT` statements inserts a value into each of the five columns in table team. We must do this because when we defined team, we declared that none of its columns could contain NULL.

The first two `INSERT` statements name the columns explicitly. The first, which inserts a record for the Chicago Cubs, names the columns in the order in which we declared them in the `CREATE TABLE` statement with which we created table team. The second `INSERT` statement changes the order of the columns. As you can see, the `INSERT` statement does not care what order the columns appear in, as long as the values given in the `VALUE` clause appear in the same order as do the columns named in the `column_name` clause.

As we noted earlier, if a column in table `table_name` accepts NULL, you can exclude it from the `column_name` clause. If you do so, SQL will insert NULL into that column.

The third `INSERT` statement, which inserts a record for the Chicago White Sox, does not use a `column_name` clause. When an `INSERT` statement does not include a `column_name` clause, SQL assumes that the `VALUE` clause will contain a value for each column in table `table_name`, and that the values will appear in the same order as did the columns in `CREATE TABLE` statement with which you created table `table_name`.

As a note of caution, we believe it is worthwhile always to name the fields explicitly within an `INSERT` statement. If you do so, then the statement will continue to work even if you use the `ALTER TABLE` instruction to change the schema of the table.

Transfer values from other tables

The second form of the `INSERT` statement transfers values from one or more tables into another. It has the following syntax:

```
INSERT INTO table_name
    [ (column_name [, ... ] ) ]
    SELECT select_statement
```

This form of the `INSERT` statement replaces the `VALUES` clause with a `SELECT` statement. (The `SELECT` statement, as you may suspect, selects data from tables; the selected data are bundled into rows that the statement returns. We describe it later.) The rows that the `SELECT` statement returns are inserted into table `table_name`.

The columns that the `SELECT` statement returns must correspond with the columns in table `table_name`, both in data type and in domain. If a column cannot accept a NULL value, the `SELECT` statement must not return NULL for that column.

We give some examples of the `INSERT` statement when we discuss the `SELECT` statement, later.

Do a mass insertion

The SQL standards describe only the two forms of the `INSERT` statement given above. However, most SQL packages include a third form that enables you to insert data into a table from a file.

The syntax for this form of the `INSERT` statement is specific to the SQL package you are using. Under MySQL, this form of the `INSERT` statement has this syntax:

```
LOAD DATA INFILE 'file_name'
    INTO TABLE table_name
    FIELDS TERMINATED BY 'term_char'
    LINES TERMINATED BY 'term_char'
    ( column_name [, ... ] )
```

`file_name` names the file that holds the data to be loaded. Each row in the file must hold exactly one record to be inserted into the table in question.

`table_name` names the table into which the data will be loaded.

The `FIELDS TERMINATED BY` and `LINES TERMINATED BY` clauses give, respectively, the character that terminates a column (field) within a row and the character that terminates the line (row).

Finally, the optional *column_name* clause names the columns into which data will be loaded. If this clause is not included, then MySQL assumes that each row in file *file_name* holds exactly one field for each column in table *table_name*, and that the fields come in the same order as do the columns in table *table_name* (as set by the CREATE TABLE statement that initially created the table).

The script in Listing 3-5, loads data into the tables in our baseball database:

Listing 3-5: **Loading Data**

```
LOAD DATA LOCAL INFILE 'bb_team.data'
    INTO TABLE team
    FIELDS TERMINATED BY ','
    LINES  TERMINATED BY '\n'
    (team_name, city, stadium, league, division);

LOAD DATA LOCAL INFILE 'bb_game.data'
    INTO TABLE game
    FIELDS TERMINATED BY ','
    LINES  TERMINATED BY '\n'
    (home_team, visiting_team, home_team_runs,
     visiting_team_runs, game_date, game_number);
```

The following gives a few rows from file bb_team.data, so you can see how data must be laid out in a file for mass loading. Baseball fans may note that the information here is obsolete; that is because we are using information from the year 1992:

```
Orioles,Baltimore,Camden Yards,A,E
Red Sox,Boston,Fenway Park,A,E
Angels,Anaheim,Anaheim Stadium,A,W
White Sox,Chicago,Comiskey Park,A,W
```

Please note that when you load data from a file, you do not have to enclose character data between quotation marks. This is a major difference from the INSERT statement.

Selecting Data from the Database

To this point, we have discussed how to build a database, and how to load data into it. The next step is to retrieve data from the database. The SQL statement SELECT selects data from the database.

In our opinion, the SELECT statement is the heart of the relational database. Everything else in this book—from the relational theory that preceded this chapter, through database design, to the C and Java programming, to database administration—are all aimed toward this one simple, yet vital, action of selecting data from the database.

As you will see, the SELECT statement can be extraordinarily complex. However, if you can master the SELECT statement, you will have mastered the one most important feature of SQL—and of the relational model.

SQL and relational calculus

In Chapter 2, we discussed relational algebra and relational calculus. These mathematical systems serve as the bases for all languages with which we interrogate relational databases, including SQL.

Both the relational calculus and the relational algebra modify existing relations in order to build a new relation. They differ, however, in how they describe the relation to be built. Relational algebra is *prescriptive*: it defines discrete actions with which you can modify one or more existing relations in order to build a new relation. On the other hand, relational calculus is *descriptive*: it enables you to name one or more existing relations, and then to describe the relation that you want built from it, without prescribing in detail how that relation is to be built.

SQL's SELECT statement is based upon relational calculus: it is descriptive rather than prescriptive. However, it also contains features drawn from relational algebra, to help you deal with knotty problems.

One-table selection

This section describes the SELECT statement gradually. We begin with its simplest form, and gradually work our way to its more complex forms.

Each step of the way, we show the syntax of the SELECT statement, with a portion added to reflect the complication that we are discussing at the moment. In this way, we will lead you gradually to an understanding of this most useful of statements.

The column clause

To begin, the SELECT statement in its simplest form has this syntax:

```
SELECT column_name
FROM   table_name
```

column_name names a column within the database.

table_name names the table within which that column resides.

For example, the script in Listing 3-6, selects the contents of column `team_name` from table team in database `baseball`:

Listing 3-6: **Selecting a Team Name**

```
SELECT  team_name
FROM    team;
```

When executed under MySQL, this returns the following data:

```
team_name
Orioles
Red Sox
Angels
White Sox
   ...
```

Selecting multiple columns

Now that you've seen the `SELECT` statement in its simplest form, you can try something slightly more complex.

You can use the `SELECT` statement to select multiple columns from within your database. The syntax to do that is:

```
SELECT  column_name [ , ... ]
FROM    table_name
```

For example, the script in Listing 3-7 selects the name of the team and its league from our `baseball` database:

Listing 3-7: **Selecting Team Name and League**

```
SELECT  team_name, league
FROM    team;
```

When executed under MySQL, this statement prints the following on your screen:

```
team_name       league
Orioles         A
Red Sox         A
Angels          A
White Sox       A
   ...
```

In Chapter 2, when we discussed relational algebra, we described an operation called *project*, which selects attributes from a relation. The above form of the SELECT statement simply implements the relational project operation.

One note: Under most implementations of SQL, a solitary asterisk * in the *column_name* clause is a synonym for all columns in the table or tables named in the FROM clause. For example, the program:

```
SELECT *
FROM   game
```

selects every column from table game.

Building a new table

You may have noticed that the output of the SELECT statement is in the form of rows and columns: one column for each column named in the *column_name* clause of the statement, and one row for each row in the table from which we are selecting data. This is a very important point: Just as each operation in the relational algebra and the relational calculus creates a new relation as its product, so, too, the SELECT statement creates as its product a new table. The columns of this new table are defined by the *column_name* and FROM clauses of the table. The rows are defined in the WHERE clause, which are described in detail later.

This new table is not added to your database. Rather, it is returned to whatever program used the SELECT to select data from the database. As we noted earlier, you can embed a SELECT statement within an INSERT statement to populate a table within your database.

The script in Listing 3-8 adds a new table to the baseball database and uses a SELECT statement to populate it:

Listing 3-8: **Adding a New Table**

```
CREATE TABLE temp_team (
    team_name CHAR(15) NOT NULL,
    league    CHAR(1)  NOT NULL
);

INSERT INTO temp_team (team_name, league)
    SELECT team_name, league
    FROM   team;
DROP TABLE temp_team;
```

The INSERT statement funnels the output of the SELECT statement into the newly created table temp_team.

Please note that the number of columns within the SELECT statement, and the type of each column, must match those of the table into which its output is being funneled; otherwise, the SQL engine will complain.

Constants and expressions

The SELECT statement can do more than just retrieve data items that already reside within the database. If you wish, you can also use constants and arithmetic expressions as data items within the *column_name* clause of a SELECT statement.

When we add this feature to the syntax of the SELECT statement, it appears as follows:

```
SELECT column_name | constant | expression  [ , ... ]
FROM   table_name
```

The bar character | here means *or*—that is, a given item named within the *column_name* clause must be a column name, or a constant, or an arithmetic expression. The *column_name* clause can mix items of different types: one item can be a constant, a second can be a column name, and a third an arithmetic expression.

We discuss both constants and arithmetic expressions later, when we introduce the WHERE clause to the SELECT statement. However, the following example gives you a taste of how they would be used in the *column_name* clause. This example, Listing 3-9, selects rows from table game, doubles the number of runs scored by the home team, and adds a constant:

Listing 3-9: **Select**

```
SELECT home_team,
       home_team_runs,
       'this is a constant',
       home_team_runs * 2
FROM   game;
```

The asterisk * here is the multiplication operator; thus, the phrase home_team_runs*2 multiplies the value of column home_team_runs by 2.

The output begins as follows:

```
home_team    home_team_runs   this is a constant   home_team_runs * 2
Blue Jays    5                this is a constant   10
Indians      1                this is a constant   2
Brewers      2                this is a constant   4
Tigers       4                this is a constant   8
Twins        5                this is a constant   10
Yankees      0                this is a constant   0
   . . .
```

The constant `this is a constant` is embedded in each row of the table that the `SELECT` statement returns to the screen; and the number of runs scored by the home team is doubled.

The following section discusses constants at greater length.

The restrictive WHERE clause

So far, we have used the `SELECT` statement to select individual columns from a table. Each of our examples has selected every row from a table. The `SELECT` statement, however, enables you to build a filter with which you can define the rows that you want to select from the table.

You may remember from our discussion of relational algebra in Chapter 2 that relational algebra includes an operation called *restrict*. This operation examines an individual row (or, to use the technical term "tuple") within a relation, and checks whether the row meets the criteria that you set; if the row meets those criteria, it inserts that row into the relation it is building. The `SELECT` includes a clause, called the `WHERE` clause, that implements the restrict operation.

The following gives the syntax of the `SELECT` statement, including this new clause:

```
SELECT column_name | constant | expression [ , ... ]
FROM   table_name
[ WHERE restrict_expression ]
```

The rest of this section describes the `restrict_expression`. We must warn you that what follows introduces several concepts. However, much of the power of SQL resides in its ability to understand subtle and complex restrictive expressions; therefore, a little time spent with this section will pay big dividends in terms of your ability to use relational databases well.

That being said, let's begin with some definitions.

An *expression* is a phrase of code that uses an operator to modify either a constant, or the data in a column, or the product of another expression. A SQL program can use an expression to calculate a value that the program uses to control the selection of data from the database. Thus, an expression appears most often in the `WHERE` clause of an `INSERT`, `DELETE`, or `SELECT` statement.

Before we show how expressions are used within a `WHERE` clause, we must first introduce two of the elements that comprise an expression: *constants* and *operators*.

Constants

SQL, like most other languages, lets you use constants within an expression. Constants come in four different flavors: numeric, string, date/time, and symbolic.

Numeric constants

A *numeric constant*, as its name implies, is a number. Such a constant can be either an integer constant or a floating-point constant.

You must prefix a negative numeric constant with a `-`. You may prefix a positive number constant with a `+`, but you do not have to do so.

An *integer constant* is, as its name implies, an integer. For example, the following are all integer constants:

```
1      +15     36793561879035160       -273
```

Note that a numeric constant does not contain commas, no matter how long it is.

A *floating-point* constant encodes a floating-point number. It contains a decimal point and it may also contain an `E` to indicate an exponent. For example, the following are floating-point constants:

```
1.0     3.1416     97.15E-8     -33.333E97
```

SQL implements some rules about how it performs arithmetic upon constants, and what constants can be compared with which columns:

- ✦ If you perform arithmetic upon two integer constants, the result has type `INTEGER`.

- ✦ If you perform arithmetic upon two floating-point constants, the result is of type `FLOAT`.

- ✦ If you perform arithmetic upon a floating-point constant and an integer constant, the result is of type `FLOAT`.

- ✦ You can compare an integer constant (or the result of performing arithmetic upon two integer constants) only with a column that has an integer data type, for example, `INTEGER` or `SMALLINT`.

- ✦ You can compare a floating-point constant (or the product of performing arithmetic upon a floating-point constant and another numeric constant) only with a column that has a floating-point data type, for example, `FLOAT` or `DOUBLE`.

Some database packages lift these restrictions; that is, they let you compare an integer constant with a floating-point column, or vice versa. However, you should not assume that a database package does lift this restriction until you check its documentation.

String constants

A *string constant* is, as its name implies, a string.

The 1992 ANSI/ISO standard for SQL requires that a string constant be enclosed between apostrophes (aka *single-quotation marks*). A literal apostrophe within a string constant must be escaped by inserting an extra apostrophe before it. For example:

```
'This is an apostrophe '' within a string constant'
```

Most database packages also let you enclose string constants between quotation marks (aka *double-quotation marks*). In this instance, there is no need to escape apostrophes. For example:

```
"This is an apostrophe ' within a string constant"
```

Again, not every database package recognizes string constants that are enclosed between quotation marks. If you are not sure whether your database package does so, check its documentation.

Please note that database packages differ with regard to how they handle case when they compare data with string constants. Some packages, such as MySQL, do not by default take case into account when they compare strings; whereas other packages, such as Sybase, do take case into account. For example, the SELECT statement

```
SELECT * FROM team WHERE name = 'CUBS'
```

will not return anything when run under Sybase, but it will return the row for the "Cubs" when run under MySQL.

Date and time constants

A *date and time constant* is a string that describes a date or a time. You can compare these constants with the contents of columns that have a date data type or a time data type.

Unfortunately, the format of a date or time string varies, depending upon your locale and the database package you are using. Most database packages recognize the format MM/DD/YYYY for dates in the United States, and the format DD/MM/YYYY for dates in Europe. For example, if you're checking whether column birthdate is set to August 27, 1952, use the expression

```
birthdate = '08/27/1952'
```

in the United States, and the expression

```
birthdate = '27/08/1952'
```

in Europe.

Some SQL packages recognize constants of the form August 27, 1952, or Aug 27, 1952; others do not. Check the documentation that comes with your database package to see what constants it does and does not recognize.

Symbolic constants

Finally, most database packages implement *symbolic constants*. A symbolic constant represents some value that is constant to the system as it is being used right now. For example, a symbolic constant can name the person who is using the system now, or today's date.

Unfortunately, symbolic constants also vary wildly from one database package to another. For example, DB2 represents today's date as the constant CURRENT DATE, whereas Oracle represents it as the constant SYSDATE and Informix as the constant TODAY.

Symbolic constants are very useful, but these differences among packages make symbolic constants very difficult to use in a portable manner. Before you use a symbolic constant in any of your SQL programs, be sure to check the documentation that comes with your package.

Operators

An operator is the verb of an expression: it tells the expression what to do. SQL includes operators that perform arithmetic, and operators that perform comparisons. An arithmetic operator yields a number as it's output, whereas a comparison operator yields a logical result (either TRUE, FALSE, or NULL).

We first discuss the arithmetic operators, and then we discuss the wide range of comparison operators.

Arithmetic operators

SQL recognizes these arithmetic operators:

+	Addition
-	Subtraction
*	Multiplication
/	Division

The above operators are recognized by every implementation of SQL. Some implementations of SQL recognize their own proprietary operators, such as the following:

%	Modulus
||	Concatenate strings

Arithmetic operators can be used only on numeric data types, not on strings, dates, or any other nonnumeric type.

Comparison operators

To begin, the following operators let you compare SQL expressions:

=	Equal
<>	Not equal
<	Less than
<=	Less than or equal
>	Greater than
>=	Greater than or equal

Most packages also recognize the operator != for not equal, although this is an extension to the SQL92 standard.

Each expression that is built around a comparison operator returns a logical value as its result — that is, TRUE, FALSE, or NULL. For example, the following compares the value of the numeric column home_team_runs with the numeric constant 5:

```
home_team_runs = 5
```

If home_team_runs equals 5, then this expression evaluates to TRUE. If home_team_runs equals a number other than 5, then this expression evaluates to FALSE. If, however, home_team_runs is not set to any number at all — if it is NULL, in other words — then this expression evaluates to NULL. In Chapter 2, we discussed the relational model's three-tiered logic; here you see it in action.

SQL lets you use the comparison operators to compare strings as well as numbers. The equality operator =, when used between two strings, indicates whether the strings are identical. For example, the following checks whether the value of column title equals the title of this book:

```
title = 'Linux Database Bible'
```

If title does equal Linux Database Bible, then this expression evaluates to TRUE. If title equals a string other than Linux Database, then this expression evaluates to FALSE. If, however, title is NULL, then the expression evaluates to NULL. The inequality operators also indicate whether one string is lexically greater than or less than the other — that is, whether one string comes earlier in the alphabet than the other. Please note that most database packages use ASCII values when comparing text. This means, among other things, that if a database package takes the case of text into account, then capital letters will be regarded as coming earlier lexically than do lower-case letters; thus, you may have the odd result of a string that begins with 'Z' has a lower lexical value than a string that begins with 'a'. Also, strings that contain punctuation marks and digits may not compare as you think they should. For more information on how text is ordered and compared, be sure to check the documentation that comes with your database package.

We provide further examples of these operators in action later.

BETWEEN

The operator BETWEEN, as its name implies, gives you an easy way to check whether a column lies within a range of values. Its syntax is:

```
column BETWEEN element AND element
```

For example, if home_team_runs is a numeric column, you can use the following expression to determine whether its value lies between 1 and 10, inclusive:

```
home_team_runs BETWEEN 1 AND 10
```

This is equivalent to saying:

```
home_team_runs >= 1 AND home_team_runs <= 10
```

You can use BETWEEN to check whether a string lies between a given lexical range. For example, the following expression checks whether a given team's name begins with any of the first five letters of the alphabet:

```
name BETWEEN 'A%' AND 'E%'
```

Note the use of the % as a wildcard character. Under SQL, the % represents an indefinite amount of text of any kind. Thus, A% represents any string that begins with a capital A. We discuss wildcards at greater length later, when we introduce the operator LIKE.

You can also use BETWEEN to check whether a date lies between two other dates. For example, the following checks whether the value of column birthdate lies in the first six months of 1952:

```
birthdate BETWEEN '01/01/1952' AND '06/30/1952'
```

The date constants must conform to those recognized by the database package.

Please note that an element used in a BETWEEN operation is usually a constant, but it can be an expression. However, it is unusual to use an expression in this operation, because if an element logically evaluates to NULL, it is difficult to predict just what the outcome will be. This is partly due to ANSI/ISO SQL's rules governing how BETWEEN handles NULL expressions being quite convoluted, and partly because they are inconsistently implemented across database packages.

IN

The operator IN checks whether the value of a column matches any value in a list. It has the following syntax:

```
column IN ( element, element, ... )
```

Every element in the list must match the type of column — either numeric, text, or date. For example, the following checks whether the value of column home_team_runs equals any of three given values:

```
home_team_runs IN (1, 3, 5)
```

This is equivalent to the expression:

```
home_team_runs = 1 OR home_team_runs = 3 OR home_team_runs = 5
```

Again, the following expression checks whether column first_name has any of five values:

```
first_name IN ('Marian', 'Ivan', 'George', 'Catherine',
'Richard')
```

An element in the list can itself be an expression. Usually, this is more trouble than it is worth. However, there is one exception to this rule: sometimes you may wish to use another SELECT statement to build the list of values used by the IN clause. We will give an example of this below, when we discuss sub-SELECTs.

LIKE

The operator LIKE is used only with strings. It checks whether a string matches a given pattern of strings. It has the following syntax:

```
column LIKE pattern
```

pattern combines string constants with wildcard characters. SQL recognizes two wildcard characters:

%   Match zero or more characters

_   Match any one character

If you are familiar with the UNIX shell, then % is equivalent to the shell's wildcard character *, and _ is equivalent to the shell's wildcard character ?. For example, the following expression checks whether the column title contains the string Linux:

```
title LIKE '%Linux%'
```

If `title` is set to a title that contains the string `Linux`, then this expression evaluates to TRUE; if it contains a title that does not contain the string `Linux`, then this expression evaluates to FALSE; and if it does not contain a title, then this expression evaluates to NULL. The above expression matches all of the following titles:

```
Linux Database Bible
The Linux Data Base Bible
Linux Databases
Forever Linux
The World's Greatest Linux Releases
The Great Big Book of Linux Programming Tips
Linux
```

If you wanted to match the string *something* `Linux` *something*, you would use the following expression:

```
title LIKE '%_% Linux %_%'
```

The wildcard character _ matches any one character — unlike %, it does not match zero characters — so the above expression forces `LIKE` to match only the book titles that have at least one character to the left of `Linux` and at least one character to the right.

One problem arises: How do you escape the wildcard characters — that is, how would you match a string that contains a literal % or a _ within it? In most instances, this is not a problem. The % character matches any range of characters, including % itself, and _ matches any single character, including an _. What you cannot do is embed an % or an _ within a string, and expect `LIKE` to treat it as a constant.

SQL2 describes a clause called `ESCAPE`, with which you can define a character that escapes a wildcard character — that is, prefixing the wildcard with the escape character tells `LIKE` to treat the wildcard as a literal character. For example, to see whether column title holds the string *something* `%%Linux%%` *something*, you could use the following expression:

```
title LIKE '% @%@%Linux@%@% %' ESCAPE '@'
```

In this example, the expression uses the `ESCAPE` clause to declare that the character @ is the escape character, and then uses the @ to escape the wildcard character %. Note that the first and last instances of % are unescaped, and so remain wildcard characters.

The problem with this approach — apart from the fact that it is extremely clumsy — is that many implementations of SQL do not recognize it. The unfortunate fact is that for all practical purposes, you cannot use `LIKE` to match exactly a string that contains % or _.

IS

We must consider one last operator: the IS operator. IS is not exactly a comparison operator; rather, it checks whether a given column is set to NULL.

You may recall from Chapter 2, when we discussed the relational model, that missing data are indicated with NULL. NULL is not a value; rather, it is a flag that indicates the absence of a value. Any comparison with NULL returns NULL—even when you compare NULL with NULL.

So far, so good; but this does raise a problem: How can you write an expression to tell whether something is NULL? After all, it is a problem if the expressions

```
FOO = NULL
```

and

```
FOO <> NULL
```

both evaluate to NULL rather than to TRUE or FALSE—neither tells you whether FOO is NULL or not.

To get around this problem, SQL introduces a special operator: IS. This operator examines whether a variable is or is not NULL. It is guaranteed always to evaluate to TRUE or FALSE—never to NULL. For example, to determine whether, in a given row, column ssn is NULL, use the expression:

```
ssn IS NULL
```

Likewise, to determine whether, in a given row, column ssn is not NULL, use the expression:

```
ssn IS NOT NULL
```

The IS operator could, in theory, be used to check whether the logical result of a comparison operation was NULL. However, a comparison operation returns NULL only if one of the columns being compared is itself NULL. Thus, it makes sense simply to examine whether the column is NULL, rather than to examine the result of an expression that includes the column.

Assembling an expression

As we noted at the beginning of this section, an expression in a SQL WHERE clause evaluates whether the contents of a given column within your database match a criterion that you set. Thus, when an expression is used in a WHERE clause, it yields a logical value—TRUE, FALSE, or NULL. As we show later, this result governs whether a given SQL statement is executed for a given row within your database.

Every expression is built around an operator—the verb of the expression. An operator, in turn, operates upon one or more operands. An operand can be a column (or to be more exact, the data in a column), a constant, or the output of another expression. A *simple* expression is one whose operands consist only of columns or constants; however, if one or more of the expression's operands is another expression, then the expression is said to be *complex*.

Because an operand can be another expression, you can stack expressions within each—or *nest* the expressions. Thus, although SQL offers only a handful of operators and constants, you can build very elaborate tests for the contents of one or more columns within your database—a complex expression can be complex indeed.

Simple expressions

Now that we have introduced what an expression is, we begin to circle back and show how expressions are used within a WHERE clause.

A simple expression compares two columns, or compares a column with one or more constants. For example, if column home_team_runs holds a numeric value, the following checks whether its value is less than or equal to 5:

```
home_team_runs <= 5
```

The script in Listing 3-10, demonstrates this:

Listing 3-10: **Comparison With a Constant**

```
SELECT  home_team, home_team_runs
FROM    game
WHERE   home_team_runs <= 5;
```

If column home_team_runs for a row contains a value that is less than or equal to 5, this expression returns TRUE. If home_team_runs within that row is set to a value that is greater than 5, this expression returns FALSE. If, however, home_team_runs is set to no value at all—if it is NULL, in other words—then this expression returns NULL.

In addition to comparing a column's value with a constant, an expression can compare the values of two columns. For example, the following expression checks whether home_team_runs in the row now being examined holds a value that is greater than that held by visiting_team_runs:

```
home_team_runs > visiting_team_runs
```

The script in Listing 3-11 demonstrates this:

Listing 3-11: **Comparing Two Columns**

```
SELECT   home_team, game_date
FROM     game
WHERE    home_team_runs > visiting_team_runs;
```

If the value to which `home_team_runs` is greater than the value to which `visiting_team_runs` is set, then this expression returns TRUE.

If the value to which `home_team_runs` is less than the value to which `visiting_team_runs` is set, then this expression returns FALSE.

If, however, either `home_team_runs` or `visiting_team_runs` has no value at all — is NULL, in other words — then this expression returns NULL.

Or, consider the column `home_team`, which is set to a string data type. We can see if `FIRSTNAME` is set to the value `Yankees`, `White Sox`, or `Brewers`:

```
home_team IN ('Yankees', 'White Sox', 'Brewers')
```

The script in Listing 3-12 demonstrates this:

Listing 3-12: **Comparison With a List of Constants**

```
SELECT   home_team, game_date
FROM     game
WHERE    home_team IN ('Yankees', 'White Sox', 'Brewers');
```

If `home_team` is set to `Yankees`, `White Sox`, or `Brewers`, this expression returns TRUE. If it is set to any other string, this expression returns FALSE. If, however, `home_team` is NULL — if it has no value at all — then this expression returns NULL.

At the risk of being repetitive, we must emphasize that SQL expressions implement the relational model's three-tiered logic: any expression can return TRUE, FALSE, or NULL. When you write an SQL expression, you must be prepared for the fact that it can return one of three logical results, not just one of two as with most other computer languages.

Complex expressions

As we noted earlier, a *complex expression* is one in which an operand is itself an expression. In most instances, the subexpression involves an arithmetic operator.

For example, consider again this expression:

```
home_team_runs > visiting_team_runs
```

Let's say, however, that we wanted to find all games in which the home team scored at least twice as many runs as the visiting team. To determine this, we must first divide `visiting_team_runs` by two, and then compare the result with `home_team_runs`, as follows:

```
home_team_runs > ( visiting_team_runs / 2 )
```

Listing 3-13 demonstrates this:

Listing 3-13: **A Simple Arithmetic Expression**

```
SELECT  home_team, game_date
FROM    game
WHERE   home_team_runs > ( visiting_team_runs / 2 );
```

The parentheses indicate that you want the arithmetic operation performed before the comparison is performed. In the above example, this is not necessary, but the parentheses do make the expression easier to read.

For a slightly more complicated example, consider the following complex expression. This is another expression that checks whether the home team scored at least twice as many runs as the visiting team:

```
( visiting_team_runs * 2 ) <= home_team_runs
```

And another way is:

```
( home_team_runs - visiting_team_runs ) <= home_team_runs
```

Or again:

```
( home_team_runs - ( visiting_team_runs * 2 ) ) >= 0
```

Listing 3-14 demonstrates this last example:

Listing 3-14: A More Complex Arithmetic Expression

```
SELECT  home_team, game_date
FROM    game
WHERE   (home_team_runs - ( visiting_team_runs * 2 )) >= 0;
```

This last example demonstrates how expressions can be nested within each other. Here, the left operand of the >= expression is a - (subtraction) expression; and the right operand of that subtraction expression is itself a multiplication expression.

If either home_team_runs or visiting_team_runs were NULL, then its expression (even an arithmetic expression) would also yield NULL—after all, multiplying or dividing NULL yields NULL—and that, in turn, would render the entire expression NULL.

Please note that the expression

```
( home_team_runs / visiting_team_runs ) >= 2
```

also appears to select the games in which the home team scored twice as many runs as the visiting team. However, it has a bug: if the visiting team is shut out (that is, it scores no runs), then this expression may attempt to divide by zero—which is, of course, impossible.

Most SQL engines protect you against this problem: that is, they will exclude all rows in which visiting_team_runs is zero, rather than attempt to divide by zero and crash. However, this expression does not correctly handle games in which the visiting team was shut out, so it is buggy.

AND and OR

One last subsection, and then our introduction to expressions is complete.

You can use the logical operators AND and OR to couple expressions together. Each of these logical operators takes two operands. Each returns a logical value, depending upon the logical value of its operands. Chapter 2 gives the truth tables for AND and OR operations; you may wish to review them quickly.

As an example, consider the baseball game we described above. In Listing 3-14, we were interested in whether the home team scored twice as many runs as the visiting team; however, let us now change that to examine whether the winning team—home or visitors—scored at least twice as many runs as the losers.

The following complex expression discovers this:

```
( ( home_team_runs * 2 ) <= visiting_team_runs )
    OR
( ( visiting_team_runs * 2 ) <= home_team_runs )
```

Listing 3-15 demonstrates this:

Listing 3-15: **Comparison Using Keyword OR**

```
SELECT  home_team, game_date
FROM    game
WHERE   ((home_team_runs * 2) <= visiting_team_runs)
        OR
        ((visiting_team_runs * 2) <= home_team_runs);
```

The above expression returns TRUE if the home team scored at least twice as many runs as the visiting team, or vice versa. In games in which the winner did not score twice as many runs as the loser, both subexpressions will return FALSE, and the overall expression therefore will also return FALSE. Of course, if either `home_team_runs` or `visiting_team_runs` is NULL, then the entire expression evaluates to NULL as well.

Consider further that we are interested in every game in which the winning team scores twice as many runs as the losing team, and in which more than six runs were scored. The script in Listing 3-16 is an example of how to do this:

Listing 3-16: **Comparison Combining Keywords AND and OR**

```
SELECT  home_team, game_date
FROM    game
WHERE   (((home_team_runs * 2) <= visiting_team_runs)
        OR
        ((visiting_team_runs * 2) <= home_team_runs))
        AND
        ((visiting_team_runs + home_team_runs) >= 6)
```

Note the use of parentheses to make clear just which operands are associated with which operators.

This expression in the WHERE clause yields TRUE if the winning team scored twice as many runs as the loser, and both teams together scored at least six runs. If either of those conditions is false, then the expression as a whole yields FALSE. Once again, if either `home_team_runs` or `visiting_team_runs` is NULL, then the expression as whole is NULL.

One way to avoid having an expression return NULL is to check for NULL explicitly. As you recall, you can use the operator IS to check for NULLity. For example, consider the example given immediately above. If we wish to avoid having it return NULL, we can explicitly check for NULL. Strictly speaking, we should not have to do so, as columns home_team_runs and visiting_team_runs were created with the NOT NULL clause, and so cannot contain NULL; however, this is a good "defensive programming" practice, particularly when a column can contain NULL. The script in Listing 3-17 checks for NULL in either column:

Listing 3-17: **Checking for NULL**

```
SELECT   home_team, game_date
FROM     game
WHERE    home_team_runs IS NOT NULL
         AND
         visiting_team_runs IS NOT NULL
         AND
         (((home_team_runs * 2) <= visiting_team_runs)
          OR
          ((visiting_team_runs * 2) <= home_team_runs))
          AND
         ((visiting_team_runs + home_team_runs) >= 6);
```

As you can see, this expression is built around three AND expressions. The first AND expression

```
(home_team_runs IS NOT NULL
     AND
 visiting_team_runs IS NOT NULL)
```

confirms that home_team_runs and visiting_team_runs is not NULL. If either is NULL, then this AND expression is FALSE. The second AND expression

```
(((home_team_runs * 2) <= visiting_team_runs)
    OR
 ((visiting_team_runs * 2) <= home_team_runs))
    AND
 ((visiting_team_runs + home_team_runs) >= 6);
```

performs our runs-scored computation.

The third AND cements the two together. If either of the columns is NULL, or if the runs scored do not match our criteria, then the expression as a whole is FALSE. In this way, we ensure that our expression will always be TRUE or FALSE. As you can see, it is rather a bother to check continually for NULLity in our expressions; such, however, is the price SQL extracts for supporting NULL.

This concludes our introduction to expressions—and to restrictive WHERE clauses. You will see many examples of restrictive WHERE clauses throughout the rest of this book. We urge you to take a good look at them because mastering the restrictive WHERE clause is one of the most important steps toward mastering SQL.

Multitable selections

Our discussion of the SELECT statement to this point has been limited to selecting data from a single table. However, much of the power of the SELECT statement lies in the fact that you can use SELECT data from more than one than table.

To use more than one table in a SELECT statement, we must add two elements to its syntax:

✦ The FROM clause must name each of the tables whose data we are using.

✦ The WHERE clause must contain an expression that shows how the tables are joined.

With these additions, the syntax of the SELECT statement now appears as follows:

```
SELECT column_name|constant|arithmetic_expression
       [ , ... ]
    FROM table_name [ , ... ]
    [ WHERE [ restrict_expression ]
        [ join_expression] ]
```

The *join_expression* indicates the joins between tables. Usually, this gives the foreign keys that link the tables.

Two-table join: An example

The best way to grasp how a multiple-table join works is to see it in action. The script in Listing 3-18 prints out all games played in Comiskey Park:

Listing 3-18: **Comiskey Park Games**

```
SELECT  stadium, home_team, visiting_team,
        home_team_runs, visiting_team_runs, game_date
FROM    team, game
WHERE   stadium = 'Comiskey Park'
            AND
        team.team_name = game.home_team;
```

The output begins as follows:

```
Comiskey Park  White Sox  Angels  5  1  06-08-1992
Comiskey Park  White Sox  Angels  4  2  06-09-1992
Comiskey Park  White Sox  Angels  3  2  06-10-1992
Comiskey Park  White Sox  Angels  0  4  06-11-1992
     . . .
```

The clause `team.team_name = game.home_team` is the *joinexpression* — it shows how the tables `team` and `game` are joined. We included the name of the table in this clause to make it clearer, although we did not have to, as the names of the columns are not ambiguous.

At this point, you may be asking yourself exactly what this statement is doing. If you remember our discussion of relational algebra from Chapter 2, you can see that the above `SELECT` statement translates into the following algebraic actions with which it builds its output:

1. It uses the Cartesian-product operation to build a temporary table whose contents combine the contents of tables `game` and `team`.

2. It then uses the restrict operation to build a second temporary table from the table built in step 1. This new temporary table contains only the rows in which column `stadium` equals the string constant `Comiskey Park`.

3. It again uses the restrict operation to build a third a temporary table from the table built in step 2. This newer temporary table contains only the rows in which the value of column `team_name` equals that of column `home_team`.

4. Finally, the SQL engine uses the project operation to build yet another temporary table — this time, from the table built in step 3. This newest temporary table consists of columns `stadium`, `home_team`, `visiting_team`, `home_team_runs`, `visiting_team_runs`, and `game_date`, in that order.

The final temporary table — the one built using the project operation — is the one that the SQL engine formats and displays on your screen. The SQL engine then throws away all of the temporary tables that it built during this process.

We should point out that the above process describes what is happening logically within the SQL engine. However, the SQL engine may not go through those steps literally. Rather than literally building the four temporary tables described above, the SQL engine uses some short cuts and optimizations to speed the processing of your SQL statement and to reduce the amount of memory used. In particular, the engine will try to make best use of any indices that that you have built for the tables named in the `FROM` clause.

Two-table join: Another example

Let's try another example of two-table joins. The script in Listing 3-19 selects every game that the White Sox lost at home (that is, scored fewer runs) when playing teams in the American League East:

Listing 3-19: White Sox Losses

```
SELECT   home_team, home_team_runs, visiting_team,
         visiting_team_runs, game_date, league, division
FROM     game, team
WHERE    home_team = 'White Sox'
             AND
         home_team_runs < visiting_team_runs
             AND
         game.visiting_team = team.team_name
             AND
         division = 'E';
```

The output begins as follows:

```
White Sox  2  Blue Jays  6  05-22-1992  A  E
White Sox  0  Blue Jays  9  08-26-1992  A  E
White Sox  0  Orioles    2  05-15-1992  A  E
White Sox  2  Orioles    7  05-16-1992  A  E
White Sox  2  Orioles    3  07-20-1992  A  E
White Sox  1  Red Sox    2  07-04-1992  A  E
White Sox  2  Yankees    4  08-15-1992  A  E
```

Unions

As you may have guessed from the above examples, SELECT statements can become rather complex. In fact, it is quite possible to write a SELECT statement that is too complex to be readily understood; and this means, in turn, that you cannot debug it because you cannot readily understand just what it is supposed to do.

One key to writing SELECT statements, as with writing any kind of computer program (or any kind of book), is to break the statement down into smaller, simpler pieces, each of which you can debug individually.

For example, consider again the script in Listing 3-19. This script selects every game that the White Sox lost at home against an Eastern Division opponent. This script has some complexity to it, but basically it is a straightforward statement. However imagine that we wished to find every game that the White Sox lost against

Eastern Division teams, whether at home or on the road. Some thought will show that it is not possible to write a simple SELECT statement to execute this query. That is because we must somehow ensure that the White Sox—whether the home team or the visitors—scored fewer runs than their opponents, and there is no way to do that without using an "if" operator, which SQL does not support.

So, what can we do? Does this mean that SQL is not relationally complete—that it cannot even execute simple, everyday questions? No. In fact, SQL gives us an elegant way to solve this problem: the UNION clause.

The UNION clause cements together into one table the output of two or more SELECT statements. This clause lets you tackle complex problems by writing a series of simple SELECT statements, and then cementing them together. With the addition of this clause, the syntax for the SELECT statement appears as follows:

```
SELECT column_name | constant | arithmetic_expression [ , ... ]
    FROM table_name [, ... ]
    [ WHERE [ restrict_expression ] [ join_expression ] ]
[ UNION
SELECT select_statement ]
```

Consider, for example, the baseball problem we stated just above. The UNION clause lets us write two simple SELECT statements—one for the White Sox as the home team, the other for the White Sox as the visitors—then cement the results together. The following SELECT statement implements this strategy:

```
SELECT   home_team, home_team_runs, visiting_team,
         visiting_team_runs, game_date, league, division
FROM     game, team
WHERE    home_team = 'White Sox'
             AND
         home_team_runs < visiting_team_runs
             AND
         game.visiting_team = team.team_name
             AND
         division = 'E'
UNION
SELECT   home_team, home_team_runs, visiting_team,
         visiting_team_runs, game_date, league, division
FROM     game, team
WHERE    visiting_team = 'White Sox'
             AND
         home_team_runs > visiting_team_runs
             AND
         game.home_team = team.team_name
             AND
         division = 'E'
```

As the above example shows, each SELECT statement that you join with the UNION clause must request exactly the same set of columns from your database, and in the same order. In other words, the column_name and FROM clauses of each of the SELECT statements must be exactly the same.

No UNIONs: A work-around

Unfortunately, some database packages, including MySQL, do not support `UNION`s. However, all is not lost. There is a work-around for `UNION`—a temporary table. The script in Listing 3-20 uses a temporary table to mimic a `UNION`:

Listing 3-20: **Mimicking a UNION**

```
CREATE TABLE sox_lose (
    home_team           CHAR(15) NOT NULL,
    visiting_team       CHAR(15) NOT NULL,
    home_team_runs      SMALLINT NOT NULL,
    visiting_team_runs  SMALLINT NOT NULL,
    game_date           CHAR(10) NOT NULL,
    league              CHAR(1)  NOT NULL,
    division            CHAR(1)  NOT NULL
);

INSERT INTO sox_lose (home_team, visiting_team, home_team_runs,
                      visiting_team_runs, game_date, league, division)
    SELECT  game.home_team, game.visiting_team, game.home_team_runs,
            game.visiting_team_runs, game.game_date, team.league,
            team.division
    FROM    game, team
    WHERE   home_team = 'White Sox'
                AND
            home_team_runs < visiting_team_runs
                AND
            game.visiting_team = team.team_name
                AND
            division = 'E';

INSERT INTO sox_lose (home_team, visiting_team, home_team_runs,
                      visiting_team_runs, game_date, league, division)
    SELECT  game.home_team, game.visiting_team, game.home_team_runs,
            game.visiting_team_runs, game.game_date, team.league,
            team.division
    FROM    game, team
    WHERE   visiting_team = 'White Sox'
                AND
            home_team_runs > visiting_team_runs
                AND
            game.home_team = team.team_name
                AND
            division = 'E';

SELECT  *
FROM    sox_lose;

DROP TABLE sox_lose;
```

At first glance, the script appears to be complex; but it's really quite straightforward:

✦ The CREATE TABLE statement creates a table called sox_lose. This table has the same number and type of the columns that we are selecting with our two SELECT statements. For the sake of convenience, we give the columns the same names as those of the columns being selected.

✦ The first SELECT statement selects the games in which the White Sox are the home team. It is embedded within an INSERT statement, which writes the output of the SELECT statement into the new table sox_lose.

✦ The second SELECT statement selects the games in which the White Sox are the visitors. It is embedded within an INSERT statement that writes its data statement into the new table sox_lose.

✦ The third SELECT statement reads the contents of sox_lose and writes them to the screen.

✦ Finally, the DROP TABLE statement throws away sox_lose when we are done with it, as we do not want it cluttering up the database now that we have no more use for it.

The use of temporary tables gives you a way to work around the absence of support for the UNION clause. In this way, you can break seemingly intractable selections into a set of small, discrete SELECT statements that you can debug and run separately.

ORDER BY: Sort output

In our examples so far, the data that we have selected from our databases have appeared in no particular order. However, the SELECT statement includes a clause with which you can sort the output of a selection.

The ORDER BY clause to the SELECT statement sorts the output of the SELECT statement. You can sort by more than one column, and you can sort by either ascending or descending order. When we add this clause to the syntax of the SELECT statement, it appears as follows:

```
SELECT column_name | constant | arithmetic_expression [ , ... ]
    FROM table_name [, ... ]
    [ WHERE [ restrict_expression ] [ join_expression ] ]
    [ ORDER BY column_name [ ASC|DESC ] [, ... ] [ ASC|DESC ] ]
[ UNION
SELECT select_statement ]
```

The script in Listing 3-21 selects team names from the baseball database without sorting:

Listing 3-21: **Unsorted Teams**

```
SELECT   team_name, league
FROM     team;
```

This script gives the following output:

```
Orioles      A
Reds         A
Angels       A
White Sox    A
```

The next script, Listing 3-22, sorts the output into alphabetical order:

Listing 3-22: **Alphabetical Sorting**

```
SELECT   team_name, league
FROM     team
ORDER BY team_name;
```

It gives the following output:

```
Angels       A
Astros       N
Athletics    A
Blue Jays    A
   . . .
```

You can also sort by more than one column. Listing 3-23 demonstrates this:

Listing 3-23: **Sorting by Multiple Columns**

```
SELECT   home_team, visiting_team
FROM     game
ORDER BY home_team, visiting_team;
```

The output of this script is as follows:

```
Angels          Athletics
Angels          Athletics
Angels          Athletics
Angels          Athletics
Angels          Athletics
Angels          Athletics
Angels          Blue Jays
        . . .
```

As you can see, the ORDER BY clause first sorted the entire output by the first column you named (in this case, home_team); then for each value of the first column sorted by the value of the second column you named (in this case, visiting_team).

By default, the ORDER BY clause sorts data by ascending order. For string types, this means sorting by lexical (alphabetical) order; for number types, by numeric value; and for date types, from earlier dates to later. You can, however, specify descending order, which reverses each of these criteria. For example, Listing 3-24 replicates Listing 3-23, except that the output is written in descending order:

Listing 3-24: **Sorting in Descending Order**

```
SELECT   home_team, visiting_team
FROM     game
ORDER BY home_team DESC, visiting_team DESC;
```

Its output is:

```
Yankees         White Sox
Yankees         White Sox
Yankees         White Sox
Yankees         White Sox
Yankees         White Sox
Yankees         White Sox
Yankees         Twins
        . . .
```

The keyword ASC tells the ORDER BY clause to sort into ascending order. Now, you may ask why such a keyword is needed, given that ascending order is the default? The reason is that you can mix your sorting: you can specify that some columns be sorted into ascending order and others into descending. The script in Listing 3-25 demonstrates this:

Listing 3-25: **Mixed Sorting**

```
SELECT  home_team, visiting_team
FROM    game
ORDER BY home_team DESC, visiting_team ASC;
```

Its output is:

```
Yankees      Angels
Yankees      Angels
Yankees      Angels
Yankees      Angels
Yankees      Angels
Yankees      Angels
Yankees      Athletics
   . . .
```

As you can see, the names of the home teams are in descending order, whereas the names of the visitors are in ascending order.

ORDER BY and UNIONs

SQL restricts how you can sort the data generated by a SELECT statement that contains a UNION clause.

In brief, only the last SELECT clause within the SELECT statement can have an ORDER BY clause. This ORDER BY clause then affects the entire SELECT statement. For example, the script in Listing 3-26 sorts the output of the example SELECT statement with which we demonstrated the UNION clause. The modified SELECT statement would read as follows:

Listing 3-26: **UNIONs and ORDER BY**

```
SELECT  home_team, home_team_runs, visiting_team,
        visiting_team_runs, game_date, league, division
FROM    game, team
WHERE   home_team = 'White Sox'
            AND
        home_team_runs < visiting_team_runs
            AND
        game.visiting_team = team.team_name
            AND
        division = 'E'
```

Continued

Listing 3-26 *(continued)*

```
UNION
SELECT  home_team, home_team_runs, visiting_team,
        visiting_team_runs, game_date, league, division
FROM    game, team
WHERE   visiting_team = 'White Sox'
            AND
        home_team_runs > visiting_team_runs
            AND
        game.home_team = team.team_name
            AND
        division = 'E'
ORDER BY home_team, visiting_team, game_date;
```

This restriction makes sense, given that it makes no sense to sort the output of a SELECT clause before you mix it with the output of other SELECT clauses.

DISTINCT and ALL: Eliminate or request duplicate rows

You may have noticed that most of the previous examples returned multiple iterations of a given row. For example, Listing 3-23, which selects the names of teams from table game, returns the following:

```
Angels   Athletics
Angels   Athletics
Angels   Athletics
Angels   Athletics
Angels   Athletics
Angels   Athletics
Angels   Blue Jays
      . . .
```

that is, it returns one pair of team names for each game played.

In many situations, however, you will not want to build a table that consists of multiple iterations of the same row. Rather, often you will want just one copy of every unique row that your SELECT statement generates. The keywords DISTINCT and ALL enable you to control whether a SELECT statement outputs every row or only one copy of each unique row.

The keyword DISTINCT tells the SQL engine to throw away duplicate rows. The keyword ALL tells the SQL engine to retain them. When we add this keyword to our syntax for the SELECT statement, it appears as follows:

```
SELECT [ DISTINCT|ALL ]
        column_name | constant | arithmetic_expression [ , ... ]
    FROM table_name [, ... ]
    [ WHERE [ restrict_expression ] [ join_expression ] ]
    [ ORDER BY column_name [, ... ] [ ASC|DESC ] ]
[ UNION
SELECT select_statement ]
```

For example, consider Listing 3-27, which adds the keyword DISTINCT to the SELECT statement:

Listing 3-27: **Omitting Duplicate Rows**

```
SELECT  DISTINCT home_team, visiting_team
FROM    game
ORDER BY home_team, visiting_team DESC;
```

This outputs the following:

```
Angels      Yankees
Angels      White Sox
Angels      Twins
Angels      Tigers
Angels      Royals
Angels      Red Sox
Angels      Rangers
   . . .
```

As you can see, duplicate rows have been eliminated: the script printed only one copy of each unique row that the SELECT statement generated.

The keyword ALL has the opposite effect: it tells the SQL engine not to throw away duplicate rows. You will not need to use this keyword with a SELECT statement that stands by itself, because the SELECT statement's default behavior is to retain duplicate copies of rows. However, you may need to use ALL in a SELECT statement that contains a UNION clause, because the default for a UNION is to throw away duplicate rows.

Please note that some database engines — in particular, Informix — use the keyword UNIQUE as a synonym for DISTINCT.

Outer joins

Consider the script in Listing 3-28:

Listing 3-28: **Join Two Tables**

```
SELECT  DISTINCT home_team, team_name
FROM    game, team
WHERE   home_team = team_name;
```

It generates the following:

```
Angels      Angels
Athletics   Athletics
   . . .
```

"But wait a second," you may be thinking. "What happened to the National League teams?" The National League teams are missing because of how the SELECT statement works. As you recall, the SELECT statement begins its work by building a Cartesian product of the tables that are named in the FROM clause of the SELECT statement. As it happens, the data we loaded into table game only contains information about American League games, the Cartesian product of tables game and team excludes the rows in team that describe National League teams.

This can be a serious problem, because many of the most important questions you will ask of a database will concern data that is missing: knowing that something did not occur can be as important as knowing that something did occur.

Fortunately, SQL2 gives us a way around this problem: the outer join. An *outer join* in effect tells the SQL engine to diddle with the output of the Cartesian product so that it contains a row for every row in a given table, regardless of whether it is joined with a row in the other table. The rows that have no counterpart in the other table are extended with NULL.

If we rewrote Listing 3-28 to use an outer join, it would output something similar to this:

```
Angels     Angels
NULL       Astros
Athletics  Athletics
Blue Jays  Blue Jays
NULL       Braves
Brewers    Brewers
NULL       Cardinals
   . . .
```

The column to the left gives the value of column `home_team`; the column on the right gives the value of column `team_name`. Because `game` holds no data for National League teams, the SQL engine replaces column `home_team` with NULL to fulfill the outer join.

Types of Outer Joins

Outer joins come in three types:

Left outer join	The table to the left of the join expression is outer-joined to the table to the right of the join expression.
Right outer join	The table to the right of the join expression is outer-joined to the table to the left of the outer-join expression.
Full outer join	Combine both left- and right outer joins.

When we join column `home_team` with column `team_name`, the types of outer-join would have these effects:

✦ A left outer join means that every row in `game` appears in a row in the output, regardless of whether it could be joined to a row in table `team`.

✦ A right outer join means that every row in `team` appears in a row in the output, regardless of whether it could be joined to a row in table `game`.

✦ A full outer join means that every row in either `team` or `game` appears in a row in the output, regardless of whether a row in either could be joined to a row in the other.

Notation of outer joins

As you can see, outer joins greatly increase the range of queries that you can write.

So much for the good news. The bad news is that the notation for outer joins varies wildly among database packages. This section discusses some of the more commonly used syntaxes.

Sybase

Sybase indicates an outer join by attaching an asterisk to the comparison operator used in the *join_expression*. The asterisk goes to the left of the operator to indicate a left outer join; to the right of the operator to indicate a right outer join; and an asterisk on both sides of the operator indicates a full outer join. For example, the following is the SELECT statement from Listing 3-28 using a Sybase-style left outer join:

```
SELECT  DISTINCT home_team, team_name
FROM    game, team
WHERE   home_team *= team_name;
```

The same, but using a right outer join:

```
SELECT  DISTINCT home_team, team_name
FROM    game, team
WHERE   home_team =* team_name;
```

And the same again, but using a full outer join:

```
SELECT  DISTINCT home_team, team_name
FROM    game, team
WHERE   home_team *=* team_name;
```

Oracle

Oracle uses an entirely different notation: it uses a parenthesized plus sign in the `join_expression`, instead of an asterisk, but it places that symbol after the table that is to be NULL extended. In effect, Oracle's notation reverses the notation used by Sybase.

For example, the following is the `SELECT` statement from Listing 3-28 using a left outer join:

```
SELECT  DISTINCT home_team, team_name
FROM    game, team
WHERE   home_team = team_name (+);
```

The same, but using a right outer join:

```
SELECT  DISTINCT home_team, team_name
FROM    game, team
WHERE   home_team (+) = team_name;
```

And the same again, but using a full outer join:

```
SELECT  DISTINCT home_team, team_name
FROM    game, team
WHERE   home_team (+) = team_name (+);
```

Informix

Informix is yet another notation: it indicates an outer join by inserting keyword `OUTER` into the `FROM` clause. `OUTER` prefixes the name of the table to be outer-joined.

The terminology *left outer join* and *right outer join* are not very descriptive when applied to the Informix notation; rather, the Informix notation can indicate a full or a partial outer join. For example, the following rewrites Listing 3-28 to outer-join table `team` to table `game` using Informix notation:

```
SELECT  DISTINCT home_team, team_name
FROM    game, OUTER team
WHERE   home_team = team_name;
```

The following outer-joins game to team:

```
SELECT  DISTINCT home_team, team_name
FROM    OUTER game, team
WHERE   home_team = team_name;
```

And the same again, but implementing a full outer join:

```
SELECT  DISTINCT home_team, team_name
FROM    OUTER game, OUTER team
WHERE   home_team = team_name;
```

The Informix notation marks outer joins more clearly than does the notation used by Oracle or SQL Server. On the other hand, the notation is less specific: that is, if you prefix a table with OUTER, Informix outer-joins it to every other table named in the FROM clause, whereas the Oracle and SQL-Server notations let you outer-join a table to some tables, and not to others.

MySQL

MySQL uses a peculiarly convoluted notation for outer joins. It implements the key-word JOIN, with which you can define the join. We do not describe this clause in detail; however, the script in Listing 3-29 rewrites Listing 3-28 to use a MySQL-style left outer join:

Listing 3-29: **MySQL Left Outer Join**

```
SELECT  DISTINCT game.home_team, team.team_name
FROM    team
LEFT JOIN game ON team.team_name = game.home_team
ORDER BY team_name;
```

Note that we inserted the clause LEFT JOIN to define the left outer join between tables team and game. Note, too, that we excluded table game from the FROM clause; if we had included game in the FROM clause, the MySQL parser would complain of a syntax error.

You can follow the JOIN clause with a WHERE clause that further restricts the query. For example, Listing 3-30 adds a WHERE clause to Listing 3-29 to limit output to games in which the visiting team is the White Sox:

Listing 3-30: **Adding WHERE**

```
SELECT  DISTINCT game.home_team, team.team_name
FROM    team
LEFT JOIN game ON team.team_name = game.home_team
WHERE   game.visiting_team = "White Sox"
ORDER BY team_name;
```

Each of the notations for outer joins has its strengths and weaknesses. The biggest weakness of each, however, is that none is recognized by any other package. Clearly, this is one of the biggest limitations in porting SQL from one database package to another.

We must note, too, that some database packages do not support outer joins. In particular, PostgreSQL first released support for outer joins in the winter of 2001; most editions of PostgreSQL that are in use on Linux systems do not support outer joins at all.

Functions

As we noted at the beginning of this section, the `column_name` clause of the `SELECT` statement can include items other than the names of columns. We also mentioned that it can include constants and arithmetic expressions. Another item that can be included in `column_name` clause are functions.

A *function* is a block of code that is executed by the database engine and that returns a single value. Most functions take one argument: the name of the column whose data are to be analyzed. (Some functions take multiple arguments; we discuss several examples later.) Consider, for example, the script in Listing 3-31, which demonstrates the output of the summary function `SUM()`.

Listing 3-31: **SUM() Function Output**

```
SELECT  SUM(home_team_runs),
        SUM(visiting_team_runs),
        SUM(home_team_runs) + SUM(visiting_team_runs)
FROM    game
WHERE   home_team = 'White Sox';
```

The output is:

```
353          280          633
```

As you can see, the expression

```
SUM(home_team_runs)
```

counted the runs the home team scored (in this instance, the White Sox); the expression

```
SUM(visiting_team_runs)
```

counted the runs scored by the visiting teams; and the expression

```
SUM(home_team_runs) + SUM(visiting_team_runs)
```

returned the sum of all runs scored by both teams.

When we take summary functions into account, the syntax of the SELECT statement appears as follows:

```
SELECT [ DISTINCT|ALL ] column_name | constant | arithmetic_expression | \
        function ( column_name ) [, ... ]
    FROM table_name [, ... ]
    [ WHERE [ restrict_expression ] [ join_expression] ]
    [ ORDER BY column_name [, ... ] [ ASC|DESC ] ]
[ UNION
SELECT select_statement ]
```

Relational-database packages implement different suites of summary functions. However, practically every database package implements the following functions. We present them as MySQL implements them.

SUM(), AVG()

Summary function SUM() adds up the contents of the column given it as an argument. Summary function AVG() gives the average (that is, the mean) of the column given it as an argument.

The script in Listing 3-32 extends Listing 3-31 to demonstrate AVG():

Listing 3-32: **AVG()**

```
SELECT  SUM(home_team_runs),
        SUM(visiting_team_runs),
        SUM(home_team_runs) + SUM(visiting_team_runs),
        AVG(home_team_runs),
        AVG(visiting_team_runs),
        AVG(home_team_runs) + AVG(visiting_team_runs)
FROM    game
WHERE   home_team = 'White Sox';
```

Its output is:

```
353      280      633      4.7703      3.7838      8.5541
```

MIN(), MAX()

Summary function MIN() returns the minimum value in the column passed to it as its argument. Summary function MAX() returns the maximum value in the column passed to it as its argument.

Listing 3-33 demonstrates these functions. It gives the minimum and maximum values scored by the home and visiting teams when the White Sox were at home.

Listing 3-33: MIN() and MAX()

```
SELECT  MIN(home_team_runs),
        MIN(visiting_team_runs),
        MAX(home_team_runs),
        MAX(visiting_team_runs)
FROM    game
WHERE   home_team = 'White Sox';
```

This returns:

```
0      0      19      11
```

The minimum number of runs scored by either home team or visiting is zero, as you would expect. The maximum number of runs the White Sox scored in a game at home was 19; the maximum number of runs scored against them at home that season was 11.

COUNT(), COUNT(*)

The summary functions COUNT() and COUNT(*) count the number of rows generated by a given SELECT statement.

These two forms of counting differ in that COUNT() takes a column name as its argument, whereas COUNT(*) counts the rows without regard to any given column. However, these two functions behave exactly the same — each counts the number of rows that the SELECT statement generates — so there is no reason ever to use COUNT(). We will limit our examination to COUNT(*).

You may wonder what use it is to know the number of rows that a given SELECT statement generates. The answer is that this information can answer a wide range of questions, most of which begin with the phrases "How often . . .?" or "How many . . .?" For example, suppose you wished to know how many times the White Sox were shut out at home. The script in Listing 3-34 uses COUNT(*) to find the answer:

Listing 3-34: **Shutouts**

```
SELECT   COUNT(*)
FROM     game
WHERE    home_team = 'White Sox'
            AND
         home_team_runs = 0;
```

And the answer is:

   5

That is, the White Sox were shut out at home five times.

GROUP BY clause

As you can see, the summary functions can be quite useful when you wish to generate a simple summary of the rows within a table. Suppose, however, that you wanted to summarize only a subset of the rows of a table? Is there a way to do that with a summary function?

The answer is yes, there is a way. The GROUP BY clause enables you to organize the output of a SELECT statement into groups, each of which is summarized individually by a summary function.

Syntax of groupings

The syntax of the GROUP BY clause is exactly like that of the ORDER BY clause: you can follow the keywords GROUP BY with the names of one or more columns. Commas must separate multiple column names. The SQL engine groups its output by the values of the columns, in the order in which you name them, and then invokes each summary function that you've named in the *column_name* clause for each of the subgroups so generated.

When we take summary functions into account, the syntax of the SELECT statement appears as follows:

```
SELECT [ DISTINCT|ALL ] column_name | constant | arithmetic_expression | \
        function ( column_name ) [ , ... ]
    FROM table_name [, ... ]
        [ WHERE [ restrict_expression ] [ join_expression ] ]
        [ GROUP BY column_name  [, ... ] ]
        [ ORDER BY column_name  [, ... ] [ ASC|DESC ] ]
[ UNION
SELECT select_statement  ]
```

For example, consider the example program in Listing 3-34, which counted the number of times that the White Sox were shut out at home. Now suppose that you want to know how many times every team was shut out at home. You could write 26 SELECT statements, one for each team; or you could use a GROUP BY clause to tell the SQL engine to group together each team's games and count each group individually. The script in Listing 3-35 does this:

Listing 3-35: **COUNT(*) and GROUP BY**

```
SELECT   home_team, COUNT(*)
FROM     game
WHERE    home_team_runs = 0
GROUP BY home_team;
```

The output is:

```
Angels        5
Athletics     4
Blue Jays     4
Brewers       1
    . . .
```

You can combine the GROUP BY and ORDER BY clauses. For example, the script in Listing 3-36 generates the same output as Listing 3-35 except that the output is in descending order:

Listing 3-36: **Descending Order**

```
SELECT   home_team, COUNT(*)
FROM     game
WHERE    home_team_runs = 0
GROUP BY home_team
ORDER BY home_team DESC;
```

The output is:

```
Yankees       3
White Sox     5
Twins         5
Tigers        4
Royals        5
    . . .
```

Aliases for columns

At this point you may be asking whether there is a way to order the output of this SELECT statement by the number of times the team was shut out, not by the name of the team? This is a real problem; after all, you cannot put the COUNT(*) function into the ORDER BY clause. However, it can be done — if we use an alias for a column name.

SQL lets you use the number of a column clause as an alias for the column's name in GROUP BY and ORDER BY clauses. A column's number is determined by the order in which the columns are named in SELECT statement's *field_name* clause. In Listing 3-36, home_team is column 1, and the output of the function COUNT(*) is column 2. This method enables you to identify a column that does not have a name because it was built by an expression or by a function.

For example, Listing 3-37 sorts by the count of shut outs:

Listing 3-37: **Descending Order on an Expression**

```
SELECT   home_team, COUNT(*)
FROM     game
WHERE    home_team_runs = 0
GROUP BY home_team
ORDER BY 2 DESC;
```

Here, the clause ORDER BY 2 tells the SQL engine to sort the output by the contents of the second column, which is the column built by the COUNT(*) function. The output is:

```
Rangers      7
Angels       5
White Sox    5
Twins        5
     . . .
```

So, now we can easily see that the Rangers were the team that was shut out most often at home.

Another way to use aliases is to assign a string as an expression's name, and then use that name throughout the rest of the SELECT statement. To assign a name to an expression, use the keyword AS.

For example, the script in Listing 3-38 rewrites Listing 3-37 to use a string as an alias for the COUNT(*) function:

Listing 3-38: String Alias

```
SELECT   home_team, COUNT(*) AS shutouts
FROM     game
WHERE    home_team_runs = 0
GROUP BY home_team
ORDER BY shutouts DESC;
```

The output of this script is the same as that of Listing 3-37; but this script has the advantage of being more readable.

This ability to alias an expression comes in very handy as you begin to write complex SELECT statements.

Other functions

In this section, we concentrated on the most commonly used functions — those that summarize data for an entire column. However, most database packages offer a rich set of functions. These include trigonometric functions; functions that analyze or transform text; functions that format date and time data; and other, miscellaneous functions.

IFNULL()

One of the most useful of these miscellaneous functions is the IFNULL() function. IFNULL() lets you set what the query returns should a given expression be NULL.

IFNULL() takes two arguments: the first argument is the expression to be evaluated, and the second argument is the value to be printed should the first expression evaluate to NULL. The type of the second argument must match that of the first; that is, if the first argument is an expression that outputs a string, then the second argument must be a string, whereas if the first argument is an expression that outputs a numeric value, then the second argument must be a number.

For example, Listing 3-39 rewrites Listing 3-29 to use IFNULL():

Listing 3-39: Demonstrating IFNULL()

```
SELECT  DISTINCT team.team_name, IFNULL(game.home_team_runs, -1)
FROM    team
LEFT JOIN game ON team.team_name = game.home_team
ORDER BY team_name;
```

Because home_team_runs is a numeric column, the second argument to IFNULL() must also be a number. When run, this script outputs the following:

```
Angels        8
Angels       10
Angels        4
Angels        3
     .   .   .
Brewers       0
Brewers      15
Cardinals    -1
Cubs         -1
Dodgers      -1
Expos        -1
     .   .   .
```

Instead of printing the string NULL in instances where the database holds no game information for a given team, the engine now prints -1.

IFNULL() is particularly useful in cases in which a database engine returns an otherwise legal value to indicate NULL. For example, some engines return zero if an integer column is NULL; if zero is a legal value in that column, then you need to use IFNULL() to map NULL to another, unused value.

Some database packages use the name ISNULL() instead of IFNULL(); however, the syntax and the behavior is the same.

Adding new functions

Many database packages let you code new functions and add them to the database engine. Both PostgreSQL and MySQL support this feature.

The method for coding a function and adding it varies quite a bit from one database package to the next. In most instances, you must be a fairly accomplished C programmer. For more information, consult the documentation that comes with your database package.

Sub-SELECTs

Earlier, we described the UNION clause to the SELECT statement. This clause enables us to link SELECT statements; it enables us to easily perform tasks that would be difficult or impossible without it.

SQL also enables you to nest SELECT statements: an expression within a SELECT statement's WHERE clause may itself be a SELECT statement. These nested SELECT statements are not used often, but they do let you answer some questions that would otherwise be difficult or impossible to answer.

To take a simple example: let's say that you wanted to find the teams in the American League East that had been shut out at home. You could write a `SELECT` statement similar to the following:

```
SELECT  home_team
FROM    game, team
WHERE   home_team_runs = 0
            AND
        home_team = team_name
            AND
        league = 'A'
            AND
        division = 'E'
ORDER BY home_team DESC
```

You could also do this with a subquery:

```
SELECT  home_team
FROM    game, team
WHERE   home_team_runs = 0
            AND
        home_team IN (
            SELECT  team_name
            FROM    team
            WHERE   league = 'A'
                        AND
                    division = 'E' )
ORDER BY home_team DESC
```

As you can see, the subquery is embedded within an `IN` expression in the `WHERE` clause; the team names that this subquery returns comprise the body of the `IN` expression.

These two `SELECT` statements are equivalent; each produces the same output. The only difference is that the one that uses the subquery is significantly slower than the one that does not.

Given that subqueries are by their nature inefficient, why should we use them? The answer is simple: you shouldn't, except to perform queries that can be performed in no other way.

The great majority of `SELECT` statements do not require a sub-`SELECT`. The most important exceptions are the `SELECT` statements that are embedded within a `DELETE` or (as we shall see) an `UPDATE` statement.

Because a `DELETE` or `UPDATE` statement can modify only one table at a time, a `SELECT` statement embedded within one of these two statements cannot use a *join_expression* — the work performed by the *join_expression* must be replaced by a sub- `SELECT`. We give examples later.

Note Not all database packages support sub-SELECTs.

SELECT: Conclusion

This concludes the introduction to the SELECT statement. Congratulations for having come with us this far! You have now passed the most difficult and complex part of working with a relational database. Believe it or not, the rest is downhill from here.

We do not claim that this section presented every facet of the SELECT, but what you learned here will enable you to perform the great majority of the selection tasks that you will need to operate your databases.

Modifying the Data Within a Database

So far, you have learned how to create a database, how to put data into it, and how to extract data from it. Now we examine how to modify the data that already resides within a database: either by deleting rows or by changing them. These statements are not used often; but when you do use them, it is important that they be fashioned correctly.

We also discuss how SQL enables you to bundle changes into transactions, to help preserve the integrity of your database.

COMMIT and ROLLBACK: Commit or abort database changes

Let's say that while you were loading a file of data into your data, your system crashed. A crash at such a time can leave the database in a very confused state; among other things, you will have no easy way to determine just how much of the file you were loading had, in fact, been loaded. Mechanisms that are meant to preserve relational integrity may now begin to work against you when you try to repair your tables by hand. Fortunately, ANSI/ISO SQL has a mechanism with which you can protect your database against erroneous or "broken" updates or inputs: transactions.

Under ANSI/ISO SQL, when you begin to work with your database, the SQL engine opens a transaction. During the transaction, the engine logs all changes you make to your database into a temporary area. All "logged" changes to your database together comprise the body of the transaction.

If you issue the SQL statement COMMIT, the SQL engine copies all of its logged changes into the permanent database. If, however, you issue the SQL statement ROLLBACK, the SQL engine throws away all changes made since the beginning of the transaction. In either case, it opens a new transaction and begins the process again.

The syntax of the COMMIT statement is very simple:

```
COMMIT
```

And the syntax of the ROLLBACK statement is equally simple:

```
ROLLBACK
```

As you can see, transactions enable you to add changes to your database in discrete groups: you can check whether a change had the effect you wanted before you modify your database.

Transactions in interactive environments

Transactions are also important in an interactive environment, in which a user may assemble several inputs or modifications of the database, all of which must dovetail. If any of the items are missing or erroneous, none of the items should be entered into the database. SQL transactions give you a means by which your input program can ensure the integrity of the data being entered before your database is modified.

Another problem that can arise is when more than one user is entering data simultaneously. Users can "step on each other's toes" by making contradictory modifications to the database. For example, a database application that manages reservations must prevent two users from simultaneously booking two different people into the same seat.

Transactions will help you guard against this situation; but they can also complicate matters. When a user opens a transaction, the SQL engine in effect makes a copy of the database for his input program; the input program throughout its transaction is working with the database as it was when the transaction opened. However, during that time another user may have modified the database in a way that contradicts the information the user is entering during his transaction. The input program will have no way of discovering this until it attempts to commit the transaction—when one of the SQL statements fails, for no reason that the user can discover. The situation is called a *race condition*, because more than one person is racing to put mutually exclusive data into the database, the loser being the one whose data are rejected.

The lesson is that transactions should be designed to lessen the chances that users will step on each other's toes. This means that rather than piling changes into one huge transaction, transactions should be small and discrete. Unfortunately, on a multiuser system, the problem of users contradicting each other will never go away entirely; but you can work to reduce the number of times it occurs, and to make it easy to recover from such a problem when it does occur.

Open transactions upon exiting

Another problem that the SQL engine faces is what it should do if the program that is issuing SQL statements exits with a transaction open. Relational database packages differ in this regard.

Some engines will attempt to determine the program's state when it exited: if the program crashed or otherwise exited abruptly, the engine will roll back the transaction; however, if the program was shut down intentionally, it will commit the transaction.

Other engines simply roll back the transaction regardless of whether the input program exited intentionally or not.

Some commercial SQL packages, including Informix, automatically commit every SQL statement unless you explicitly open a transaction.

DELETE: Remove rows from tables

The simplest modification you can make to a table in your database is to delete some of its rows. The SQL statement DELETE, as its name suggests, deletes rows from a table. Its syntax is as follows:

```
DELETE FROM table_name
  [WHERE expression  ]
```

The FROM clause names the table from which rows are to be deleted. The WHERE clause lets you identify the rows to be deleted.

If you use DELETE without its WHERE clause, by default it removes every row in table table_name. For example, the statement

```
DELETE FROM team
```

removes every row from table team.

The WHERE clause introduces an expression with which you can identify the rows to be deleted. expression is a standard SQL expression, as we described for the SELECT statement. For example, the following statement deletes from table team all teams in the National League East:

```
DELETE FROM team
WHERE league = 'N' AND division = 'E'
```

Likewise, if you wanted to delete all teams whose home cities' names lie in the first half of the alphabet, you could use the following statement:

```
DELETE FROM team
WHERE city BETWEEN 'A%' AND 'M%'
```

As with the SELECT statement itself, the WHERE clause of the DELETE statement can also contain a SELECT statement. For example, the following enables you to delete from table game every game that involves an American League team:

```
DELETE FROM game
WHERE home_team IN (
    SELECT DISTINCT team_name
    FROM    team
    WHERE   league = 'A'
)
```

Deletions and transactions

Deletions, like INSERT and UPDATE statements, are controlled by transactions. This has saved many a user from blowing a gaping hole into the middle of his database.

Consider, for example, that you wished to remove every game from table game in which the California Angels is the home team. You began to type the following statements:

```
DELETE FROM game
WHERE home_team = 'Angels';
```

However, your finger slipped when you went to press the Return key at the end of the first line: by accident you pressed the semicolon ;, then Return (after all, the keys are close to each other), and so by accident issued the statement:

```
DELETE FROM game;
```

Despair! You have deleted every row from table game: the work of years of patient transcribing from *The Sporting News* is gone! (Naturally, you did not make a backup.) To confirm this horrible fact, you type:

```
SELECT * FROM game;
```

You see nothing: the data in table game has been wiped out.

If your database package supports transactions, the answer is simple—type:

```
ROLLBACK;
```

Voilà! That which was lost is now found—the deleted rows are undeleted. You could confirm it by again typing:

```
SELECT home_team, visiting team FROM game;
```

This returns:

```
Angels      Yankees
Angels      Yankees
Angels      Blue Jays
Angels      Blue Jays
    . . .
```

All is well again. (Now go and make that backup, while you have a chance.)

Unfortunately, not every database package supports transactions. In particular, MySQL does not support transactions unless transactional support is specifically compiled into the MySQL engine.

Deletions and relational integrity

When we discussed the CREATE TABLE statement earlier in this chapter, we noted that some implementations of SQL let you set the default action that the engine should take when a deletion violates relational integrity. SQL's ON DELETE clause lets you determine whether the deletions will cascade through the database, set any referring foreign-key columns to NULL, or bar the deletion should integrity be violated. MySQL does not implement this feature of SQL. However, if it did, the deletion of a row from table team would be controlled by how we had set the ON DELETE clause for the foreign keys in table game.

UPDATE: Modify rows within a table

The last major SQL statement that we consider is UPDATE. This statement modifies the contents of a row or rows within a table. The syntax of this statement is as follows:

```
UPDATE table_name
SET column_name = expression [, column_name = expression ]
[ WHERE expression ]
```

table_name names the table whose rows are to be modified.

The SET clause names the columns that are to be modified, and the value to which each is to be set. You can use an expression to define the value to which each is to be set.

The WHERE clause introduces an expression that enables you to define which rows are to be updated. If this clause is not used, the UPDATE statement modifies every row in the table—assuming that it does not violate any of the referential integrity clauses you entered when you defined the table. For example, the following statement

```
UPDATE team
SET name = 'Old MacDonald'
```

sets the last name of every team's name to Old MacDonald—should you ever wish to do such a thing.

Suppose, for example, that the New York Yankees decided to change their name to the Highlanders (which name the team had before World War I). To do so, you would use this script:

```
INSERT INTO TEAM VALUES (
    'Highlanders', 'New York', 'Highlander Stadium', 'A', 'E');
COMMIT;

UPDATE game
    SET home_team = 'Highlanders'
    WHERE home_team = 'Yankees';
COMMIT;

UPDATE game
    SET visiting_team = 'Highlanders'
    WHERE visiting_team = 'Yankees';
COMMIT;

DELETE FROM team
    WHERE team_name = 'Yankees';
```

A few points in this script should be emphasized:

✦ We inserted a new row into table team to describe Highlanders to the database. We did this to avoid violating referential integrity, as table game has two foreign keys that refer table team.

✦ We used the COMMIT statement to commit the changes to our database after each INSERT or UPDATE statement. It may have been wiser to wait until all statements had executed successfully before we committed the changes to the database; but in this instance, we preferred to save the output of each statement individually.

✦ Only when a new team had been added to table team and all modifications made to table game do we remove the record that describes the now-obsolete Yankees.

✦ If we had used a unique number to represent a team, instead of the team's name itself, then updating the name of a team would not be a big deal—all we would have to do is change the name of the team in table team, and all would be well. In this database, we did not use a unique number to link the tables because in fact team names almost never change. However, teams do change their names from time to time (for example, the Houston Astros were originally named the Colt .45s); if we expect team names to change with any frequency at all, then the numeric link is the better choice.

Such mass modifications are performed only rarely. More often, the UPDATE statement is used to repair or complete an individual record. For example, the following statement repairs a score that is (or rather, should have been) erroneous:

```
UPDATE  game
SET     visiting_team_runs = 7
WHERE   home_team = 'Padres'
            AND
        game_date = '10-7-1984'
```

Views

As the next stop on our "nickel tour" of SQL, we look at views. We discussed views briefly in Chapter 2, but now we explore them in a little more detail.

A view, as its name implies, lets the user view a body of data within the database. In this, it resembles the SELECT statement. However, a view is stored within the database; in this, it resembles a table. In effect, a view is a SELECT statement that is stored within the database.

To create a view, use the statement CREATE VIEW. It has the following syntax:

```
CREATE VIEW view_name
    [ ( column_name [, i , ... ) ]
    AS SELECT select_statement
```

The *view_name* gives the view's name. The name must be unique for the database within which you are creating it.

The optional *column_name* clause enables you to name each column within the view.

The AS SELECT clause identifies the SELECT statement with which data are selected from the database. This can be any form of a legal SELECT statement.

To use a view, simply embed it within the FROM clause of a SELECT statement, the same as if it were the name of a table. For example, Listing 3-40 builds a view and executes it. This view prints the total number of runs scored by a given team at home.

Listing 3-40: **A View**

```
CREATE VIEW home_team_runs AS
    SELECT  home_team, SUM(home_team_runs)
    FROM    game
    GROUP BY home_team;

SELECT * FROM home_team_runs;
```

Views are useful for letting users passively view data. They are also used for building sets of data that can be downloaded to other programs (for example, spreadsheets or *applets*) for further viewing or manipulation. We make further use of views later in this book.

As you may recall from Chapter 2, E. F. Codd stated that a truly relational database must permit updates through views; however, most database packages do not yet support this feature.

Not all database packages support views; in particular, MySQL does not support them.

Stored Procedures and Triggers

Stored procedures and triggers are the final topic for this chapter.

A *stored procedure* is a function that is stored within the database, just like the summary functions that are built into the SQL engine. You can use a stored procedure just like a summary function, except that a stored procedure may return more than one column. Stored procedures are useful because they let you move into the database the routines by which the database itself is accessed. They also make it much easier to write a complex SELECT statement.

A *trigger* is a portion of code that is stored within the database, and which is executed when a given table is modified. The code that forms the body of the trigger can be a script of SQL statements, or it can be a shell script, or it can mix the two. For example, you can use a trigger to update the database automatically, to enforce referential integrity, to bump counters, or perform other useful "housekeeping" tasks. In some instances, triggers can also be used to interact with programs outside the database; for example, if a given condition occurs within the database, then update a log or send mail to the database administrator.

Triggers and stored procedures usually are written in scripting languages that are created by the database vendor. These scripting languages vary wildly among vendors, both in their power and in their syntax. Thus, if you intend to move a database from one database package to another, then bear in mind that all of the code with which you implemented your stored procedures and triggers has to be rewritten.

On this note, we conclude our introduction to SQL. This is by no means an exhaustive discussion of this complex and useful language. However, you now know enough to perform most query tasks with SQL, although no doubt you will need practice before you feel comfortable with it.

Summary

This chapter introduces Structured Query Language (SQL).

The discussion began with the history of SQL, the standards that define SQL, and its disadvantages and advantages. SQL is most useful as a reasonably powerful, standard language for interrogating relational databases. However, no two implementations of SQL are exactly alike, and these differences make SQL scripts difficult to port from one implementation to another.

The terminology of SQL varied a bit from that used in relational theory: column is used as a rough equivalent of attribute; row is used in place of tuple; and table is used instead of relation.

SQL is a query language rather than a fully featured programming language; it does not include many features of a general-purpose language, such as loops, if statements, or ways to manipulate or redirect input or output. SQL usually is embedded within another program or language such as in a SQL interpreter or in a program written in another language (for example, C or Java).

SQL recognizes a large number of keywords — the exact number varies from standard to standard and from implementation to implementation. SQL is not case sensitive.

SQL recognizes data types that encode text, binary numbers, and specialized data (for example, dates, time, money, and binary large objects). The assignment of data types to the columns within a table requires some thought. In particular, two rules apply:

The data type must be able physically to hold every value within the column's domain. For example, if a column holds an attribute that is numeric and has 355,000 members, you must use type INTEGER — type SMALLINT will not be able physically to hold every member of the domain.

The data types of a column that is a foreign key must be exactly the same as the data type of the column in the table to which it is linked. For example, if a foreign key references a column that is of type INTEGER that key must also have type INTEGER.

We then examined each basic SQL statement in turn:

- ✦ CREATE — Create a database, a table, or an index.
- ✦ GRANT — Grant permissions to a user on a given database or table.
- ✦ INSERT — Insert rows into a table.

✦ SELECT — Select data from a database.

✦ DELETE — Delete rows from a table.

✦ UPDATE — Modify one or more rows within a table.

✦ COMMIT — Commit changes to the database.

✦ ROLLBACK — Throw away all changes made since either the beginning of the program, or the last COMMIT or ROLLBACK statement.

The discussion of the SELECT statement also introduced the subject of SQL expressions, including operators, constants, and functions.

Views are SELECT statements that are stored permanently within the database itself. The columns of a view can be included within another SELECT statement, just like the columns of a table.

Stored procedures are functions that are stored within the database, just like the summary functions that are built into the SQL engine.

Triggers are SQL expressions that are stored within the database, and which are executed when a given action is taken upon a given table or tables.

✦   ✦   ✦

Designing a Database

In Chapter 2, we discussed data, relations, integrity, query language, and the other features that comprise the relational model for databases. In Chapter 3, we introduced IBM's Structured Query Language (SQL), which is the relational query language used almost universally by relational databases.

In this chapter, we discuss how to execute a database project. The chapter is in two sections.

The first section discusses how to plan and execute a database project. Here, we emphasize what you need to do to execute a project successfully within a real-world organization.

The second section discusses the art and craft of database design. We discuss how to translate a real-world problem into a set of tables that manage your application properly.

Planning and Executing a Database Project

There are two critical steps to a successful database project: planning the project and executing the project. A dependable, consistent recipe for planning and executing a project is frequently referred to as a *methodology*. Having something you can refer to and use as a methodology goes a long way toward ensuring a usable project plan and increases the likelihood of efficient project execution.

What is a methodology and why have one

A methodology is a sequence of tasks structured for a desired outcome particular to an art or science. Using a proven, dependable method for planning and executing projects results in better control over achieving goals, timing, and cost. It provides a way to "box" a project in terms of cost, cost versus time, or just time. A committed business sponsor embraces a proven methodology; an uncommitted business sponsor does not accept anything but its own opinion, or at least does not commit to the effort to adequately plan the project.

A good methodology provides a clear picture of the present situation, establishing the reason or reasons why change is needed; articulates the desired goal; and provides the route and milestones that guides the progression to reach the goal from the existing situation.

That being said, a word to the wise is appropriate. To paraphrase General Dwight D. Eisenhower: Don't confuse the plan with the project. A comprehensive project plan has little bearing on the actual project progression. The future has no respect for the present. Reality has no respect for the ideal.

A practical methodology for a developing a plan

A methodology for a developing a viable database project plan has three components. Each component needs to be completely understood by the entire project team. The third component — Planning the Tasks — doesn't need to be intimately understood by the business sponsor, but it does have to be accepted. The three components are:

1. Defining and understanding the goal or desired outcome

2. Describing and understanding the existing situation

3. Planning the tasks for reaching the desired goal given the existing situation

Defining and understanding the goal

An organization needs a *vision*, something to give it a purpose, defining just what it is that the organization does better than any other organization. To fulfill this vision requires a strategy. Putting a strategy into action is done through tactics. A project is a tactic and there has to be a rationale for using a tactic.

Regardless of whether you think of the business rationale as the strategy for the business vision, or of the business strategy as the rationale for the project, the project is really the, or perhaps one, tactic for implementing the strategy. This goal component is critical because it gives a reason for the existence of the project. A well-defined goal gives vitality and purpose to the project. A poor (ill-chosen, ill-defined, or nebulous) goal consumes resources that are better used elsewhere, if at all.

Describing and understanding the existing situation

A useful technique for defining the goal is to assess the existing environment, system, and work situation. When you can put down on paper the problem(s) created by the existing system (sometimes called "feeling the pain") and how this situation prevents the business from executing on its business strategy and therefore fulfilling its vision, you have the goal and rationale for the project.

However, assessing the existing situation is also one of the two ingredients of the plan. With a careful assessment and clear understanding, it is possible to know what the plan should consist of. It enables the plan to be efficient and to avoid consuming time, material, and people unnecessarily.

A vital part of understanding the existing situation is to discern what problem a potential project can solve and what problem it cannot solve. For example, automating some business processes because they are consuming too much time when done manually frequently means that the *processes are broken* and *not* that they are too slow. Too often, a software project computerizes a really bad business process, which just moves the problem down the line.

Planning the tasks

This is where you connect the assessment and understanding of the existing situation with the goal. You will need to identify the roles (the grouping and classification of the skills) that the project will need before you can figure out which people will fill the roles. Break the plan into tasks small enough that your available resources can accomplish them, preferably one person per task. If at all possible, never define a task that depends on two people simultaneously. You'll probably find tasks that can occur in parallel, though.

Set a milestone for each task, and have a task (or design) review at that milestone. It is always helpful to just mull over the results in a group. This is another place where the project leaders and/or project champions are important for their attitude and ability to inspire and lead. These milestone reviews must be productive, and there is a real danger of them becoming blame-storming sessions, or at least feel like it to the person whose milestone is being analyzed.

Impediments to a successful project

As you might expect, there are numerous obstacles to a successful project. Not all of them are in the details of the project progress, either. We touch on just a few of the pitfalls that can be created before the project actually gets under way.

The goal statement

Not getting a clear, unambiguous articulation of the desired goal is an easy error to make. After all, what does a clearly stated goal look like? Isn't stating, "Create a new order-entry system on time and under budget" an articulation of a clearly understood goal? The problem is the nebulous nature of the phrase "new order-entry system." A clear goal would refer to the specifications that are *agreed upon* to be met. These specifications are not even necessarily the technical/performance specifications. It is impossible to have a successful project when the business goals are not clearly defined and stated, that is, what is to be gained by the organization.

A second problem with even a clear goal is the question of whether the goal is achievable. If achieving the project goal is not within the capability of the organization, then the project will fall short of success.

A third problem is having a project that is without a clear *organizational* advantage. This is exclusive of the remark above about what the organization will gain. What is meant here is that the organization must gain something from the project that clearly increases (or improves) the delivery of the service or product that it produces.

Competition among several projects for limited resources, personnel, and financing, however well planned each may be, is a problem if the organization cannot select vital projects.

No prioritization of competing goals presents problems with projects because it means that the organization is either unable to decide which projects are the *most important* and therefore should get allocated the limited resources, or that the organization has unrealistic expectations of what it takes to complete a project successfully.

A project/organization that cannot distinguish among its musts, needs, and wants cannot focus on the essential elements of a project. The essential elements of a project are those requirements that bring the most return. This is another symptom of an organization that cannot prioritize. This can be the result of not understanding the organization's goals, the project goals, or how the project fits into the organization's overall strategy.

Not getting a clear, unambiguous understanding of the existing situation will inevitably lead to proposing and providing a solution that does not sufficiently address (solve) the problems that the organization is dealing with. The result is an unsuccessful project, and bad feelings all around.

Not understanding the process for achieving that goal given the existing situation reflects a communication problem. A project kickoff meeting, or maybe a couple of meetings having different focus, is the solution for this problem. One meeting where the project sponsors are in attendance should focus on the business processes that will change and what the impact of those changes will be. A second meeting with the project team should focus on the architecture of the project, the tasks, and the project deliverables.

A lack of focus on the part of project sponsors and project managers will kill a project by neglect and lack of support through difficulties, or by a thousand small changes. See the section on Change Control/Management for related problems.

Unrealistic expectations always kill a project. One of the first responsibilities of the project sponsor (and a project leader) is to keep changing or unrealistic expectations in check. This is an *ongoing* effort; it should never cease. Setting realistic expectations is an often-overlooked key to acceptance of the completed project. Don't let it get to the point of "I thought it was going to. . . ."

A successful project requires

At a high level, a successful project needs support, and agreement on the need and the importance of meeting that need. This is manifested by:

✦ A clear benefit to the organization

✦ Realistic expectations on the part of the receivers of the project, and the people paying for the project

✦ A project champion who maintains visibility, enthusiasm, focus

✦ Clear, honest (honest!) communication

✦ Focus

✦ Change control and management of requested changes

✦ Timely access to resources

✦ A willing acceptance of the results

✦ An end

Although you'll rarely find all of these elements present, you should use the foregoing list as part of a checklist for gauging the project risk. Some of these points need to be part of the project plan as the responsibility of a project role. For example, there is a need for change control in a project, so this should be considered as some of the ongoing project tasks and a resource should be assigned responsibility for change management. As another example, although communication is everyone's responsibility, it is especially the responsibility of the project leader.

Getting to first base – Phases and components of the plan

A project plan should consist of some or all of the following:

✦ Business problem definition

✦ Proposed solutions with a cost/benefit analysis of the proposed solutions

✦ Chosen solution and rationale

✦ Project objectives and organization

✦ Project team makeup with major organization representatives

✦ Critical success factors (don't overlook these!)

✦ Project scope

✦ Project planning assumptions

✦ Detailed project plan and milestones

✦ Project risks and issues

✦ Project contingencies

The idea is to plan well enough that the project participants know, understand, and agree with the goals and the process. After the plan is complete and the project gets underway, the project plan as a document becomes much less useful.

Establishing the need of the organization

The very first bit of information that's established is the organization's need for a project. This should be developed as part of a planning cycle that looks at the present state of the organization, compares it to the desired state of the organization, and from the difference, identifies the needs of the organization. Establishing the need is part of the diagnoses.

The pressures for an organization to change originate in a number of places, and include:

✦ Regulatory compliance pressure, for example, collecting new state and local taxes

✦ Competitive pressure

✦ Organizational efficiency

✦ Market pressures for new products

You should make it a point to know the pressure for the project. The more that the pressure is outside the control of the organization, the more likely that the project will proceed. This is true especially for pet projects — for example, department initiated projects — as compared to projects that are mandated by higher levels in the organization.

Knowing the driving force for the project enables you to identify the people who have the biggest stake in seeing that the project is successful, as well as identifying those people who are unconcerned, maybe even antagonistic, toward the project.

Establishing the relative benefit as compared to other needs of the organization

This should be called *the compelling reason to proceed.* You may not be able to make this choice, but you should be aware of, and put into the project documentation, what other projects similar to this project existed at the time and why this one was chosen over them. Knowing this will aid your communicating in a meaningful way with the project sponsor, and the business areas that may be waiting their turn. It could be that one of these projects becomes more important even before your project is complete.

Evaluating and analyzing the organizational environment

This is part of the diagnosis of the problem. It also forms a part of the plan of action. Don't be surprised to find that there are underlying organizational issues that should be solved before resorting to a technical solution.

Putting together a list of questions for a questionnaire

The best way to get this information is to write down as many questions as you can think of that have to do with the organization. What you really want is to get unrehearsed answers from people "high up" in the organization, higher than even the project sponsor, if at all possible. Analyze the responses so that you can understand and convince anyone that you understand the issues about the organization's perspective of the project; you should be able to develop a history from the answers. By analyzing and comparing responses, you will be able to discover any discrepancies between attitudes and expectations at the highest level of the organization as compared to the project level of the organization. You are looking for *hidden pitfalls* and *hidden opportunities for success*. You need to understand what will solve the problem.

Where you see the word "problem" or "issue" in the following questions, replace it with a statement of the actual problem, for example, "order fulfillment errors." Get the person you're interviewing to give their definition of the problem, and use that definition when you talk to them.

✦ Has the organization, or you, had experience solving this kind of problem before? If yes, what is your perspective on the results? Where they good or bad results? Was your expectation fulfilled?

✦ How does this problem make you lose sleep?

✦ When did this problem become apparent to you, and how did it become apparent?

✦ Can you give me your perspective on the current business process? What problems have resulted from this?

✦ What do you expect to gain (or lose) by solving this problem?

✦ How do financial factors contribute to this problem?

✦ Who else are you aware of who has also addressed, even solved, this problem?

✦ Are there internal or external factors that could cause the problem to get worse or go away?

✦ Are there advantages to leaving well enough alone?

✦ Can you name the parts of the organization that are affected by the problem? How about the unaffected areas? Who has the biggest stake?

✦ Do you see a downside to addressing this problem now? What makes this a particularly good or bad time to address this problem?

✦ Do you think that the organization is prepared to solve this problem? (The answer to this question can be very revealing!) What might work against efforts to address this problem?

✦ Could you suggest what unintended side effects the organization might experience as a result of solving this problem? What do you recommend to avoid or to minimize them?

Establishing the project with a plan

This involves project plan and strategy, and project scope.

Project plan and strategy

The project strategy and plan come after determining the "gap," the difference between the existing situation and environment and the desired situation and environment. Establishing the strategy comes from knowledge of the kinds of solutions — technical and organizational — that are available and what the scope of the project is.

Project scope

Establishing the project scope — the extent of what is to be achieved — should come from questions and analysis of the responses. Here's a list of questions that you can begin with. Add to this list and use it to formally put a "box" around the project. Keep a copy of the responses. Don't ask technical questions of nontechnical people or you'll have them designing the solution blindly.

Where does the data come from and who supplies it?

✦ Does it come from customers?

✦ Does it come from suppliers, governments, internally?

✦ How much of this is already captured in existing systems? Is there documentation for this?

Is a new application definitely needed; how has this been determined?

✦ Is there an existing application that can be used as a model?

✦ Does modifying an existing application look feasible?

✦ Are there off-the-shelf solutions? How would they be integrated? Who would do the integration? Are there internal staff members who are knowledgeable enough to handle it?

Is integration with existing systems needed because that's where the data will come from?

> ✦ How many systems? How old are they? Are their interfaces proprietary? Can the data format be changed or does this project need to reformat/translate the data?
>
> ✦ When will the interface specifications be available? Who do you get them from? Will it cost money?
>
> ✦ Who will write the interfaces? Will it have to be planned into this project?

Do you have to coordinate and integrate with concurrent projects?

> ✦ When will the interface specifications be available?
>
> ✦ Who will write the interfaces?

Is this a departmental/location/and so on infrastructure improvement?

> ✦ Are hardware purchases to be made out of the project budget?
>
> ✦ What is the timing of the purchases?
>
> ✦ Who is responsible for installation?
>
> ✦ Is there a list of qualified vendors?
>
> ✦ Has anyone already contacted vendors and made any commitments?

What end-user software is needed?

> ✦ How many users are there now? How many users will there be in one, two, and three years?
>
> ✦ If any end-user software needs to be purchased, who is buying it?
>
> ✦ Is it budgeted for in the departments where it will be installed?

Training Issues

> ✦ How many users are there now? How many users will there be in one, two, and three years?
>
> ✦ Who is responsible for developing the end-user training? Who is responsible for conducting the end-user training? When will it occur?
>
> ✦ Who is responsible for DBA training? When will that occur? Who will be trained? Is this enough considering the number of users and criticality of the system?

Help Desk Staffing and Training

✦ How many help desk people are needed considering the number of users?

✦ Who is responsible for developing the help desk staff training? Who is responsible for conducting the help desk staff training?

End-User Desktop

✦ Are new desktop PCs going to be needed based on the quantity and age of the current systems? Are the existing desktop PCs adequate for the expected end-user software? How many users are there now? How many users will there be in one, two, and three years?

✦ Who is responsible for specifying the desktop PCs? Who is responsible for purchasing the desktop PCs? Who is responsible for installing and supporting them?

Project Staffing

✦ Are third-party consultants being used for development? Where will they sit? What computers and other equipment are required for them?

✦ Who is responsible for which deliverables and when (doesn't require a lot of detail at this point)?

✦ Does it generate management reports? What reports? Describe them!

✦ Are there regulatory requirements? Please identify those that are applicable.

Change control

You need, at minimum, some acknowledgment that things may change during the project. If you don't expect to be affected by changes, at least put in a section that says, "I don't have a reasonable expectation that any changes will impact this project." Then, update your résumé.

Project hardware and software

Determining the needs of the project for either or both hardware and software require some design work to be done, usually only at an architectural level (as opposed to a detailed level). Some of the requirements may seem to jump out at you, but be sure that it's not you just making presumptions about a solution before all of the investigation (assessments) is complete.

Determining the hardware and software needs

This is more information gathering. Use the following lists to help you start on the questions that you will need to ask. You should always be developing questions as you go. It is especially helpful to make a list of the things that you want answered based on the rough scope that you developed earlier. Planning is an iterative practice, stopping only when asking questions begins to draw blank stares!

Computer/server

Although not a hardware question per se, you need to ask about administration of the servers if you're using existing hardware. If you specify new hardware, then administration will become an issue that you'll need to cover in your plan. Be very aware that database administration requires a different role than server administration does.

Vendor and model number

Amount of RAM and type (is it error correcting?)

Number and type of processors

BIOS or Firmware version

Disk storage systems

Number and size of disks

Disk types

Is a RAID (redundant array of independent disks) storage system attached? What is the RAID level?

What other disk drive interfaces/controllers are used

Controller types, for example, SCSI

Tape/tape backup

Tape drive types, that is, tape media

Tape drive capacity and speed

Operating system

Linux version and vendor (be very specific)

Compiler version

Connectivity

Network configuration; protocols, topology, wiring infrastructure

Is dial-up (remote) access available?

Is ftp available to other servers or to the outside world (maybe through a firewall)?

Are other Linux/UNIX workstations connected?

Software needs

The solution architecture will determine the direction you go here when looking at software. For example, does the architecture specify a client-server solution? Is there data to be accessed that resides on a mainframe? Is this a Web-based solution? Is this a server-only solution? Are you developing only the middle tier of a much larger project? Are you replacing an existing RDBMS and not changing the architecture? You can see from even this simple list that your questions need to be developed from the architecture, which, in turn, is developed from the strategy for solving the problem.

RDBMS

Because this is a book about Linux databases, we provide just a few questions to get you started! Look at the chapters on specific databases for more questions.

What is the licensing cost? What is the annual maintenance?

How much data is anticipated (this is for sizing the RDBMS) and what is its expected growth over one and two years?

Is data from an existing RDBMS being migrated? How will this be accomplished? Is there a bulk data-loading utility? How long will it take?

How is security controlled at the database level?

Does the RDBMS have backup utilities? How are they managed? Are there Database Administrators available to take on the additional work?

Who will administer the RDBMS (who will be the DBA) and what administrative tools are available?

What are the APIs for the RDBMS? Is a Java (JDBC), or ODBC, or Perl DBI, or C/C++ API available? Is CGI available?

What version of SQL is supported; for example, is it fully ANSI SQL-92 compliant?

Middleware

If the high-level solution architecture is leaning toward a multitier solution, you will have to answer questions such as those that follow. Although this list may seem short, it will get long if you have a multitier solution.

How will data access/security be controlled? Will it be through the application?

Is the database server to reside on an inner tier and will it be executing CGI?

If this is a Web-based solution, is there a Web server to be selected, too? Do you need one or more firewalls? Where is the database with respect to the firewall? (You can add a whole bunch more questions about Web servers!)

Will a mainframe be involved? Is mainframe connectivity an issue? If so, to which system (machine type/database type)? (Add more gateway questions here, if a database gateway is needed to access mainframe based data.)

Application development

For application development, a high-level description of the application is needed. You should be aware that there are only two choices for software: buy it or develop it. Even at a high level, the choice to buy or develop is readily apparent based on cost, availability (or time to develop), and features. What you really need here from the solution architecture is what portions of the solution will be purchased and what will be developed. Between these are the interface specifications (yes, even software has interfaces) that will have to be spelled out in the design. Even if you're purchasing a complete solution, you'll probably have interfaces to existing systems. It's pretty rare not to have this requirement.

Answer these following:

> Which language development tools are anticipated: C/C++; Perl; PHP; Java? For which portion of the solution will it be used?
>
> Will CGI be used?
>
> Are dynamic Web pages required by the solution, or will simpler static pages be used?
>
> What HTML editors/Web-page development environment will be needed?
>
> Are there graphical or image development and manipulation tasks?
>
> Which browser will be used?
>
> What Java version will be used? Java Beans?
>
> Is a transaction monitor needed for distributed databases? Is one available for Linux?
>
> What database-specific development tools are missing? Are ODBC libraries, JDBC classes, or Perl DBI classes needed?

Implementation strategy and design

The design requires a conceptual design document followed by an application/process flow diagram. Following those documents, any software that is required can be specified by its "place" in the design and the "work" that it has to accomplish.

If custom software is called for, its specifications can be developed just as if you were purchasing off-the-shelf software. The only difference is that you have to write it and support it! The methods and techniques for partitioning and specifying software at a more detailed level are left for you to research; there is plenty of literature on system engineering (this subject), both theoretical and practical.

Ultimately, you will have a functional specification for every module and subsystem in the design. When you hold design reviews, you are comparing what has been implemented with the specifications.

Concept design

The conceptual design should provide the strategy for implementing the system functions, the modules in which the functions are placed; that is, how the system functions are partitioned among the components of the design. It is helpful to begin with a diagram of showing/illustrating all the primary system functions and features and how they relate to each other, further breaking this down until the individual modules are shown. From these lowest-level diagrams the entire system will have been specified and ready for implementation.

Use the concept design documentation for design reviews, analyzing the impact of feature changes both to the schedule and the other functions. To be truly useful, it should provide a high-level, easily comprehended view of all aspects of the module.

Data-flow diagrams

Data-flow diagrams show the flow and interaction of data through the application. It shows the data needed at each interface point in the system (where modules connect) and provides the guidance to determine the information and business rules required to process the data and pass it on to the next step. Make sure that these diagrams show all of the programs, tables, user output (to reports, or to a PC), and interfaces to other systems affected by each modules. Again, to be truly useful it should be easily comprehended, yet comprehensive.

Module logic-flow diagrams

This document should outline the logic of the program. Use an agreed upon pseudo-code format to specify the logic within the module. Don't get into syntax issues here; that is, don't write it in an actual programming language. This is not a language-specific document! This information along with the data-flow diagram shows how the program works. This must agree with the module functional specification because it becomes part of the module functional specification.

Functional specification

The following sections describe functional specifications.

Module description

Briefly describe the purpose (what part of the overall design) and primary functions of each module; for example, provides a GUI object, validates data according to business rules, implements security.

Design strategy

Describe the approach used to create the module based on the higher level specifications. List every assumption, for example, constant values, frequency of execution, volume of data, made about the specification in addition to the interface specification (the input/output part).

Detailed specification

Proved a detailed functional description of the module based on the higher level specifications. Describe in detail the transformations, validations, modifications of each input datum, the interdependencies among data, format, and representation of data, return values, and so forth. Be especially diligent about side effects!

Database data sources

For each database data source (table, command line, file, and the like) the following information should be provided: data source physical name; data source type; is it manipulated by using insert, update, delete, select; and so forth.

Database logical design: Entity relationship diagrams

A reasonably experienced database designer, a DBA, or a system engineer can develop the logical design by following industry practices and by using the information from all of this design documentation. From the logical design they can produce the physical design.

Plan for the logical design to evolve; maybe relationships will change among entities or as new entities are identified. The physical design will change, too, especially the data types/sizes. But, of course you will have design reviews of all of these changes, won't you?

A data dictionary

The data dictionary is the document that defines the entities (tables), attributes, and intertable and intratables relationships — for example, primary key, foreign key, and so on. A useful data dictionary contains enough information that a developer and database administrator can write correct programs that access the data without illogical results (that they make sense from a business perspective), and can modify, create, and delete data without creating integrity problems, as well as supply data to others.

The following sections in this chapter discuss database design in much more detail. For now, use this list as a starting point:

Entity name	The business entity that this table models.
Table name	The unique identifier for each table.
Column name	The unique identifier for the table column.
Attribute name	The attribute (property or characteristic) of the entity being modeled by the column.
Column data type	The column's physical data type, for example integer, char (10), or decimal (10.2).
Nullable	Whether or not this attribute can be NULL and still be valid.

Default value	What, if any, the default value is for this attribute.
Domain	The domain for this attribute (the range of valid values, if it's easily described).
Description	A description of how the column is used.
Data source	The system plus table plus column(s) from which this datum is gotten. It may give a filename, position, and length if the source is from a file and not a system. It may give a variable name in a program if from an application, so the application name should be provided.
Business rules applied	Shows how this value is derived or how this attribute value is used.

User interface and report layouts

It has been reported that user interface design ends up taking at least 50 percent of the total design and implementation effort. When you consider the amount of data validation that needs to take place for just about every data entry field on a screen for a typical interactive windowing application, this number doesn't seem so outrageous.

GUI layouts

A mock-up of the screen layout should be provided. For each data item on the screen, a detailed description that addresses, at a minimum, the following, is needed:

Title/description, Default value, Validation rules (minimum and maximum values, and the like), Maximum input length, Maximum display length, Calculations, Dependencies with other fields, Button/check box/edit box type of interface element, Confirmation upon validation.

Also, for efficient GUI design, every form must fit into a seamless flow for information entry. You also need to user control and flow via such items such as buttons (OK, Cancel, and so on), navigation to other screens, and tab order from field to field.

Report layouts

Report layouts are significantly easier than GUI design. After all, reports are output only. Nevertheless, the report layout needs to be carefully considered so that the data is displayed so as to convey the *maximum information* in the least amount of time. The information should be readily comprehended. Start with a mockup of the report and address the following:

✦ Report header information

✦ Report column descriptions

✦ Field calculations

✦ Sorting options

✦ Printing options

People resources and project roles

There are project roles and there are people. People fill a role according to the task in the project. When planning a project, the project is divided into tasks that essentially map to individual roles. The project architecture determines which roles are needed. The project plan determines when and for how long.

These are major roles that can appear on a database project. There can be many more roles depending on the scope of the project. The following descriptions are meant only as a guide for you to use; it is not necessary to find a person whose skill and experience exactly matches the role description below.

Primary roles

The Director of Enterprise Information Architecture possesses insight into short and long-term business requirements and strategies. Creates and supplies the enterprise level vision and strategies. Cultivates and maintains sponsorship for mission critical initiatives.

Skills: Is a people person (this person may be above you, so you have no choice!).

The Sponsor Representative represents the goals of the project sponsor to the project, articulating the problem to be solved. Provides the definitions of business data requirements and business rules; arranges for organizational experts needed by the project, validates correctness and completeness of the project strategy. Provides approval at project milestones, approves specifications as they develop and evolve. As a primary receiver of the completed project, this role defines tactical and/or strategic data requirements and priority of information needs.

Skills: Knowledgeable about the subject area, has the ability to communicate clearly, and is focused on results. Has access to executives.

The System Architect possesses broad knowledge of computer and information systems and information delivery, and has the perspective to relate to other information technology disciplines. Develops (the project's) system architecture, assigning responsible roles for the implementation, integrated with information delivery strategies that are consistent with organizational goals and experience. Has an understanding of the disparate project requirements for the varying user groups and the related source systems to ensure a cohesive strategy across initiatives. Provides reliable technical planning and control. Contributes to the project plan, especially for personnel resource assignment. Conducts, participates in, and approves designs at design reviews

Skills: Information system design expertise. Depending on the project, a solid foundation in Web, mainframe, and client-server technologies is required. Should have current knowledge of emerging tools and techniques in information delivery; should be viewed as an expert.

The IT Project Manager manages the organization's information system development projects, including external and internal project coordination; project planning development and tracking; status reporting; issue tracking; resources; and deliverables. Has knowledge of existing systems and the people responsible for those systems. Ensures that all projects are in accordance with organization's strategic efforts.

Skills: System development project management (presumes interpersonal and communication skills have been proven!).

The Project Leader is directly responsible for the start-to-finish implementation of specific information system development projects. Manages project definition, scope, requirements, resources, and implementation. This person, in conjunction with other functional groups, assigns and coordinates the personnel resources for the project, coordinates interviews, schedules design reviews, coordinates schedules and resources for design testing, acceptance testing, and so on.

Skills: System development project management with a strong customer focus. Because the person filling this role has the primary responsibility for the project team's functioning, excellent team-building and intrapersonal communication skills are needed.

The End-User Tool Expert manages all aspects related to the installation/configuration, deployment, and the effective utilization/implementation of all designated end-user software. May develop user documentation and training materials. Provides end-user training in accessing and using the database. Consults with users on an ongoing basis for the duration of the project. May be responsible for end-user, or for "train the trainer" training when that part of the project is reached. Contributes to the design and specification of the end-user tool(s).

Skills: Hands-on end-user tool installation, configuration, and training. Should have taken training/certification offered by software vendors if an off-the-shelf solution is used. Substantial overall PC and Web skills are a plus. Depending on the project, software development experience may be needed. Needs extensive knowledge of the logical and physical contents of the database. Must also possess strong verbal, written, and analytical skills.

The Mainframe System Programmer or Administrator ensures that mainframe processing performs as designed, provides detail system knowledge, and serves as the primary contact/interface to mainframe system owners/support personnel. Because mainframes still are a distinctly different species of computer system from Linux systems, this role has distinctly unique purposes. A broad understanding of mainframe system(s) functionality, data contents, business rules, and system interdependencies and interfaces is absolutely needed.

Skills: Solid technical skills on the source system platforms, including programming and data access experience; strong analytical abilities.

The Database Administrator (DBA) is responsible for all aspects relating to the installation, configuration, use, and monitoring of the Linux database software and/or the specific database. Provides project-level support by advising on and performing logical database design; indexing strategies; physical implementation strategies and trade-offs; overall database/application tuning; end-user database access; database security; and backup and disaster recovery strategies. In conjunction with the Data Modeler, creates the data dictionary for the project and maintains the data dictionary after the project is complete.

Skills: Linux RDBMS-specific design, performance monitoring, database utilities, SQL language. Overall, needs a strong relational database knowledge. Extensive practical hands-on DBA experience. May need experience with mainframe data access, as well.

The Data Modeler analyzes the requirements and develops the logical data requirements project. Translates logical data requirements into a physical design. Because this role is one of the two best suited for creating the data dictionary, it creates the data definitions, relationships, and business rules. Provides documentation to the rest of the project. Contributes to the detailed design specification.

Skills: Overall, strong relational database knowledge with formal training. Conversant in data-modeling theory and experienced in data-modeling practice. Familiarity with data-modeling tools is preferred.

The Linux System Administrator manages all aspects related to the installation/configuration and utilization of all primary server related hardware and software (operating system, network software/protocols, backup and recovery software, and so on). Coordinates and/or performs all physical server configurations modifications with regards to kernel OS modifications, expanding storage and memory capacity, and general maintenance upgrades. Also performs basic administrative tasks as required for end-user access at the operating system level.

Skills: Extensive Linux/UNIX system administration experience.

The Programmer/Analyst understands and provides analysis and business processes, information flow, data requirements, unique data characteristics. Conducts and evaluates results of interviews with end users and peers in other business groups to devise specifications for programs (software). Implements these specifications as program modules. Directs the efforts of programmers. Tests and debugs programs and more complex systems.

Skills: Good oral skills; works well with diverse personalities; is capable of clear written communication. Knowledgeable about information system design, modeling, programming languages, and computer hardware and software. Keeps abreast of developments in information technologies.

The End-User Liaison works closely with the end users, representing their needs, and has an understanding of how they accomplish their tasks. Understands business processes, which is especially important when the processes are broken. Can communicate with end users, explaining and exploring alternatives, new business process and work flow. Contributes to the design and specifications of the end-user tool(s) for the project.

Skills: Good oral skills; works well with diverse personalities; is capable of clear written communication.

The Network Engineer keeps abreast of developments in network technologies; protocols, topologies, wiring (or wireless) application interfaces (for example, Web browsers), network performance, network solutions, analyzing trade-offs. Knowledge of the organization's network infrastructure.

Skills: Education and experience in networking (design, installation, and maintenance) and computer communication.

Customer resources

The goal of obtaining personnel availability information is to ensure that *all* the resources needed to make the project successful are available for the duration of the project. These people, once identified, will be relied upon for critical project activities.

Document any resource concerns, such as availability, experience, or suitability, that may adversely affect the outcome of the project. For example, concurrent responsibility for multiple projects by a key staff member that might interfere with this project.

Use the following questions to evaluate your resources, whether or not they are internal (from your own organization) or are external (maybe a customer's organization or an outsourcing firm). Add to this list as the project scope dictates.

✦ Who is the project manager and how many simultaneous projects will the manager have?

✦ Will there be a dedicated Linux system administrator for the duration of this project?

✦ Will there be a dedicated DBA for the duration of the project?

✦ How many (qualified) application/middleware/Web developers will be working on the project? What are their individual qualifications (list products, other projects, and so on) and their experience with such tools and languages as C, C++, Java, Perl, CGI/PHP, Web Servers (Apache), JDBC, RDBMS experience (design and programming) especially with Linux databases.

✦ What will be the makeup of the test group that performs the system test?

✦ Which, if any, system integrators will help with the development? How many people from the system integrator will be needed and are their qualifications available?

✦ What support requirements are anticipated from other parts of the organization; for example, performance analysis and tuning, application migration, client tools?

Testing the system

System testing is driven by the system architecture. The System Architect is the person most responsible for developing the system test plan. From the system test plan, and the functional requirements come the test plans for the constituent elements of the system. The System Test Plan describes the procedure(s) for system testing, testing approach and philosophy for the system testing process.

The System Test plan specifies the testing environment from a hardware and software perspective (which hardware platforms, networked in what way, which software operating systems and tools, configuration parameters, and so on). The testing environment needs to be kept constant so that no variables are introduced that are not part of the plan, creating unreliable and nonrepeatable results.

All customer requirements must be addressed in the System Test Plan, one by one. Each requirement is described and how it is tested and verified. Unusual test conditions need to be explained. Inputs for each test must be specified and what outcomes indicate pass or fail. Any particular preloading of the database and what this data signifies is also defined here.

Bug tracking and identification are essential parts of this test plan. The plan must specify how this is accomplished and what the process is for regression testing once a fix is made.

Testing the system components

From the system test plan and the functional requirements come the test plans for the constituent elements of the system, usually referred to as a *unit test*. The system component developers (whether software or database or hardware) and the System Architect develop the unit test strategy, that is, what constitutes proof that the unit meets the requirements and that it functions without error.

The unit test documentation should state the purpose of the test, the modules required, and the requirements to verify. From these the unit test procedure is developed. The test procedure specifies how the test is conducted and what constitutes success.

Final acceptance testing

The final acceptance test is developed with the help of the System Architect, the Business Sponsor, End-User Liaison, the Project Manager, and Project Leader(s). Needless to say, this is the acid test for the project. The final acceptance test specifies the proof that is needed for the project to end and the users take it over. In the final acceptance test plan, the system and software configuration and scenario necessary confirm that the system meets the needs of the users. Typically, the scenario is a scripted business process using real-life data.

Change control

Change happens, you just don't want it to happen to your project. However, change requests will seem like a blizzard by the time you reach the testing phase. The best strategy is to assume that a change can be valid, it just has to have the support of the project sponsor. Probably the most difficult changes to manage are those that come through the sponsor or the sponsor's liaison. The implication is that you cannot refuse them because "they should be easy to do. . . ." You'll need to treat these especially carefully, meaning that you have to be diligent in documenting why these are a really bad idea.

Objectives of change control

Unless the requested change is to eliminate features that were going to consume an inordinate amount of resources, changes will at least make the project take longer. This doesn't mean that change is bad; just that change is, well, time-consuming. What you really want is to make sure that the only changes that are implemented are those that (a) fix a bug or correct an error in the specifications that prevents the project from meeting its (prioritized) goals and those that (b) are fully funded. Essentially, the change control team must make sure that the benefits clearly outweigh the costs of the change. Be on guard for death by a million small changes "making things better."

So, you'll need criteria to help the change control team evaluate the change requests in a timely and efficient manner. Here is a list of questions to which you'll need the answers for each proposed change.

Change evaluation criteria

Where did the change request originate? Does it reflect a strategic change of the organization?

Is the requested change outside of the project scope? Would it change the justification for the project?

Is there valid justification included in the request? Has there been written approval from the sponsor provided?

In what way is the change essential to the project at this time? What is the risk to the project by not going ahead at this time?

What is the impact to the project plan? What is the quantified cost and schedule impact? Make sure that the cost considers the diversion of resources from other tasks. Does it save time, money, or resources?

How does this change affect the critical path?

What would the side effect be if this change is implemented?

Are other systems or projects affected by this change, dependent on it, adversely affected by it? Have the other change control team(s) been made aware of this change request? Have they made a decision?

Planning for the operation's manual documentation

Regardless of whether or not the project will be supported internally, a users operating manual is necessary. You should think of this manual as having all of the information necessary to install, configure and run the system *as delivered*. This includes requirements for operational support, hardware requirements, software requirements, network configuration, software installation, and hardware installation.

It should be comprehensive, even to the point of including information that is easily obtained elsewhere. Nothing that is obvious to the project team will be obvious to those who follow. You can consider the manual as a receiver for all of the procedures; if it's not in the manual, you just might be the one who's put in the hot seat to fix a problem! Make sure that known problems are listed with solutions and workarounds!

Following is a categorized list of information that should be provided.

Support requirements

Availability of application (when it should be available for users as opposed to, say nightly maintenance)

Software versions and release Levels (for example, which versions of the software work together on what hardware) — when you use open-source software, you need to know from where you got it and where to get it again

Installing open-source software (for example, will you be using RPM?)

Help desk support and problem management (who to call with when a given problem occurs)

Dial-up access for after hours or off-site support

Network support requirements and information for network support persons

How to monitor the "vital signs" of the system — error log files, CPU usage, disk usage, disk performance, memory and paging performance; Linux system monitoring tips should be included

Linux system configuration requirements

Here's a short list of items that are often overlooked because you've started development on an existing system.

Desktop environment; Window manager; startup and shutdown; network interface and TCP/IP configuration; assigning users; group assignments; default umask; security and passwords (aging, and so on); programs including execute permissions; backup device configuration (all device configurations); OS kernel parameters

Linux backup and recovery procedures

Backup and recovery is seen as something to be done later. Usually, later is too late! Picture yourself explaining to the project sponsor why the strategic vision has to be put on hold for a while so that you can put the pieces back together.

You should back up system files, user files (maybe even home directories), and the application files. You must determine how often each needs to be backed up. Write this down and put it into the documentation for the system. Send it to the system administrators. Then secure the backups tapes (don't throw them into a box in your desk). You need to be able to get to them quickly.

You have only done half of the job. Now, write a recovery procedure and practice it. Many organizations have found to their dismay that their backups are actually blank!

Application installation and maintenance

The procedures for installing and maintaining the application and/or system are the second most important project deliverable (the first being the system). You must be detailed and comprehensive. Rewrite this document until it is flawless. It helps to have someone who is a capable writer. Make sure you address every step from obtaining the software, confirming the configuration of the hardware, compatibility of other required software, if and how to maintain the software, identifying compatibility problems, and so on.

Linux RDBMS installation and management

Most of this is available from the open-source supplier (thankfully!). However, you may find yourself augmenting this documentation to fill in the gaps, and pulling together the tools needed for efficient management. For many of the open-source products there is a lack of DBMS management utilities, backup and recovery tools, and monitoring tools that are common with proprietary Linux databases.

From Project Plan to Tables

As the previous section demonstrates, designing and managing a database project is a complex task that involves a considerable range of skills.

This section focuses on a key part of part the database project: designing the database. This is the most important single task in a database project, for these reasons:

✦ The database's design controls the rest of your work. A database that is soundly designed will make the rest of your tasks easier, if only because you will not have to work around flaws or inconsistencies in the database.

✦ If you intend to use your database for years, you probably will have to update it — both to fix bugs and to add new features. A soundly designed database is robust: it withstands change more easily than one that contains dead ends and contradictions.

✦ Furthermore, a well-designed database is, by itself, the best way to explain your ideas to the people who will maintain the database after you have moved on to other projects. The design of your database — both the structure of each table and the interactions among tables — describes how you view the real-world entity that your database reflects.

The literature on the relational database offers any number of methods for translating entities and events into tables. Some of these are quite elaborate. In our experience, however, a designer can achieve good results by applying a few common-sense principles — and by tempering those principles with art and with experience.

The rest of this section discusses the principles; the remainder of the chapter presents you with some examples that walk you through the designing of two example databases.

What does it mean to "design" a database?

Before we discuss what it means to design a database, let's quickly review just what a database is.

✦ A *database* is an orderly body of data and the software that maintains it. In the relational model for databases, which we use as our principal way of thinking about databases, a database is composed of relations.

✦ A *relation* consists of one or more attributes, each of which holds data drawn from a single domain of data.

✦ A *domain* describes one aspect of an entity or event in the real world.

✦ The *attributes* that comprise a relation are related to each other, so that together they portray an entity or event in the real world. If a relation is a mosaic that portrays an entity or event, then each of its attributes is a tile in the mosaic.

✦ Relations can be joined to each other through *foreign keys*. A foreign key is a combination of one or more attributes that are present in two or more relations. These shared attributes join relations together, just as a set of characters that appear in more than one novel join the novels together into a single work.

✦ Through foreign keys, a group of relations can be linked together to form a whole that models a complex, real-world system — that is, they form a database. If one relation is a mosaic that portrays an entity or event, a database is a series of such portraits, when joined together, portray an entire system of entities.

To use another simile, the craft of the database designer is like that of the mechanical engineer. An individual relation is like a gear or bolt that is designed to perform a simple task; and a database is like a machine that assembles many gears and bolts into a whole that performs a complex task. The engineer must design each part so that it is simple, efficient, and easily understood, yet it dovetails with its neighboring parts. The engineer must design the whole so that parts work together efficiently, with no extraneous parts and with all parts easily accessible so that the machine can be repaired easily.

The art of the engineer — and of the database designer — lies in this balancing of the requirements of the whole and of the parts.

As the above description illustrates, designing a database has two aspects:

✦ Designing each relation so that it fully yet efficiently portrays the real-world entity or event you have in mind.

✦ Designing the system of relations and how they join, so that together they portray the real-world system that your database models.

Of course, most databases are not so elevated; most are simple and straightforward. But as the examples that come later in this chapter show, even a simple database requires thought if you want to do it well.

The steps of designing a database

The following steps describe how we design a database. Our approach is empirical rather than theoretical; however, each step builds directly upon the theory we presented in Chapter 2.

Step 1: Articulate the problem

The first step in designing a database is to articulate the problem, and to write a requirements document. This is the most important task that you will undertake as a database designer. A well-analyzed project probably can withstand a badly designed database; but the best database design in the world must fail if the analysis that underlies it is faulty.

Step 2: Define the information you need

After you have articulated the problem, the next step is to ask, "What information do I need to solve this problem?"

In this step, you must name the entities that you must model to solve the problem. In the literature on databases, this process often is called "defining the problem space." We prefer to think of it as *naming the objects that reside within the problem space*.

Consider, for example, a system to catalogue your comic book collection. Your requirements document is very simple: "Record all information for identifying the comic books in my collection." To solve this problem, you must store information about the following entities:

- ✦ Each comic book publisher; for example, DC or Marvel.
- ✦ Each title of which you have an issue; for example, *Green Lantern* or *Fantastic Four*.
- ✦ Each issue of a comic book that you possess; for example, *Fantastic Four*, December 1966.
- ✦ Each person who worked on an issue you possess; for example, Gil Kane, Jack Kirby, Steve Ditko, or Stan Lee.

These are the entities that you will model in your database. These entities, and how they relate to each other, define how you will think about your database. The rest of your work is to describe these entities and how they fit together.

Step 3: Decompose the entities

After the entities that will comprise the database are identified, we must decompose each entity into the data elements that define it. (In the literature of databases, the term "decompose" does not mean to rot; rather, it means to disassemble a composition into its constituent parts.)

For example, in our comic book example, one of the identified entities is a comic book title. To identify a title, we need to record the following the data elements:

- ✦ The publisher
- ✦ The title's name
- ✦ The month and year the title began publication

We could record other information about a title; for example, whether it is published monthly or bimonthly. However, the elements we listed here are sufficient to solve the problem we articulated in phase 1, which is to catalogue our personal comic book collection.

The problem statement will, in fact, guide us in choosing the data elements we wish to gather and store. For example, suppose that one of the entities in our database is *person*. For a database that catalogues our comic book collection, it is sufficient to record the person's name. We may also wish to record the person's specialty (writer, editor, penciller, inker, or whatever), but not much else is needed. However, for a database that records information about people who have cancer, we will need to record many additional data elements:

✦ Identifying information, such as name, address, telephone number, and e-mail address.

✦ Demographic information, such as date of birth and sex.

✦ Biographical information, such as the industry in which the person works; the person's use of alcohol, tobacco, and recreational drugs; and the person's hormonal and reproductive histories.

As you can see, the definition of an entity is dictated by the problem that our database is attempting to solve.

Our ability to decompose entities will depend, in turn, in how much we know about the problem area we are dealing with. If you already know the "problem domain" with which this database deals, then this phase may require just some reflection on your part. If you do not know the problem domain — or if the problem domain is complex, as in our cancer example — you must research the topic and consult with experts to ensure that you have decomposed the entities properly.

Step 4: Design the tables

After we have defined the entities that we are modeling and have written down the data elements that we must record to describe each entity sufficiently, we must translate these entities into tables. It is in this phase that the craft of the database designer shines brightest.

From this point forward, we speak of tables instead of relations because we are moving from theory into the real world of code that we must actually implement.

To begin, each of your designs must state the following for each table:

✦ The attributes (columns) within the table.

✦ The table's primary key.

✦ The table's foreign keys, should it have any.

✦ The indices that we build for the table, if any.

You also have to state each column's data type; for example, whether it is an integer or a string, and if it is a string, how long it must be.

If we have done our work well in the first three phases of this task, designing the tables is straightforward — most of the entities that we defined in phase 2 will translate into one table; and each table's columns will be those defined in phase 3. However, some entities do not require their own table; and some do require more than one table.

Rules for translation

So, what are the rules by which we should translate entities into tables? There are two:

Our first rule is this: *The columns in a table must be existentially related to each other*. Please pardon our use of the adverb "existentially," but that word does express best the fact that the columns must be essential to the entity we are modeling, and not peripheral to it.

For example, if we are writing a database for an automobile dealership, we will want to record the fact that a given person owns a given model and make of automobile. To an auto dealer, the kind of car a person drives is an essential part of his definition of a person — to the auto dealer, "car" is existentially related to what a person is. However, not even an auto dealer will want to record in the definition of "person" how many cylinders the car has. The number of cylinders is existentially related to the car, not to the person, and therefore should be put into the table with which we describe cars, not into the table with which we describe persons. The person table will have a foreign key that "points" to the kind of car the person drives.

Our second rule is: *avoid redundancy*.

This refers to redundancy of columns, as well as to redundancy of entities within tables. If possible, each entity should appear once and only once within the database. If the table requires multiple iterations of one or more columns, that column probably describes an entity on their own and it should be broken out into its own table. Likewise, if our design requires that an entity be described in more than one row, we probably should break that entity's columns into a table of their own.

For example, suppose that your database must record information about a person, including a person's address. You can either move the address columns into a separate table, or you can add them to the table that holds the other data that describe a person. If we only want to record the person's current address, and don't care about any other address at which the person has lived, then it makes sense to add the address columns to the person table. However, there are two circumstances in which we should break the address into its own table:

> ✦ *A person has lived at more than one address*. We may be interested in storing all of the person's addresses. For example, an epidemiologist may wish to see whether a person has lived near a uranium mine or a high-tension power line. We could create separate columns for each address — for example, a column

named address1, a second column named address2, and so on through the number of addresses we wished to store. However, this is wasteful and clumsy—redundant, in other words. To store all of the addresses at which a person has lived, we should move the address columns into their own table.

✦ *More than one person probably lives at an address.* We can add the same address again and again to the person table of each person who lives at that address; but this, too, is redundant. This is not as gross an example of redundancy as having multiple address columns within the person table, but it is a redundancy nonetheless. If it is likely that more than one person in our database will live at the same address, and this fact interests us, then we should break addresses into their own table.

Methods of joining tables

The example of person and address raises the question of how tables are joined to each other.

As we noted in Chapter 2, tables are joined through a foreign key: one table holds a column whose value "points" to one or more tuples in another relation. Tables can be joined in any of three manners:

✦ *One-to-One*—Here, a row in one table has one and only one counterpart in the other table. For example, if each person had one and only one address, this would be a one-to-one join. We would join the two tables either by putting a foreign key in the "person" table that points to the address table, or vice versa—or simply move the address columns into the person table, as we had originally planned.

✦ *One-to-Many*—Here, each record in one of the tables can point to many records in the other table. For example, in our person-address example, one person can have many addresses, or many persons can have one address. If one person can have multiple addresses, we would put into the address table a foreign key that points to the person table; thus, multiple records in the address table could point to the same record in person. If one address can be held by multiple persons, then we would put into the person table a foreign key that points to the address table; thus, multiple records in the person table can point to the same record in person.

✦ *Many-to-Many*—Here, each record in each table can point to many records in the other table. In our person/address example, a many-to-many join occurs when each person can have many addresses and many persons can hold each address. In this situation, putting a foreign key into the person table or the address table will not work: as each person can hold multiple addresses, and an address can be held by multiple persons, each table would need multiple foreign keys—one for each address or person being pointed to. This, of course, is highly redundant, and therefore will not do.

To build a many-to-many join, you must insert a third table into the database to hold the keys of the rows being joined. In our example of the person and address tables, we would create a third table that consists of two columns: one holds a foreign key that references the person table, and the other a foreign key that references the address table. Each record in this third table links one person with one address; thus, we can link a person to as many addresses — and an address to as many persons — as we like.

Such "utility" tables within a relational database are quite useful. It is not a good idea to let them proliferate, but they can make for a cleaner design by helping you to avoid polluting a table with multiple instances of the same column.

Normal form and normalization

So far so good: we want to make each table hold only the columns that are "existentially" part of the entity it is modeling; and we want to avoid redundancy within the database. The question now arises: "Is there a method by which we can analyze our tables to avoid redundancy?" The answer is yes, thanks again to the work of E. F. Codd.

Codd proposed a process called *normalization*, by which a database is translated into "normal form." The literature recognizes many levels of normal form; the higher the level, the closer the database approaches to the "pure" relational form. However, four levels of normalization are used most commonly:

✦ First normal form

✦ Second normal form

✦ Third normal form

✦ Boyce-Codd normal form (BCNF)

There are other levels beyond this, but the four mentioned here are quite sufficient for most work. In the following sections, we introduce each normal form briefly, and then discuss how we use normalization to design tables. But before we do that, we must introduce one last notion: that of functional dependency.

Functional dependency

The idea of a normalized database depends on the idea of functional dependency. This is a simple concept: in brief, it states that the value of one column depends upon the value of another.

For example, consider an automobile manufacturer, Acme Motors. Acme builds two varieties of car: one has six cylinders, and one has four. Each make of car that Acme manufactures comes in one of these two varieties; for example, the Banshee and Thor have six cylinders, whereas the Zeus, Odin, and Loki have four. If we build a database that describes Acme's products, the column that gives the number of cylinders functionally depends upon the column that gives the car's make, because the make determines the number of cylinders a car has, not vice versa.

Functional dependency is another way of expressing our "existential" rule for database design. After all, true functional dependency reflects the nature of the entity or event that the table reflects: every functional dependency in our database should, in some way, reflect a functional dependency in the real world.

Much of the process of normalization—and much of what goes under the term "normal form"—is simply the process of identifying functional dependencies, and organizing tables around them.

Now we ready to introduce the types of normal form.

First normal form

First normal form states that every column contains a scalar. A scalar is an atomic data type—that is, a data type that cannot be reduced mathematically to a collection of simpler data types. Thus, to achieve first normal form, a column cannot hold a structure or another table.

As you will recall from Chapter 2, this is part of the definition of a relational database. To be called relational, a database must adhere to first normal form.

Second normal form

For a table to conform to second normal form, each of its columns that is not part the primary key must depend irreducibly upon the key. A table will not conform to second normal form if its primary key consists of more than one column, and one or more of its non-key columns depend upon part of the primary key, but not all of it.

For example, consider a table that describes telephone numbers. It consists of three columns: area code, telephone number, and the town in which the telephone number is located. Some sample telephone numbers are:

```
AreaCode  Number   Town
312       3825968  Chicago
312       3287448  Chicago
```

The primary key of this table is the area code plus the telephone number. As it happens, however, the name of the town does not irreducibly depend upon the primary key—an area code always lies within a town (as is the case with area code 312 and Chicago) or a town lies entirely within a given area code. Thus, the town depends not upon the entire primary key, but on only part of it—that is, the area code.

To put this table into second normal form, we must break it into two tables:

```
AreaCode  Number
312       3825968
312       3287448
```

and:

```
AreaCode  Town
312       Chicago
```

As you can see, this reduction to second normal form eliminates the redundant appearance of "Chicago" within the table. It also brings the table into line with our common-sense rule of avoiding redundancy in a database.

Third normal form

For a table to conform to third normal form, it must adhere to first and second normal form; furthermore, every column must be independent from every other column, except for the column (or columns) that comprise a primary key. In other words, a table cannot contain a key that controls some of the columns in that table, but not all of them.

Earlier, we mentioned an example of an auto-dealership database, in which the person table also mentioned the make and model of the automobile that the person currently owns. We considered whether to add the number of cylinders of the car's engine to that database's person table, but we rejected the idea because it would violate our rule of existential integrity — that is, we would have a nonperson column grafted onto a table that was describing a person. Adding cylinders to a person table would also violate third normal form, because the cylinders column would depend not upon the table's primary key, but upon the car column. Our database would be sounder if we broke the car and cylinder columns into a separate car table.

Relational theorists have proven that a database can always be transformed into third normal form without losing information (although this proof is beyond the scope of this book.)

Boyce-Codd normal form

The Boyce-Codd normal form (BCNF) is a more robust statement of the third normal form. A table adheres to BCNF if and only if every column within the table functionally depends *only* upon the table's primary key.

The simple definition of BCNF subsumes first, second, and third normal forms. With this single rule, we can gauge whether a table truly adheres to the relational model. BCNF is easier to demonstrate than it is to explain, so we give an example momentarily.

Normalization

As you can see, we now have a simple rule by which we can gauge the "relationality" of the tables in our database. The process of normalization is a pencil-and-paper task by which we can turn a bag of columns into a neatly dovetailed set of tables.

For example, let's suppose that we are designing a database that will hold a bookstore's inventory. Among other things, our database must describe books; and a description of a book can include these columns:

✦ Title

✦ Authors

✦ Price

✦ ISBN number

✦ Year of publication

✦ Publisher

✦ Publisher's address

Our initial design includes all of these columns within a single table. We will make the ISBN number the table's primary key because that is a simple number that is assigned to one and only one book. This gives us the following table:

```
CREATE TABLE book (
    isbn             CHAR(20)      NOT NULL,
    title            VARCHAR(255)  NOT NULL,
    authors          VARCHAR(255)  NOT NULL,
    price            INTEGER       NOT NULL,
    publicationYear  INTEGER       NOT NULL,
    publisherName    VARCHAR(128)  NOT NULL,
    publisherAddress VARCHAR(255)  NOT NULL,
    PRIMARY KEY (isbn)
)
```

However, when we apply the rule of BCNF, we see that one column—publisher's address—does not depend upon the ISBN number directly; rather, it depends upon the name of the publisher. If the publisher were to move, the publisher's address would change, without affecting the other columns in the table. This violates BCNF; thus, we will divide columns `publisher_name` and `publisher_address` into their own table—`publisher`—that we join to table book table through a foreign key. The revised design now appears as follows:

```
CREATE TABLE book (
    isbn         CHAR(20)      NOT NULL,
    title        VARCHAR(255)  NOT NULL,
    authors      VARCHAR(255   NOT NULL,
```

```
    price                INTEGER      NOT NULL,
    publicationYear      INTEGER      NOT NULL,
    PRIMARY KEY (isbn)
    FOREIGN KEY (publisher.publisherName)
)
CREATE TABLE publisher (
    publisherName      VARCHAR(128) NOT NULL,
    publisherAddress   VARCHAR(255) NOT NULL,
    PRIMARY KEY (publisher_name)
)
```

So far, so good. However, when we look again at table book, we see that each book can have an indefinite number of authors — most have one or two, but some can have as many as six or more. We could create separate columns within book table for each possible author — called, say, author1, author2, and so on — but that would be adding redundant columns to this table, which violates the rule of avoiding redundancy. Therefore, we will divide authors into their own table, which joins authors with books. This satisfies the many-to-many relationship between authors and books — that is, each book can have multiple authors, and each author can have written multiple books. Our revised design now appears as follows:

```
CREATE TABLE book (
    isbn                CHAR(20)     NOT NULL,
    title               VARCHAR(255) NOT NULL,
    price               INTEGER      NOT NULL,
    publicationYear     INTEGER      NOT NULL,
    PRIMARY KEY (isbn)
    FOREIGN KEY (publisher.publisherName)
)
CREATE TABLE publisher (
    publisherName      VARCHAR(128) NOT NULL,
    publisherAddress   VARCHAR(255) NOT NULL,
    PRIMARY KEY (publisher_name)
)
CREATE TABLE authorBook (
    authorName         VARCHAR(255) NOT NULL,
    isbn               CHAR(20)     NOT NULL,
    PRIMARY KEY (authorName, isbn),
    FOREIGN KEY isbn REFERENCES book
)
```

If we were a publisher and needed more information about an author than just the author's name, we would create an additional table to hold that information, and join it to table author-book through a foreign key. However, because we are writing a database for a bookstore rather than for a publisher, the author's name is all the information we need: we do not want to cross the thick black line we've drawn around this project unless we absolutely must.

At first glance, this design may seem to be more convoluted than our initial design, which simply dumped all of the columns into a single table. However, as you get further into this book, you will see that a normalized relational database is both easier to program and easier to maintain than one that is not normalized. A normalized relational database withstands change better than one that is not normalized. The effort you spend in designing your relations well will pay great dividends over the life of the database.

Step 5: Write domain-integrity rules

As the last step in designing a database, we write down the database's domain-integrity rules. These rules check whether the data being written into the database are consistent with the nature of the domain of which our database is a model.

For example, if we design a table that holds an address, we may wish to write a domain-integrity rule that states that no address can have the ZIP code 00000 because there is no such ZIP code; thus, no address can have it.

Domain-integrity rules are not part of the database *per se*. Rather, we implement them in software. These rules are useful because they will help us prevent non-sense from being written into the database.

This phase is the last in the process of database design. It is also an ongoing phase: as you work with your database, you will discover more and more rules that govern domain integrity, and you will work some or all of them into the software with which you manage your database. No database project is ever really ended; ways to improve the database appear continually.

The art of database design

In his book *The Mythical Man-Month* (Addison-Wesley, 1982), Frederick Brooks wrote, "[T]hat system is best in which one can specify things with the most simplicity and straightforwardness." It is not difficult to be either simple or straightforward—the trick is to be both at the same time.

Think of your database as being a machine for the storage and manipulation of data. A well-designed machine works efficiently: no part is extraneous, each part is as simple as possible, every part works well with all of the others.

Unlike a machine, however, you often have to revise your database while it is in day-to-day operation. Think of rebuilding an airplane while it is in flight, and you will have an idea of some of the problems that can afflict a database manager. Much of the art of database design comes in the balancing of simplicity and straightforwardness: often, you will have to choose whether to perform a task with a few simple tables, or one more complex table. Here, experience is your best guide. The examples in the following chapter sections, show some instances when we had to select one approach or the other.

Designing a database is a creative act. Like most truly creative acts, it is easy to do—but difficult to do well. The difficulty makes it challenging; the creativity makes it fun. The following examples suggest the difficulty and the creativity of database design.

Building a Simple Database: The Baseball Example

Now, at last, we use the theory that we have presented to design a database.

We begin with a simple example: a small database to hold the scores of baseball games. We already used this database in Chapter 3, when we introduced SQL, but here we discuss how we came to design the database in the way that we did.

Step 1: Articulate the problem

In this example, we want to build a system that records information about baseball games. We are not interested in modeling a baseball game in all of its complexity: runs, hits, errors, fielding chances, earned runs, the names of the winning and losing pitchers—none of this interests us at this time. The task we set ourselves is very simple: *Record the score of each official game played by two major league teams.*

Note the words "official" (which excludes exhibition games and spring training) and "major league" (which excludes amateurs and minor leagues). Note, too, that we are just recording the score of the game—no other statistic. Our problem statement draws a very thick, very black line around this project.

Step 2: Define the information we need

Now that we have articulated the problem, our next step is to ask, "What information do we need to solve this problem?" In this example, we need to record information about two entities:

✦ The game itself.

✦ The teams that played the game.

The database will also name other entities, in particular the city in which a team plays and the stadium in which it plays. However, the problem-statement does not require that we gather detailed information about these entities, so our database will not describe them in detail. We discuss this in step 4.

Step 3: Decompose the entities

Our next step is to decompose each of these entities into its constituent elements. Each game consists of:

✦ The names of the teams that are playing the game.

✦ The number of runs that each team scored.

✦ The day the game was played.

✦ Because teams sometimes play double headers (that is, they play two games on the same day), we also must record whether the game was the first or second game played on a given day.

In baseball, one team is the home team and the other is the visiting team. This information is important, as the rules of baseball give the home team a distinct advantage. Thus, we must not only name the two teams that are playing, we must also note which team is the home team. A game's importance depends upon whether it is played during the regular season or during the playoffs, so we need some way to determine whether a game is a regular season game or a playoff game.

For each team, we need to record information by which it can be identified:

✦ The name of the team.

✦ The team's home city or state.

✦ The name of the stadium in which the team plays.

We also want to record the league and the division in which a team plays; by counting the number of games that each team has won, we will be able to compute which team wins its division during the regular season.

This last point, in truth, is peripheral to our original problem statement; however, we can add a great deal of functionality to our little database by adding this one column, so we will add it. Still, we must be careful to avoid "creeping feature-itis" — a fatal disorder that occurs when attractive little features creep into our minds, attach themselves to the project, and their accumulated mass eventually drags the project into the mud.

Step 4: Design the tables

Now that we have decomposed each entity into the data elements that comprise it, our next step is to design tables to hold those elements. At this point, relational theory comes into play. The following subsections name each table and its columns. For each column, we will note whether it is forbidden to hold NULL. We will also give each table's keys.

As we noted in the previous subsection, our database comprises two entities: baseball teams, and the games they play. We will define one table for each.

Teams

Table team describes a baseball team:

```
CREATE TABLE team (
    team_name CHAR(15) NOT NULL,
    city      CHAR(15) NOT NULL,
    stadium   CHAR(30) NOT NULL,
    league    CHAR(1)  NOT NULL,
    division  CHAR(1)  NOT NULL,
    PRIMARY KEY (team_name)
);
```

Column team_name names the team in question; for example, Cubs or Brewers.

Column city names the home city or state of the team, for example, Chicago or California.

Column stadium names the stadium in which the team plays when it is at home; for example, Wrigley Field.

Column league names the league in which the team plays. In this instance, it will be "National" or "American." Minor leagues, for example, the International League or the Pacific Coast League, are beyond the scope of our database's problem statement, but could easily be inserted into this column.

Finally, column division names the league division that the team is in, that is, East, Central, or West.

This table has no foreign keys. It has one primary key, the name of the team. It is unusual to use a name as a primary key because of the practical consideration that keys often are values that are entered into the system by users, and users often mistype or misspell strings. However, the table team is a static table—that is, its data changes infrequently—and the names of the teams are well known; so in this instance, it is acceptable to use a name as a primary key.

We mentioned earlier that both city and stadium are entities unto themselves. However, we do not model these entities within tables of their own because we are only interested in their names. If other columns interested us about the city—say, the number of other professional sports teams that it supports, or its population, or the state in which it is located—then it would make sense to divide city into its own table. But we are not interested in those columns, so it makes no sense to put city into its own table. Adding these extraneous columns would smudge the thick black line we have drawn around the project.

The same applies to stadium— as well as to league and division, which are also entities in themselves. The good database designer, like any good engineer or scientist, likes to wield Occam's Razor, and does not multiply entities unnecessarily.

Games

Table `game` gives the score of each game, as follows:

```
CREATE TABLE game (
    home_team           CHAR(15) NOT NULL,
    visiting_team       CHAR(15) NOT NULL,
    home_team_runs      SMALLINT NOT NULL,
    visiting_team_runs  SMALLINT NOT NULL,
    game_date           CHAR(10) NOT NULL,
    game_number         SMALLINT NOT NULL,
    PRIMARY KEY (home_team, game_date, game_number),
    FOREIGN KEY (home_team) REFERENCES team
);
```

Columns `home_team` and `visiting_team` names the teams that play the game. Each is a foreign key that joins this table to table `team`.

Columns `home_team_runs` and `visiting_team_runs` give the number of runs scored by each team. The winning team is the team that has scored more runs.

Column `game_date` gives the date the game was played. Because teams occasionally play two games on the same day, column `game_number` gives the number of the game — either one or two. The primary key combines the date, the number of the game, and home team.

We record the names of the visiting and home teams separately, in part because we want to be able to see where the game was played, and in part because the rules of baseball give the home team a distinct advantage. This may seem to violate our rule that forbids redundancy; but it does not, because each team fulfills a very different role in the game. We could break the teams into a separate table, but we would still have to have two foreign keys to that table — one for home team and one for visiting — so doing so doesn't gain us anything.

We need the number of the game so that we can distinguish among games played by the same teams on the same day; if we did not make that distinction, we could not build a primary key for this table. Another way to solve this problem is to record the time that each game started, because a team never plays two games simultaneously.

Indices

As we noted above, designing a set of indices must balance speed of lookup against cost of building the index and the disk space it consumes.

Indices should be built for all of the columns with which users will be performing look-ups — but no more than that. As a rule of thumb, you should give every key an index; after that you must use your best judgment.

Before people begin to use a database, it is difficult to predict just what columns will be used in look-ups. (If you could know ahead of time just what queries users would want to make on a database, you would not need a relational database.) Fortunately, you can build and drop indices without affecting the structure of the database, so you don't have to get your suite of indexes exactly right before you begin.

For this database, we will build the following indices:

```
CREATE UNIQUE INDEX index1 ON team(name);
CREATE        INDEX index2 ON game(home_team);
CREATE        INDEX index3 ON game(visiting_team);
CREATE UNIQUE INDEX index4 ON game(home_team, game_date, game_number)
CREATE        INDEX index5 ON game(visiting_team, game_date, game_number)
```

As you can see, a column can be used in more than one index. We give each index a name. Naming an index lets us manipulate it later, in case we wish to alter or drop it. The names do not have to be descriptive, or even imaginative; hence, our names index1, index2, and so on.

Step 5: Write domain-integrity rules

Table team is static, and is only used to look up information. We do not need any rules for it, except that the information be accurate.

Table game requires these rules:

✦ A team never plays itself, therefore, columns home_team and visiting_team must never be identical.

✦ A team can never have a negative number of runs, therefore, columns home_team_runs and visiting_team_runs must never be less than zero.

✦ A baseball game can never end in a tie, therefore, columns home_team_runs and visiting_team_runs must never be equal.

✦ Teams never play more than two games on a given day, so column game_number must always equal one or two.

No doubt we will think of other rules as we gain experience in working with our database, but these will give us a good start.

Building a More Complex Database: The Library Example

In this section, we design a more extensive database that tackles a real-world problem — tracking the books in the collection of a multibranch public library.

Our task is to design an information system for a multibranch library. Our library is a lending library—that is, it lends books to users. Each user keeps the books that the user has borrowed for a fixed period of time or less, and then returns them.

The library's collection has one or more copies of each book, with the copies being distributed across one or more branches.

The library has a body of users, each of whom can borrow books from any of the branches. A user can borrow a book for two weeks. If the user returns it late, the user pays a fine.

Again, we will walk through the steps of designing a database for this problem. This problem is considerably more complex than the baseball score problem, and our database's design will reflect this complexity.

Step 1: Articulate the problem

As with our simple example, we begin by articulating the problem: *The library must record who has possession of any given book at any given time.* This statement tells us what the system must do. It also gives us a method by which we can gauge whether our system is successful: it will be successful if it can tell us who has possession of any book right now.

Step 2: Define the information we need

Now that we have articulated our problem, we ask what information we need to solve the problem—that is, what entities inhabit the problem space. To answer the question of who has possession of a given book at a given time, we need information about the following entities:

✦ What can be possessed (in this case, the books).

✦ Who or what can possess a book at any given time (in this case, the library and its patrons).

✦ Which "possessor" possesses each book.

So far, so good. However, each of these entities—the possessor, the possession, and the action of possession—can be further divided. After all, a possessor can be a user or a library, and the act of possession involves borrowing items and returning them. So, our next step is to take each item of information that we need, and decompose it into its constituent parts.

Step 3: Decompose the entities

As we have seen, our library system needs to manage information about three entities: the possession, the possessor, and the act of possession. The next step is to decompose each entity into its constituent elements.

The possession

The possession is something that can be possessed — in this case, a book. For the sake of simplifying our example, we'll ignore the fact that libraries also handle other materials, such as videotapes, DVDs, CDs, and periodicals.

A book has many features — its size, its weight, the number of color plates, and so on — but for our system we are interested just in the information with which the book can be identified. If you look over the book in your hands, you can see that it can be identified in the following ways:

- ✦ By title
- ✦ By author's names
- ✦ By publisher
- ✦ By city and year of publication
- ✦ By ISBN number

In addition, a book will have been assigned either or both of the following numbers to a book:

- ✦ Library of Congress number.
- ✦ Dewey Decimal System number.

Some books are not suitable to be borrowed by minors. Our description of a book must flag this fact.

Finally, we want to record the price of book. This will let us recover its cost should it be lost.

The above data identify a book title. However, a library system can have multiple copies of the same title. Therefore, to identify an individual volume — that is, a physical book — we need all of the above information, plus the number that uniquely identifies a given copy of the title.

Each copy will be "owned" by a given branch of the library. So, we must identify the branch to which the copy belongs. For example, the Chester A. Arthur branch library may have three copies of the *Linux Database Bible*, whereas the Rutherford B. Hayes branch may have only two. How we will do this must await our detailing how we will describe each branch of the library.

Finally, we need to record the copy's status. A copy may be discarded, or it may be marked as lost or stolen. We could mark a copy as being unavailable by simply removing its record from the database. However, as you recall from Chapter 2, if we remove a given record from our database, we must also remove all records that reference it; this is necessary to maintain database integrity. Thus, if we remove a record that describes a book, we must also remove the records that reference it; which means that, in effect, we will forget all transactions that involved this book.

We could purge all of this information from our system, but it would be unwise to do so. An information system should not only tell us the current state of the entity it models; it should also be an archive that we can explore to discover the state of our entity in times past, and so discover how the entity is changing over time. For this reason, we want to mark the status of books that are no longer in our library, so that our system can "remember" the transactions that involve them.

The possessor

A library or a user can possess a book. So, we need to decompose each of these separately.

As we noted earlier, our library consists of a number of different branches. Each branch can be described many ways, such as by the name of the architect who designed it; however, some study and reflection shows that a branch library can best be identified in the following ways:

✦ Its name

✦ Its address

✦ Its telephone number

Strictly speaking, all we need to identify a branch library is its name (assuming that the name is unique within the library system). However, we will include address and telephone number as a convenience to the persons who will use our system.

A user is a person who has permission to borrow books at our library. Our library system, then, needs information with which it can identify a person. It also needs the information with which it can contact a person—in case, say, the user doesn't return a book that the user has borrowed. Some thought and study show that our library system needs to record the following information by which the library can identify and contact a user:

✦ Name

✦ Address

✦ Telephone number

✦ Social Security number

✦ Date of birth

✦ User's status

We need to record date of birth in order to determine how old the user is—our library restricts some materials from access by minors.

The "status" datum indicates whether a user is allowed to borrow books. The user, after all, may have become ineligible—the user may have moved away, or died, or lost his or her privileges (perhaps the user borrowed some books that the user never returned).

To borrow books, a person must apply for and receive a library card. After a user possesses a card, a user can borrow a book from any of the library's branches.

We mention the library card apart from the user, because a user can have many library cards during his or her lifetime. Furthermore, the user may lose his or her card and be issued a replacement; in this case, we will want the system to disallow borrowing by anyone who possesses the first card (after all, the card may have been stolen) but still permit borrowing with the replacement card. The only way to meet this criterion is to have the library apply a unique number to each card. Our library system will have to record the following information about a library card:

✦ The identification number of the card.

✦ The fact that a given card is possessed by a given user.

✦ The status of the card.

✦ The date the card is issued.

Again, the "status" datum indicates whether a card can be used. A card may have been reported as being lost or stolen, or the library may have withdrawn it from circulation—for example, it may have become worn out and the library may have issued a replacement.

We record the date the card is issued so that we can retire cards after a defined number of years.

In our description of library branches and users, we mentioned that we need to record the address and the telephone number for each. Both address and telephone number can be decomposed further. We will do so because our system will be able use some of the information that is embedded within each.

An address can be decomposed into these elements:

✦ Street address

✦ Apartment or unit number

✦ City

✦ State

✦ ZIP code

We assume that all addresses are within the United States.

Some of the address elements can be decomposed further. For example, we could decompose the street address into the number, the street name, and the direction (for example, 1234 N. Main St.); however, for our library system that would be overkill.

A telephone number can be decomposed into these elements:

✦ Area code

✦ Number

Again, we assume that all telephone numbers are within the United States.

The act of possession

Someone or something will always possess a book: either a user will have borrowed it, or it will be in a library branch.

As we noted earlier, a user can borrow a book from any branch of the library. The user can also return a book to any branch. If a book is returned to a branch other than the branch that "owns" that book, the book must be transferred to its home branch before it can be borrowed again.

We can assume that if a book has not been borrowed or is not being transferred from one branch to another, that it is residing in its home branch. Thus, to define who has a book at any given time, we must record when the book changes hands. A book can change hands in three different ways: when a user borrows it, when a user returns it, and when a book is transferred from one branch to another.

The following discusses each of these events.

To describe a "borrowing" event, we need the following information:

✦ The book being borrowed.

✦ The user who borrowed the book.

✦ The date it was borrowed.

We do not record where the book was borrowed from, because we assume that a book is always borrowed from its home branch.

To describe a "return" event, we need the following information:

✦ The book being returned.

✦ The date it was returned.

✦ The branch to which it was returned.

We do not need to record who returned the book, because we already know who borrowed it.

To describe a "transfer" event, we need the following information:

✦ The book being transferred.

✦ The branch from which it was transferred.

✦ The date it was transferred.

We assume that a book is always transferred to its home branch.

One last event must be described: a fine.

As we noted earlier, a user must pay a fine for every day that the user keeps a book longer than the normally allowed borrowing period. When a user pays a fine, we must record the fact, and to do so, we need the following information:

✦ The user paying the fine.

✦ The date he paid the fine.

✦ The amount of the fine.

Step 4: Design the tables

Our next step is to design tables to hold those elements.

The possession

As we noted above, "possession" consists of two entities: the book titles that our library houses, and the copies of each title (that is, the physical books).

Table `title` describes a book title:

```
CREATE TABLE title (
    title_id_number INTEGER     NOT NULL    AUTO_INCREMENT,
    title           VARCHAR(255) NOT NULL,
    author          VARCHAR(128) NOT NULL,
    isbn            CHAR(20)     NULL,
    loc_number      CHAR(20)     NULL,
    ddn_number      CHAR(20)     NULL,
    adult_flag      CHAR(1)      NULL,
    publisher       VARCHAR(128) NULL,
    city            VARCHAR(64)  NULL,
    year            INTEGER      NULL,
    price           INTEGER      NULL,
    PRIMARY KEY (title_id_number);
);
```

Column id_number gives a unique identifier for the title. The keyword AUTO_INCREMENT is used by MySQL to automatically assign a unique value in this column whenever a record is inserted into the database.

Columns title and author give the title and author of the book.

Columns isbn, loc_number, and ddn_number give, respectively, the book's ISBN number, Library of Congress number, and Dewey Decimal number. Most books will not have all three numbers set; older books will not have an ISBN number. For this reason, we permit these fields to be set to NULL.

Column adult_flag flags whether this an adult title. Minors cannot borrow adult books.

Columns publisher, city, year, and price give information about the book's publication. We permit these to be NULL because they may not be known, and they are not essential to identifying a title.

This table has one primary key, column id_number. It does not reference any other tables, so it has no foreign keys.

With regard to the data type we assigned to each column, we made our best guess as to how much storage each column would require. Some columns, such as loc or adult_flag, consist of a fixed number of characters; these we set to CHAR. Other columns can vary in length; these we set to type VARCHAR, after estimating what the maximum amount of text each would hold.

Table copy describes a copy of a book:

```
CREATE TABLE copy (
    title_id_number  INTEGER NOT NULL,
    copy_number      INTEGER NOT NULL,
    branch_code      CHAR(5) NOT NULL,
    PRIMARY KEY (title_id_number, copy_number),
    FOREIGN KEY (title_id_number) REFERENCES title,
    FOREIGN KEY (branch_code) REFERENCES branch
);
```

Column title_id_number gives the key of the title, as set in table title.

Column copy_number gives the number of this copy of the book.

Column branch_name gives the name of the branch that "owns" this copy.

The number of the book's title and the copy number must together identify the book uniquely. For that reason, we made this pair of columns the table's primary key.

Columns `title_id_number` and `branch_name` are declared to be foreign keys, because each references a column in another table. As you can see, a column can be used in more than one table — `title_id_number` is both a foreign key and part of this table's primary key.

The possessor

Two entities can possess a book: a user and a library branch.

A library branch is described in one table. A user is described in two tables: one describes the user himself, whereas the other describes the library card with which a user can borrow books.

Table `branch` describes a branch of our library:

```
CREATE TABLE branch (
    branch_code CHAR(5)      NOT NULL,
    branch_name VARCHAR(64)  NOT NULL,
    street      VARCHAR(64)  NOT NULL
    city        VARCHAR(32)  NOT NULL,
    state       CHAR(2)      NOT NULL,
    zip         CHAR(5)      NOT NULL,
    area_code   CHAR(3)      NOT NULL,
    phone       CHAR(7)      NOT NULL,
    PRIMARY KEY (branch_code),
);
```

Column `branch_code` gives a brief mnemonic code that uniquely identifies the branch library. This is a primary key, and is the field that other tables use for their foreign keys to join themselves to this table.

Column `name` gives the branch's name. Each branch must be named uniquely. As there are only a few branches, this is not difficult to do.

Columns `city`, `street`, `state`, and `zip` give the branch's address.

Columns `area_code` and `phone` give the telephone number of the branch. Most branches have a number of telephone extensions, but all have only one main number.

When we decomposed the concept of a branch in the previous section, we discussed the fact that an address is an entity unto itself and could be broken out into its own table. However, there is a one-to-one relationship between address and the entity that is at that address (user or branch); therefore, we decided that breaking addresses into their own table — and setting up the mechanism for relating them, policing the integrity between the two tables, and so on — would be more trouble than it was worth. For that reason, we simply embedded the branch's address within its table. The same holds true for telephone number.

Column `branch_code` is the primary key. Because this table references no other tables, it has no foreign keys.

Table `user` describes a user of the library, that is, someone who has permission to borrow books.

```
CREATE TABLE user (
     first_name    VARCHAR(32)  NOT NULL,
     middle_init   CHAR(1)      NULL,
     last_name     VARCHAR(32)  NOT NULL,
     birthdate     DATE         NOT NULL,
     ssn           CHAR(9)      NOT NULL,
     street        VARCHAR(32)  NOT NULL,
     unit          VARCHAR(32)  NULL,
     city          VARCHAR(32)  NOT NULL,
     state         CHAR(2)      NOT NULL,
     zip           CHAR(5)      NOT NULL,
     area_code     CHAR(3)      NOT NULL,
     phone         CHAR(7)      NOT NULL,
     status        CHAR(1)      NOT NULL,
     PRIMARY KEY (ssn)
);
```

Columns `first_name`, `middle_init`, and `last_name` respectively give the user's first name, middle initial, and last name. Note that `middle_init` can be NULL, because some people do not have a middle name.

Column `birthdate` gives the date the user was born. Our system will use this date to compute whether the user is a minor.

Column `ssn` gives the user's Social Security number.

Columns `street`, `unit`, `city`, `state`, and `zip` give the user's address — respectively, the street number and name, unit or apartment number, city, state, and ZIP code. Column `unit` can be NULL, because some users live in single-family homes that do not have unit numbers.

Columns `area_code` and `phone` give the user's telephone number.

Column `status` flags the user's status — whether the user is active or inactive. A user can become inactive for any number of reasons: the user may have moved away from our community; the user may have died; or the user may have unpaid fines or have a book that is long overdue. The "middleware" that we write for this application will cover setting and unsetting a user's status.

Column `ssn` is this table's only primary key. We use Social Security number as the primary key because each person in the United States past the age of one year must have a Social Security number, and a Social Security number is unique to each person (in theory, at least).

This table does not reference any other tables, so it has no foreign keys.

As you can see from our address and telephone-number columns, we have given the same name to every column that holds the same type of information. For example, tables `user` and `branch` each have a column that gives ZIP code; and in each instance, we named that column `zip`. Although it is not required, it is a good rule of thumb to give the same name to columns that hold the same information. A consistent scheme for naming columns will make it much easier to code your database and to interrogate it.

Table `card` identifies a library card. One user may have held many library cards over the years that the user has patronized our library; after all, cards wear out, are run through the wash, and are lost or stolen. We record information about the card apart from information about the user because we want to ensure that bogus cards are not in circulation, and to ensure that each user has only one card that is active at any given time.

```
CREATE TABLE card (
    card_id_number  INTEGER NOT NULL AUTO_INCREMENT,
    ssn             CHAR(9) NOT NULL,
    date_issued     DATE    NOT NULL,
    status          CHAR(1) NOT NULL,
    PRIMARY KEY (card_id_number),
    FOREIGN KEY (ssn) REFERENCES user
);
```

Column `id_number` gives a unique number that identifies this card. Because we use the keyword `AUTO_INCREMENT`, so the database will automatically generate this number for us.

Column `ssn` gives the Social Security number of the user whose card this is. This column is the foreign key that joins this table to table `user`.

Column `date_issued` gives the date that this card was issued to this user. A card can remain in use only for a set period of time — say, five years — after which it must be replaced.

Column `status` gives the status of the card: whether it is in use, expired, lost, or stolen. A card that is not active cannot be used to borrow a book. If a card's status indicates that it has been lost or stolen, our system will notify the branch's security person should someone try to borrow a book with that card.

Act of possession

An "act of possession" occurs whenever a book leaves the possession of one entity (library or user) and enters the possession of another. There are three such acts:

✦ A user borrows a book from a library.

✦ A user returns a book to a library.

✦ A book is transferred from one library branch to another.

We assume that a user can borrow a book only from the book's "home" library. We also assume that a user cannot loan a book to another. Even if this were allowed, there is no way that we can trace such transfers, so we will ignore them.

Borrowing a book and returning it are two halves of the same event, so we will use one table to record both:

```
CREATE TABLE borrow (
    card_id_number   INTEGER NOT NULL,
    title_id_number  INTEGER NOT NULL,
    copy_number      INTEGER NOT NULL,
    borrow_date      DATE    NOT NULL,
    return_date      DATE    NULL,
    PRIMARY KEY (card_id_number, title_id_number, copy_number,
                 borrow_date),
    FOREIGN KEY (card_id_number) REFERENCES card,
    FOREIGN KEY (title_id_number, copy_number) REFERENCES copy
);
```

Column `card_id_number` gives the unique identification number of the library card with which the book was borrowed. This column is a foreign key to its namesake column in table `card`.

Columns `title_id_number` and `copy_number` identify the book being borrowed. They form a foreign key to their namesake fields in table `copy`.

Columns `borrow_date` and `return_date` give, respectively, the dates that the book was borrowed and returned. `return_date` must allow a NULL value, because it will be NULL when the book is borrowed and will remain so until the book finally is returned.

When the user borrows a book, the library application creates a record for table `borrow`. It initializes the columns `card_id_number`, `title_id_number`, `copy_number`, and `borrow_date`, which together form the table's primary key. Note that `title_id_number` and `copy_number` do not form a primary key because a given copy of a book will be borrowed many times over the years. Our design assumes that the same person cannot borrow the same book more than once on the same day, which (we think) is not too restrictive a rule.

When the user returns the book, the system looks up every record in the system for which `title_id_number` and `copy_number` equals those of the book, and for which `return_date` is NULL. The system then initializes `return_date` to the date the book was returned. We do not use `card_number` to look up the book because books are often returned in book drops or carrels, and no card is available. Also, a book may have been returned and its return not recorded (the borrower may have snuck the book back into the library to avoid a fine), so more than one "borrow" event may be open for a given book at a given time.

If a user wishes to renew his or her borrowing of a book, the system simply marks the current borrowing has having been returned, and opens a new borrowing for the same user and same copy.

As we noted in our analysis section, a user can return a book to any branch library; however, a book can be borrowed only from its home branch. When a book is returned to a library other than its home branch, the book must be returned home. This means that the book must be transferred from one branch to another.

Because we have a well-organized library system, all books that are being returned to their home branches are first returned to the central branch, where they are sorted and sent back out to their appropriate branches. This means that a book that is being transferred will be moved twice: once from the branch to which it was returned to the central library, and once from the central library to its home branch.

We could record a "return" event in one table; however, we prefer to record each time the book changes hands, because this procedure may change in the future. Therefore, we design our transfer table as follows:

```
CREATE TABLE transfer (
    title_id_number      INTEGER NOT NULL,
    copy_number          INTEGER NOT NULL,
    send_branch_code     CHAR(5) NOT NULL,
    receive_branch_code  CHAR(5) NOT NULL,
    transfer_date        DATE    NOT NULL,
    PRIMARY KEY (title_id_number, copy_number,
                 send_branch_code, receive_branch_code,
                 transfer_date),
    FOREIGN KEY (title_id_number, copy_number) REFERENCES copy,
    FOREIGN KEY (send_branch_code) REFERENCES branch,
    FOREIGN KEY (receive_branch_code) REFERENCES branch
);
```

Columns `title_id_number` and `copy_number` together identify the volume that is being transferred. These form a foreign key to table `copy`.

Column `send_branch_code` identifies the branch that is surrendering possession of the book. Column `receive_branch_code` identifies the branch that is receiving possession of the book. Both are foreign keys to table `branch`.

Finally, `transfer_date` gives the date that the book was transferred. We assume that the book was sent and received on the same day.

This table has only one primary key, which is comprised of all the columns in the table. Our system will be able to trace the movement of a book through the system, until it arrives back at its home branch. This tells us who has the book right now — or at least tells us who last accepted responsibility for the book.

This design does not trace the book while it is in the possession of the truck driver who is transporting it. Our design simply assumes that whoever received the book last still has possession of it until it is logged as having been received by someone else. For valuable objects such as jewelry, cash, or medical specimens, a system should log every time the object changes hands; but that would be overkill in our library system.

Fines

One last item of information needs to be described: when a user keeps a book too long, the user must pay a fine.

When a user returns a book, the system will check whether the book is overdue. If it is, the system will compute the user's fine and whether the user paid it. We may wish to add an additional flourish — if the user has any unpaid fines, the system will not allow the user to borrow books.

The length of time that a user is allowed to keep a book, and the amount of the fine, will vary from time to time, as the library's policy changes. When we code this part of our library system, we must enable administrators to change these values without having to write code or recompile the system.

Our fine table looks like this:

```
CREATE TABLE fine (
    card_id_number  INTEGER NOT NULL,
    title_id_number INTEGER NOT NULL,
    copy_number     INTEGER NOT NULL,
    return_date     DATE    NOT NULL,
    paid_date       DATE    NOT NULL,
    amount          INTEGER NOT NULL,
    PRIMARY KEY (card_id_number, title_id_number, copy_number,
                 date_levied),
    FOREIGN KEY (card_id_number) REFERENCES card,
    FOREIGN KEY (title_id_number, copy_number) REFERENCES copy,
    FOREIGN KEY (card_id_number, title_id_number, copy_number,
                 return_date)
  REFERENCES borrow
);
```

Column `card_id_number` identifies the library card with which this book was borrowed. This is a foreign key that joins this table to table `card`.

Columns `title_id_number` and `copy_number` identify the book that was overdue. These columns form a foreign key that join this table to table `copy`.

Column `return_date` gives the date that book was returned. We also use this date to mark when the fine was levied — the system will levy the fine as soon as the book is recorded as having been returned. This column, plus `card_id`, `title_id_number`, and `copy_number`, form a foreign key that joins this table to table `borrow`. We do this because we want to be able to trace back the fine to the borrowing event for which the fine was levied.

Column `paid_date` gives the date upon which the user paid the fine.

Column `amount` gives the amount of the fine. We assume that the amount of the fine and the amount paid are the same.

The primary key for this table combines the columns `card_id_number`, `title_id_number`, `copy_number`, and `return_date`. This assumes that the same person may keep the same book overdue more than once. It also assumes that the same person will not return the same overdue book more than once on the same date. We record the date paid separately from the date the fine was levied, because the user may not pay on the spot.

Two design considerations should be discussed further.

First, because the table `fine` shares so many columns with table `borrow`, why don't we simply add the columns for recording a fine to the borrow column and be done with it? This is a reasonable thing to do. However, most books are returned on time; in these instances, the disk space we allocate to hold information about fines will be wasted. As our library handles hundreds of thousands of borrowing transactions a year, that will add up to quite a bit of disk space that is initialized to NULL.

Furthermore, when a user tries to borrow a book, we want to determine whether the user has any unpaid fines before we let the user borrow the book. If we graft the fine information onto the `borrow` table, we will have to pull up all of the user's borrowing transactions, recompute whether they were on time, and then determine whether the fines were paid for them all. In a large database, this can be a huge query, and the last thing we want is to make the system slow. We could speed this transaction by inserting flags into table `borrow` to mark whether this transaction involved a fine and whether the fine was paid, but this tramples on the notion of data normalization. We should violate normalization only if we have a very good reason for doing so.

When we move the fine information into its own table, then this look-up becomes very simple: when the user tries to borrow a book, we check whether there are any records in table `fine` in which the column `card_id_number` matches that of the user's library card and in which column `paid_date` is NULL. This is a quick transaction that requires no recomputation whatsoever. Thus, it is best to move the fine information into its own table.

One last consideration: When we design our system, we must give the librarian the ability to cancel a fine. For example, a person may have returned a book on Saturday, when the book was due, by dropping it into a book drop, but it may not be logged in as returned until the following Monday or Tuesday. The user returned it on time, but we want to prevent a fine being levied against the user because of the library's delay in logging the book.

Indices

As with our simple example, the indices that we create for this database must balance the improved performance that an index brings, with the cost of making and maintaining the index.

For our first pass, we will build indices for most keys, as follows:

```
CREATE UNIQUE INDEX index1  ON title (title_id_number);

CREATE UNIQUE INDEX index2  ON copy (title_id_number, copy_number);
CREATE        INDEX index3  ON copy (title_id_number);
CREATE        INDEX index4  ON copy (branch_code);

CREATE UNIQUE INDEX index5  ON branch (branch_code);

CREATE UNIQUE INDEX index6  ON user (ssn);

CREATE UNIQUE INDEX index7  ON card (card_id_number);
CREATE        INDEX index8  ON card (ssn);

CREATE UNIQUE INDEX index9  ON borrow (card_id_number, title_id_number,
                                       copy_number, borrow_date);
CREATE        INDEX index10 ON borrow (card_id_number);
CREATE        INDEX index11 ON borrow (title_id_number, copy_number);

CREATE UNIQUE INDEX index12 ON transfer (title_id_number, copy_number,
                                         send_branch_code, receive_branch_code,
                                         transfer_date);
CREATE        INDEX index13 ON transfer (title_id_number, copy_number);

CREATE UNIQUE INDEX index14 ON fine (card_id_number, title_id_number,
                                     copy_number, date_levied);
CREATE        INDEX index15 ON fine (card_id_number);
```

We did not build indices on the following keys, because, in our opinion, they will not be involved in many transactions:

```
branch.branch_name
transfer.branch_code
transfer.receive_branch_code
fine.title_id_number, fine.copy_number
fine.card_id_number, fine.title_id_number, fine.copy_number, fine.return_date
```

In addition to indices built on keys, we add one additional index:

```
CREATE        INDEX index16 ON fine (card_id_number, paid_date);
```

This index will help us to find when a user has unpaid fines: in these instances, the column fine.paid_date will be NULL. This illustrates that even though a column can hold NULL cannot be used in a key, it is correct to build indexes for such columns. In this instance, the system will look up a user's unpaid fines every time a user attempts to borrow a book, so we very much want to find the instances where `fine.paid_date` is NULL, and we very much want to build an index for this column so that we can make this look-up as fast as possible. This set of indices gives us a good start toward having a database that is fast, yet efficient. As with our baseball database, we can — and probably will — change our array of indices over time, as experience shows us where the bottlenecks lie.

Note that MySQL does not allow you to build an index on a column that can be NULL; however, most relational database packages do let you do so — which can be quite useful, as this example shows.

Step 5: Write domain-integrity rules

At this point, we've finished most of the work of designing our database. However, one major task remains: to write domain-integrity rules for our database.

The domain-integrity rules are rules that we will implement in software, to help prevent nonsense from being written into the database. These rules are in addition to the rules of database integrity that apply by default. Study of the library problem and of our system suggests these rules:

✦ No rules should directly involve tables `title`, `copy`, `branch`, or `user`. These are semistatic tables into which information is inserted only occasionally.

✦ A user can have only one library card at a time. If the user reports a library card as having been lost or stolen, the status on the user's current entry in table card must be changed to an appropriate value to render the card unusable.

✦ Before a book can be borrowed, the status of the card must be checked. If the card has expired, the user must be denied the loan. If the card has been reported as stolen, appropriate authorities must be notified.

✦ A user cannot borrow the same copy of the same book twice in one day. We could add a "number" column to table `borrow` that would allow a user to do so, but we would have to track an additional column to account for a situation that occurs very rarely; it is not worth it.

✦ Finally, the system automatically levies fines for books that are returned late. Clerks can override fines at their discretion, under appropriate circumstances. For example, if a book has lain in a book-return bin for several days before being logged back into the system, any fine that occurred during that period could be waived.

As with our indices, our suite of domain-integrity rules probably is not complete. Experience — in the form of bug reports and customer complaints — will show us the rules that we missed. However, the above rules will give us a good start on building a robust, useful application.

Summary

This chapter discusses how to design and execute a database project.

The chapter first discusses the planning and execution of a database project. The emphasis is on project management: the steps needed to ensure that the project is planned, designed, built, tested, and maintained correctly, on time, and within budget. This requires not only engineering skills, but also a fair amount of people skills, as well as skill in maneuvering within an organization.

The chapter then discusses the art and craft of database design in translating the requirements of real-world project into a set of tables. Designing a relational database has five phases:

✦ **Step 1: Articulate the problem.** In this phase, write a brief, simple, and precise statement of the problem that the database is to solve. This phase should result in a requirements document to guide the building of our database application.

✦ **Step 2: Define the information needed.** In this phase, the entities that live within the "problem space" that was defined in phase 1 are written.

✦ **Step 3: Decompose the entities.** In this phase, the columns that comprise each entity named in phase 2 are written. Most entities will have more columns than we have paper to write them on; the problem we are trying to solve, as articulated in phase 1, dictates the columns we select.

✦ **Step 4: Design the tables.** In this phase, the bag of columns that we wrote in phase 3 are turned into a set of tables. We have found two rules to be helpful when organizing columns into tables:

Columns should be "existentially" related to each other. That is, a table should contain only the columns that are part of the real-world entity that the table reflects.

The database as a whole should avoid redundancy: no table should contain more than one instance of a column, and no entity should be described in more than one record.

These two rules are summarized in the principle of Boyce-Codd normalization, which states that every column within a table should functionally depend only upon the table's primary key.

✦ **Step 5: Write domain-integrity rules.** After the tables that comprise our database are designed, we must write down rules to help preserve the domain-level integrity of our database. These rules help to protect our system from writing into the database data that cannot occur.

Database design is a craft best learned by doing. To illustrate these principles, this chapter walks through two real-world examples of database design.

✦   ✦   ✦

Deciding on Linux Databases

✦   ✦   ✦   ✦

In This Chapter

Evaluating your data
requirements

Assessing your
existing data

Environmental factors

✦   ✦   ✦   ✦

Before you can make a choice about which Linux
database is best for your needs, you will need to have a
firm understanding of the criteria for choosing one database
product over another. That is the subject of this chapter.

The criteria proposed in this chapter cover three rather broad
perspectives of an organization:

✦ Current data requirements—that is, the requirements
  from this point forward

✦ Existing data—that is, from legacy systems that are
  being replaced

✦ The environment in which the database will be
  operated—for example, the technical infrastructure,
  which may include evaluating the skills of the personnel
  who are expected to administer the database.

Evaluating Your Data Requirements

Clearly, with respect to choosing a DBMS, an organization
must gain an understanding of the data to be managed. In this
section we will take a look at how functions of an organization
depend upon data (and therefore databases), and how the data
itself and the use of the data changes from function to function.
Implicit in this discussion is the need for ongoing assessments
of how well the organization makes use of its database assets,
what is redundant and what is missing, and whether the existing database infrastructure is a hindrance or a help.

Not as clear to many organizations just starting out using databases as a strategic asset is that there is more to the decision than this. There is also the environment—business and technological—in which the database is to be used. How will it benefit the organization? Who will own it? There are also issues surrounding the migration of old data to new database platforms. How will the old data fit into the new database schema? How can we move the data? These are frequently significant hurdles in the way of effective use of legacy data.

Business categories of organizational data

The data that organizations manage can be classified in many ways. Let us look at some possible classification of data for a typical organization.

Administration

This includes information on the personal information and benefits of employees, information on job applicants, the personnel hierarchy, departments, and the classification of employees.

Administrative information tends to be organized as a series of records with similar format that is related hierarchically and by basic classification. This sort of data is well suited to both relational and object databases. It could be queried with basic SQL relational queries, object-oriented path expressions, or collection queries.

If not already in formal databases, such information is often found in spreadsheets, proprietary human-resource and contact-management software, or even in flat directories and listings. Converting to a generalized database is usually a straightforward task.

Human resources, departmental leadership, and executive decision-makers use administrative data, as do employees, to examine benefit information.

Financial information systems

Financial information systems encompass the majority of the applications that one will find in organizations of almost any size. Financial data includes these three major areas.

General ledger

The general ledger contains the accounting transactions, primarily from accounts payable and accounts receivable, as it applies to the corporation as a whole. An organization that tracks and accounts for the expenditures and receipts in a way that is compliant with accepted accounting practices, such as the Financial Accounting Standards Board (FASB), and regulatory requirements, such as Securities and Exchange Commission (SEC) and Internal Revenue Service (IRS) rules, it does so primarily through a general ledger application. The general ledger is the place where every accounting transaction ultimately ends up. For example, it is in the general ledger that an organization sets up budgets; compares actual expenditures and receipts to budgeted expenditures and receipts; determines profitability; records depreciation and appreciation; records balance accounts; and shows stockholder equity. The author has even seen general ledgers being used for the recording of the amount of industrial waste (yes!) generated because this was a required report by regulatory bodies.

Accounts payable

Accounts payable contains the transactions for obligations, that is, purchases of material, employee compensation, money owed to vendors, and the payments that are made for each of these obligations. Typically, a voucher number that approves the payment for an obligation identifies an account payable transaction.

The accounts payable systems include such information as the vendors to whom the payments are made (including government agencies for obligations such as sales, use, and income taxes); the payments themselves; when the payment cleared; who approved the payment; which department is being charged with the payment; and which general ledger account(s) should be credited/debited with the payment. The actual list of attributes and entities involved is rather lengthy.

Accounts receivable

The other side of the coin is the accounts receivable, the monies owed to the organization. Primarily, these will be the customers. Again, the general ledger accounts to be credited/debited with the receipt will be of importance here. Other important information contained in an accounts receivable system are credit history, payment history, credit rating, what was purchased, customer information (contact names, addresses, phones, and so on).

Accounting data tends to be organized in tabular format organized by date and basic categories; for example, what part of the organization and which general ledger account.

For some organizations, accounting data is particularly dependent on currency and exchange rates. This can be an onerous restriction, as many companies found out when the European Union adopted the unified currency, the euro, in 1998.

If not already in formal databases or specialized financial packages, many organizations manage their accounting data with interlinked spreadsheets. In fact, the advent of the spreadsheet program VisiCalc on the Apple in the early 1980s, was one of the first computer developments to affect organizations of every size and profile, as many of them adopted the computerized version of the classic spreadsheet model for their financial records and projections.

Choosing database formats and management systems for accounting data is typically a very serious task with numerous factors to consider. The eventual choice often has great consequences for other database decisions. For the larger organizations, the choice is most often for an off-the-shelf package that provides a turnkey (ready-to-run) solution encompassing and integrating virtually all of the functional areas imaginable, including Personnel; Accounts Receivable; Accounts Payable; Sales Order Entry; General Ledger; Timekeeping and Payroll; Purchasing, Material, and Resource Planning; Shipping, Distribution, and Warehouse.

Analysts, comptrollers, and management at all levels use accounting data in the decision-making process.

Product

Product data includes specifications, part numbers, pricing, categorization, and descriptions of the various products put out by an organization. Although clearly relevant to manufacturers of various kinds, products can also be used abstractly to denote services, government functions, nonprofit concerns, and the like.

Product data tends to consist of distinct records using complex categories, and incorporating unstructured data such as textual descriptions, pictures, and schematics. In manufacturing firms, it is often highly integrated with the operational data that pertains to the processes for developing, producing, and supporting these same products.

The incorporation of nonstructured data introduces some challenges. Luckily, object and universal databases provide approaches to simplifying the management of such data. Increasingly, product data is geared toward "enabling" those applications that produce online catalogs and that support e-commerce.

It is not at all unusual to find product design and manufacturing data in specialized file formats. These files may be comprised of schematic drawings and parts lists. To integrate these files with a relational database management system (RDBMS), you would store a pointer, such as a URL or file system directory path, to the file(s) as one of the attributes of a database record used in a product manufacturing application. Another scenario is to have some product data actually exist only in marketing and sales material intended for internal or public distribution. In this event, there's an obvious risk of losing track of when or where such information can be found. But, such is the real world! Product information is used by marketing and line-of-business staff and manufacturing management to direct day-to-day activities, and by executives to determine overall enterprise strategy. Customer support agents use product information to help customers.

Marketing and customer data

Marketing data includes survey and product-registration responses, competitor and marketplace information, and information on prospective customers.

Marketing data very often consists of collections of data in a variety of schemes and formats, and from numerous sources. It can be difficult to mold it all into a unified structure, but such efforts bring great benefits, as businesses have lately discovered. Frequently, the data used by marketing is purchased from vendors who specialize in this kind of service. For example, one can send out a list of customers and receive back this list with additional information such as income, age, marital status, and so on. A second source of marketing data comes from surveys of every kind imaginable. Survey data can be somewhat more difficult to manage with the usual RDBMS structures because so much of it is textual in nature, for example free-form text responses to questionnaires. However, with the appropriate preprocessing, even this kind of data can be made accessible in a practical way in a RDBMS.

Marketing data is usually entirely intended for statistical analysis, and this requirement has a significant bearing on the chosen database management system (DBMS). Some analytical techniques, such as data mining, work most effectively on flat-file layouts that are, interestingly enough, the antithesis of RDBMS practice. So, having a system that can export (produce) a flattened (fully denormalized) version of an organization's customer data for analysis by some specialized statistical applications is valuable. If not already in a formal database, marketing data is often found in flat tables, or incorporated into customer-relations systems.

Customer data has traditionally been a synthesis of data from marketing to accounting, but recent management theory highlights the importance of handling customers in a holistic manner, and there is an entire series of industries that has emerged to provide tools for this purpose. These industries go by names such as Customer-Relationship Management (CRM), Consumer Affairs, and Customer Master File applications. Even though there are subtle differences between processes and approaches in each segment, the key data managed includes customer contact information and purchase histories as well as records of customer complaints, comments, and requests for help; demographics; psychographics (attitudes); responses to marketing promotions; and so on. If not already in formal databases, customer data is usually found in custom software such as call-center toolkits, with various approaches to implementing a database management system.

Customer data is used by marketing research, advertising, sales, and customer support to streamline customer contact, improve the efficiency of marketing and promotion activities, and it is analyzed by management to determine customer trends and anticipate crises and improve market positioning.

Operations

Operational data is very hard to generalize. Between broad categories of organizations, it changes dramatically in character. Even within one vertical segment, transportation, for instance, the operational details of a given organization tend to be as distinct as a fingerprint. Most generally, operational data incorporates asset and equipment inventories, and the parameters and rules for general management process. In manufacturing firms, it includes job scheduling and supply chain management data. In the airline industry, it includes seat-maps, flight and maintenance schedules, and crew assignments. In universities, it includes course listings and schedules, along with student registrations, faculty assignments, grades, and grade-point averages. And so on.

Operational data takes many forms and comes from many sources. The process of gathering, preparing, and managing this data usually depends on the systems employed in managing other types of organizational data.

In some industries, a good deal of operational data consists of business rules, which come with their own peculiar database demands. For instance, business rules could be aggregated into an inference-engine in order to automate many line-of-business decisions. In this case, the rules would often be encoded into a format based on formal logic, which might be familiar to those of you who have worked with the prolog computer language. In highly regulated industries the business rules might to a large extent originate outside the organization.

Line-of-business staff and general management use operational data. It is usually the key information that drives enterprise strategy and market positioning.

Research and development

Some organizations gather large amounts of research data. Universities, think tanks, consultancies, government, healthcare organizations, and armed forces are a few examples. Research and development data comes from scientific experiments, surveys, and product testing.

Research and development data often comes in tabular form, with mathematical relationships. It is usually managed with highly specialized applications with powerful statistical and scientific analysis facilities.

Research and development (R&D) data is used by line-of-business staff to inform daily decisions and marketing for product promotion and general public relations. Quality assurance personnel use R&D data to make decisions about product readiness and manufacturing process.

Electronic document management

Documents are often neglected in a discussion of organizational data, but this is an unfortunate oversight. Documents, a vast category, as you might imagine, range from employee handbooks to product manuals, from marketing white papers to shareholder reports. The big impediment to managing documents electronically with the same flexibility as is found in RDBMS is that, from the perspective of available database management systems, documents are essentially unstructured.

Documents come in varying levels of structure, although recent trends encourage greater structure for documents. They can be imagined in a hierarchy from document class or template, to individual document, and further down to subsections and document fragments. This suggests a structure similar to nested containers or a collection of trees (a *grove*).

Managing documents is a great problem in computer science. Some industries, such as airline manufacturing, have tackled the problem with great commitment and at great cost, while for other organizations, document management is not a concern. The growth of the Web is boosting the appreciation of document management as companies struggle to arrange their documents in a coherent form online, internally for employees, within a group of partners, or with the public. Doing so inexpensively and securely requires great attention to document-management issues, and modern tools, including DBMS products, provide improved document support.

Assessing Your Existing Data

If you are evaluating a Linux database for your department or small enterprise, you may already have an overall database methodology, or you may just have data scattered about a clutch of small DBMSs, proprietary software, flat documents, spreadsheets, and Web-site material. This is a typical arrangement that suits many businesses. However, there are good reasons for an organization to want to develop an overall database strategy. The basic problem is that with the data disorganized, gathering data for such basic processes as budgeting and employee orientation involves undue effort and expense.

A recent catch phrase in Information Technology (IT) is the enterprise information portal (EIP). This is the idea of designing a unified set of intranet sites that enable employees to access enterprise information using searches, site maps, categories, and hierarchies. While EIPs are technically more the interest of very large organizations whose vast collections of internal data make such portals somewhat of a necessity, the idea is useful to organizations of all sizes.

Some organizations are driven to a more formalized database structure by the advantage of using universal connectivity to enable mobile users to access the databases using the emerging class of personal communications devices. The huge success of the 3COM Palm Pilot and the move of such technology into cellular phones, pagers, and other such appliances, has encouraged database vendors to develop versions designed to work on such small-scale devices. This allows great flexibility of information access and entry if all the organization's data is stored in an applicable universal database, or in a framework that allows easy export to small-scale operating system databases such as the database built into 3COM's PalmOS.

Environmental Factors

If you are planning a database strategy, you should consider several factors beyond your existing data.

Network infrastructure

Client-server DBMSs are currently the most common, including commercial products such as Oracle, Sybase, and Adabas, as well as Open Source (see Chapter 1) products such as MySQL and PostgreSQL. In fact, all the DBMSs more closely examined in later chapters of this book are of client-server architecture. Such DBMSs have a server module that maintains the actual persistent data store, and that provides a network interface to which various client applications can connect.

The first issue that this opens is that of network security. If you are to use a client-server database, it is important to ensure that only authorized users can connect to the database server. If not, a malicious person, or cracker, might be able to access your data. But network security is important even if you are not using all the network facilities of your DBMS. Many DBMSs leave the network port open, even if the clients are configured on the same machine as the server. In this case, a cracker could scan the ports on the server, isolate the DBMS address and port, and use various methods to gain access.

The general solution to this is to make sure that your DBMS servers are behind a firewall. This is no different from any other networked machine, but inexperienced system administrators sometimes forget to protect their DBMS server. Many databases are set up as part of Web information systems on the Internet that are completely unprotected.

Figure 5-1 shows how a security breach of the Web server can allow unauthorized access to the DBMS from an outside attack, in this case from the World Wide Web. In Figure 5-2, with the same components in a different configuration, the DBMS is much more secure from unauthorized access from outside. Note that in this case the internal network could still be a source of a security breach. We presume that in both cases the intent is to allow the internal network to get through the firewall to the Web, so this has not changed in either case. Normal security precautions are required in either event to secure the database via log-in identifiers and secure passwords.

Crackers with access to your networks present another danger: they may use snooping devices to compromise your passwords. This makes encrypted passwords, as well as such authentication methods as S/Key and biometrics, important. In fact, encrypting all network traffic is usually a good idea to prevent sophisticated crackers from reading sensitive data right off the wires.

Remember that even if a cracker cannot get your passwords or snoop on your data, they may still employ a denial-of-service attack to disrupt your systems. The best defense for this is rapid detection of denial-of-service attacks.

Apart from security, you will want to make sure that your network is robust enough to handle the volume of traffic that your applications will be generating between clients and servers. You will want to arrange some sort of failure-recovery procedure, ranging from automatic approaches such as clustering and redundant hardware to failure detection and instant administrator alert for remediation.

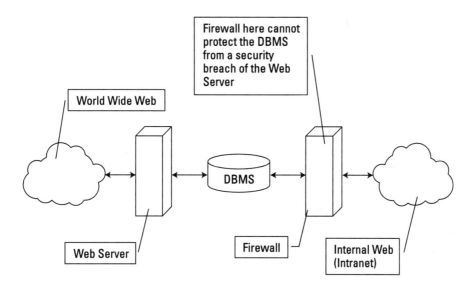

Figure 5-1: Outside firewall

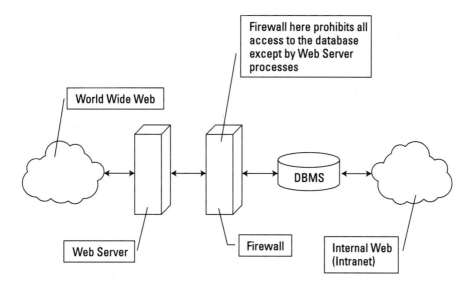

Figure 5-2: Inside firewall

Technical staff

All databases that see any use require maintenance. When deciding on a database strategy it is important to consider who will be maintaining the databases. Despite Oracle Corporation's efforts to make the operating system obsolete, DBMSs still need to run on an operating system. It is important to be sure that you have experienced system administrators to maintain the operating system. For Linux databases, it should be enough to have technical staff with experience in UNIX, including some knowledge of security. Naturally, specialized Linux support is even better, and the availability of specialized Linux systems administrators increases with the popularity of the operating system.

DBMS software requires varying levels of expertise for administration. Some, such as the large enterprise databases are legendary in their need for specialized training and experience. This is understandable as many of them are themselves as complex as operating systems. Minor changes in the administration of such systems can have far-ranging effects on performance. Currently, Open Source DBMSs are not as demanding of maintenance staff, but that is because they have fewer complex features. As they gain more features, this will be less and less the case.

One possibility is to hire a consultant for OS and DBMS management. In fact, many more data-center specialists, and even Internet Service Providers (ISPs), are looking to host database servers entirely for their clients.

Another possibility is to employ third-party training to prepare administrators for the anticipated introduction of new technology, especially those who are novices with Linux and/or UNIX. Again, this is a quickly growing area in Linux, with the various certification and training efforts announced recently, and the major DBMS vendors have long had extensive training and certification networks. There is much less available for Open Source databases.

Organizational processes

You must also consider what processes are in general use in your organization. These processes determine how your data is updated, how reports are generated, and with what external systems your data must interact.

For instance, if you use Electronic Data Interchange (EDI) in your cooperation with vendors and partners, you will need to consider the ease and expense with which your data can be exported to EDI formats.

Other organizational matters, such as the processes of hiring and terminating employees, are relevant. To take these events as examples, hiring an employee might mean giving the employee access to particular portions of the database, while terminating an employee would involve removing all simple opportunities for sabotage or theft of data. Your DBMSs should support user and account management systems that readily incorporate into your organizational process.

Cross-platform issues

Your database strategy might involve several DBMSs and host operating systems. If so, it is important to consider issues that may occur while trying to integrate these systems, such as internal data representations and encoding of data exchanged between subsystems.

Issues such as backup and security are also significantly affected by cross-platform issues. There are many software and hardware solutions for turnkey cross-platform backup, but they can be very expensive and many organizations choose to simply roll their own with scripts. The question of available expertise comes up again in these contexts.

Summary

In this chapter we have presented an organization from the perspective of the need to decide on a Linux database. We have proposed that there are three areas that need to be considered: existing data and uses of the data; data from obsolete applications; and the environment — physical and organizational — in which the data is managed.

When an organization is evaluating its data requirements for the present and the near term, it is necessary to understand the distinction between the data needs and the uses of the data by parts of the organization.

When an organization needs or desires to make use of data from old systems, it is of prime importance to determine how the old data will fit into the new structure, whether it is an accounting system or a human resource system. It may be that the old data is left as is because the cost to convert it to the new system is too high.

The third area that is of importance when considering a Linux database is the environment in which the database will be used. For example, the fact that it will run under Linux can prove to be a substantial obstacle for an organization that has a corporate standard of using Microsoft products only. From a technology perspective, the introduction of a new operating system and network protocol (Linux with TCP/IP) can mean additional training for an organization that doesn't have personnel with the required skills besides the issues of cross-platform access to the data. A third area that almost seems implicit when considering a Linux database is when an organization starts allowing customers and suppliers to have access to some portion of the organization's formerly inaccessible data, and the security infrastructure that such a change in doing business requires.

✦   ✦   ✦

Identifying Your Requirements

This chapter will help you to understand the process of building a database system, and help you to identify the needs and requirements of database systems in general. It provides a general set of guidelines to follow while planning, selecting, installing, and configuring your database system. Greater detail is given about much of this information in later chapters, but this chapter helps you to look at the big picture and to address common database issues in a general way.

Introduction to the Database Management Life Cycle

The database management life cycle is a general set of steps involved in designing, planning, and building a database system. This cycle can be extended to reach various levels of system setup and design depending on your specific needs.

If you are starting from scratch, you may want to extend the database management life cycle down to the level of choosing and setting up your hardware. If your shop is already set up, and if you are just beginning to build a new application, then a lot of the lower-level decisions may already have been made for you.

Either way, your goal is the same, you want to build a database system that meets all of your requirements and conforms to all of your constraints. After all, the important thing is that you end up with a system that does what you want it to do. These steps help you address the issues involved in building a good database system.

State your goal

Take a step back and try to look at the problem as a real-life situation, not as a new computer or database, project. This is a crucial step in designing your system. It is too easy to begin designing a project by getting right into the guts, forgetting all about the real-world problem that you are trying to solve.

Stating the goal of your system identifies for you the main objective of your project. This goal is the one thing that you must keep in mind with each decision that you make that is related to this project.

For example, let's look at a human resources database system. A human resources database system should not be designed so that it stores personal information about employees in one table and the departmental information about the organization in another table, even though the two tables can be joined to relate each person to the department that he or she works in. Ultimately, that may be the implemented solution. It will give the user the information they want, but it is not the goal of the system. The real goal of the human resources database is to make it easy for users to find the information that they need to know the employees in their organization.

As a developer, you will have plenty of opportunities later to make decisions about how your data will be best organized in the database. Right now, we are simply trying to figure out why we want a database system, and what we want it to do for us as people.

Identify constraints

Your system must accomplish your goal — that is the most important thing. Once you identify your goal, it's time to think in more detail. Start deciding on the guidelines that you will follow while trying to build a system that accomplishes your overall goal. Keep a detailed list of your constraints, and document the reasons that you have for putting each constraint on your project.

Constraints, in this context, should not be thought of as limitations; instead, think of them as guidelines that you are setting for yourself to follow. The guidelines are just another part of your design, and if you find that a constraint limits your ability to meet your end goal, then you should consider redefining that constraint. Also, remember that these constraints are not to be set in stone. When an alternative design better fits the solution to your problem, you should use it.

Organizational constraints

Define any organizational guidelines that you are required to follow early in your design. If your organization already has a database server in place that you are required to use, then note that as a constraint. If your project has a deadline, or budget, then you should make notes of them also. All of these factors will need to be considered when defining the solution to your problem. Identifying them now will help you to know exactly what you have to do later.

Organizational constraints are usually easy to define, and hard to change. Stating them clearly in the early design stages of your system will help you to avoid backtracking when you get into the later development phases of building your database system.

Application constraints

You also need to define other guidelines that will be required of your system. Now is a good time to figure out what types of client programs will be used to access the data in your database.

In general, you need to lay out how you expect the system to work. Define the client machines, in terms of hardware, operating system, and network protocols. Figure out what language the client applications are going to be written in, and what protocols the client applications will use to communicate with the database server.

If your system will be run on the Web, then the only client you have accessing the database may be the machine running your Web server. You will still need to know what type of system it is, and decide what language you will use to write the applications. You will have to decide whether you are going to use server-side CGI (Common Gateway Interface) programs or servlets, or whether you will use client-side Java applets that will be downloaded and run from the user's machine. There are a whole variety of things to consider when building a Web-based database system, and they are covered in more detail in later chapters.

As you can see, there are many factors that must be considered when building a client-server database application. Defining strong guidelines for the application up front will help you tremendously when you finally get to start the development of your project.

Layout requirements

Now that you have a detailed list of constraints, you can start to lay out your requirements, and begin designing your database system. You may want to lay out a few possible solutions, and then discuss them with others in your organization to see which solution will be best to use. Communicating your ideas with others will help you to see things that you won't notice on your own, and will also give you fresh insight to the problem at hand.

Remember to have your constraints and overall project goal handy when you are working on and discussing the different solutions. At this point, they are the rules that you have decided to follow, and straying from them now will cause you a lot of confusion during the later stages of design and development.

Now, you can begin to think in more technical detail. At this point, you know what you need to do, and it's time to start thinking about how you are going to do it. I know that's what you have wanted to do all along, so go ahead and have a go at it!

If you don't already have a database server, then it's time to figure out which one you want to use for the project. Choosing a database server is another important decision that can get very complicated. Choosing a database to meet your needs is discussed in detail in Chapter 7. In general, you want to select a database that fits well into your organization and that addresses the needs and constraints of your problem comfortably. You should also pick a product that will expand to meet your future needs.

You also have to decide which programming language the application software will be written in, and how that software is going to communicate with the database. Chapter 13 discusses several different languages and protocols that can be used to communicate with the databases from client applications. Remember to be practical when making these decisions. If your research tells you that a particular language is best for a project, but you don't have anyone around that knows how to program that language, then it will probably not be the best solution for your organization. You are going to have to live with your decisions for a long time, so try to make comfortable ones.

At this point, you know what database server you are going to use, what language your client applications are going to be written in, and how your client applications are going to communicate with the database server. Now it's time to move on to the next level of detail, finalizing your requirements.

Finalize your requirements

This is the part of designing that seems the most practical to developers. Now that we have the goal of our project laid out, and we have identified the tools that we will use to meet our goal, it is time to determine whether what we plan to do is possible. After we decide our design is possible, we have to determine whether it's a practical solution, and then try again to identify any areas that can be improved. The idea here is to torture test your design. If there is a potential problem, you will want to find it at this stage of your development.

You begin by thinking about how you will store the data in the database. Get to know your data, identify obvious relationships, and begin to lay out some possible table configurations. Draw diagrams of these layouts, and define the relationships of the data. Talk to the future users of the system and make sure that you understand the data well, and how it all fits together.

If your design is good, all of this planning will be carried over directly into the later development stages of your project. If you discover that your design is not good, or that it will not meet your end goal, then be happy that you found out now. It is much easier to identify problems before they happen, than it is to have something sneak up on you when you think that you are almost done with the project. Just imagine how you will feel if you have to throw away a few hundred, or even thousand, lines of code. That's when you will wish that you had spent more time planning.

During this step, you should finalize many aspects of your system. You should know what database server you will use, and what type of machines the client applications are going to run on, and the language that you are going to write the software in. You should also know and understand the data that your system is being designed to store.

Now that you have all of this, you are ready to move on. Don't feel bad about the amount of time that you spent on this part of your project—it will have been well worth it when you are finished.

Plan your execution process

You are almost ready to start building your system. But before you jump in, you need to outline your plan of development. You think that you have already done too much planning for this project, and planning how you will implement your plan sounds silly. It is really a small step, and you would probably have done it anyway, without even realizing that you were outlining your development plan. We are just suggesting that you pay a little closer attention to something that you were already going to do.

Now is when you make a schedule for what needs to be done in order to implement your design, and to make a timeline of when you expect to have different stages of your project finished. If you have a development team, you can divide the work, assigning different sections of the project to your developers. If you are doing all of the work yourself, it will still help you to divide the work into distinct parts. That way you will have several short-term goals to focus on, and will feel some accomplishment each time you complete one.

These steps will help you to manage your time and to figure out when different stages of your project need to be completed. If you are working for someone else it might be nice to show them this plan so that they know what you are doing, and when to expect the different phases of your project to be completed.

Build the system

Now, the moment that you have all been waiting for—let's start developing the database system! At this point, you will know exactly what to do. Because every system is so different, there really isn't that much to say. You have planned everything out so carefully that you know exactly what you need to do. Now, all you have to do is start it.

We suggest that you stick as close as possible to your plan, and that you document any deviations from it very carefully. This part of your project should be straightforward, and you can concentrate on all of the little details. Isn't it nice to not have to worry about the big picture as you do your day-by-day development? This is just one of the great advantages of starting with a good design, and planning well for its execution. If you ever need to know what to do next, just take a look at your schedule. Everything should be right there, clearly laid out for you.

Assessing the Requirements of Your Database Installation

The requirements of your database installation are based on the needs of your system. If your system is going to hold many gigabytes of data, then you are going to need a lot of disk space. If you want people to have access to your data from other machines, then you will need some form of remote access. The requirements of your database installation are specific to the problem that you have already set out to solve.

What is a database server?

In general, a database server is just a set of programs on a computer, with an area on that computer's hard drive that these programs will use to store data. In the most basic form, that's all a database server is. In practice though, a database server can be a very complicated system that is capable of doing all sorts of things.

One of these programs is usually called a *daemon,* and it waits on your computer, listening for requests that will be sent to it. When the program receives a request, it interprets that request, and responds to whoever made the request accordingly. The request usually asks the database to do something, and the response is the database's reply to that request.

There are other programs on the computer that are related to the database and that do other things. A program that allows users to directly interact with the database almost always comes with a database server. It is commonly called an SQL monitor, and it is how you access the database server manually in an interactive way. The SQL monitor usually lets you type in commands that get sent directly to the database server, and then display the database server's reply back to you.

There may also be other utility programs that are part of the database server. They may be programs that help you to do things like copy large amounts of data to or from the database, or programs that help you to back up your data, or simply programs that start and stop the database server safely. Now you can see how your database server is starting to look like a little more than a program and a section of your hard drive.

Read the documentation

Each database has its own set of installation requirements. Regardless of which database system you are installing, you should always start by carefully reading the system requirements and installation documentation.

The people who wrote the software thought the documentation was important enough to write, and we all know how much developers dislike writing documentation, so you can be fairly certain that the information there is important enough for you to read.

Set up a user account

Database servers allow remote access to your computer. By design, they are supposed to allow only known users to perform specific tasks on your system. But like any software, if it is not correctly configured, the program can give complete access to your database, or to your entire computer system, to anyone who knows how to take it.

Most of the database servers that we are covering in this book run on your system under a special user account. This account is given full rights to the parts of your computer that have to do with the database system, and is not given any rights to other areas of your system. This is a good way to have your system set up, and it will protect against unauthorized access to both your machine and your database.

Having your database server run as a separate and dedicated user provides two benefits. First, it prevents users of your database from gaining unauthorized access to your machine by putting them into a controlled environment.

 Note   Remember that the users of your database are not only the people to whom you have issued database accounts; users include anyone who even uses some client software to connect to your database.

If you have a Web database application set up, then the user of your database can be anyone on the Web. If one of these users figures out a way to compromise your database system, they may be able to gain access to your machine through the database server. Having your database run as a special user will limit what they can do to your system should this ever happen.

A second benefit that having the database server run as a special user account is that administration of the Linux system is made slightly easier. Many RDBMS systems run the query processes against the data as the login account used for installing the database. Typically, an account is created solely for this. So, when using system utilities that display user activity the database activity is easier to identify and monitor when the processes are owned by a single user account, that of the RDBMS. This is as opposed to database processes having the current login user identification that is more difficult to use when trying to identify which, if any, of the running Linux processes are database processes.

Assess disk space

The database server needs disk space. Each database system needs enough disk space to store its server and utility programs, documentation, and configuration information, as well as additional space to store the data that you are planning to keep in your database, plus index space and temporary space needed by query processes, and possibly table temp space for user queries and application queries. If there will be application programs using the database, the application developers need to provide the requirements for temporary space consumed by the queries. Make sure that you take into consideration multiple queries running simultaneously!

Each database server has its own space requirements for the system program and configuration files. You should be able to find out how much space is required by reading the documentation that comes with your database server.

Cross-Reference

We will discuss all of these issues in depth when we get to the second part of this book.

For the purpose of assessing whether or not an existing configuration of mass storage is sufficient you only need a rough idea how much space the database will require for its system programs, configuration files, and the minimum database storage area. We're talking about 3:1 or 4:1 initial estimates. If the estimated need is 60 percent or more of what is available, it is best to conclude that you don't have nearly enough storage space! Knowing how much space the database system needs, and roughly how much data you want to store in your database, will give you enough information to decide whether or not you can support the system. There are ways to calculate exactly how much space you will need for your data and database, but they go beyond the scope of this section of the book. For now you need only a rough calculation. That will be enough to determine whether some existing mass storage will work for you.

Classification of Information and Data Needs

Data comes in all different shapes and sizes. It is helpful for you to know all you can about your data before you set up a database system to store it. You should find out what type of data will be stored in your database, as well as how the user intends to manipulate the data and what the user expects to gain from having the data in a database.

Amount of data and data growth

It is an imperative that you know how much data you will need to store in your database, and how the data is expected to grow over the anticipated lifetime of both the database and the applications that use the database. The term "database" is meant here to cover both the logical database as well as the particular instance of the Linux RDBMS. This information is necessary for you to plan not only for the data storage needs over the years, but also for back up and recovery strategies, migration strategies, application planning, the number of users that can be supported, and so forth.

Different types of data grow at different rates. Some databases hold a set amount of data, and the size of the database rarely ever grows or shrinks. In this type of situation, you have a fixed-size database. This type of database is easy to plan for (although not really very common)

A second type of database is one that grows and shrinks regularly. This type of database may store transaction information of some sort, or some type of information that varies frequently, but not at a necessarily set rate. These databases are hard to plan for, and even though you have extra room today, it is uncertain whether you are going to have it tomorrow. Pay close attention to the variations in this type of database, or you will have problems.

Another common use of a database system is as a data repository. This is where data gets added to the database but is almost never removed. A repository-style database might hold customer information, your Web site log data, or some other information that is used for archival purposes. These databases grow as data is collected, and would lose value if it were removed. At the same time, these databases usually hold important information, and are expected to keep it there. Be sure to perform regular backups, and make sure that this database always has enough room to grow.

Importance of data

Importance of data is not about whether or not you need the data. Rather, it is about how replaceable your data is. Asking about data replaceability can bring a different answer than asking about whether you need the data to begin with.

Determining the importance of your data is a necessary step in deciding what features you need in a database server. If your data is a collection of all the work that you have done over an amount of time, then your data is probably very important, and will need to be treated as such.

Storing data of this nature involves frequent backups of the database and very high security for the server that it runs on. The programs that access the data will need to be very carefully planned out, and care should be taken to make sure that the data in the database maintains its integrity and stays safe.

On the other hand, if your data is something that you keep in a database for convenience, then it may not be as important, or it may be very replaceable. Maybe you are just putting the data in a database so that it can be easily searched or referenced against. In this case, you are using the database for its capability to easily perform complex searches on your data, or the database's capability to relate this data to some other information that you have stored somewhere else. In some cases, the data may not even be your own, but it might be something that you download from a public data repository regularly.

If this is the case, then someone else is already making sure that the data is accurate, and properly archived. If you completely lost your database it might take you longer to restore from a dump, or backup, than it would to for you to re-create the database from scratch. This is especially true if you have scripts written that automatically handle the updating of the data from a downloaded file. In this situation, frequent backups would do you very little, if any, good at all.

Common database activity

What do you want to do with your data once you have it in the database? This is another factor that will help you determine the features that you want in a database system.

Two common types of database systems are transaction systems and decision support systems. Each type has different features that are important to it. Defining what type of system you plan to implement will help you make better decisions for your specific needs.

In transaction-based systems, full data recovery and uninterrupted service are probably the most important features. With transaction-based systems the data stored in the database changes frequently, and without administrator interaction over periods of time. That makes the data very hard to recover in case of a failure.

Consider the classic bank account example. Would you want your bank's database server to go down before it had a chance to record a transaction in which you just withdrew several hundred dollars from your savings account? Maybe, but what if you were making a deposit? In that case, we are sure that you will want to know that your bank has the capability to fully recover from any type of database failure.

Data repository and decision-support systems are usually much easier to recover in case of a database failure than are transaction-based systems. Sometimes it might even be faster to re-create a data repository from scratch, than to restore the data from the database's logs and backups. However, in these types of systems, it is very important to be able to perform complex queries on your data, and get the information back very quickly.

Decision-support systems are commonly used to help people make important decisions. If you are a retailer and you track where your customers live, possibly by asking for their zip code at the checkout, then every day you collect a lot of data. Is the data very important to you? Maybe, but will your business come to a screeching halt if you lose it? Probably not, but there must be a reason why you are collecting it. If you are trying to expand your customer base, you might use this data to find out in what geographical areas you might be able to find new customers. If your business wants to focus on customer support, you might use the information to target your current customer base when advertising specials or sending out coupons. Thousands of different searches could be done on your data, and you will want a system that makes that as pain free as possible.

Odds are that your database needs fall somewhere between these two types of systems. Join the club — most database developers try to find ways to make their systems use the best features of both types of systems. It's not always easy, but deciding where you fit between these two types of systems will help you to make some very important decisions when setting up and configuring your database server and system.

Choosing the Proper System and Setup

Deciding which is the proper hardware for your system is heavily based on all of the decisions that you have made so far. The hardware you will use to run your database system is what brings your plan, ideas, design, and programs to life. All of the planning that you have done so far will be for nothing if you implement it on inadequate hardware.

The main areas that you need to focus on when deciding the hardware requirements for your system are processor, memory, disk storage, and backup media. The important thing to remember when configuring your system is that you want to keep it balanced. Don't put all of your resources in one area of your system and starve another. Your system will only perform as well as its weakest point. A good goal is to try to use about 85 percent of the total capacity of each resource in your system.

Processor

You only need enough processing power so that you can use the other components in your system. Having a super processor in your machine won't help you very much if slow disk access and low memory resources never let it work at more that 20 percent of its full capacity.

It is very hard to predict what kind of processor load your system will be under after it's up and running, so you are going to have to estimate your needs. If you can, you should talk to other people that are running similar systems, and ask them what they recommend. At the same time, don't feel too bad if you have to make a blind estimate on your own. Modern processor speeds are very fast, and any one that you choose will most likely be enough to get you well on your way.

Memory

Memory is another tricky factor to consider when building your system. It never hurts to have too much memory, but adding memory to your machine will not always be the solution to poor database performance.

Follow the guidelines laid out in the documentation for your database server carefully for specific memory configurations. The memory needs of different database servers varies, and the server's documentation should give you guidelines to follow on how much memory is adequate in your environment. Memory needs are mostly based on the structure of your data and the types of operations you will be performing on it. We will discuss memory issues related to each database server in more detail when we talk about configuring database servers later in the book. For now, it should be enough for you to set your system up and watch it run. If you notice that your system often needs to use swap space, then adding memory will probably improve your database system performance. If your system never needs to use swap space, you most likely have enough memory, and should spend your time trying to optimize processing and disk I/O.

Disk storage

Disk I/O is a huge portion of your database's overall function. The database server is constantly reading information from the disk into memory, and writing new information back to the database on the disk. After all, the disk is where your data is being stored, so being able to access the disk quickly will improve the performance of your database system.

The efficiency with which your database server can read and write data to and from the disk has a big impact on your database's overall performance. The major problem with having data stored on a disk is that it is read and written to and from the disk sequentially. This is fine when reading small amounts of data, the read head runs over the disk to pick up the data that it wants and it's done. But when you have a lot of data that you want to read from the disk, you have to wait while one device does all the work.

You can understand the problem if you think of it like the checkout line at a grocery store. When there is one cashier (disk drive) checking out all of the customers (data) in the store, the line (data) moves very slowly. But when another cashier opens an additional cash register the line moves faster. Adding disks to your database system is like opening another cash register in a grocery store. All of the data, or customers, are free to move through the checkout line much faster. If you have a lot of data going to and from your disks, you will see a major gain in performance by spreading that data out over several different disks.

There are two types of configurations that you can use to spread the data in your database out over multiple disk drives. You can use multiple individual disk drives, or a RAID (Redundant Array of Independent Disks) system. RAID is a group of individual small disks that act, and interface, as one single large disk. There are different types, or levels, of RAID configurations. Each configuration has its advantages and disadvantages, and lends itself to different situations.

Single drives

Multiple individual disk drives are nice to use when setting up a database system because you can configure the server to use them exactly how you want it to. You can have full control over what parts of the database are placed on the different drives, giving you a lot of control over how the database performs its physical reads and writes to the disks.

However, with all the freedom and control to configure the disks the way you want, comes the hassle of having to setting it all up, which leaves room for error. Configuring your database system to use multiple disk drives effectively is a lot of work, and if not done properly can actually reverse the performance benefit that we are trying to gain. The specific configuration for each of database server is different.

Another advantage to using multiple disk drives for your database is the capability to mirror your data. Mirroring is the concept of storing a single piece of data on more than one disk. This way, if one disk fails, the data is still available from another disk. Mirroring will not directly help with database performance — it may actually slow your database down — but it will help drastically with data recovery, especially in case of a disk failure. The performance loss with disk mirroring is only associated with writing data, because it has to be put on two disks each time a single piece of data needs to be saved. In most database situations, the cost in performance of mirroring is happily paid for by the added recoverability that results from having your data in more than one place.

RAID

RAID systems are nice for the opposite reason. With RAID you don't have to worry about configuring every detail of the disk access yourself, the RAID controller takes care of that for you. There are different types of RAID setups. The advantage that we are expecting to gain come from the capability to stripe data, which is when you spread the data out on more than one disk, and mirroring, which we just talked about. There are a few different types of RAID, called levels, and you will want to choose the one that provides both striping and mirroring of your data.

Raid level 1+0 is a common choice for a database system. It gives you the advantages of both striping and mirroring, with minimal performance penalty. RAID level 0 is disk striping. It offers maximum performance, but no recovery features. RAID level 1 is disk mirroring, where you have the same piece of data stored on more than one disk. Level 1 offers the best performance, and most complete fault tolerance of all the fault-tolerant RAID configurations. To find more detailed information about the different RAID levels, use your favorite Internet search engine to search for "RAID Definition."

The combination of RAID levels 1 and 0 provide an optimal environment for a database system. The price you pay for RAID 1+0 is in disk space. To have all your data stored in two places at the same time, you need double the disk space. That means that the nice new 200GB disk array that you just bought has now been chopped in half, and will now only be able to store 100GB of the data that you need to put into your database.

Again, with RAID all of the striping and mirroring is configured when the disk array is set up, so once it's configured you get to access the entire array just like it was one huge drive on your system. This is a great advantage, if you want the performance and security of having your data mirrored, but don't want to spend a lot of time configuring your database and a bunch of separate disk devices.

It is important to remember that when you use RAID, all of your data on that device is treated the same way. When your RAID does both striping and mirroring, any piece of data that is stored on that device will also be both striped and mirrored. Setting up individual drives yourself will give you the finer level of control in deciding exactly what data needs to be striped, and what needs to be mirrored. With this finer level of control you can sometimes save disk space, and still increase performance at the same time.

Backup media

The data that you store in your database is probably important to someone that you work for. With that in mind, you will want to take good care of the data to ensure that you never lose any of it, ever, no matter what happens.

A good way to prevent losing the data in your database is to back it up regularly. Most database servers have complex backup systems, and some vendors even guarantee, that if you follow their guidelines exactly, you will never lose any data.

In general, there are two different types of backup procedures. Incremental backups, in which you only save the information that has changed since you made the last backup, and full backups, in which you save all of the information in your database at that point in time. Most backup plans that offer full, up-to-the-minute recovery use a combination of the two methods. Commonly, you will make full backups at regular set intervals, and make incremental backups at intermediate points between your full backups. This will allow you to do a full restoration from your last full backup, and then apply the changes that were made with the remaining incremental backups.

Backups should be made on media that is separate, or removable, from your database system. That way, if you lose the disk drives or the entire machine the database is on, you will not lose the data with it. Some common media for database backups are tapes and disks. Disks are becoming more attractive as they get cheaper, but tape also has some good characteristics that make it a desirable media for backing up your data. There are also media such as CD-ROMs and DVDs that can be used for backing up your data, but they are not as commonly used. As of now DVD is more often used as a means of archiving data, but as prices drop and DVD writers become more accessible, they may begin to work their way into the mainstream for backing up data.

Disk

Disk drives are also nice for backing up your data. Disks are very fast to write to and do not need to be loaded onto the machine before they can be used. The downside of disk drives for backing up data is that they stay inside your machine when they are not being used. This is a problem if your machine fails, and your only source of backup data is sitting inside it.

A better idea is to store your incremental backups on disk, and then use tape as the media for your full database backups. This way you will benefit from the speed and convenience of doing the more frequent backups to the faster disk drives. Additionally, you will not lose the security of having your full backups on the more stable media and removed from your machine.

Tape is also nice for backing up your database because you can take it away from your machine, and store it in a safe environment. That way, if your machine fails, and you have a backup on tape, you can load it onto another machine, and recover your data to be used from there. This will protect you from more serious failures and natural disasters that prevent data recovery from any of the drives that that data were originally stored on.

The downside of tape is that it is slower to write to and read from than disk, and less convenient to use. If you want to back up or restore from tape, someone has to physically load it onto the machine and leave it there while the data is copied back onto the disks. Speed is another reason why you might find it better to use tape for the less frequent backups, and rely on disks for the more common backup operations.

Summary

In this chapter we examined the primary activities and information that are used in planning and choosing a database system.

The greatest amount of effort is devoted to developing the requirements that are necessary for meeting the organization's goal that will, in part, be met through the use of a Linux database.

After addressing the organizational issues, we discussed some of the elements of the plan for choosing and installing a Linux database. Typically, an assessment of the data storage requirements are next in the list of important information to have on hand. The data storage needs are, for the most part, independent of the particular RDBMS and the operating system. The data drives the specifications. In most cases you'll find that high performance disk systems are the single greatest cost in a new database implementation; second only to the cost of application development. Over the long run, it is the administrative costs of the database(s) that are the largest — DBA, Linux System Administrator, and application support, for example.

Third, we looked at some classifications of information and the particular data needs and uses for some common functional areas in an organization. This information can be used when developing a strategic plan for the organization's data.

Finally, we looked at the hardware that would be expected to have available for a database system. Once again, it is the disk systems that take the majority of the discussion. RAID systems can have a large impact on database performance, and on implementation cost.

✦   ✦   ✦

Choosing a Database Product

This chapter explores several Linux-based DBMSs, evaluating the suitability of each.

Overview of Choosing Database Products

This section describes the features and design characteristics that should guide your choice of a Linux DBMS. Let's examine the basic characteristics important to all modern database management systems (DBMS).

Architecture

DBMSs follow a client-server architecture. In a client-server architecture, all database processing occurs on a server, which carries out that processing in response to requests from clients, a database administrator, or database operator. Most frequently, client and server run on separate hardware — and even operating system — platforms, connected only by means of a network.

A client-server architecture has a number of advantages over a peer-to-peer or dumb-tube-to-mainframe scheme from a database point of view.

- ◆ It reduces network load, because much of the processing occurs on the server.

- ◆ It frees the clients to carry out other, more immediate tasks, such as handling the intricacies of a GUI (graphical user interface).

✦ If fully implemented, it allows DBMSs to handle some of the processing load that might otherwise fall to the operating system. For instance, many DBMSs provide data and user controls beyond those offered by their operating system platforms.

Clearly, therefore, the more thoroughly and efficiently a DBMS implements a client-server architecture, the better a candidate it is for any environment.

Relationship modeling and the relational model

A critical factor in evaluating a DBMS for use is the way in which a DBMS represents the relationships between and among items of data. Why do so many DBMSs follow this standard? Two reasons appear frequently in the literature. First, the relational model is simple and easy to implement; that is, defining schemas that accord with this model needs no complex logic or analysis of underlying data. Second, the relational model can link successfully to most categories of problems. That is, tables related by common fields represent most scenarios as effectively as do more complex structures for representing data, such as those found in network or hierarchical DBMSs.

Tip   Where do more recent developments such as object-oriented databases (OODB) fit into this picture? Unless you must store complex data structures, such as those involved in geographical or geophysical applications, must process large volumes of data in real time, or must provide tools such as natural-language searching and reporting, it's unlikely that you need to turn to OODBMSs.

Hardware and operating system platforms

As you might expect, a database's performance depends largely on its underlying platform. Therefore, let's review a few tried-and-true performance-related maxims.

RAM

It's a cliché, but it achieved that status by being so very true — you can never have too much memory. Data-intensive applications like those this book discusses make this more a fact of implementation life. Pay close attention to what the various DBMSs you're considering suggest as memory requirements. Then, count on at least doubling the suggested amounts.

Tip   One must, of course, exercise common sense in this regard. For instance, the Linux 2.2.x and 2.3.x kernels can only deal with up to 4GB of RAM, and then only with some patches that introduce other issues.

CPU

As with memory, so with processor — more is better. Not more capacity, but more speed. And the more flashy features a particular DBMS offers, the more you can be sure that you'll need a fast processor to take full advantage of those tools.

Operating system

This one's a relative no-brainer. Even more than other categories of applications, DBMSs depend on the operating system's capability to provide disk, caching, and network services efficiently, and features such as multithreading and multitasking, which can make or break a database's efficiency record.

UNIX has long dominated the DBMS platform market. Because UNIX offers capabilities such as support for many simultaneous client connections, superior I/O and memory management, and process management that enables administrators to quickly intervene to correct CPU bottlenecks and gridlock, major database vendors such as Oracle and Sybase have supported it for years. The porting of DBMSs from these and other vendors to x86-, RISC-, and SPARC-based UNIX, that is, to some flavor of Linux, must be viewed as a perfectly natural evolutionary step. Consequently, you can feel comfortable that the DBMS you choose will work hand-in-glove with any Linuxlike operating system (OS) it claims to support. Read the labels, and you'll do fine.

SQL standards

SQL standards and their impact on the choice of a database are not, unfortunately, as clear-cut as are questions relating to operating system platforms. Three SQL standards need to be considered: SQL-89, SQL-92, and SQL3.

✦ SQL-89 can be viewed as the lowest common denominator of DBMS capabilities. For example, this standard initially offered the ability to invoke SQL commands only from the programming languages: COBOL, FORTRAN, Pascal, and PL/I. Further, SQL-89 implemented checks on referential integrity only as an option.

If a suite you're investigating offers SQL-89 compliance and no more, do not consider it for your environment.

✦ SQL-92 goes well beyond its predecessor, adding a number of important features to DBMSs, including support for:

  • SQL agents, or utilities, that themselves generate SQL statements

  • Connections from client to server being managed by SQL agents

  • A much broader variety of human languages

  • Advanced data types such as Binary Large Objects (BLOBs)

Tip Examples of BLOBs include multimedia files such as audio and streaming video. Often, BLOBs have no defined structure that can be interpreted by a database, but rather are known only by their size and location.

Does a downside exist? Indeed, it does. Even today, many DBMSs, particularly open source products, are not fully SQL-92 compliant. What's more, the new standard, SQL3, which adds even more capabilities such as user-defined data types, has yet to be addressed, let alone fully implemented, by many DBMS vendors.

Therefore, in choosing a database application, try to determine the degree to which the application meets the SQL-92 standard and the timeframe in which its creators anticipate it will implement SQL3.

Tip If your environment must organize and track large amounts of object-oriented items, keep an eye on the SQL3 standard and the Linux DBMSs implementing it. That standard deals largely in object-oriented extensions to SQL.

Stored procedures, triggers, and rules

Stored procedures, triggers, and rules are DBMS terms for what we might call *library functions*, or *utilities*.

Stored procedures have been defined as collections of SQL statements and procedural logic that reside on the DBMS server. They are considered database objects. As a result, clients can run these pieces of canned code simply by sending a request to the server.

Triggers, as their name suggests, cause an action to take place within the database when certain predefined conditions occur. For instance, a trigger might be initiated by a user deleting a record, and might function by requesting confirmation of the deletion.

Rules refer to a special type of trigger that verifies data before inserting it into a database. So, for example, your DBMS might include a rule that ensures that the server would not accept a user-entered date such as February 31.

While it's clear that stored procedures, triggers, and rules are very useful, powerful tools for a database administrator (DBA), they should not play the primary role in choosing a DBMS for several reasons. One reason is that capabilities vary greatly from vendor to vendor, and even from release to release. Another reason is the great difficulty or impossibility of porting stored procedures and triggers from one DBMS to another.

Two basic DBMS functions are (a) the DBMS's capability to support and carry out referential integrity efficiently, or the capability of a database to accurately match values in key fields across tables and two-phase commit, and (b) the practice of storing data in a way that helps to ensure the recovery of data that may have been in transit at the point of a platform crash.

Specifically, look for a DBMS that supports referential integrity and that can apply it to primary keys as well as to columns, and even to entire domains, without the use of indices.

Operating system-related performance issues

Many DBMSs, among them Oracle8*i* for Linux, can bypass the OS's native file system and go directly to the raw disk, or raw space of the physical disk partition. Raw space is unformatted space. Thus, because it doesn't have to call upon the operating system to act as a middleman for input or output, the database server encounters less I/O overhead. Ergo, faster disk I/O and a faster DBMS.

Nonetheless, there are several drawbacks to this technique:

✦ Often, when a DBMS uses raw disk, it also requires special utilities to be backed up. That is, a simple "tar" won't suffice.

✦ Linux, like UNIX, can use some raw, or unformatted, disk as swap. When a single physical storage device houses both file system, that is, formatted space, and raw space that contains swap, some flavors of Linux permit no other use of any leftover raw space.

However your OS reacts to the combination of swap and file system on a single physical drive, it's certain that a large amount of raw space given over to swap lessens the amount available to a DBMS's I/O.

So, in evaluating Linux databases, pay attention to the degree to which and the way in which they manipulate raw disk space. Remember that everything has a price; don't accept poorer overall system performance or more difficult backups for database performance that may improve only slightly over what it would have been without the ability to manipulate raw space.

Means of multiprocessing

Many flavors of Linux and other Intel, RISC, or SPARC UNIXs support multiprocessing or parallel processing, which is spreading an operating system's processing load across several CPUs. In evaluating databases and their platforms, what matters isn't so much that an OS can multiprocess, but rather *how* it multiprocesses, and how much of this parallel processing can be controlled by a DBMS server.

If your OS will not give up to an application server the task of allocating system resources, no choice or problem exists. But if your OS permits a database server to allocate resources to its own processes, such as queries, you're not necessarily gaining anything. DBMS servers that typically do this sort of job:

✦ Have been written and compiled specifically for parallel query processing, and act by breaking up a query into smaller subqueries that execute concurrently on different processors.

✦ Therefore require a query manager to oversee the distribution of subqueries and the reassembling of subquery results into a coherent whole that can be presented to a user.

✦ As a result, may present more overhead and certainly more expense.

Only if lightninglike response time is critical in your environment should a database server's capability to carry out parallel processing be a factor in choosing a DBMS.

Managing connections

DBMS servers manage client connections and allocate resources to them in three ways. When you evaluate a database candidate for your environment, a particular suite's connection management method must be considered.

The three client connection management techniques are:

✦ Process-per-client

✦ Threading

✦ Some combination of per-client and threading

Process-per-client

This approach, as its name suggests, gives every database client its own process for the client connection. So, if your DBMS server happens to be handling 30 clients at a given moment, rest assured that your OS has been presented 30 separate additional processes. It's easy to see the disadvantages of this technique.

First, process-per-client gobbles up your resources, with each client grabbing one or more processes. Further, process-per-client DBMSs tend also to be RAM gluttons, using as much as 2MB per client.

Also, as a result, more interprocess communication, with its attendant overhead, takes place.

Process-per-client does have definite advantages, though. The biggest advantage is that client connections that operate as individual processes reside in their own process address space in memory, and thereby receive built-in protection from misbehaving processes that share space. In addition, process-per-client can be more readily and efficiently managed by multiprocessing operating systems running on multiple CPUs.

Tip Earlier versions of Oracle used process-per-client. However, Oracle8*i* for Linux has full multithreading capabilities, as do many of the Linux DBMSs discussed later in this chapter.

Threading

Threading views individual client connections, and even the DBMS server, as individual threads, and runs them all in the same address space.

Tip Just what is a thread? An informal definition: a path or track through memory, like a line in a connect-the-dots game that links data and instructions pertaining to a particular task. A more formal and more Linux-related definition: a lightweight process that executes more quickly and demands fewer system resources than a "true" or "heavyweight" process, because the thread requires less management.

Threading also has its own process scheduler, thereby freeing any application that employs it from reliance on an operating system's process-management mechanisms. Because they rely less on OS services, threaded applications also port more easily.

Does threading have any disadvantages? Yes, the most significant being the fact that threaded applications don't distribute resources even-handedly. Threading can instead monopolize a CPU, leaving other threads languishing in line until the gluttonous one relinquishes the processor.

Combining process-per-client and threading

In an attempt to provide the best of both worlds, some DBMSs use a combination of process-per-client and threading. Among Linux databases, Oracle8*i* stands out in this category.

Oracle for Linux uses a multithreaded agent called a *listener*. Here's how the listener-initiated processing of a client connection works:

1. The listener establishes client/server connections by assigning client requests for services to another agent called a dispatcher.

2. The dispatcher sends requests from the client to a server queue.

3. A server process takes the message off the queue, executes the request inside the database server engine, and starts the response on its way back to the client, again using the server queue.

Such a scheme can maintain a protected processing environment like that enjoyed by process-per-client, without having actually to allocate a process for every connection. However, as can happen with so many categories of tasks, this queue can back up, and result in delays in servicing client requests.

Evaluating client connection-management methods

Correlating candidate DBMSs' client connection-management techniques with the suitability of the suite to your environment must begin with an overview of system resources. If, for example, you're lucky enough to have CPU and RAM to burn, client connection-management need not play a significant role in your DBMS selection process. If, on the other hand, and as is too often the case in the real world, you must implement in a limited setting, connection management becomes a more important question in evaluating database candidates.

Note   All of the Linux DBMSs covered in detail in this book—MySQL, PostgreSQL, and Oracle8*i*—have multithreading capabilities built in.

Administrative and other tools

Think of them as necessary frills. Any DBMS that you're considering should, ideally, bundle administration and monitoring tools with itself. Tools to look for include those that expedite:

✦ Backing up and restoring a database

✦ Carrying out user administration

✦ Fine-tuning and maintaining DBMS security

✦ Fine-tuning DBMS performance

Government Security Standards

Government and other security standards are set forth by the National Computer Security Council, a subsidiary organization of the National Security Agency, in the document *Trusted Computer System Evaluation Criteria* (DOD standard 5200.28-STD, December 1985). The standards are definable as follows.

✦ D-level security: A nonsecure system or application

✦ C-level security: Some security provisions; includes:

• C1: User log-on required, group IDs also permitted

• C2: Individual log-on with password required; audit mechanisms available

✦ B and A levels: Provide mandatory control with access based on standard Department of Defense clearances

Most UNIXlike operating systems offer C1 security by default, and can be upgraded to C2 without undue effort. Therefore, the Linux DBMSs we're examining either do or can closely monitor user activity, age passwords, detect intruders, and so on. But as you probably have guessed, there's a price for this additional security. Such databases are more expensive and perform more poorly, because they demand so many additional system resources to be capable of accomplishing the additional security they offer.

Even more attractive is a database suite of bundled tools that enable you to monitor the database's cache usage, disk access efficiency, and processor usage.

 Tip   Of the Linux DBMSs covered in detail in this book, Oracle8*i* and PostgreSQL offer at least some of the monitoring tools just mentioned.

Security techniques

All Linux DBMSs worth considering offer security at the database, table, column/field, and row/record levels. Such databases can prevent at all these levels:

✦ Damage to data due to collisions or overlapping of modification attempts

✦ Unauthorized access

✦ Unauthorized modification

However, this doesn't make these DBMSs hack-resistant. Should you need to at least approach that ephemeral goal, consider a DBMS that complies with such government security standards as C2 and B1.

Overall performance

In evaluating database candidates, compare their performance. Request performance statistics from vendors for the same task. For instance, you might ask the MySQL Project, PostgreSQL Inc., and Oracle Corporation for mean response time to a simple query when ten or more clients connect to a server.

Capability to interface

You should consider whether, and how easily, the DBMS you're evaluating can interface with application programming interfaces (APIs) and with executable libraries for such applications as data communications, graphics, and drag-and-drop capabilities. Should your users need to interweave data derived from a Linux database with tools such as Microsoft Access or PowerPoint, the selected database must, at a minimum, have the capability to save query results as flat ASCII files whose fields are delimited only by white space. Even more useful would be the capability to export directly in Access or other Microsoft or Windows-compatible formats.

General design and performance questions

Finally a number of general questions that pertain to database functionality and the overall DBMS model (relational, network, or object-oriented), or to specific application characteristics that best fulfill the criteria implied in the question should be examined.

DBMS Models

Here are brief definitions of the three most significant DBMS models.

✦ Relational: based on a model developed by E.F. Codd. RDBMSs enable the definition of data structures, storage and retrieval operations, and integrity constraints; and data and relations between data organized by tables, records, and fields. RDBMSs use key fields to enable automatically indexed searches for specific values of that field.

✦ Network: model in which each record type can have multiple parent relationships; for example, a record type called inventory relating to both a customer and a product record type. Also called multirelational model.

✦ Object-oriented: model that requires data to be stored as objects, and to be interpreted only using methods similar to those of object-oriented programming. OODBMs preserve relationships between similar objects, as well as references between objects. OODBMs often provide queries that execute more quickly because of a lack of need for joins due to capability to retrieve an object without a search by means of its object ID.

Of the three Linux DBMSs covered in detail in this book, PostgreSQL and Oracle8*i* offer significant object-oriented capabilities. MySQL provides such capabilities only through add-on tools. Although all three rely heavily on the relational model, they also offer some features that are more typically associated with the network model, such as the capability to support very large databases being accessed by multiple simultaneous users in a client-server environment.

Note   Check out new releases of these products—recently released or about to be released as of this writing—Oracle9*i*, PostgreSQL 7.1.2, and MySQL 3.23.

Fields

If a Linux DBMS has multiple occurrences of a few data items in slightly different contexts, the relational DBMS model will most likely best serve your needs.

Percentage of multimedia or other BLOB data

Will multimedia data, such as video and sound, be what your DBMS tracks? If so, you'll need an application that can work according to the object-oriented model.

Speed of updates

The more critical response time is to your DBMS, the more it needs to rely on the classic relational model for databases.

Frequency of schema modification

If your database design must be changed frequently, your needs will be best met by a DBMS that adheres to the relational model. Such suites handle schema changes more readily than network or object-oriented databases.

Size of database

Will your database have to store and manipulate a very large number of records? Also, do you anticipate that the schema of this database will be relatively unchanging? If so, your needs may be best served by a DBMS that follows the network model.

Number of simultaneous transactions and user sessions

Do you anticipate numerous users accessing your databases simultaneously? Will each user perform a multitude of modifications to those databases? If so, your environment would be best served by a DBMS that adheres to the network or multi-relational model.

Choosing a DBMS

When choosing a DBMS, you have several options.

MySQL

The MySQL Web site at `www.mysql.com` lists what this DBMS's creators consider important in a database system. The site emphasizes these points about the product:

✦ Capability to handle very large bodies of data, as well as databases that contain BLOBs

✦ Adherence to the SQL standard

✦ Availability of libraries and client programs

✦ Multithreaded, client-server architecture

✦ Multiuser nature

Its developers created and tested MySQL in an environment that included:

✦ A significant percentage of tables containing more than 7 million records

✦ Approximately 10,000 tables

✦ More than 40 databases

✦ At least 100GB of data

Like all open source products, MySQL remains very much a work in progress. Also like its open source peers, and as the figures above state, MySQL offers production capabilities. Even better, the price is right; MySQL, again like its open source companions, can be obtained for little to no cost.

Oracle

Among other things, Oracle Corporation intends its DBMS Oracle8*i* to compete with such market staples as the DBMSs that run under Windows NT. One of Oracle's senior Linux development managers has pointed out that the Linux community itself has expressed the need for broadly relevant applications and the user community at large has been skeptical about Linux because of the lack of a variety of applications from which to choose.

Oracle Corporation addressed both concerns by the original port of its DBMS to Linux and by a commitment to an ongoing enhancement of the ported product and to full support from Oracle Corporation, including such as free upgrades.

Specifically, Oracle Corporation points to these features to demonstrate that Oracle8*i* for Linux is an enterprise-ready product:

✦ A database development environment

✦ An applications development environment

✦ Open Database Connectivity (ODBC) libraries

✦ Support for multiprocessing

✦ Support for Apache, the world's most widely used Web-server application

To offer these and other features, Oracle8*i* relies largely upon a design paradigm called Optimal Flexible Architecture (OFA). Oracle Corporation considers OFA to be a set of configuration guidelines that permit the creation of fast, reliable databases that require little maintenance. Specifically, OFA attempts to facilitate the administration of data and schema growth, control of multiple databases, and routine administrative task backups. OFA also attempts to minimize fragmentation in both data and schema storage, as well as to organize software and data in such a way as to avoid bottlenecks and poor performance.

However, the ways in which OFA attempts to accomplish these admirable goals may themselves create at best overhead and at worst problems. Consider these points made in various areas of Oracle8*i* documentation.

✦ Hardware costs should be minimized only when doing so does not conflict with operational considerations.

✦ Oracle8*i*'s practice of separating categories of files into independent directory subtrees minimizes the extent to which files in one category can be affected by operations on files in other categories.

✦ Spreading Oracle8*i* databases and software across more than one drive minimizes the impact of drive failures on those databases and software.

On paper, each point seems completely sound. But in the real world, each may introduce complications as thorny as the circumstances they intend to preclude. For example, a large, heavily subdivided database might result in a file subsystem that proliferates to the point of gobbling up too large a percentage of the OS's inodes. Or, the reliance on RAID might introduce expense and administrative complexity that other means of protecting the integrity of the DBMS might not. In a nutshell, Oracle8*i*'s admirable attention to processing efficiency and database integrity make it somewhat ill-suited, despite its many strengths, to small environments or small, simple collections of data.

PostgreSQL

In a very real sense, PostgreSQL combines the strengths of both MySQL and Oracle8*i* for Linux, without the (admittedly, in many environments, minor) drawbacks of either.

PostgreSQL, the open source incarnation of Ingres, evolved in an academic environment. In its developers' own admission, PostgreSQL "had not been exposed to the full spectrum of real-world queries." As a result, its growth since 1995 has emphasized adding or improving:

✦ Commercial-style features such as telephone support

✦ SQL functionality that was missing

✦ Support for complex data types

✦ Support for complex queries

✦ Transaction support

✦ Locking

✦ SQL conformance

The following list of some of PostgreSQL's features demonstrates the DBMS's part-commercial, part-open source persona.

✦ Multicolumn indexes are available

✦ Multiple index types are available, including B-Tree and hash

✦ ODBC drivers are available

✦ Online backup is supported

✦ Online documentation is available

✦ Online recovery is available

✦ Parallel querying is supported

✦ Read-only databases are available

✦ Row-level locking is available

✦ Shared SQL cache

✦ Several operating systems supported, including FreeBSD, NetBSD, Linux x86, Linux Alpha, Linux SPARC, SGI Irix 5.3, Solaris SPARC, and Solaris x86

✦ Several programming languages supported, including C, C++, Java, Perl 4, Perl 5, Python, and Tcl

Candidates

This section discusses the strengths and weaknesses of commercial Linux database suites and open source Linux DBMSs.

Commercial products

More commercial Linux DBMSs than you might imagine exist. This section reviews the pros and cons not only of this category, but also of individual representatives of it.

 Note   A DBMS belongs in the commercial category if it does not make source code available, or if it offers that code only at additional cost.

Strengths of commercial products

Most of the products here offer sophisticated management tools such as the capability to administer remotely via the Internet. Many also support features critical to e-business applications, including the capability to handle BLOBs, multimedia data, and streaming. In addition, these products make available GUI-based development toolkits and environments that surpass the capabilities of similar open source tools. For these reasons, and if your environment requires object-oriented or network DBMS features, you must consider commercial database management systems.

Weaknesses of commercial products

It's said that in real estate the three most important criteria are location, location, and location. In business, that might be paraphrased as cost, cost, and cost. None of the commercial Linux DBMSs we review here is inexpensive. If yours is a small environment with relatively simple data management requirements, you may want to forgo commercial database management systems.

Sample commercial products

Now, let's look at 12 commercial Linux DBMSs.

ADABAS/D

Adabas/D, a product of Software AG of Frankfurt, Germany, provides a professional database system that fully implements the relational model by supporting domains, primary keys, referential integrity, stored triggers and procedures, and updatable join views.

ADABAS/D has been ported to Linux since 1997. Among its features of primary interest to business environments are:

✦ Capability to increase data space areas without shutdowns or reorganization

✦ Low cost compared to other commercial alternatives

✦ Silent operation without permanent supervision

✦ Balanced B* trees to optimize storage allocation

✦ Scalability on multiprocessor systems

✦ Multithreaded architecture

✦ Record-level locking

✦ Support for C, C++, and COBOL

✦ Support for the standards ANSI, SQL-92, and OFA

✦ ODBC support

✦ JDBC support

✦ Includes a Perl Version 5.4 tool

✦ Includes a Tcl/TK interface

✦ Remote Control, a graphical database administration tool, which can be used in an intranet or via the Internet, and which permits remote database installation and server configuration

✦ GUI front-end for queries on all supported platforms

✦ WebDB, an integration of Internet and intranet HTML documents with the DBMS's file system

✦ Supported operating systems include SUN Solaris 2.5 or higher, SCO UnixWare, and Linux

See www.softwareag.com for more information.

Caché

Caché calls itself a "postrelational" database, and relies on both a transactional paradigm and the multidimensional DBMS model. Its significant components include:

✦ Caché Distributed Cache Protocol (DCP), a networking technology that dynamically distributes the database across the network in response to processing demands

✦ Caché Object Server that permits direct use of Caché Objects by Java, ActiveX, and C++ language processors and development tools

✦ Caché ObjectScript, a built-in scripting language designed for enterprise-class transaction processing

✦ Caché SQL Server, that provides access to databases by either SQL or ODBC

✦ Caché Studio, a GUI-based development environment

✦ Caché WebLink, that provides connectivity between Caché and Web servers for Web-based transaction processing applications

✦ Object-Oriented functionality, including support for inheritance and multiple inheritance; support for multimedia and application-specific data; and support of popular object languages and technologies including Java, ActiveX, and C++

✦ Visual Caché, to automate the creation of Microsoft Visual Basic forms and to link Caché database objects with these VB forms

See www.e-dbms.com/cache for more information.

DB2 Universal Database for Linux

IBM's DB2 Universal Database for Linux, the Intel port of the company's longstanding DBMS, includes these significant features.

✦ A multimedia, Web-ready relational DBMS

✦ A performance monitor

✦ A Perl driver for the Perl Database Interface

✦ Connection enhancements such as connection pooling

✦ DB2 Control Center, administrative interface that can be run from any Java-enabled Web browser

✦ Increased table/column limits

✦ Lightweight Directory Access Protocol (LDAP) support

✦ OLE DB Container Support

✦ Replication capability for BLOBs

✦ Support for JDBC and SQLJ

✦ Stored procedures

✦ Unicode support

Tip DB2 Personal Developer's Edition can be downloaded at no charge, but may only be used only for the evaluation, demonstration, testing, and development of application programs. Although there is no time limit on its evaluation, it cannot be used in a production environment.

See www.ibm.com/software/data/db2/linux for more information.

Empress Suites for Linux

Empress Software, which has provided database products for Linux since 1995, offers three products:

✦ Empress E-Commerce Database Toolkit for development and deployment of e-commerce applications

✦ Empress Embedded Database Toolkit for developers of embedded systems; features a fast RDBMS with a small footprint

✦ Empress Web Database Toolkit for the creation of interactive, data-driven Web pages

At the core of each of these Toolkits lies the Empress RDBMS, a compact SQL-database engine. Empress RDBMS has these significant features:

✦ Capability to add, drop, and redefine attributes to a table without unloading and reloading data

✦ An extended transaction mechanism that allows multiple transactions to be named and nested within each other

✦ ANSI SQL database

✦ Automatic two-phase commit to help ensure data integrity during transactions

✦ Data-transfer and data-loading utilities

✦ Extended objectlike capabilities such as Persistent Stored Modules, User-Defined Functions, and User-Defined Procedures

✦ Fully distributed, client-server, and multiserver architectures across heterogeneous networks

✦ Fully integrated report writer to produce custom-formatted reports

✦ Interactive, embedded SQL

✦ Kernel-level C and FORTRAN interfaces to the database engine

✦ Kernel-level X Window System interface access for more efficient GUI-based operations

✦ Recovery utilities to restore databases in the event of a major failure

✦ Referential constraints and range checks built in to the data dictionary

✦ Strong integrity and recovery features

✦ Support for numerous universal data types including text, float, and bulk

Tip   Empress Software offers free, 30-day evaluations of all its Linux suites.

See `www.empress.com/` for more information.

FrontBase

Billed on its Web site as "the only enterprise-level relational database server with zero-administration," FrontBase, which is available for Linux platforms such as Red Hat Linux, SuSE Linux, YellowDog Linux, and Solaris, offers these significant features.

✦ Capability to back up live databases

✦ Access privileges at the record level

✦ Block mode, on-the-fly encryption

✦ Built-in mirroring ability

✦ Conservation of storage by using the UTF-8 standard for data representation

✦ Exclusive use of Unicode 2.0 for all character data

✦ Full compliance with the SQL-92 standard, including full integrity constraint checking built into the server

✦ In-memory table caching

✦ Multicolumn B-tree indexing

✦ Reliance on sockets for client-server communication, thereby providing support for a variety of client platforms

✦ Remote management ability from any Web browser

✦ Stored procedures

✦ Streaming, on-the-fly encryption of client-server communications

✦ Support for gigabyte BLOBs

✦ Support for gigabyte character-type field values

✦ Support for streaming QuickTime content

✦ Support for terabyte databases

✦ Tool to migrate MySQL databases

See `www.frontbase.com` for more information.

Informix SE

On its Web site, Informix Corporation emphasizes Informix SE's performance, data consistency, client-server capabilities, standards adherence, and ease of administration. Among the suite's specific features that support these claims are:

✦ A variety of indexing options that can involve indexes covering one to eight fields, as well as B+ tree indexing options that include unique and clustered indexes

✦ Built-in client-server connectivity by means of libraries that preclude the need for any additional networking products

✦ Maintenance of data consistency by means of audit trails, transaction logging, locking procedures, and isolation levels

✦ Meets SQL-92 entry-level requirements

✦ Native language support based upon the X/Open XPG3 specification

✦ No need for OS kernel modification in order to provide such features as shared memory or the use of raw devices

✦ Permits a maximum character field size of 32,511 bytes

✦ Permits a maximum key size of 120 bytes

✦ Permits a maximum of 32,767 columns per table

✦ Permits a maximum of 1 billion rows per table

✦ Permits a maximum record length of 32,767 bytes

✦ Reliance on the native Linux file system for simplification and speed of data storage and retrieval

✦ Supplies utilities that migrate Informix SE data in ASCII format to other Informix databases

✦ Support for a number of levels of read-only isolation control, such as an SQL SELECT FOR UPDATE request's precluding other SELECT FOR UPDATE transactions' locking records already being updated

✦ Support for entity integrity by enforcing acceptable data values for fields

✦ Support for integrity constraints, stored procedures, and triggers

✦ Support for referential integrity, for example by ensuring that information about an entry in a master table remains intact as long as corresponding information still exists in a detail table

✦ The capability to automatically determine the fastest way to retrieve data from a table, based on the capability to collect and calculate statistics about specific data distributions during nonpeak processing hours in order to provide a means to avoid bottlenecks during heavy loads

✦ The capability to lock at the row, table, or database levels

✦ The capability to restore tables or even an entire database, in the event of a system failure, based on audit trails

✦ Two levels of access privileges to help to ensure database security: database privileges that permit creating tables and indices, and table privileges that allow such tasks as modifying, inserting, and deleting data

See www.informix.com for more information.

Ingres II

Ingres II for Linux remains available only as a beta release. However, that beta version, available for free download, includes features such as:

✦ IngPerl, that is, Ingres database access by means of Perl scripts

✦ Interfaces for C

✦ Internet-publishing capabilities

✦ Row-level locking

✦ Support for BLOBs

✦ Variable page size

✦ An embedded SQL precompiler

✦ C2 security auditing

✦ Query and reporting tools

✦ Terminal monitors

However, the beta of Ingres II does not include other features offered by the commercial version of Ingres II, such as enhanced security, that is, tools for establishing security beyond C2, networking utilities, object management tools, or Ingres' Visual DBA tool. Finally, this beta has several known bugs that are as yet unresolved, the most significant of which are:

✦ Syscheck, the Ingres II system-requirement checking utility, that tries to determine whether the machine on which Ingres II is running has sufficient resources, always reports such resources to be available, whether or not they are in fact available

✦ Ingres II cannot run under Red Hat Linux 5.0 or earlier, because of incompatibility problems between the glibc library versions offered by the OS and required by the DBMS.

Tip   Ingres II for Linux will be of interest, for the foreseeable future at least, primarily to application developers who have facility with GNU development tools and Apache Web Server.

See `www.cai.com/products/ingres.htm` for more information.

InterBase

Despite Inprise Corporation's January 2000 announcement that it planned to release InterBase 6, which it calls the Open Source Database, in true open source form, the release has not yet occurred. As a result, we must still consider InterBase a commercial or quasi-commercial product. InterBase 6 remained in beta release as late as May 2000, and was released as a production tool for Linux and Solaris only in July 2000.

Regardless of such sticky points, however, InterBase 6 deserves consideration as a Linux enterprise DBMS, because it offers features such as:

✦ An integrated graphical user interface called IBConsole, through which an InterBase server can be created and managed, or with which you can create and administer databases on that server

✦ A Replicator that facilitates replication and synchronization between multiple InterBase databases that have similar structure

✦ A services API that enables you to write applications that monitor and control InterBase servers and databases; possible tasks can include:

- Backup and restore
- Shutdown and restart
- Garbage collection
- Scanning for invalid data structures

- Creating, modifying, and removing user entries in the security database

- Managing software activation certificates

✦ Improved warnings regarding status of current transactions and of SQL statements; including in the latter:

  - API calls that will be replaced in future versions of the product

  - Pending database shutdown

  - SQL expressions that produce different results in different InterBase versions

  - SQL statements with no effect

✦ New data types SQL DATE, TIME, and TIMESTAMP

✦ Support for Delphi 5

✦ Support for large exact numerics — that is, NUMERIC and DECIMAL data types with 10 to 18 digits of precision — stored as 64-bit integers

✦ Support for read-only databases

✦ Support for SQL-delimited identifiers; that is, for database object names that are delimited by double quotes

✦ The capability to back up and restore a database to or from multiple files

✦ The concept of dialects that enable users to move ahead with new features, such as delimited identifiers, large exact numerics, and the SQL DATE, TIME, and TIMESTAMP data types, that are incompatible with older versions of InterBase

✦ The new `EXTRACT()` function to retrieve date and time information

See `www.interbase.com` for more information.

KE Texpress

Texpress, a DBMS suite that follows the object-oriented model, offers an engine that includes such features as:

✦ A nested relational database model that, in turn, supports complex object definitions without the need to decompile those objects in order to modify them

✦ A network communication layer that supports direct communications — that is, remote function calls — as well as both TCP/IP-based network communications and serial line connections

✦ An object-based method of indexing that results in unusually quick retrievals

✦ Fully integrated support for European languages through 8-bit extended ASCII, and for Asian languages through multibyte character sets such as Chinese and Japanese

✦ No practical limits on database size other than those imposed by the hardware and operating system platforms

✦ Security features that include user accounts and object privilege levels

✦ Support for indexing individual words, numbers, and field values, as well as complex data types such as dates and times

✦ Support for object-oriented database structures that offer such features as text attributes, multivalued fields, nested tables, and object references

See www.kesoftware.com for more information.

Oracle8*i* for Linux

Oracle Corporation considers Linux one of the fastest growing operating system platforms in the enterprise environment, and cites the OS's millions of users as the reason for its commitment to Oracle on Linux. Consequently, the Oracle8 and Oracle8*i* DBMSs, as well as Oracle DBMS suite components such as Application Server, Jserver, and WebDB, have been made available to the Linux community.

This commitment to Linux as an enterprise platform is reflected by the features that are new in Oracle8*i*, including:

✦ Improved security, including setting time limits to or keeping histories of passwords, and the capability to disable a user account if the attempt to connect to it involves three invalid password entries

✦ Improvements to parallel processing through commands such as CREATE INDEX and CREATE TABLE AS SELECT

✦ Support for object-oriented and relational DBMS features such as nested tables, VARRAYs, and object views

✦ Tables and indices that can extend across partitions

✦ Tables of up to 1,000 fields

✦ Tables stored as indices, that is, in B

✦ Treive format

✦ The new data types BLOB, BFILE, and CLOB, as well as a larger maximum size for the traditional data type VARCHAR, whose value can now reach 4,000 bytes

✦ Updatable views that can employ triggers based on the INSTEAD OF clause

See www.oracle.com for more information.

Sybase Adaptive Server Enterprise

Adaptive Server Enterprise (ASE) for Linux, Sybase Corporation's entry in the commercial Linux DBMS derby, offers many attractive features, including:

✦ A Logical Memory Manager (LMM) with which you can assign database objects directly to named caches

✦ A Logical Process Manager (LPM) that allows you to assign CPU resources to individual applications

✦ A tool known as a Resource Governor, whose job it is to prevent runaway queries and their system resource gluttony

✦ An asynchronous prefetch operation that helps maximize query speed

✦ The capability to carry out index modification under nontransactional locks, so as to expedite such modifications

✦ Clustered indices that help ensure fast retrieval and updating

✦ Database engine internal parallelism, including parallel query execution and parallel sorts

✦ Fully multithreaded architecture

✦ Precluding the storing of duplicate values for keys in both disk and memory

✦ Storing all statistics data in catalog tables that can be accessed directly by users to whom those statistics might be useful

✦ Support for block I/O as a means of improving performance by reducing actual, physical I/O

✦ Support for table partitioning in order to provide parallel processing

✦ Support for up to 31 fields in an index

✦ Task prioritization to attempt to ensure optimum response times

✦ Task prioritizing that can provide more system resources to high-priority transactions

✦ Three types of locking models: page locking on the data page; row-level locking in data pages; and transaction-duration locks on both data and index pages

See www.sybase.com for more information.

Unify DataServer

Release 7 of Unify DataServer for Linux adds features such as the following to those that one would expect from a basic relational DBMS:

✦ An industry-standard ODBC interface

✦ Backup verification

✦ Enhanced ANSI SQL standard compliance

✦ Enhanced stored procedures and triggers

✦ Support for backup files larger than 2GB

✦ Support for B-tree and hash indices greater than 2GB

Web site: www.unify.com

Open source products

As you might imagine, many DBMSs available for Linux are themselves open source software. This section discusses suites that are representative of the available open source software.

A DBMS belongs in the open source category if it makes the source code for the suite available at no additional cost.

Strengths of open source products

The greatest strength of open source database management systems is their price. All of the DBMSs discussed here can hold their own in any comparison with similarly structured commercial products. All can be freely downloaded. All offer complete source code at no additional cost, thereby providing the opportunity to customize the suites. When compared to the licensing and other costs of suites such as those from Oracle or Sybase, open source Linux DBMSs present the same advantages as do all open source products: functionality and reliability at little to no cost.

Weaknesses of open source products

No open source DBMS that we reviewed is anything less than a fully functional, versatile suite. However, few of these products offer more than minimal management tools. In addition, to be used to greatest benefit, each open source DBMS we examined requires significant, if not intimate, knowledge of C and Linux. If your environment requires quick, easy loading, configuration, and management of a DBMS, or such features as remote DBMS management capabilities, open source Linux databases may not be for you.

Sample open source products

This section summarizes five open source Linux DBMSs.

CodeBase for Linux

CodeBase 6, an *x*Base -compatible database engine for C or C++ programmers, has these significant features:

✦ Enables the query of millions of records in a second

✦ Can perform bulk appends, edits, and deletes

✦ Exposes its low-level API to provide the ability to customize applications

✦ Permits the creation of individual tables with a maximum size of 8.6 million terabytes; that is, 9,223,372,036,854,775,808 bytes

✦ Places no limit on the number of tables per database

✦ Provides full multiuser record locking

✦ Supports multithreaded standalone or client-server applications

✦ Supports the *x*Base file standard, thereby providing compatibility with FoxPro, dBASE and Clipper data files

See www.sequiter.com/products for more information.

db.linux

Centura's db.linux stands alone among all the DBMSs we reviewed as a suite that enables developers to build applications for e-business and information appliances. Yes, you can now have your database on your hand-held computer. Centura's most significant characteristics in accomplishing that feat are:

✦ A C API that includes a library of more than 150 functions, and that is compatible with any ANSI C-compliant compiler, such as GNU C

✦ A data definition language (DDL) that is largely based on the C programming language

✦ A thread-safe, reentrant code architecture that provides support for multithreaded applications and numerous multiple simultaneous user sessions

✦ Enables up to 16,777,215 records to be stored as a single file; that is, as a table or record type, in db.linux parlance

✦ Autorecovery from transaction logs

✦ Compound keys

✦ Limits the number of fields in a record only by the maximum record size

✦ Optional support for read, write, and exclusive locks

✦ Permits records of up to 32K in size

✦ Provides for up to 256 record types per database, for an allowable maximum of 4,294,967,040 records per database

✦ Requires only about 200K of RAM, or about 40K if data access is read-only

✦ Support for B-Tree indices, pointer-based navigation, and efficient caching

✦ Support for features of both the relational and network database models

✦ Timestamp support

✦ Transaction logging

See www.centurasoft.com/dblinux for more information.

MiniSQL/mSQL

MiniSQL 3.0, the most recent incarnation of the mSQL open source DBMS which became available on February 15, 2001, retains and satisfies its progenitor's design goal: to provide high-speed access to small data sets. Mini SQL goes well beyond mSQL, however, in the capability to accommodate high-end applications that involve as many as 1 million records.

MiniSQL was programmed to accomplish this latter goal through better handling of complex queries and large data sets. Specifically, MiniSQL was designed with these criteria in mind: to comply more fully with the ANSI SQL-92 specification, to provide better performance for simple operations, and to provide rapid access to large databases and complex operations. MiniSQL seeks to fulfill these criteria with:

✦ W3-mSQL 2.0, a second-generation Web interface package that provides a complete scripting language and full access to the mSQL API within an HTML tag

✦ Enhanced indexing that includes, for example, the capability to define multiple indices for every table, and the capability to include as many as ten fields in any such index

✦ Enhancements to authentication of users connecting across the Internet, including configuration, management of user groups, definition of secure areas, and creation of authorized users through a graphical interface accessed by means of a Web browser

✦ Storing indices in a series of B-tree structures that are mapped into the virtual memory address space of the mSQL server process, thereby helping to ensure extremely fast retrieval of key data

✦ Support for a variable-length character data type, which permits an unrestricted amount of data to be inserted into a field by using an overflow buffer scheme to hold data beyond the specified size of the field

✦ The introduction of *candidate rows abstraction* to expedite query processing; candidate rows abstraction enables a module performing a query request to also request matching rows as well as the physically next row from tables that have been identified as candidates that might fulfill selection criteria specified in the query; think of this technique as an analog to the prediction and predication used by CPUs to "guess" which data will be required next and to retrieve that data in anticipation of its being needed

See www.hughes.com.au/ for more information.

Tip It's anticipated that upcoming releases of MiniSQL will support more data types, such as DATE/TIME and CURRENCY, which have been defined in the most recent SQL standards, as well as data types such as BLOB, which are most often found in large commercial DBMSs.

MySQL

MySQL's most important design goals were ease of use, robustness, and speed. The MySQL Web site offers benchmark test results that demonstrate that this compact, deceptively simple DBMS can handle very large databases at least an order of magnitude faster than can many commercial database management systems. Furthermore, since 1996, MySQL has been developed and tested in an environment that presents 500 tables with more than 7 million rows, about 100GB of overall data, more than 10,000 tables, and more than 40 databases.

More than any of its open source or commercial peers, MySQL requires a comfortable familiarity with the Linux command-line environment and with manipulating C source code. But if you have these skills, you may need look no further for a DBMS than this Goliath in David's clothing of a database.

See www.tcx.se/ for more information.

PostgreSQL

PostgreSQL, which operates under a University of California at Berkeley-style rather than a GPL license, is nonetheless, as one reviewer has termed it, "about as open as open source gets."

Tip A Berkeley-style license allows anyone to use source code in any way, as long as that use is accompanied by an appropriate copyright notice. The GPL license goes further in attempting to ensure the right always to have access to GPL source code, by requiring that once software has been licensed as GPL, any subsequent distributed versions must also be GPL.

Among the suite's most attractive characteristics are:

✦ A GUI-based administrative tool

✦ A permissions syntax that resembles Linux file access permissions

✦ A reasonable degree of compliance to the SQL-92 standard

✦ An impressive set of data types for fields, including all standard SQL data types; a handful of integer sizes; several floating-point and fixed-decimal-point types; both fixed- and variable-length strings; more esoteric data types such as Boolean, time interval, and autonumber; multidimensional array types; two-dimensional geometric-shape types that can represent polygons, circles, and the like; and, in an admirable thoroughness, even data types specifically intended for IP addresses and Classless Interdomain Routing or CIDR blocks

Tip   CIDR attempts simultaneously to represent multiple IP addresses. Rather than advertise a separate route for each destination in a group, a router that uses CIDR can use what's called a supernet address to advertise a single aggregate route that represents all intended destinations. This technique therefore reduces the size of routing tables, the internal address books of routers, which store network and internetwork routes.

✦ Its availability in the big three of Linux distribution formats: Red Hat's RPM, Debian, and .tgz

✦ Its being bundled with several popular Linux distributions, including Red Hat's

✦ Its parsimonious use of system resources; for example, using only about 1.1MB RAM for the server daemon, in comparison to the approximately 950KB needed by a common Linux shell such as bash

✦ SQL functions and algebraic operators that handle PostgreSQL's more esoteric data types, such as the time interval data type

✦ Support for more sophisticated query constructs such as subselects

✦ Support for transaction commit and rollback

✦ Support, albeit support that results in rather slow processing, for BLOBs

✦ The combination of operating system platforms with which it can work, including, on the server side, Linux, FreeBSD, and most major UNIX variants, and, on the client side, all these as well as Windows 95, 98, and NT

✦ The relative simplicity of its installation

See `www.postgresql.org` for more information.

Recommendations

If this were a multimedia publication, we would insert a drum roll at this point. Taking into account all the evaluative premises we've discussed in this chapter, we've arrived at a single recommendation for Outstanding DBMS in both the commercial and open source categories.

Commercial product   Our recommendation for a commercial Linux DBMS is Oracle8*i*. We chose this product because it is among the most fully featured DBMSs in either the commercial or the open source categories, and, as importantly, because of Oracle Corporation's commitment to Linux. That commitment must surely help guarantee the continued high quality of this product.

Open source product   Our recommendation for an open source Linux DBMS is PostgreSQL. This suite's intriguing set of data types; capability to incorporate clients from the Microsoft side of the fence; commendably miserly use of system resources; GUI-based administrative tool pg_access, which is remarkable among open source database management systems; and its handy distribution formats and bundling options, make it eminently suited to a variety of environments as well as easily obtained, installed, and configured.

Summary

When choosing a DBMS, investigate for each candidate, in as much detail as possible and practical, these factors.

✦ Adherence to SQL standards

✦ Administrative tools

✦ Architecture

✦ Handling of stored procedures, trigger, and so forth

✦ Hardware and operating system platforms and any constraints these might impose

✦ Performance-related issues such as multi-threading capabilities and connection management techniques

✦ Relational model

✦ Security techniques

✦   ✦   ✦

Installation and Configuration

Installation

This chapter discusses installing Linux-based databases, highlighting the most significant tasks involved with loading each of MySQL, Oracle8*i*, and PostgreSQL.

MySQL

As the MySQL Project states on its Web site, an important goal of the open source database is ease of use. That ease is reflected in the installation process for the server. Table 8-1 describes MySQL's component programs, and Table 8-2 outlines MySQL's environment variables.

Tip   Individual MySQL programs each take different options. However, each also offers the option help, with which you can obtain a full list of a particular command's other options.

Table 8-1
MySQL Programs

Program	Purpose
make_binary_release	Creates a binary release of a compiled MySQL, which could then, for instance, be sent by ftp to other locations
msql2mysql	Shell script that converts mSQL programs to MySQL
myisamchk	Utility to check, display information on, optimize, or repair MySQL tables
mysql_install_db	Script that creates MySQL grant tables and the default privileges those hold
mysqlaccess	Script that checks access privileges, matching specific host/user/database combinations
mysqladmin	Administrative utility that handles such tasks as creating or dropping databases
mysqld	MySQL server daemon
mysqldump	Utility that dumps a MySQL database to a file, either as SQL statements or as tab-separated text
mysqlimport	Utility that imports text into databases by means of the MySQL statement LOAD DATA INFILE
mysqlshow	Utility that displays information about databases, tables, fields, and even indices
replace	Utility used by msql2mysql
safe_mysqld	Script that starts the mysqld daemon with safety features such as the capability to restart the server or to log runtime information

Table 8-2
MySQL Environment Variables

Variable	Contains
MYSQL_DEBUG	Options available for debugging MySQL
MYSQL_HISTFILE	Name of file which stores client command history; default: $HOME/mysql_history
MYSQL_PWD	Default MySQL password
MYSQL_TCP_PORT	Default TCP/IP port number
MYSQL_UNIX_PORT	Default Linux socket used for connections to local host
TMPDIR	Directory where MySQL's temporary tables and files reside

Sockets and Ports

Sockets and ports, as they occur in this and other data communications contexts, refer not to physical devices but to virtual devices.

A socket is a mechanism, which originated in Berkeley UNIX, for creating a virtual connection between processes. In effect, sockets act as conduits between standard I/O and networked communications facilities. Sockets are established and maintained by the operating system library function called, logically enough, `socket()`, which creates a communications end point (either origin or destination as the case may be), and returns an integer value which acts as a file descriptor for that point or socket. Each socket receives a socket address; that address consists of a TCP/IP port number and the local host's network address.

A TCP/IP port is also a channel or channel end point. TCP/IP running on Ethernet media, as it almost invariably does, uses port numbers to distinguish between different channels on the same network interface on the same computer. As a result, every data communications or communications-related application has a unique port number associated with it. The file `/etc/services` defines these port numbers. Some TCP/IP application-level protocols, such as telnet or HTTP, have specific default ports, but can also be configured to use other ports.

Requirements and decisions

Installing MySQL begins by reviewing its requirements and then deciding which of its forms to load.

Operating system

While it has been written to and tested under Solaris from Sun Microsystems and Red Hat Linux, MySQL should compile and run under any operating system that includes functioning POSIX threads and a C++ compiler.

Tip

Threads, also sometimes called lightweight processes, are similar to Linux processes, but are not processes themselves. To understand POSIX threads, one must understand the idea of thread synchronization. When a thread creates a new thread, a situation arises that is unlike that produced when a process creates a new process. In the latter case, the new processes, or child processes, begin execution at the same point as their creators or parents, but take different paths through system resources. However, it is possible for parent and child threads to execute concurrently, introducing the further possibility of their interfering with one another. Therefore, the POSIX thread standard was developed to provide two-thread synchronization techniques, in an effort to preclude a child thread's interfering with either its parent or its siblings.

Tip If all you need to do is to compile MySQL client code, you can forgo the POSIX threads and just ensure the C++ compiler.

MySQL has been reported to compile successfully on these operating system/thread package combinations:

✦ AIX 4.*x* with native threads

✦ BSDI 2.*x* with the included MIT-pthreads package

✦ BSDI 3.0, 3.1, and 4.*x* with native threads

✦ FreeBSD 2.*x* with the included MIT-pthreads package

✦ FreeBSD 3.*x* with native threads

✦ Linux 2.0+ with LinuxThreads 0.7.1 or glibc 2.0.7

✦ NetBSD 1.3/1.4 Intel and NetBSD 1.3 Alpha

✦ OpenBSD 2.5 or higher with native threads

MySQL version

As is the case with open source software in general, MySQL evolves constantly. Consequently, the first choice you have to make before you install the DBMS is that between a development release or a stable release.

The MySQL Project recommends that if you are installing MySQL for the first time, or if you are porting it to a system for which there is no binary distribution, that you use the most recent development release. The Project bases this recommendation primarily on the fact that this release provides crash-simulation and benchmark tests. Otherwise, the Project recommends the latest binary available for your hardware/operating system combination.

Source (to compile) or binary (executable to run)

Your second decision regarding which MySQL format to load is closely related to the first. Clearly, if a binary distribution exists for your platform, you'll most likely choose to install that, even if you're implementing MySQL for the first time, because such installs are less complicated than those of a source distribution. However, if for any reason you need to look at or modify MySQL's C and C++ source code, then you'll have to work with a source distribution. As the MySQL Project puts it, source code is always the ultimate manual. To aid you in making this binary versus source decision, we review the MySQL naming scheme here.

MySQL release numbers consist of three integers and a suffix. Thus, you might encounter a release name like

```
mysql-4.37.21-beta
```

Here's how to interpret such a release name.

✦ The first number, or 4 in our example, describes file format. All MySQL releases whose names begin with the same number can be counted on to have the same format. Furthermore, this number alerts the database administrator to the fact that, should he or she carry out an upgrade of MySQL, existing tables must be converted to the new format.

✦ The second number, or 37 in our example, represents the release level. Ordinarily, MySQL offers two such levels for every release: a stable branch and a development branch. Again, citing our example and assuming that release level 37 represents the stable branch, we can assume that the development branch for this same release is numbered 38.

✦ The third number, or 21 in our example, defines a version number within a release level, and is incremented by 1 for each new distribution.

✦ The suffix, `beta` in our example, expresses the stability of the overall release. Possible suffixes are:

- **alpha:** The release contains large amounts of new code that hasn't been fully tested, but that holds no known bugs.

- **beta:** All new code in the release has been tested. To graduate from alpha to beta, a MySQL release must go without any reported fatal bugs for at least one month.

- **gamma:** A MySQL gamma release equates to what most commercial software houses call, simply, a release. That is, a gamma release has existed and been played with and in general banged on for quite some time, without demonstrating any significant problems.

- no suffix: The release has been run for an appreciable time at different sites under different operating system/hardware combinations, with no bugs or only platform-specific bugs reported. It's this last state that the MySQL Project calls a stable release.

Tip   The MySQL Project does more than run new releases of the DBMS through a set of standard tests and benchmarks. It also modifies those tests over time to check for all previously reported bugs. Further, whether to provide bug fixes or new features, updates to the suite appear frequently. Luckily, you need not download a new release in order to determine whether it's right for your environment. The News section of the MySQL Web site describes the contents of each new release in detail.

Anatomy of a MySQL binary distribution

Should you choose to implement a MySQL binary distribution, you'll create, as a part of that process, the directories outlined in Table 8-3.

Table 8-3
Directories Created for MySQL Binaries

Directory	Contains
bin	mysqld, the MySQL server, as well as MySQL client applications
data	Log files, databases
include	Include (header) files
lib	Libraries that MySQL requires
scripts	mysql_install_db, the shell script that controls installing MySQL
share/mysql	Error message files
sql-bench	Benchmark test suite

Anatomy of a MySQL source distribution

Working with a source distribution of MySQL means:

1. Preparing the environment
2. Compiling the source
3. Installing the compiled suite

Linux daemons

Like so many significant Linux applications that rely on the client/server model, MySQL implements its server as a daemon. A daemon (pronounced like the word demon) is simply a Linux process that runs continuously in the background, and whose only reason for being is to handle periodic service requests of a particular type. A daemon can also forward such requests to other processes if needed. Important Linux daemons include:

✦ crond, the daemon that manages jobs scheduled by means of the operating system feature called cron

✦ ftpd, the ftp application server

✦ httpd, a Linux system's Web server (most frequently the open source product Apache)

✦ inetd, the TCP/IP daemon

✦ initd, which initializes the operating system

✦ telnetd, the telnet application server

By default, that installation places files in a number of subdirectories in the path /usr/local, as outlined in Table 8-4.

Table 8-4
Directories Created for a MySQL Source Installation

Directory	Contains
bin	Applications and scripts for MySQL clients
include/mysql	Include; that is, C or C++ header files
info	MySQL documentation in Info format
lib/mysql	C or C++ libraries that MySQL draws upon
libexec	mysqld, the MySQL daemon or server
share/mysql	Error message files
sql-bench	Benchmark and crash-simulation test suites
var	Database and log files

Tip *Info format* refers to the GNU project's preferred online reference, which is in texinfo format, a widely available format for Linux online documentation. Similar to the online manual or *man*, info nonetheless goes beyond that classic UNIX/Linux help feature by offering capabilities for cross-referencing, indices, and easy integration with emacs, a text editor much beloved by Linux mavens.

Requirements for installing MySQL

To install either type of MySQL distribution, you need:

✦ The GNU file uncompression utility gunzip to expand the compressed files that make up the distribution

✦ Preferably the GNU version of the OS command tar

✦ Experience in working with these Linux commands:

```
cd
gunzip
ln
make
tar
```

Tip GNU, a recursive abbreviation that stands for the phrase *GNU's Not UNIX*, is the nickname, as it were, of the Free Software Foundation's project to provide a freely distributable replacement for UNIX. Sound like Linux? Well, yes and no. GNU software and Linux interact often, but are not identical. For instance, most Linux distributions offer emacs, the GNU editor that first saw the light of day in the mid-1980s, in addition to the more traditional UNIX universe text editor vi. Equally as popular as emacs is the GNU C compiler, gcc, a widely used tool in Linux software development.

✦ A Linux kernel of version 2.0 or higher

✦ A minimum of 16MB RAM

✦ A minimum of 80MB free disk space

Header Files

C and C++ header files, also often called include files, demonstrate the modularity that helps to make these languages so powerful. Such files, whose names are of the format something.h,

✦ Contain code for such things as input and output

✦ Make that code available to programmers

✦ Are read by a preprocessor, a front-end to C compilation, which inserts the code header files contain into the code being compiled at the point at which the header file is named in the latter.

A classic example of a header file is stdio.h, which deals with the C library of input and output functions. A portion of stdio.h on one of our machines looks like this.

```
#ifndef _STDIO_INCLUDED
#define _STDIO_INCLUDED

#ifndef _SYS_STDSYMS_INCLUDED
#   include <sys/stdsyms.h>
#endif /* _SYS_STDSYMS_INCLUDED */

#include <sys/types.h>

#ifdef __cplusplus
extern "C" {
#endif

#ifdef _INCLUDE__STDC__

#   define _NFILE       60
#   define BUFSIZ       1024
#   define _DBUFSIZ     8192

/* buffer size for multi-character output to unbuffered files */
#   define _SBFSIZ      8
```

Preparation

The MySQL Project prefers that downloads take place from one of its many mirror sites, rather than from its home base. Check `www.mysql.org` for a complete listing of these mirrors; there are dozens around the world.

Installing

This section details installing both binary and source MySQL distributions.

Installing a binary distribution

This example of installing a MySQL binary distribution is straight from the DBMS's documentation. Table 8-5 elaborates on the example, which assumes:

✦ Bourne shell prompts

✦ That you've logged in as or su'ed to the superuser account, thereby ensuring that you have the write permissions needed to carry out the installation, which involves creating directories and writing files to them

```
# cd /usr/local
# gunzip < mysql-VERSION-OS.tar.gz | tar xvf -
# ln -s mysql-VERSION-OS mysql
# cd mysql
# scripts/mysql_install_db
# bin/safe_mysqld &
```

Static

MySQL binary distributions use a form of linking compiled modules known as static. Statically linked executables:

✦ Are less finicky than dynamically linked code about version questions in the context of OS libraries

✦ Are anywhere from slightly to significantly bigger than dynamically linked code

✦ Can in some cases be slightly faster than dynamically linked code

What distinguishes static from dynamic linking? Both refer to pointers, with a dynamic link being a pointer, called at runtime, that helps the executable find its way back to where it started in a series of nested procedures. Static linking does much the same job, but its pointers are defined at compilation.

What does this imply about MySQL? Because user-defined functions can't interact with statically linked programs, C or C++ programmers thinking of writing code to customize MySQL need to be aware that if they do so, they'll have to recompile the suite with dynamic linking, especially if MySQL must interact with Perl, Perl 5.004_03 or higher.

Table 8-5
Commands Used to Install MySQL Binary Distributions

Command or Command Fragment	Indicates
cd /usr/local	Change to the path /usr/local, the preferred root of the MySQL file subsystem.
gunzip	Run the GNU file uncompress utility.
<	Take input for gunzip not from standard input but rather from the file to the right of this symbol, the input-redirection indicator.
mysql-VERSION-OS.tar.gz	The complete name of the MySQL distribution you're about to install, which indicates: In the VERSION parameter, the release name of MySQL
	In the OS parameter, the operating system for which the distribution was compiled With the suffix .tar, that the file is an archive in a format readable only by the operating system command tar
	With the suffix .gz, that the tar file has itself been compressed with the GNU utility gzip
|	That the commands to either side of the symbol, which is called the pipe symbol, interact with no further intervention needed, with the command to the left of the pipe automatically handing its output to the command on the right of the pipe. In our example, this means that the unzipped MySQL distribution immediately is handed off to the command tar.
tar xvf –	Which, with the indicated qualifiers x, v, and f, knows that: It should extract filesIt should operate in verbose mode, that is, report on every file it processes
	It takes its input from operating system standard input, which, in this case, means the other side of the pipe with gunzip
ln –s mysql-VERSION-OS mysql	Use the operating system command ln to create a symbolic link, in effect an alias, for the unzipped, unarchived binary distribution, under the new directory name mysql.

Command or Command Fragment	Indicates
cd mysql	Change to the mysql directory ln made available.
scripts/mysql_install_db	Run the installation script housed in the subdirectory scripts.
bin/safe_mysqld &	Test the success of the installation by starting a single-user version of the MySQL server daemon in background.

In list form, these commands translate into the following installation steps:

1. Pick the directory in which you want to unpack the distribution, and move into it. Our example unpacks the distribution under the path /usr/local.

2. Download a distribution file, which exists on the MySQL mirrors as a compressed tar file with a name of the form mysql-VERSION-OS.tar.gz, where VERSION represents a release number such as 3.45.67, and OS holds the operating system flavor that the distribution supports, such as pc-Linux-gnu-i586 for GNU-based Linux OSs running on Pentiums or higher.

3. Unpack the distribution and create the root of the MySQL file subsystem:

```
# gunzip < mysql-VERSION-OS.tar.gz | tar xvf -
# ln -s mysql-VERSION-OS mysql
```

4. Change to the MySQL path.

```
# cd mysql
```

In this path, you see several files and subdirectories. The most important subdirectories are:

- bin, which houses both the MySQL server daemon and MySQL client software

- scripts, which contains the installation shell script mysql_install_db that is used to set up permissions for access to the server and its files.

5. Create the MySQL grant tables (necessary only if you haven't installed MySQL before):

```
# scripts/mysql_install_db
```

Tip

If you would like MySQL to start automatically when you boot your machine, you can copy support-files/mysql.server to the location where your system has its startup files. Depending on your Linux flavor, you may first, though, need to create a password for the mysqladmin account with a command like this:

```
mysqladmin -u root password []
```

substituting the new password for this account for []. In addition, you'll have to add a line like the following to your startup file (usually the file `/etc/rc.d/rc.local`):

```
mysql.server start
```

6. Ensure that the environment variable `PATH` includes the path to your MySQL installation. Check the contents of `PATH` with the command `env` (for both the Bourne and C shells).

Should the resulting display not include the MySQL path, add that to your environment with commands such as these.

- For the Bourne shell: `PATH=$PATH:/usr/local/mysql export PATH`
- For the C shell: `setenv PATH=$PATH:/usr/local/mysql`

Caution

Should you want to use mysqlaccess with a MySQL distribution installed to a non-standard location, you must explicitly include the path to this utility in your environment, just as you did with the overall MySQL path. But the way in which you make MySQL aware of the location of this utility differs. You must edit the shell script `mysqlaccess`; look, at or about line 18, for the text `MYSQL = '/usr/local/bin/mysql'; #` path to mysql executable; and change the path to contain your MySQL implementation's real location.

7. Initialize and test your distribution in safe mode.

```
# bin/safe_mysqld &
```

Installing a source distribution

Installing a MySQL source distribution closely resembles loading the DBMS's binary.

1. Decide whether you want to unpack the distribution. Ensure that you have both read and write privileges for the directory you choose.

2. Move to the chosen directory with the command `cd`.

3. Get a MySQL source distribution file from one of the suite's Internet sites. These files exist as compressed tar archives, and have names such as mysql-VERSION.tar.gz, where VERSION is a version number.

Tip

Note the difference between the naming conventions for MySQL binary distributions and its source distributions. The former contains an operating system indicator; the latter does not.

4. Unpack the distribution into the directory to which you just changed, with a command such as this:

```
# gunzip < mysql-VERSION.tar.gz | tar xvf -
```

Such a command creates a directory named mysql-VERSION as it unpacks the distribution file.

5. Change into the top-level directory of the unpacked distribution, with a command like this.

```
# cd mysql-VERSION
```

6. Configure and compile in sequence, with commands such as these:

```
# ./configure --prefix=/usr/local/mysql
# make
```

Why configure first and only then compile? With MySQL, as with much open source software and Linux itself, configuration involves defining many runtime parameters, which the compilation then includes in the executable.

As a result, an administrator should always confirm the success of a compilation or "build" before proceeding with other tasks.

Installing by means of Red Hat Package Managers

As noted earlier in this chapter, much of MySQL development takes place under Red Hat Linux. Consequently, and because of the nature of that OS, MySQL may also be installed with a Red Hat-specific tool called RPM or the Red Hat Package Manager.

Currently, MySQL RPMs are being built under Red Hat 5.2 but are compatible with other versions of Linux that support RPM and use glibc.

Include the following RPMs in your installation.

MySQL-VERSION.i386.rpm	The MySQL server
MySQL-client-VERSION.i386.rpm	The standard MySQL client
MySQL-bench-VERSION.i386.rpm	Benchmark and other tests. If you load this, you must also load the Perl and msql-mysql-modules RPMs.
MySQL-devel-VERSION.i386.rpm	Libraries and include files needed to compile MySQL client features such as Perl modules
MySQL-VERSION.src.rpm	Source code for all the above packages

Use a command such as this from the Red Hat prompt to carry out a standard minimal installation; that is, to install only the MySQL server daemon and clients:

```
# rpm -i MySQL-VERSION.i386.rpm MySQL-client-VERSION.i386.rpm
```

The RPM-based installation of MySQL writes primarily to the path /var/lib/mysql. This type of load also creates entries in the system startup file /etc/rc.d/ that will start the MySQL server daemon automatically when the installation completes, and after that every time the OS boots.

PostgreSQL

This discussion of installing PostgreSQL assumes that you download, configure, and compile source code.

Caution

As you'll find if you choose to download PostgreSQL from any of the many mirrors on which it resides, the suite is not public domain software. Rather, the University of California holds copyright to it, but permits its use under the licensing terms set out in the file `ftp://ftp.postgresql.org/pub/README`.

Requirements

To create a PostgreSQL executable, you must have the following:

✦ Experience in working with the operating system commands `gunzip`, `tar`, and `mv`

✦ GNU make

Caution

PostgreSQL will not compile with any other version of make. Luckily, many Linux OSs offer GNU make as the default compilation-control tool. But on some Intel UNIX systems, GNU make exists as the command `gmake`.

Tip

You can determine which flavor of make your system includes with the command `gmake -version`. Should the resulting display not indicate GNU make, that tool can be downloaded from the Web site of the GNU Organization at `ftp://ftp.gnu.org`. Or, as another alternative, simply try plain old "make"; there are few Linux systems on which that standard tool won't do the job.

✦ An operating system from the list of supported platforms at `www.postgresql.org/docs/admin/ports.htm`

✦ An absolute minimum of 8MB RAM, with as much more as you can manage, up to 96MB

✦ Free disk space as follows:

- 30MB for source during compilation

- 5MB for the installation directory

- 1MB for an empty template database

- 20MB if you want to run regression tests

Tip

To find out where you stand on free disk space, use the command `df -k`. This syntax reports disk space allocated per file system in KB.

Obtaining PostgreSQL

PostgreSQL can be obtained from

✦ `www.pgsql.com/pg_goodies/`, as either a single CD which contains the most current stable release, or as a subscription entitling you to three CDs

✦ `ftp://ftp.postgresql.org/pub/CURRENT/`

As of late February 2000, the downloadable PostgreSQL source distribution took up more than 7.5MB. In an effort to facilitate downloading, the PostgreSQL group now splits distributions into several smallish files. Don't be confused by the similarity in these files' names. You need to download them all.

The names of these files follow these conventions:

✦ docs.tar.gz: PostgreSQL documentation

✦ support.tar.gz: PostgreSQL source for interfaces; libraries

✦ test.tar.gz: PostgreSQL test suite

✦ base.tar.gz: remaining PostgreSQL source

Preparation

Get ready to install PostgreSQL by setting a number of environment variables.

✦ Ensure that the PATH on your system includes the location of the PostgreSQL bin directory, typically /usr/local/pgsql/bin. To see PATH's current value, simply type `env`.

✦ Whatever shell you use, be it bash, C, or some other, should you need to modify the contents of PATH, do so like this:

- For the Bourne shell: `PATH=$PATH:/usr/local/pgsql/bin export PATH`

- For the C shell: `setenv PATH=$PATH:/usr/local/pgsql/bin`

✦ Or, to ensure that PATH can find PostgreSQL from system startup rather than just for the current session, put the following line in your startup file, which can be either .bash_profile for shell-specific characteristics, or /etc/profile for a global profile that affects all user sessions on a system:

`PATH=$PATH:/usr/local/pgsql/bin`

✦ Ensure that PostgreSQL man pages and HTML documentation can be accessed with the following environment setting:

`MANPATH=$MANPATH:/usr/local/pgsql/man`

> **Tip**
> Since not all Linux systems use the environment variable MANPATH, you may have to check the contents of the file /etc/man.conf to determine if this path to online documentation has been properly defined. Current versions of "man" read /etc/man.conf to set MANPATH.

Table 8-6 offers operating system-specific preparation tasks.

<table>
<tr><td colspan="3" align="center">Table 8-6
OS-Specific Factors in Preparing to Install PostgreSQL</td></tr>
<tr><td>**OS**</td><td>**File**</td><td>**Task**</td></tr>
<tr><td>NetBSD</td><td>rc.local</td><td>**Edit to contain the line** `su postgres -c "/usr/local/pgsql/bin/postmaster -S -D /usr/local/pgsql/data"`</td></tr>
<tr><td>SPARC Solaris 2.5.1</td><td>rc2.d</td><td>**Edit to contain the line** `su postgres -c "/usr/local/pgsql/bin/postmaster -S -D /usr/local/pgsql/data"`</td></tr>
<tr><td>FreeBSD 2.2</td><td>/usr/local/etc/
rc.d/pgsql.sh</td><td>**1. Edit to contain the lines:**
`bin`
`!/bin/sh [ -x /usr/local/pgsql/bin/`
`postmaster ]`
`&&`
`{su -l pgsql -c 'exec`
`/usr/local/pgsql/bin/postmaster -`
`D/usr/local/pgsql/data -S -o -F >`
`/usr/local/pgsql/errlog'`
`& echo -n ' pgsql'}`
placing line breaks as shown here.

2. Set file permissions so that the root user has all forms of access, but members of the superuser group, and all other users, can only read and execute, with this command.
`chmod 755`
`/usr/local/etc/rc.d/pgsql.sh`

3. Assign file ownership to the superuser with this command.
`chown root`
`/usr/local/etc/rc.d/pgsql.sh`</td></tr>
<tr><td>Red Hat Linux</td><td>/etc/rc.d/init.d/
postgres.init</td><td>**1. Add a file of this name, using the example supplied under** `contrib/Linux/` **in the PostgreSQL source.**

2. Make a symbolic link to this file from the `file /etc/rc.d/rc5.d/`
`S98postgres.init`.</td></tr>
</table>

Installation

To install PostgreSQL from scratch, or to upgrade from an earlier release of the DBMS, take these steps.

1. Create the PostgreSQL superuser account, under which the server runs. This account should have only "average" file access rights, and in many installations is called simply postgres. Building and compiling the PostgreSQL server need not be done under this account, but can be if you wish. In any case, when this account needs to come into the installation process, you'll be prompted to log in as this database (as opposed to operating system) superuser.

Tip Running PostgreSQL as root, bin, or any other OS user account with special access rights is a security risk; don't do it. The postmaster will refuse to start as root.

2. Configure the PostgreSQL source code, specifying, if need be, such parameters as the path in which building and installation should take place, as well as particular features to install or operating characteristics to be taken on by the executable. Do all this simply by changing into the src subdirectory of the source code file system, and typing:

   ```
   ./configure
   ```

   followed by any options you might need. (Most first-time installations require few, if any, options.). For a complete list of options, type:

   ```
   ./configure --help
   ```

   Some of the more commonly used PostgreSQL configuration options are:

   - enable-multibyte: Allows the use of multibyte character encoding; primarily for Asian languages
   - prefix=BASEDIR: Defines a nondefault home directory in which to install PostgreSQL (default is /usr/local/pgsql)
   - with-odbc: Builds a set of Open Database Connectivity (ODBC) drivers
   - with-perl: Builds a Perl interface PostgreSQL extensions to Perl
   - with-tcl: Builds interface libraries for and programs that use Tcl/Tk

Tip Perl, as it always does, must be installed into a specific point in the overall file system, ordinarily /usr/lib/perl. Therefore, to carry out this PostgreSQL installation task, you need root file access permissions. As an alternative, the PostgreSQL project recommends installing the DBMS without Perl at first, and building and integrating that language interface with PostgreSQL at a later time.

3. Compile PostgreSQL with the simple command:

   ```
   gmake
   ```

Tip Once again, "plain old make" is an alternative that few Linux systems will reject.

The compilation process can take anywhere from 10 to 60 minutes. When it completes successfully, you see this display:

```
All of PostgreSQL is successfully made. Ready to install.
```

4. If you're upgrading an existing PostgreSQL implementation, back up your existing database by using this syntax:

```
pg_dumpall > db.out
```

Caution

Make sure that users do not modify or otherwise update data in any PostgreSQL database as you're backing up that database. The PostgreSQL group recommends that, in order to avoid this potentially very destructive combination of circum-stances, you bring down the postmaster (the communications channel between a PostgreSQL server and its clients); edit the permissions in the file /usr/local/pgsql/data/pg_hba.conf to allow only you on; and bring the postmaster back up.

5. Again only if you're upgrading an existing PostgreSQL implementation, kill any running, nonupgraded database server. Type:

```
ps ax | grep postmaster
```

or

```
ps -e | grep postmaster
```

to obtain the process ID number or numbers of running postmasters. Your output from ps should look something like this.

```
263   ?   SW    0:00 (postmaster)
```

Then enter another command, similar to that shown here, but with the generic parameter pid replaced by the actual process ID you learned from ps and grep:

```
kill pid
```

or, in keeping with the sample output above

```
kill 263
```

6. Install the PostgreSQL executable files and libraries. Type:

```
gmake install
```

Caution

Do this step as the user who will own the installed executables. This need not be the database superuser, however.

7. If necessary, tell your system how to find the newly installed PostgreSQL shared libraries. Use a command that follows one of these examples:

For the Bourne shell:

```
LD_LIBRARY_PATH=/usr/local/pgsql/lib
export LD_LIBRARY_PATH
```

For the C shell:

```
setenv LD_LIBRARY_PATH /usr/local/pgsql/lib
```

8. Create the database installation, that is, working template PostgreSQL data files. To do so:

First, log in to PostgreSQL under the database (not operating system) superuser account.

Enter the series of command shown in this example:

```
mkdir /usr/local/pgsql/data
chown postgres /usr/local/pgsql/data
su - postgres
/usr/local/pgsql/bin/initdb -D /usr/local/pgsql/data
```

Caution

If you ran `gmake` (or `make`) as the OS root user, you'll have to be or take on the identity of that user while doing the `mkdir` and `chown` just mentioned.

The –D option to the database initialization utility defines where PostgreSQL will store data. Any path can be supplied for this parameter; you need not limit its value to a location under the installation directory. But the value defined for –D must be a path to which the database superuser has write permission.

9. Test your installation; start up the database server in the foreground with a command like this.

```
/usr/local/pgsql/bin/postmaster -D /usr/local/pgsql/data
```

10. If you are upgrading from an existing installation, don't forget to dump your data back in.

```
/usr/local/pgsql/bin/psql -d template1 -f db.out
```

Oracle8*i*

This section investigates working with the Oracle8*i* Installer.

Requirements and preparation

Oracle8*i* requires:

✦ At least 400MB free disk space

✦ At least 32MB RAM

✦ Linux 2.0.34 or higher

✦ GNU C Library version 2.0.7 or higher

Preparing to load Oracle8*i* involves the tasks described below.

LINUX environment setup

Before you can install Oracle8i, you must ensure that the operating system offers the DBMS the environment the latter needs. Those needs occupy two categories:

✦ Kernel parameters

✦ Environment characteristics

Kernel parameters

Oracle8i requires a number of specific values for operating system kernel parameters. Should your kernel not offer these, you must recompile the OS to make them available. Table 8-7 describes these parameters and the values Oracle8i expects of them.

Table 8-7			
Linux Kernel Parameters Required by Oracle8i			
Characteristic	*Parameter*	*Value Required for Oracle8i*	*Description*
Identifiers for shared memory	SHMMNI	100	Number of shared memory identifiers
Minimum size of shared memory segments	SHMMIN	1	Minimum size, in bytes, of a single, shared memory segment
Semaphore identifiers	SEMMNI	70	Number of semaphore set identifiers in the OS
Semaphores	SEMMNS	200	Number of semaphores available in the OS
Semaphores per set	SEMMSL		Maximum number of semaphores per semaphore set; should equal the maximum number of Oracle processes anticipated
Shared memory	SHMMAX	4294967295	Specifies the maximum allowable amount of shared memory; has no impact on other kernel resources
Shared memory and processes	SHMSEG	10	Maximum number of shared memory segments that a process can call upon

Tip Semaphores are protected variables used to restrict access to shared resources such as disk storage in multiprocessing environments. Semaphores track free units of the resource, track whether or not a resource is available, and make a resource available again after a process has finished using it, thereby ensuring that only one process can use a semaphore at any given time.

Environment characteristics

Whether through environment variables or simply by means of commands, you must ensure that Oracle8*i*'s environment has the characteristics outlined in Table 8-8.

Table 8-8
Oracle8*i* Environment Characteristics

Feature	Significance	Value
DISPLAY	Environment variable which defines machine name and monitor type for a user station	Set to values appropriate to stations from which users will connect to the Oracle8*i* server
LD_LIBRARY_PATH	Location of Oracle8*i* shared libraries	Set to $ORACLE_HOME/lib
LINUX user account for installation	Oracle8*i* requires an operating system user account dedicated solely to installing and upgrading the DBMS	Must be a member of the group set up for the OSDBA
LINUX user groups	Oracle8*i* must have an operating system user group for each of the database administrative roles it entails; thus, a group must exist for the Oracle System Database Administrator (OSDBA) role and for the Oracle System Operator (OSOPER) role	dba and oper respectively
Local `bin` directory	Directory that houses shared Oracle8*i* software	Default: /usr/local/bin
Mount Points	Must exist at the same level of the directory structure. One for Oracle8*i* itself; three more for template database	At least four
ORA_NLS33	Required for databases which use character sets other than US7ASCII	Set to $ORACLE_HOME/ocommon/ nls/admin/data.

Continued

Table 8-8 *(continued)*

Feature	Significance	Value
ORACLE_HOME	Root of the Oracle8*i* file subsystem	Set to the directory where Oracle8*i* will be installed
ORACLE_SID	Instance name of the Oracle Server; each Oracle instance running on a given machine must have a unique SID	Set to a string of four characters or fewer
ORACLE_TERM	Definition of terminal characteristics for Oracle8*i* similar to those found in the operating system terminal definitions file /etc/termcap	Set as appropriate to your environment
oratab file	Information about Oracle instances or running copies of the Oracle8*i* server	Defaults to value supplied during installation
PATH	Search path for Oracle8*i*	Must include $ORACLE_HOME/bin, /bin, /usr/bin, and /usr/local/bin
Permissions assigned to files at their creation	Set with the OS command umask	Set to 022
SRCHOME	Home directory for Oracle8*i* source	Leave undefined until done running the Installer; if SRCHOME is set, the Installer searches the location SRCHOME specifies for software to install
TMPDIR	Installation temporary directory	Must be set to a directory with at least 20MB available space, to which the oracle account has write permission; default: /usr/tmp

Tasks to perform as the user root

Log in as the operating system root user and carry out the following tasks to set up your environment for the Oracle8*i* Server:

1. Configure the kernel for Oracle8*i*. In particular, set up LINUX Interprocess Communication (IPC) parameters to accommodate Oracle8*i*. You can determine a system's current shared memory and semaphore values, and their ID numbers and owners, with this command:

```
ipcs
```

2. Set the kernel parameters as outlined in Table 8-7.

3. Create mount points. The Oracle8*i* Server requires at least four. Further, all mount points defined for Oracle8*i* must follow a pattern like that shown here:

```
/oracledb2
```

This example assumes that Oracle8*i* software was installed under a path called /oracledb1. In other words, mount point names must:

- Share the same root as the Oracle installation directories to which they correspond

- Have as their final character a digit that has incremented by one any digit associated with the Oracle pathname

4. Create LINUX user groups for database administrators and operators. The Installer assigns Oracle DBA and OPERATOR privileges to LINUX groups during Installation. Oracle knows these groups as OSDBA and OSOPER respectively. Members of these groups have DBA or OPERATOR privileges on the Oracle system by virtue of their membership in the corresponding operating system user groups. Therefore, the groups to which you assign these roles must exist before you begin installing.

Tip

You can name the database administrative group anything you like. But if you call it something other than dba, the Installer will relink the executable that it's creating. If you plan to designate a separate group for the OSOPER group, create that group also. The Installer offers the group that you designate as OSDBA as the default choice for the OSOPER group. If you accept the default, there is effectively no OPERATOR role, because its privileges are simply a subset of the DBA privileges already assigned to the group.

5. Create a LINUX user account whose sole purpose is to own the Oracle8*i* software that you're installing. You *must* run the Installer under this account, which should have these characteristics.

- Login Name: Can be anything; referred to in Oracle8*i* documentation as the oracle account

- Default Group ID (GID) for the OSDBA group

- Home Directory: Should share a file subsystem with all other Oracle8*i* user home directories; need not, however, exist under the ORACLE_HOME directory

- Shell: Default shell for working with Oracle8*i*; can be any of /bin/sh, /bin/csh, or /bin/ksh, but defaults to /bin/sh, the Bourne shell

> **Tip**   Sites with multiple Oracle servers may install them under the same oracle user account, or under separate user accounts. If multiple installations share an oracle account, the DBAs for each installation have access to the other installations.

6. Create a local bin directory in order to provide a common environment for Oracle8*i* users. This directory should be outside the ORACLE_HOME path. Typically, /usr/local/bin takes this role for Oracle8*i* implementations. Wherever you place an Oracle user common environment, make sure that every Oracle user has this directory in his or her PATH and has execute permission on the directory.

7. Create the oratab file. While the oracle user account owns this file, the file lives in a directory that requires root user privilege if it is to be manipulated. Run the shell script orainst/oratab.sh provided on the Oracle8*i* distribution CD-ROM to create the oratab file and set its permissions.

Tasks to perform as the user oracle

Log in to the oracle account and perform these tasks:

1. Set the permissions to be assigned automatically to newly created files. Use this syntax:

```
umask 022
```

This command ensures that members of the oracle user's OS user group, and all other users on the system, have read and execute, but not write permission, to all files the Installer creates.

> **Tip**   Use the `umask` command to check current settings for file-creation masks.

2. Set environment variables in the .profile or .login file of the oracle user account before firing up the Installer.

   For the Bourne shell, use syntax that follows this pattern:

```
VARIABLE NAME=value
export VARIABLE NAME
```

   For the C shell, use syntax that follows this pattern:

```
setenv VARIABLE NAME value
```

   You must set all environment values specified in Table 8-8.

3. Update the environment. After setting environment variables, update the environment in the current shell session, following one of these patterns:

   For the Bourne or Korn shell:

```
$ ./.profile
```

   For the C shell:

```
$ source .login
```

Installing

Take these steps to install Oracle8*i*. But note first that:

✦ The volume management software originated with Sun Microsystems' Solaris, but is now available in many Linux flavors. Oracle's Product Installation CD, in RockRidge format, will be mounted automatically to the mount point /cdrom/oracle as soon as you place it in its drive, thereby allowing you to begin the Oracle8*i* Installer immediately.

✦ If your OS doesn't offer this volume management software, you must mount the CD-ROM manually. Therefore, you must be logged in as, or use the command su to take on the identity of, the operating system superuser.

The steps we list here assume that you must mount the Oracle8*i* CD manually, and begin with that task.

1. Become the root user. If one does not already exist, create a directory that will act as a mount point for the CD-ROM. Use commands similar to these, substituting a path name for the CD mount point that's appropriate to your environment.

   ```
   $ su root
   # mkdir directory_for_CD_mount
   ```

2. Mount the CD-ROM drive to the appropriate mount point directory; then drop the shell you started as the superuser. Again, use commands similar to those here, but supply parameters appropriate to your environment.

   ```
   # mount /dev/OS_designation_of_cd_drive
   directory_for_CD_mount
   # exit
   ```

3. Use the command su to temporarily become the oracle user.

4. Change directories to the mount point that you just created, with a command such as this:

   ```
   cd directory_for_CD_mount
   ```

5. Launch the Installer in character mode with this command:

   ```
   ./orainst
   ```

Tip   Basic navigation techniques needed to work in character mode with the Oracle8*i* Installer include the Tab key, which moves you forward through screens; arrow keys, which move you between fields; and the spacebar, which selects fields.

Initial installer prompts

An Oracle8*i* Installer session consists of a series of prompts, each displayed in its own window. These prompts appear regardless of the task you are performing or the products that you are installing. This section describes these initial Oracle8*i* Installer prompts.

Installation Type/README Files	The Installer offers a choice between a custom or default installation. If you choose default, the Installer displays the settings it will use and asks you to confirm them.
Installation Activity Choice	Allows you to specify why you want to use the Installer; includes: Install, Upgrade, or De-Install Software; Create/Upgrade Database Objects; Perform Administrative Tasks

Installation options

The Installer offers two types of installation activities:

✦ Install New Product, which can be done with or without creating database objects

✦ Add/Upgrade Software

An Oracle8*i* server can be loaded with either of these options.

Installation location

If you've set the environment variable ORACLE_BASE before starting the Installer, that tool prompts you to confirm the values of ORACLE_BASE and ORACLE_HOME. If ORACLE_BASE is not set, the Installer prompts you for a software mount point, as well as for the ORACLE_HOME directory.

Installation log files

To record its work, the Oracle8*i* Installer creates four log files. These files track:

✦ Actions taken that affect the operating system

✦ Actions that rely on the Installer makefile

✦ Actions that use SQL statements

✦ General Installer actions

By default these logs reside under $ORACLE_HOME/orainst.

Tip   Installation logs from an immediately previous invocation of the Installer are not overwritten; instead, they are saved under names in the pattern of somelog.old.

Install source

At this Installer prompt, you must specify whether you are installing from CD-ROM or from a staging area, that is, another area of a system or a network file structure. If you specify a staging area, you'll be prompted again, this time to say whether the staging area is temporary or permanent. Be sure to enter the correct response to this latter prompt, because the Oracle8*i* Installer deletes temporary staging areas as it finishes with them during installation.

National language support

At this prompt, you can specify a language other than U.S. English in which screen messages from Oracle8i should be displayed.

Tip
Any definition of display language that you make with the National Language Support prompt can be overridden. Users or client applications can also set this parameter.

Location of the root.sh script

The Installer creates a shell script called root.sh in $ORACLE_HOME/orainst. The operating system superuser must run this script immediately upon installation's completing.

Tip
Should root.sh already exist, the Installer will prompt you to learn whether it should append new commands to the existing script or to create a new script. Oracle Corporation recommends doing the latter in most cases and suggests appending to an existing script only on those occasions when specific Oracle8i characteristics must be preserved.

Software asset manager

In the prompt labeled Software Asset Manager, select the Oracle8i products to install from the Available Products window; then just click Install.

Tip
In addition to letting you pick products, the Software Asset Manager tracks space available in the directory, that is, in ORACLE_HOME, where those products will be placed. Also, this window provides detail on some product categories. So, for instance, if you want to know what specific products fall under the banner Protocol Adapters, then you need only double-click the category name in graphical mode, or select it and press Enter in character mode.

Caution
Among the items listed in the Available Products window is the Oracle8i Installer itself. Be sure to select this product if you anticipate installing documentation that applies to all Oracle8i products regardless of their OS platform, or if you simply want to have the Installer more easily accessible on your hard drive.

OSDBA group

In this window, you choose the operating system user group that will receive Oracle DBA privileges. This setting defaults to the group to which the oracle user belongs.

OSOPER group

Here, you can give Oracle8i OPERATOR privileges to a distinct Linux user group, or allow them to default to the group you specified as OSDBA.

Instance name

Use this prompt to set the Oracle8*i* SID to:

✦ A string no more than four characters long

✦ In single-instance installations, a string whose value is the same as that of the DB_NAME initialization parameter

Database creation prompts

If you use the Oracle8*i* Installer to create a database, you'll see another series of prompts, as discussed in this section.

Storage type

In this window, you can specify whether databases will be stored on raw devices or within a file system.

Tip   Under Linux, a raw device is one that has not been formatted to hold files. Frequently, raw devices house such resources as swap space. Oracle8*i* somewhat breaks this OS convention by allowing you to place databases on a raw device.

Number of mount points

At this prompt, you must say whether you want the Installer to adhere to the recommendation from Oracle Corporation to spread database objects across at least three mount points. While the Installer won't object if you define only a single mount point, or mount points on a single drive, Oracle Corporation strongly recommends that you spread your database across at least three devices. If you take this option, both the template database that you're creating and the log files spread out over the mount points you specify.

Mount point locators

Oracle Corporation recommends that the database mount points you define to this prompt differ from software mount points you provided to the initial Installer prompts.

Character set

Here, you define the character set in which the database will function and store data. As you might imagine, the default is US7ASCII.

Caution   If you specify a database character set other than the default, you must also have set the environment variable ORA_NLS33 during preinstallation. If you haven't, an error may occur. Further, be aware that once it's defined through the Installer, a storage character set cannot be changed without recreating the database. A loophole does exist, though. Oracle8*i* allows clients to use a character set other than the storage set.

National character set

In this prompt, you can define a second character set for use with specially declared fields. Otherwise, this parameter defaults to the database storage character set.

SYS and SYSTEM user passwords

Oracle Corporation strongly recommends that you use this prompt to change both these built-in Oracle8*i* accounts' passwords.

The dba and operator group passwords

To connect to an Oracle8*i* database as either a system/database administrator (SYS-DBA) or system/database operator (SYSOPER), a user must:

✦ Be a member of the operating system group or groups to which you assigned DBA or OPERATOR roles

✦ Enter the passwords you supply to this Installer prompt

Installing documentation

Oracle8*i* documentation, in both operating system-specific and in generic, product-related forms, arrives with the Oracle8*i* distribution set either:

✦ For OS-specific documentation, on the Oracle8*i* CD-ROM

✦ For product documentation, on a separate CD-ROM

Both categories ordinarily are loaded during an Installer session. Product documentation, however, must be installed during its own, separate Installer session.

Tip   An Oracle8*i* distribution CD offers both operating system-specific and product documentation in HTML and PDF formats.

To install operating system-specific documentation, simply choose LINUX Documentation from the Available Products window during an overall Installer session. To install product documentation, however, you must take these steps:

1. Verify that the Installer exists on your file system. If it does not exist on your file system, load it.

2. Start the Installer from the hard drive rather than from the CD.

3. At the Installation Activity prompt, choose Install, Upgrade, or De-Install Software.

4. At the Installation Options prompt, choose Install Documentation Only.

5. Indicate HTML, PDF, or both formats for the documentation you're loading.

6. From the Software Asset Manager, select Oracle8*i* Product Documentation.

7. Click Install, or, in character mode, select Install and press Enter.

Summary

When installing a Linux DBMS, pay particular attention to these factors:

✦ Disk and memory requirements

✦ Whether to install a pre-compiled executable or to obtain and configure, by compiling, specific to your environment

✦ Kernel characteristics needed by your chosen DBMS

✦ Environmental characteristics your selected DBMS must have

✦ Installation and configuration tasks which must be carried out as the user root

✦   ✦   ✦

Configuration

Preparing to set up a database under Linux starts where such preparation would under any OS — with the analysis and structuring of the data the DBMS must manipulate.

Effective Schema Design

A database that relies on an inefficient schema is of as little use as a building whose blueprints fail to depict all rooms or entrances. This section discusses techniques that can contribute to effective schema, or data dictionary, design.

Data modeling

Modeling data as the first or one of the first steps in database design seeks to ensure accurate abstractions of data. Such modeling attempts to understand the inherent nature of the data to be processed, apart from any situational or operational qualifiers that might affect the data. So, data modeling uses techniques such as end-user and operator interviews in an attempt to identify and completely correctly define required data, while at the same time precluding duplicate data items.

You can choose from a number of data modeling techniques. I review the most significant of these techniques here.

Object modeling

An object model is a collection of facts or groups of facts (that is, words and phrases) that describe the environment in which the database must function. These facts, in turn, serve as the basis for identifying individual data items.

Logical modeling

Upon completion of an object model, that model is often converted into tables that define the logical relationships between areas of data that the database must reflect. This process of modeling the database logic takes place in spite of the fact that the model may not yet contain all the data items that the DBMS will ultimately house.

Physical modeling

Physical modeling is the keystone of schema design, because it involves creating the initial schema based on the relationships and entities defined during object and logical modeling.

During physical modeling, it is even more critical than at earlier design stages to analyze data definitions as they are being supplied, to help preclude

✦ Erroneous data

✦ Field data types that are not consistent across tables

✦ Fields that may not be available to all applications

✦ Missing data

✦ Redundant data

Table 9-1 summarizes data modeling as presented.

Table 9-1
Data Modeling

Stage of Modeling	Task	Helps Ensure...
Defining the overall database structure	Create an object model	that all entities with which the DBMS must deal will be identified
	Create a logical model	that all relationships between entities, which will influence the manner in which the database can manipulate data, will be identified
	Use the logical model as the basis for creating a physical model	physical model, by incorporating not only data and relationship definitions but also constraints such as the manner in which operator skill levels or equipment might affect the accuracy of data input, helps ensure a complete and correct schema
Implementing the database structure, that is, the schema	Use the physical model as a template	

Accurate modeling not only helps to ensure an accurate database, but it also helps provide for

✦ Less correction and redesign down the road

✦ The independence of the database from hardware or operating system platforms

✦ The capability of the database to work seamlessly with applications other than the DBMS that must manipulate it

Further, such a step-by-step approach helps to ensure input from and feedback to end-users, in turn thereby assuring them a shorter, smoother learning curve.

Normalization

It's not necessary to be scrupulous in applying relationship theory to data modeling. On the other hand, understanding and employing normalization techniques can benefit the schema that results from the data-modeling process.

Table 9-2 summarizes what I consider the most important normal forms to keep in mind when modeling your data.

Table 9-2 Normalization	
This Normal Form	**Involves This Type of Relationship**
Second Normal Form (two functional dependencies; that is, a single field from a record in either of two tables will reflect the relationship)	A one-to-one relationship, in which, for example, Table A and Table B have the same data item serving as the key, and from which, therefore, only one record in Table B will match any given record from Table A
First Normal form (one functional dependency)	A one-to-many or many-to-one relationship, in which, for example, a number of records in Table B might match any given record from Table A
No Normal Form (that is, no functional dependencies)	A database without relationships

Joins

Another way of looking at relationships between tables is to examine them as joins. A join can be defined like this: If you have two tables, one called Table Y and the other Table Z, which have a field in common, a new table will result when a join is carried out on these two. For example, consider the table designs depicted in Figure 9-1.

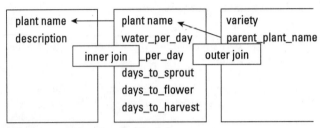

Figure 9-1: An example of a join

This design presents the possibility for both an inner join and an outer join, which reflects, respectively, a one-to-one and a one-to-many relationship. Based on those relationships and the sample data shown in Figure 9-2, new tables would result from each of these joins' being carried out, as shown in Figure 9-3.

dahlia	dahlia	cactus
colorful, good for	1 ounce	dahlia
cutting	6 hours	
	45	
	65	

Figure 9-2: Sample data for joins

| cactus dahlia | 65 days to flower | colorful, good for cutting |

Figure 9-3: The result of joins

Data definition language

While syntax differs from DBMS to DBMS, all Linux databases possess a critical feature: the data definition language DDL. The appropriate DDL must be used in building a schema. In general, the DDL enables you to identify to the database application:

  ✦ Tables

  ✦ Fields within tables

✦ The nature of the data to be contained within those fields (that is, field length and data type)

✦ The field that will serve as the key for each table

✦ Any additional indexing to be applied to tables

✦ Relationships between tables

Data manipulation languages and schema design

It may seem to be putting the cart before the horse to discuss data manipulation in a section on schema design. However, the nature of the data manipulation language that your Linux DBMS makes available can influence how you structure your data in the first place.

Any data manipulation language (DML) should provide the capability to:

✦ Insert data

✦ Delete data

✦ Update or modify data

✦ Retrieve or display data

Table 9-3 summarizes the most significant ways in which the nature of a DML can impact your schema design.

Table 9-3
Data Manipulation Languages' Effects on Schemas

This DML Function	Often Perceived by Users As	And Therefore
Insert	Uncomplicated	Need have little effect on schema design
Remove	Uncomplicated	Need have little effect on schema design
Update/Modify	Uncomplicated	Need have little effect on schema design
Retrieve/Query	Unclear, because users may not know what to look for, or they may state their requests for data subjectively or in a disorganized way	Requires schemas to be set up to cause the relationships between data items to be immediately apparent to the user

Because of the difficulty many users have in clearly formulating requests for data, data manipulation languages, or *query languages,* have been designed to take up this slack. However, a well-designed schema can help do the same, by highlighting the relationships between data items.

Database query languages and schema design

Literature on relational databases frequently discusses three major types of database query language:

✦ Procedure-oriented

✦ Tuple- or record-oriented

✦ Domain- or table-oriented

A procedural query language, such as IBM's SQL, uses keywords such as SELECT, FROM, and WHERE to create joins. A tuple- or table-oriented query language uses variables, conditions, and formulas; one such language, QUEL, the query language of INGRES, might begin to construct a query in this way.

```
range of p is PLANT_DESCRIPTION range of v is VARIETIES
retrieve
(p.plant_name, p..plant_description, v.variety,
v.parent_plant_name)
```

Finally, a domain-oriented query language uses its variables and expressions to bridge domains rather than to bridge relationships.

One can see that the differences in how these categories of query languages operate might present constraints to schema design similar to these:

✦ The procedural type of query language, being perhaps the most straightforward type of query language, focuses easily on relationships and thereby aids in cross-table schema building.

✦ The record-oriented type of query language, being as much table- as relationship-oriented, affects schemas by focusing designers' attention on the structure of individual tables.

Capacity Planning

You cannot effectively plan a database or create its schema without considering the demand for system resources that the database will make. This section discusses three categories of such demands: storage, memory, and processing.

Storage

In addition to defining your database's schema for complete and accurate storage, manipulation, and retrieval of data, you must also:

✦ Consider the demand for storage such administrative aspects of the DBMS as log files will make. How big might such files become? How often does the DBMS allow you to trim them?

✦ Consider the demand for storage such user-related features of the DBMS as individual and group profiles will make.

✦ Carefully note the record size of each table as you define your schema, in order to have a sound basis for extrapolating the amount of disk storage data files will take up as actual data is entered into them.

Ask yourself questions such as:

✦ How many tables do I really need to accurately represent my data and the relationships among the data?

✦ How closely and to what degree of detail must I monitor activity in the database?

✦ At about what rate do I anticipate the volume of data stored will grow?

The answers to these questions will influence maintenance of your database, the performance required of your database, and how I/O hardware must be configured to serve your database efficiently. For instance, if you anticipate seven tables in a database that must be monitored only once a month, and whose volume of data stored is expected to grow only at the rate of about ten percent annually, there's little need to fine-tune either DBMS or the I/O or data communications upon which it relies. The DBMS's initial settings should suffice.

RAID

Using a form of RAID (redundant array of inexpensive disks), to spread data across a number of physical drives can improve database throughput, which is notorious for its lackadaisical nature, by relying on parallel data access across multiple files. From the point of view of the database administrator, only one logical drive exists; thus, striping as we've just described it or other RAID techniques need introduce no complications to managing a database, even though, physically, data may be spread across several drives.

Figure 9-4 depicts an example of RAID as it can be implemented in Linux DBMSs.

```
raiddev/dev/md0
        raid-level          0
        nr-raid-disks       2
        nr-spare-disks      0
        chunk-size          4
        persistent-superblock       1
        device              /dev/hda 5
        raid-disk           0
        device              /dev/hda 6
        raid-disk           1
```

Figure 9-4: Striping and mirroring under MySQL

As MySQL interprets it, striping involves placing the first block of data to be stored in your database on the first disk in your RAID array, then writing the second block to the second such disk, and so on. Under such a scheme, if the size of a typical write operation is less than or precisely equal to the defined stripe size, your database will perform much better, with throughput significantly reduced.

Tip

Striping's effectiveness has a very direct relationship to the particular flavor and release of Linux that underlies it. The folks at MySQL as well as other Linux database gurus recommend benchmarking your DBMS with different stripe sizes in order to determine which size provides optimal database performance. Note also that the exact way in which striping parameters are defined, as well as the number of disks involved, can give performance differences several orders of magnitude apart from one another. Finally, the decision to use random or sequential access in defining striping can also affect performance improvements.

Another technique recommended by several Linux DBMS vendors seeks to further ensure data reliability and DBMS up-time by combining RAID levels 0 and 1, that is, by using both striping and mirroring in implementing your database. Should you take this path, remember that you will need twice the number of drives you otherwise would have employed. For example, to mirror a database that had been implemented on a four-drive array, you would need an additional four drives, or a total of eight. Of course, in such an implementation, cost can quickly become a determining factor.

A third storage option that is available for most Linux DBMSs combines striping all data with the striping and mirroring data that is the most difficult to recover or reconstruct (for example, schemas and logs).

Tip

Whatever form of RAID or mirroring you settle on, remember that the larger the array and volume of data handled, the more likely you will be to require additional software tools to manage that volume efficiently. Also remember that the more your database is weighted toward write operations, that is, toward addition and modification rather than toward retrieval, having a high number of drives may impede database performance. The larger the number of writes, the more time the DBMS and OS require to update parity and other RAID management information

Defining Inodes

An inode can be defined as a data structure holding information about files in a UNIX or Linux file system. Every file on such systems has its own inode, which helps not only to identify the file within the operating system but also within the particular file system in which the file lives.

Every inode identifies:

✦ The physical device in which the inode resides

✦ Locking information for the file the inode documents

✦ Access mode for the file the inode documents

✦ Type of file the inode documents

✦ Number of links to the file the inode documents

✦ The user and group IDs of the file the inode documents

✦ The number of bytes in the file the inode documents

✦ Access and modification times for the file the inode documents

✦ The time the inode itself was last modified

✦ Addresses of the file's blocks on disk

That is, an inode does everything and more than one of its analogs, a record in a File Allocation Table, does. For those of you who are curious about very small details, a file's inode number can be found using the `-i` option to the command `ls`.

Perhaps the simplest, but certainly in the case of relatively small databases the most efficient, way of optimizing disk usage by your database is to mount the file system within which the database resides with the *noatime* option. This option directs the operating system to forego updating an inode's last access time, thereby avoiding at least a few some disk seeks, and resulting in better disk and DBMS performance.

Memory

Memory requirements for Linux DBMSs, while not exorbitant, are not trivial either. A minimum of 48MB is required for RAM. Swap space requires three times the amount of physical RAM.

Tip   In systems with more than 1GB RAM, the amount of swap space required can, as a rule, be reduced to 1.5 to 2 times the amount of RAM.

Also remember that some Linux DBMSs may have to be compiled and that such tasks, that is, large GNU C Compiler (*gcc*) compilations, heavily stress memory. Therefore, in designing your schema, in order to help preclude unnecessary demands on memory, make every effort to keep it as tight as it is correct.

> **Tip**   Another aspect of memory management that can plague a Linux DBMS involves shared memory. If you have not compiled shared memory support into your kernel, you need to recompile Linux to add this feature in order to avoid core dumps that might otherwise result when certain DBMS administrative utilities are run.

Examples of demands on memory: MySQL

Every connection to a MySQL database server uses several thread-specific memory spaces:

✦ A stack, whose default size is 64K

✦ A connection buffer

✦ A result buffer

Both the connection buffer and result buffer are dynamically allocated, and can grow to provide for the maximum number of packets permitted.

MySQL supports up to 4GB RAM, managing it through a 32-bit memory space. As a result, none of MySQL's operations involve memory mapping. Rather, every request doing a sequential scan over a table allocates a read buffer. Further, all joins are done in one pass, with most joins handled without the need for temporary tables. Any tables that might be required are by default memory-based, that is, heap tables.

Almost all of MySQL's parsing and calculating is done in local memory, with memory allocated only for unexpectedly large strings, and the relevant index and data files opened only once for each concurrently-running thread. For each such thread, a table structure, column structures for each column, and a buffer of size (3×n) is allocated, with *n* representing maximum row length.

Table handlers for all active tables reside in cache and execute as First In, First Out (*FIFO*) operations. Ordinarily, such a cache contains 64 entries.

Given these and other similar characteristics of MySQL, conciseness in schema design becomes even more imperative than usual, especially for servers whose hardware platforms offer less than generous memory.

Processors

To design your database for optimum performance and to configure it and its OS platform for the same, you must keep in mind, not only demands on memory, but also on processors.

As much as possible, configure your database server with an optimum number of concurrent users, that is, a number that will allow it to dovetail its handling of user requests without short-changing any individual user on processing power.

For CPU-intensive databases and their applications, use either thread-scheduling utilities provided by the DBMS, or operating system tools such as nice, to optimize use of the processor and achieve greater throughput.

Queries that must examine large numbers of rows, which are therefore CPU-intensive, can benefit from being run in parallel. If your DBMS supports multiple CPUs, enabling parallel query execution could benefit overall performance.

Note Examples of operations that can benefit from parallel execution include joins of large tables, substantial aggregations, and the sorting of large result sets.

Redundancy and backup

In database parlance, *redundancy* can refer either to the capability of a database server to run as many operations as possible in parallel, or to the immediate availability of one or more duplicate copies of the database which can be brought online immediately in order to minimize downtime. Backup, of course, simply refers to the capability to provide the latter form of redundancy.

If possible under your Linux implementation, consider using either multiple backup devices or permitting your database server to use parallel I/O to increase the speed of backup and restore operations. When each backup device can be written to or read from concurrently, especially in environments with very large databases, multiple backup devices can decrease the time required for backup and restore operations.

Initial Configuration

Successfully configuring an RDBMS under Linux requires a solid grasp of certain basic concepts and commands. I begin this section by reviewing those Linux features.

Linux concepts and commands

Those of you with a long familiarity with Linux can, if you like, proceed to the next section. Those of you new to the OS, however, can expedite your configuring a database under it by reviewing the concepts and commands discussed here.

Case sensitivity

Linux is case sensitive; the great majority of your typed conversations with Linux commands will be rendered in lowercase. So, for instance, you must distinguish between the filenames database.log and Database.log; be assured, Linux will do so.

Executable scripts

Under the Bourne shell, the default command-line interface for most flavors of Linux, a special syntax must be used to run user-written command files or shell scripts. That syntax is:

```
./script_name
```

For example, to run a script called db_cleanup from the directory where the script lives, you could type:

```
./db_cleanup
```

To run that same script from a directory other than its native one, you would type something similar to this.

```
/directory/where/the/script/lives/db_cleanup
```

Tip   To preclude voluminous typing such as that in the previous example, include the path or paths where database maintenance scripts are likely to be housed in your PATH environment variable.

Wildcard characters

In the Linux universe, as in the Microsoft, the characters ? and * act as *wildcards*; that is, they replace, respectively:

✦ A question mark (?) replaces a single occurrence of any character.

✦ An asterisk (*) replaces any number of occurrences of any character or characters.

Table 9-4 provides some examples of using wildcards under Linux.

Table 9-4 Linux and Wildcards	
Linux Interprets the Pattern	**As Meaning**
a*	any string, of any number of characters, whose first character is a lowercase a. The patterns a, aa, ab, abc, a1drgnkj73, and aA would all match this notation.

Linux Interprets the Pattern	As Meaning
a?	any string, of no more than two characters, whose first character is a lowercase a. The patterns a, aa, ab, a5, ak, and aA would all match this notation.
*b	any string, of any number of characters, whose last character is a lowercase b. The patterns b, ab, bb, dcb, a1drgnkj73b, and Bb would all match this notation.
?b	any string, of no more than two characters, whose last character is a lowercase b. The patterns ab, bb, 4b, and +b would all match this notation.
c*d	any string which begins with a lowercase c, contains any number of other characters after that, and ends in a lowercase d. The patterns c32[59umynljd, ca'p84od, and cd would all match this notation.
c?d	any string which begins with a lowercase c, contains any single occurrence of another character after that, and ends in a lowercase d. The patterns c2d, c0d, cyd, and cd would all match this notation.

Symbols

Linux gives special significance to the characters discussed in this section, and carries out specific actions when it encounters those characters.

Slash

By itself, or at the beginning of a pathname, the forward-slash character (/) indicates the root directory to Linux. Within a path, slashes separate directory, subdirectory, and file names.

Dollar sign

Like the forward slash, the dollar sign ($) has two meanings to Linux:

✦ It can be used as a command-line prompt for "ordinary" users, that is, users other than the superuser root.

✦ It can be used with environment variables, to tell the shell to deal, not with the variable name itself, but with the value stored under that name. For example, if the environment variable PATH, which defines the areas of the file system in which Linux will look for data or commands, contains the value /usr, then the value of $PATH is /usr.

Ampersand

The ampersand (&) tells Linux to place a job in background processing, freeing your station for other, foreground work while still plugging away on the background job, and tracking it, as it does all tasks, by means of a Process Identification Number (PID).

For instance, if you wanted to run a shell script called does_a_lot, which ordinarily takes about four minutes to complete, but didn't want to tie up your machine for that length of time, you could use this command.

```
./does_a_lot &
```

In response, Linux would issue a message like that shown in Figure 9-5, and then return control of your station to you.

Figure 9-5: Linux lets you know that it's accepted a job into background.

Pipe

Should you need to combine Linux commands in such a way as to automatically pass the output of one command to another, which will use that data as input, you need to use a pipe (|).

In the example below, we've piped the output of the ls -l command, which produces a long listing of files in the current directory, to the command grep, which searches for the pattern trek in any of the files in that listing, and produces output like that in Figure 9-6.

```
ls -l | grep 'vulcan*'
```

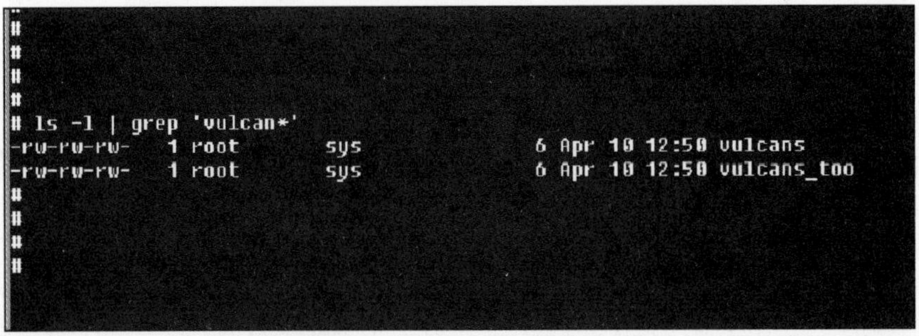

Figure 9-6: Piping from ls to grep to find files whose names contain the string vulcan.

Output redirection

If you need to send a Linux command's output somewhere other than to its default destination (almost always the monitor, known in Linux as *standard output*), you can do so with a single greater-than symbol (>).

For example, to store the output of the ls command in a file called list_of_databases, in the current directory, you could use this syntax:

```
ls *.db > list_of_databases
```

Caution   Note that, if the indicated output file already exists, such a command completely overwrites it.

Output redirection by appending

To store the output of the ls command in a file called list_of_databases, in the current directory, and at the same time avoid replacing earlier contents of that file, use this syntax:

```
ls *.db >>  list_of_databases
```

The double greater-than symbol (>>) causes Linux to append to, rather than replace, existing file contents.

Input redirection

Should you need to take a command's input from somewhere other than its default source, the less-than symbol (<) tells Linux to do so. For instance, the echo command ordinarily expects its input from the keyboard. But, if you want to display standardized text, you could place that text in a file, and redirect the file's contents to echo. Figure 9-7 illustrates this technique.

```
#
# cat 4input
To all database users:

The database server will come down in 10 minutes.
Please save your work and disconnect from this server.


#
# wall < 4input

Broadcast Message from root (ttyp1) Mon Apr 10 13:08:41...
To all database users:

The database server will come down in 10 minutes.
Please save your work and disconnect from this server.
```

Figure 9-7: Frequently used messages can be supplied to commands with input redirection.

Semicolon

If need be, or simply to speed up typing and execution, Linux commands can be strung together one after another, by separating them with a semicolon (;) like this.

```
clear; cd /; ls -l | grep '*db'
```

Colon

In the context of system and database administration, the colon (:) has two significant roles.

Colons separate fields in the Linux password file /etc/password. For example, in the following line, colons enable us to distinguish that the user in question has the login name jason, no password, and the home directory /home/httpd/logs, among other things.

```
jason::18:2::/home/mysql/jason:/sbin/sh
```

Colons separate fields in the values associated with the environment variable PATH, which in turn defines those areas of the file system that Linux will automatically examine for data or programs requested by a user. In the following PATH, those areas include the directories associated with the DBMS.

```
PATH=/usr/sbin:/usr/bin:/home/oracle8
```

Basic Linux tasks

To configure any DBMS under Linux, you must carry out a number of common operating system administrative tasks, as described in this section.

Logging in as the superuser or root

Root user privileges, that is, privileges usually available only to a Linux system administrator, allow you to carry out tasks denied to most users. These tasks include altering processing priorities, changing file and directory access and execution permissions, and creating user accounts.

Because the root login conveys such extensive powers, it is usually restricted to system administrators. Contact your system administrator for the required login name and password should you need to function, however temporarily, as root.

Altering processing priorities

Assume that you're in the midst of compiling, that is, configuring by means of a gcc compilation, a Linux DBMS. Assume further that this task is taking far longer than you had anticipated. You can speed up this or any other command by raising its processing priority, making it of more immediate importance to the OS and CPU.

To do this, you'd need to be logged in as root. If that's the case, you'd only need to do one more thing — issue the command nice with the following syntax.

```
nice -- 10 gcc my_database
```

This command would lower by 10 the nice number associated with the indicated command, thereby raising that command's processing priority. Linux sees the hierarchy of execution as having an inverse relationship to nice numbers, with lower numbers denoting higher priorities.

Changing file and directory access permissions

Linux organizes file access permissions into three groups of three permissions. It offers read, write, and execute permission for files and directories to the owner of the file or directory, members of the owner's user group, and everyone else on the system, also often called "world."

The letter x in a long listing of files indicates the capability to execute. The capability to modify the contents of a file or directory will always be indicated by the letter w in such a listing, while permission to read a file, which includes being able to see its name in listings, is denoted by an r in the output of ls. The first three columns of the output of ls -l apply to the owner of a file or directory, the center three columns to users who are members of the owner's user group, and the last three columns to all other users of a system. Table 9-5 summarizes how these permissions relate to one another and to the overall status of a file.

Table 9-5
Changing Linux File Permissions

This Syntax	*Allows You to*
chmod (+/– r or w or x)u filename	Add (+) or remove (–) any or all of read, write, or execute permission to a file for the user who is that file's owner.
chmod (+/– r or w or x)g filename	Add (+) or remove (–) any or all of read, write, or execute permission to a file for members of that file's owner's user group.
chmod (+/– r or w or x)w filename or chmod (+/- r or w or x)o filename	Add (+) or remove (–) any or all of read, write, or execute permission to a file for the user population at large, that is, for the world or others.
chmod 7xx or x7x or xx7 filename	Add all possible permissions to the indicated user. The octal digit 7 translates to binary as 111, which three digits can be read as "enable read, write, and execute permissions."
chmod 6xx or x6x or xx6 filename	Add read and write permissions to the indicated user. The octal digit 6 translates to binary as 110, which three digits can be read as "enable read and write, but not execute, permissions."

Continued

Table 9-5 *(continued)*	
This Syntax	*Allows You to*
chmod 5xx or x5x or xx5 filename	Add read and execute permissions to the indicated user. The octal digit 5 translates to binary as 101, which three digits can be read as "enable read, but not write, permission. Also enable execute permission."
chmod 4xx or x4x or xx4 filename	Enable only read permission for the indicated user, because the octal digit 4 translates to binary as 100.

Tip Pluses (+) and minuses (−) may be combined in a single command. For example, `chmod +w-xg myfile` would add write permission but remove execute permission to the file myfile for members of the owner's user group. Similarly, `chmod 700` would grant all available types of permissions to a file's owner, but deny those same permissions to members of the owner" user group, as well as to the user population at large.

Creating user and group accounts

You can use the Linux utility groupadd to restrict access to database administration functions to designated users. For example, Oracle8*i* recognizes the Linux user groups dba and oper, in the OS group file /etc/group, as the groups that were granted Oracle DBA, or database administrator, and Oracle OPER, or database operator, privileges. Use a command similar to the one below to create these groups if they're not already present on your system.

```
$ groupadd -g 101 dba
```

Oracle documentation refers to the database administrator and operator groups as OSDBA and OSOPER respectively.

Setting default file access permissions

The Linux command umask sets default access permissions on all newly created files on a system. In carrying out database administration, you're likely to use the value 022 most frequently, to give read and directory search, but not write permission, to specific users. To apply such permissions to any new files created under the login name db_user, enter the following in the .profile or .login file of that user account:

✦ For the Bourne or Korn shells, add `umask 022` to .profile

✦ For the C shell, add the same line to the file .login

Setting environment variables

Every Linux shell has what are called environment variables. Such variables hold values that define the characteristics of a user session. For example, Linux environment variables specify, among other things, the printer you use, your file permission settings, and the colors displayed on your monitor.

Environment variables for a Linux DBMS are usually set in the .profile or .login file of the login account or accounts which connect to the database server. The appropriate file is read automatically when you connect to that server, and its contents applied to your database session.

To set an environment variable in the Bourne shell, use the following syntax: variable_name=value; export variable_name. (Of course, the terms "variable_name" and "value" here are generic ones, and must be replaced by actual environment variable names or values.) For example, the command line below sets the home directory for Oracle to /usr/app/oracle/product/805 by means of the syntax *variable=*, and then makes the shell aware of that value by means of the command *export*.

```
ORACLE_HOME=/usr/app/oracle/product/805; export ORACLE_HOME
```

To set an environment variable in the C shell, a somewhat different syntax is needed. This syntax does not require the command export. For instance, the line below accomplishes, with only the setenv command, what the Bourne shell needed two commands to do.

```
setenv ORACLE_HOME /usr/app/oracle/product/805
```

Tip When you change the values of environment variables, you can ensure that those new values will be in force immediately by executing the .profile or .login file. Should you not do so, you'll have to reboot your Linux database server to make such changes take effect.

For the Bourne or Korn shell, type:

```
$ . .profile
```

For the C shell, enter:

```
% source .cshrc
```

Creating mount point directories

While not all Linux DBMSs require it, the administration of your file system can benefit if you create a mount point directory that will act as the highest level of your DBMS directory structure. Should you take this step, make sure that:

✦ The name of the mount point you create is identical to that which was originally assigned to your DBMS software

✦ The DBMS administrator user account has read, write, and execute privileges on any database mount point directories you create

Generic configuration tasks

With such Open Source products as MySQL and PostgreSQL, *configuration* is almost completely synonymous with *installation*. That is, configuration of such DBMSs involves:

✦ Obtaining the appropriate distribution

✦ Unpacking the distribution into the appropriate directory

✦ Changing your working directory to the uppermost level of the distribution subsystem

✦ Compiling and simultaneously configuring, by means of options supplied to the compilation

✦ Initializing and testing the configured DBMS

Vendor-specific configuration

This section discusses vendor-specific configuration tasks relating to three widely used Linux DBMSs: MySQL, PostgreSQL, and Oracle8*i* for Linux.

MySQL

To begin to configure MySQL, you must first select a directory to house it and then unpack the distribution file.

Configuration Options

Examples of common configuration options include:

✦ Compiling only client libraries and executables while foregoing server compilation

✦ Compiling to place log, and even database, files in a specific directory

✦ Compiling to produce a statically linked executable (sometimes recommended for speed)

✦ Compiling to suppress or require use of default, or non-null, values

✦ Compiling to require a specific character set for data and sorting

✦ Compiling to provide debugging

✦ Compiling to provide for or preclude multithreading

Note MySQL's default distribution format is a binary release linked with the option -static. Such linking helps ensure that the administrator need not worry about system library versions.

A program linked with the -static option is slightly bigger than a dynamically linked executable, but it is also slightly faster — an estimated 3 to 5 percent faster. However, a statically linked MySQL executable presents a problem in that it will not accept user-defined functions (UDFs). If you plan to use such C or C++ add-ins with MySQL, you must compile the application yourself, using dynamic linking.

.gz distribution files

Dealing with the GNU analog to zipped files means taking the steps below.

1. Pick the directory under which you want to unpack the distribution.

Note Make sure you have both read and write privileges for the directory you choose.

2. If you're not already there, move to that directory by using the command cd.

3. Get a MySQL source distribution file from one of MySQL's Internet sites. These files exist as compressed tar archives, and have names such as mysql-VERSION.tar.gz, where VERSION is, of course, a version number.

4. Unpack the distribution into the current directory with a command similar to this:

```
$ gunzip < mysql-VERSION.tar.gz | tar xvf -
```

Such a command creates a directory named mysql-VERSION as it unpacks the distribution file.

5. Change to the top-level directory of the unpacked distribution, with a command similar to this:

```
$ cd mysql-VERSION
```

6. Configure the release and compile everything, with commands similar to these:

```
$ ./configure --prefix=/usr/local/mysql
$ make
```

Tip When you configure MySQL, you can simultaneously specify configuration and runtime options. Run ./configure --help for a list of such options.

7. Complete the installation with this command:

```
$ make install
```

8. If you've not previously installed MySQL, create grant tables for it with a command similar to this:

```
$ scripts/mysql_install_db
```

9. After installation completes, initialize and test your database by starting the MySQL server with a command like the one below. In this sample command, the parameter BINDIR represents the directory in which the MySQL server has been installed, called in this example, safe_mysqld; the default value for this parameter and for that directory is /usr/local/bin.

```
$ BINDIR/safe_mysqld &
```

Tip   If you recognized the name safe_mysqld as representing a daemon process, give yourself a few extra points, and reflect for a moment on the fact that it makes sense to run the MySQL or any other Linux database server as a daemon. What's more, in the circumstances just cited, note that starting this daemon should not fail unless another MySQL server was already running.

RPM (Red Hat Package Manager) distribution files

If your MySQL source distribution exists as an RPM file, you must run the following command before beginning the installation and testing sequence just outlined. Carrying out this command creates a binary RPM file that you can then install:

```
$ rpm --rebuild MySQL-VERSION.src.rpm
```

Compiling and linking

Should you compile and link MySQL yourself, the way in which you do so affects its speed and overall performance. This section lists what I feel to be the most important aspects of MySQL's configuration.

MySQL uses LinuxThreads on Linux. If you are using an old Linux version that doesn't have glibc2, you must install LinuxThreads before trying to compile MySQL. LinuxThreads can be obtained from www.mysql.com/Downloads/Linux.

If you compile the MySQL server yourself rather than using the make and other installation files cited in the previous section, you can create a server which will run 10 to 30 percent faster if you use a C compiler such as pgcc or the Cygnus CodeFusion compiler.

You'll create a faster MySQL executable if you link with the option -static.

Compiling and configuring for multiple MySQL servers

Should you need or want to run more than one MySQL server simultaneously from the same machine, there are specific steps you must take.

Tip   You can determine sockets and ports used by currently executing MySQL servers with this command.

```
$ mysqladmin -h hostname --port=port_number variables
```

If a MySQL server is running on the port whose number you supplied, this command displays several important configuration variables for that server, including the socket name.

You also need to edit any initialization scripts that you're using to start and/or kill MySQL servers automatically, to take into account the fact that there is now more than one such server.

You don't have to recompile a new MySQL server just to start with a different port and socket. You can change the port and socket to be used by specifying them at runtime as options to safe_mysqld, with a command similar to this.

```
$ /full/path/name/of/safe_mysqld --socket=file_name --
port=port_number
```

Implementing multiple database servers to manipulate the same database is a potentially dangerous step, especially if your operating system platform doesn't support fault-free file locking. Much preferable is configuring subsequent database servers to use their own individual database directories, with the safe_mysgld run-time option:

```
--datadir=/full/path/name/of/the/directory/to be used
by/safe_mysqld
```

Creating Multiple Database Servers

Here is one example of when you might want to create multiple database servers on the same platform: the need to test a new DBMS release while leaving an existing production implementation undisturbed. Another example: an Internet service provider (ISP)'s need to provide unique database server implementations for a number of customers.

Running multiple simultaneous MySQL servers begins with compiling those servers to use distinct TCP/IP ports and sockets in order to ensure that each server "listens" to the appropriate "conversation," that is, receives and responds to only those requests made by its own clients.

I begin by assuming that one MySQL server already exists and has been configured to use the default TCP/IP port and socket. That being true, you would then use something similar to the following multipart command.

```
$ ./configure --with-tcp-port=port_number --with-unix-
socket=file_name --prefix=/usr/local/mysql-3.22.9
```

In such a command, the parameters port_number and file_name must differ from the default values presented to the previously implemented MySQL server. Furthermore, the parameter prefix should define a directory different than the one under which the existing MySQL installation lives.

PostgreSQL

This section discusses specific steps needed to install and configure PostgreSQL.

Tip   As was the case with MySQL, a complete list of PostgreSQL configuration parameters can be displayed with the command:

```
$ ./configure --help
```

Basic installation

Table 9-6 summarizes important PostgreSQL configuration parameters.

Table 9-6 PostgreSQL Configuration Options	
This Option	*Allows You to*
--prefix=PREFIX	install architecture-independent files in PREFIX; default is /usr/local/pgsql
--bindir=DIR	install user executables in DIR; default is EPREFIX/bin
--libdir=DIR	install object code libraries in DIR; default is EPREFIX/lib
--includedir=DIR	install C header files in DIR; default is PREFIX/include
--mandir=DIR	install man documentation in DIR; default is PREFIX/man
--disable-FEATURE	not include FEATURE in compiled PostgreSQL
--enable-FEATURE[=ARG]	include FEATURE [ARG=yes]
--with-PACKAGE[=ARG]	use PACKAGE [ARG=yes]
--without-PACKAGE	not use PACKAGE
--enable and --with options recognized	specify the location of libraries to be included in the compilation, by using the syntax --with-includes=dirs
look for header files for tcl/tk, and so on, in DIRS	specify the location of tcl/tk header files that might be needed for the compilation, by using the syntax --with-libraries=dirs
look for additional libraries in DIRS	specify the location of Perl libraries that might be needed for the compilation, by using the syntax --with-perl
build Perl interface and plperl	create an interface to Perl modules by using the syntax --with-odbc

This Option	Allows You to
build ODBC driver package	create a library of ODBC drivers by using the syntax --with-odbcinst=odbcdir
`--with-CC=compiler`	use specific C compiler
`--with-CXX=compiler`	use specific C++ compiler
`--without-CXX`	prevent building C++ code

Figure 9-8 depicts a typical PostgreSQL file subsystem structure.

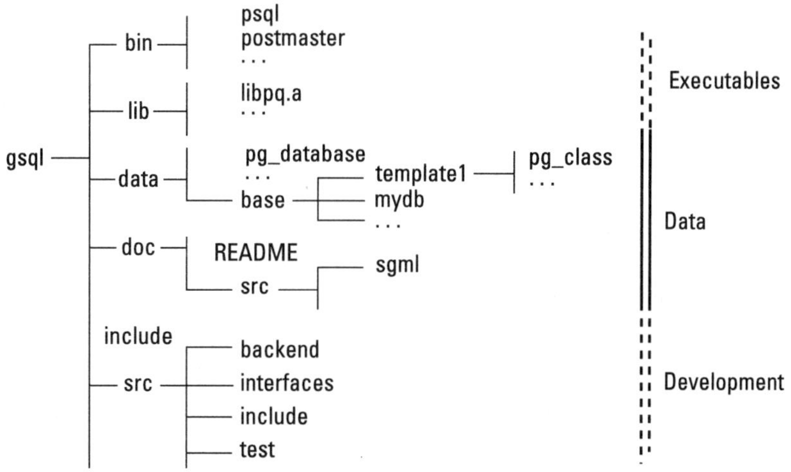

Figure 9-8: A default PostgreSQL file structure

As was the case with MySQL, installing PostgreSQL begins with obtaining the binary PostgreSQL distribution, in this case from `ftp.postgresql.org`. Once in hand, you must unpack, and begin to distribute the contents of, this compressed tar file with the following commands.

```
$ gunzip postgresql-7.0.tar.gz
$ tar -xf postgresql-7.0.tar
$ mv postgresql-7.0 /usr/src
```

Your next step is to build PostgreSQL with a make. Building PostgreSQL requires GNU make; no other form of this utility will do the job. To test for GNU make type this command:

```
$ gmake --version
```

If it turns out that you must obtain GNU make, you can do so from
ftp://ftp.gnu.org.

Before you begin the make, ensure that you have sufficient disk space. PostgreSQL
needs:

✦ About 30MB for the source file tree during compilation

✦ About another 5MB for the installation directory

✦ About 1MB for the initial empty database

✦ About 20MB should you want or need to run regression tests on the database
   at some point

Use this command to check for the amount of disk space available to PostgreSQL:

    $ df -k

Then take these steps to install the application.

1. Create the PostgreSQL superuser account under which the server will run.

2. Configure the PostgreSQL source for your system. During this step, you can
   specify the installation path for the build process and make choices about
   what gets installed.

3. Change to the src subdirectory and enter this command:

       $ ./configure

   At this point, you can include any options you want to configure into
   PostgreSQL.

4. Compile the server with this command:

       $ gmake

Note   The compilation process can take anywhere from 10 to 60 minutes.

Assuming that the compile completed without error, you can run the regression
test suite to verify that PostgreSQL will function according to specs on your server.

Tip   The Administrator's Guide should probably be your first reading if you are com-
           pletely new to PostgreSQL, as it contains information about how to set up
           database users and authentication.

Configuring automatic startup at boot time

While the PostgreSQL server can be run successfully from nonprivileged accounts
without root intervention, it may nonetheless be convenient or more secure to configure it to start automatically at bootup.

Most Intel UNIX systems have a file called either:

```
/etc/rc.local
```

or

```
/etc/rc.d/rc.local
```

in which the commands needed to accomplish autostart should be placed.

 Caution postmaster, that is, the PostgreSQL server, must be run by the PostgreSQL superuser (postgres) and not by the OS root, or any other, user.

Table 9-7 summarizes operating system-specific commands to automate starting the PostgreSQL server.

Table 9-7
Autostarting the PostgreSQL Server

Operating System	File	Commands
NetBSD	`rc.local`	`$ su postgres -c "/usr/local/pgsql/bin/postmaster -S -D /usr/local/pgsql/data"`
SPARC Solaris	`rc2.d`	`$ su postgres -c "/usr/local/pgsql/bin/postmaster -S -D /usr/local/pgsql/data"`

FreeBSD 2.2	`/usr/local/etc/rc.d/pgsql.sh`	`#!/bin/sh`
		
		`[ -x /usr/local/pgsql/bin/postmaster ] && {`
		
		`su -l pgsql -c 'exec /usr/local/pgsql/bin/postmaster -D/usr/local/pgsql/data -S -o -F > /usr/local/pgsql/errlog' &`
		
		`echo -n ' pgsql'}`
		
		`chmod 755 /usr/local/etc/rc.d/pgsql.sh`
		
		`chown root:bin /usr/local/etc/rc.d/pgsql.sh`

Red Hat Linux	`/etc/rc.d/init.d/postgres.init` **must be added**	

Creating a test database

To fully test your PostgreSQL implementation, create a test database with which you can tinker. Use this command:

```
$ createdb testdb
```

Then connect to that database with this command:

```
$ psql testdb
```

In response, you'll receive the PostgreSQL prompt from which you can enter SQL commands and otherwise experiment.

Oracle8*i*

Of the databases with which I worked while preparing this book, Oracle8*i* for Linux is perhaps the most sophisticated, and certainly the most complex, making demands of and interacting with its OS platform in ways that neither MySQL nor PostgreSQL do. So, I begin the discussion of Oracle8*i* with a summary of its most significant requirements (Table 9-8).

Table 9-8
What Oracle8*i* Needs from Linux

Category	Factor	Description	What Oracle8i Considers a Default
Linux Kernel Parameters	SHMMAX	maximum allowed value for shared memory	4294967295
	SHMMIN	minimum allowed value for shared memory	1
	SHMMNI	maximum number of shared memory segments allowed	100
	SHMSEG	maximum number of shared memory segments to which a user process can attach	10
	SHMMNS	maximum amount of shared memory that can be allocated systemwide	
	SEMMNS	number of semaphores allowed	200
	SEMMNI	number of semaphore set identifiers in the system; SEMMNI determines the number of semaphore sets that can be created at any one time	70

Category	Factor	Description	What Oracle8i Considers a Default
Linux Kernel Parameters	SEMMSL	maximum number of semaphores that can be in one semaphore set	Equal to or greater than the value of the PROCESSES initialization parameter; should also equal the maximum number of Oracle processes
Mount Points			At least four mount points, all at the same level of the directory structure; one is for the software, three are for an OFA-compliant database
OS Groups for Oracle	OSDBA	database administrator	dba
	OSOPER	database operator; may exist as own group or as a user who is a member of the	oper
	OSDBA group		
OS Account		dedicated solely to installing and upgrading the Oracle system; the account must be a member of the group used by OSDBA	
Oracle bin Directory		directory for software shared among Oracle users	/usr/local/bin
oratab file		information about Oracle instances	
file masks permission		use OS command `umask 022`	creates file access
Environment Variables	DISPLAY	machine name and monitor of the station from which you are connecting to the server	

Oracle Corporation recommends that you do not include /usr/ucblib in your LD_LIBRARY_PATH. If you require /usr/ucblib in LD_LIBRARY_PATH, make sure it appears after /usr/ccs/lib in the search order

Continued

Table 9-8 (continued)

Category	Factor	Description	What Oracle8i Considers a Default
Environment Variables	LD_ LIBRARY_ PATH	needed by Oracle products using shared libraries	must include $ORACLE_ HOME/lib.
	ORACLE_TERM	required by all character mode and Motif mode Oracle products	
	ORACLE_SID	specifies the instance name, or *server ID (SID)* of the Oracle Server; must be unique for each Oracle instance running on a given machine; Oracle Corporation recommends using four characters or fewer	
	ORACLE_HOME		set to the directory where the Oracle software will be installed; recommended: $ORACLE_BASE/product/release
	ORACLE_BASE	the directory at the top of the Oracle file structure	recommended: software_mount_point/app/oracle
	PATH	search path	must include all of: $ORACLE_HOME/ bin /bin /usr/bin /usr/local/bin
	SRCHOME	directory housing source code	unidentified at install; if SRCHOME is set, the Installer defaults to the location it specifies to find software to install

Category	Factor	Description	What Oracle8i Considers a Default
	TWO_TASK	an alternate database for certain objects	should be undefined at Install; If you set TWO_TASK and are creating database objects, the Installer attempts to place them in the database specified by TWO_TASK.
	TMPDIR		A directory with at least 20MB of available space where the Oracle account has write permission; the default location on Linux is /usr/tmp

Tasks that must be carried out as the root user

This section outlines the half-dozen steps that must be taken by the superuser to configure the operating system to accept Oracle8*i*.

1. Configure Linux kernel for Oracle. Set Linux kernel Interprocess Communication *(IPC)* parameters to accommodate the shared memory required by the Oracle8*i* Server. (You won't be able to start this server if the system hasn't been configured with enough shared memory.)

   Type the command:

   ```
   # ipcs
   ```

   to display the operating system's current shared memory and semaphore segments. Then set the kernel parameters listed below as defined in Table 9-8.

   - Maximum size of a shared memory segment (SHMMAX)

   - Maximum number of shared memory segments in the system (SHMMNI)

   - Maximum number of shared memory segments a user process can attach (SHMSEG)

   - Maximum amount of shared memory that can be allocated system-wide (SHMMNS)

2. Create mount points. An Oracle8*i* Server must have at least four mount points — one for the DBMS software, and at least three more for database files. All such mount point names, whatever their use, should follow the pattern /pm, where p is a string constant and m is a fixed-length key to distinguish between mount points.

3. Create OS groups for database administrators. The Oracle Installer assigns database administrator and operator privileges to operating system user groups during installation, calling these categories of privileges OSDBA and OSOPER, respectively. Members of the groups to which these privileges are assigned these groups automatically, therefore, have the corresponding privileges under Oracle. So, the groups you wish to use for these roles must exist before you start the Installer.

On most Intel UNIX platforms, use a command of this type to create such groups if they do not already exist.

```
# grpadd oracledba oracleoper
```

4. Create an OS account to own Oracle software. Because the operating system user account you've set up for oracle itself owns the Oracle distribution, you must run the Installer under this account. Therefore, you must first ensure that the account exists and is defined appropriately.

Under most Intel Linux operating systems, the utility useradd allows you easily to create this or any other user account. Follow the specifications set out in Table 9-9 for the oracle user account.

Table 9-9
Characteristics of the oracle User Account

Parameter	Value
Login Name	Can be anything, but make it mnemonic, for example, oracle.
Default Group Identification (GID)	Can be anything, but make it mnemonic, for example, OSDBA or OPER as appropriate.
Home Directory	Choose a home directory consistent with other user home directories. Note also that the home directory of the oracle account should not share the same value as the ORACLE_HOME directory.
Login Shell	Can be the Bourne shell (/bin/sh), the C shell (/bin/csh), or the Korn shell (/bin/ksh).

Tip Sites with multiple Oracle servers may install them under the same oracle account or under separate accounts. If multiple installations share an oracle account, the DBAs for each installation have access to the other installations. If this presents security problems, install each Oracle system under a different oracle account.

5. Create a local bin directory. With Oracle, as is true of all software, a common environment expedites administration. Such an environment should include a database-specific bin directory for shared software, which is outside the ORACLE_HOME directory. To create this common environment, take these steps.

a. Create a local bin directory, such as /usr/local/bin, with commands similar to these. (Of course, the exact nature of your file system's structure will dictate the precise parameters you must supply to such commands.)

```
# cd /usr
# mkdir local
# cd local
# mkdir bin
```

b. Ensure that this newly created directory appears as part of the PATH of every user who must work with Oracle, and that those users have execute permissions on the directory.

c. Copy the oraenv (or coraenv under the C shell) and dbhome configuration scripts to the newly created local bin directory. You can also copy or move other software that you want all users to be able to access to this directory.

6. Create the oratab file. An important Oracle8*i* administrative file, the oratab file, contains information about Oracle instances, that is, individual Oracle sessions. The oracle user account owns oratab. However, the file lives in a directory that requires root privileges. Therefore, when creating the file or setting permissions on it, you must run the script cdrom_mount_point/orainst/oratab.sh in order to manipulate the /etc directory appropriately.

Tasks that must be carried out as the user oracle

A number of Oracle configuration tasks can be carried out from a login to the oracle account. These include setting permissions for newly created files, setting environment variables, and updating the environment.

1. Set new file permissions. Use the `umask` command both to check and to set file masks, that is, default permissions assigned to files at their creation.

To check existing file masks, simply type:

```
umask
```

If the OS reports anything other than a value of 022, use the following command to set masks to that value:

```
umask 022
```

This command ensures that all users on a system, other than the owner of a file, can read and execute, but not write to, newly created files, including those the Oracle Installer creates.

2. Set environment variables. Use the syntax shown below as appropriate to your shell to set the environment variables outlined above in Table 9-8.

For the Bourne shell, enter commands whose syntax follows this pattern:

```
variable_name=value
export variable_name
```

For the C shell, use a command of this pattern:

```
setenv variable_name value
```

Because there are so many possible values for this environment variable, they have a table of their own — Table 9-10. ORACLE_TERM identifies the terminal definition resource file to be used with the Installer.

Table 9-10
Typical ORACLE_TERM Settings

Terminal Type	ORACLE_TERM Setting
AT386 console	386
AT386 xterm	386x
UnixWare terminal	386u
Solaris x86 xterm	386s
Data General 200	dgd2
Data General 400	dgd4
IBM High Function Terminal and aixterm (color)	hftc
IBM High Function Terminal and aixter (monochrome)	hft
hpterm terminal and HP 700/9x terminal	hpterm
IBM 3151 terminal	3151
vt220 terminal	vt220

3. Update the environment. Once you've properly defined all environment variables in .profile or .login as appropriate to your shell, you can immediately update the environment so that the current, active shell session reflects the characteristics just specified.

For the Bourne or Korn shell, use this command:

```
$ ./.profile
```

For the C shell, type this command:

```
$ source .login
```

Running the Oracle Installer

The Oracle Product Installation CD-ROM is in RockRidge format. Of course, you must have root privileges to mount or unmount the CD-ROM.

Caution Preclude damage to the CD or the drive by unmounting the medium before removing it from that drive.

Take these steps to prepare to run the Oracle Installer.

1. Place the Product Installation CD-ROM in the CD-ROM drive.

2. Log in as the root user and create a CD-ROM mount point directory, with a command of this pattern:

```
# mkdir cdrom_mount_point_directory
```

3. Make the newly created mount point directory readable, writable, and executable for all users with a command similar to this.

```
chmod 777 cdrom_mount_point_directory
```

4. Mount the CD-ROM drive on the mount point directory and exit the root account, with commands such as these:

```
# mount options device_name cdrom_mount_point_directory
# exit
```

A more specific Linux example might use this syntax.

```
# mkdir /cd
# chmod 777 /cdrom
# mount -t iso9660 /dev/cdrom /cd
# exit
```

5. Start the Installer with these steps:

   • Log in as oracle user.

   • Issue commands of the following patterns.

```
$ cd cdrom_ mount_point_directory/orainst.
$ ./orainst
```

Caution Do not run the Installer as the root user. Doing so would assign file ownerships and permissions appropriate to that user, and thereby possibly deny access to others.

Table 9-11 describes some navigational details of working with the Installer.

Table 9-11	
Navigating Within the Oracle Installer	
Keystroke	**Action Produced**
Tab key	Move to next block
Arrow keys	Move between fields
Spacebar	Selects current fields

Tip   The Installer can record responses from one installation session, and then apply those to subsequent installations, enabling them to be carried out noninteractively, in what Oracle calls silent mode.

Installer screens

An Oracle Installer session consists of a series of prompts, each displayed in its own window. The first such window enables you to choose a default or a custom installation.

If you decide upon both a default installation and the simultaneous creation of a database, the Installer copies prebuilt data files to the specified mount points, thereby building a database, creating control files, and — perhaps most important — saving the time that would otherwise be needed to load and run data dictionary creation scripts.

If you simply choose a default installation, the Installer will display and ask you to confirm the settings it plans to use.

Tip   The default path assumes that you are installing from CD-ROM. If you are installing from a network drive or from some other form of what Oracle refers to as a staging area, you cannot use the default installation path.

Installation log files

The Oracle Installer creates four log files in which it records the current installation session's activities. These logs store information regarding:

✦ The Installer's manipulation of the operating system

✦ The Installer's own activities

✦ Activities related to Oracle SQL

✦ Activities related to installation makefiles

If you accept the default presented by the Installer at this point, all of these logs will be placed in the directory $ORACLE_HOME/orainst. Should earlier versions of the logs exist, the Installer will first rename them as *xxx*.old before creating the current log set.

Install source

The next Installer prompt window asks you whether you are installing from CD-ROM or from a staging area. If you indicate the latter, you'll be prompted a second time, to specify whether the staging area is temporary or permanent, because the Installer deletes temporary staging areas as it installs.

National language support

Should you need to use a language other than U.S. English for messages from Oracle8*i*, you can specify it with this prompt screen. Be aware, though, that this default language can be overridden by settings supplied by users or even client applications when a session is initiated. Note also that the Installer itself operates only in U.S. English.

The root.sh script

The script root.sh, created by the Installer in the $ORACLE_HOME/orainst directory, must be run by the root user after installation. If the Installer detects a previous copy of this script, it will prompt you to learn whether it should append new actions to it, or to create a new root.sh. Tell the Installer to create a new file.

Software asset manager

Oracle's Installer tool, called Software Asset Manager, monitors the storage required by the DBMS features you select, comparing that to space available in the destination ORACLE_HOME directory. Therefore, as you choose what you want to install from the Asset Manager's Available Products window, you might receive further Installer prompts pertaining to available disk space.

Tip   The Software Asset Manager groups many products under categories such as Protocol Adapters or Precompilers, and denotes these categories with a plus sign to the left of the name. To expand a category name to reveal its component products, simply double-click the name. Or, in character mode, select it and press Enter.

OSDBA group

In its next prompt screen, the Installer displays choices available for the user group that will be granted Oracle DBA privileges; this parameter defaults to the primary user group of the oracle account.

OSOPER group

As it did for the database administrator, the Installer prompts you to choose a group which will be granted Oracle OPERATOR privileges. This parameter defaults to the group you specified as the OSDBA group. Should you go along with this default, no separate user group will receive operator privileges. If you do choose a group other than dba, Oracle's default administrator group, the Installer will accept your choice but have to relink the DBMS executable.

Instance name

An Oracle8*i* instance name, defined in the environment variable ORACLE_SID, is, in single-database installations, supplied the same value as the DB_NAME initialization parameter. In other scenarios, you should supply an instance name that is not only a unique identifier, but also no more than four characters long.

Database creation

The following prompts appear only if you use the Installer to create a database.

Number of mount points

When installing the Oracle8*i* server, follow the recommendation of Oracle Corporation to spread your database across at least three independent devices. When you accept this default in the Number of Mount Points prompt screen, control and redo log files are also spread across the mount points you specify.

Mount point Locators

Oracle Corporation recommends that the database mount points you specify in this window differ from the software mount point you defined to the initial Installer prompt. Table 9-12 summarizes the default size and placement for the sample or demonstration database the Installer will create.

Table 9-12 Sample Database Summary			
File	*Default Size*	*Minimum Size*	*Default Location*
Control Files	50KB	database-dependent	db_mount_point[1-3]/ oradata/db_name/ control0[1-3].ctl
Redo Log Files	500KB	100KB	db_mount_point[1-3]/ oradata/db_name/ redosid0[1-3].log
SYSTEM	80MB	5MB	db_mount_point1/oradata/ db_name/system01.dbf
ROLLBACK	15MB	1MB	db_mount_point1/oradata/ db_name/rbs01.dbf
TEMP	550KB	260KB	db_mount_point1/oradata/ db_name/temp01.dbf
USERS	1MB	200KB	db_mount_point1/oradata/ db_name/users01.dbf
TOOLS	25MB	1MB	db_mount_point1/oradata/ db_name/tools01.dbf

Character set

This Installer prompt screen enables you to specify the character set in which the database will be stored; the default is US7ASCII. Change this only after careful consideration. To choose any character set other than the default requires having set the environment variable ORA_NLS33 during preinstallation to a matching value. A nondefault character set cannot be changed without recreating the database it affects.

National character set

The *national* character set for which the Installer next prompts you affects only specially declared columns; it defaults to the character set you specified as the database character set.

SYS and SYSTEM user passwords

The Installer prompt screen for the Oracle8*i* (as opposed to operating system) user accounts SYSTEM and SYS shows defaults of *manager* and *change_on_install* respectively. Use this screen to supply passwords for both these accounts that are appropriate for your environment.

The dba and operator group passwords

Next, the Installer asks whether you want to set passwords for the operating system user groups to whom you granted database administrator and operator privileges. Set these passwords, because doing so enables authentication on attempts to connect to the Oracle8*i* server as either user.

Multithreaded server

Configuring the Oracle8*i* server to act as a Multithreaded Server *(MTS)* allows you to keep to a minimum the number of processes and amount of memory certain types of database applications will demand. Oracle Corporation considers MTS best suited for systems running applications with few long-running transactions, such as Oracle InterOffice. On the other hand, Oracle considers MTS not well suited for systems supporting long-running transactions, such as those found in decision-support applications. Keep these caveats in mind when responding to this Installer prompt.

Installing documentation

Oracle documentation can be either operating system-specific or product-related, with the latter type sometimes referred to as generic. The distribution CD houses operating system-specific documentation, thereby allowing this document category to be installed during the overall software installation. Product documentation, on the other hand, occupies its own CD-ROM, and therefore requires a separate Installer session to be loaded. However, both categories of Oracle8*i* documentation are provided in both HTML and PDF formats.

To install operating system-specific documentation, simply choose Linux Documentation, in addition to whatever other products you wish to load, from the list of available products presented to you at the early stages of the installation.

Verifying the Installer's work

After installation completes, the Oracle8*i* Installer automatically returns to the Software Asset Manager screen from which you can verify that all products selected show as having been installed.

Configuring Oracle8*i*

Completing installation doesn't mean you've also completed setting up Oracle8*i*. After completing an Installer session, certain configuration tasks must still be done.

Tasks to perform as the root user

To begin configuring Oracle8*i*, log in to the operating system as root. Then carry out the tasks described in this section.

The root.sh script

Running the root.sh script created by the Installer in the $ORACLE_HOME/orainst directory sets file permissions for Oracle products, and performs other configuration activities.

Run this script with commands similar to these:

```
# cd $ORACLE_HOME/orainst
# ./root.sh
```

root.sh will ask you to confirm the environment before it performs any actions, thus allowing you to terminate the script should you need to reset anything in the environment. If you terminate the script, you must rerun it, but you do not need to rerun the Installer.

root.sh informs you of its progress as it works, and may also prompt for such parameters as usernames.

The catrep.sql script

If you're installing Oracle8*i* for the first time, you must run the script catrep.sql, found in the $ORACLE_HOME/orainst directory, to give the DBMS the capability to replicate.

Create additional Linux accounts

Should more than one user of your system need to exercise database administrative privileges, each such user must have his or her own account affiliated with the OSDBA user group. Any additional such accounts that are needed should be created at this point with the utility useradd.

Verify database file security

Ensure that your newly installed DBMS adheres to the file modes and ownerships recommended by Oracle Corporation. Table 9-13 outlines these modes and ownerships.

Table 9-13
Oracle File Security

Area of the DBMS	Recommended Characteristics
All common system files and installation files	Owned by the user account oracle
All common system files and installation files	Should provide read, write, and execute privileges to all members of the OSDBA user group
Any files or directories in an Oracle installation	Should not provide write access to any user not a member of the OSDBA user group

Automate database startup and shutdown (optional)

Oracle Corporation considers automating database startup optional, but strongly recommends automating the capability to shut down the DBMS as a means of protecting the suite from errors or corruption caused by improper shutdown. Two scripts, dbshut and dbstart, found in the $ORACLE_HOME/bin directory, automate database shutdown and startup, respectively. Both scripts reference the same records in the oratab file, and must, therefore, pertain to the same database or set of databases. As Oracle Corporation points out in its Administrator's Guide, you cannot have dbstart automatically fire up databases sid1, sid2, and sid3, but have dbshut close only sid1 and sid2.

Set up dbstart and dbshut to be called at bootup by taking these steps:

1. Edit the file /etc/oratab, whose entries take the format:

   ```
   ORACLE_SID:ORACLE_HOME:{Y|N}
   ```

   where Y or N specify respectively using or not using dbstart and dbshut to start up and shut down the database. Change the value for every database whose launching and closing you wish not only to automate but to link to operating system startup to Y.

2. If it doesn't already exist, create a file called dbora in the directory /etc/rc.d/init.

3. At the end of the file dbora, place entries similar to those shown in the example below. Be sure to use full path names.

   ```
   # Set ORA_HOME to the location of dbshut
   # Set ORA_OWNER to the user id of the owner of the Oracle
   database
   ORA_HOME=/u01/app/oracle/product/8.0.5
   ORA_OWNER=oracle
   ```

```
# Test for the presence of the script dbstart in ORA_HOME
if [! -f $ORA_HOME/bin/dbstart -o ! -d $ORA_HOME]
then
echo "Oracle startup: cannot start"
exit
fi
# Assuming dbstart is in the right place ...
case "$1" in
'start')
# Start the Oracle databases
su - $ORA_OWNER -c $ORA_HOME/bin/dbstart &
;;
'stop')
# Or, stop the Oracle databases in background after becoming
the user ORA_OWNER
su - $ORA_OWNER -c $ORA_HOME/bin/dbshut &
;;
esac
# Link dbora to operating system startup with a command
appropriate to
# your environment, like this.
ln -s /etc/rc.d/init.d/dbora /etc/rc0.d/K10dbora
```

After specifying startup and shutdown options, your work as root to install Oracle8*i* is finished.

Summary

Getting ready for any Linux DBMS means:

✦ Understanding and using effective schema design, which in turn requires understanding at least some of normalization theory

✦ Having a clear picture of your intended platform's resources, and of how much those resources might have to grow to accommodate your growing databases

✦ Grasping and being able to use correctly the basic Linux concepts and commands, such as chmod and groupadd, needed to install any Linux DBMS

✦ Reviewing vendor-specific installation instructions

✦   ✦   ✦

Interaction and Usage

Interacting with the Database

As a Linux database administrator, you will need to interact with your DBMS in a number of ways. This section discusses three commonplace, but still essential, operations:

✦ Dumping a database

✦ Importing text files into a database

✦ Displaying database summary information

Interacting with MySQL

MySQL offers command-line utilities by means of which you can dump the contents of one or more databases; import text into a MySQL database in order to populate its tables; and display database, table, and field names.

Dumping a database

You must use the utility mysqldump to dump one or more MySQL databases in order to back them up or to transfer them to another MySQL server. Such dumps can include the MySQL statements needed to create or populate the tables involved.

The three commands below are each examples of generalized syntax for the mysqldump utility.

```
# mysqldump [OPTIONS] database [tables]
# mysqldump [OPTIONS] --databases [OPTIONS]
DB1 [DB2 DB3...]
# mysqldump [OPTIONS] --all-databases
[OPTIONS]
```

Table 10-1 summarizes this syntax.

Table 10-1
mysqldump Syntax

Syntax	Effect
`# mysqldump [OPTIONS] database [tables]`	Dumps out the contents of the specified database and tables, according to the options given if any
`# mysqldump [OPTIONS] --databases [OPTIONS] DB1 [DB2 DB3. . .]`	Dumps out the contents of the specified databases, according to the options given if any
`# mysqldump [OPTIONS] --all-databases [OPTIONS]`	Dumps out the contents of all databases, according to the options given if any

Caution

If you don't supply table names or use the `--databases` or `--all-databases` options, mysqldump will output everything in every database.

Here's a lineup of what I consider to be the most useful of mysqldump's options.

✦ `mysqldump --add-locks` — Locks tables before and unlocks tables after each table dump; provides faster inserts

✦ `mysqldump –A` or `mysqldump --all-databases` — Dump all databases

✦ `mysqldump --allow-keywords` — Create column names that include keywords; functions by causing mysqldump to begin each column name with the appropriate table name

✦ `mysqldump –C` or `mysqldump –compress` — Compress all information that passes between client and server; assumes both client and server support compression

✦ `mysqwldump –B` or `mysqldump –databases` — Dumps several databases, without the need to supply table names, because all arguments are regarded as database names

✦ `mysqldump –F` or `mysqldump --flush-logs` — Flush all MySQL log files before starting the dump

✦ `mysqldump –f` or `mysqldump –force` — Complete the dump even if SQL errors occur during the dump

✦ `mysqldump –h` or `mysqldump --host= named host` — Dump from the active MySQL server to the named host; the default value for the named host parameter is localhost

✦ `mysqldump –l` or `mysqldump --lock-tables` — Lock all tables before beginning the dump

✦ `mysqldump -d` or `mysqldump --no-data`—Write no row information; useful when only a dump of the structure of a table is needed

✦ `mysqldump -ppassword` or `mysqldump --password=password`—Connects to the mysql server with the permissions associated with the supplied password before beginning the dump

✦ `mysqldump -q` or `mysqldump -quick`—Carries out dump without buffering; dumps directly to standard output

✦ `mysqldump -u user name` or `mysqldump --user=user name`—Connects to the MySQL server as the indicated user before doing the dump; default for username—operating system login name of current user

✦ `mysqldump -w` or `mysqldump --where="condition"`—Dumps only those records specified by the condition stated in the where clause, whose single quotes are required

Tip

One can use the `where` option of mysqldump to do an ad hoc display of records sharing a specific characteristic, while at the same time transferring those records to another MySQL database, with syntax like this:

```
mysqldump --database_of_gardening --
where=plant_name='zinnia' | mysql
--host=far_away_machine -C db_of_gardening
```

Importing text files

The command-line interface to MySQL's LOAD DATA statement is mysqlimport. Most of the options that this utility accepts are identical to those of that statement.

Launch mysqlimport with a command of this general syntax.

```
# mysqlimport [options] database ASCII file 1 [ASCII file 2]
[ASCII file 3]
```

Caution

Be careful in naming, or deciding upon, files that mysqlimport may have to work with. The utility mysqlimport strips off any extension from the name of a file to be imported, and uses the result to decide which table in the indicated database will receive the text file's contents. So, if you want to import data from a file called veggies.txt into a table called comestibles in a gardening database, you must first rename the text file to comestibles.txt. Otherwise, mysqlimport will place the results of the importing in a new table called veggies.

Table 10-2 summarizes the most useful of mysqlimport's options.

Table 10-2
mysqlimport Options

Option	Effect
-C or --compress	Compress all information as it moves between client and server; assumes that both support compression.
-d or --delete	Remove all existing data from a table before importing text file
-f or --force	Ignore errors such as those generated by a text file not having a corresponding, pre-existing table in a database. Causes mysqlimport to attempt to continue the import beginning with the next text file available, if any. Without this option, mysqlimport will exit if a table doesn't exist to receive the contents of a text file.
-h host_name or --host=host name	Import data to the MySQL server on the host indicated by the host name parameter.
-i or --ignore	Ignore, that is do not import, input records whose key fields' values duplicate those of existing records.
-L or --local	Get input files locally, that is, from the active MySQL client. This option is needed if you wish to override mysqlimport's default behavior of obtaining text files from the MySQL server on the default host, that is, on the machine specified by the OS parameter localhost.
-l or --lock-tables	Lock ALL tables, that is, preclude any write operations to those tables, before importing text files. Therefore ensures that all tables on the server contain the same data, that is, that those tables are synchronized.
-r or --replace	Replace existing rows whose key fields have unique values duplicated in input records with those input records.

The code sample below demonstrates mysqlimport, after first using mysql itself to create an empty database and table into which the contents of a text file can be placed. Such a file can be created in any of the editors Intel UNIX makes available. Finally, MySQL's response to these commands is in italics; Table 10-3, which follows this sample, elaborates upon it.

```
$ mysql -e 'CREATE TABLE trek_good_guys(id INT, name
VARCHAR(20))' trek_trivia
$ mysqlimport --local trek_trivia trek_good_guys.txt
trek_trivia.trek_good_guys: Records: 2  Deleted: 0  Skipped: 0
Warnings: 0
```

Table 10-3 **Understanding mysqlimport**	
Command Fragment	**Means**
`mysql -e`	Start MySQL, execute the command encased in single quotes, and then quit, that is, end the MySQL session.
`'CREATE TABLE trek_good_guys (id INT, name VARCHAR(25))'`	Create a new table called trek_good_guys. Further, define two fields for that table: an integer field called id and a variable-length character field called name, whose maximum length can be no more than 25 characters.
`trek_trivia`	Create the indicated table and fields in the new database called trek_trivia.
`mysqlimport -local`	Import data from the local host. . .
`trek_trivia trek_good_guys.txt`	. . .to the database called trek_trivia from the ASCII file called trek_good_guys.txt.

Assuming that the contents of trek_good_guys.txt look like this:

```
001     Captain James T. Kirk
002     Constable Odo
```

an inquiry of the newly created and loaded table might look like this. Again, MySQL's output from the command you enter is italicized.

```
$ mysql -e 'SELECT * FROM trek_good_guys' trek_trivia
+------+---------------+
| id   | name          |
+------+---------------+
| 001  | Captain James T. Kirk |
| 002  | Constable Odo |
+------+---------------+
```

Tip I've done and shall continue to do my best to reproduce both the content and the look of MySQL's responses. However, that look may vary slightly depending upon such OS characteristics as terminal definitions.

Displaying database summary information

The command-line utility mysqlshow gives a thumbnail sketch of existing databases and their tables, and of those tables' columns or fields.

Watch Out for What's Missing

Be aware that, if you do not supply a:

✦ Database name to mysqlshow, information on all matching databases will be displayed

✦ Table name to mysqlshow, information on all matching tables in the indicated or in all databases will be displayed

✦ Column name to mysqlshow, information on all matching columns and column types in the indicated or in all tables will be displayed

Note also that in the most recent versions of MySQL, mysqlshow will display information only on databases, tables, and columns for which you have the necessary read privilege.

Invoke mysqlshow with generalized syntax similar to this:

```
$ mysqlshow [OPTIONS] [database [table [column]]]
```

Interacting with PostgreSQL

This section reviews the PostgreSQL utilities that enable you to dump the contents of one or more databases, import text as data for a database, and display database summary information.

Dumping a database

PostgreSQL offers two utilities that can dump the contents of databases: pg_dump and pg_dumpall.

pg_dump

pg_dump places the contents of a PostgreSQL database into a *script* file (that is, a file that is in ASCII form, that holds query commands, and that can be used to reconstruct the database on the local or some other host).

More specifically, pg_dump generates queries that re-create all user-defined types, functions, tables, indices, aggregates, and operators. Finally, pg_dump copies out all data as text so that it can be copied in again easily or even dumped into a text editor for further massaging.

pg_dump's generic syntax comes in two flavors.

```
pg_dump [ dbname ]
pg_dump [ -h host ] [ -p port ] [ -t table ] [ -a ] [ -s ] [ -u
] [ -x ] [ dbname ]
```

Table 10-4 describes what we consider the most useful pg_dump options.

<table>
<tr><td colspan="3" align="center">Table 10-4
pg_dump Syntax</td></tr>
<tr><td>**Command
or Fragment**</td><td>**Example**</td><td>**Effect**</td></tr>
<tr><td>dbname</td><td>pg_dump trek_trivia</td><td>Dumps the contents and schema of the database trek_trivia to standard output</td></tr>
<tr><td>-a</td><td>pg_dump -a trek_trivia</td><td>Dumps only the contents, and not the schema, of the database trek_trivia to standard output</td></tr>
<tr><td>-s</td><td>pg_dump -s trek_trivia</td><td>Dumps only the schema, and not the data, of the database trek_trivia to standard output</td></tr>
<tr><td>-t table</td><td>pg_dump –t starships trek_trivia</td><td>Dumps only the schema and data of the table starships in the database trek_trivia to standard output</td></tr>
<tr><td>-u</td><td>pg_dump -t starships -u trek_trivia</td><td>Dumps only the schema and data of the table starships in the database trek_trivia to standard output, after prompting for a PostgreSQL username and password</td></tr>
<tr><td>-x</td><td>pg_dump –t starships –x trek_trivia</td><td>Dumps only the schema and data of the table starships in the database trek_trivia to standard output, and withholds any user- or permission-related information from the dump</td></tr>
<tr><td>-h host</td><td>pg_dump –h 207.102.233.251 –x trek_trivia</td><td>Connects to the postmaster, that is, to the PostgreSQL server, on the machine indicated by the given IP address, and withholds any user or permission related information from the dump; host names may also be supplied for this parameter</td></tr>
<tr><td>-p port</td><td>pg_dump –p 2345 –x trek_trivia</td><td>Connects to the postmaster by means of the specified TCP/IP port or local socket file extension to which the postmaster listens, and withholds any user or permission related information from the dump; port number defaults to 5432</td></tr>
</table>

However you structure its command line, pg_dump can write either to an ASCII file or to standard output, as these examples demonstrate:

```
% pg_dump
% pg_dump > trek_out
```

Tip   Should pg_dump return errors, your best bet is to ensure that you have permissions adequate to the dump. An easy way to check this is to do a simple query of the database in question from psql.

pg_dumpall

pg_dumpall does just what its name suggests; it dumps all existing PostgreSQL databases into a single script file. As a result, it does not recognize the arguments dbname or -t table.

Otherwise, its syntax and behavior are identical to those of pg_dump as we've just presented them.

Importing text files

Just as it relies on the OS concept of redirecting output to place the results of a dump in an ASCII file, so PostgreSQL leans on the mirror-image idea of redirecting input to import the dumped information. Let's go back to my example of the former and enlarge upon it to illustrate the latter.

I created a text file called trek_out with this command:

```
% pg_dump > trek_out
```

To reload this information to a new database, I need only issue this command:

```
% psql -e next_gen < db.out
```

Displaying database summary information

PostgreSQL offers the utility vacuumdb to enable you to clean or simply to analyze a PostgreSQL database. vacuumdb's generalized syntax in its most usable form and as it pertains to such analysis looks like this:

```
vacuumdb [ --analyze | -z ] [ --alldb | -a ] [ --table 'table
[ ( column [,...] ) ]' ] [dbname ]
```

Table 10-5 elaborates on vacuumdb.

Table 10-5
Using vacuumdb as a Database Analysis Tool

Command or Fragment	Example	Effect
`-z` or `--analyze`	$ vacuumdb --analyze firstdb	Prepare statistics on the database firstdb that the PostgreSQL optimizer can use
`-a` or `--alldb`	$ vacuumdb --analyze --alldb	Analyze all databases on the local host
`-t` or `--table` table name or column name	$ vacuumdb --analyze --table 'starships(classification)' trek_trivia	Work only with the column classification in the table starships of the database trek_trivia
`-h` or `--host` host name or IP address	$ vacuumdb –h library --analyze firstdb	Work with the database firstdb running under the postmaster on the remote machine whose host name is library
`-p` or `--port` port number	$ vacuumdb –p 2345 --analyze firstdb	Work with the database firstdb running under the postmaster that listens at the port numbered 2345
`-U` or `--username` username	$ vacuumdb –U adhoc --analyze firstdb	Work with the database firstdb, with the identity and privileges associated with the PostgreSQL user adhoc
`-W` or `--password`	$ vacuumdb –W --analyze firstdb	Work with the database firstdb, after prompting for a PostgreSQL password

Tip   If vacuumdb returns the simple message

```
VACUUM
```

it's telling you it had no problems. If, however, it displays something similar to

```
vacuumdb: Vacuum failed.
```

it's telling you something went wrong. Again, your best debugging bet is to check, and if need be adjust, the database, table, and column permissions.

Interacting with Oracle8*i*

Despite being such a formidable DBMS, Oracle8*i* lacks two major features:

✦ The capability to dump either data or schema into an ASCII file, substituting instead the utilities EXPORT and IMPORT, which handle data or data definitions in internal binary Oracle8*i* format.

✦ A command-driven means of obtaining summary statistics for any level of a database, substituting instead a number of GUI-based monitoring capabilities.

Navigating the Server Console

This section discusses the administrative functions of using a Linux DBMS server console.

MySQL

Every MySQL server relies on the utility mysqladmin to carry out all management of the DBMS. The generalized syntax for this utility is:

```
# mysqladmin [OPTIONS] command [command-option] command ...
```

Table 10-6 summarizes the most useful commands that you can pair with mysqladmin.

Table 10-6
mysqladmin Commands

Command	Effect
create databasename	Create a new database
drop databasename	Delete a database and all its tables
kill id,id,	Kill mysql clients by supplying the process ID associated with those clients, in turn obtained with the command process list
ping	Use ping to determine if the daemon mysqld still runs
processlist	Display a list of all active client sessions currently being serviced by mysqld
shutdown	Stop the MySQL server
status	Display server status information

Tip   All the commands described in Table 10-6 can be abbreviated. For instance, mysqladmin stat would produce the same output as mysqladmin status.

Status information available under mysqladmin includes:

✦ Uptime, that is, the number of seconds the MySQL server has been running

✦ Threads, that is, the number of active clients

✦ Questions, that is, the number of queries from clients since the most ercent launching of the MySQL server or daemon, mysqld

✦ Slow queries, that is, queries whose execution has needed more than a predefined number of seconds

✦ Opens, that is, how many tables are currently open under mysqld

✦ Flush tables, that is, the number of flush, refresh, and/or reload commands that have been carried out since mysqld was most recently started

✦ Open tables, that is, the number of tables currently open

✦ Memory in use, that is, memory allocated directly by mysqld, and only available when the MySQL server was started with the option `--with-debug`

✦ Max memory used, that is, the maximum memory mysqld can allocate; similar to Memory in use, Max memory used is only available when the MySQL server was started with the option `--with-debug`

Output from mysqladmin stat might look similar to this:

```
Uptime: 10077  Threads: 1  Questions: 9  Slow queries: 0
Opens: 6  Flush tables: 1  Open tables: 2  Memory in use: 1092K
Max memory used: 1116K
```

Table 10-7 gives examples of the mysqladmin commands I've discussed.

Table 10-7
Examples of mysqladmin Commands

Command	Example	Result
`create` databasename	mysqladmin CREATE DATABASE IF NOT EXISTS pittsburgh_pirates	Creates the empty database pittsburgh_pirates if that database does not already exist. Note that because MySQL implements databases as directories, which, in turn, contain files corresponding to tables in the database, CREATE DATABASE creates only a directory under the MySQL data directory. It does not place any files, that is, tables, in that created directory.

Continued

Table 10-7 (continued)

Command	Example	Result
drop databasename	mysqladmin DROP DATABASE IF EXISTS pittsburgh_pirates	Deletes the database pittsburgh_pirates if that database exists. DROP DATABASE returns the number of files that were removed; normally, this value is three times the number of tables in the database, because each table is represented by a .MYD, a .MYI, and an .frm file.
kill id	mysqladmin kill 3456	Terminates the client session whose process ID is 3456.
ping	mysqladmin –u root ping	Temporarily takes on the identity of the root user before pinging the MySQL daemon.
processlist	mysqladmin proc	Displays a list of all MySQL processes currently running.
shutdown	mysqladmin shut	Stops the MySQL server.
status	mysqladmin stat	Displays status information for the MySQL server.

PostgreSQL

PostgreSQL, because it is so closely interwoven with languages such as Tcl/Tk, offers a means of carrying out administrative tasks that its Open Source peer MySQL does not. This GUI-based tool is called pgaccess.

pgaccess enables you to manage or edit tables, define queries, and carry out dozens of DB administration functions. In fact, the list of pgaccess features is so long that I only outline the most valuable of them.

Cross-Reference For specifics on or practice with pgaccess, consult the CD-ROM that accompanies this book, or visit the PostgreSQL Web site at: www.postgresql.readysetnet.com.

pgaccess's syntax couldn't be simpler. In general, it's this:

```
pgaccess [ database name ]
```

Now for the roll call of some of the more impressive of pgaccess's capabilities. This tool can:

✦ Access record sets with a query widget

✦ Add new records, saving them with a right-click

✦ Build, edit, and save queries with a visual tool that supports drag and drop

✦ Call user-written scripts

✦ Create tables through an assistant

✦ Delete or design views

✦ Delete records simply by pointing and then pressing the Delete key

✦ Dynamically adjust row height when editing

✦ Edit in place, that is, when viewing query results

✦ Execute VACUUM

✦ Load or save reports from/to a database

✦ Perform ad hoc queries such as

```
select * from starships where classification=[parameter
"Please enter a starship class, for example, Intrepid
class."]
```

✦ Open multiple tables for viewing, presenting as it does so a user-configurable maximum number of records

✦ Open user-defined forms

✦ Open any database on any host at a specified port and under a specified username and password

✦ Rename or delete tables.

✦ Resize columns by dragging their vertical grid lines

✦ Retrieve information such as owner, field characteristics, and more for specified tables

✦ Run action queries such as those which insert, update, or delete

✦ Save queries as views

✦ Save table definitions

✦ Save view layouts

✦ Save preferences, in the file .pgaccessrc under the PostgreSQL file subsystem

✦ Specify sort orders

✦ Specify ad hoc filters such as

```
like position="Catcher"
```

✦ View the results of select queries

Oracle8*i*

As one might expect of such a high-powered commercial DBMS, the nuances of Oracle8*i*'s administrative capabilities far outnumber those of either MySQL or PostgreSQL. However, those many capabilities can be executed with only one tool: Server Manager. This section gives an overview of that tool.

Server Manager

Server Manager, Oracle's database administration tool, exists in both a GUI-based and a command line-based form. Server Manager can be used to:

✦ Administer both local and remote databases

✦ Administer multiple databases

✦ Dynamically execute SQL, PL/SQL, and Server Manager commands

✦ In its GUI-based incarnation, concurrently perform multiple tasks

✦ Perform common DBMS administrative tasks such as server startup, shutdown, backup, and recovery

Tip   In its GUI persona, Server Manager can support Motif-based desktop managers such as XFree86, the most widely used PC desktop which is X Windows based.

Using Server Manager in graphical mode

Not only Server Manager itself but also a number of views of the databases you intend to manage must be present on your machine before you can use this tool.

Tip   You must install Server Manager views for each database you wish to administer, even if you implement only one copy of Server Manager.

An Oracle8*i* script, CATSVRMG.SQL, which is included with Server Manager on the Oracle8*i* distribution media, creates these Server Manager views, and is run automatically during installation. To verify that appropriate Server Manager views have been installed, check the version information in Server Manager's Administration window or issue the following query:

```
SM$VERSION (SELECT * FROM sm$version
```

Privileged operations

As you might expect, you must have privileges appropriate to the administrative task you want to carry out if Server Manager is to work for you. In particular, because many of Server Manager's windows include information selected from data dictionary tables, you need the SELECT ANY TABLE system privilege to fully utilize Server Manager's interface.

Starting Server Manager

On most Intel UNIX platforms, Server Manager is started with this command from the OS prompt:

```
$ svrmgr
```

Server Manager's copyright window, its first to appear upon startup, disappears in seven seconds, but you can also remove the window by one of the following methods:

✦ Pressing any key

✦ Clicking anywhere in the window

Next, you'll see Server Manager's Connect dialog box, through which you can connect to an Oracle instance, that is, a running image of the Oracle8*i* server.

Tip   You can also jump directly to a specific Server Manager window when you start the Manager, a technique that Oracle calls launching in context. A context launch can be carried out with a command similar to this:

```
$ svrmgr connect
```

Server Manager's anatomy

Server Manager's graphical interface has three major components: Administration Manager, SQL Worksheet, and System Monitors.

Administration Manager, Server Manager's most important component and the one you're likely to use most often, divides database administration into these categories, among others:

✦ Backing up and recovering a database

✦ Controlling security

✦ Managing a replication environment

✦ Managing instances and sessions

✦ Managing storage

✦ Viewing schema objects

Each of these groups offers its own menus and dialogs.

Think of SQL Worksheets as an Oracle8*i* analog to more traditional, spreadsheet application worksheets. SQL Worksheets are associated with particular databases and enable you to enter SQL statements, PL/SQL code, and Server Manager commands, or to run Oracle8*i* scripts on the fly, with the results of those entries automatically being reflected in the active database component.

Note   According to Oracle Corporation, PL/SQL is a *full-fledged application program-ming language that integrates features such as data encapsulation, structured parameter passing, and exception handling with support for distributed comput-ing,* as well as with a programming environment that extends SQL to enable build-ing applications that include multiple procedures and functions. Or, in a nutshell, PL/SQL combines multiple procedural steps with SQL statements.

These worksheets also keep a history of commands you use, thereby allowing you to edit and rerun commands conveniently.

As you've no doubt guessed, Oracle8*i*'s System Monitors gather and display database performance statistics. Among the significant System Monitors are:

✦ **Dispatcher** — Monitors Oracle8*i* sessions

✦ **File I/O** — Monitors any shared servers

✦ **Library Cache** — Monitors overall I/O

✦ **Lock** — Keeps system statistics

Server Manager menus

Server Manager offers four main pull-down menus:

✦ File

✦ Edit

✦ Window

✦ Help

The File menu items allow you to open or close Server Manager windows and cre-ate new connections. It offers these selections:

✦ **Connect** — Displays the Connect dialog box to connect to an instance and open an Administration window for that database

✦ **Administration Window** — Brings the associated Administration window for-ward, or displays a new Administration window

✦ **New Worksheet** — Starts a new SQL Worksheet.

✦ **Monitor** — Displays the Monitor dialog box, which allows you to choose a System Monitor to start

✦ **Close** — Closes the current window

✦ **Exit** — Exits Server Manager

Tip The Administration window, New Worksheet, and Monitor menu items are only available from a window connected to an instance. These items display a window associated with that connection.

The Edit menu contains standard editing commands most frequently used when editing text in the SQL Worksheet. The Window menu displays the names of all open Server Manager windows, allowing you to bring a window to the foreground simply by selecting it in the Window menu. From the Help menu, you can access the Server Manager online Help system.

Connecting to an instance

You can connect to an Oracle instance by using Server Manager's Connect dialog or choosing Connect from Server Manager's File menu.

The Connect dialog box allows you to specify:

✦ **Username** — Oracle username for the database to which you wish to connect

✦ **Password** — Appropriate password

✦ **Service Name** — SQL*Net service name for the database to which you wish to connect

✦ **Connect As** — Pop-up menu containing Normal, SYSOPER, and SYSDBA

Opening new windows

From Server Manager's File menu, you can open new windows within Administration Manager, an SQL Worksheet, or a System Monitor. When you open a new window, it is associated with the instance and username of your current window.

Using Server Manager in line mode

For the Linux traditionalists among us, Server Manager also offers a command-line interface.

Starting Server Manager in line mode

Server Manager is started in line mode by typing the following at the operating system prompt:

```
$ svrmgrl
```

To start Server Manager in line mode and to have it execute a script immediately upon launching, use a command similar to this:

```
svrmgrl command=@some_oracle8_script
```

Working with Server Manager in line mode

Here's a precis of working with Server Manager in line mode.

Single-line Server Manager commands need no terminators. On the other hand, Server Manager commands may span lines if each such line terminates in a back-slash (\ ) to indicate continuation.

Server Manager also accepts single- or multiple-line SQL statements, but, unlike its handling of multiline Manager commands, doesn't require you to end multiline SQL statements in any continuation character. Rather, to complete an overall SQL statement, whatever its length, end it in either a semicolon (;) at the end of the statement itself, or a forward slash (/) on its own last line of the SQL command sequence.

Scripts are run by using the @ command. For instance, to run a script called BASE-BALL_STATS.SQL, you'd type this command.

```
@baseball_stats
```

If you don't provide a script name, Server Manager will prompt for one.

```
SVRMGR> @
Name of script file: test
```

Tip   Many Server Manager commands available in line mode can also be used in an SQL Worksheet.

Table 10-8 summarizes the Server Manager commands that are most useful in line mode.

Table 10-8
Summary of Server Manager Commands

Command	Use	Requirements	Syntax	Meaning
@ (at symbol)	Run scripts containing SQL, PL/SQL, and Server Manager commands	You must have previously created the script and stored it as an operating system file.	@ command = script	Run the command whose name you specify in the parameter script.
CONNECT	Connect to a database	Only valid username/password combinations can successfully connect. Users connecting as SYSOPER or SYSDBA must have privileges appropriate to accessing the SYS schema.	CONNECT [user] [password] [path to image] [SYSOPER] [SYSDBA]	*user:* Any valid Oracle username for the current database; *password:* password corresponding to the specified username; *path to image:* A valid specification for an instance/database combination; *SYSOPER:* connect as the system operator; *SYSDBA:* connect as the database administrator; examples: CONNECT; CONNECT scott/tiger; CONNECT scott/tiger AS SYSDBA
DISCONNECT	Disconnect from an Oracle server	You must be connected to a database.	DISCONNECT	Drop the current connection.
EXIT	Exit Server Manager line mode	None	EXIT	Quit line mode.
HOST	Execute an operating system command without exiting linemode	None	HOST cat INIT.ORA	Escape to the OS command line and display the Oracle initialization file.

Continued

Table 10-8 (continued)

Command	Use	Requirements	Syntax	Meaning
SET	Set or change characteristics of the current command-line mode session	None	SET [parameters]	CHARWIDTH integer: Sets column display width for CHAR data; ECHO: ON enables echoing of commands entered from command files. OFF, thedefault, disables echoing of commands; INSTANCE instance-path: Changes the default instance for your session to the specified instance path; LOGSOURCE pathname: Specifies the location from which archive logs are retrieved during recovery; LONGWIDTH integer: Sets column display width for LONG data; MAXDATA integer: Sets maximum data size; NUMWIDTH integer: Sets column display width for NUMBER data; RETRIES integer: Sets number of retry attempts used with the STARTUP command; STOPONERROR ON: If a command file incurs an error, terminate.
SHOW	Show settings currently in effect	None	SHOW	ALL: All settings except for ERRORS, PARAMETERS, and SGA (System Global Area); AUTORECOVERY: If autorecovery is enabled; CHARWIDTH: Column display width for CHAR data; DATEWIDTH: Column display width for DATE data; ECHO: If commands from command files are echoed; INSTANCE: The connect string for the default instance. Returns the value LOCAL if SET INSTANCE has not been used; LOGSOURCE: Archive log location; LONGWIDTH: Column display width for LONG data; MAXDATA: Maximum data size; NUMWIDTH: Column display width for NUMBER data; PARAMETERS: Current values for one or more initialization parameters; RETRIES: Number of retries that will be attempted when restarting an instance in parallel mode; SERVEROUTPUT: Displays ON if output from stored procedures and functions is enabled. Otherwise, displays OFF; SPOOL: If spooling is enabled, displays the name of the output spool file. Otherwise, displays OFF; STOPONERROR: If not errors encountered during execution of command files will stop execution of the file; TERMOUT: If output to the terminal is enabled

Command	Use	Requirements	Syntax	Meaning
SHUTDOWN	Shut down a currently running Oracle instance, optionally closing and dismounting a database	You must be connected to a database as INTERNAL, SYSOPER, or SYSDBA. You cannot be connected via a multithreaded server.	SHUTDOWN	*ABORT:* Fastest possible shutdown. Does not wait for calls to complete or users to disconnect. Does not close or dismount the database, but does shut down the instance. Requires instance recovery on next startup; *IMMEDIATE:* Does not wait for completion of current calls, prohibits further connects, and closes and dismounts the database. Finally, shuts down the instance. Does not wait for connected users to disconnect. Does not require instance recovery on next startup; *NORMAL:* Waits for currently connected users to disconnect, prohibits further connects, and closes and dismounts the database. Finally, shuts down the instance. Does not require instance recovery on next startup. NORMAL is the default.
STARTUP	Start an Oracle instance with any of several options, including mounting and opening a database	You must be connected to a database as INTERNAL, SYSOPER, or SYSDBA. You cannot be connected via a multithreaded server.	STARTUP	*FORCE:* Shuts down the current Oracle instance (if it is running) with SHUTDOWN ABORT, before restarting it, and therefore should normally not be used; *RESTRICT:* Only allows Oracle users with the RESTRICTED SESSION system privilege to connect to the database; *PFILE=filename:* Causes the specified parameter file to be used while starting up the instance; *MOUNT:* Mounts a database but does not open it; *OPEN:* Mounts and opens the specified database; *EXCLUSIVE:* Specifies that the database can only be mounted and opened by the current instance; *PARALLEL:* Must be specified if the database is to be mounted by multiple instances concurrently; *SHARED:* same as PARALLEL

Basic Operations

This section offers a more detailed discussion of common Linux DBMS administrative tasks.

MySQL

This section looks at MySQL's most important administrative features:

✦ Starting the server

✦ Stopping the server

✦ Starting the client

✦ Stopping the client

✦ Creating and deleting databases

✦ Basic security provisions and permissions

✦ Connecting remotely

Starting the server

You can start the MySQL server, that is, the daemon mysqld, in either of two ways.

1. Run the script mysql.server. Most often, this script runs at system startup and shutdown. But when invoked at the command prompt, it can take the arguments start or stop, as these examples illustrate:

```
# mysql.server start
# mysql.server stop
```

In most implementations the script mysql.server is housed in either the subdirectory share/mysql under the main MySQL directory, or the subdirectory support-files of the MySQL source file subsystem.

2. Run the script safe_mysqld, which tries to determine the proper options for the MySQL server daemon mysqld, and then runs the daemon with those options.

In the opinion of many DBMS-saavy folks, running safe_mysqld is the more reliable option.

Before the script mysql.server launches mysqld, it changes directory to the MySQL installation directory, and then itself invokes safe_mysqld. As a result, you may need to edit the script if you've installed to a nonstandard path. Modify mysql.server to use the OS command cd to change to the directory appropriate to your installation before the script runs safe_mysqld. You can, of course, also modify mysql.server to pass any other needed or nonstandard options to safe_mysqld.

Stopping the server

When used in its most common form, the script mysql.server stops the MySQL server by sending a signal to it with the command:

```
mysql.server stop
```

You can also take down mysqld manually with this command:

```
mysqladmin shutdown
```

In addition, you can add appropriate stop (or start) commands to the shell initialization file /etc/rc.local. For example, you could append the following:

```
/bin/sh -c 'cd /usr/local/mysql ; ./bin/safe_mysqld &'
```

Or, if you wish to control the MySQL server globally, you can do so by placing a file called my.cnf in the /etc directory as shown here:

```
[mysqld]
datadir=/usr/local/mysql/var
socket=/tmp/mysqld.sock
port=3456
[mysql.server]
user=mysql
basedir=/usr/local/mysql
```

Table 10-9 defines each line in this sample my.cnf file.

Table 10-9 Understanding my.cnf	
Line	**Effect**
[mysqld]	Identifies all lines that follow until the next line encased in square brackets is encountered as pertaining to the MySQL server daemon mysqld
datadir=/usr/local/mysql/var	Defines the path /use/local/mysql/var as the location of MySQL's data directory
socket=/tmp/mysqld.sock	Defines the file whose full path name is /tmp/mysqld.sock as the TCP/IP socket MySQL's protocols will use

Continued

Line	Effect
Table 10-9 *(continued)*	
port=3456	Defines the port number 3456 as the TCP/IP port MySQL's protocols will use
[mysql.server]	Identifies all lines that follow until the next line encased in square brackets is encountered as pertaining to the script mysql.server
user=mysql	Identifies the user mysql as the user under whose permissions the script will run
basedir=/usr/local/mysql	Identifies the path /use/local/mysql as the starting point which the script will use in seeking DBMS files and commands when it runs

Debugging starting and stopping

However you start mysqld, if it fails to launch correctly, look in the data directory, typically /usr/local/mysql/data for a binary distribution or /usr/local/var for a compiled source distribution, for log files. Such files usually have names of the forms host_name.err or host_name.log, where host_name is the name of your server host.

After you've located these files, use the OS command `tail` to copy the last few lines of each; for example:

```
$ tail doli.err
$ tail doli.log
```

Examine these garnered lines for any references to path-related problems. Failure of mysqld to start properly usually is related to mysqld's being unable to find the MySQL data directory where it expects that directory to be.

What safe_mysqld Wants

safe_mysqld normally can start a server that was installed from either a source or a binary version of MySQL, even if these exist in nonstandard locations. However, safe_mysqld expects one of the following conditions to be true:

✦ The server daemon mysqld and the databases it will present must exist in subdirectories of the directory from which safe_mysqld is invoked.

✦ Should it not find mysqld and its databases relative to its working directory, safe_mysqld must be able to locate them by absolute pathnames, such as /usr/local/libexec or /usr/local/var.

If it turns out that pathing problems have caused mysqld to fail to start correctly, you should then determine what options mysqld expects, and what its default path settings are, by invoking the daemon with the --help option. Then, you can correct any errors by specifying appropriate pathnames as command-line arguments to mysqld.

Tip Normally you only need to tell mysqld the full path name of the base directory under which MySQL was installed. The sample command below, which assumes you're running it from the directory in which the daemon lives, illustrates this process.

```
$ ./mysqld --basedir=/usr/local --help
```

The error

```
Can't start server: Bind on TCP/IP port: Address already in use
```

indicates that some other program, or even another instance of the MySQL server, is already using the TCP/IP port or socket mysqld is trying to access. To correct this problem, take these steps.

1. Run the operating system command ps to determine if another mysqld server is running.

2. If such a superfluous server is running, stop it with the OS command

   ```
   kill PID
   ```

   replacing the generic parameter PID with the process ID number reported by ps for the superfluous server.

3. If no extra copies of mysqld are running, rerun ps, this time looking for such processes as telnet or ftp. It's a pretty good bet that one of these is using the port or socket mysqld wants.

Tip Should it be safe_mysqld that fails to start properly, even when invoked from the MySQL installation directory, it, too, can be modified. Just supply the correct path to mysqld and any other path names it needs to function correctly.

Starting the client: connecting to the server

Starting a MySQL client is synonymous with causing that client to connect to its MySQL server. Do so with a command like this:

```
$ mysql trek_trivia
```

Replace the fictitious database name trek_trivia with the name of the database you wish to access.

mysql is a simple SQL shell that is usable either interactively or in batch fashion. When used interactively, mysql displays the results of any queries to it as an ASCII table. When used in a batch mode, that is, through a script of some kind, mysql presents its results in a tab-separated format.

Table 10-10 summarizes MySQL's most useful options.

Table 10-10 mysql Options		
Option	*Sample Syntax*	*Effect*
-B or --batch	mysql --batch	Display results separated by tabs, with each record on a new line.
-C or --compress	mysql --compress	Use compression in client/server exchanges.
-D or --database=name	mysql --database= eastern_thought	Start mysql with the indicated database (eastern_thought in this example) already loaded.
-e or --execute=command	mysql -e 'CREATE TABLE trek_good_guys(id INT, name VARCHAR(20))' trek_trivia	Starts mysql, executes the indicated command, and then quits.
-h or --host=...	mysql –h=some_machine	Connects to the indicated host, in this example one named some_machine.
-H or --html	mysql --hyml	Produces HTML output.
-ppassword or --password=...	mysql -pabcdef	Connect to the MySQL - server with the privileges associated with the indicated password.
-q or --quick	Print results one record at a time, rather than caching them first.	-t or --table
mysql -t < some_query > some_output_file	Present output in table format. Because such format is the default, this option is only useful when running mysql in batch mode.	-u or --user= ...
mysql -u root	Connect to the MySQL server and with the privileges of the indicated user.	-w or --wait
mysql --wait	Should the attempt to connect to the MySQL server abort, wait a bit, and then retry connecting.	

You must distinguish mysql commands from mysql options. Table 10-11 discusses the most important mysql commands, and gives examples of each.

	Table 10-11 Important mysql Commands	
Command	**Example**	**Effect**
connect	mysql connect	Reconnects to the active server, with the (optional) database specified by the argument db=. Or, connect to the MySQL server on the host indicated by the optional argument host=.
exit	mysql exit	Terminates the mysql session.
source	mysql source some_file_name	Executes the SQL script file whose name is given as an argument.
status	mysql status	Displays status information on the MySQL server.
use	mysql use pittsburgh_pirates	Uses the named database.

Tip   Any mysql command can be run from either the operating system command line, with the initial keyword mysql, as illustrated in Table 10-8, or from within a mysql session, at the mysql prompt mysql>.

Stopping the client

From the system administrator's perspective, a MySQL session is nothing more than a user-initiated process running under Linux. As such, you have two methods available for terminating a MySQL client.

1. Use the operating system command ps to obtain the process ID or PID of the MySQL client you wish to kill; then supply that PID to the kill command to terminate the session. Figure 10-1 below illustrates.

```
#
#
#
#
# kill 6135
kill: 6135: The specified process does not exist.
#
#
#
#
# _
```

Figure 10-1: By the time we supplied the appropriate process ID to the command kill, the process in question, that is, the client session, had already ended.

2. Use the mysql commands process list and `kill` to terminate the client.

Creating and deleting databases

In MySQL, you can create or delete databases from the operating system command line with the utility mysqladmin, or from within a MySQL session.

From the OS command line, use syntax similar to this:

```
# mysqladmin CREATE DATABASE IF NOT EXISTS pittsburgh_pirates
```

Such a command would create a new, empty database called pittsburgh_pirates if no such database already exists.

From within a MySQL session, use a command similar to this at the mysql prompt to accomplish the same thing.

```
mysql> CREATE DATABASE IF NOT EXISTS pittsburgh_pirates
```

Basic security provisions

To use the mysql client to set up new users, you must be logged in as the root user to the same machine on which mysqld runs. In addition, you must have ensured, prior to the login in question, that the root user has the insert privilege for the mysql database and also has the more general reload privilege.

MySQL offers two means of establishing new users and defining their access privileges within MySQL:

✦ Using GRANT statements at the mysql prompt

✦ Manipulating MySQL grant tables directly

The following code fragment illustrates using GRANT statements to establish new users and their MySQL privileges:

```
$ mysql --user=root
mysql> GRANT ALL PRIVILEGES ON *.* TO someone@somewhere
IDENTIFIED BY 'their_password' WITH GRANT OPTION;
mysql> GRANT ALL PRIVILEGES ON *.* TO someone@"%" IDENTIFIED BY
'their_password' WITH GRANT OPTION;
mysql> GRANT RELOAD,PROCESS ON *.* TO admin@localhost;
mysql> GRANT USAGE ON *.* TO dummy@localhost;
```

Table 10-12 elaborates on these commands.

Table 10-12
The GRANT Command

Example	Effect
$ mysql --user=root mysql	Connect to MySQL as the root user.
mysql> GRANT ALL PRIVILEGES ON *.* TO someone@somewhere IDENTIFIED BY 'their_password' WITH GRANT OPTION;	Give the user someone, who connects from the host called somewhere, all available privileges on all databases. Furthermore, allow them to grant privileges to other users, but require them to connect to MySQL with a password.
mysql> GRANT ALL PRIVILEGES ON *.* TO someone@"%" IDENTIFIED BY 'their_password' WITH GRANT OPTION;	Give the user someone, no matter from where the user someone connects, all available privileges on all databases. Furthermore, allow them to grant privileges to other users, but require them to connect to MySQL with a password.
GRANT RELOAD,PROCESS ON *.* TO admin@localhost;	Define a user who can connect to the MySQL server on the local machine, that is, on localhost, without having to supply a password. Assign this user the administrative privileges reload and process. These privileges enable a user to reload or refresh a database, or to flush a number of its features such as logs. However, this command does not give the defined user any database-related privileges.
GRANT USAGE ON *.* TO dummy@localhost;	Define a user who can connect to the MySQL server on the local machine, that is, on localhost, without having to supply a password. However, give this user the ability to do absolutely nothing; the USAGE privilege assigns no privileges.

The second means of adding or modifying user privilege information is to use the INSERT command directly to modify MySQL's user table, and then to use the RELOAD command to refresh MySQL's grant tables. To grant an existing user additional or new privileges, use GRANT statements similar to these:

```
$ mysql --user=root mysql
mysql> GRANT SELECT,INSERT,UPDATE,DELETE,CREATE,DROP
ON trek_trivia.*
TO somebody@somehost IDENTIFIED BY 'captain';
mysql> FLUSH PRIVILEGES;
```

To modify an existing user's privileges using GRANT statements, use commands similar to these:

```
$ mysql --user=root mysql
mysql> INSERT INTO user (Host,User,Password)
VALUES('localhost','somebody',PASSWORD('captain'));
mysql> INSERT INTO db
(Host,Db,User,Select_priv,Insert_priv,Update_priv,Delete_priv,
Create_priv,Drop_priv)
VALUES('localhost','trek_rtivia','somebody','Y','Y','Y','Y','Y'
,'Y');
mysql> FLUSH PRIVILEGES;
```

Tip   There are three utilities on the MySQL Web site in the Contrib directory that you can also use to insert, change, and update values in grant tables: xmysqladmin, mysql_webadmin, and xmysql.

Connecting remotely

To connect to MySQL on a remote machine, use syntax similar to this:

```
$ mysql -h library -u ref_desk
```

Having connected, you're ready to carry out tasks such as:

✦ Verifying connections

✦ Verifying requests

✦ Securing connections

The MySQL Project has a number of concerns about and recommendations for ensuring the security of remote connections to a MySQL server. When running MySQL, follow these guidelines whenever possible.

✦ Learn the MySQL access privilege system. The GRANT and REVOKE commands are used for restricting access to MySQL. Do not grant any more privileges than are necessary. Never grant privileges to all hosts.

✦ Try mysql –u root. If you are able to connect successfully to the server without being asked for a password, you have problems. Set a root password.

✦ Use the command SHOW GRANTS and check to see who has access to what. Remove those privileges that are not necessary using the REVOKE command.

✦ Consider having your application connect to the database using a different username than the one you use for administrative purposes. Do not give your applications any more access privileges than what they need.

Verifying connections

When you attempt to connect to a MySQL server, the server accepts or rejects the connection based on your identity and whether or not you can verify your identity by supplying the correct password. If not, the server denies access to you completely. Otherwise, the server accepts the connection, and waits for requests.

Your identity is based on two pieces of information—the host from which you connect and your MySQL username.

The server accepts the connection only if a user table entry matches your host name and username, and you supply the correct password.

The following example illustrates how several combinations of Host and User values in user table entries apply to incoming connections–

```
'thomas.loc.gov'
'fred'
fred, connecting from thomas.loc.gov
'thomas.loc.gov'
''
Any user, connecting from thomas.loc.gov
'%'
'fred'
fred, connecting from any host
'%'
''
Any user, connecting from any host
'144.155.166.177'
'fred'
fred, connecting from the host with IP address 144.155.166.177
```

Tip   In an effort to preclude hacking attempts based upon this syntax, MySQL will not match host names that start with digits and a dot.

When a connection is attempted, the server looks through the sorted entries and uses the first match found.

Verifying requests

After you establish a connection, the server enters stage 2. For each request that comes in on the connection, the server checks whether you have sufficient privileges to perform it, based on the type of operation that you wish to perform. This is where the privilege fields in the grant tables come into play. These privileges can come from any of the user, db, host, tables_priv, or columns_priv tables. The grant tables are manipulated with GRANT and REVOKE commands.

For administrative requests (shutdown, reload, and so on), the server checks only the user table entry, because that is the only table that specifies administrative privileges. Access is granted if the entry allows the requested operation and denied otherwise. For example, if you want to execute mysqladmin shutdown but your user table entry doesn't grant the shutdown privilege to you, access is denied without even checking the db or host tables. (They contain no Shutdown_priv column, so there is no need to do so.)

For database-related requests (insert, update, etc.), the server first checks the user's global (superuser) privileges by looking in the user table entry. If the entry allows the requested operation, access is granted. If the global privileges in the user table are insufficient, the server determines the user's database-specific privileges by checking the db and host tables.

Securing remote connections

To make a MySQL system secure, follow these suggestions.

1. Use passwords for all MySQL users. Remember that anyone can log in as any other person.

```
$ mysql -u root mysql
mysql> UPDATE user SET Password=PASSWORD('new_password')
WHERE user='root';
mysql> FLUSH PRIVILEGES;
```

2. Don't run the MySQL daemon as the UNIX root user. mysqld can be run as any user. You can also create a new UNIX user mysql to make everything even more secure. If you run mysqld as another UNIX user, you don't need to change the root username in the user table, because MySQL usernames have nothing to do with UNIX usernames. You can edit the mysql.server script to start mysqld as another UNIX user. Normally this is done with the su command.

3. Check that the UNIX user that mysqld runs as is the only user with read/write privileges in the database directories.

4. On UNIX platforms, do not run mysqld as root unless you really need to. Consider creating a user named mysql for that purpose.

5. Don't give the process privilege to all users. The output of mysqladmin process list shows the text of the currently executing queries, so any user who is allowed to execute that command could see whether another user issues an UPDATE user SET password=PASSWORD('not_secure') query. mysqld reserves an extra connection for users who have the process privilege, so that a MySQL root user can log in and check things even if all normal connections are in use.

6. Don't give the file privilege to all users. Any user that has this privilege can write a file anywhere in the file system with the privileges of the mysqld daemon! To make this a bit safer, all files generated with SELECT . . . INTO OUTFILE are readable by everyone, and you can't overwrite existing files. The file privilege may also be used to read any file accessible to the UNIX user that the server runs as. This could be abused, for example, by using LOAD DATA to load /etc/passwd into a table, which can then be read with SELECT.

7. Finally, you can launch mysqld with command line options that affect security. Table 10-13 summarizes what we consider the most important such options.

Table 10-13
mysqld Security-Related Options

Option	Effect
--secure	IP numbers returned by the `gethostbyname()` system call are checked to make sure that they resolve back to the original host name. This makes it harder for someone on the outside to get access by pretending to be another host. This option also adds some sanity checks of host names.
--skip-grant-tables	Causes the server not to use the privilege system at all. This gives everyone full access to all databases! (You can tell a running server to start using the grant tables again by executing mysqladmin flush-privileges or mysqladmin reload.)
--skip-name-resolve	Host names are not resolved. All Host column values in the grant tables must be IP numbers or localhost.
--skip-networking	Don't allow TCP/IP connections over the network. All connections to mysqld must be made via UNIX sockets. This option is unsuitable for systems that use MIT-pthreads, because the MIT-pthreads package doesn't support UNIX sockets.

PostgreSQL

This section details PostgreSQL's most important administrative features:

✦ Starting and stopping the server

✦ Starting and stopping the client

✦ Creating and deleting databases

✦ Basic security provisions and permissions

✦ Connecting remotely

Starting and stopping the server

PostgreSQL enables you to launch or stop both multi- and single-user servers.

Multiuser server

postmaster, the PostgreSQL multiuser backend to the database server, manages conversations between client and server, and allocates memory and other system resources. postmaster does not itself interact with the user; furthermore, it must be started as a background process. And, only one postmaster should be running within a file subsystem at any given time. However, you can run more than one postmaster if each occupies its own directory and uses a distinct port number.

Generic syntax to start postmaster with its most useful features looks similar to this:

```
postmaster [ -D data directory ] [ -N maximum number of servers
] [ -i ] [ -p port number ]
```

Here's a rundown of this syntax and its effects.

✦ **-D data directory**—Identifies the root of the set of database directories

✦ **-N maximum number of servers**—Sets the maximum number of server processes that the postmaster may start; default is 32, but can be set as high as 1024

✦ **-I**—Permits TCP/IP connections

✦ **-p port**—Identifies the TCP/IP port or local socket file extension on which the postmaster should listen

These sample commands start a multiuser postmaster:

```
% nohup postmaster >logfile
#Starts postmaster on the default port, sending system messages
#regarding the launch to a file in the active directory called
#logfile
% nohup postmaster -p 1234 &
#Starts postmaster on the indicated port
```

To stop a multiuser server, use a command similar to this:

```
% kill -15 process ID of the server you want to kill
```

Such syntax will stop postmaster, but not before it can release system resources such as shared memory.

Startup Scripts

Startup scripts, commonly known as rc files, can be used to kickstart software that should be up and running as soon as a Linux machine boots. One example of using such a file to start the PostgreSQL postmaster might be:

```
#
#! /bin/sh
# postgresql    This is the init script for starting up the
PostgreSQL server
# Version 6.5.3-2 Lamar Owen
# description: Starts and stops the PostgreSQL backend daemon
that handles all database requests.
# processname: postmaster
# pidfile: /var/run/postmaster.pid
#
```

```
# Source function library.
. /etc/rc.d/init.d/functions

# Get config.
. /etc/sysconfig/network

# Check that networking is up.
# Pretty much need it for postmaster.
[ ${NETWORKING} = "no" ] && exit 0

[ -f /usr/bin/postmaster ] || exit 0

# This script is slightly unusual in that the name of the daemon
(postmaster)
# is not the same as the name of the subsystem (postgresql)

case "$1" in
  start)
        echo -n "Checking postgresql installation: "
        # Check for the PGDATA structure
        if [ -f /var/lib/pgsql/PG_VERSION ] && [ -d /var/lib/
pgsql/base/template1 ]
        then
        # Check version of existing PGDATA

                if [ `cat /var/lib/pgsql/PG_VERSION` != '6.5' ]
                then
                        echo "old version. Need to Upgrade."
                        echo "See /usr/doc/postgresql-
6.5.3/README.rpm for more information."
                        exit 1
                else
                        echo "looks good!"
                fi

        # No existing PGDATA! Initdb it.

        else
                echo "no database files found."
                if [ ! -d /var/lib/pgsql ]
                then
                        mkdir -p /var/lib/pgsql
                        chown postgres.postgres /var/lib/pgsql
                fi
                su -l postgres -c '/usr/bin/initdb --pglib=/usr/
lib/pgsql --pgdata=/var/lib/pgsql'
```

Continued

Continued

```
        fi
        # Check for postmaster already running...
        pid=`pidof postmaster`
        if [ $pid ]
        then
                echo "Postmaster already running."
        else
                #all systems go -- remove any stale lock files
                rm -f /tmp/.s.PGSQL.* > /dev/null
                echo -n "Starting postgresql service: "
                su -l postgres -c '/usr/bin/postmaster -i -S -
D/var/lib/pgsql'
                sleep 1
                pid=`pidof postmaster`
                if [ $pid ]
                then
                        echo -n "postmaster [$pid]"
                        touch /var/lock/subsys/postgresql
                        echo $pid > /var/run/postmaster.pid
                        echo
                else
                        echo "failed."
                fi
        fi
        ;;
  stop)
        echo -n "Stopping postgresql service: "
        killproc postmaster
        sleep 2
        rm -f /var/run/postmaster.pid
        rm -f /var/lock/subsys/postgresql
        echo
        ;;
  status)
        status postmaster
        ;;
  restart)
        $0 stop
        $0 start
        ;;
  *)
        echo "Usage: postgresql {start|stop|status|restart}"
        exit 1
esac

exit 0
```

Single-user server

The command `postgres` starts a single-user database server. A single-user server need not be run in the background and offers different arguments than its multiuser peer.

Generic syntax for the most useful postgres single-user server features looks similar to this:

```
postgres [ -D data directory ] [ -E ] [-S sorting memory size ]
[ -e ] [ -o output file ] [ -s ] [database name ]
```

Let's look more closely at this lineup.

- ✦ **-D data directory** — Specifies the root of the set of database directories
- ✦ **-E** — Echoes all queries
- ✦ **-S sorting memory size** — Specifies the amount of memory available to sorting and hashing operations before disk caches will be drawn upon
- ✦ **-e** — If supplied, this option passes dates to and from the client in European or dd-mm-yyyy format
- ✦ **-o OutputFile** — Sends all debugging and error output to the indicated file
- ✦ **-s** — Places statistics, including time of run, at the end of each query
- ✦ **database name** — Specifies the name of the database to be served out by postgres; defaults to the value of the USER environment variable

Caution
While the postgres backend most frequently runs directly from the shell rather than in background, don't run it in this way, that is in foreground, if multiple post-masters, each servicing an individual PostgreSQL server, access the same set of databases intended for the postgres backend you're working with.

pg_ctl

PostgreSQL offers another utility, pg_ctl, with which you can start, stop, restart, or find the status of a postmaster. Its generic syntax comes in four flavors:

```
pg_ctl [-w] [-D datadir][-p path] [-o "options"] start
pg_ctl [-w] [-D datadir] [-m [s[mart]|f[ast]|i[mmediate]]] stop
pg_ctl [-w] [-D datadir] [-m [s[mart]|f[ast]|i[mmediate]]] [-o
"options"] restart
pg_ctl [-D datadir] status
```

Table 10-14 elaborates on these syntax elements.

Table 10-14
Understanding pg_ctl

Element	Effect
-w	Waits for the database server to come up.; times out after 60 seconds.
-D datadir	Specifies database location.
-p path	Specifies the path to the postmaster executable image.
-o options	Specifies options to be passed directly to postmaster. Options usually are embedded in single or double quotes to ensure that they are passed to postmaster as a group.
-m mode	Specifies the shutdown mode: *smart* or *s*—smart mode: wait for all clients to log out; *fast* or *f*—fast mode: rolls back active transactions; *immediate* or *i*—immediate mode: aborts backend processes, necessitating database recovery at next startup.
start	Starts postmaster.
stop	Shuts down postmaster.
restart	Restarts postmaster, that is carries out a complete stop/start cycle.
status	Shows postmaster's current status; output is of the form: `pg_ctl: postmaster is running (pid: 1234567)` In addition to running, a postmaster's status may be reported as sleeping.

Some examples of pg_ctl's use follow. All assume the default PostgreSQL prompt.

✦ `> pg_ctl start`—A no-frills startup

✦ `> pg_ctl -w start`—Starts postmaster but blocks any requests to it until it has been confirmed to be running

✦ `> pg_ctl -p /usr/local/pgsq/bin/postmaster start`—Starts postmaster with the full path of its binaries specified

✦ `> pg_ctl -o "-p 5433" start`—Starts postmaster on a specific port

The following are some examples of stopping a postmaster with pg_ctl:

✦ > pg_ctl stop — No-frills stop

✦ > pg_ctl -m smart stop — Stops postmaster after waiting for all clients to log out

The following examples use pg_ctl to restart a postmaster:

✦ > pg_ctl restart — No-frills restart

✦ > pg_ctl -w restart — Restarts postmaster after blocking any requests to it until postmaster is confirmed to have shut down and to have restarted. The "w" stands for "wait," appropriately enough, and precludes abrupt and possibly problematic disconnecting of clients that are still engaged in completing a transaction.

Finally, to use pg_ctl to get some basic information about a postmaster's status, use the following command:

```
> pg_ctl status
```

Such a command might produce output similar to this:

```
pg_ctl: postmaster is running (pid: 13718)
options are:
/usr/local/src/pgsql/current/bin/postmaster
-p 5433
-D /usr/local/src/pgsql/current/data
-b /usr/local/src/pgsql/current/bin/postgres
-N 32
```

Starting and stopping the client

A single command, psql, initiates or terminates PostgreSQL client sessions. Its generic syntax looks like this:

```
psql [ options ] [ database name [ user name ] ]
```

As this syntax indicates, you supply the name of the database to which you wish to connect. You can use these options to make the connect more efficient:

✦ hostname of the PostgreSQL server to which you wish to connect

✦ port number on the PostgreSQL server through which you wish to connect

✦ username under which you wish to connect

psql accepts these parameters under the respective options:

✦ -d: database

✦ -h: host

✦ -p: port

✦ -U: user

Tip   Be careful in supplying these psql options and their arguments. Should an argument be presented to psql that it cannot understand, psql assumes that argument is a database or username, which might induce errors.

For example, the command

```
$ psql blues_db
```

results in a display similar to this:

```
Welcome to psql, the PostgreSQL interactive terminal.

Type:  \copyright for distribution terms
       \h for help with SQL commands
       \? for help on internal slash commands
       \g or terminate with semicolon to execute query
       \q to quit

blues_db=>
```

At the prompt, which as shown above includes the name of the active database, a user may type queries or commands. Some of the most useful psql commands include:

✦ \connect (or \c) [database name [user name]]—Connect to a new database under the indicated user name, first closing the existing connection.

✦ \H—Toggle HTML output format for queries on, or off if this format is already in use.

✦ \i file—Takes as input from the indicated file commands to be executed.

✦ \l or \list—Lists all databases and their owners that are on the server.

✦ \q—Quits psql.

Creating and deleting databases

PostgreSQL offers a number of commands that pertain to creating and deleting databases; this section explores them.

initdb

initdb creates a new PostgreSQL database installation; that is, a new collection of postgres databases that are all:

✦ Administered by the same user

✦ Distributed by a single postmaster

Generic syntax for initdb that reflects its most significant options is:

```
initdb [ --pgdata=data directory or -D data directory ] [ --
pwprompt or -W ] [ --pglib=directory name or -L directory name]
```

Let's examine these parameters more closely.

✦ --pgdata=data directory or -D data directory—Specifies where in the file system the database should be stored

✦ --pwprompt or -W—Causes initdb to prompt for the password of the database superuser

✦ --pglib=directory name or -l directory name—Tells initdb where to find initialization files

To create a database system, you:

✦ Create the directories in which the database data will live.

✦ Generate shared catalog tables; that is, tables that don't belong to any particular database.

✦ Create the template1 database, which, as its name suggests, serves as the blueprint for all new PostgreSQL databases that you create thereafter. template1 houses tables that supply such facets as built-in data-type definitions.

Caution Never run initdb as root. You cannot run the database server as root, but at the same time, that server needs to access files initdb creates. Therefore, running initdb as root might assign ownership of needed files to root, and thereby block access to those files for other users. What's more, during initialization, before users or access controls have been created, postgres will only connect under the account that will own the server process.

initlocation

The command initlocation establishes a secondary PostgreSQL storage area. initlocation takes only one argument: a directory or full path name.

A sample of initlocation looks similar to this:

```
initlocation /usr/local/src/pgsql/current/data2
```

Caution   To use `initlocation`, you must be logged in as the database superuser.

Tip   On some platforms, that is, on those flavors of Linux that use the bash shell, a near-doppelganger for the Bourne shell, you can also create a secondary database storage area at least partially from the operating system, as the following example shows.

```
$ export PGDATA2=/opt/postgres/data
$ initlocation PGDATA2
```

Alternatively, you could use absolute paths:

```
$ initlocation /opt/postgres/data
```

dropdb

As its name suggests, the command `dropdb` deletes an existing postgres database. The generic syntax of its most useful elements is:

```
dropdb [ -h host name or -- host host name] [ -p port number or
--port port number] [ -U user name or - username user name] [ -
W or -- password] [ -i or --interactive] dbname
```

These parameters have these effects:

- ✦ `-h` or `-host` — Host name of the machine on which the postmaster controlling the database to be deleted is running
- ✦ `-p` or `-port` — TCP/IP port or local socket file extension on which the post-master controlling the database to be deleted listens
- ✦ `-U` or `-username` — User name under which you wish to connect in order to delete a database
- ✦ `-W` or `-password` — Force a prompt for the database superuser password
- ✦ `-i` or `-interactive` — Issues a verification prompt before doing anything destructive
- ✦ `dbname` — Name of the database to be removed

If you see the message

```
DROP DATABASE
```

after running `dropdb`, you'll know that the database you told it to delete was indeed removed. However, if you see this message :

```
dropdb: Database removal failed.
```

you'll know that `dropdb` failed.

Tip

Because `dropdb` destroys an existing database, it only stands to reason that you must be either the database superuser or the owner of the database to be deleted to run `dropdb`.

`dropdb` is actually a shell script wrapper around the SQL command `DROP DATABASE`, which, in turn, runs under `psql`. As a result:

✦ `dropdb` must be able to find `psql`

✦ A database server must be active on the host `dropdb` and `psql` target

✦ All default settings and environment variables used by `psql` or the PostgreSQL client library libpq will apply to `dropdb`

Here are a few examples of using `dropdb`:

✦ `$ dropdb eastern_thought`—Deletes the database eastern_thought on the default PostgreSQL server

✦ `$ dropdb -p 5678 -h pets -i cats`—Deletes the database cats, which runs under the postmaster on host pets, which listens at port 5678; results in a display similar to this:

```
Database "cats" will be permanently deleted.
Are you sure? (y/n) y
DROP DATABASE "cats"
DROP DATABASE
```

Basic security

PostgreSQL is nothing if not straightforward in its naming of its most important user management tools—`createuser`, executed as CREATE USER, and `dropuser`, executed as DROP USER.

createuser

`createuser` creates a new postgres user. Only users with the account characteristic usesuper enabled, that is, only users who can temporarily take on superuser privileges, can create new postgres users. `createuser` is actually a shell script wrapper that can be run under `psql` for the SQL command `CREATE USER`. Therefore, `createuser` requires that

✦ It must be able to find `psql`

✦ A database server must be running on a targeted host

✦ Any default settings and environment variables available to `psql` and the libpq front-end library be applied to `createuser`

`createuser`'s general syntax is quite simple:

```
createuser [ options ] [ user name ]
```

`createuser`'s most important options are:

- ✦ `-h host name` or `--host host name`—Host name of the machine on which you wish to create a user
- ✦ `-p port number` or `--port port number`—TCP/IP port or local UNIX domain socket file extension on which the postmaster for the database in which you wish to create a user listens
- ✦ `-d` or `--createdb`—Creates a new user who can create databases
- ✦ `-D` or `--no-createdb`—Creates a new user who cannot create databases
- ✦ `-a` or `--adduser`—Creates a new user who can create other users
- ✦ `-A` or `--no-adduser`—Creates a new user who cannot create other users
- ✦ `-P` or `--pwprompt`—Causes `createuser` to issue a prompt for the password of user being created
- ✦ `username`—Name of the postgres user being created, which must be unique among all postgres users; you will be prompted for a username if you fail to specify it from the command line when running `createuser`

Now let's look at some examples of using `createuser`.

- ✦ `$ createuser tom`—Creates a new user tom on the default database server; produces the following display:

```
Is the new user allowed to create databases? (y/n) n
Shall the new user be allowed to create more new users? (y/n) n
CREATE USER
```

- ✦ `$ createuser -p 5678 -h nirvana -D -A wheeley`—Creates the user wheeley using the postmaster on the host nirvana, which listens to port 5678, and bypasses prompts concerning wheeley's capability to create databases or other users by supplying the `-D` and `-A` options; results in this display:

```
CREATE USER "wheeley" NOCREATEDB NOCREATEUSER
```

As you've probably deduced, the message

```
CREATE USER
```

indicates that `createuser` ran successfully. Had it encountered any problems, you'd instead have seen something similar to this.

```
createuser: creation of user "username" failed
```

dropuser

dropuser removes an existing postgres user and the databases owned by that user. Only users with usesuper set can destroy postgres users.

Like its counterpart that expedites adding users, dropuser is a shell script wrapper around the SQL command DROP USER that runs from psql. As a result, dropuser must:

✦ Be able to find psql

✦ Be able to connect to a database server at any indicated host

✦ Apply to itself any default settings and environment variables available to psql and the libpq front-end library

dropuser's syntax mirrors that of createuser:

```
dropuser [ options ] [ username ]
```

These are the parameters usable with dropuser:

✦ -h host name or --host host name — Name of the machine on which post-master runs through which dropuser will work

✦ -p port number or --port port number — TCP/IP port or local UNIX domain socket file extension on which the postmaster listens for connections

✦ -i or --interactive — Prompts for confirmation before actually removing a user

✦ username — Name of the postgres user to be removed, which name must exist in the postgres installation; you will be prompted for a name if none is specified on the command line

The next two examples illustrate how dropuser is used:

✦ To remove user leo from the default database server

```
$ dropuser leo
```

✦ To remove user elmo using the postmaster listening at port 3456 on the host called federation, but only after prompting for and receiving confirmation

```
$ dropuser -p 3456 -h federation -i elmo
User "elmo" and any owned databases will be permanently
deleted.
Are you sure? (y/n) y
DROP USER "elmo"
DROP USER
```

As the last example above indicates, the response

```
DROP USER
```

tells you that `dropuser` executed successfully. The message

```
dropuser: deletion of user "elmo" failed
```

would have told you something had gone wrong, and that elmo had not been deleted as a PostgreSQL user.

pg_passwd

The utility pg_passwd manipulates some of PostgreSQL's password file functionality, one of the suite's several supported security mechanisms.

Entries in the password file must adhere to the conventions used for identity authentication in the PostgreSQL configuration file pg_hba.conf. Its format is:

```
host db 123.45.67.250 255.255.255.255 password passwd
```

In such a line:

- ✦ The first field represents the host to which a user may be authenticated
- ✦ The second field represents the database to be accessed
- ✦ The third and fourth fields indicate that a user may connect from the IP address 123.45.67.250 and the subnet address 255.255.255.255, that is, any subnet
- ✦ The fifth field indicates that a password will be required
- ✦ The final field specifies that any of the passwords found in the PostgreSQL password file will be accepted

The PostgreSQL password file uses the same format as the operating system password files /etc/passwd and /etc/shadow. Thus, the PostgreSQL password file consists of records made up of two fields.

- ✦ The first field contains a username
- ✦ The second field holds the accompanying, encrypted password

Such records might look similar to this:

```
some_one:/wnsargset6435
somebody_else:/ v398476h#e+wq::/home/somebody_else:/bin/tcsh
```

> **Tip** The second, more extensive sample above also defines a home directory and default shell for the user in question.

Given these supporting files and formats, running pg_passwd looks similar to this:

```
% pg_passwd passwd
Username: some_one
Password:
Re-enter password:
```

When pg_passwd runs in this way, it does more than change the PostgreSQL password of the indicated user. It also causes the previous version of the DBMS password file to be renamed to passwd.bk.

User authentication

In PostgreSQL, authentication means that the server and postmaster ensure that the user requesting access to data is in fact who the user claims to be. All users who invoke postgres must be cleared to do so. However, verification of the user's actual identity can take place in either of two ways.

1. From the user shell: A backend server started from a user shell notes the user's effective, as opposed to OS login, ID, and changes the identity of the user attempting to connect to PostgreSQL to that of the user postgres. However, the retained, effective user ID serves is used as the basis for subsequent access control checks. No other authentication takes place.

2. From the network: When PostgreSQL is distributed, any of its users by definition have access to the TCP/IP port at which the postmaster listens. As a result, such implementations must include a configuration file pg_hba.conf file which specifies what authentication method will be used. These definitions, in turn, rely on the nature of the host attempting the connection and the database that host is attempting to access.

Authentication types

PostgreSQL supports several authentication methods for both UNIX and TCP/IP domain sockets:

✦ **trust** — The connection is allowed unconditionally.

✦ **reject** — The connection is rejected unconditionally.

✦ **crypt** — The user must supply a password, which is transmitted to the server encrypted, using the operating system call crypt(3), and at the server it is compared to that user's password as it appears in the pg_shadow table. If the passwords match, the connection is allowed.

✦ **password** — The user must supply a password, which is, however, transmitted to the server in the clear, where it is compared to the user's password as it appears in pg_shadow. If the passwords match, the connection is allowed. An optional password file may be specified after the password keyword, which is used to match the supplied password rather than the pg_shadow table.

The following example illustrates some of the effects of these authentication methods on the PostgreSQL password file.

```
# Trust any connection via Unix domain sockets.
local    trust
# Trust any connection via TCP/IP from this machine.
host    all     127.0.0.1        255.255.255.255         trust
# This machine cannot be trusted in any way.
host    all     192.168.0.10    255.255.255.0           reject
# This machine can't encrypt, so passwords will be sent in
clear.
host    all     192.168.0.3     255.255.255.0
password
# These machines must send encrypted passwords.
host    all     192.168.0.0     255.255.255.0           crypt
```

Access control

Postgres provides mechanisms to enable users to limit the access that other users can have to their data.

Tip   Database superusers, that is, users who have the environment variable pg_user.usesuper set, silently bypass all access controls, with two exceptions: manual system catalog updates are not permitted if the user does not have pg_user.usecatupd set, and destruction of system catalogs (or modification of their schemas) is never allowed.

Available categories of access include:

✦ Access privilege — Used to limit reading, writing and setting of rules on classes; usually handled by grant or revoke

✦ Class removal and schema modification — Commands that destroy or modify the structure of an existing class, such as alter, drop table, and drop index, only operate for the owner of the class. In addition, such operations are never permitted on system catalogs.

Connecting remotely

As it does with connections to local postmasters, PostgreSQL handles remote connections by what it calls host-based access control. That is, remote connections rely on the configuration file pg_hba.conf, in the PGDATA directory of the PostgreSQL implementation, to control who can connect to where from where.

When Some Encryption Is Better Than None

While crypt(3) is a weak encryption algorithm, some encryption is better than none at all. Most Linux distributions now understand encrypted passwords. More to the point for us:

✦ PostgreSQL supports a number of variants of the MD5 encryption algorithm in addition to crypt(3).

✦ Oracle8*i* supports these encryption algorithms:

• DES (standards-based encryption)

• DES40 (for international encryption)

• RSA RC4 (a very secure, very fast encryption method)

• SSL

✦ MySQL supports both crypt(3) and SSH

Connections made via the Internet or using TCP/IP within an Intranet rest on pg_liba.conf records of the following format.

```
host database TCP/IP address TCP/IP mask authentication method
```

The TCP/IP address that appears in such a record is logically anded, that is, made part of a Boolean expression that translates as both this and this must be true, to the specified TCP/IP mask, and then compared to the TCP/IP address and mask of the client attempting to connect. If the two values are equal, the remainder of the record in question comes into play, defining the method by which the attempt will be authenticated. Should a connection address/mask combination match more than one record, the first such matching record in pg_liba.conf will be used.

Oracle8*i*

This section examines the most important administrative features of Oracle8*i:*

✦ Starting the server

✦ Stopping the server

✦ Starting the client

✦ Stopping the client

✦ Creating and deleting databases

✦ Basic security

✦ Connecting remotely

Starting and stopping the server

Whether you're operating in a graphical or command-line environment, starting and stopping an Oracle8*i* server, that is, an instance or running copy of the server executable, needs almost no effort.

Starting and stopping in Server Manager GUI mode

To start an Oracle8*i* instance in the graphical Server Manager mode, take these steps.

1. Open an SQL Worksheet.

2. Enter a command such as:

   ```
   STARTUP
   ```

   or

   ```
   STARTUP RESTRICT
   ```

   or

   ```
   STARTUP PFILE=some_file
   ```

Refer to Table 10-8 for details on the parameters available to STARTUP.

Starting and stopping in Server Manager line mode

To start an Oracle8*i* instance in the command-line Server Manager mode, simply enter the STARTUP command and any appropriate options at the Server Manager prompt; for example:

```
svrmgr> STARTUP
```

Refer to Table 10-8 for details on the parameters available to STARTUP.

Starting and stopping the client

As is the case with all the DBMSs I've discussed, "starting and stopping a client" under Oracle8*i* is synonymous with "a client connecting to or disconnecting from a server." Whether that's done from the graphical or line modes of Server Manager, it involves the CONNECT and DISCONNECT commands. Consult Table 10-8 for syntax and parameters for each.

Tip   In line mode, if you omit either or both of the parameters *username* and *password*, Server Manager prompts for them.

Tip   In an SQL Worksheet, if you omit the *username* parameter, Server Manager brings up the Connect dialog box.

Creating and deleting databases

Oracle Corporation recommends the following sequence of steps for creating and deleting a database in Server Manager GUI mode:

1. Make complete backups of all existing databases before creating a new database. Backup should include parameter files, datafiles, redo log files, and control files.

2. Any Oracle8*i* database launches by using a parameter file. Each database on your system should have at least one customized parameter file that corresponds only to that database. To create a parameter file for a new database, use the Linux command `cp` to make a copy of the parameter file that Oracle8*i* provided on the distribution media.

3. As part of creating a new database, inspect and edit at least the following parameters of the new parameter file, which should contain the parameters

   ```
   DB_NAME
   DB_DOMAIN
   CONTROL_FILES
   DB_BLOCK_SIZE,
   DB_BLOCK_BUFFERS
   PROCESSES
   ROLLBACK_SEGMENTS
   LICENSE_MAX_SESSIONS
   LICENSE_SESSION_WARNING
   LICENSE_MAX_USERS
   ```

   supplied with values appropriate to your hardware, operating system, and DBMS implementations.

4. If you have other databases, check the instance identifier of the one you're creating. An Oracle8*i* instance identifier must match the value of `DB_NAME` to preclude confusion with other instances during concurrent operations.

5. Start Server Manager; connect to the server as an administrator.

6. Start an instance to be used with the database you're creating by using Server Manager's Startup Database dialog box. In this dialog, choose the Startup Nomount radio button. Upon selecting this button, the instance starts.

Tip   When an instance starts before a database has been created, only a System Global Area and background processes exist for that instance.

7. To create the new database, use the SQL command `CREATE DATABASE`, optionally setting parameters within the statement to name the database, establish maximum numbers of files, name the files and set their sizes, and so on. When you execute a `CREATE DATABASE` command, Oracle performs the following operations:

   • Creates datafiles

   • Creates control files

- Creates redo log files

- Creates SYSTEM tablespace and SYSTEM rollback segment

- Creates data dictionary

- Creates users SYS and SYSTEM

- Specifies the character set in which data will be stored

- Mounts and opens the database for use

Caution   Make sure that the datafiles and redo log files that you specify do not conflict with files of another database.

8. Make a full backup of the new database to ensure that you have a complete set of files from which to recover it.

Creating and deleting in line mode

Command syntax similar to that outlined in Table 10-8 is all that's needed to create a database in Oracle8*i* Server Manager line mode. The following example illustrates this process:

```
CREATE DATABASE mukachevo
LOGFILE
GROUP 1 ('mukachevo_log1a', 'mukachevo_log1b') SIZE 500K,
GROUP 2 ('mukachevo_log2a', 'mukachevo_log2b') SIZE 500K,
DATAFILE 'mukachevo_system' SIZE 10M;
```

The items and information in the example statement above produce a database with the following characteristics:

✦ Names the file mukachevo

✦ Assigns a SYSTEM tablespace to one 10MB datafile named mukachevo_system

✦ Receives two online redo log groups, each containing two 500KB members

Parameters that can be supplied to CREATE DATABASE include:

✦ DB_NAME and DB_DOMAIN—Local name component and logical location within a network structure respectively, which together form a database name that is unique within a network. DB_NAME must be a string of no more than eight characters. During database creation, the value of DB_NAME is recorded in the datafiles, redo log files, and control file of the database. Later attempts to start an instance of or with this database must match DB_NAME. DB_DOMAIN typically equals the name of the organization that owns the database, as in University of Pittsburgh. So, a value for DB_NAME might be

enrollment.pitt

✦ CONTROL_FILES—Include the CONTROL_FILES parameter; set its value to a list of control filenames to use for the new database. Make sure that the filenames listed to CONTROL_FILES match no existing filenames, unless you want Oracle to reuse or overwrite those files.

Oracle Corporation strongly recommends at least two control files, each of them stored on a separate physical drive, for every database you create. Follow these guidelines for such files:

List at least two filenames for the CONTROL_FILES parameter.

Place each control file on separate physical disk drives by fully specifying filenames that refer to different disk drives for each filename.

✦ DB_BLOCK_SIZE—Default data block size for any Oracle8i server depends on operating system block size, but usually equals either 2K or 4K. Only when dealing with a system with a lot of memory and speedy drives, but with a small operating system block size, should that block size be increased.

✦ DB_BLOCK_BUFFERS—Number of buffers in the buffer cache in the System Global Area. Larger cache size reduces the number of disk writes needed to record modified data. On the downside, though, a large cache may take up too much memory and might induce memory paging or swapping, or even thrashing. Estimate the number of data blocks that your application uses most regularly; include table, index, and rollback processing in this estimate, which is a rough approximation of the minimum number of buffers the cache should have. Typically, between 1000 and 2000 buffers suffice.

Thrashing, one of the more descriptive data processing terms, refers to a system's swapping data in and out of memory so frantically and frequently that the system slows or even hangs.

✦ PROCESSES—The maximum number of operating system processes that can connect to Oracle simultaneously. Must include 5 for background processes and 1 for each user process. So, if you anticipate 35 concurrent users, set PROCESSES to at least 40.

✦ ROLLBACK_ SEGMENTS—A list of the rollback segments an instance acquires at database startup

Rollback segments refers to a system's swapping data in and out of memory so frantically and frequently that the system slows or even hangs.

✦ LICENSE_MAX_ SESSIONS and LICENSE_MAX_USERS—Set a limit on the number of concurrent sessions and concurrent users respectively that can connect to a database. Examples are:

```
LICENSE_MAX_SESSIONS = 50
LICENSE_MAX_USERS = 30
```

Basic security

Oracle8*i,* wisely, in my opinion, relies largely on Linux to provide database security. That is to say, it makes full use of such OS features as file ownership, group accounts, and the capability of a program to change its user ID upon execution. Furthermore, databases can be accessed solely through the Linux technique of shadow passwords. Finally, Oracle8*i* also imposes special authorizations on the database executable.

File ownership

The security of an Oracle8*i* database profits from ownership of all files involved by a user at the Database Administrator or DBA level of permissions. Such ownership helps to ensure that less knowledgeable users cannot, inadvertently or otherwise, do such things as change access permissions for, rename or move, or otherwise alter the nature of Oracle8*i* data, executable, or configuration files.

Groups and users

To create Oracle8*i* users and user groups from Linux, so that those users can be controlled by the OS files /etc/passwd and /etc/group, and so that Oracle executables can be divided, as they were intended to be, into two sets: those executable by any user on the system, or what Linux calls the user type other, and those executable by DBAs only, Oracle Corporation recommends these specific steps:

1. Before installing the Oracle server, create a database administrators' group (dba) and assign the root and oracle software owner IDs to this group. Programs executable by dba only have permission 710. That is, the files containing dba-executable programs can be read from written to, or run by their owner, read but nothing else by members of the owner's user group, and are completely invisible in every way to all other users on the system. And the latter is a good thing, too, because Server Manager system-privileged commands are assigned automatically to the dba group when the Oracle8*i* server is installed.

2. Again, before installing the server, add a Linux user group that consists of users permitted limited access to Oracle8*i* utilities, and assign group ownership of those utilities to this oracle group ID. Publicly executable programs such as SQL*Plus should be executable by this group. Overall, set permissions on such files to 710.

Caution Even though both the oracle software owner and root user should belong to the dba group, the oracle software owner should not be a member of the group to which the operating system user root, often called the superuser, belongs. The only member of the OS root group should be the superuser.

Security for utilities

Oracle Corporation makes these suggestions for protecting Oracle8*i* utilities.

✦ Keep all executables in the bin subdirectory of the main Oracle directory. Give ownership of these files, and of the bin subdirectory in which they live, to the oracle software owner.

✦ Give all user utilities, such as sqlplus, the permission 711, so that every operating system user can at least access the Oracle server.

✦ Give all DBA utilities, such as Server Manager, the permission 700 so that no one other than the DBA user, usually the same as the oracle software owner, even knows that these files exist.

Security for database files

Oracle Corporation makes these recommendations for securing Oracle8*i* database files.

✦ The oracle software owner should also own all database files. Set permissions on these files to 600, ensuring that the files will be readable and writeable only by their owner, and invisible to all other users.

✦ Similarly, the oracle software owner should also own directories containing database files. Set permissions on these directories to 600 as well.

✦ To allow users other than the oracle software owner to access database files and directories protected in this way, turn on the set user ID or setuid bit of these files. This gives other users temporary access to the files by temporarily giving those users some of the permissions of the file owner. Use this command to set the UID bit for these files:

```
$ chmod 6751 $ORACLE_HOME/bin/oracle
```

✦ Then use the Linux command `ls`; you should see a display similar to this. As long as the first ten column positions of this output, that is, the `-rwsr-s--x`, appear as they're shown, you've been successful in this task:

```
-rwsr-s--x 1 oracle dba  443578 Nov 19 13:09 oracle
```

Connecting remotely

Users can access any Oracle8*i* database across an intranet or the Internet if:

✦ An Oracle8*i* password file exists

✦ Remote users have an identity defined in that file as well as in the operating system passwd and shadow files

✦ The remote user either connects to the database with the parameter `INTERNAL` or launches an Oracle application that uses the database

Given this ability of users to connect remotely, the importance of other Oracle administrative tasks such as starting and stopping the server, starting and stopping clients, and managing security becomes paramount.

Summary

Installing and configuring any Linux DBMS requires you to be comfortable with:

✦ Navigating the server console

✦ Starting and stopping the server

✦ Starting and stopping the client

✦ Creating and deleting databases

✦ Providing basic security

✦   ✦   ✦

Linux Database Tools

This chapter discusses administrative tools available to the Linux DBMSs this book examines.

Vendor-Supplied Tools

This section reviews tools supplied by PostgreSQL and MySQL.

Open source tools: PostgreSQL

Although many of PostgreSQL's administrative tools operate in command-line mode, a few exist that provide a GUI interface to administrators. This section summarizes a graphical tool for managing PostgreSQL databases: kpsql.

The third-party product, kpsql, from Mutiny Bay Software at `www.mutinybaysoftware.com/kpsql.html`, is specific to PostgreSQL, and provides a tool similar to Oracle's Server Manager Worksheets. kpsql's features include:

- ✦ Bookmarks
- ✦ Color syntax highlighting for its internal editor
- ✦ Drag-and-drop functionality
- ✦ KDE desktop integration
- ✦ Online Help for PostgreSQL and general SQL questions
- ✦ Query results displayed in HTML tables
- ✦ Search and replace capabilities in its internal editor
- ✦ The capability to execute multiple SQL statements
- ✦ The capability to redirect query output to a file
- ✦ The capability to cancel running queries

kpsql requires:

✦ KDE 1.1+ or higher

✦ PostgreSQL 6.4+ or higher

✦ Qt 1.44+

Caution Be aware that downloads from the Mutiny Bay Web site aren't always tidy. For example, when we downloaded kpsql, we saw the binary stream that is the executable on our PC's monitor as the transfer progressed.

Such GUI-based features can help even the most command-line-challenged, Windows-wedded DB administrator comfortably monitor his or her PostgreSQL implementation.

Open source tools: MySQL

MySQL is even more command-line oriented than PostgreSQL. MySQL offers several significant tools, which are outlined in Table 11-1.

Table 11-1
Selected MySQL Tools

Tool	Use	Sample Syntax
myisamchk	Describes, checks, optimizes, or repairs MySQL tables.	`$ myisamchk [options] table_name` **Significant options:** `-a, --analyze`: **Analyze the distribution of keys.** `-d, --description`: **Displays basic information about the specified table.** `-e, --extend-check`: **Does a very extensive check of the specified table.** `-f, --force`: **Overwrites existing temporary files.** `-i, --information`: **Displays statistics for the specified table.**

Tool	Use	Sample Syntax
		`-l. --no-symlinks`: Causes MvSOL to forego following symbolic links when repairing a table.
		`-r, --recover`: Recovery mode, that repairs numerous database problems.
		`-o. --safe-recover`: Recoverv mode that uses a slower, but in a few cases, more reliable, repair method.
		`-s, --silent`: Silent mode; writes output only upon errors.
		`-S, --sort-index`: Sorts the index in high-low order; used to optimize seeks and make table scanning by key faster.
		`-R index_num, --sort-records=index_num`: Sorts records according to an index, the latter specified by a number. You can determine index numbers with the command `SHOW INDEX`.
		`-u, --unpack`: Unpack a table that was packed with myisampack.
		`-w, --wait`: Wait if a table is locked.
make_binary_release	Creates a binary release of a compiled MySQL. Such files then can be transferred to other users, local or remote, via FTP or other such mechanisms.	`$ make_binary_release`
msql2mysql	Shell script that converts mSQL programs, that is, scripts or SQL files from mSQL, the precursor of MySQL, to MySQL. Handle most but not all such files.	MySQL's documentation suggests this two-step process for using msql2mysql. 1. Run the utility on the msql source. This requires the replace program, which is distributed with MySQL. 2. Recompile.

Continued

Table 11-1 *(continued)*

Tool	Use	Sample Syntax
mysqladmin	Carries out administrative tasks such as creating or dropping databases, reloading the grant tables, flushing tables to disk, and reopening log files.	`$ mysqladmin command [command-option] command ...` Significant commands: `create db_name`: **Create a new database of the specified name.** `drop db_name`: **Delete the specified database and all its tables.** `flush-hosts`: **Flush all cached hosts.** `flush-logs`: **Flush all logs.** `flush-tables`: **Flush all tables.** `flush-privileges`: **Flush all grant tables.** `processlist`: **Display list of active threads in server.** `refresh`: **Flush all tables; close and then immediately reopen logfiles.** `shutdown`: **Stop the MySQL server.**
mysqlbug	Script to be used to file bug reports with the MySQL mailing list.	The MySQL Group states, "We encourage everyone to use the mysqlbug script to generate a bug report (or a report about any problem), if possible. mysqlbug can be found in the scripts directory in the source distribution, or, for a binary distribution, in the bin directory under your MySQL installation directory."
mysqldump	Dumps a MySQL database into an output file which can consist of either SQL statements or tab-separated text.	`$ mysqldump [options] database [tables]` Significant options: `--add-locks`: **Use** `LOCK TABLES` **before and** `UNLOCK TABLE` **after each table dump.** `-A, --all-databases`: **Dump all databases.**

Tool	Use	Sample Syntax
		`-C. --compress`: Compress all information between the client and the server if both support compression.
		`-B. --databases`: Dump several databases. All name arguments are regarded as database names.
		`--delayed`: Insert rows with the `INSERT DELAYED` command.
		`-e, --extended-insert`: Use multiline `INSERT` syntax for more compact and faster inserts.
		-F, --flush-logs: Flush log files on the MySQL server before starting the dump.
		`-f, --force`: Dump even if SQL errors occur during a table dump.
		`-h, --host=`: Dump from the MySQL server on the named host.
		`-l, --lock-tables`: Lock all tables before starting the dump.
		`-d, --no-data`: Write no record information for a table. In effect, a dump of the schema only.
		`-q, --quick`: A quick dump, that is, unbuffered and sent directly to standard output.
mysqlimport	Imports text files into MySQL tables.	`$ mysqlimport [options] database_name` (to be imported to) `text_iunput_file` (to be imported from)
mysqlshow	Displays information about MySQL databases, tables, columns and indices.	`$ mysqlshow [options] [database [table [column]]]`
replace	Utility used by msql2mysql, but which also has more general applicability. Changes strings in place in files or on standard input. Used to modify strings.	`$ replace a b b a -- file1 file2`

Particularly significant to any DBMS administrator are:

✦ myisamchk, since it contributes to table integrity

✦ mysqladmin, since it is central to day-to-day administrative tasks

✦ mysqlimport, since it allows the manager to bring text files into MySQL tables easily

✦ mysqlshow, needed if you want to see stats on the components of MySQL databases

Third-Party Tools

This section summarizes a number of third-party tools for Linux databases, from both commercial and open source suppliers. We've chosen those tools we feel might be of greatest use to database administrators.

Brio.Report

Brio.Report, a component of a larger suite called Brio ONE, provides DBMS reporting and management tools that can, with one exception, be run from Windows clients.

✦ Author: Brio Technology (some components acquired from SQRIBE Technologies)

✦ Web site: www.brio.com

✦ Distribution method: Professional sales, commercial licenses

✦ Source available: No

Brio.Report, billed on the Brio Technology Web site as an industrial-strength enterprise-reporting suite, includes components such as the following, which function in heterogeneous environments that include Linux DBMSs.

✦ Brio.Report Builder: A Windows-based graphical development tool that allows you to create enterprise and business-to-business reports. It includes a graphical query builder that supports multiple queries and nested subqueries as well as report features such as load lookups, report headers and footers, and exception notification.

✦ Brio.Report Viewer: A report-viewing utility for Windows clients that displays screen previews of reports prior to printing.

✦ Brio.Insight: A Web browser plug-in that provides optional Web-based interactive analysis and report-viewing capabilities for data delivered within reports produced by means of the Brio SQR Server.

✦ Brio.Report SQR Server: A report-processing and data-manipulation tool that provides native access to more than 60 combinations of databases and operating environments. The latest version of SQR Server has been enhanced to support features such as XML input and output, and access to multidimensional databases. SQR Server also enables you to add procedural language and control to SQL queries and commands.

✦ Brio.Report Personal SQR: A single-user, Windows-based emulation of SQR Server. Personal SQR allows you to test applications locally on non-Linux clients before implementing them on a back-end SQR Server.

C/Database Toolchest

The C/Database Toolchest in effect allows the addition of DBMS capabilities to existing, and large at that, collections of data. The libraries provided with the Toolchest offer more than 150 database management functions, including file operations such as create, open, and close; and record operations such as add, find, modify, and delete. What's more, the Toolchest gives you template programs that illustrate how each such function operates.

✦ Author: Mix Software

✦ Web site: www.mixsoftware.com/

✦ Distribution method: Retail

✦ Source available: Yes

The Toolchest includes both C and C++ libraries and a simple interface. Together, these enable you to use the libraries' database management functions to support such tasks as:

✦ Converting to and from dBASE data files

✦ File operations like create, open, close

✦ Indexing

✦ Locking

✦ Record operations such as add, find, modify, and delete

✦ Viewing and compressing databases

Finally, the C/Database Toolchest offers LDM, a database manager that accomplishes interactive creation and editing of databases.

SQL or SQR?

No, you didn't just misread that acronym. By SQR, Brio Technology means *Structured Query Reporting*.

CoSORT

CoSORT, the first independently-developed, standards-based, platform-independent database sorting utility, bills itself as *the world's fastest, and most widely licensed, commercial-grade sort package for UNIX systems.*

✦ Author: The CoSORT Company

✦ Web site: www.iri.com/external/products/products.html

✦ Distribution method: FTP

✦ Source available: N/A

CoSORT is a collection of utilities for file sorting; for one-pass extraction, sorting, summarization, and reporting; and, for providing sort functionality within databases, data warehouses, and application programs. CoSORT helps speed up database loads with a minimal time-sorting algorithm employed by a software architecture that transfers records directly through memory and that can make use of direct Sequential Multiprocessing (SMP), that is, parallel CPU, capabilities if they exist on CoSORT's platform.

CoSORT supports many file sizes, record formats, and data types, including alphanumeric and binary forms; C and COBOL numerics; EBCDIC; zoned decimal; floating point; currency; and Julian and multinational timestamps. It can input from or output to new or existing files, tape or optical devices; standard input and to standard output pipes and applications.

CoSORT includes several standalone end-user utilities, among them a mainframe-based sort control language called sortcl, which can perform tasks such as:

✦ Cross-table matching (joins)

✦ Field selection and extraction

✦ Field-level data-type translations

✦ Mathematical and expression evaluations

✦ Multikey comparisons

✦ Record grouping and filtering

CoSORT also includes:

✦ Automatic and manual resource tuning tools that can be used to fine-tune CPU, memory, and disks as CoSORT calls on them

✦ Command-line conversion tools that build UNIX and NT sortcl scripts from mainframe sort control files

✦ Full hardcopy and searchable electronic documentation, online man pages and scripting samples, with example calls presented in C, COBOL, and FORTRAN

CoSORT supports most flavors of Linux, Solaris, and Interactive UNIX.

DBMS/COPY for UNIX/Linux

DBMS/COPY is a tool that allows administrators to transfer data between DBMSs and databases with dissimilar record structures. The tool accomplishes this by directly reading and writing databases' native binary files.

✦ Author: Conceptual Software, Inc.

✦ Web site: www.conceptual.com/

✦ Distribution method: N/A

✦ Source available: N/A

DBMS/COPY directly reads and writes the native binary files of over 80 DBMSs. In addition, the package provides record filters, variable subsetting, and computational tools. DBMS/COPY considers its capability to transfer data that involves dissimilar numeric, date, and time data types among its most useful features. The package also offers:

✦ A Spreadsheet Grabber that enables data to be pulled from within a spreadsheet

✦ An ASCII Data Dictionary builder

✦ An ODBC query builder

OpenAccess ODBC and OLE DB SDK

These development kits act as middleware, providing standardized APIs that in turn can be used to create ODBC-compliant drivers and OLE-compatible, that is, "plug-and-play"-based access tools, for a number of data sources.

✦ Author: Automation Technology, Inc.

✦ Web site: www.odbcsdk.com

✦ Distribution method: FTP

✦ Source available: No

Note   OpenAccess is free for individual use (commercial pricing is available on request).

OpenAccess provides tools to make a data source accessible by means of standard SQL from a number of environments, such as:

✦ Desktop applications

✦ Networked enterprise applications

✦ Web servers

✦ XML servers

The newest releases of these developers' kits include:

✦ Enhanced error checking and error reporting

✦ Optimized memory management and client/server protocol

✦ Support for multithreading by all components of the OpenAccess SDK

✦ Support for native OLE DB 2.0, including full SQL support, for local and client/server configurations

✦ Support for SQL Server 7.0 Distributed Queries

OpenLink Virtuoso

Virtuoso, middleware designed for e-business, acts to simplify the creating of XML data from existing HTML files, and from SQL-compliant databases.

✦ Author: OpenLink Software

✦ Web site: `www.openlinksw.com/`

✦ Distribution method: FTP and retail

✦ Source available: Yes

 Note   OpenLink Virtuoso is free for individual use (commercial pricing is available on request).

OpenLink Virtuoso is a virtual database engine that enables you to view, update, or manipulate the data stored in dissimilar databases from a single ODBC, JDBC, UDBC, or OLE-DB connection. Among the databases Virtuoso supports are:

✦ DB2

✦ Informix

✦ Oracle

✦ SQL 92-compliant DBMSs

✦ Sybase

Summary

Management tools that accompany or coexist with Linux DBMSs occupy two categories:

✦ Tools provided by vendors, such as the command-line utilities offered with MySQL

✦ Tools presented by third parties, such as Brio.Report and CoSORT

Within either category, a variety of functions can be found.

IV

Programming Applications

Application Architecture

◆ ◆ ◆ ◆

In This Chapter

What is a database
application?

The three-tier model

Organization of tiers
into programs

◆ ◆ ◆ ◆

To this point, we have discussed what a database is, and
how to install and administer several popular database
packages. In this and the next few chapters, we discuss how
to program applications that work with your database. Our
discussion begins with a description of the architecture of an
application that works with a database. Subsequent chapters
describe in detail how to code an application.

If you are familiar with object-oriented programming or with
networking, much of the material in this chapter will be familiar to you—although you may be unfamiliar with some of the
details of working with databases. If you are not familiar with
networking or object-oriented programming, some of the
ideas that we present may strike you as novel or difficult. In
either case, all will become clear as we progress into this
chapter.

By the way, as you read this chapter, you may gain the impression that you must design and build every aspect of the
database application on your own. Fortunately, this is not the
case: libraries and tools will help you with many of the tasks
that we describe below. However, we speak as if you are building every aspect of the application on your own, because the
better you understand the task that a tool or library must
execute, the better able you will be to decide whether a given
tool can do that job, and the better you will know how to
use it.

What Is a Database Application?

A database application is a program that is used to manipulate data contained in a database.

The application insulates the user from the details of the
database. The user should not know or care which data elements are stored in what tables or columns, what data types

are used, or how much storage is available. Users should think only about doing their job: entering data correctly or extracting the data that is needed.

Likewise, the application insulates the database from the user. The application lets the user do what the user needs to do, but it also stops the user from doing what the user should not do.

In brief, a database application enables users to perform sophisticated tasks on a complex database with a minimum of fuss — and without harming themselves, the database, or you.

Evolution of the database application

Building a database application, like designing a database, is in theory a simple task: it accepts input from a user, applies domain logic to the input, translates the input into SQL calls, then passes those SQL calls to the database engine for execution.

However, building a robust application — one that has no holes or cracks in it, doesn't break down, doesn't trash the database, and doesn't permit the user to fill it with nonsense — is not easy, because of the wealth of details to which you must pay attention.

Fifteen years ago, writing an application was a relatively straightforward task. Every person who used the application logged into the machine that held both the database and the application. In most cases, this was a large, multiuser machine that ran some flavor of UNIX. The application was a monolithic program that contained all of the code needed to perform all of the application's tasks — from drawing data-entry screens to interacting with the database's engine.

Since then, however, four major shocks have occurred to upset this way of working.

Networks

The first shock was the advent of networks.

Suddenly, a user could log into the machine from a remote site. Furthermore, database servers could begin to talk with each other, albeit crudely, to exchange data.

Developers began to work with the idea that an application could be two programs — one that ran on a personal computer and the other that ran on a server machine — and so the idea of "client-server architecture" was born. This idea grew slowly, mainly because each manufacturer advocated its own proprietary networking protocol, but the seeds were planted that grew into today's networked environment.

The Internet

The next shock was the Internet. Although the Internet has been around since the 1960s, its existence became widely known only in the late 1980s. Many people were amazed to discover that the worldwide computer network they dreamed of building, already existed. It's as if Henry Ford designed the Model T, then discovered that the government had already built the interstate highway system. Overnight, machines and users at widely scattered sites began to exchange data. Bodies of data could be made accessible to the public at large.

Furthermore, the public discovered that the federal government had created a set of networking protocols that were robust, flexible, and proved to work—and that were in the public domain. The computer world woke up one day not only to discover that it had a worldwide network, but that that network had an excellent protocol to which local networks could also adhere.

The Web

Then came the World Wide Web. The Web brought two powerful enhancements to the Internet: graphics and the idea that bodies of data could link themselves to each other through universal resource locations (URLs). By inviting the public to come and view a company's wares, the Web turned the Internet from a preserve of hackers and academics into a commercial bonanza.

Companies wanted tools that would permit users to download data-entry templates and enter information directly into databases. These led to the creation of HTML forms and CGI interpreters; and then the Java language and Java applets. (If some of these terms are not clear to you, don't worry—we explain them in this chapter.) Suddenly, the ability to break a database application into modules that could be relocated over a wide-area network became a necessary part of any database package.

Intranets

The final shock was the idea of applying the Internet's protocols to internal networks—to *intranets*, as they are called. Building a mini-Internet within one's enterprise had great appeal: the tools already existed, users were familiar with the Internet's standards, and the intranet could be plugged into the Internet itself with a minimum of trouble. The intranet brought great power, but this power had a price: the writing and administration of database applications suddenly became much more complex.

Costs and benefits

As you can see, since the early 1990s, the database application has evolved from a monolithic program that runs on one machine, to a cluster of programs that are scattered across a network, and that can be made accessible to users around the globe.

It is fair to say that the world of database applications is still trying to cope with these changes. New ways of organizing, distributing, and presenting data appear almost weekly. These changes bring great power to users and programmers; but they also multiply the details that an applications programmer must manage.

Fortunately, engineers have created a model to help us manage the building and administration of a database application: the three-tier model. In the following section, we explore the three-tier model and discuss a few of the many ways in which it can be implemented on a computer network.

The Three-Tier Model

The three-tier model divides a database application into three sections, or tiers. Each tier receives data, and performs a well-defined task upon it. If all goes well, the tier then forwards the data; if an error occurs, it returns an error to the data source.

In theory, no tier duplicates the work performed by any other tier. In practice, of course, there will be some blurring of the tasks that each tier performs; but a well-designed database application will avoid such blurring as much as possible.

The tiers of the three-tier model are described in the following sections.

Bottom tier: Access to the database

This tier is the "data source"—that is, the software that controls access to the data themselves. It comprises the database engine, plus drivers and networking software with which your application accesses the engine. These almost always come from third-party providers. We also place in the bottom tier the code with which your application converses with the data source.

This tier receives instructions from the tier above it, and executes them. It then receives the engine's reply to those SQL statements—data, or an acknowledgment that the statements were processed, or an error statement—and returns that reply to the tier above it.

Middle tier: Business logic

The middle tier contains business logic. "So what," you may be asking, "is business logic?"

You may remember that, when we discussed database design in Chapter 4, we defined step 5 of designing a database as the task of writing domain-integrity rules. In the phrase "domain integrity," the word "domain" refers to a domain of knowledge, for example, baseball or librarianship; and "integrity" refers to the soundness of the data being entered. Thus, a *domain-integrity rule* is a rule that helps to ensure that the data being entered are sound with regard to the area of knowledge with which the database is concerned.

For example, in our baseball database, a domain-integrity rule would ensure that a user could not enter a tie score, or give a team a negative number of runs.

A domain-integrity rule can be prescriptive as well as prohibitive. For example, if you are writing a database for a hospital's heart-transplant program, one domain-integrity rule will tell the database to mark the donor patient as having died the day his heart is transplanted into another patient. Or, in our library example in Chapter 4, if a person tries to borrow a book that was previously borrowed and whose return was not recorded, the database application marks the book as having been returned, and then lets the current user borrow it. Thus, a domain-integrity rule may force your application to modify the database on its own in order to keep the database synchronized with reality.

As we noted in Chapter 4, the domain-integrity rules are not part of a relational database per se. Rather, they must be implemented separately, as part of the application. The set of domain-integrity rules, when taken together, are called the database application's *domain logic* or *business logic*—usually the latter.

Some experimental databases are experimenting with incorporating business logic directly into the database; this is particularly true of the object-relational databases. However, the typical commercial relational database currently does not have this capacity.

The middle tier is where the application's business logic is implemented. This tier accepts instructions from the tier above it, and compares the domain-integrity rules that are programmed into it. The middle tier then forwards data to the bottom tier for interaction with the database; and it forwards to the top tier what the bottom tier returns in reply—data or an acknowledgment that the instructions were processed— and forwards it to the tier above it.

Top tier: User interface

The top tier holds the user interface. It displays data and instructions on the user's screen, accepts what the user types or clicks, and forwards it to the middle tier for processing. It then displays what the middle tier returns to it—either data or an error message.

The term *presentation logic* is used to describe the design that underlies the user interface. The presentation logic encompasses all of the many details of the interface, such as:

✦ How the interface is broken into screens

✦ How the screens flow into each other

✦ How fields are arranged within each screen

✦ How error messages and information messages are presented

✦ The rules for which graphical widget to use, if any

✦ How color is used

✦ How icons and graphics are used

How the tiers relate to each other

Each tier performs a task that is both well defined and discrete.

No tier should duplicate work performed by any other tier. No tier should have any knowledge of the other tiers. Rather, all a tier should know is that it receives data from the tier above it, does something to those data, and forwards the modified data to the tier below it. It then receives in reply something from the tier below it, and returns that something to the tier above it.

The top and bottom tiers should be contextless — that is, neither should have any knowledge of what is in your database, or how your database is structured. The top tier should simply receive input from the user, process it, and forward it to the middle tier. Likewise, the bottom tier should receive instructions from the middle tier, execute them, and return the results to the middle tier. The middle tier should be the only tier that knows about the content and structure of your database; thus, it should contain all of the logic with which your data are processed.

We must emphasize that the tiers of the three-tier model are logical. The software that comprises the bottom tier almost always are programs that run on their own machine; the top and middle tiers may be lumped into one large program, or broken into two programs, or even broken into more than two separately running programs. Later, we discuss in detail how the pieces of the three-tier model can be organized.

Benefits of the three-tier model

The three-tier model for database applications offers several significant benefits:

✦ **Easier design** — By organizing an application into tiers, each of which performs one well-defined task, we make each module easier to design. It's easier for a human being to think clearly about a complex task by dealing with it one piece at a time.

✦ **Easier implementation** — Each piece can be written separately, and debugged separately. Because each piece performs one well-defined task, problems are easier to isolate and fix. If the design is sound, then all of the debugged pieces should fit together to form the full application, just as the pieces of a jigsaw puzzle fit together to form a picture.

✦ **Reusability** — Database applications perform the same tasks repeatedly. After we have built and debugged a module to perform a task reliably, we can use it repeatedly to perform the same task in other applications.

✦ **Distributability** — When an application is a set of programs that talk with each other, we can distribute those programs over a network. This lets the labor of managing an application be shared among the machines in the network. It also enhances the reusability of our code, because we can place one piece of our application onto one machine and funnel the input from several other machines into it.

Three-tier model: An example

In Chapter 3, we presented some simple database applications: our example SQL scripts. At first glance, a script is too simple to fit into the three-tier model. However, let's look more closely at what actually would occur were we to invoke the MySQL interpreter to interpret one of our examples:

✦ When we invoke the interpreter, which is named `mysql`, its first task is to establish contact with the SQL engine. Under MySQL, the engine is a daemon named `mysqld`.

✦ `mysqld` receives the name of the database, the login, and the password from the `mysql` interpreter. The server checks the login and password, and confirms that the user has permission to connect to the database.

✦ The interpreter `mysql` then begins to read and execute the SQL instructions from our script. It translates each raw SQL statement into a call in MySQL's call-level interface (CGI); then it passes that call to the engine, to execute.

✦ If the daemon `mysqld` discovers an error in any statement, it notifies the interpreter, which then prints an error message.

✦ When the script has concluded, the interpreter closes contact with the engine and exits.

So, even the interpretation of simplest of all database applications — a SQL script — involves communication among three separate software entities: the script, the interpreter, and the database engine.

So, how do these entities relate to the three-tier model?

✦ The bottom tier is comprised of the `mysqld` server, which executes our SQL instructions, and the `mysql` interpreter, which turns SQL statements into CLI calls to the database engine.

✦ The top tier is the script itself.

✦ And the business logic of the middle tier? It resides in our heads. When we work directly with SQL, we must do all our domain-level checking by hand, without the assistance of software.

As you can see, the three tiers are present even in an extremely simple application—logically present, that is, even if not present physically as a body of code.

Organization of the Tiers

The three-tier model is a template with which we organize our work. Although we organize a database application into three tiers, it does not follow that a database consists of three separately running programs: rather, all three tiers may be bundled into one program; or two tiers may be broken into one program and the third tier into another; or one program may contain the top tier and part of the middle tier, and a second program contain the rest of the middle tier.

Our point is that the tiers are conceptual rather than physical. Thinking about your application as being formed of three tiers—however those tiers are coded into programs—will help you to design a program that is both easier to build and easier to maintain.

An application can implement its tiers in many ways. This section presents a few of the commoner ways in which the tiers of the three-tier model are implemented.

Clients and servers

When tiers are implemented as separate programs, the programs often are organized into clients and servers. You probably are familiar with clients and servers; but in case you are not, the following defines them briefly:

✦ A client is a program that issues a request for a service.

✦ A server is a program that receives a request for a service from a client, and executes it.

✦ In general, a server can service multiple clients simultaneously. A server may also be a client; as part of its work, it may issue a request for service from another server.

So, how does this relate to the three-tier model? As follows:

✦ The top tier is always a client.

✦ The middle tier can be both a client and a server: it fields requests from the top tier, and it requests services from the bottom tier.

✦ The bottom tier is almost always a server: it fields requests from the middle tier.

Machines vs. programs

One problem with the terminology *client* and *server* is that the terms are used ambiguously. As described here, it means a set of programs that interact with each other. However, these terms are also used to describe machines. In this context, the client usually is a PC that is running a flavor of Windows and is being used by a human being, whereas the server is a machine that is running UNIX or Windows NT, and that provides services via a network to a cluster of client machines.

Client programs are usually run on client machines, and server programs can be run on server machines — but not always. Both client and server programs can be run on a single machine; for example, when you run the X Window System on your Linux, you are running both client programs and a server program on the same box. However, if your Linux box is plugged into a network that includes other boxes that run X programs, then you can invoke clients from those other boxes and run them on your console through your machine's X server.

And so it is with the tiers of a database application. If all three tiers are implemented as separate programs, you may run all three tiers on your local box; or you may run the top tier alone on your box, and request service from a middle-tier server that is located elsewhere on your network, which, in turn, requests services from a bottom tier located on a third machine; or you may run any permutation of this architecture. For the most part, when we speak of clients and servers, we refer to programs that can be distributed across one or more machines, rather than the machines themselves. When we mean machines rather than programs, we say so specifically.

Fat versus thin clients

The tiers of the three-tier model are logical entities. Physically, each tier can be implemented either as separate programs, or they can be bundled together into one large program.

When a client program has more than one tier built into it, it often is called a *fat client*. Contrariwise, when the client program contains only the top tier, with the other tiers run as one or more server programs, then the client sometimes is called a *thin* or *skinny client*.

So why, you ask, should it matter how the tiers are bundled, so long as the three tiers are implemented somehow? Actually, it can matter a great deal — but not because of any issue that is intrinsic to designing a database application. Rather, this is an administration issue.

Every time you alter your database or the logic of a tier, you must give an altered copy of the application to every person who uses it. When all users log into your machine and use one executable program to access your database, then a fat client works quite well. If, however, your users are running that fat client on their PCs and accessing the database over a network, then you must somehow put a copy of that fat client into each user's hands every time you modify it. As you can imagine, replacing these fat clients can be quite a problem.

Because the middle tier is the only one that knows about your database, it is the tier that is most likely to change frequently. Thus, if you can implement the middle tier within a server program, and put the top tier into a skinny client, then you will have to replace only the one copy of the server program to make most alterations available to every user of your application.

As a rule of thumb, if your users are running over a network, then the skinnier you can make the client, the better. We discuss this issue in more detail later in this section, when we discuss programming the user interface.

Drivers

In our discussion of the three-tier model, we speak of the bottom tier as accessing the database's engine directly. However, it is becoming common to have a driver stand between the database engine and the application.

The most commonly used drivers are built around Microsoft's Open Database Connectivity (ODBC) application-program interface (API) and Sun's Java Database Connectivity (JDBC) API. The following introduces each of these APIs, and shows how their drivers fit into the architecture of a database application.

ODBC

As we noted in Chapter 3, SQL instructions are passed to a SQL engine through a call-level interface (CLI).

This is a set of calls that are implemented in one or more languages (often C), that pass SQL statements directly to your database package's engine.

So far, so good. However, as we noted in Chapter 3, the ANSI/ISO standard for SQL defines a syntax for SQL itself, but it does not define the syntax for the CLI. Thus, each relational database package has its own CLI, and no two are compatible.

As you can imagine, this situation is a serious obstacle to porting a database application from one relational database package to another. It also complicates writing a multitier application that works with more than one brand of relational database package.

To alleviate this situation, a group of software companies led by Microsoft Corporation formed a consortium to design a common CLI for all relational databases. The result is the ODBC API.

In ODBC, an ODBC driver stands between the database and the application. The application issues calls in the ODBC CLI; the driver receives these calls, translates them into the CLI expected by the target database package, and then forwards those database-specific calls to the database's engine. Thus, each database package, and each major release of each package, needs its own ODBC driver. For example, an ODBC driver is needed for Informix release 5; a different driver is needed for Informix release 6; and yet another for Oracle release 7.

ODBC is a major step toward opening up database connectivity, as it was meant to do. However, implementations of ODBC use two architectures that are mutually incompatible. One architecture is client oriented; the other is server oriented. The following explains these two architectures.

ODBC client-oriented architecture

In the client-oriented architecture, the ODBC driver (or drivers) reside on the user's computer — usually a PC that is running some version of Microsoft Windows. Each ODBC driver uses the database vendor's proprietary networking software to connect to the database engine. Because an application may work simultaneously with two or more "brands" of database, this architecture uses an ODBC driver manager to ensure that a given ODBC call is directed to the correct driver, and thus to correct database. The driver manager is linked directly into the application; the driver manager, in turn, loads at runtime the drivers that it needs.

For example, consider an application that is working with Informix. In the client-oriented architecture, the ODBC driver manager on the client's Windows machine loads the Informix ODBC driver. The ODBC driver translates the ODBC calls into Informix ESQL calls, and forwards them to the copy of I-NET (Informix's networking tool) that resides on the client's machine. I-NET, in turn, talks across to the Informix engine that resides on the server machine.

Under this architecture a user must purchase an ODBC driver manager for each of the user's PCs. Furthermore, for each brand of database with which each PC works, the user must purchase a copy of the appropriate ODBC driver and a copy of the database vendor's proprietary networking software.

ODBC server-oriented architecture

Some companies support ODBC systems that use a server-oriented architecture. In this architecture, the ODBC driver on the client machine communicates with an ODBC server on the server machine. The server makes the translation from ODBC to the database-specific CLI, not by the driver.

The server-oriented architecture differs from the client-oriented architecture in three key aspects:

✦ The client machine does not need the database vendor's proprietary networking software to communicate with the engine. Standard networking software is sufficient.

✦ The client machine needs only one general ODBC driver. This driver does not translate ODBC; rather, it simply communicates with the ODBC server.

✦ The server machine needs no more than one ODBC driver for each "brand" of database that it supports.

A company that implements the server-oriented architecture still must make a major investment in software, but less than what is required by the client-oriented architecture. Such a system is considerably easier to set up and manage than is one that uses the client-oriented architecture.

JDBC

The JDBC API is a set of objects that are written in the Java programming language. JDBC is, in effect, the Java counterpart to ODBC.

The JDBC API, like ODBC, works by passing calls to a JDBC driver. Like ODBC, however, JDBC uses two different architectures to talk with the database engine:

In one architecture, the JDBC driver talks directly to the database engine. The JDBC driver translates JDBC instructions into the CLI recognized by the brand of database to which the JDBC driver is talking.

In the other architecture, the JDBC driver talks to an ODBC driver or server. The JDBC driver translates its JDBC instructions into ODBC calls, and it depends upon the ODBC driver or server to manage the task of talking with the database engine.

The JDBC-to-engine architecture is specific to a given brand of relational database; the JDBC-to-ODBC architecture is more general purpose, in that one JDBC driver will, in theory, talk with all ODBC drivers or servers.

From Tiers to Programs

The Web has become the "gold standard" for providing users with access over a network to a body of information. Providing access to a database over the Web has become an extremely important aspect of the Web, to record information collected from users and to take orders for goods. The graphical capabilities of the Web format give companies a way to build front-end clients that are complex, easy to use, and centrally stored, yet available to many users over Internet.

The rest of this section introduces the three major ways with which a Web page can interact with a database: through a common gateway interface (CGI) program, through an applet, and through a servlet.

Common Gateway Interface

As you may recall from our earlier discussion of fat versus thin clients, we want to reduce as much as possible the number of copies of any program that comprises a database application. Ideally, we would have only one copy of every program, with that copy located on a machine that we control; thus, when we modify the database or fix a bug, all we have to do is replace that one copy, and the modification or bug fix is immediately available to all users.

The strategy of using one centrally located copy of a program is relatively easy to do for the middle and bottom tiers of a database application: they can be implemented as centrally located servers. However, the top tier — the tier with which the user interacts — must run on the user's machine. This is not a problem if all users log into the machine on which the database is stored; however, when users are scattered across a network, putting a copy of the updated program into users' hands can be a problem.

One way to do this is to use the CGI. In this model, an HTML form that gathers data from a user is stored on a central server machine, and is downloaded to a user's machine every time a user requests the form's URL. The data that the user writes into the form is then downloaded to a program that is located on your central machine; the program is responsible for processing the data, interacting with the database, and constructing the HTML that is returned to the user. Thus, CGI lets you have one copy of a top-tier program, with that copy used by everyone across the network.

CGI programs are quite useful: they are simple to write and maintain, and they can perform a wide range of tasks. However, CGI has two serious limitations:

✦ CGI severely restricts what you can do on the client's machine. Some tasks are best performed by the client rather than by the server; for example, checking what a user has input for consistency and correctness is best performed on the client side, rather than submitting what the user enters to the server and having the server discover the error. A CGI program can be supplemented with a script written in JavaScript or a similar scripting language, to pass onto the client tasks that are best performed on the client side but that cannot be executed in HTML. However, this approach raises problems with regard to the different ways that browsers implement scripting languages.

✦ A CGI program is stateless; that is, it receives a form from the user, processes it, writes output to the browser, then dies. It does not "remember" what the user has done from one form to the next; all it knows are the data that the browser sends to it. Thus, if the execution of a task requires a user to work with a number of forms, the browser and the server may be passed a large number of data back and forth; and the CGI program must parse and interpret a large number of parameters. Thus, a CGI program can become impossibly difficult once it involves more than a fairly small number of forms.

As you can see, CGI programs can be quite useful; but they can have limitations that are addressed by the other methods of working over the Web: applets and servlets.

Applets

An applet is a program that is downloaded to a Web browser. The browser invokes another program, or "engine," to execute the applet, and then incorporates the output it receives from that program into the page that it displays to the user.

An applet gives a programmer access to the entire range of graphical and communications functionality that are built into the browser's engine. Thus, you can embed within a Web page an applet that performs a complex task — an animation, say, or a complex interaction with the user. And although the applet performs complex tasks, the browser interprets it; therefore, one applet can be run under every operating system and microprocessor upon which the browser has been implemented.

Like a CGI script, an applet gives you a way to build a top-tier program that is centrally stored yet is available to all users on the network. An applet is requested from within an HTML document, and is downloaded by the same server that downloaded the page. Thus, you can store one copy of an applet, and have that one copy used by every user on your network. However, applets remove the limitations that are built into CGI:

✦ An applet can use a socket to plug itself into a middle-tier server. The only restriction is that this server must reside on the same machine as the HTTP server with which you downloaded the applet.

✦ The middle-tier server can be programmed to remember the applet's state. The applet can interact with the server on a field-by-field basis, rather than in batch mode. Furthermore, because it is written in a fully featured language, you can build low-level error checking into the applet.

✦ Finally, an applet has access to the full range of graphical objects that reside in the engine; this lets you program complex graphic tasks, such as dragging objects.

Java is the most popular language for writing applets. However, other applet systems are also in use; Flash applets, in particular, are becoming quite popular. One major advantage offered by Java is that its JDBC API lets an applet interact directly with a database on a remote server.

For example, a user who is working with a Web browser asks an HTTP server on a given server for an HTML page; this page, in turn, has a request for an applet built into it.

When the user begins to work with the applet, the applet begins to exchange information with the database via JDBC driver. The JDBC driver either works through an existing ODBC driver or communicates directly with the database.

This architecture is of almost Byzantine complexity, but in practice it works quite smoothly. It is possible to build the middle tier into an applet, and to make the applet a fat client; however, such an applet could well be very large and take a long time to download. In practice, the more functionality that can be off-loaded onto a middle-tier server, the better.

Servlet

A servlet resembles an applet: it is a small, discrete program that holds business logic. Unlike an applet, however, a servlet is not uploaded to the client machine. Rather, the servlet is managed by the HTTP server with which the user's browser is working. When a user requests a service of the servlet, the Web server invokes the servlet and passes data between the browser and the servlet.

Servlets have one major disadvantage: they consume resources on the machine that is running your Web server. However, they have a huge advantage: because they are run on a single machine that you control, you do not have to worry about having to run your code on a variety of client machines, many of which you do not have available for testing. With a servlet, you can write your code, test it, and prove that it works before you put it into production.

PHP is a popular language for writing servlets.

Cross-
Reference

We introduce PHP and give an example of coding servlets in Chapter 13.

Summary

This chapter introduces the architecture, or structure, of database applications. To begin, we introduced the three-tier model for database applications. This model views an application as being comprised of three tiers:

✦ A bottom tier, which interacts with the database.

✦ A middle tier, which contains all business logic — that is, the logic that manages domain-level integrity and that manages the passage of data into and out of the database.

✦ A top tier, which interacts with the user.

The tiers can be organized in a number of different ways: either lumped into one large program; or as individual programs that communicate with each other; or any combination thereof.

A network introduces another level of complexity to the organization of tiers into programs. It may well be that a program that contains the top tier is run on the user's machine, and that the top tier communicates with a program that resides on a central machine and that contains the middle and bottom tiers of the application. In this case, the tiers are said to use a client/server architecture. The client — in this case, the program on the user's machine that holds the top tier — sends requests for services to the centrally located program that holds the middle and bottom tiers. The program on the user's machine is the client, because it requests services; the program on the centrally located machine is the server, because it executes requests for services from one or more clients.

If more than one tier is included within the client program, it is said to be a fat client. A thin or skinny client is one that contains only the top tier — that is, it only contains the user interface.

As a rule of thumb, a skinny client is preferable to a fat client, so as to reduce the number of copies of a given program that are in circulation. However, there are exceptions to this rule.

In many instances, the bottom tier will communicate directly with the database engine. However, it may also use one or more drivers that stand between the engine and the application's bottom tier. Two of the more common are drivers that use the ODBC protocol, or the JDBC protocol. Using drivers makes it easier to write an application that can work with more than one "brand" of relational database package.

Finally, giving the Web access to a database is becoming more and more important. The three most common methods by which a database can interact with the Web are through the CGI, Java applets, and servlets.

✦   ✦   ✦

Programming Interfaces

The most basic form of access for the majority of database users is through the tried-and-true command-line client tool. This seems to hold true for just about every product on any platform. Much of this is expected and, it turns out, very efficient for database administrators (DBA) and technical support staff for these databases. We say client tool because database server products are actually distinct computer programs that operate quite independently of the tools and utilities that interact with them.

End-user access is another matter, entirely. However familiar the end users become with the arcane commands and seemingly obscure tools that some of the database vendors have you use to get information into and out of their products, the most productive environments are the sole reserve of well-thought-out and implemented application programs.

To support these productivity-enhancing tools, database vendors usually provide one or more industry-standard Application Programming Interfaces (API) for their product. It is common to have a preferred API for use with databases and even operating systems. For the Microsoft Windows product line, the API of choice (theirs, not yours) for client access is ODBC using C/C++ or possibly Visual Basic as the programming language. The advantage of using a standard database API is that, in theory, the database can be switched to any other having the same API without impacting the database application.

For each standard database API there needs to be specific database drivers that act as the functional layer that translates the more generic API and the particular way each database implements the API; the under-the-hood stuff. So, if we consider MySQL as the database, there needs to be a specific MySQL driver for DBI (Perl), a different driver for ODBC (C/C++), a third for JDBC (Java), and so on.

The following is a quick rundown of some common combinations of language and industry-standard database APIs:

✦ DBI with Perl

✦ ODBC with C/C++

✦ JDBC with Java

If an industry-standard API is not available, then the remaining option is a call-level interface (CLI) offered as a library for a specific language. An example of a language-library interface is PHP and its available drivers. Call-level interfaces expose more of the internal operations of the database servers, and so is sometimes the preferred choice.

It bears repeating, though, that if all else fails the command-line tools and utilities are capable of performing everything that can be done, however frustrating and time-consuming it may seem.

This chapter discusses the main industry-standard database APIs, an example of how to use the command-line client tool that ships with MySQL, and an example of a language-library interface using PHP. We make use of PHP with MySQL in the chapter on Web-enabled database applications.

One final word of warning, being compliant with a standard API in no way means that the database implements every function or method in the API, let alone that every database vendor implements the same API the same way. Read the vendor-supplied documentation very carefully.

Basic Database Connectivity Concepts through an API

Before moving on to more specific examples of database connectivity, we present a brief discussion of some basic concepts. First, we discuss what is necessary to connect to a typical database. Next, we discuss disconnecting from a typical database. And, finally, we discuss some basic ways to interact with databases. This discussion is a general discussion of database connectivity and may vary depending on the unique situation.

Connecting to a database

Basic database connectivity is achieved by supplying a database name, the machine location of the database, and the name and password of a valid user (username parameter). The username and password have to have already been made known to the database security process by having been preassigned by a database administrator for that database—in other words, the user must already exist. Upon successful connection (the login process completed successfully implying that the username parameter and the password parameter were correct) the application will have a valid (non-NULL) pointer to a data structure that represents the database session. This data structure holds detailed information necessary for subsequent database operations that occur *during the same session*. The application doesn't directly use this detailed information.

Disconnecting from a database

Log out of the database using the same username that was used when logging into the database (implicitly used by way of the "handle" to the database), which frees the memory structure that was allocated for the connection.

SQL Statements

The fundamental relational database operations that are needed when using a custom application are:

✦ Create (Insert) new records

✦ Update existing records

✦ Read (Select) records

✦ Delete existing records

All significant application functions (as far as the database is concerned) must be implemented from one or more of these fundamental operations.

Prepared (SQL) Statements

Several APIs can preprocess a SQL statement prior to the statement being executed. This preprocessing can, in some cases, significantly speed up the database access portions of the application. Statements that are candidates for being prepared are those that are executed frequently with little or no change to the statement.

Stored Procedures

Some APIs have special ways of executing and managing the results of stored procedures. Stored procedures can implement several SQL statements within themselves, so special handling of stored procedure results is often necessary.

Retrieving Metadata

Metadata is information about data, or data about data. In database terms, metadata consists of information about the structures that make up the database, for example, the table names, the relationships between the tables, the attribute (column) names of the tables, the sizes and data types of the attributes. For a large number of database applications, this metadata is not used because the application knows ahead of time what to expect at each and every step of the way. The metadata is embedded in the application by design.

However, if an application allows ad hoc access to the database, it is mandatory that the application query for and examine the metadata for every result set in order to be able to present the data to the user without masking or otherwise obscuring the information contained therein.

Transactions

For multiple concurrent user databases (those of any interest) there is the concept of a transaction. For this chapter, the two transaction operations are:

✦ Commit a change to the database

✦ Rollback a change to the database

From the perspective of an end user, a transaction consists of all of the fundamental operations that must successfully complete as a unit. So, the deletion of a single record from one table may be a transaction. However, if a record in each of three different tables must either all be successfully updated together (three update operations) or none at all, then the transaction consists of all three update operations taken together, one after another.

API and Code Examples

This section lists the functions and provides examples for some of the more common APIs. The lists are complete lists of the functions for ODBC, DBI, MySQL C++, CLI, and the PHP MySQL interface. Although counterparts exist for practically all databases, we use MySQL because it is widely available and supported on Linux and because it is open source software.

ODBC and C/C++

The ODBC API goes back to the early 1990s when Microsoft implemented it from a preliminary specification for a CLI from X/Open and a similar specification from the SQL Access Group. The most recent version of ODBC (currently in the 3.x revision) is compliant with both the X/Open CAE Specification "Data Management: SQL Call-Level Interface" and ISO/IEC 9075-3:1995 (E) Call-Level Interface (SQL/CLI). ODBC interfaces are implemented by a platform-specific driver manager and by database-specific drivers. Be aware that a specific database driver may be compliant with only a subset of the standard. Read the documentation carefully.

C/C++ most often uses ODBC libraries, supplied either by a third party or by the vendor of the database. Alternatively, some vendors supply a CLI interface. Table 13-1 shows a list of ODBC functions.

Table 13-1
Alphabetical List of ODBC Functions

Function	Description
SQLAllocHandle(HandleType, InputHandle, *OutputHandle)	Obtains one of either an environment, connection, statement, or descriptor handle.
SQLAllocConnect(EnvironHandle, *ConnectionHandle)	Allocates the memory (data structure) for a connection handle.
SQLAllocEnv(EnvironmentHandle)	Allocates the memory (data structure) for an environment handle.
SQLAllocStmt(ConnectionHandle, *StatementHandle)	Allocates memory (data structure) for a SQL statement handle and associates it with an existing connection handle.
SQLBindCol(StatementHandle, ColNumber, C_DataType, *Value, ValueMaxSize, *ValueSize_Indicator)	Assigns storage (data structure) for a result column and specifies the data type.
SQLBindParameter(StatementHandle, ParamPostionNumber, ParamType, C_DataType, SQL_DataType, ValueSize, DecimalDigits, *Value, ValueBufferSize, *ValueSize_Indicator)	Assigns storage (data structure) for a parameter in a SQL statement. One of these is required for every bound parameter.

Continued

Table 13-1 *(continued)*	

Function	*Description*

`SQLBrowseConnect(`
`ConnectionHandle,`
`*BrowseReqString,`
`BrowseReqStringSize,`
`BrowseResult,`
`MaxSizeOfBrowseResult,`
`*ActualSizeOfBrowseResult,`
`)`
	Used for making browsing the available data sources. Returns successive levels of connection attributes and valid attribute values. When a value is specified for each connection attribute, connects to the data source.

`SQLBulkOperations(`
`StatementHandle,`
`OperationType`
`)`
	Performs bulk insertions and bulk bookmark operations; for example, update, delete, and fetch by bookmark.

`SQLCancel(`
`StatementHandle`
`)`
	Stops SQL statement processing.

`SQLCloseCursor(`
`StatementHandle`
`)`
	Closes an (open) cursor on a statement handle.

`SQLColAttribute(`
`StatementHandle,`
`ColNumber,`
`Attribute,`
`*CharValue,`
`CharValueMaxSize,`
`*CharValueActualSize,`
`*NumericValue`
`)`
	Retrieves various descriptor information about a column in the result set.

`SQLColumnPrivileges(`
`StatementHandle,`
`*CatName,`
`CatNameSize,`
`*SchemaName,`
`SizeOfSchemaName,`
`*TableName,`
`SizeOfTableName,`
`*ColumnName,`
`SizeOfColumnName`
`)`
	Returns, as a data set, a list of columns and associated privileges for one or more tables.

Function	Description
SQLColumns(StatementHandle, *CatName, CatNameSize, *SchemaName, SizeOfSchemaName, *TableName, SizeOfTableName, *ColumnName, SizeOfColumnName)	Returns the list of column names for the specified table in the specified database.
SQLConnect(ConnHandle, *DataSourceName, SizeofDataSourceName, *UserName, SizeOfUserName, *Password, SizeOfPassword)	Connects to a specific database driver by using the predefined data source name, and passes the user ID, and password.
SQLCopyDesc(DestinationDescriptorHandle SourceDescriptorHandle,)	Used for copying descriptor information from one handle to another.
SQLDataSources(EnvironHandle, Selection, *DataSourceName, MaxSizeOfDataSourceName, ActualSizeOfDataSourceName, *DataSourceDriverDesc, *MaxSizeOfDataSourceDriverDesc, *ActualSizeOfDataSourceDriverDesc,)	Returns the list of available (predefined ODBC) data sources on the local machine.

Continued

Table 13-1 *(continued)*

Function	Description
SQLDescribeCol(StatementHandle, ColNumber, *ColName, ColNameMaxSize, *ColNameActualSize, *SQL_DataType, *ColSize, *DecimalDigits, *NullableCol)	Returns various characteristics for one specific column of a result set.
SQLDescribeParam(StatementHandle, ParamMarketNumber, *SQL_DatatType, *ValueSize, *DecimalDigits, *Nullable)	Returns the information for a specific column (or expression) in a SQL statement.
SQLDisconnect(ConnectionHandle)	Closes the connection.
SQLDriverConnect(ConnHandle, WindowHandle, *ConnectionInd, SizeOfConnectionInd, *ConnectOut, MaxSizeOfConnectOut, *ActualSizeOfConnectOut, DriverMgrCompletionMode)	Connects to a specific driver by connection string or requests that the Driver Manager and driver display connection dialog boxes for the user, which means that the user has to make the choices.
SQLDrivers(EnvironmentHandle, Selection, *Description, DescriptionMaxSize, *DescriptionSize, *Attributes, AttributesMaxSize, *AttributesSize,)	Returns the list of installed drivers and their respective characteristics.

Function	Description
SQLEndTran(HandleType, Handle Action)	Commits or rolls back all active transactions since the last commit for a specific connection or environment handle.
SQLError(EnvironHandle. ConnHandle, StatementHandle, *SQLStateValue, *NativeErrorCode, *ErrorMessage, *ErrorMessageMaxSize, *ErrorMessageActualSize.)	Retrieves status, warning and error information for the most recently completed ODBC function.
SQLExecDirect(StatementHandle, SQLQueryString, QueryStringLength)	Executes a statement, possibly using previously defined positional parameter values.
SQLExecute(StatementHandle)	Executes a successfully prepared statement, that is, using SQLPrepare.
SQLFetch(StatementHandle)	Advances a cursor to the next row in a result set and retrieves data.
SQLFetchScroll(StatementHandle, FetchType, RowNumber)	Returns some scrollable result rows from a result set.

Continued

	Table 13-1 *(continued)*	
Function	*Description*	
SQLForeignKeys(StatementHandle, *PKCatName, PKCatNameSize, *PKSchemaName, SizeOfPKSchemaName, *PKTableName, SizeOfPKTableName, *FKCatName, FKCatNameSize, *FKSchemaName, SizeOfFKSchemaName, *PKTableName, SizeOfFKTableName,)	Returns a list of column names that are the foreign keys (if they exist) for a specified table in a specified database.	
SQLFreeConnect(ConnectionHandle)	Releases the data source connection and associated data storage.	
SQLFreeEnv(EnvironmentHandle)	Releases the environment data storage.	
SQLFreeHandle(HandleType, Handle)	Releases an environment, connection, statement, or descriptor handle (and data structure).	
SQLFreeStmt(StatementHandle, Option)	Terminates statement processing, discards pending results and, optionally, frees all resources associated with the statement handle.	
SQLGetConnectAttr(ConnectionHandle, Attribute, *Value, ValueMaxSize, *ActualBytesWritten)	Returns the current value of a specific connection attribute.	

Function	Description
SQLGetConnectOption(ConnectionHandle, Option, *Value)	Gets the current value of the specified connection attribute (option).
SQLGetCursorName(StatementHandle, *CursorName, CursorNameMaxSize, *CursorNameActualSize)	Gets the cursor name associated with the specified statement handle.
SQLGetData(StatementHandle, ColNumber, C_DataType, *Value, ValueMaxSize, *ValueSizeIndicator)	Returns part (for long datum) or all of one column of one row of a result set.
SQLGetDescField(DescriptorHandle, RecordNum, Identifier, *Value, ValueMaxSize, *StrLen)	Returns the value of a specified single descriptor field.
SQLGetDescRec(DescriptorHandle, RecordNum, *ParamName, NameMaxSize, *NameActualSize, *ParamDataType, *ParamDataSubType, *ByteLenOfParam, *Precision, *Scale, *IsNullable)	Returns the values of multiple descriptor fields.

Continued

Table 13-1 (continued)	
Function	**Description**
SQLGetDiagField(HandleType, Handle, RecordNum, FieldIdentifier, *Value, MaxSizeOfValue, *ActualSizeOfValue)	Returns additional diagnostic information (a single field of the diagnostic data structure).
SQLGetDiagRec(HandleType, Handle, RecordNum, *SQLStateValue, *NativeErrorCode, *ErrorMessage, ErrorMessageMaxSize, ErrorMessageActualSize)	Returns current values of some commonly used diagnostic information.
SQLGetEnvAttr(EnvironmentHandle, Attribute, *Value, ValueMaxSize, *ActualBytesWritten)	Returns the value of a specified environment attribute.
SQLGetFunctions(ConnectionHandle, Function, *Supported)	Returns supported driver functions. (*Supported can point to a single value or to a list of values.)
SQLGetInfo(ConnectionHandle, InformationType, InformationValue, InformationValueMaxSize, *InformationValueSize)	Returns information about the specified database driver and data source.

Function	Description

`SQLGetStmtAttr(`
`StatementHandle,`
`Attribute,`
`*Value,`
`ValueMaxSize,`
`*ActualValueSize`
`)`
	Returns the current value of a specific statement attribute.

`SQLGetStmtOption(`
`StatementHandle,`
`Option,`
`*Value`
`)`
	Gets the current value of a specific statement attribute (option).

`SQLGetTypeInfo(`
`StatementHandle,`
`SQLDataType`
`)`
	Returns, as a data set, information about supported data types for the current data source

`SQLMoreResults(`
`StatementHandle`
`)`
	Determines whether or not there are more result sets available and, if there are, initializes processing for the next result set.

`SQLNativeSql(`
`ConnectionHandle,`
`*SQLStringInput,`
`StringInputLength,`
`*SQLStringOutput,`
`StringOutputMaxSize,`
`*StringOutputActualSize`
`)`
	Returns the text of an SQL statement as translated by the driver and that will be presented to the data source for execution.

`SQLNumParams(`
`StatementHandle,`
`*ParamMarkerNumber`
`)`
	Returns the number of parameters in a prepared SQL statement.

`SQLNumResultCols(`
`StatementHandle,`
`*NumResultCols`
`)`
	Returns the number of columns in the result set for the statement handle.

`SQLParamData(`
`StatementHandle,`
`*Value`
`)`
	Used with `SQLPutData` to supply parameter data at query execution. See `SQLPutData`.

Continued

Table 13-1 *(continued)*

Function	Description
SQLParamOptions(StatementHandle, NumberOfRows, *RowIndex)	Associates a set of bound parameter values with a statement, for example for bulk inserts. Superseded in later versions.
SQLPrepare(StatementHandle, *SQLQueryString, QueryStringSize)	Sends a query to a data source for preparation and later execution. Use SQLExecute to cause the query to actually run.
SQLPrimaryKeys(StatementHandle, *CatName, CatNameSize, *SchemaName, SizeOfSchemaName, *TableName, SizeOfTableName,)	Returns the list of column names that make up the primary key for a table.
SQLProcedureColumns(StatementHandle, *ProcCatName, ProcCatNameSize, *ProcSchemaName, SizeOfProcSchemaName, *ProcName, SizeOfProcName, *ColName, SizeOfColName)	Returns the list of input and output parameters, as well as the columns that make up the result set for the specified procedures.
SQLProcedures(StatementHandle, *ProcCatName, ProcCatNameSize, *ProcSchemaName, SizeOfProcSchemaName, *ProcName, SizeOfProcName,)	Returns the list of procedure names that have been registered on a specific data source.

Function	Description
SQLPutData(StatementHandle, *Value, ValueSize_Indicator)	Sends part (for very large datum) or all of a data value for a parameter. See SQLParamData.
SQLRowCount(StatementHandle, RowCount)	Returns the number of rows affected by an insert, update, or delete.
SQLSetConnectAttr(ConnectionHandle, Attribute, *Value, ValueLength)	Sets the specified connection attribute to the specified value.
SQLSetConnectOption(ConnectionHandle, Option, Value)	Sets the value of the specified connection attribute (option).
SQLSetCursorName(StatementHandle, *CursorName CursorNameSize)	Names a cursor of a specified statement.
SQLSetDescField(DescHandle, RecordNum, FieldIndentifier, *Value, ValueSize)	Sets the value of a single descriptor field.

Continued

	Table 13-1 *(continued)*
Function	*Description*
SQLSetDescRec(DescriptorHandle, RecordNum, ParamDataType, ParamDataSubType, ByteLenOfParam, Precision, Scale, *Data, *StrLen, *IsNull)	Sets values of multiple descriptor fields.
SQLSetEnvAttr(EnvironmentHandle, Attribute, *Value, SizeOfAttribute)	Sets the value of an environment attribute.
SQLSetParam(StatementHandle, ParameterNum, C_DataType, SQL_DataType, SizeOrPrecision, Scale, *Value, *ValueSize)	Associates a parameter in a SQL statement with variables in the calling application.
SQLSetPos(StatementHandle, RowNum, OperationType, LockType)	Positions a cursor within a row set, refreshes data in the row set, or updates or deletes data in an updatable result set.
SQLSetStmtAttr(StatementHandle, Attribute, *Value, ValueSize)	Sets the value of a statement attribute.

Function	Description
SQLSetStmtOption(StatementHandle, Option, Value)	Sets the current value of a specific statement attribute (option).
SQLSpecialColumns(StatementHandle, RowIdentifier *CatName, CatNameSize, *SchemaName, SizeOfSchemaName, *TableName, SizeOfTableName, RowIdentifierScope, CanBeNullable)	Returns information about the set of columns that uniquely identifies a row in a specified table.
SQLStatistics(StatementHandle, *CatName, CatNameSize, *SchemaName, SizeOfSchemaName, *TableName, SizeOfTableName, IndexType, PagesAndCardinalityAccuracy)	Returns statistics about a single table in a specified database, and the list of indexes associated with the table.
SQLTablePrivileges(StatementHandle, *CatName, CatNameSize, *SchemaName, SizeOfSchemaName, *TableName, SizeOfTableName,)	Returns a list of tables and the privileges associated with each table in a specified database.

Continued

Table 13-1 *(continued)*

Function	Description
SQLTables(StatementHandle, *CatName, CatNameSize, *SchemaName, SizeOfSchemaName, *TableName, SizeOfTableName, TableType, *SizeOfTableType)	Returns the list of table names (catalog) stored in a specific data source.
SQLTransact(EnvironmentHandle, ConnectionHandle, Action)	Causes either a commit or rollback of all active transactions since the last commit. Superseded by SQLEndTran().

DBI and Perl

Perl applications use the Perl DBI interface module and one of the database drivers.

The DBI is a database access module for the Perl Language. It defines a set of methods, variables, and conventions that provide a consistent database interface independent of the actual database being used. The DBI sends the method, calls to the driver, which, in turn, sends it to the database server for actual execution. The DBI is also responsible for the dynamic loading of database drivers, error checking/handling, and other duties. There are database interfaces for the specific databases available for Linux. The module for a particular database is referred to as a DBD (database driver). These drivers are implementations of the DBI methods written by using the private interface functions of the corresponding database server. Table 13-2 and Table 13-3 illustrate these concepts.

Table 13-2
Perl Documentation Notations and Conventions

DBD	Meaning
DBI	Static top-level class name
$dbh	Database handle object
$sth	Statement handle object

DBD	Meaning
$drh	Driver handle object
$h	Any of the $dbh, $sth, or $drh handle types
$rc	General Return Code (Boolean: true = OK; false = error)
$rv	General Return Value
@ary	List of values returned from the database, typically a row of data
$rows	Number of rows processed
$fh	A file handle
undef	NULL values are represented by undefined values in Perl
\%attr	Reference to a hash of attribute values passed to methods

Table 13-3
Commonly Used Perl DBI Methods

Method	Description

`@driver_names = DBI->`
`available_drivers;`
`@ driver_names = DBI->`
`available_drivers ($quiet);`
	Returns a list of all available drivers by searching for DBD::* modules through the directories in @INC. By default, a warning will be given if some drivers are hidden by others of the same name in earlier directories, unless this behavior is inhibited by passing a true value for $quiet.

`@data_sources = DBI->`
`data_sources ($driver_name);`
`@ data_sources = DBI->`
`data_sources ($driver,`
`\%attr);`
	Returns a list of all data sources (databases) available via the named driver. If not already loaded, the driver will be loaded. The value of the DBI_DRIVER environment variable is the default if $driver is empty or undefined. The attributes are driver dependent.

`$dbh = DBI->connect`
`($data_source, $username,`
`$auth, \%attr);`
`$dbh = DBI->connect`
`($data_source, $username,`
`$password)`
	Attempts to create a connection to the specified data_source and returns a database handle object if the connect succeeds. The attributes, if needed, are driver dependent.

Continued

	Table 13-3 *(continued)*	
Method	**Description**

`$dbh = DBI->connect_cached`
`($data_source, $username,`
`$password)`
`$dbh = DBI->connect_cached`
`($data_source, $username,`
`$password, \%attr)`
	Attempts to create a connection to the specified `data_source` and returns a database handle object if the connect succeeds. The database handle returned will be stored in a hash associated with the given parameters for efficiency of further connection attempts. If a previously cached database handle has been disconnected, or if the `ping()` method fails, then a new connection is created. The attributes are driver dependent.

`DBI->trace($trace_level)`
`DBI->trace($trace_level,`
`$trace_filename)`
	Enables DBI trace information for all. To enable trace information for a specific handle use the similar `$h->trace` method described elsewhere.

`$rc = $dbh->do($statement);`
`$rc = $dbh->do($statement,`
`\%attr);`
`$rv = $dbh->do($statement,`
`\%attr, @bind_values);`
	Prepare and execute a single statement. Returns one of either the number of rows affected, -1 if not known or not available, or This method is typically most useful for non-`select` statements that either cannot be prepared in advance (because of a limitation of the driver), or which do not need to be executed repeatedly. It should not be used for `select` statements because it does not return a statement handle, so you can't fetch any data.

`$ary_ref = $dbh->`
`selectall_arrayref`
`($statement);`
`$ary_ref = $dbh->`
`selectall_arrayref`
`($statement, \%attr);`
`$ary_ref = $dbh->`
`selectall_arrayref`
`($statement, \%attr,`
`@bind_values);`
	Combines `prepare`, `execute`, and `fetchall_arrayref` into a single call, returning a reference to an array of references to arrays for each row of data fetched.

Method	Description

`@row_ary = $dbh->`
`selectrow_array ($statement);`
`@row_ary = $dbh->`
`selectrow_array`
`($statement, \%attr);`
`@row_ary = $dbh->`
`selectrow_array ($statement,`
`\%attr, @bind_values);`
	Efficiently combines `prepare`, `execute`, and `fetchrow_array` into a single call. In a list context, this returns the first row of data from the statement. In a scalar context, this returns the first field of the first row. The `$statement` parameter can be a previously prepared statement handle.

`$ary_ref = $dbh->`
`selectcol_arrayref`
`($statement);`
`$ary_ref = $dbh->`
`selectcol_arrayref`
`($statement, \%attr);`
`$ary_ref = $dbh->`
`selectcol_arrayref`
`($statement, \%attr,`
`@bind_values);`
	In a single call, this combines `prepare`, `execute`, and `fetch` one column from all the rows of a result set. It returns a reference to an array that contains the values of the first column from each row.

`$sth = $dbh->`
`prepare($statement)`
`$sth = $dbh->prepare`
`($statement, \%attr)`
	Prepares a single statement for subsequent later execution by the database engine. This returns a reference to a statement handle object.

`$sth = $dbh->`
`prepare_cached`
`($statement)`
`$sth = $dbh->`
`prepare_cached`
`($statement, \%attr)`
`$sth = $dbh->`
`prepare_cached`
`($statement, \%attr,`
`$allow_active)`
	Similar to prepare except that the statement handle returned will be stored in a hash associated with the `$dbh` for efficiency of subsequent `prepare` calls using the same parameter values.

`$rv = $sth->bind_param`
`($p_num, $bind_value);`
`$rv = $sth->bind_param`
`($p_num, $bind_value,`
`$bind_type);`
`$rv = $sth->bind_param`
`($p_num, $bind_value,`
`\%attr);`
	The `bind_param` method can bind (assign/associate) a value with a placeholder, indicated with a ? character in the prepared statement. As some drivers do not support placeholders, check the driver documentation carefully.

Continued

Table 13-3 *(continued)*	

Method	Description

`$rc = $sth->`
`bind_param_inout ($p_num,`
`\$bind_value, $max_len)`
`$rv = $sth->bind_param_inout`
`($p_num, \$bind_value,`
`$max_len, \%attr)`
`$rv = $sth->`
`bind_param_inout ($p_num,`
`\$bind_value, $max_len,`
`$bind_type)`
	Typically a call to a stored procedure, enables values to be output from, or updated by, the statement. The `$bind_value` must be passed by reference. The value in the `$bind_val` variable is read when execute is called.

`$rv = $sth->execute`
`$rv = $sth->execute`
`(@bind_values)`
	Executes the (prepared) statement. Returns either `undef` if an error occurs or true if successful regardless of the number of rows affected.

`$rc = $sth->bind_col` `($col_num, \$col_variable);`	Binds an output column of a `select` statement to a Perl user variable.

`$rc = $sth->bind_columns`
`(@list_of_refs_to_`
`vars_to_bind);`
	Calls `bind_col` for each column of the `select` statement.

`$rc = $sth->finish;`	Good for housekeeping, this method indicates that no more data will be fetched from this statement handle before it is either executed again or destroyed.
`@row_ary = $sth->` `fetchrow_array;`	Gets the next row of data as an array holding the field values.

`$ary_ref = $sth->`
`next`
`fetchrow_arrayref;`
`$ary_ref = $sth->fetch;`
	The quickest way to retrieve data; gets the row of data as a reference to an array holding the field values. Use in conjunction with `$sth->bind_columns`.

`$hash_ref = $sth->`
`fetchrow_hashref;`
`$hash_ref = $sth->`
`fetchrow_hashref ($name);`
	Retrieves the next row of data as a reference to a hash containing field name/field value pairs.

Method	Description

`$tbl_ary_ref = $sth->`
`fetchall_arrayref;`
`$tbl_ary_ref = $sth->`
`fetchall_arrayref`
`($slice_array_ref );`
`$tbl_ary_ref = $sth->`
`fetchall_arrayref`
`($slice_hash_ref );`
	Retrieves, as a reference to an array containing one reference per row, all the data resulting from a prepared and executed statement handle.

`$rv = $sth->rows;`	Returns either the number of rows affected by the last command that had an effect on any rows, or -1 if unknown or unavailable.
`$rc = $dbh->commit;`	Commits the most recent series of database changes since the last commit or rollback. Check the documentation to find out whether the target database supports transactions.
`$rc = $dbh->rollback;`	Undoes the most recent series of database changes if the database supports transactions. Check the documentation to find out whether the target database supports transactions.

`$sql = $dbh->quote($value);`
`$sql = $dbh->quote($value,`
`$data_type);`
	Quotes a string literal for use as a literal value in a SQL statement by escaping any special characters (such as quotation marks) contained within the string and adding the required type of outer quotation marks.

`$rc = $h->err;`	Returns the native database engine error code (may be a string) from the last driver function called.
`$str = $h->errstr;`	Returns the native database engine error message from the most recent function.
`$rv = $h->state;`	Returns an error code in the standard SQLSTATE five-character format. Refer to the driver documentation for the exact values returned.
`$rc = $dbh->disconnect;`	Disconnects the database from the database handle.

Using the interface

We demonstrate some common uses of DBI with a simple mysql interface and wrap up DBI with an example of how to retrieve metadata using some of these features of DBI. We show how to connect to a database, retrieve results, perform transactions, and disconnect from the database. Our example demonstrates connecting to a database, preparing a query, executing the query and extracting and manipulating the metadata stored in attributes of the statement handle.

Connecting to a database

The following example supplies a database name and the machine location of the database, supply the name of a valid user (`username` parameter) and the correct password for that user to the database using DBI. The username and password have to have already been made known to the database security process by having been pre-assigned by a database administrator for that database. Upon successful connection (the login process completed successfully implying that the username parameter and the password parameter were correct) the application will have a valid (non-NULL) pointer to a data structure that represents the database session. This data structure holds detailed information necessary for subsequent database operations that occur *during the same session*. The application doesn't directly use this detailed information.

Perl DBI example:

```
$con1 = DBI->connect ( $data-source-name, $login_name,
$login_password) || die $DBI::errstr;
```

Disconnecting from a database

Log out of the database using the same username that was used when logging in to the database (implicitly used by way of the "handle" to the data), then free the memory structure that has been allocated for the connection.

Perl DBI example:

```
$con1->disconnect || warn $dbh->errstr;
```

Retrieving results

The following is how results are retrieved.

```
$stmt1 = $con1->prepare ( q/Select name from Customer/ )
$rs = $stmt1->execute;
```

Updating rows

```
$sth = $dbh->prepare($statement)
$rc = $dbh->do($statement)
```

Prepared (SQL) statements

```
$sth = $dbh->prepare($statement) || die $dbh->errstr;
```

Transactions

The documentation that comes with the Perl DBI module recommends using the eval{} method for transaction processing. eval evaluates the statements within the block at runtime. So, in this case, $statement1 can change prior to the eval; however, when we reach this block it is executed (evaluated). For example:

```
eval {
    $sth1=$dbh->prepare($statement1)
    $sth2=$dbh->prepare($statement2)
    $sth3=$dbh->prepare($statement3)
    $sth4=$dbh->prepare($statement4)
    $sth1-> execute
    $sth2-> execute
    $sth3-> execute
    $sth4-> execute
};
if ($@) {
    # $@ contains $DBI::errstr if DBI RaiseError caused die
    $dbh->rollback;
    # add any other application specific error handling code
here
}
else {
    $dbh->commit;
}
```

The preceding code prepares several SQL statements and then executes them. If an error occurs, the database rolls back; otherwise the statements are committed.

Retrieving metadata

The following program illustrates connecting to a database and retrieving the metadata about a particular table. It is run from the shell prompt and outputs the create table statement necessary to reproduce the table. Although not so useful in itself, we use the same concepts to facilitate a more complex application in Chapter 16. Its purpose is to illustrate how some of the common DBI methods are used to manipulate data in a database.

```perl
#!/usr/bin/perl
#######################################################
#                                                     #
# meta_get.pl <tablename>                             #
#    get column information about a table             #
#                                                     #
#######################################################


use DBI;  # Use the DBI module (must be installed first)
use strict; # Use strict perl to be safe



###################################
# Database variables         #
###################################
my $dbname='order_entry_db';
my $user='dba';
my $password='dba2pass';
my $dbd='mysql';


# connect to database

my $dbh=DBI->connect($dbname, $user, $password, $dbd);

#if connection fails... print error string
if (!$dbh) {
  print "ERROR: $DBI::errstr\n";
}


# check usage; if incorrect let user know
my $num=@ARGV;
if($num=1) {

  #######################################
  #                                     #
  # Interface with Database             #
  #                                     #
  #######################################

  # Assign table to be looked at
  my $table=$ARGV[0];

  # build query
  my $query="select * from $table where 1=0";

  # prepare query
  my $sth=$dbh->prepare("$query");

  # execute query
  my $error=$sth->execute;
```

```
############################################
#                                          #
# Extract   metadata                       #
#                                          #
############################################

# if no columns, table does not exist;
if(! $sth->{NAME}) {
  print "$table does not exist\n";
  $dbh->disconnect();
  exit;
}


# reference column name, type, and precision
my $columns=$sth->{NAME};
my $types=$sth->{TYPE};
my $precisions=$sth->{PRECISION};

# Create a lookup for known values of type
 my @type_desc=('unknown','char',
'unknown','unknown','integer',
'unknown','unknown','unknown','unknown','date');

############################################
#                                          #
# Format and output metadata     #
#                                          #
############################################


# Strict requires variables to be defined
my $num_of_col=@$columns;
my $ii=0;
my $column=undef;
my $type=undef;
my $precision=undef;

# output first part of create statement
print "create table $table (\n";

# foreach  column print the ddl statement

foreach $column (@$columns) {

  # get type by using the description lookup above
  # and the statement handle  attributes

  $type=$type_desc[shift @$types];
  # precision is a direct statement handle attribute
  $precision=shift @$precisions;
```

```
        # print column name;
        print "\t $column $type";

        # if char print number of chars


        if($type=~ m/char/) {
          print "($precision)";
        }

        # if not last column, print new line

        if ($ii < $num_of_col) {
          print ",\n"
        }

        # keep track of column we're on
        $ii++;
    }

    # finish up table statement
    print "\n);\n";


    ######################################
    #                                    #
    # Gracefully exit program            #
    #                                    #
    ######################################


    # close the statement handle
    $sth->finish;

} # if usage wrong, print usage
else { die "Usage meta_get.pl <tablename> "; }


# disconnect from database
$dbh->disconnect();
```

Upon executing this script, we get the create statement used to create the table.

```
$ metaget.pl customer
create table customer (
    customer_id char(20),
    first_name char(20),
    middle_initial char(20),
```

```
last_name char(20),
address_line_1 char(20),
address_line_2 char(20),
city char(20),
state char(20),
zip char(20),
phone_number char(18),
premium_shipped char(20),

);
```

We see that the preceding perl program takes a customer's name and returns the create statement necessary for creating the table. The code uses the perl DBI functions access this information.

Java and JDBC

The API for use with Java is JDBC — Java Database Connectivity. JDBC is part of the standard Java distribution. It consists of a set of classes and interfaces written in the Java programming language. JDBC provides a standard API for that makes it possible to write database applications using a pure Java API. Java applications will use JDBC and one of the JDBC libraries for the particular database(s). The libararies come in four levels of compliance, with level 4 being a native-protocol pure Java driver. The least-compliant level, Level 1, is the JDBC-ODBC bridge plus ODBC drivers. This class of database drivers was initiated in order to get acceptance of Java for database applications off of the ground.

JDBC Essential Package

java.sql	Provides the JDBC package. JDBC is a standard API for executing SQL statements. It contains classes and interfaces for creating SQL statements, and retrieving the results of executing those statements against relational databases. JDBC has a framework in which different "drivers" can be installed dynamically to access different databases.

Interface

Array	The mapping in the Java programming language for the SQL type ARRAY.
Blob	The representation (mapping) in the Java programming language of an SQL BLOB.
CallableStatement	The interface used to execute SQL stored procedures.
Clob	The mapping in the JavaTM programming language for the SQL CLOB type.
Connection	A connection (session) with a specific database.

DatabaseMetaData	Comprehensive information about the database as a whole.
Driver	The interface that every driver class must implement.
PreparedStatement	An object that represents a precompiled SQL statement.
Ref	JDBC 2.0 A reference to an SQL structured type value in the database.
ResultSet	A ResultSet provides access to a table of data.
ResultSetMetaData	An object that can be used to find out about the types and properties of the columns in a ResultSet.
SQLData	The interface used for the custom mapping of SQL user-defined types.
SQLInput	An input stream that contains a stream of values representing an instance of an SQL structured or distinct type.
SQLOutput	The output stream for writing the attributes of a user-defined type back to the database.
Statement	The object used for executing a static SQL statement and obtaining the results produced by it.
Struct	The standard mapping for an SQL structured type.

Class

Date	A thin wrapper around a millisecond value that enables JDBC to identify this as a SQL DATE.
DriverManager	The basic service for managing a set of JDBC drivers.
DriverPropertyInfo	Driver properties for making a connection.
Time	A thin wrapper around java.util.Date that enables JDBC to identify this as a SQL TIME value.
Timestamp	This class is a thin wrapper around java.util.Date that enables JDBC to identify this as a SQL TIMESTAMP value.
Types	The class that defines constants that are used to identify generic SQL types, called JDBC types.

Exception

BatchUpdateException	An exception thrown when an error occurs during a batch update operation.

DataTruncation	An exception that reports a DataTruncation warning (on reads) or throws a DataTruncation exception (on writes) when JDBC unexpectedly truncates a data value.
SQLException	An exception that provides information on a database access error.
SQLWarning	An exception that provides information on database access warnings.

Using JDBC

The following example takes advantage of Java graphics capabilities to generate a summary bar graph of the transactional data in our simple database. It loads our specific database driver (in this case mm.mysql-2.0.1). It then creates a drawing space. Next it connects to the database. Finally, it selects summary data about revenue and plots bar graphs on it. It uses the Java try-catch syntax to catch errors along the way.

```
File PlotRevenue.java :
import java.applet.Applet;
import java.awt.*;
import java.sql.*;


/*
 * The PlotRevenue program summarizes the data with a simple database
 *
 */

public class PlotRevenue extends Applet {


    /***************************
     * initialize variables    *
     ***************************/

    public static int width=1000;
    public static int height=750;
    public static int border_width=50;
    public static int shift=50;
    public static int bar_width = 100;
    public static int total_revenue=0;


    /***************************
     * Resize plot             *
     ***************************/
    public void init() {
    resize(width,height);
    }
```

```
/***********************************************
 *   Paint the plot using data from database    *
 ***********************************************/

public void paint(Graphics graph) {

    // First try to load driver to database
    try {

        Class.forName("org.gjt.mm.mysql.Driver");
    }
    // if error print
    catch (Exception error) {
        System.err.println("Unable to load driver.");
        error.printStackTrace();
    }

    // Everything's okay try to connect
    try {
        Connection connection =
DriverManager.getConnection("jdbc:mysql://localhost/order_entry?user=dba&passwor
d=dba2pass");


        // Draw the graph and its border.

        graph.setColor(Color.white);
        graph.fillRect(0,0,width,height);
        graph.setColor(Color.black);
        graph.drawRect(border_width,border_width,width-2*border_width,height-
2*border_width);


        // try to use the connection we created
        try {

            // Simple read from the database

            Statement query = connection.createStatement();
            ResultSet results = query.executeQuery("select Order_Date,
sum(Extended_Price) from Order_Header natural join Order_Detail group by
Order_Date ");

                // Initialize shift to zero to keep
                // plot from shifting on redraw
                shift=0;

                // While we have results and space
```

```
          while (results.next() && shift < width) {

              shift=shift+2*bar_width; //shift bar over

              // set color for text
              graph.setColor(Color.red);

              //print the months below each bar
              graph.drawString(results.getString(1),shift+10,height-10);

              //if the amount is too great scale and let user know

              total_revenue=Integer.parseInt(results.getString(2))/100;
              if ( total_revenue >  height-2*border_width) {
                  graph.drawString("(Not to
scale)",shift+10,border_width+20);
                  total_revenue=height-30;
              }

              //print the totals in dollars above each bar

graph.drawString(results.getString(2),shift+10,border_width+height-
total_revenue-20);

              // Set color to blue for bars
              graph.setColor(Color.blue);

              // Draw the bars
              graph.fillRect(shift+10,border_width+height-total_revenue,
                         bar_width,total_revenue-2*border_width);
          }


          // Close everything
          results.close();
          query.close();
          connection.close();

      }

      //if Statement creation failed let print an error
      catch (SQLException error) {
          System.out.println("Error: " + error.getMessage());
      }

  }
  //if connection fails print an error and stack trace.
  catch (SQLException error) {
      System.out.println("Error: " + error.getMessage());
      error.printStackTrace();
```

```
      }


    }
  }
```

The HTML document to display this applet is as follows:

```
<!DOCTYPE HTML PUBLIC "-//W3C//DTD HTML 4.01 Transitional//EN">
<html>
  <head>
    <title>Revenue</title>
  </head>

  <body>
    <h1>Revenue</h1>

    <APPLET CODE="PlotRevenue.class" WIDTH=150 HEIGHT=25>
            </APPLET>

    <hr>
    <!-- Created: Thu Oct  5 02:46:04 EDT 2000 -->
    <!-- hhmts start -->
    Last modified: Mon Oct 30 23:02:13 EST 2000
    <!-- hhmts end -->
  </body>
</html>
```

When you use the applet viewer, you see the following applet appear.

```
    $ appletviewer  revenue.html
```

PHP and MySQL

Rasmus Lerdorf developed PHP in 1994, and used it on his home page to keep track of who was browsing his résumé. The first public version, known as the Personal Home Page Tools, consisted of a parser that only understood a few macros and a number of utilities implementing common home page features, such as counters and guest books. The parser was rewritten in 1995, MySQL support was added, and the package was renamed PHP/FI Version 2, the FI coming from an HTML form interpreter.

The product eventually evolved and the parser was rewritten from scratch, forming the basis for PHP Version 3. Either PHP/FI or PHP3 ships with a number of commercial products such as C2's StrongHold Web server and Red Hat Linux. Estimates based on numbers provided by NetCraft place PHP in use on more than 1 million sites around the world, a number that compares favorably with Netscape's server product.

MySQL functions allow you to access MySQL (www.mysql.com/) database servers (as shown in Table 13-4). In order to have these functions available, you must compile PHP with MySQL support by using the `--with-mysql` option. If you use this option without specifying the path to MySQL, PHP will use the built-in MySQL client libraries. Users who run other applications that use MySQL (for example, running PHP3 and PHP4 as concurrent Apache modules, or `auth mysql`) should always specify the path to MySQL: `--with-mysql=/path/to/mysql`. This will force PHP to use the client libraries installed by MySQL, avoiding any conflicts.

Table 13-4 The MySQL Database API for PHP	
Database API	**Description**
mysql_affected_rows	Get number of affected rows in previous MySQL operation
mysql_change_user	Change logged in user of the active connection
mysql_close	Close MySQL connection
mysql_connect	Open a connection to a MySQL server
mysql_create_db	Create a MySQL database
mysql_data_seek	Move internal result pointer
mysql_db_query	Send a MySQL query
mysql_drop_db	Drop (delete) a MySQL database
mysql_errno	Returns the numerical value of the error message from previous MySQL operation
mysql_error	Returns the text of the error message from previous MySQL operation
mysql_fetch_array	Fetch a result row as an associative array
mysql_fetch_field	Get column information from a result and return as an object
mysql_fetch_object	Fetch a result row as an object
mysql_fetch_row	Get a result row as an enumerated array
mysql_field_flags	Get the flags associated with the specified field in a result
mysql_field_name	Get the name of the specified field in a result
mysql_field_len	Return the length of the specified field
mysql_field_seek	Set result pointer to a specified field offset
mysql_field_table	Get name of the table that the specified field is in
mysql_field_type	Get the type of the specified field in a result
mysql_free_result	Free result memory

Continued

<table>
<tr><th colspan="2">Table 13-4 (continued)</th></tr>
<tr><th>Database API</th><th>Description</th></tr>
<tr><td><code>mysql_insert_id</code></td><td>Get the id generated from the previous INSERT operation</td></tr>
<tr><td><code>mysql_list_dbs</code></td><td>List databases available on a MySQL server</td></tr>
<tr><td><code>mysql_list_fields</code></td><td>List MySQL result fields</td></tr>
<tr><td><code>mysql_list_tables</code></td><td>List tables in a MySQL database</td></tr>
<tr><td><code>mysql_num_fields</code></td><td>Get number of fields in result</td></tr>
<tr><td><code>mysql_num_rows</code></td><td>Get number of rows in result</td></tr>
<tr><td><code>mysql_pconnect</code></td><td>Open a persistent connection to a MySQL Server</td></tr>
<tr><td><code>mysql_query</code></td><td>Send a MySQL query</td></tr>
<tr><td><code>mysql_result</code></td><td>Get result data</td></tr>
<tr><td><code>mysql_select_db</code></td><td>Select a MySQL database</td></tr>
<tr><td><code>mysql_tablename</code></td><td>Get table name of field</td></tr>
</table>

Linux Shell Scripts and Piping

Most Linux databases have a command-line interface that can also be used in Linux shell scripts. The basic approach is to create an executable shell script having command lines in it that look identical to the same command as if it were entered interactively. For example, a MySQL script may look like (`$SHELL_PROMPT>` is the prompt for whatever OS platform is being used):

```
$SHELL_PROMPT >mysql -h <host> -u <user> -p<password> -N <
batch_file_of_mysql_commands.sql
```

or

```
$SHELL_PROMPT> mysql -N < batch_file_of_mysql_commands.sql >
batchfile.out
batch_file_of_mysql_commands.sql
select * from customers where last_update_date<='1999-12-31';
```

Some Notes about Performance

Finally, we offer some tips and concepts to help you steer clear of performance degradation. It is probably more typical to worry about performance issues when they arise, however, having a clear understanding of some basic concepts can avoid some pitfalls later on — and potentially a lot of tuning and rewriting. The following are some typical performance degradations and ways of avoiding them.

Connecting to a data source

The process of connecting to a data source is expensive in terms of end-user time. So, efficient connection management has an impact on application performance. Implement your application to issue a connect request the least number of times possible You should use statement handles to manage multiple SQL statements instead of connecting and disconnecting several times to execute SQL statements. SQL statement objects provide access methods and data storage for SQL statements. Perl may be an exception to this, as the Perl DBI module provides an efficient cache for use with multiple connections to the same data source (refer to the description for `DBI->connect_cached` in `Perldoc`). However, reusing one handle is still guaranteed to be the most efficient.

A common mistake is to issue multiple connect requests rather than the preferred (and probably intended) use of multiple SQL statement objects to the same database connection. For example, to optimize performance, applications that are designed as separate modules should pass the already established connection object pointer (or handle) between them, instead of passing the database name, username, and password, and connecting and disconnecting repeatedly.

For transaction processing in which multiple SQL statements must all complete as a unit or none complete at all, it may be necessary to create multiple statement objects simultaneously using the same connection object in order to have the multiple SQL statements be able to commit or rollback the transaction as intended.

Using column binding

Performance may also be improved by binding result set columns to application variables, for example, an application-managed data structure. The reason to use column binding is that many database drivers are implemented to take advantage of binding result information directly from the data source into the user's buffer; the driver can use the bound columns directly instead of going through an intermediate buffer. This will reduce the number of method or function calls that the application will need to perform.

SQL queries that return result sets require the use of specific methods depending on the API. For example, in Perl DBI, the method that is needed for queries that return results, that is, Select. . .From. . . queries, itself returns a result set object. However, the ODBC API uses a different approach for determining, at runtime, whether or not a query returned any results.

Executing calls with SQLPrepare and SQLExecute versus direct execution

Certain ODBC, JDBC, and Perl DBI methods or functions are more efficient than others at executing queries depending on both the query type and how frequently it is used.

For ODBC, the use of SQLPrepare and SQLExecute is intended for multiple executions of a statement that uses parameter markers, whereas the use of SQLExecDirect is intended for a single execution of a SQL statement. Therefore, for better performance, use SQLPrepare and SQLExecute for queries that are executed more than once, and use SQLExecDirect for queries that are executed only once. In transactional applications that use embedded SQL extensively, for example, for order-entry applications, the use of parameterized queries is widespread in order to implement data entry. In these applications the combination of SQLPrepare and SQLExecute is dictated, although it is possible to create query statements on the fly by using only string copy and string concatenation functions.

Transactions and committing data

Committing data is I/O-intensive and, consequently, is slow. When a connection is initially made to a database, autocommit on is the typical default mode. The application presumes that any changes have been successful. This means that any changes to the database by each SQL statement are committed immediately upon successful completion of the statement without the explicit action of the application. There are two implications to this: First, transactions are at the statement level. To implement transactions across statements requires that the commit mode be set to manual. Then, the application issues an explicit method or function to commit the changes. Second, if there is no chance of corruption if a statement does not complete successfully, that is, database recoverability is ensured, turning autocommit off can improve performance because the I/O for a commit is not performed for every single SQL statement.

Summary

This chapter summarizes some APIs and interfaces that are common to a database on Linux MySQL. It provides a few examples that use the API's basic functionality. Included are lists of the functions to these databases. For the most part, we described APIs that are common to the UNIX environment. We mentioned one very common API—ODBC—because of its pervasiveness in the industry. In the remaining chapters in this part, we build applications using two of these interfaces. Which interface should be chosen is determined by the task at hand. If you are going to be accessing the database via a Windows machine, then using the ODBC driver is a good solution. However, if the application is a Web application or a Linux desktop application, then some of the more modern APIs may be better suited for the task.

✦ ✦ ✦

Programming APIs – Extended Examples

◆ ◆ ◆ ◆

In This Chapter

ODBC

JDBC

Perl DBI

◆ ◆ ◆ ◆

This is the second of two chapters on programming an interface to a relational database. In the previous chapter, we presented synopses of a number of popular APIs with which you can work with a relational database. These APIs included ODBC, JDBC, Perl DBI, and PHP.

This chapter discusses in greater detail how to code the ODBC, JDBC, and Perl API interfaces. We present a number of example programs, and walk you through how they work.

Open Database Connectivity

As we noted in previous chapters, a consortium of software companies led by Microsoft Corporation designed the Open Database Connectivity (ODBC) protocol. This protocol provides a universal call-level interface through which applications can work with relational databases.

Linux purists will look with skepticism at anything originating from Redmond, Washington, but the fact is that ODBC is a truly open, well-designed standard. Commercial development of ODBC drivers has centered around the DOS/Windows for the same reason that Willie Sutton robbed banks — because "that's where the money is." However, ODBC is available under Linux, both to access databases that are running under Linux, and to let applications that are running under Linux access databases that are running under other operating systems.

In the previous chapter, we presented ODBC in the abstract. This chapter describes how to install and configure ODBC under Linux to access the MySQL database, and walk you through example program that work with MySQL.

Structure of an ODBC application

Chapter 12 presented the ODBC's architecture. To review quickly, an ODBC application has three parts: application code, the driver manager, and one or more drivers.

✦ The application code is what you, the programmer, write. It contains your user interfaces, SQL, and business logic.

✦ The driver manager is linked into the application. As its name implies, it is responsible for loading and unloading ODBC drivers, and for passing data between each driver and the application.

✦ The ODBC driver is responsible for communicating with a data source. The ODBC standard defines a data source as being a repository of data plus the network interface used to access those data. A *repository of data* usually is a relational database, but it may be any source of data—for example, an archive of news articles. The driver itself is implemented as a shared library that the driver manager loads into memory upon request. The driver receives statements from the application via the ODBC driver manager, translates each statement into the CLI expected by the data source, forwards the statements to the data source, and then receives replies from the data source that it returns to the application. The application can request that more than one driver be loaded into memory simultaneously, with each driver being used to communicate with a different data source.

To an application program, the ODBC driver is invisible: the application never explicitly loads or frees a driver. Rather, the application tells the driver manager to open a connection to a data source; the driver manager loads the appropriate driver, uses the driver to establish a connection to a data source, and returns a handle with which the application can work with the data source. When the application closes the connection to that data source, the driver manager drops the driver and frees the memory allocated for it.

At first glance, this structure may seem overly complex; in fact, it is quite efficient. The driver manager handles tasks that are common across all data sources, while the driver handles tasks for the data source. Because the drivers are implemented as shared libraries, you can add new drivers or update existing drivers without having to change your application at all—not even relink it.

Installing and configuring ODBC under Linux

ODBC is used mostly under Windows. However, at least two ODBC driver managers are available for Linux, and drivers are available for a number of databases, including MySQL, PostgreSQL, and most commercial databases.

In the following two subsections, we describe how to install and configure an ODBC driver manager and an ODBC driver. Much of the description is specific to the software that we use in these examples; however, you should be able to use these descriptions as a template for installing and configuring the ODBC software that you wish to use with your application.

Installing a driver manager

As of this writing, two principal ODBC driver managers are available for Linux:

✦ iodbc—This driver manager is maintained by OpenLink Corporation, which is one of the first ODBC companies to support Linux. It is based on an open-source driver manager written by programmer Ke Jin. iodbc consists of a C library that is linked to an application.

✦ unixODBC—This driver manager attempts to reproduce the ODBC driver-management system used by Windows. It provides a GUI that a user can use to select ODBC drivers and define data sources that can be used by applications.

In this section, we work with the iodbc driver manager. We chose iodbc partly because we are familiar with it, and partly because its simplicity makes it easier to use.

We first describe the archives that must be downloaded and where they can be found. We then describe how to install the software and how to configure the software and your environment to use the software.

Downloading archives

To load a precompiled version of iodbc onto your Linux system, point your browser to the URL: http://www.iodbc.org/.

On this Web page's left frame, select the entry for the OpenLink iODBC software development kit (SDK) binaries. When the SDK menu appears in the right frame, select two entries: one for the generic installation script, and one of the Linux SDKs for your Linux system. Be sure to select the one compiled with the appropriate libraries, for example, glibc2.

Installing software

After you have downloaded the archives, you're ready to install them, as follows:

1. su to the superuser root.

2. Create the directory in which you want the iodbc software stored. We suggest /var/iodbc, although you may have another place you prefer. Move the archives into this file.

3. Enter the directory into which you are installing iodbc. Type the command:

   chmod +x install.sh

   to make the installation script executable.

4. Type install.sh to install the software. This script dearchives the bits, creates the directory odbcsdk, backs up previously installed iodbc software, and dearchives the bits into subdirectory odbcsdk. It also builds two scripts with

which you can set your environment for running iodbc: `openlink.csh`, which works with the C shell, and `openlink.sh`, which works with the Bourne or bash shells.

5. Execute these commands:

```
rmdir bin
mv odbcsdk/*
```

This compensates for a bug in the installation script that causes it to build the wrong directory path into scripts `openlink.csh` and `openlink.sh`.

6. Type the command `exit`, to cease having root permissions. Then copy script `openlink.sh` or `openlink.csh` (depending upon which shell you're running) into the configuration file for your shell. If you are running `bash`, be sure to copy it into file `$HOME/.bashrc` instead of into `$HOME/.bash_profile`; otherwise, some key environmental variables (for example, `LD_LIBRARY_PATH`) will not be set properly.

That's all there is to it. Now you are ready to install the ODBC driver.

Installing an ODBC driver

This section presents examples that work with the MySQL database. MySQL provides an ODBC driver, called MyODBC, that works with the MySQL database. We describe how to download MyODBC and how to configure it.

The descriptions in this section are tailored for MyODBC. However, you should be able to use them as a template for installing an ODBC driver for your database of choice.

Downloading archives

The first step is to obtain a copy of the ODBC driver. In this example, we work with the MyODBC driver; so, if a copy of MyODBC is not included with your Linux release (and some do not include it), point your browser to URL:

```
http://www.mysql.com
```

When the page appears on your browser, scroll the left frame until you see Downloads; click it.

When the Downloads page appears, scroll the right frame until you see MyODBC; click it.

When the MyODBC download page appears, scroll the right frame until you see MyODBC for UNIX. Click the appropriate entry for the archive that you want. If you want an installable archive of precompiled bits, click the entry for Binary RPM of MyODBC. In this example, we use MyODBC 2.50.36; however, the version may well have changed by the time you read this.

Note that you may have to upgrade your edition of MySQL to use the current distribution of MyODBC. For example, we are running SuSE Linux 7.0, which comes with MySQL 3.22 on its disks; however, to run MyODBC 2.50.36, we had to upgrade the MySQL client software to release 3.23. Fortunately, MySQL client 3.23 works with server release 3.22, so we could avoid a more painful server upgrade. If you are not sure whether the MyODBC bits you have downloaded work with your release of MySQL, check the documentation that comes with the bits; or simply attempt to install and see if the rpm command complains of software mismatches.

Installing the software

After you have downloaded the software, the next step is to install it. This is quite simple: just su to the superuser root, and then type the command:

```
rpm -i archivename
```

where archivename gives the name of the archive that you have just downloaded. The rpm manager will take care of installation for you. If rpm complains of any software mismatches, you will have to resolve them first, and then try again to install.

By default, rpm installs the MyODBC driver into directory /usr/local/lib. It installs the (somewhat sparse) documentation for MyODBC into directory /usr/doc/packages/MyODBC. It also installs into /usr/doc/packages/MyODBC an example ODBC initialization file, called odbc.ini; we discuss this file in the following section.

Preparing the initialization file

At this point, you have installed both the ODBC driver manager and one or more ODBC drivers, and you have set your environment so that any applications you run will be able to find the shared libraries for the ODBC driver manager. One last step remains, however: to prepare an ODBC initialization file.

Before an application can connect with a data source via ODBC, the application must pass a large amount of information to the ODBC driver manager. Among other things, it must tell the driver manager what database it wishes to open, the location of the driver to use, and the port through which the database is accessed.

With most ODBC packages, initialization information is passed through an initialization file. The name and layout of this file vary from one ODBC package to another; but most packages base their initialization files on the Windows format, which has the following structure:

✦ The initialization file has the suffix .ini.

✦ Initialization is given in the form of a *NAME=VALUE* pairs, much as environmental variables are defined in your .profile file.

✦ The initialization file can hold multiple sets of initializations. Each initialization set gives the information needed to connect to a given data source. Each set of initializations is headed by a data source name (DSN), which is given in square brackets.

For example, the following adapts the example MyODBC initialization file to define a data source that accesses our baseball database:

```
[baseball]
Driver   = /usr/local/lib/libmyodbc.so
Server   = localhost
Port     = 3306
Database = baseball
Socket   = /tmp/mysql.sock
```

✦ [baseball] — The data source name. In this example, we have given the data source the same name as our database, but we did not have to do that. The only requirement is that the data source name be unique within the initialization file.

✦ Driver — The path name for the shared library of the ODBC driver needed to connect to this data source.

✦ Host — The name or IP address of the machine upon which the database resides. In this example, the database is running on the same box that we are using, so set Host to localhost.

✦ Database — The database with which you will be interacting; in this case, baseball.

✦ Port — The port through which the database is accessed. This is set to 3306, which is the default port used by MySQL.

✦ Socket — The socket file through which MySQL is accessed.

Note that this initialization file does not include some information needed to access the data source; in particular, it does not hold the user's login or password. Our application will pass those data to MySQL when we open the connection to the data source, as you will see in the next section.

When you have finished modifying the initialization file, copy it into file .odbc.ini in your home directory.

After you have created the ODBC initialization file, all you have to pass to the driver manager is the data source name, the login identifier (as set on the remote system) of the user who is connecting with the data source, and that user's password. This assumes that the user has permission both to connect to the remote system, and has appropriate permissions for manipulating the database. What these permissions are, and how to set them, varies from one database package to another; for details, see the documentation for the database package with which you wish to work.

Compiling an ODBC application

It has taken us a while to get this far, but we finally have our ODBC software installed and configured. However, one last preliminary task remains before we can write code: we must describe how to compile and link an ODBC application.

The following gives the command line for compiling a simple ODBC program:

```
cc -s -o exeFile -I/var/iodbc/include srcFile.c -L/var/iodbc/lib -liodbc
```

In this example, `-o exeFile` names the executable that we wish to create, and `srcFile.c` names the file of C code that we wish to compile.

Option `-s` tells the C compiler to use shared libraries instead of statically linking a library into the executable.

Option `-I/var/iodbc/include` names the directory that holds the header files that came with the iodbc SDK. Remember that /var/iodbc is the directory into which we installed the iodbc SDK earlier in this section; if you install it elsewhere, then use the name of that directory instead.

Option `-L/var/iodbc/lib` names the directory that holds the iodbc libraries that came with the iodbc SDK. As with the header files, /var/iodbc is the directory into which we installed the iodbc SDK; if you install it elsewhere, then name that directory instead.

Finally, option `-liodbc` tells the linker to link library iodbc.so into the executable that it builds.

Basic program structure

Finally, we are finished with our preliminaries: we have installed and configured ODBC software, we have prepared our initialization file, and we have compiled our ODBC programs. Now, we are ready to write some code.

To begin our examination of ODBC, we look at the elements that appear in every ODBC application, which include:

- ✦ Allocation of resources
- ✦ Loading an ODBC driver
- ✦ Opening a connection to a database
- ✦ Executing SQL statements
- ✦ Handling errors
- ✦ Closing the database connection
- ✦ Freeing resources

Each of these tasks is performed by calling one or more functions defined in the ODBC CLI.

Listing 14-1 presents an example ODBC program. You should look over this program now, although we do not expect you to understand it yet. Subsequently, we explain what each call does:

Listing 14-1: **A Basic ODBC Program**

```c
#include <stdio.h>
#include <stdlib.h>
#include <string.h>
#include "sql.h"
#include "sqlext.h"

/***********************************************************************
 * Check the value returned by a function. If it indicates an error,
 * call SQLError() to retrieve details about the error, print the output
 * and exit; otherwise, just return.
 ***********************************************************************/
void
check_return( RETCODE rc,
              HENV    henv,
              HDBC    hdbc,
              HSTMT   hstmt )
{
    UCHAR   state_str[SQL_MAX_MESSAGE_LENGTH];
    SDWORD  native_error;
    UCHAR   error_msg[SQL_MAX_MESSAGE_LENGTH];
    SWORD   error_msg_avail = SQL_MAX_MESSAGE_LENGTH - 1;
    SWORD   error_msg_len;
    RETCODE local_rc;

    if (rc != SQL_ERROR && rc != SQL_SUCCESS_WITH_INFO)
    {
        return;
    }

    local_rc = SQLError (henv,
                         hdbc,
                         hstmt,
                         state_str,
                         &native_error,
                         error_msg,
                         error_msg_avail,
                         &error_msg_len);

    if (local_rc != SQL_SUCCESS && rc != SQL_SUCCESS_WITH_INFO)
    {
        fprintf(stderr, "Uninterpretable error; exiting\n");
        exit (EXIT_FAILURE);
    }

    if (rc == SQL_SUCCESS_WITH_INFO)
    {
        fprintf (stderr, "Warning %s: %s\n", state_str, error_msg);
        return;
    }
```

```
        fprintf (stderr, "Fatal Error %s: %s\n", state_str, error_msg);
        exit (EXIT_FAILURE);
}
/* ------------------------------------------------------- */
int main(void)
{
    HENV    henv = SQL_NULL_HENV;
    HDBC    hdbc = SQL_NULL_HDBC;
    HSTMT   hstmt = SQL_NULL_HSTMT;
    RETCODE rc;

    char    buf[257];
    short   buflen;

    printf ("Initialize the environment structure.\n");
    SQLAllocEnv (&henv);

    printf ("Initialize the connection structure.\n");
    SQLAllocConnect (henv, &hdbc);

    printf ("Load the ODBC driver.\n");
    rc = SQLDriverConnect (hdbc,
                           0,
                           "DSN=baseball;UID=mylogin;PWD=mypassword",
                           SQL_NTS,
                           (UCHAR*) buf,
                           sizeof (buf),
                           &buflen,
                           SQL_DRIVER_COMPLETE);
    check_return (rc, henv, hdbc, hstmt);

    printf ("Initialize the statement structure.\n");
    SQLAllocStmt (hdbc, &hstmt);

    /* Now, do something */

    printf ("Create table table \"foo\".\n");
    rc = SQLExecDirect (hstmt, "CREATE TABLE foo (bar INTEGER)", SQL_NTS);
    check_return (rc, henv, hdbc, hstmt);

    printf("Insert values into table \"foo\".\n");
    rc = SQLExecDirect (hstmt, "INSERT INTO foo(bar) VALUES (1)", SQL_NTS);
    check_return (rc, henv, hdbc, hstmt);

    rc = SQLExecDirect (hstmt, "INSERT INTO foo(bar) VALUES (2)", SQL_NTS);
    check_return (rc, henv, hdbc, hstmt);

    rc = SQLExecDirect (hstmt, "INSERT INTO foo(bar) VALUES (3)", SQL_NTS);
    check_return (rc, henv, hdbc, hstmt);
```

Continued

Listing 14-1 *(continued)*

```
    printf ("Drop table \"foo\".\n");
    rc = SQLExecDirect (hstmt, "DROP TABLE foo", SQL_NTS);
    check_return (rc, henv, hdbc, hstmt);

    /* We're done: free resources and exit */

    printf ("Free the statement handle.\n");
    SQLFreeStmt (hstmt, SQL_DROP);

    printf ("Disconnect from the data source.\n");
    SQLDisconnect (hdbc);

    printf ("Free the connection structure.\n");
    SQLFreeConnect (hdbc);

    printf ("Free the environment structure.\n");
    SQLFreeEnv (henv);

    printf ("Goodbye!\n");
    exit (EXIT_SUCCESS);
}
```

When this program is compiled and run, you should see the following:

```
Initialize the environment structure.
Initialize the connection structure.
Initialize the statement structure.
Create table table "foo".
Insert values into table "foo".
Drop table "foo".
Free the statement handle.
Disconnect from the data source.
Free the connection structure.
Free the environment structure.
Goodbye!
```

The following subsections describe each task that this program performs.

Header files

The beginning of the program declares five header files. Three files — stdio.h, stdlib.h, and string.h — are standard C header files that are familiar to all C programmers.

Header files sql.h and sqlext.h declare the ODBC-specific prototypes, types, and constants. sql.h holds declarations that are specific to SQL, whereas sqlext.h holds declarations that extend the SQL standard. These header files are included as part of the iodbc driver manager's development kit; they reside in directory include under the directory into which we installed the development kit.

The names of the ODBC-specific header files may vary from one ODBC driver manager to another. For more information, check the documentation that comes with the driver manager that you are using.

Allocation of resources

At the risk of oversimplification, a program that uses ODBC consists of the allocation and freeing of resources:

✦ When the program begins, it allocates and initializes the ODBC environment.

✦ Each time the program connects to a new data source, it allocates and initializes the resources for communicating with that data source.

✦ Each time it executes a SQL statement for a given data source, the program allocates resources for executing the statement.

✦ When a statement has finished processing, the program frees the resources set aside for that statement.

✦ When a program has finished working with a given data source, it closes the connection with that source and frees the resources used to communicate with it.

✦ When the program has finished, it frees the resources allocated for the environment, and exits.

For each of these entities — environment, data source, and statement — the ODBC driver manager allocates resources and returns a handle: an environment handle for the environment, a connection handle for the data source, and a statement handle for the statement.

The declarations

```
HENV    henv = SQL_NULL_HENV;
HDBC    hdbc = SQL_NULL_HDBC;
HSTMT   hstmt = SQL_NULL_HSTMT;
```

declare the variables that will hold the handles to our three sets of resources: environment, database connection, and statement. Each of the types — HENV, HDBC, and HSTMT — is a typedef for a void*. We also initialized each to NULL, using the appropriate manifest constant for each.

To allocate resources for the ODBC environment, we call the following function:

```
RETCODE SQLAllocEnv (HENV* henv)
```

This function allocated the resources for the ODBC environment, and writes into variable `henv` the handle for the environment. The program then passes this handle to other ODBC calls. An ODBC application will only call this function once, as all ODBC connections share the same environment.

Function `RETCODE SQLAllocConnect (HENV henv, HDBC* hdbc)` allocates resources for a connection to a data source. It writes into variable `hdbc` the handle of the data connection. Note that you can open an indefinite number of connections simultaneously (although our example program uses one).

In Listing 14-1 we used these functions in the following calls:

```
SQLAllocEnv (&henv);
SQLAllocConnect (henv, &hdbc);
```

Note that your application should not fool around with the internals of an environment, connection, or statement — unless, of course, you are hell-bent on writing an application that is both buggy and nonportable.

Connecting to a data source

ODBC offers several functions with which a program can connect to a data source. Our example programs use `SQLDriverConnect()`, which loads the appropriate ODBC driver and connects to the data source. This call has the following syntax:

```
RETCODE SQLDriverConnect (
                HDBC    hdbc,
                HWND    windowhandle,
                UCHAR*  connect_string,
                SWORD   connect_string_length,
                UCHAR*  complete_connect_string,
                SWORD   complete_connect_string_max,
                SWORD*  complete_connect_string_length,
                UWORD   completion_flag )
```

hdbc is the handle to the database connection, as allocated by a call to `SQLLAllocConnect()`.

windowhandle is a handle for a window that can be used to ask the user for the connection string. This is strictly a Windows feature; under Linux, this always should be zero.

connect_string gives the text of the connection string. This string consists of a set of *variable=value* pairs, just like the ODBC initialization file for the data source. The connection string must at least give the data source name and the password. Type UCHAR is a typedef for `unsigned char`.

connect_string_length gives the length of *connect_string*, in bytes. Type SWORD is a typedef for `short`. The constant SQL_NTS indicates that *connect_string* is a C-style NUL-terminated string.

complete_connect_string gives the address of a place where the ODBC driver can write the complete connect string; that is, the connect string that has been "fleshed out" with definitions drawn from the initialization file. This buffer must be at least 255 bytes long.

complete_connect_string_max gives the length, in bytes, of the array to which *complete_connect_string* points.

complete_connect_string_length points to a variable into which the ODBC driver can write the length of the text it has written into the buffer to which *complete_connect_string* points. If the complete connection string is longer than the value given in *complete_connect_string_max*, the driver truncates it.

Finally, *completion_flag* gives a flag that tells the driver what to do if the connection string is not complete. It recognizes the following values:

✦ SQL_DRIVER_PROMPT—Display a prompt box that shows the user the connection string values. The user must confirm them before the driver will attempt to connect to the remote data source. The prompt box is displayed regardless of whether or not the connection string is complete (that is, contains all information needed to load the driver and connect to the data source).

✦ SQL_DRIVER_COMPLETE—If the connect string contains all information needed to load the driver and connect, then do so. Otherwise, display a prompt box and ask for more information.

✦ SQL_DRIVER_COMPLETE_REQUIRED—The same as SQL_DRIVER_COMPLETE, except that all fields that are not necessary to connecting to the data source are grayed out.

✦ SQL_DRIVER_NOPROMPT—If the connection string is not complete, fail.

Most Linux ODBC drivers do not use prompt boxes, so all four of these flags are, in effect, the same as SQL_DRIVER_NOPROMPT. In our program, we invoked this function as follows:

```
rc = SQLDriverConnect (hdbc,
                0,
                "DSN=baseball;UID=mylogin;PWD=mypassword",
                SQL_NTS,
                (UCHAR*) buf,
                sizeof (buf),
                &buflen,
                SQL_DRIVER_COMPLETE);
```

Note the format of the third argument, which gives the connection string. As you can see, it consists of three *variable=value* pairs, which are separated by semicolons. Variable DSN names the data source; the ODBC driver manager uses this string to find the settings for the data source as defined in the user's ODBC initialization file. Variable `UID` gives the user identifier, and variable `PWD` sets the user's password. If you wish, you can also set other ODBC variables, or even override one or more settings that are in the user's ODBC initialization file.

Allocation of statement resources

After we have connected to the database, we can allocate resources for a SQL statement. To do so, call function `SQLAllocStmt()`, as follows:

```
RETCODE SQLAllocStmt(HDBC hdbc, HSTMT* hstmt)
```

hdbc gives the handle for the database connection that we obtained by calling `SQLAllocConnect()` and initialized through a call to `SQLDriverConnect()`.

hstmt points to the variable into which the ODBC driver can write the handle for this newly allocated statement. In our program, we call it as follows:

```
SQLAllocStmt (hdbc, &hstmt);
```

For each database connection, we can allocate multiple statements. Some we execute asynchronously — that is, "in the background" — whereas others we can execute synchronously.

Handling errors

As you probably noticed, each of the ODBC calls returns a value of type `RETCODE`. This value indicates if the called function succeeded; the program should (under most circumstances) check this value before it proceeds to the next call.

An ODBC call returns one of the following codes to indicate whether it succeeded:

- ✦ `SQL_SUCCESS` — The call succeeded.
- ✦ `SQL_SUCCESS_WITH INFO` — The call succeeded, but the driver wishes to give the application some extra information.
- ✦ `SQL_NO_DATA_FOUND` — Either a request for information (that is, a SELECT statement) returned no data, or the application has retrieved all data.
- ✦ `SQL_ERROR` — An error occurred. The application can request a detailed description of the error.
- ✦ `SQL_INVALID_HANDLE` — A call used an invalid handle.
- ✦ `SQL_STILL_EXECUTING` — This value is returned if a statement is being executed asynchronously, and the application has requested information about its status.

Many calls return values in addition to these. If a function returns `SQL_ERROR` or `SQL_SUCCESS_WITH_INFO`, you can call function `SQLError()` to obtain further information. This function call has the following syntax:

```
RETCODE SQLError ( HENV        henv,
                   HDBC        hdbc,
                   HSTMT       hstmt,
                   UCHAR*      sql_state_string,
                   SDWORD*     sql_native_error,
                   UCHAR*      error_message,
                   SWORD       error_message_maximum,
                   SWORD FAR*  error_message_actual)
```

henv, *hdbc*, and *hstmt* give the handles for, respectively, the ODBC environment, the data-source connection, and the statement. Depending upon the nature of the error being checked, *hstmt* or *hdbc* may be NULL.

sql_state_string points to a character array into which SQLError() can write a string that describes the SQL state. This string is a four-digit number prefixed with one or more alphabetic characters. The ODBC standard defines the errors that can be associated with any given ODBC call, to help you with debugging your program.

sql_native_error points to a variable into which SQLError() can write the native error code. This error code is specific to the data source. SDWORD is a typedef for long.

error_message points to a character array into which SQLError() can write a string that describes the error.

error_message_maximum gives the length of this character array.

error_message_actual points to a variable into which SQLError() writes the length of the message it wants to write into error_message. If this value exceeds that of *error_message_maximum* — that is, the message the driver wishes to write exceeds the memory your application has allocated to hold it — then SQLError() truncates the message so that it will fit into *error_message*.

We have written function check_return() to check the return value of each ODBC call. This function calls SQLError() as follows:

```
local_rc = SQLError (henv,
                     hdbc,
                     hstmt,
                     state_str,
                     &native_error,
                     error_msg,
                     error_msg_avail,
                     &error_msg_len);
```

We call check_return() after practically every ODBC call, to trap errors and to print a diagnostic message should something go wrong.

Executing SQL statements

Now that we have allocated resources, connected to the database, and figured out how to handle errors, we can now do something with our database. As you can imagine, ODBC offers a wealth of calls for interacting with a database. We explore these in our later examples; for our first example, we look at the most elementary of these calls: SQLExecDirect(). This function takes a SQL statement in the form of text, and executes it directly upon the database. SQLExecDirect() takes the following syntax:

```
RETCODE SQLExecDirect (
              HSTMT   hstmt,
              UCHAR*  statement_text,
              SDWORD  statement_length)
```

hstmt gives the handle of the SQL statement, as set by a call to SQLAllocStmt().

statement_text gives the address of the character array that holds the statement to be executed.

statement_length gives the length of *statement_text*, in bytes. The constant SQL_NTS indicates that *statement_text* is a C-style NULL-terminated string.

In Listing 14-1, we use this call as follows:

```
rc = SQLExecDirect (hstmt, "CREATE TABLE foo (bar INTEGER)", SQL_NTS);

rc = SQLExecDirect (hstmt, "INSERT INTO foo(bar) VALUES (1)", SQL_NTS);
rc = SQLExecDirect (hstmt, "INSERT INTO foo(bar) VALUES (2)", SQL_NTS);
rc = SQLExecDirect (hstmt, "INSERT INTO foo(bar) VALUES (3)", SQL_NTS);

rc = SQLExecDirect (hstmt, "DROP TABLE foo", SQL_NTS);
```

Each of these calls passes a string literal as *statement_text*. The first call creates a table, called foo. The next three insert an integer into foo. The last drops table foo.

Free resources and disconnect

After we have finished manipulating our database, we must close the connect and free resources. We do this in the opposite order from that in which we allocated and opened them.

Our first task is to free the statement. To do so, we use the call SQLFreeStmt(), which has the following syntax:

```
RETCODE SQLFreeStmt (HSTMT hstmt)
```

where *hstmt* gives the statement handle.

The next step is to disconnect from the data source. To do so, we call SQLDisconnect(). It has the following syntax:

```
RETCODE SQLDisconnect (HDBC hdbc)
```

where *hdbc* gives the data-source handle.

Next, we free the sources allocated to the data-source connection by calling SQLFreeConnect(). It has the following syntax:

```
RETCODE SQLFreeConnect (HDBC hdbc)
```

where *hdbc* gives the data-source handle.

Finally, we free the resources allocated to the ODBC environment by calling SQLFreeEnv(). It has the following syntax:

```
RETCODE SQLFreeEnv (HENV henv)
```

where *henv* gives the environment handle.

Listing 14-1 calls them as follows:

```
SQLFreeStmt (hstmt, SQL_DROP);
SQLDisconnect (hdbc);
SQLFreeConnect (hdbc);
SQLFreeEnv (henv);
```

Binding a variable to a parameter

At this point, you have seen the framework for an ODBC program. To review, a program consists of these steps:

1. Initializing the ODBC environment.
2. Initializing a data source and opening a connection to it.
3. Initializing a statement.
4. Executing one or more instructions upon the data source.
5. Checking return values for errors.
6. Freeing resources, and exiting.

Now that you have seen how to structure an ODBC program and how to use it to manipulate a data source, we can start doing some real work.

Listing 14-1 calls function SQLExecDirect() to create a table and to populate it. This is fine if you only wish to execute static SQL instructions, which can be compiled directly into your program. However, in most instances, you will want to use variables to build SQL statements on the fly.

ODBC gives you a way to do this. Under ODBC, building a SQL statement on the fly is a two-step process:

1. *Prepare a SQL statement.* Each variable within the SQL statement is bound to a variable in your application

2. *Execute the statement.* The value of each variable within the SQL statement is read from its corresponding variable in your application.

Listing 14-2 demonstrates how to prepare and execute a SQL statement. Most of Listing 14-2 is a re-creation of Listing 14-1, so we print here only the lines of code that illustrate how to prepare, bind, and execute a statement:

Listing 14-2: **Preparing a SQL Statement**

```
printf ("PREPARE an INSERT statement.\n");
rc = SQLPrepare (hstmt, "INSERT INTO foo VALUES ( ? )", SQL_NTS);
check_return (rc, henv, hdbc, hstmt);

printf ("Bind a variable to the ? within the INSERT statement.\n");
rc = SQLBindParameter (hstmt,
                       (UWORD) 1,
                       SQL_PARAM_INPUT,
                       SQL_C_SLONG,
                       SQL_INTEGER,
                       (UDWORD) 0,
                       (SWORD) 0,
                       &value,
                       0,
                       NULL);
check_return (rc, henv, hdbc, hstmt);

for (value = 1 ; value <= 3 ; value++)
{
    printf ("Insert value %d into table \"bar\".\n", value);
    rc = SQLExecute (hstmt);
    check_return (rc, henv, hdbc, hstmt);
}
```

Prepare the statement

To begin, we used function `SQLPrepare()` to prepare a statement. This function has the following syntax:

```
RETCODE SQLPrepare (
                HSTMT   hstmt,
                UCHAR*  statement_text,
                SDWORD  statement_text_length)
```

hstmt is the handle of the statement we are preparing, as returned by a call to `SQLAllocStmt()`. *statement_text* gives the text of the statement being prepared.

statement_text_length gives the length, in bytes, of *statement_text*. The constant `SQL_NTS` indicated that *statement_text* is a C-style NUL-terminated string. In our example

```
rc = SQLPrepare (hstmt, "INSERT INTO foo VALUES ( ? )", SQL_NTS);
```

the statement contains one `?`. The question mark is a marker that tells `SQLPrepare()` that a variable will be used to pass data into or out of the statement at that point. The usual practice is to bind a variable to each marker, although this is not strictly necessary—Listing 14-10 demonstrates how to exchange data with a marker on the fly.

Bind a variable to a marker

To bind a variable to a parameter marker, we call the ODBC function `SQLBindParameter()`. It has the following syntax:

```
RETCODE SQLBindParameter(
                HSTMT    hstmt,
                UWORD    marker_number,
                SWORD    parameter_type,
                SWORD    C_data_type,
                SWORD    SQL_data_type,
                UDWORD   column_precision,
                SWORD    column_scale,
                PTR      parameter_address,
                SDWORD   maximum_length,
                SDWORD*  parameter_length)
```

hstmt gives the handle for the statement being manipulated. The handle must have been returned by a call to function `SQLAllocStmt()`.

marker_number gives the number of the marker to which you are binding the parameter. The `?` markers are counted from left to right, as they appear in the statement, counting from one.

parameter_type flags the type of the parameter, as follows:

✦ SQL_PARAM_INPUT—Data are being passed from the parameter into the statement.

✦ SQL_PARAM_OUTPUT—Data are being passed from the statement into the parameter.

✦ SQL_PARAM_INPUT_OUTPUT—Data are being passed from the parameter into the statement, then from the statement into the parameter.

C_data_type gives the type of the C variable that you are binding to the parameter marker. The recognized C data types are:

SQL_C_BINARY	SQL_C_TIMESTAMP	SQL_C_SSHORT
SQL_C_DOUBLE	SQL_C_CHAR	SQL_C_USHORT
SQL_C_TIME	SQL_C_SLONG	SQL_C_DEFAULT
SQL_C_BIT	SQL_C_ULONG	SQL_C_STINYINT
SQL_C_FLOAT	SQL_C_DATE	SQL_C_UTINYINT

The iodbc driver manager declares these constants in header file sqlext.h. Other driver managers may declare them elsewhere. These constants may vary from one ODBC driver manager to another. Most are self-explanatory. For details, check the documentation that comes with the ODBC driver manager that you are using; or if the documentation is minimal (as is the case with iodbc), read the header files themselves.

SQL_data_type gives the SQL data type of the parameter marker to which the variable is being bound. It must be one of the following:

SQL_BIGINT	SQL_LONGVARBINARY	SQL_NUMERIC
SQL_FLOAT	SQL_TIMESTAMP	SQL_VARBINARY
SQL_SMALLINT	SQL_CHAR	SQL_DECIMAL
SQL_BINARY	SQL_LONGVARCHAR	SQL_REAL
SQL_INTEGER	SQL_TINYINT	SQL_VARCHAR
SQL_TIME	SQL_DATE	SQL_DOUBLE
SQL_BIT		

The iodbc driver manager declares these constants in header file sql.h. Most are self-explanatory. Again, these may vary from one driver manager to another; check the driver manager's documentation for details.

Continuing with the discussion of the arguments passed to SQLBindParameter(), *column_precision* gives the column's precision.

column_scale gives the column's scale.

parameter_address gives the address of the variable that is being bound to the parameter marker.

maximum_length gives the length, in bytes, of the variable to which *variable_address* points.

Data are being passed from the statement into the parameter. The parameter is used only if its type is SQL_PARAM_INPUT or SQL_PARAM_INPUT_OUTPUT.

parameter_length gives the length in bytes of the buffer to which *parameter_address* points. This is a pointer rather than an integer because it is possible to bind a structure to a given parameter marker; in this case, *parameter_length* points to an array of SDWORDs, each of which gives the size of one field within the structure. (This is used, for example, to pass data to a stored procedure.) For most common input variables, this can be set to NULL.

In our example, we call SQLBindParameter() as follows:

```
rc = SQLBindParameter (hstmt,
                       (UWORD) 1,
                       SQL_PARAM_INPUT,
                       SQL_C_SLONG,
                       SQL_INTEGER,
                       (UDWORD) 0,
                       (SWORD) 0,
                       &value,
                       0,
                       NULL);
```

Execute the Statement

Finally, we call SQLExecute() to execute the prepared statement. This function has the following syntax:

```
RETCODE SQLExecute(HSTMT hstmt)
```

hstmt is the handle of the statement, as set by a call to function SQLAllocStmt(). In Listing 14-2, we call SQLExecute() within a loop, as follows:

```
for (value = 1 ; value <= 3 ; value++)
{
    printf ("Insert value %d into table \"bar\".\n", value);
    rc = SQLExecute (hstmt);
    check_return (rc, henv, hdbc, hstmt);
}
```

Each iteration of the loop inserts into the database the value that is written into variable value.

After this loop has finished executing, Listing 14-2 frees its resources and closes up shop, as we described earlier in this section.

Reading data returned by a SELECT statement

The previous subsection examined how to bind a variable to a ? parameter marker within a SQL statement. This works well when passing data into a database, say via an INSERT or UPDATE statement; however, this mechanism does not address how to deal with SELECT statements, which do not use variables.

ODBC automatically creates a mechanism, called a *cursor*, for managing the data that a SELECT statement returns. Cursors let you read one record at a time, parse the record, and work with the data that the record contains. In some instances, you can move backwards or forwards within the cursor, to reread records.

ODBC also lets you read data directly from columns, by binding a variable to a column. The following subsections demonstrate both methods.

Reading data from a cursor

Listing 14-3 demonstrates how to read data from a cursor. Most of this program repeats code given in Listing 14-1 and 14-2. The following gives the code that demonstrates fetching data, and then returning it.

Listing 14-3: **Reading Data from a Cursor**

```
rc = SQLExecDirect (hstmt, "SELECT max(bar) FROM foo", SQL_NTS);
check_return (rc, henv, hdbc, hstmt);

printf ("FETCH the output of the SELECT statement.\n");
rc = SQLFetch (hstmt);
check_return (rc, henv, hdbc, hstmt);

printf ("Get the data returned by the FETCH statement.\n");
rc = SQLGetData (hstmt, 1, SQL_C_ULONG, &value, 0, NULL);
check_return (rc, henv, hdbc, hstmt);

printf ("\nThe maximum value in table \"bar\" is %d.\n\n", value);

printf ("Cancel further processing of the cursor.\n");
rc = SQLCancel (hstmt);
check_return (rc, henv, hdbc, hstmt);
```

When run, this program prints the following:

```
Build a table.
Insert values into the table.
Execute a SELECT statement. Note—no cursor declaration.
FETCH the output of the SELECT statement.
```

```
Get the data returned by the FETCH statement.
The maximum value in table "bar" is 3.
Cancel further processing of the cursor.
Blow away table "foo".
Goodbye!
```

The first step is to call SQLExecDirect() to execute a SELECT statement. This function was introduced in the previous subsection.

Next, we call SQLFetch() to fetch a row that the SELECT statement selected from the database. This function has the following syntax:

```
RETCODE SQLFetch (HSTMT hstmt)
```

hstmt gives the handle for the statement in question. Note that you do not have to declare a cursor or execute it explicitly—ODBC automatically spools the output of a SELECT statement into a cursor.

Finally, we call function SQLGetData() to move the fetched data into variables. This function has the following syntax:

```
RETCODE SQLGetData(
            HSTMT    hstmt,
            UWORD    marker_number,
            SWORD    C_data_type,
            PTR      variable_address,
            SDWORD   maximum_length,
            SDWORD*  parameter_length)
```

These variables are the same as their counterparts in function SQLBindParameter(), with one exception: parameter marker_number does not indicate a parameter marker within the statement (after all, there are none); rather, it gives the number of the column from which data are being retrieved. The columns are identified in order, from left to right, counting from one.

After we have printed the value fetched from the database, we call function SQLCancel() to abort further processing of the statement. The syntax of this function is:

```
RETCODE SQLCancel (HSTMT hstmt)
```

hstmt gives the handle for the statement in question. We must call this function to close the cursor before we begin to close down our program. Another way to handle close a cursor is to fetch data within a loop until SQLFetch() returns SQL_NO_DATA_FOUND. This "drains" the cursor, at which point the ODBC driver then closes the cursor automatically, thus eliminating the need to call SQLCancel(). We demonstrate this in Listing 14-5.

Bind a variable to a column

Listing 14-4 demonstrates how to bind a variable to a column. The relevant code is as follows:

Listing 14-4: **Binding a Variable to a Column**

```
rc =
  SQLExecDirect (hstmt,
            "SELECT team_name FROM team WHERE city = 'Boston'",
            SQL_NTS);
check_return(rc, henv, hdbc, hstmt);

printf ("Bind a column to a character variable.\n");
rc = SQLBindCol (hstmt, 1, SQL_C_CHAR, team_str, 50, NULL);

printf ("FETCH the output of the SELECT statement.\n");
rc = SQLFetch (hstmt);
check_return (rc, henv, hdbc, hstmt);

printf ("\nThe team in Boston is the %s.\n\n", team_str);

printf ("Cancel further processing of the cursor.\n");
rc = SQLCancel (hstmt);
check_return (rc, henv, hdbc, hstmt);
```

When compiled and run, Listing 14-4 prints the following:

```
Execute a SELECT statement.
Bind a column to an integer variable.
FETCH the output of the SELECT statement.

The table "team" has  26 rows.

Cancel further processing of the cursor.
Execute another SELECT statement.
Bind a column to a character variable.
FETCH the output of the SELECT statement.

The team in Boston is the Red Sox.

Cancel further processing of the cursor.
Goodbye!
```

First, the program executes a call to SQLExecDirect(), to execute a SQL SELECT statement. Next, it calls function SQLBindCol() to bind a variable to one of the columns that is selected. The syntax of this function is as follows:

```
RETCODE SQLBindCol (
            HSTMT    hstmt,
            UWORD    marker_number,
            SWORD    C_data_type,
            PTR      variable_address,
            SDWORD   maximum_length,
            SDWORD*  parameter_length)
```

These parameters are the same as for functions SQLGetData(). Note that in the call:

```
rc = SQLBindCol (hstmt, 1, SQL_C_CHAR, team_str, 50, NULL);
```

parameter team_str points to a 50-character array; and parameter maximum_length gives the number of bytes in the array.

The program then calls SQLFetch() as before; except that in this instance, the fetch automatically copies the data into the variable that is bound to the first column returned by the SELECT statement. We do not have to call SQLGetData() to move data from the fetched row into the variable. Again, the program calls SQLCancel() to cancel further processing of the statement.

Error handling in a SELECT statement

We mentioned earlier that the function SQLFetch() returns SQL_NO_DATA_FOUND to indicate that a cursor is empty. It also returns SQL_NO_DATA_FOUND if a SELECT statement returns no rows at all.

Listing 14-5 demonstrates this. The relevant code is as follows:

Listing 14-5: **Demonstrate SQL_NO_DATA_FOUND**

```
printf ("Execute a SELECT statement that will fail.\n");
rc = SQLExecDirect (hstmt,
                "SELECT team_name FROM team "
                "WHERE city = 'Indianapolis'",
                SQL_NTS);
check_return (rc, henv, hdbc, hstmt);

printf ("Bind a column to the output.\n");
rc = SQLBindCol (hstmt, 1, SQL_C_CHAR, team_str, 50, NULL);
```

Continued

Listing 14-5 *(continued)*

```
printf ("FETCH the output of the SELECT statement.\n");
rc = SQLFetch (hstmt);
check_return (rc, henv, hdbc, hstmt);

if (rc == SQL_NO_DATA_FOUND)
{
    printf ("\nIndianapolis has no team.\n\n");
}
else
{
    printf ("\nThe team in Indianapolis is the %s.\n\n",
team_str);
}
```

When compiled and run, it prints the following:

```
Execute a SELECT statement that will fail.
Bind a column to the output.
FETCH the output of the SELECT statement.

Indianapolis has no team.

Cancel further processing of the cursor.
Goodbye!
```

In this case, SQLFetch() returns SQL_NO_DATA_FOUND upon its first invocation—as we expect, because Indianapolis does not have a major league baseball team.

If the SELECT statement contained erroneous code—for example, a syntax error or requesting a nonexistent column—SQLExecDirect() will return an error code, which we trap and interpret.

Retrieving multiple rows from a SELECT statement

To select multiple rows under ODBC, you must do the following:

✦ Execute a SELECT statement.

✦ Fetch data that are spooled in a cursor.

✦ Continue fetching until the FETCH statement indicates that the cursor is drained.

Listing 14-6 gives an example of how to do this. The relevant code is as follows:

Listing 14-6: **FETCHing**

```
rc = SQLExecDirect (hstmt,
                    "SELECT team_name FROM team "
                    "WHERE city = 'Chicago'",
                    SQL_NTS);
 check_return (rc, henv, hdbc, hstmt);

 printf ("Bind a column to the output.\n");
 rc = SQLBindCol (hstmt, 1, SQL_C_CHAR, team_str, 50, NULL);

 printf ("FETCH the output of the SELECT statement.\n\n");
 while (1)
 {
     rc = SQLFetch (hstmt);
     check_return(rc, henv, hdbc, hstmt);

     if (rc == SQL_NO_DATA_FOUND)
     {
         break;
     }
     else
     {
         printf ("%s.\n", team_str);
     }
 }
```

When Listing 14-6 is compiled and run, it prints the following:

```
Execute a SELECT statement.
Bind a column to the output.
FETCH the output of the SELECT statement.

White Sox.
Cubs.
Goodbye!
```

We already introduced the functions SQLExecDirect(), SQLBindCol(), and SQLFetch(); their use in this code fragment should be clear by now. The only real difference from Listing 14-5 is that the function SQLFetch() is enclosed within a while loop, and the value it returns is checked to see whether the cursor is "drained." Again, we do not have to declare a cursor — ODBC builds one for us automatically, regardless of the number of rows that the SELECT statement returns.

Handling NULL values

NULL values present a problem for ODBC programs: that is, how do you represent a value that by definition is unrepresentable?

The solution is straightforward: If a column can hold a NULL value, ODBC returns two variables for that column. The first variable holds the value within the column, and the second holds a flag that indicates whether the column's value is NULL. You can examine the flag, and then act appropriately.

Listing 14-7 demonstrates how to do this. The relevant code is as follows:

Listing 14-7: **Detecting and Handling NULL**

```
rc = SQLExecDirect (hstmt,
                    "SELECT  DISTINCT team.team_name, game.home_team "
                    "FROM    team "
                    "LEFT JOIN game ON team.team_name = game.home_team "
                    "WHERE   city = 'Chicago' "
                    "ORDER BY team_name",
                    SQL_NTS);
check_return (rc, henv, hdbc, hstmt);

printf ("Bind columns to the output.\n");
rc = SQLBindCol (hstmt, 1, SQL_C_CHAR, team_name, 20, NULL);
rc = SQLBindCol (hstmt, 2, SQL_C_CHAR, home_team, 20, &home_team_null);

printf ("FETCH the output of the SELECT statement.\n\n");
while (1)
{
    rc = SQLFetch (hstmt);
    check_return(rc, henv, hdbc, hstmt);

    if (rc == SQL_NO_DATA_FOUND)
    {
        break;
    }
    if (home_team_null == SQL_NULL_DATA)
    {
        printf ("%s:—NO RECORD IN TABLE 'GAME'\n", team_name);
    }
    else
    {
        printf ("%s:—%s\n", team_name, home_team);
    }
}
```

When compiled and run, this program prints the following:

```
Execute a SELECT statement.
Bind columns to the output.
FETCH the output of the SELECT statement.
```

```
Cubs:—NO RECORD IN TABLE 'GAME'
White Sox:—White Sox
Goodbye!
```

In the above example, we realize that because table `game` describes only games played by American League teams, any attempt to join table `team` to a record for a National League team in table `team` will return NULL. Thus, our `SELECT` statement uses an outer join between tables `team` and `game`. (As you may have noticed, MySQL uses nonstandard syntax for declaring an outer join.

Because column *home_team* may be set to NULL, we have to set a NULL flag for that column. To set a flag for a NULL-able field, we must pass the address of a flag variable (a DWORD—that is, a long) as the last parameter in function `SQLBindCol()`. For example:

```
rc = SQLBindCol (hstmt, 2, SQL_C_CHAR, home_team, 20, &home_team_null);
```

We could assign such variables for both fields, regardless of whether they are NULL-able, but it makes sense only to do so for the fields that are NULL-able— assuming that our program has that knowledge built into it.

Handling user input

ODBC offers a number of ways to incorporate user input within a SQL statement. The most straightforward way is simply to build a string that holds the input, and then execute it. Listing 14-8 is an example of this. The relevant lines of code are:

Listing 14-8: **User Input**

```
while (1)
{
    if (!get_city (t_city))
    {
        break;
    }

    sprintf (statement,
                "SELECT team_name FROM team WHERE city = '%s'",
                t_city);

    printf ("Execute the statement.\n");
    rc = SQLExecDirect (hstmt, statement, SQL_NTS);
    check_return (rc, henv, hdbc, hstmt);

    printf ("Bind a column to the output.\n");
    rc = SQLBindCol (hstmt, 1, SQL_C_CHAR, team_str, 50, NULL);
    check_return (rc, henv, hdbc, hstmt);
```

Continued

Listing 14-8 *(continued)*

```
    printf ("FETCH the output of the SELECT statement.\n\n");
    for (number_rows = 0; ; number_rows++)
    {
        rc = SQLFetch (hstmt);
        check_return (rc, henv, hdbc, hstmt);

        if (rc == SQL_NO_DATA_FOUND)
         {
            if (number_rows == 0)
            {
                printf ("No teams found.\n");
            }
            break;
        } else {
            printf ("%s.\n", team_str);
        }
    }
}
```

The following gives an example session with this program:

```
Enter the name of the city ('q' to quit): Chicago
Execute the statement.
Bind a column to the output.
FETCH the output of the SELECT statement.

White Sox.
Cubs.
Enter the name of the city ('q' to quit): Indianapolis
Execute the statement.
Bind a column to the output.
FETCH the output of the SELECT statement.

No teams found.
Enter the name of the city ('q' to quit): q
Goodbye!
```

Function get_city(), which is not shown here, uses the standard C functions printf() and gets() to accept input from the user. If the user types **q**, the function exits. All of the ODBC calls have already been introduced, and should be familiar by now; but to review briefly:

✦ The program constructs a SELECT statement.

✦ It calls SQLExecDirect() to execute the statement.

✦ It calls `SQLBindCol()` to bind a variable to the one column in the `SELECT` statement.

✦ It calls `SQLFetch()` to read the rows in the cursor that the ODBC driver builds, and to return them one by one.

As you can see, passing user input to an ODBC program is relatively easy.

Transactions

It is straightforward to commit or rollback a transaction under ODBC. However, ODBC also gives you the ability to set the default manner in which a data source handles transactions; and this points to some of ODBC's more powerful extensions. Listing 14-9 shows how to execute a transaction with ODBC. The relevant portion of code is as follows:

Listing 14-9: **Executing a Transaction**

```
printf ("Turn off autocommitting of data.\n");
rc = SQLSetConnectOption (hdbc, SQL_AUTOCOMMIT, SQL_AUTOCOMMIT_OFF);
check_return (rc, henv, hdbc, hstmt);

rc = SQLExecDirect (hstmt, "SELECT count(*) FROM game", SQL_NTS);
rc = SQLBindCol (hstmt, 1, SQL_C_SLONG, &number_rows, 0, NULL);
check_return (rc, henv, hdbc, hstmt);

while (1)
{
    rc = SQLFetch (hstmt);
    check_return (rc, henv, hdbc, hstmt);

    if (rc == SQL_NO_DATA_FOUND)
    {
        break;
    }
    else
    {
        printf ("Table \"games\" has %d rows.\n", number_rows);
    }
}

printf ("Delete everything from table \"game\"\n");
rc = SQLExecDirect (hstmt, "DELETE FROM game", SQL_NTS);
check_return (rc, henv, hdbc, hstmt);

printf ("Roll back the transaction\n");
rc = SQLTransact (henv, hdbc, SQL_ROLLBACK);
check_return (rc, henv, hdbc, hstmt);
```

Continued

Listing 14-9 *(continued)*

```
rc = SQLExecDirect (hstmt, "SELECT count(*) FROM game", SQL_NTS);
rc = SQLBindCol (hstmt, 1, SQL_C_SLONG, &number_rows, 0, NULL);
check_return (rc, henv, hdbc, hstmt);

while (1)
{
    rc = SQLFetch (hstmt);
    check_return (rc, henv, hdbc, hstmt);

    if (rc == SQL_NO_DATA_FOUND)
    {
        break;
    }
    else
    {
        printf ("Table \"games\" has %d rows.\n", number_rows);
    }
}
```

In this example, we:

✦ Turn off autoexecution of transactions, so a statement's changes to the database will not be committed automatically.

✦ Count the rows in table game.

✦ DELETE every row from table game, and again count them to ensure that they are gone.

✦ Roll back the transaction, and then count them one last time to ensure that the rows have reappeared.

This example introduces two new ODBC calls: SQLSetConnectOption(), and SQLTransact().

SQLTransact(), as its name implies, executes a transaction. Its syntax is:

```
RETCODE SQLTransact (
                HENV    henv,
                HDBC    hdbc,
                UWORD   transaction)
```

henv and *hdbc*, respectively, give the handles to the ODBC environment and the connection with which you are working. transaction is a flag that indicates the type of transaction to be performed. It must be one of the following constants:

✦ `SQL_COMMIT` — Commit the transaction to the database.

✦ `SQL_ROLLBACK` — Roll back the transaction.

`UWORD` **is a typedef for** `unsigned short`.

Databases and ODBC drivers vary as to whether they autocommit transactions. If they do autocommit data, then every SQL statement is committed to the database as soon as it is executed; rolling back a transaction has no effect upon the contents of the database. The ODBC call `SQLSetConnectOption()` lets you set a default option for your connection. It has the following syntax:

```
RETCODE SQLSetConnectOption (
              HDBC    hdbc,
              UWORD   option,
              UDWORD  parameter)
```

hdbc is the database connection whose option you are setting.

option is a constant that identifies the option you are setting.

parameter is the value to which you are setting the constant. The nature of this parameter varies from one option to another — in some instances it is a flag, whereas in others, it is a pointer or a file handle. `UDWORD` is a typedef for `unsigned long`.

The range of options that can be set with this call are too many to cover here; for details, see a reference book on ODBC. In this instance, however, you can use this call to determine whether a database autocommits an SQL statement. To manipulate autocommitting, set the option to `SQL_AUTOCOMMIT` and set the parameter to either `SQL_AUTOCOMMIT_OFF` or to `SQL_AUTOCOMMIT_ON`, depending upon whether you want to turn autocommitting off or on, respectively.

SQL interpreter

Our final ODBC example, Listing 14-10, implements a generalized SQL interpreter. We show all of the source code for it:

Listing 14-10: **An ODBC-based SQL Interpreter**

```
#include <stdio.h>
#include <stdlib.h>
#include <string.h>
#include "sql.h"
#include "sqlext.h"
/* ------------------------------------------------------- */
```

Continued

Listing 14-10 *(continued)*

```c
int
get_statement( char* sql_buffer )
{
    char  buffer[200];
    char* semi_ptr;

    sql_buffer[0] = '\0';

    while (1)
    {
        printf ("OK> ");
        fflush (stdout);

        gets(buffer);

        if (!strcmp(buffer, "exit") ||
            !strcmp(buffer, "Exit") ||
            !strcmp(buffer, "EXIT"))
        {
            return (0);
        }

        strcat (sql_buffer, buffer);
        strcat (sql_buffer, " ");

        /* semicolon indicates end of SQL statement */
        if ((semi_ptr = strchr (sql_buffer, ';')) != NULL)
        {
            *semi_ptr = '\0';
            fprintf (stderr, "%s\n", buffer);
            fflush (stderr);
            return (1);
        }
    }
}
/* -------------------------------------------------------- */
void
check_return( RETCODE rc,
              HENV    henv,
              HDBC    hdbc,
              HSTMT   hstmt )
{
    UCHAR   state_str[SQL_MAX_MESSAGE_LENGTH];
    SDWORD  native_error;
    UCHAR   error_msg[SQL_MAX_MESSAGE_LENGTH];
    SWORD   error_msg_avail = SQL_MAX_MESSAGE_LENGTH - 1;
    SWORD   error_msg_len;
    RETCODE local_rc;
```

```
    if (rc != SQL_ERROR && rc != SQL_SUCCESS_WITH_INFO)
    {
        return;
    }

    local_rc = SQLError (henv,
                         hdbc,
                         hstmt,
                         state_str,
                         &native_error,
                         error_msg,
                         error_msg_avail,
                         &error_msg_len);

    if (local_rc != SQL_SUCCESS && rc != SQL_SUCCESS_WITH_INFO)
    {
        fprintf(stderr, "Uninterpretable error; exiting\n");
        exit (EXIT_FAILURE);
    }

    if (rc == SQL_SUCCESS_WITH_INFO)
    {
     fprintf (stderr, "Warning %s: %s\n", state_str, error_msg);
        return;
    }

    fprintf (stderr, "Fatal Error %s: %s\n", state_str, error_msg);
    exit (EXIT_FAILURE);
}
/* ------------------------------------------------------- */
main (void)
{
    HENV    henv = SQL_NULL_HENV;
    HDBC    hdbc = SQL_NULL_HDBC;
    HSTMT   hstmt = SQL_NULL_HSTMT;
    RETCODE rc;

    char    sql_statement_text[1000];
    char    fetch_buffer[1000];
    SWORD   number_cols;
    SWORD   i;
    char    column_name[50];
    SWORD   type;
    SWORD   scale;
    SWORD   nullable;
    UDWORD  precision;
    SDWORD  null_indicator;

    char    buf[257];
    short   buflen;
```

Continued

Listing 14-10 *(continued)*

```
SQLAllocEnv (&henv);
SQLAllocConnect (henv, &hdbc);
rc = SQLDriverConnect (hdbc,
                       0,
                       "DSN=baseball;UID=mylogin;PWD=mypassword",
                       SQL_NTS,
                       (UCHAR *) buf,
                       sizeof (buf),
                       &buflen,
                       SQL_DRIVER_COMPLETE);
check_return (rc, henv, hdbc, hstmt);

rc = SQLAllocStmt (hdbc, &hstmt);
check_return (rc, henv, hdbc, hstmt);

while (1)
{
    if (!get_statement (sql_statement_text))
    {
        break;
    }

    rc = SQLExecDirect (hstmt, sql_statement_text, SQL_NTS);
    check_return (rc, henv, hdbc, hstmt);

    rc = SQLNumResultCols (hstmt, &number_cols);
    check_return (rc, henv, hdbc, hstmt);

    if (number_cols == 0)
    {
        continue;
    }

    while (1)
    {
        rc = SQLFetch (hstmt);
        check_return (rc, henv, hdbc, hstmt);

        if (rc == SQL_NO_DATA_FOUND)
        {
            break;
        }

        for (i = 1 ; i <= number_cols ; i++)
        {
            rc = SQLDescribeCol (hstmt,
                                 i,
```

```
                                (UCHAR *) column_name,
                                sizeof (column_name),
                                NULL,
                                &type,
                                &precision,
                                &scale,
                                &nullable);
            check_return(rc, henv, hdbc, hstmt);

            printf ("%s: ", column_name);

            rc = SQLGetData (hstmt,
                                i,
                                SQL_CHAR,
                                fetch_buffer,
                                sizeof (fetch_buffer),
                                &null_indicator);
            check_return (rc, henv, hdbc, hstmt);

            if (null_indicator == SQL_NULL_DATA)
            {
                printf ("NULL\n");
            }
            else
            {
                printf ("%s\n", fetch_buffer);
            }
        }
        printf ("\n");
    }
}

    SQLFreeStmt (hstmt, SQL_DROP);
    SQLDisconnect (hdbc);
    SQLFreeConnect (hdbc);
    SQLFreeEnv (henv);

    printf ("Goodbye!\n");
    exit (EXIT_SUCCESS);
}
```

The following gives a brief session with this program, after it has been compiled
and run.

```
OK> select team_name from team where city = 'Chicago';
team_name: White Sox
team_name: Cubs
OK> exit
Goodbye!
```

To begin, function `get_statement()` uses some standard C library calls to retrieve the user's input. Function `check_return()` has not changed from our other example ODBC programs. The program also allocates resources and connects to the data source in the usual way.

The heart of the program is a `while` loop. It calls `get_statement()`, which returns a SQL statement. The program calls `SQLExecDirect()` to execute the SQL statement. We introduced this function earlier in this section, and it should be familiar by now.

The program then calls `SQLNumResultsCols()` to count the number of columns that is returned by the SQL statement just executed. This function has the following syntax:

```
RETCODE SQLNumResultsCols(
            HSTMT  hstmt,
            SWORD* number_of_columns)
```

hstmt is the handle of the statement that was just executed.

number_of_columns points to a variable into which this function can write the number of columns returned by the newly executed statement. `SWORD` is a typedef for `short`. Listing 14-10 calls it as follows:

```
rc = SQLNumResultCols (hstmt, &number_cols);
```

If the call to `SQLNumResultCols()` indicates that the statement returns no columns, the program has no more work to do with this statement; it continues the `while` loop and waits for the user to enter another statement.

If, however, the statement is returning one or more columns, then the program processes what the statement returns. To process the statement, it must determine the type of data being returned by each column, prepare a receptacle for it, fetch the data, move the data into the receptacles, and dispose of the data.

First, the program calls `SQLFetch()` to fetch a row returned by the `SELECT` statement. Then, for each column in the row the program does the following:

✦ Calls `SQLDescribeCol()` to read a description of the column.

✦ Calls `SQLGetData()` to get the appropriate column and place it into a variable.

✦ If the value is NULL, it prints the column's name and the string `NULL`; otherwise, it prints the column's name and its value.

`SQLDescribeCol()` returns a description of a column in a fetched row. Its syntax is:

```
RETCODE SQLDescribeCol(
            HSTMT    hstmt,
            UWORD    column_number,
            UCHAR*   column_name,
            SWORD    column_name_max,
            SWORD*   column_name_actual,
            SWORD*   sql_data_type,
            UDWORD*  column_precision,
            SWORD*   column_scale,
            SWORD*   nullable)
```

hstmt gives the handle of the newly executed statement.

column_number gives the number of the column in the fetched row, counting from one.

column_name points to a character array into which the ODBC driver can write the name of the column whose description is being retrieved.

column_name_max gives the length in bytes of the allocated space to which *column_name* points.

column_name_actual points to a variable into which the function can write the actual length of the column name, in bytes. If the value written *column_name_actual* is greater than that in *column_name_max*, the function truncates the column name.

sql_data_type points to a variable into which the function can write a constant that identifies the column's SQL data type.

column_precision points to a variable into which the function can write the column's precision.

column_scale points to a variable into which the function can write the column's scale.

nullable points to a variable into which the function can write a flag that indicates whether the column can be set to NULL.

Listing 14-10 calls `SQLDescribeCol()` as follows:

```
rc = SQLDescribeCol (hstmt,
                     i,
                     (UCHAR *) column_name,
                     sizeof (column_name),
                     NULL,
```

```
                           &type,
                           &precision,
                           &scale,
                           &nullable);
```

If the value returned by SQLDescribeCol() indicates that no error occurred, the program calls SQLGetData() to get the data. As we noted earlier, this function lets us retrieve the data in a fetched row on the fly, without first having to bind the column to a parameter. The syntax for this function is given above. For each column, regardless of its type, we call SQLGetData() as follows:

```
              rc = SQLGetData (hstmt,
                              i,
                              SQL_CHAR,
                              fetch_buffer,
                              sizeof (fetch_buffer),
                              &null_indicator);
```

Argument *i* gives the number of the column, from one through the value returned by function SQLNumResultcols().

The third argument to SQLGetData() gives the SQL data type of the column being fetched. Because we always declare it to be of type SQL_CHAR — that is, a character string — the data are returned in the form of a string, regardless of the type it has within the database. The ODBC driver makes this conversion automatically.

From this point on, the program is trivial: it prints the column's value as returned by SQLGetValue(), and then reexecutes the loop. The program cleans up and closes its allocated resources in the usual manner.

This concludes our brief tutorial on ODBC. The examples given above provide you with templates for programming many common tasks. However, the ODBC standard offers many features that we do not have space to explore here:

✦ *Interrogate the driver* — ODBC drivers will vary, depending upon their capacities. ODBC offers a suite of functions with which you can interrogate the driver. You can discover the level of ODBC the driver implements, and whether it supports a given function. Data that describe the driver are sometimes called driver-level metadata. We discuss these further in the following section, when we introduce JDBC.

✦ *Interrogate the data source* — ODBC includes a suite of functions with which you can interrogate the data source. It also lets you set options in the data source.

✦ *Interrogate the database* — You can interrogate the database, to discover the database's schema (that is, the tables and columns that comprise it), column privileges, primary and foreign keys, stored procedures, table privileges, and statistics (for example, the size of a row in each table and the number of rows in a table). Data about the data source or the database are sometimes called data source-level metadata.

✦ *Set the type of cursor* — In all of the examples, we used a "vanilla" cursor: we read one row of data at a time until the cursor was drained. ODBC, however, lets you use a number of kinds of cursor. These include the scrollable cursor, which lets you scroll backward and forward through the cursor's contents.

✦ *Examine the results of a SELECT* — ODBC lets you check the results of a `SELECT` statement before you begin to manipulate its output. It lets you count the number of columns and rows the statement returns, and it describes each column and its attributes.

✦ *Retrieve blocks of data* — ODBC lets you retrieve blocks of data. You can retrieve multiple values for selected columns, or multiple rows en bloc. The data can be written into a structure, an array, or an array of structures.

✦ *Sending blocks of data* — ODBC lets you upload a block of data at once. If you wish, you can break the data into chunks and reassemble it within the database. This is useful for extremely large data types, such as images or sounds.

Java Database Connectivity

Java Database Connectivity (JDBC) is a protocol that Sun Microsystems designed to be the Java equivalent of ODBC; that is, a protocol with which Java applications and applets can exchange data with a data source. The data source usually is a relational database, although — again, like ODBC — JDBC can exchange information with any type of data repository for which a JDBC driver has been written.

In the previous chapter, we introduced the JDBC standard, and gave some examples of how to program it. This chapter delves into JDBC in a little more depth. We describe the structure of JDBC and give an example of how to install a JDBC driver. We introduce the objects and interfaces that comprise JDBC, and walk through some coding examples. In particular, we show how JDBC reproduces the functionality of ODBC.

Structure of JDBC

Because Sun designed JDBC to be a Java equivalent to ODBC, it is not surprising that JDBC and ODBC are quite similar. Like ODBC, a JDBC implementation consists of two parts: a driver manager, which manages the loading of drivers and connecting to a data source, and a driver, which actually passes data between the application and the data source.

If you read the previous section on ODBC, much of what appears in this section will already be familiar to you. The most important differences between JDBC and ODBC are largely because of differences between their parent languages — Java and C.

To summarize briefly, JDBC calls are simpler than corresponding ODBC calls, in large part because JDBC takes advantage of the features built into the Java language. For example, both ODBC and JDBC allocate and free resources for connections and statements; however, because Java encapsulates connections and statements within objects, JDBC does not need to assign a unique handle to each connection and statement that it creates.

Unlike ODBC, JDBC does not have an explicit mechanism for running statements asynchronously. Instead, JDBC uses Java's multithreading capability to supply that functionality. Likewise, JDBC does not need ODBC's elaborate mechanism for handling errors: Java's error-throwing mechanism is more than sufficient to handle errors that may arise during the execution of a program.

In brief, if you are at all familiar with ODBC and Java, you will find it easy to learn JDBC.

Installing a JDBC driver

Installation and configuration of JDBC is much simpler than installing and configuring ODBC, principally because the driver manager is already built into Java: it comes as part of the standard set of objects included with every Java distribution.

To run a JDBC program, all you need to do is install and configure a copy of the JDBC driver for the data repository that you wish to interrogate.

Likewise, support for JDBC is built into the standard Java development kit: you do not have to install a special software development kit to develop JDBC programs.

In this section, we describe how to install and configure the MM MySQL JDBC driver. The details of driver installation vary from one driver package to another, but you should be able to use this example as a template for installing a JDBC driver for the data source that interests you.

Installing the driver

The first step to installing a JDBC driver is to obtain a copy of it. To get a copy of the MM MySQL JDBC driver, do the following:

1. Point your browser to the MySQL home page:

   ```
   http://www.mysql.com
   ```

2. When the page appears, scroll the left frame until you see the entry for Downloads; click it.

3. When the Downloads page appears, click the entry for JDBC in the right frame.

4. Click the driver you prefer. We selected mm.mysql.jdbc-1.2c.tar.gz; however, by the time you read this, more releases and drivers should be available.

After you have downloaded the driver, the next step is install the driver:

1. `su` to the superuser root and create the directory in which you want to keep the JDBC driver. We suggest directory /var/jdbc, although you may prefer to put it elsewhere.

2. `cd` to the directory you just created, then move the archive into this directory.

3. Dearchive the driver with the following command:

```
tar xvzf mm.mysql.jdbc-1.2c.tar.gz
```

This command installs the driver into subdirectory mm.mysql.jdbc-1.2c.

That's all there is to it: installation is now complete.

Configuring the driver

After you have installed the JDBC driver, you don't have to perform any special configuration of the driver itself. All you need to do is add to the environmental variable `CLASSPATH` the name of the directory into which you installed the driver.

For example, if you installed the MM JDBC driver into directory /var/jdbc, and you are using the bash shell, then add the following instruction to file ~/.bashrc:

```
export CLASSPATH=/var/jdbc/mm.mysql.jdbc-1.2c:$CLASSPATH
```

If you are using sh, insert the following into file ~/.profile:

```
CLASSPATH=/var/jdbc/mm.mysql.jdbc-1.2c:$CLASSPATH
export CLASSPATH
```

Again, that's all there is to it. No further configuration is needed.

Elements of the JDBC standard

Now you're ready to start writing code and to run JDBC programs. We first introduce you to the elements of the JDBC standard; then we walk you through some examples.

To begin, the JDBC standard describes 11 classes and 8 interfaces. The rest of this subsection summarizes them briefly.

Objects

The following 11 classes define the specialized data types used by a JDBC program. They also implement the driver manager.

DataTruncation

JDBC throws an object of this type when it truncates data that it was to write into the database. Its constants flag aspects of the data-truncation event.

Date

This class describes a date, in the form of year, month, and day. It is analogous to the SQL DATE type. This class contains methods for turning a string into a date, and date into a string.

DriverManager

This class is the cornerstone of the JDBC package. It provides services analogous to those provided by the ODBC driver manager: it loads a driver and establishes a connection with a given data source at a given URL. Its most important method is getConnection(). We discuss this more fully later.

DriverPropertyInfo

This class holds information that describes a given JDBC driver. It is of interest only to advanced programmers.

NullData

An object of class NullData is used to indicate that a given datum is NULL. Its variables indicate which column of those returned is set to NULL.

Numeric

This class encodes the SQL data types NUMERIC and DECIMAL values, for Java's native data types have no analogue. These SQL data types are discussed in Chapter 3. In brief, each defines a fixed-point number; that is, a number with a fixed number of digits to the left and to the right of the decimal point.

The methods for this class let you convert a numeric data type into one of Java's native data types, compare Numeric objects, and perform arithmetic upon Numeric objects.

SQLException

This class describes an error that occurred while attempting to execute a SQL statement. Its methods return information about the error and describe the state of the SQL system. If a SQL statement generates multiple errors, these errors are chained; this class has methods that permit you to read the error messages in order.

SQLWarning

This class describes a warning that the database engine generated while attempting to interpret a SQL statement. A given SQL statement can generate multiple warnings. If so, these warnings are chained; this class has methods that permit you to read the warnings in order.

Time

This class describes time, in the form of hour, minute, and second. It is analogous to the SQL TIME type. This class contains methods that convert a formatted string into time, and convert time into a formatted string.

Timestamp

This class defines an exact moment in time. A timestamp consists of seven elements: year, month, day, hour, minute, second, and fraction of second. The precision of the fraction depends upon the precision of your machine and database. This class has methods that convert a timestamp to a string, convert a formatted string into a timestamp, and compare timestamps for equality.

Types

This object holds constants that identify SQL types. Each data type defined by the ANSI-2 constant is represented by a constant, for example, LONGVARCHAR or FLOAT. Constant NULL indicates whether a type is NULL.

Interfaces

The JDBC interfaces define how an application or applet will communicate with the database. Each defines a template that is implemented by a JDBC driver.

CallableStatement

This interface defines the class that holds a stored procedure. Its methods let you (a) register variables to hold data returned by the stored procedure; (b) retrieve data from any of a number of Java data types; and (c) test data for nullity. Stored procedures that have OUT or INOUT parameters must be precompiled into an object of this class.

Connection

This interface describes a connection to a given data source. Its methods return information about the connection and the data source, set some limitations upon the connection (for example, set it to read-only), manage transactions, and prepare calls and statements for execution.

DatabaseMetaData

Metadata are data that describe how data are organized. This interface describes a class whose dozens of methods and variables describe information about the data source—that is, the database package (for example, the name of the package), the database itself (for example, its columns), the JDBC driver, and how the package is configured.

Driver

This interface describes a JDBC driver. Its methods describe the driver, and attempt to open a connection to a given URL.

PreparedStatement

This interface describes a prepared statement. A *prepared statement* is one that is precompiled and stored within an object of class PreparedStatement. Unlike an ordinary Statement object, a PreparedStatement can be invoked multiple times efficiently.

This interface's methods "set" a parameter within the statement to a variable with a given Java type; this is roughly equivalent to binding a parameter under ODBC. As with ODBC, a ? represents a parameter within the prepared statement; parameters are addressed by index number, counting from left to right within the prepared statement.

ResultSet

This interface describes a set of data returned by executing an object of class Statement. Its many methods retrieve the next row of data from the set retrieved by the execution of the statement, and return a given column of that row as a given Java data type. One method also generates an object of class ResultSetMetaData, which is described below. The following example programs extensively use objects that implement this interface.

ResultSetMetaData

This interface describes the class that holds metadata about a given result set. Its methods let you obtain a given metadatum that describes some aspect of the result set.

Statement

This interface describes the class that holds a static SQL statement. A SQL statement is static if it does not contain parameters, and therefore it does not have to be prepared.

This interface's methods describe the limits of a statement it can execute, and the limits of the dataset it can build. It also defines methods by which a static SQL statement is executed.

A simple example

Listing 14-11 shows how to connect to a database and read data from it.

Listing 14-11: **Example JDBC Program**

```
import java.net.URL;
import java.sql.*;

class jex14_11
{
    public static void main (String argv[])
    {
        Connection con;
```

```java
    try {
        Class.forName ("org.gjt.mm.mysql.Driver");
        con = DriverManager.getConnection (
                            "jdbc:mysql://localhost:3306/baseball",
                            "mylogin",
                            "mypassword" );
    } catch ( Exception e) {
        e.printStackTrace ();
        return;
    }

    /* do a query */
    try {
        Statement stmt = con.createStatement ();
        ResultSet rs = stmt.executeQuery (
                            "SELECT team_name " +
                            "FROM team " +
                            "ORDER BY team_name" );
        while(rs.next())
        {
            System.out.println (rs.getString(1));
        }
        stmt.close ();
    } catch (Exception e) {
        e.printStackTrace();
    }

    try {
        con.close();
    } catch (Exception e) {
        e.printStackTrace();
    }
  }
}
```

If Listing 14-11 were saved into file 14_11.java, we would use the following command to compile the program:

```
javac 14_11.java
```

This builds a class named jex14_11.class. (We gave this class the prefix jex—for Java Example—because the Java compiler complains if a class's name begins with a numeral.) To run this class, type the command:

```
java jex14_11
```

Please remember *not* to put the suffix .class on the name of the class; otherwise, java will look for a class named jex14_11.class.class, and will complain that it cannot find it.

When you run jex14_11.class, you should see the following:

```
Angels
Astros
Athletics
Blue Jays
Braves
Brewers
      . . .
```

When you look over the source, you'll see that the program consists of three sections:

✦ Load the driver and connect to the data source.

✦ Execute a SQL statement and display the data it returns.

✦ Close the connection to the data source.

We examine each of these sections in turn.

Making a connection

The following block of code opens the connection with the data source:

```
try {
    Class.forName ("org.gjt.mm.mysql.Driver");
    con = DriverManager.getConnection (
                    "jdbc:mysql://localhost:3306/baseball",
                    "mylogin",
                    "mypassword" );
} catch ( Exception e) {
    e.printStackTrace ();
    return;
}
```

Method forName() obtains the objects for the MM JDBC driver.

Method getConnection() opens the connection to the data source. It can be invoked with one, two, or three arguments:

✦ The first argument must always be a String that gives the URL of the data source.

✦ The optional second argument gives the login identifier of the user who will be manipulating the database.

✦ The optional third argument gives the user's password.

The URL consists of four colon-separated fields, as follows:

1. The protocol under which the data source will be accessed. This usually is `jdbc`.

2. The subprotocol under which the data source will be accessed. Here, we give it as `mysql`, because we are working with a MySQL database.

3. The machine upon which the data source resides. Naturally, `localhost` is a synonym for the machine on which you are running the program.

4. The port through which the data source will be accessed, and the name of the data source. We use port 3306 in this example, because this is the default port for MySQL. If you assigned MySQL a different port, that port should be used here. Finally, the data-source name usually gives the name of the database, for example, `baseball`.

The JDBC protocol lets the JDBC driver define the URL string, to let driver manufacturers take advantage of existing methods of passing information to a driver. For example, OpenLink JDBC drivers read the same `odbc.ini` initialization file as ODBC drivers. With this driver, the URL string should include the same as information as you would normally pass to the ODBC driver—that is, the DSN name, your user identifier, and your password. For example, if we were using the OpenLink JDBC driver with Listing 14-11, we would invoke the `getConnection()` method as follows:

```
      con = DriverManager.getConnection (
 "jdbc:openlink://localhost:5000/DSN=baseball/" +
          "ID=mylogin/PWD=mypassword");
```

Note that the OpenLink server uses port 5000 by default.

Executing a statement

Executing a statement is quite easy, as the following block of code shows:

```
        try {
            Statement stmt = con.createStatement ();
            ResultSet rs = stmt.executeQuery (
                                "SELECT team_name " +
                                "FROM team " +
                                "ORDER BY team_name" );
            while(rs.next())
            {
                System.out.println (rs.getString(1));
            }
            stmt.close ();
        } catch (Exception e) {
            e.printStackTrace();
        }
```

Method `createStatement()` instantiates an object of type `Statement`.

Method `executeQuery()` executes a query upon the currently opened connection. JDBC automatically "spools" the data returned by the query for retrieval by the program.

Class `ResultSet` contains the data and methods needed to retrieve the data. Method `ResultSet.next()` retrieves the next row of data from the data set retrieved by the `SELECT` statement we just executed. It is roughly equivalent to the ODBC function `SQLFetch()`. This method returns a Boolean value that indicates whether a row of data was successfully retrieved. Normally, this method is used as the control expression within a while statement, as shown in Listing 14-11.

Object `ResultSet` also has a set of methods that retrieve a column's data and translates them into a Java data type. These methods together are roughly equivalent to the ODBC function `SQLGetData()`. The name of each of these methods begins with the string get, followed by the name of the Java data type into which it translates the SQL datum. For example, `ResultSet.getFloat()` retrieves an SQL datum and translates it into a Java `Float`, whereas `ResultSet.getString()` retrieves a datum and translates it into a Java `String`.

Naturally, not every SQL data type can be translated into every Java data type; for example, a SQL `VARCHAR` cannot be translated into a Java `Int`. However, the range of Java types into which an SQL data type can be translated is surprisingly broad, and (as with ODBC) every SQL data type can be translated into a Java `String`. For a table of the get methods in object `ResultSet` and the SQL data types each can handle, see JavaSoft's JDBC API manual.

Each of the get methods takes a single argument, which identifies the column whose data are being retrieved. The column can be identified either by name, or by its position within the `SELECT` statement that retrieved the data being retrieved, counting from left to right within the *column_name* section of the `SELECT` statement being executed. For example, invoking method

```
rs.getString(1)
```

retrieved data from the first (that is, the leftmost) column returned when statement

```
SELECT team_name FROM team ORDER BY team_name
```

is executed — that is, it returns the data from column team_name. The call

```
rs.getString("team_name")
```

also returns data from that column.

When method `ResultSet.next()` returned `FALSE`, it could not retrieve another row of data. As an error has not been thrown, this means that no more data remains to be retrieved. At this point, the program exits from its `while` loop and invokes method `ResultSet.close()`. This method frees the resources allocated to a `ResultSet` object, and closes the queue it had been handling.

Close the connection

Closing a connection is simplicity itself. Method `Connection.close()` closes the connection that that object had been managing:

```
try {
    con.close();
} catch (Exception e) {
    e.printStackTrace();
}
```

Modifying the database

The next example, Listing 14-12, modifies the database:

Listing 14-12: **Modifying the Database**

```
import java.net.URL;
import java.sql.*;

class jex14_12
{
    public static void main(String argv[])
    {
        Connection con;
        String upstring;

        try {
            Class.forName ("org.gjt.mm.mysql.Driver");
            con = DriverManager.getConnection (
                        "jdbc:mysql://localhost:3306/baseball",
                        "mylogin",
                        "mypassword" );
        } catch( Exception e) {
            e.printStackTrace();
            return;
        }

        try {
            /* create a table */
            Statement stmt = con.createStatement();
```

Continued

Listing 14-12 *(continued)*

```
                  stmt.executeUpdate ("CREATE TABLE mytmp (aval int)");
                  System.out.println ("created temp table");
                  stmt.close();

                  /* put some stuff into the table */
                  stmt = con.createStatement();
                  for (int i = 1 ; i < 5 ; i++)
                  {
                      upstring = "INSERT INTO mytmp values" + i + ")";
                      stmt.executeUpdate (upstring);
                      System.out.println ("added value " + i);
                  }
                  stmt.close();

                  /* read the stuff back from the temporary table */
                  stmt = con.createStatement();
                  ResultSet rs = stmt.executeQuery (
                              "SELECT aval FROM mytmp ORDER BY aval");

                  while(rs.next())
                  {
                      System.out.println(rs.getString(1));
                  }
                  stmt.close();

                  /* drop the temporary table */
                  stmt = con.createStatement();
                  stmt.executeUpdate("DROP TABLE mytmp");
                  System.out.println("dropped mytmp");
                  stmt.close();
              } catch( Exception e) {
                  e.printStackTrace();
              }

          try {
              con.close();
          } catch( Exception e) {
              e.printStackTrace();
          }
      }
}
```

To run this program, use the command:

```
java jex14_12
```

You should see the following on your screen:

```
created temp table
added value 1
added value 2
added value 3
added value 4
1
2
3
4
dropped mytmp
```

The program consists of six sections:

✦ Load the driver and connect to the data source.

✦ Create a table.

✦ Insert data into the table.

✦ Read data back from the table.

✦ Drop the table.

✦ Close the connection to the data source.

The program loads the driver, connects to the data source, and closes the connection exactly as it did in Listing 14-11. We examine the other four sections in turn.

Create a table

The following code creates a table:

```
Statement stmt = con.createStatement();
stmt.executeUpdate ("CREATE TABLE mytmp (aval int)");
System.out.println ("created temp table");
stmt.close();
```

As in Listing 14-11, this program invokes method `Connection.createStatement()` to create an object of type `Statement`.

The program then invokes method `Statement.executeUpdate()` to execute a statement that modifies the database. According to the JDBC standard, method `executeUpdate()` should be used for all SQL statements that modify the database, including `UPDATE`, `INSERT`, and `DELETE`.

This method takes one argument, which is a string that holds the SQL statement to be executed. The program then invokes method `Statement.close()`, to close the statement and free its resources.

Insert data into a table

The following code inserts data into the newly created table mytmp:

```
stmt = con.createStatement();
for (int i = 1 ; i < 5 ; i++)
{
    upstring = "INSERT INTO mytmp values(" + i + ")";
    stmt.executeUpdate (upstring);
    System.out.println ("added value " + i);
}
stmt.close();
```

A for() loop is used to build a string that holds the INSERT statement that we wish to execute. Then method Statement.executeUpdate() is invoked to execute the string. After the for() loop has exited, the program again invokes method Statement.close().

Read data from a table

The following code reads data back from the newly initialized table, and prints the data:

```
stmt = con.createStatement();
ResultSet rs = stmt.executeQuery (
                "SELECT aval FROM mytmp ORDER BY aval");

while(rs.next())
{
    System.out.println(rs.getString(1));
}
stmt.close();
```

The program invokes method Statement.executeQuery() to execute a SELECT statement and "spool" its output for retrieval. This is identical to the approach used in Listing 14-11.

Drop a table

When the program has finished working with its temporary table, it drops the table, as follows:

```
stmt = con.createStatement();
stmt.executeUpdate("DROP TABLE mytmp");
System.out.println("dropped mytmp");
stmt.close();
```

Again, the program invokes method Statement.executeUpdate() to execute the statement that modifies the database—in this case, DROP TABLE.

We should note that JDBC by definition autocommits its transactions: after a statement is executed, its effects modify the database and cannot be rolled back. JDBC does have methods that enable you modify this default and manipulate transactions; we discuss these methods later.

NULL data

As with ODBC, JDBC offers a number of ways to judge whether a datum is NULL. The easiest way is to use method `ResultSet.wasNull()`. This method returns true if the last datum returned by one of the `ResultSet.getXXX()` methods returns NULL; otherwise, it returns false.

Listing 14-13 demonstrates how to handle NULL values returned by a query. It recreates in Java what Listing 14-7 did in ODBC. Most of this program recreates what is in Listing 14-12; Listing 14-13 gives the significant portion of code:

Listing 14-13: **Handling NULL Values**

```
String team_name;
String home_team;
    . . .
try {
    stmt = con.createStatement();
    ResultSet rs =
        stmt.executeQuery (
                "SELECT  DISTINCT team.team_name, game.home_team " +
                "FROM team " +
                "LEFT JOIN game ON team.team_name = game.home_team " +
                "WHERE city = 'Chicago' " +
                "ORDER BY team_name"
        );

    while(rs.next())
    {
        team_name = rs.getString (1);
        System.out.print (team_name + ":-");

        /* get home_team; check if it's NULL */
        home_team = rs.getString(2);

        if (rs.wasNull())
        {
            System.out.println ("NO RECORD IN TABLE 'GAME'");
        } else {
            System.out.println (home_team);
        }
```

Continued

Listing 14-13 *(continued)*

```
            System.out.println("");
        }
        stmt.close();
    } catch (Exception e) {
        e.printStackTrace();
    }
```

When compiled with the command

```
javac 14_13.java
```

and run with the command

```
java jex14_13
```

this command generates the following output:

```
Cubs:—NO RECORD IN TABLE 'GAME'
White Sox:—White Sox
```

The expression `if (rs.wasNull())` tested whether the column that was previously "gotten" contained NULL; in this example, it tested the value returned by:

```
home_team = rs.getString(2);
```

Preparing a statement

Like ODBC, JDBC offers a mechanism for preparing an SQL statement. A prepared statement is, in effect, one that is precompiled. You can store it and invoke it again and again, without incurring the overhead of having the driver parse the statement and translate it into the data source's native CLI. A prepared statement is also useful for handling binary data, especially large binary objects that cannot be embedded within a text string.

JDBC has two "prepare" interfaces: one for SQL statements and one for stored procedures.

Prepared statements

Method `Connection.prepareStatement()` builds an object of type `PreparedStatement`. This method is analogous to the ODBC function `SQLPrepare()`. This method takes one argument, the SQL statement to prepare; as with ODBC, the variables are represented by a question mark.

The code in Listing 14-14 demonstrates this:

Listing 14-14: **Preparing Statements**

```
PreparedStatement prepstmt =
    con.prepareStatement("INSERT INTO mytmp values( ? )");
for (int i = 1; i < 5; i++)
{
    prepstmt.setInt(1, i);
    int rows = prepstmt.executeUpdate();
}
prepstmt.close();
```

As with ODBC, a parameter is represented by a ? within the SQL statement. The method `PreparedStatement.setInt()` links the integer variable i with the first parameter; as with ODBC, parameters are numbered from left to right within the statement.

`PreparedStatement` defines many `setXXX` methods, each of which sets a parameter to a given Java type, and one (`setNull()`) sets a parameter to NULL. The `setXXX` methods do not perform any data conversion; it is your responsibility to ensure that the Java type corresponds to the SQL data type that the parameter represents.

Calling a `setXXX` method binds the current value of the variable to the parameter. Thus, in the above example, we had to call method `setInt()` for each iteration of the `for()` loop. The method `PreparedStatement.clearParameters()` clears all parameters. Under ODBC, a variable's address is bound to a parameter; thus, whatever is read or written at that parameter is copied into memory at the bound address. Java cannot do this because, of course, it is pointer-free.

Prepared statements always return their output in an object of class `ResultSet`. Therefore, JDBC does not need a mechanism whereby a variable can be bound to a column within a `SELECT` statement, such as can be done under ODBC. Also, Java being pointer-free, this would be very difficult to do in any case.

Prepared stored procedures

The interface `PreparedStatement` executes SQL statements. To execute a stored procedure, however, requires a more complex interface. Unfortunately, MySQL does not support stored procedures, so we cannot demonstrate this; but interface works as follows:

✦ Use method `Connection.prepareCall()` to build an object of type `CallableStatement`. This object is used to execute a stored procedure — but only those that use `OUT` or `INOUT` parameters. As with a prepared SQL statement, a parameter is indicated by a ?. For example:

```
CallableStatement callstate =
  connection.prepareCall ("{call mystoredprocedure(?, ?) }");
```

✦ Use method `CallableStatement.registerOutParameter()` to tell the JDBC driver the SQL type of each parameter. The type must be defined within the JDBC class `Types`; for example:

```
callstate.registerOutParameter(Types.INTEGER, 1);
callstate.registerOutParameter(Types.VARCHAR, 2);
```

✦ Execute the call to the stored procedure. For example:

```
callstate.executeUpdate();
```

✦ Call an appropriate `getXXX` method to retrieve the datum from the parameters. For example:

```
Integer firstparam callstate.getInt(1);
String secondparam callstate.getString(2);
```

A stored procedure all of whose parameters are of type `IN` can be executed through a common `Statement` object.

General SQL statements

Our earlier JDBC examples used one method for querying the database, and another method for modifying it. The former method, `Statement.executeQuery()`, returns an object of class `ResultSet`, whereas the latter method, `Statement.executeUpdate()`, returns an integer that indicates how many rows within the database are affected by the modification.

In some instances, however, you will not know whether a SQL statement will modify the database. For these cases, JDBC includes the method `Statement.execute()`. This method returns true if the SQL statement it executes has generated a ResultSet; otherwise, it returns false.

Listing 14-15 reimplements in Java our SQL interpreter. It gives the JDBC analog of the ODBC program in Listing 14-10.

| Listing 14-15: **Java-based SQL Interpreter** |

```
import java.net.URL;
import java.sql.*;

class jex14_15
{
```

```java
public static void main(String argv[])
{
    Connection con;
    Statement stmt;
    byte sql_text[] = new byte[1000];

    try {
        Class.forName("org.gjt.mm.mysql.Driver");
        con = DriverManager.getConnection(
                            "jdbc:mysql://localhost:3306/baseball",
                            "mylogin",
                            "mypassword");
    } catch ( Exception e) {
        e.printStackTrace();
        return;
    }

    System.out.println ("Type an SQL statement, or 'quit' to exit\n");

    /* do a query */
    while (true)
    {
        try {
            stmt = con.createStatement();
            System.out.print ("Ok> ");
            System.out.flush();

            System.in.read (sql_text);
            String sql_string = new String (sql_text);

            if (sql_string.indexOf("quit") != -1)
            {
                break;
            }

            // if true, the executed statement generated a ResultSet
            if (!stmt.execute(sql_string))
            {
                // the statement did not return a ResultSet; therefore,
                // it is an UPDATE, INSERT, or DELETE statement
                System.out.println ("Database modified");
                continue;
            }

            // if we reach this point, the statement generated a
            // ResultSet: get it
            ResultSet rs = stmt.getResultSet();

            // get the MetaResult object that describes this ResultSet
            ResultSetMetaData mr = rs.getMetaData();
```

Continued

Listing 14-15 *(continued)*

```java
                    for (int i = 1 ; i <= mr.getColumnCount() ; i++)
                    {
                        int colwidth    = mr.getColumnDisplaySize (i);
                        String colname = mr.getColumnName (i);
                        int strwidth    = colname.length();

                        System.out.print (colname);

                        // pad the column with spaces
                        for (int j = 0 ; j < colwidth - strwidth ; j++)
                        {
                            System.out.print(" ");
                        }
                    }
                    System.out.println("");

                    while(rs.next())
                    {
                        for (int i = 1 ; i <= mr.getColumnCount() ; i++)
                        {
                            String colvalue;

                            int colwidth = mr.getColumnDisplaySize (i);

                            colvalue = rs.getString(i);
                            if (rs.wasNull())
                            {
                                colvalue = new String("NULL");
                            }

                            int strwidth = colvalue.length();
                            System.out.print (colvalue);

                            // pad the column with spaces
                            for (int j = 0 ; j < colwidth - strwidth ; j++)
                            {
                                System.out.print (" ");
                            }
                        }
                        System.out.println("");
                    }
                } catch ( Exception e) {
                    e.printStackTrace();
                    return;
                }
            }

        System.out.println ("\nGoodbye!");
```

```
    try {
        stmt.close();
    } catch (Exception e) {
        e.printStackTrace();
        return;
    }


    try {
        con.close();
    } catch (Exception e) {
        e.printStackTrace();
        return;
    }
  }
}
```

The following gives a brief session of running this program:

```
java jex14_15
Ok> select city, team_name, stadium from team where city = 'Chicago'
city            team_name       stadium
Chicago         White Sox       Comiskey Park
Chicago         Cubs            Wrigley Field
Ok> quit
Goodbye!
```

The program's code for connecting to the database and for disconnecting from it is the same as in our earlier examples. The heart of the program is within a single while() loop.

First, the program displays the Ok> prompt and receives the input that the user types:

```
        try {
            stmt = con.createStatement();
            System.out.print ("Ok> ");
            System.out.flush();

            System.in.read (sql_text);
            String sql_string = new String (sql_text);
```

Next, the program checks whether the user has typed quit; if the user has typed quit, it exits:

```
            if (sql_string.indexOf("quit") != -1)
            {
                break;
            }
```

Next the program invokes method `Statement.execute()` to execute the statement that the user typed. If the statement does not parse or run correctly, the method throws a `SQLException`, which is caught at the bottom of the loop.

If the statement executed correctly and did not generate a `ResultSet` (that is, the statement performed an `INSERT`, `UPDATE`, or `DELETE` operation), the program prints a brief statement and continues the `while()` loop:

```
// if true, the executed statement generated a ResultSet
if (!stmt.execute(sql_string))
{
    // the statement did not return a ResultSet;
    // it is an UPDATE, INSERT, or DELETE statement
    System.out.println ("Database modified");
    continue;
}
```

If the SQL statement that the user typed did generate a `ResultSet`, it must be retrieved and processed correctly. First, we invoke method `Statement.getResultSet()` to retrieve the `ResultSet`:

```
// if we reach this point, the statement generated a
// ResultSet: get it
ResultSet rs = stmt.getResultSet();
```

Next, we must invoke method `ResultSet.getMetaData()` to get metadata about the result set. The metadata will tell us information about the result set itself, such as how many columns comprise the set, the name of each column, and how wide each column is:

```
// get the MetaResult object that describes this ResultSet
ResultSetMetaData mr = rs.getMetaData();
```

Next, the program builds a header that consists of the name of each column. Method `ResultSetMetaData.getColumnName()` retrieves the name of a column, and method `ResultSetMetaData.getColumnDisplaySize()` retrieves a column's width. Columns are identified by the order in which they appeared in the `SELECT` statement, from left to right, counting from 1. The program uses this information to display the column's width, then pad each column with the appropriate amount of white space:

```
for (int i = 1 ; i <= mr.getColumnCount() ; i++)
{
    int colwidth    = mr.getColumnDisplaySize (i);
    String colname  = mr.getColumnName (i);
    int strwidth    = colname.length();

    System.out.print (colname);
```

```
        // pad the column with spaces
        for (int j = 0 ; j < colwidth - strwidth ; j++)
        {
            System.out.print(" ");
        }
    }
    System.out.println("");
```

Finally, the program invokes method ResultSet.next() to retrieve rows of data. If method ResultSet.wasNull() indicates that a column's datum is NULL, then the program prints the string NULL in its place. The program then uses the column's width to pad each column with the appropriate amount of white space:

```
while(rs.next())
{
    for (int i = 1 ; i <= mr.getColumnCount() ; i++)
    {
        String colvalue;

        int colwidth = mr.getColumnDisplaySize (i);

        colvalue = rs.getString(i);
        if (rs.wasNull())
        {
            colvalue = new String("NULL");
        }

        int strwidth = colvalue.length();
        System.out.print (colvalue);

        // pad the column with spaces
        for (int j = 0 ; j < colwidth - strwidth ;
j++)
        {
            System.out.print (" ");
        }
    }
    System.out.println("");
}
```

Although we did not show it here, method Statement.execute() can return more than one result set. This can happen if, for example, a SQL statement invokes more than one stored procedure, each of which generates a result set. Method Statement.getMoreResults() retrieves the next available result set. It returns true if it could retrieve another result set, or false if it could not—either because all results have been returned, or because the next result is an integer (as returned by an UPDATE statement or stored procedure).

Metadata

Listing 14-15 gave several examples of how metadata can be used within a program. JDBC defines two metadata classes, both of which are quite helpful: `DatabaseMetaData`, and `ResultSetMetaData`. We discuss each class in turn.

Database metadata

Class `DatabaseMetaData` defines several dozen methods that return information about what ODBC calls the "data source;" that is, the database itself, the database package that is managing the database, and the JDBC driver with which the program accesses the database package. Methods that return information about the package include:

✦ `getDataProductName()` — Get the name of the product.

✦ `getDataProductVersion()` — Get the version of the product.

✦ `getIdentifierQuoteString()` — The string with which an SQL identifier can be quoted. (See Chapter 3 for details on quoting, and the problems it can raise in an SQL statement.)

✦ `getTypeInfo()` — Information about the data types that this package supports.

✦ `supportsANSI92FullSQL()` — Does this package support the full grammar of the 1992 ANSI standard for SQL (SQL-2)?

✦ `supportsOuterJoins()` — Does the package support outer joins?

Methods that return information about the JDBC driver include:

✦ `getDriverMajorVersion()` — Return the number of the driver's major version.

✦ `getDriverName()` — Return the name of the driver.

✦ `isReadOnly()` — Was the database opened into read-only mode?

Methods that return information about the database itself include:

✦ `getColumns()` — Return the columns within this database.

✦ `getTablePrivileges()` — Return the privileges assigned to each table.

✦ `getProcedures()` — The names of the stored procedures in this database.

✦ `getPrimaryKeys()` — Return a given table's primary keys.

As you can see, class `DatabaseMetaData` lets you draw a portrait of the data source with which your application is conversing. This is not needed for the simple examples that appear in this chapter; but as applications grow in scope in power — and as applications can expect to converse with all manner of data sources across the Internet — these methods will prove to be extremely useful.

Result set metadata

Class `ResultSetMetaData` gives access to metadata about a given result set. Listing 14-15 uses this class to discover the number of columns in a result set, the name of each column, and the width of each column. This class also includes these methods:

✦ `getPrecision()` — Return a column's precision. This is used for columns of type `NUMERIC`, which have a fixed precision.

✦ `getTableName()` — Return the name of the table from which a column was drawn.

✦ `isNullable()` — Can this column return a NULL value?

✦ `isWritable()` — Can data be written into this column?

As you have seen, these methods prove their worth even in the simple examples shown in this section.

Other features

This section gives only the basics of working with JDBC. The many more advanced features of JDBC include methods for handling objects directly and moving large binary objects in chunks across a network. For a full description of these features, see the JDBC documentation that is available online from Sun.

We hope that this brief introduction has whetted your interest in JDBC.

Perl DBI

In the spirit of saving the best for last, we now look at the Perl Database Interface (DBI).

Perl DBI is a package of Perl objects whose attributes and methods give Perl programmers a robust means of working with data sources.

In the spirit of Perl, the design of Perl DBI blends the theoretical with the pragmatic. Perl DBI is modeled after the X/Open standard that also served as the model for ODBC and JDBC, which is why Perl DBI has much of the "look and feel" of ODBC and JDBC; however, it also extends the X/Open standard to provide services that working programmers have found to be useful.

Also in the spirit of Perl, Perl DBI gives programmers more than one way to do practically anything. This section only scratches the surface of what you can do with Perl DBI. Our goal is to familiarize you with the basics, so that you can begin on your own to explore and be productive with this most useful package.

Structure of Perl DBI

Like ODBC and JDBC, Perl DBI consists of a driver manager, which manages a program's interaction with a data source; and one or more drivers, which translate the Perl instructions into instructions in the call-level interface of the database with which you are working.

The driver manager, in effect, is built into Perl DBI: you do not need to install it or perform any configuration.

As with ODBC, Perl DBI drivers are written in the form of shared libraries that are loaded at runtime. Releases of Linux differ somewhat in the suite of drivers that they include by default; most include the driver for MySQL, and some include drivers for other relational database packages as well.

Installing and configuring a Perl DBI driver

To install a driver, simply following the directions that come with the driver for installation. In most cases, this involves executing a script that copies the bits into the appropriate directory under `/usr/lib/perl5/site_perl/5.005/`, and setting the permissions properly. No other special configuration is needed.

Some database packages created their own, proprietary Perl interfaces; for example, MySQL created the package Mysql.pm for working with MySQL through Perl. Most database vendors have now abandoned those packages, and encourage users to use Perl DBI instead; however, the packages are still included with most current distributions of Perl, so that applications that were written to use these now-obsolete packages are not orphaned.

A simple example

Installation and configuration of Perl DBI is quite simple, particularly when compared with ODBC. The rest of this section walks you through some simple examples, just as was done with ODBC and JDBC, to give you a feel for what it is like to work with Perl DBI, and to help you acquire a basic working knowledge of it. This section assumes that you have some familiarity with Perl.

To begin, Listing 14-16 opens a connection with our `baseball` database, retrieves some data from it, prints those data, and closes the connection. It re-creates in Perl, the ODBC program in Listing 14-1 and the JDBC program in Listing 14-11.

Listing 14-16: An Example Perl DBI Program

```perl
#!/usr/bin/perl -w -T
use DBI;
{
    my $dbh;
    my $sth;
    my $cmd;

    my $restype;
    my $ret_val;

    my $data;
    my @rawResults;

    # open the connection to the data source

    $dbh = DBI->connect('dbi:mysql:baseball',
                        'mylogin',
                        'mypassword' );

    if ( !defined($dbh) )
    {
        print "Cannot connect to database.\n";
        exit 1;
    }
    else
    {
        print "Success—Connected to database.\n";
    }

    # Prepare the SQL SELECT statement, and execute it.

    $cmd = "SELECT team_name " .
           "FROM team " .
           "ORDER BY team_name";

    $sth = $dbh->prepare($cmd);

    if (!defined($sth))
    {
        print "Preparation Failed\n";
        $dbh->disconnect();
        exit 0;
    }

    $ret_val = $sth->execute();

    if (!defined($ret_val))
    {
```

Continued

Listing 14-16 *(continued)*

```
        print "Execution Failed\n";
        $dbh->disconnect();
        exit 0;
    }

    # Write the retrieved data to the standard output

    $sth->dump_results();

    # Disconnect from the data source, and exit.

    $dbh->disconnect();
    exit 0;
}
```

If you read the sections on ODBC and JDBC, the program's structure should be familiar by now. In brief, the program performs these tasks:

1. Loads the database-interface package.
2. Opens a connection to the data source and obtains a handle through which the data source is accessed.
3. Prepares a SQL statement and obtains a handle through which resources related to the statement can be accessed.
4. Executes the SQL statement.
5. Retrieves the data retrieved from the data source, if any, and displays them.
6. Closes the connection to the data source and exits.

We discuss each of these tasks in turn.

Loading the DBI package

To load the DBI package, you must prefix the program with the instruction:

```
use DBI;
```

This assumes that Perl is properly installed and configured on your machine.

Opening the connection

Method `DBI->connect()` opens a connection to a data source. It takes the following arguments:

```
DBI->connect( data_source,
              login,
              password );
```

`data_source` names the data source to which a connection is to be opened. This argument consists of three colon-separated fields:

+ The first field is the string `dbi`; this is required.

+ The second field gives the name of the database driver to load. This almost always mirrors the name of the database package — in this example, `mysql`.

+ The third field is a string that identifies the data source to the driver. This string may name an entry in a configuration file, or give the name of a database, or (as seen with ODBC function `SQLDriverConnect()`) give a set of `key=value` pairs that, among other things, identify the machine on which the database resides and the port through which it is accessed.

`login` gives the login through which the user accesses the database.

`password` gives the user's password.

Method `connect()` returns a database handle, which is a reference to the object that gives access to the database. If the handle is not defined, then the attempt to open a connection to the data source has failed.

The database handle gives access to methods with which the data source can be interrogated, and to attributes that hold metadata that describe the data source. We discuss the data-source methods throughout this section, and we discuss metadata at the end of this section.

For example, in Listing 14-16 we use this method as follows:

```
$dbh = DBI->connect('dbi:mysql:baseball',
                    'mylogin',
                    'mypassword' );
```

The method `DBI->connect()` can also take an optional fourth argument, a reference to a hash of arguments to be passed to the data source. The database package defines what arguments you can set in this hash.

Please note that you can open multiple connections at the same time. The connections can either be to multiple data sources, or to the same data source.

DBI->connect() returns a reference to hash through which the data source can be accessed. The hash also contains metadata about the data source; later in this section, we describe how to use this connection-level metadata.

Preparing the statement

The next step to executing a DBI program is to prepare a SQL statement for execution. Preparing the statement means that the driver allocates resources for the SQL statement; the data source also checks the statement for correctness.

To prepare a statement, use the method prepare(), which is accessed through the database handle. This method takes one argument, the SQL statement to be prepared; and it returns one value, the handle of the statement that it has prepared. The statement handle gives access to methods with which we can execute the statement and retrieve the data that it returns. If the statement handle is not defined, then the attempt to prepare the statement failed.

In Listing 14-16, we use this method as follows:

```
$cmd = "SELECT team_name " .
       "FROM team " .
       "ORDER BY team_name";

$sth = $dbh->prepare($cmd);
```

Executing the statement

After the statement is prepared, the statement is executed. When the data source executes the statement, it returns whatever data the statement requested. The data source also sets metadata that describes how the statement affected the data source and describes the data set being returned. We describe these metadata at the end of this section.

To execute a statement, use method execute(). This method is accessed through the statement handle. It takes no arguments. This method returns a flag that indicates success or failure: the flag is set to true if execution succeeded, or to undefined if execution failed.

For example, Listing 14-16 executes the statement as follows:

```
$ret_val = $sth->execute();

if (!defined($ret_val))
{
    print "Execution Failed\n";
    $dbh->disconnect();
    exit 0;
}
```

Perl DBI offers a number of ways to pass a statement to the data source: you do not necessarily have to use methods `prepare()` and `execute()`. We discuss one alternative method when we introduce Listing 14-17.

Returning the data

After a statement has been prepared and executed, the next step is to retrieve the data that the statement requested from the data source, and make it available to the program.

Perl DBI offers you a multitude of ways to retrieve data; in Listing 14-16, we use the simplest method, `dump_results()`. This method reads each row returned when the statement was executed, formats it into a simple table, and prints the table on the standard output.

Method `dump_results()` returns the number of rows that it prints outs. It can take either no arguments, or you can pass it arguments that give the file of a handle into which the data should be written, and how it should be formatted.

In Listing 14-16, we use `dump_results()` as follows:

```
$sth->dump_results();
```

Closing the connection

Finally, the program calls the method `disconnect()` to break the connection with the database:

```
$dbh->disconnect();
```

That being done, the program exits.

Methods of execution

Listing 14-16 uses the methods `prepare()` and `execute()` to prepare a SQL statement and to execute it. Perl DBI offers other ways to pass a statement on to the data source; in particular, the method `do()` gives you a one-step way to both prepare and execute a statement.

do method

Method `do()` is accessed through the database handle. It takes one argument, the SQL statement to execute. It returns a flag that is set to true if execution succeeded, or to undefined if execution failed.

do() differs from the prepare() and execute() methods principally in that it does not return data from the data source. For this reason, do() is not suitable for executing any SQL statement that retrieves data, in particular a SELECT statement. However, it works perfectly well with any SQL statement that does not retrieve data from the database, such as an INSERT, DELETE, or UPDATE statement.

Example program

Listing 14-17 demonstrates how you can use the do(), prepare(), and execute() methods in a single program. It recreates in Perl DBI, the ODBC program in Listing 14-1, and the JDBC program in Listing 14-12.

Listing 14-17: Preparing and Executing an SQL Statement

```perl
#!/usr/bin/perl -w -T
use DBI;
sub sqlExec
{
    my ($cmd) = @_;

    my $dbh;
    my $sth;

    my $ret_val;
    my $data;
    my @rawResults;

    $dbh = DBI->connect( 'DBI:mysql:baseball',
                         'mylogin',
                         'mypassword' );

    if ( !defined($dbh) )
    {
        print "Cannot connect to database.\n";
        exit 1;
    }

    if (lc(substr($cmd, 0, 6)) ne "select")
    {
        # if true, this is not a SELECT: use "do" method.
        $ret_val = $dbh->do($cmd);

        $dbh->disconnect();

        if (!defined ($ret_val))
        {
            print ("Execution of non-SELECT statement failed.\n");
            exit 1;
```

```
            }
        else
        {
            return;
        }
    }
    else
    {
        # $cmd holds a SELECT statement:
        # prepare it, execute it, retrieve data
        $sth = $dbh->prepare($cmd);

        if (!defined($sth))
        {
            $dbh->disconnect();
            print ("Preparation of SELECT statement failed\n");
            exit 1;
        }

        $ret_val = $sth->execute();

        if (!defined($ret_val))
        {
            $dbh->disconnect();
            print ("Execution of SELECT statement failed\n");
            exit 1;
        }

        while ( $data = $sth->fetchrow_arrayref() )
        {
            push @rawResults, [ @$data ];
        }

        $dbh->disconnect();
        return \@rawResults;
    }
}
# ****************************************************************
# MAIN
# ****************************************************************
{
    my $cmd;
    my $i;
    my $results;

    sqlExec ("CREATE TABLE mytmp (aval int)");

    for ( $i = 0 ; $i < 5 ; $i++ )
    {
        sqlExec ("INSERT INTO mytmp values( $i )");
    }
```

Continued

Listing 14-17 *(continued)*

```
$results = sqlExec ("SELECT aval FROM mytmp ORDER BY aval");

for ( $i = 1 ; $i < @$results ; $i++ )
{
    my ($aval) = @{ $$results[$i] };

    print $aval . "\n";
}

sqlExec ("DROP TABLE mytmp");

exit 0;
}
```

In this example, we isolated into one subroutine, called `sqlExec()`, the code that interrogates the database. This subroutine opens the connection to the database just as we described for Listing 14-16. However, after the connection is opened, we look for the keyword `select` in the instruction to be executed; if it is not found, we use the `do()` method to execute the instruction:

```
if (lc(substr($cmd, 0, 6)) ne "select")
{
    # if true, this is not a SELECT: use "do" method.
    $ret_val = $dbh->do($cmd);

    $dbh->disconnect();

    if (!defined ($ret_val))
    {
        print ("Execution of non-SELECT statement failed.\n");
        exit 1;
    }
    else
    {
        return;
    }
}
```

If the instruction does contain the keyword `select`, then we use method `prepare()` to prepare the instruction, and method `execute()` to execute the instruction:

```
else
{
    # $cmd holds a SELECT statement:
```

```
# prepare it, execute it, retrieve data
$sth = $dbh->prepare($cmd);

if (!defined($sth))
{
    $dbh->disconnect();
    print ("Preparation of SELECT statement failed\n");
    exit 1;
}

$ret_val = $sth->execute();

if (!defined($ret_val))
{
    $dbh->disconnect();
    print "Execution of SELECT statement failed\n");
    exit 1;
}
```

When the instruction has been prepared and executed, we use method
`fetchrow_array()` to retrieve the data. This method retrieves data one row at a
time; the data are returned in the form of an array (hence, the method's name). We
push each row of data into an array; and we return a reference to the array that
holds the data:

```
    while ( $data = $sth->fetchrow_arrayref() )
    {
        push @rawResults, [ @$data ];
    }

    $dbh->disconnect();
    return \@rawResults;
}
```

To demonstrate our subroutine `sqlExec()`, the main part of Listing 14-17 executes
four SQL instructions. The first, second, and fourth instructions do not contain the
keyword `SELECT` and so are executed through the `do()` method, whereas the third
instruction does contain the keyword `SELECT`, and so is executed using the methods `prepare()` and `execute()`:

```
sqlExec ("CREATE TABLE mytmp (aval int)");

for ( $i = 0 ; $i < 5 ; $i++ )
{
    sqlExec ("INSERT INTO mytmp values( $i )");
}

$results = sqlExec ("SELECT aval FROM mytmp ORDER BY aval");
for ( $i = 1 ; $i < @$results ; $i++ )
```

```
{
   my ($aval) = @{ $$results[$i] };

    print $aval . "\n";
}

sqlExec ("DROP TABLE mytmp");

exit 0;
```

When executed, Listing 14-17 prints the following:

```
1
2
3
4
```

NULL data

As you recall, both ODBC and JDBC have problems in representing NULL because neither C nor Java has a way to represent a value that, by definition, cannot be represented. ODBC gets around the problem by initializing a separate variable that flags whether a column holds a NULL value; JDBC uses a special method, wasNull(), to test whether a column was set to NULL.

By contrast, built into the Perl language is a value that represents a nonvalue — defined. If a column is NULL, Perl DBI is set to not defined. Thus, by testing whether a variable is defined, we can determine whether it holds NULL.

Listing 14-18 demonstrates how to handle NULL with Perl DBI; it re-creates under Perl DBI the programs in Listing 14-7 and Listing 14-13. We show here only the code that is unique to this example.

Listing 14-18: **Handling NULL**

```
$results = sqlExec ("SELECT  DISTINCT team.team_name, game.home_team " .
                    "FROM team " .
                    "LEFT JOIN game ON team.team_name = game.home_team " .
                    "WHERE city = 'Chicago' " .
                    "ORDER BY team_name");

for ( $i = 0 ; $i < @$results ; $i++ )
{
    my ($team_name, $home_team) = @{ $$results[$i] };

    if (defined ($home_team))
```

```
        {
            print $team_name . "\t" . $home_team . "\n";
        }
        else
        {
            print $team_name . "\tNO RECORD IN TABLE 'GAME'\n";
        }
    }
```

As we noted earlier, the SELECT statement is designed to return a NULL value. The program calls sqlExec() to execute the SELECT statement; it then reads the array that sqlExec() returns. If $team_name is defined, the program prints it; if it is not defined, the program prints an error message.

When executed, Listing 14-18 prints the following:

```
Cubs          NO RECORD IN TABLE 'GAME'
White Sox         White Sox
```

As you can see, this program returns the same results as do the analogous ODBC and JDBC programs — but with considerably less pain.

Binding parameters

Like ODBC and JDBC, Perl DBI lets you bind parameters to positions within SQL statements.

To bind a parameter, you must place a ? in the SQL statement at the point where you want to bind the parameter. After you have used method prepare() to prepare the statement, you must use method bind_param() to bind a parameter to the one of the ? variables in the SQL statement.

bind_param() takes two arguments:

✦ The first argument gives the number of the ? from left to right within the SQL statement from left to right, counting from one.

✦ The second argument names the variable that you want to bind to that ?.

Listing 14-19 demonstrates binding variables. The program prompts you to enter the name of a city; it then prints the names of the baseball teams in that city (if any).

Listing 14-19: **Binding Parameters**

```perl
#!/usr/bin/perl -w -T

use DBI;
{
    my $dbh;
    my $sth;

    my $restype;
    my $ret_val;

    my $data;
    my @rawResults;

    my $cmd;
    my $cityName;
    my $teamName;
    my $i;

    $dbh = DBI->connect('DBI:mysql:baseball',
                        'mylogin',
                        'mypassword' );

    if ( !defined($dbh) )
    {
        print "Cannot connect to database.\n";
        exit 1;
    }

    $sth = $dbh->prepare("SELECT team_name FROM team WHERE city = ? ");

    if (!defined($sth))
    {
        $dbh->disconnect();
        print ("Preparation of SELECT statement failed\n");
        exit 1;
    }

    $sth->bind_param ( 1, $cityName );

    while (1)
    {
        print "Enter a city name: ";
        $|++;
        $cityName = <STDIN>;
        chomp ($cityName);

        if (lc ($cityName) eq 'quit')
        {
```

```
        $dbh->disconnect();
        print "Goodbye\n";
        exit 0;
    }

    $ret_val = $sth->execute();

    if (!defined($ret_val))
    {
        print ("Execution of SELECT statement failed\n");
        next;
    }

    while ( $data = $sth->fetchrow_arrayref() )
    {
        push @rawResults, [ @$data ];
    }

    if (@rawResults == 0)
    {
        print ($cityName . " has no team.\n");
        next;
    }

    for ( $i = 0 ; $i < @rawResults ; $i++ )
    {
        my ($team_name) = @{ $rawResults[$i] };
        print $team_name . "\n";
    }

    undef @rawResults;
    }
}
```

To begin, we prepare the SELECT with which we retrieve from the database the names of baseball teams. Note that it uses one ?, for the name of the city:

```
$sth = $dbh->prepare("SELECT team_name FROM team WHERE city = ? ");
```

When the statement has been prepared, the program calls method bind_param() to bind variable $cityName to the ? in the SELECT statement:

```
$sth->bind_param ( 1, $cityName );
```

As the program executes, it prompts the user to enter a city name; the program writes what the user enters into variable $cityName. When the user enters a city name, the program uses method execute() to execute the statement:

```
$ret_val = $sth->execute();
```

The program then uses `fetchrow_arrayref()` to read the data that has been retrieved:

```
while ( $data = $sth->fetchrow_arrayref() )
{
    push @rawResults, [ @$data ];
}
```

You may ask, "Why doesn't the program simply print what is returned by `fetchrow_arrayref()`?" The reason may surprise you: because only by reading the data and storing it in an array can we find out how many rows were returned by the query. (Perl DBI does not offer a method that states how many rows were returned by a SELECT statement.) When the data are read, we count the number of rows retrieved; if no rows were retrieved, then we print an error message, otherwise we print the data:

```
if (@rawResults == 0)
{
    print ($cityName . " has no team.\n");
    next;
}

for ( $i = 0 ; $i < @rawResults ; $i++ )
{
    my ($team_name) = @{ $rawResults[$i] };
    print $team_name . "\n";
}
```

After the code walks through array @rawResults and print its contents, it calls `undef` it to throw away the contents of @rawResults.

Transactions

Perl DBI defines methods with which you can execute transactions. Unfortunately, we cannot demonstrate transactions because MySQL does not support them; but they are easy to grasp.

To begin, the database object's attribute `AutoCommit` lets you set whether the database is to automatically commit the output of SQL statements. When autocommitting is turned on, the effects of every SQL statement are automatically committed to the database, even if you do not explicitly commit it.

By default, this attribute is set to 1 (on), as the ANSI standard requires. To turn off autocommitting, use the statement:

```
$dbh->AutoCommit = 0;
```

If the database supports transactions, and if AutoCommit is set to off, then you can use database methods commit() and rollback() to, respectively, commit or roll back the effects of all SQL statements executed since the last commit of data.

For example,

```
$dbh->commit();
```

commits into the database all SQL statements executed since the last call to method commit(). Likewise,

```
$dbh->rollback();
```

throws away the effects of all SQL statements executed since the last call to method commit().

Disconnecting from the database automatically commits all uncommitted data.

Metadata

This section briefly discusses how Perl DBI handles metadata.

As you may recall from our discussions of ODBC and JDBC, metadata are data that describe how data are organized. Perl DBI does not offer as rich a set of metadata as do ODBC and JDBC; however, unlike ODBC and JDBC, you do not have to issue a special call or examine a special object to read metadata — the metadata are available through attributes and methods that are built into the DBI's database and statement objects.

This subsection reviews the database metadata and statement metadata, then gives an example application that uses metadata to perform its work.

Database metadata

Perl DBI offers two principal methods for obtaining database metadata: tables() and table_info().

Method tables() returns an array that holds the names of all tables in the database.

Method table_info() returns a statement handle that retrieves detailed information about each table in the database. Each row returned by the statement has five columns:

✦ *qualifier* — The table's qualifier identifier. In most instances, this is NULL.

✦ *owner* — The name of the table's owner.

✦ *name*—The name of the table.

✦ *type*—The table's type. Among the values that can be given for a table's type are TABLE, VIEW, SYSTEMTABLE, and ALIAS.

✦ *remarks*—Miscellaneous remarks about the table.

Example of database Metadata

Listing 14-20 demonstrates how to use database metadata:

Listing 14-20: Using Metadata

```perl
#!/usr/bin/perl -w -T
use DBI;
{
    my $dbh;
    my @tables;
    my $sth;
    my $i;

    my $tQualifier;
    my $tOwner;
    my $tName;
    my $tType;
    my $tRemarks;

    $dbh = DBI->connect( 'DBI:mysql:baseball',
                         'mylogin',
                         'mypassword' );

    if ( !defined($dbh) )
    {
        print "Cannot connect to database.\n";
        exit 1;
    }

    # demonstrate method tables()

    @tables = $dbh->tables();

    foreach $tName ( @tables )
    {
        print "Table: $tName\n";
    }

    # demonstrate method table_info()

    $sth = $dbh->table_info();
```

```
    print "\nQualifier\tOwner\tName\tType\tRemarks\n";

while ( ( $tQualifier,
          $tOwner,
          $tName,
          $tType,
          $tRemarks ) = $sth->fetchrow_array() )
    {
    foreach ($tQualifier, $tOwner, $tName, $tType, $tRemarks)
        {
        if (defined ($_))
            {
            print $_ . "\t";
            }
        else
            {
            print "N/A\t";
            }
        }
    print "\n";
    }

$dbh->disconnect();
exit 0;
}
```

When this program is run with our `baseball` database, it returns the following
output:

```
Table: game
Table: team

Qualifier          Owner          Name          Type          Remarks
N/A          N/A          game          TABLE          N/A
N/A          N/A          team          TABLE          N/A
```

In this example, most of the table metadata is not set; this is a limitation of MySQL
rather than of Perl DBI.

The designers of Perl DBI acknowledge that Perl DBI offers only a limited body of
database metadata. Future releases should offer more metadata, and more ways to
obtain them.

Statement metadata

Statement metadata describe the statement that is being executed and, more
importantly, describe the data set that is returned upon execution of the statement.

Statement metadata are stored as attributes of the statement object. Unlike database metadata, you do not have to execute any methods in order to read statement metadata.

Please note that statement metadata can be read only after a statement has been prepared and executed. Furthermore, after you have finished reading data from the data set returned by a statement — either by explicitly reading every row returned by the statement, or by invoking the method finish() — the statement's metadata can no longer be read. Thus, the right time to read statement metadata is after the statement has been executed but before you start to read the data that the statement returns.

Some of the more important attributes that supply statement metadata are:

✦ NUM_OF_FIELDS — The number of columns (fields) in the data set returned by the statement.

✦ NAME — This array holds the names of each column in the data set returned by the statement.

✦ PRECISION — This array gives the size, in bytes, of each column in the data set returned by the statement. If the column holds a numeric data type (for example, an INT or a FLOAT), its precision is the number of bytes for that type. However, if the column holds an array type (for example, an array of type CHAR), then the precision gives the number of bytes in the array).

✦ NULLABLE — This array gives a flag for each column in the data set returned by the statement; the flag indicates whether the corresponding column can hold NULL, as follows: 0, the column cannot hold NULL; 1, the column can hold NULL; 2, it is not known whether the column can hold NULL.

Other attributes also hold statement metadata; for more information on them, see the documentation for Perl DBI referenced at the end of this section.

Example of statement metadata

Listing 14-21 demonstrates how to use statement-level metadata to implement a simple SQL interpreter. This program re-creates in Perl DBI the ODBC program in Listing 14-10 and the JDBC program in Listing 14-15. We reproduce it in full here; following the listing we discuss some of the program's highlights.

Listing 14-21: Perl DBI-based SQL Interpreter

```
#!/usr/bin/perl -w -T
use DBI;
{
    my $dbh;
    my $sth;
```

```perl
my $cmd;
my $ret_val;
my @column_width;
my $data;
my $i;

$dbh = DBI->connect( 'DBI:mysql:baseball',
                     'mylogin',
                     'mypassword' );

if ( !defined($dbh) )
{
    print "Cannot connect to database.\n";
    exit 1;
}

while (1)
{
    print "\nOk> ";
    $|++;
    $cmd = <STDIN>;
    chomp ($cmd);

    if (lc ($cmd) eq 'quit')
    {
        $dbh->disconnect();
        print "Goodbye\n";
        exit 0;
    }

    if (lc(substr($cmd, 0, 6)) ne "select")
    {
        # if true, this is not a SELECT: use "do" method.
        $ret_val = $dbh->do($cmd);

        if (!defined ($ret_val))
        {
            print ("Execution of non-SELECT statement failed.\n");
            exit 1;
        }
        else
        {
            print "Non-SELECT statement affected " .
                $sth->rows .
                " rows in the database.\n";
            next;
        }
    }
    else
    {
        # $cmd holds a SELECT statement:
```

Continued

Listing 14-21 *(continued)*

```perl
# prepare it, execute it, retrieve data
$sth = $dbh->prepare($cmd);

if (!defined($sth))
{
    $dbh->disconnect();
    print ("Preparation of SELECT statement failed\n");
    exit 1;
}

$ret_val = $sth->execute();

if (!defined($ret_val))
{
    $dbh->disconnect();
    print ("Execution of SELECT statement failed\n");
    exit 1;
}

for ($i = 0 ; $i < $sth->{NUM_OF_FIELDS} ; $i++)
{
    if ( length($sth->{NAME}->[$i]) > $sth->{PRECISION}->[$i] )
    {
        $column_width[$i] = length ($sth->{NAME}->[$i]) + 1;
    }
    else
    {
        $column_width[$i] = $sth->{PRECISION}->[$i] + 1;
    }
}

for ($i = 0 ; $i < @column_width ; $i++)
{
    printf "%-" . $column_width[$i] . "s",
            $sth->{NAME}->[$i];
}
print "\n";

while ( $data = $sth->fetchrow_arrayref() )
{
    for ($i = 0 ; $i < @column_width ; $i++)
    {
        printf "%-" . $column_width[$i] . "s",
                $data->[$i];
    }
    print "\n";
}
```

```
            undef @column_width;
        }
    }
    $dbh->disconnect();
    exit 0;
}
```

This example has the following structure:

1. Connect to the database and obtain a handle to the database object.
2. Prompt the user to enter a SQL statement; record what the user types.
3. Prepare and execute the SQL statement entered by the user.
4. Use statement metadata to lay out the data returned by the statement.
5. Print the data returned by the statement.

Listing 14-21 connects to the database in the same way as the other example Perl DBI programs did; there is no need to describe it further.

The body of the program consists of a `while` loop that ends only when the program exits. Each iteration of the `while` loop gathers a SQL statement from the user, prepares and executes it, and presents the results to the user.

The following code gathers the user's input:

```
print "\nOk> ";
$|++;
$cmd = <STDIN>;
chomp ($cmd);

if (lc ($cmd) eq 'quit')
{
    $dbh->disconnect();
    print "Goodbye\n";
    exit 0;
}
```

The example program uses the `prepare()` and `execute()` methods for each SQL statement, regardless of whether the statement contains the keyword `SELECT` or not:

```
$sth = $dbh->prepare($cmd);
 if (!defined($sth))
{
    $dbh->disconnect();
    print ("Preparation of SELECT statement failed\n");
    exit 1;
}
```

```
$ret_val = $sth->execute();
if (!defined($ret_val))
{
    $dbh->disconnect();
    print ("Execution of SELECT statement failed\n");
    exit 1;
}
```

After the example program has prepared and executed the SELECT statement, it reads the statement metadata to lay out how the data should be printed. If the SQL statement does not use the keyword SELECT, the example program uses the statement method rows() to print the number of rows in the database that were affected by the SQL statement, then returns to the top of the while loop:

```
if (lc(substr($cmd, 0, 6)) ne "select")
{
    print "Non-SELECT statement affected " .
        $sth->rows .
        " rows in the database.\n";
    next;
}
```

However, if the SQL statement does include the keyword SELECT, the example program reads the number of columns in the data set returned by the SELECT statement, the name of each column, and the precision (width) of each column, then builds a layout of how it should print the data:

```
else
{
    for ($i = 0 ; $i < $sth->{NUM_OF_FIELDS} ; $i++)
    {
        if ( length($sth->{NAME}->[$i]) > $sth->{PRECISION}->[$i] )
        {
            $column_width[$i] = length ($sth->{NAME}->[$i]) + 1;
        }
        else
        {
            $column_width[$i] = $sth->{PRECISION}->[$i] + 1;
        }
    }
```

Attribute NUM_FIELDS gives the number of columns returned by the SELECT statement. Attribute NAME is an array that names the columns returned by the SELECT statement; if the column holds an expression, then that expression is used as the column's name. Attribute PRECISION gives the width of each column. The example program adds one to the width of each column, to allows a bit of gutter between columns when the data are printed.

The final step is to print the data, as follows:

```
for ($i = 0 ; $i < @column_width ; $i++)
{
    printf "%-" . $column_width[$i] . "s",
            $sth->{NAME}->[$i];
}
print "\n";

while ( $data = $sth->fetchrow_arrayref() )
{
    for ($i = 0 ; $i < @column_width ; $i++)
    {
        printf "%-" . $column_width[$i] . "s",
                $data->[$i];
    }
    print "\n";
}

undef @column_width;
}
```

The first for() loop prints the header for each column; the second for() loop prints each row returned by the SQL statement. Finally, the program undefines array @column_width, to clear it out for the next statement.

The following is an example of using Listing 14-21 to work with the baseball database:

```
Ok> update team set team_name = 'Cubs' where team_name = 'foo'
Non-SELECT statement affected 1 rows in the database.

Ok> update team set team_name = 'foo' where team_name = 'Cubs'
Non-SELECT statement affected 1 rows in the database.

Ok> select team_name from team where city = 'Chicago'
team_name
White Sox
foo

Ok> update team set team_name = 'Cubs' where team_name = 'foo'
Non-SELECT statement affected 1 rows in the database.

Ok> select team_name, city, stadium from team where city = 'Chicago'
team_name       city            stadium
White Sox       Chicago         Comiskey Park
Cubs            Chicago         Wrigley Field

Ok> quit
Goodbye
```

With this, we conclude our discussion of Perl DBI. We hope that our "nickel tour" of this most useful protocol will help you to start using it, and to explore it further on your own.

For more information on Perl DBI, we recommend *Programming the Perl DBI*, by Alligator Descartes and Tim Bunce (O'Reilly & Associates, 2000). It is both authoritative and a model of clarity.

Summary

This chapter introduces the commonly used methods for interacting with a database: ODBC, JDBC, and Perl DBI.

ODBC is standard call-level interface that works across database packages. It uses an elaborate system of drivers that translate the ODBC calls to the call-level interface recognized by the database package in question. ODBC gives all of the capabilities of embedded SQL, plus numerous extensions.

JDBC is call-level interface designed by Sun Corporation for its Java programming language. JDBC re-creates most of the capabilities of ODBC; however, it simplifies some of the tasks, and offers features only available to an object-oriented language.

Perl DBI is a package prepared for Perl that manages interaction with data sources. Like JDBC, it is modeled after ODBC. It offers the flexibility and power of the Perl language, and is the interface of choice for CGI scripts.

✦   ✦   ✦

Standalone Applications

This chapter discusses standalone database applications. The goal is to present the essential characteristics of a standalone database application and to illustrate how one such application might be specified and implemented. This chapter expands somewhat on the material presented in Chapter 13 by implementing the demonstration application using Perl and the Perl DBI for MySQL, too.

Standalone Database Applications

Probably the quickest way to define a standalone database application is to simply state that the salient characteristic of a standalone application is that it is designed so that all of the user interfacing and all of the data interfacing are contained within the same program. Another way of looking at it is to say that the application is not shared with anyone (or program for that matter) else.

Prime examples of standalone applications are those found on personal computers, for example, word processors, checkbook registers, calendars, and desktop publishing programs. A checkbook register is a good example of a standalone database application because it presents data in a tabular format and makes use of a database.

An example of a simple application might be a program that removes unwanted files from your hard drive. In Linux, this shell script easily accomplishes this task:

```
#/bin/bash
rm core
rm *.old
```

When executed, this simple script removes any core (files that occur when a program fails) files in your directory as well as any *.old files. This example of an extremely simple application that performs a specific task raises several issues: What if

I don't want to remove a particular `*.old` file for some reason? Quickly, we can see this program become a much larger program that prompts for user input to ensure that the files are backed up before being removed. And eventually a modern-day application comes about.

Since the advent of the computer, the number of computer applications has grown dramatically. These applications are often placed in categories to help differentiate one from another. In fact, the example above is often not referred to as an application at all; instead, it is referred to as a script, although technically it is an application. Some of the categories into which applications are put are desktop applications, Web applications, business applications, and database applications — the categories are pretty dependent on the marketplace and on what the market leaders are doing at the time. And we can expect a whole new set of applications as computers get placed in everything. To further clarify the definition of an application, let's look at some common applications.

✦ Word processors

✦ Calculators

✦ Billing systems

✦ Reporting systems

✦ Spreadsheets

✦ Change of address forms

✦ System monitors

✦ Financial registers

✦ Project tracking tools

✦ Calendars

✦ Collaboration

✦ Administration software

✦ Computer-Aided Drafting

A very common application is the database itself. An advantage of a database is that it is an extremely flexible application that allows you to build applications on top of it. It is so flexible that applications are often built from commercial databases. In fact, a lot of new companies specialize in applications built on commercial or store-bought databases. Because this book is about databases, we can further narrow our definition of an application to only database applications. A database application is a program that interfaces with a database to perform a specific function or set of functions. As the chapter title suggests, this chapter discusses standalone applications and the next chapter discusses multiuser, multimachine applications. Let us define a standalone database application as an application that interfaces with a database and interacts with or is entirely self-contained on one computer.

Our simple standalone application is built on top of another application, specifically a database application. Although this may violate our previous definition that the program not interact with any other program, this is a small price to pay to avoid writing an actual database for our simple example. It also demonstrates and builds on materials presented in Chapter 13.

The choice of whether to buy an application or not depends on your unique situation. In some environments, developing an application in house, often referred to as a homegrown application, may have a better return on investment than in other shops. It really depends on the talent at hand. However, because you either have chosen Linux, or may choose Linux, it is highly likely that you or someone in your organization is highly talented. So, it is expected that you will be developing at least some homegrown applications. This chapter goes through the building of a simple standalone database application. The example is an application intended to facilitate or enhance the entry of orders within our example company Widget-R-Us. It is a rather simple menu system that would allow a person to update, insert, or delete information in a simple order-entry database. Building the application follows a basic strategy of design, implement, redesign. This strategy lends itself well to the real world in which an application may be built and have feature after feature added to it. It is not necessary to follow this strategy when building your own applications; you should use whatever works for you.

This chapter also discusses when to buy or, more appropriately, what not to buy. Obviously, if you don't have the talent or time to develop your own application, you are at the mercy of vendors. If you don't enjoy programming, finding someone who does — it is often a win-win situation, especially if they are interested in the problem at hand. My basic approach to buying an application is can it resolve a *real* problem that I have. I can't emphasize this enough. If you are going to build a data warehouse, buy a database built for data warehousing. If you're going to build a transactional database buy a transactional database. Spend the time to figure out what your problem is. A lot of vendors would love to sell you a hammer even if your problem is a screw. You owe it to yourself and to your organization to get this understanding. We are beginning to see a shift in the market for better tools (Linux being one of them) and with more tailored, applications. Certain software companies would rather this not be the case, but are having to change their software and operating systems to be more flexible and more feature rich.

Application architecture

The architecture of the application is the manner in which the components of the application are organized and integrated. It can vary from application to application. The architecture used for our database application is:

✦ A command-line user interface for the client

✦ The API (using Perl DBI)

✦ The database

The framework for the user interface can further be divided into metadata and menus. Figure 15-1 illustrates the architecture of the example presented here.

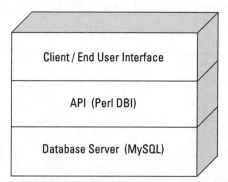

Figure 15-1: Layered application architecture

The application consists of three layers, the client interface, the API, and the database as shown in Figure 15-1. This is the architecture of our application. It is also known as a client server application; however since we've chosen to use it as a standalone application, it will only have the one user interface connecting to the one server. The user interfaces with a series of menus. This is the Client Interface. Depending on what the end user does, information is passed and processed by the database server through the API. Since the API and database are already written, all that is needed is to write the end user interface and its calls to the API.

Scope

The scope of the application is essentially a list of what to expect from the application in terms of the application's capabilities. In some organizations, this what makes or breaks your application's chance of success. Too many worthless applications survive and continue to get funded despite the scope of the application being so limited that it was a waste of resources to have created it originally. However, because the scope of the application was so well defined, the application was declared a huge success. A lot of well-known vendors rely on this stuff for success stories. That said, not determining the scope for an application at all will result in an absolute failure with the unfortunate client or end user expecting more than they're getting. So, determining the scope for an application is a balancing act. A good approach is to scope vary narrowly, but design for change. This means that features can be added at a later time, which will increase the application's success.

In defining scope it is probably easiest to start by concentrating on the end users. If you run a business, this probably means most of your employees and maybe the customers. It may mean just you; it could mean an entire organization with thousands of people, or if you worked for a well-known software company, it could mean that you have most of the world to please. Either way, talking to the end user, especially if there is a user interface involved, is a good idea.

A Lighter-Side Conversation with an End User

Application Developer: "So you're going to be in charge of taking orders?"

End User: "Yep."

A D: "What would you like the user interface to look like?"

End User: "I would like it to only run on Wednesday."

A D: "Would you like it to be a GUI?"

End User: "No, I'd rather have a latte."

A D: "Do you want a menu-driven interface?"

End User: "No, I've decided on a small latte. Thanks, though."

Notice that the end user and the developer fail to communicate at all. Although quite amusing, this should be avoided.

Sometimes the end user will not want to cooperate at all; others may be too helpful:

A D: "I've been assigned to build you an application."

End User2: "Really? I want it to have a button."

A D: "We can do a button."

End User2: "Really? Okay, but just one."

A D: "Well, then it can only do one thing."

End User2: "Okay. . .can it pop up a new button?"

A D: "Sure."

End User2: "Okay, but just one. Okay? Thanks! I can't wait!"

A D: "No problem."

Much later . . .

Ed from accounting: "We spent a million dollars on a button that brings up another button?!!!"

So, we see how the developer end user dialogs can and often do impact the scope of an application. Include the end user in the development cycle, and it will result in a better- defined project, scope, and chance of success. The other thing that will ultimately impact the project scope is the amount of time that you have to deliver the application. Ensure that there is enough time. Unfortunately, the truth is that there is never enough time. Applications that are delivered late will always have to live with a bad first impression so try to be as consistent as possible. Depending on the size of your application you may want to organize your application into smaller components and break them up so one developer, or team of developers, is not doing everything all at once, but rather working on their specific code streams. This may help you develop applications faster. On the other hand, if your resources are limited to one person it may make more sense to prioritize and begin with the most important or least-difficult application. Again, do what works for your situation.

An Example of a Standalone Linux Database Application

For our example database application, we will model a *very simple* order-entry database using a small number of related tables.

Initial database design

There are several steps to designing our database:

1. Determining the application or business function, that is, the project requirements and scope

2. Determining the minimum information that is necessary for this business function to operate (required information)

3. Understanding the *desired* information and its relationship to required information

4. Determining the source(s) of this information

5. Determining the relationships among these sources of information (creating a logical database model)

6. Creating the physical database

In the interest of brevity, I only touch on the steps that are needed to complete the example for this chapter.

Requirements

We'll assume that we held discussions with the personnel who will make use of this application. The requirements are fairly straightforward for the database design: It must hold order information for multiple orders for multiple customers. The list of products that can be ordered will be in one table. The list of customers (along with some address and telephone data) will be held in a second table. A third table will hold order header information, that is, information about the order as a whole. There is one customer per order, but multiple ordered items. The fourth and final table will hold information about individual ordered items: one record per order, per product. Figure 15-2 shows the schema for the order-entry database.

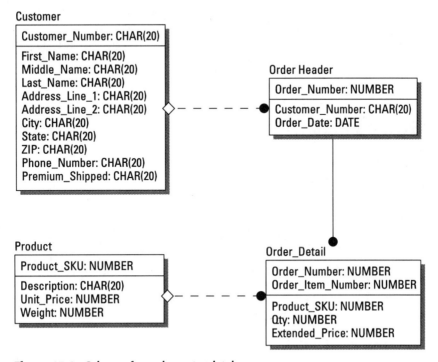

Figure 15-2: Schema for order-entry database

Figure 15-2 shows the tables required to keep track of all the orders that take place in our standalone application. The Customer table keeps track of all of the customers who order from our fictitious company. A customer can make one or more orders, which are then stored in a Order Header table. The details of the order — such as which product, how many, and the sale price — are located in Order detail. The Product table describes the product itself.

As far as the functions that the application needs to implement, we are told that the user need to accomplish three main tasks:

1. Enter new orders, customers, and products

2. Change existing orders, customers, and products

3. Delete existing orders, customers, and products

The target database for this application is MySQL, an SQL-compliant, open source, fully relational database management system product available for Linux. The essential SQL commands needed to fulfill the requirements are:

Insert	Add new records to a table
Update	Alter existing records in a table
Delete	Delete existing records in tables

We have been told that the users are not facile with SQL, so our application needs to map the task of entering new orders to the individual SQL table insert actions that MySQL uses; to map the task of altering information about an existing order to the individual SQL table update commands; and to map the listing of particular order detail to the individual SQL table select commands.

To speed up the implementation, we will not use a graphical user interface (GUI). Instead, we'll rely on a character-based menuing system as can be found on many legacy applications today. This text-menuing system, though, can be used as the foundation for a GUI-based application.

User interface

We design our applications with the end user in mind. For our example, we assume that the end user is familiar with Linux command line, but does not know (nor has any desire to know) SQL. Also, we assume that eventually our client will want this to be a GUI interface, so we will implement a simple text-menu user interface that can be modified later. In addition, we will constrain this release of our application to do three things: insert rows, delete rows, and browse the tables within our database. These series of menus direct the end user to perform a specific task. The first menu might look like the following.

```
connecting to database.....
Welcome....
Please select a table from the following list or quit[q]:
        1) Product
        2) Customer
        3) Order Header
        4) Order Detail
Make your selection:
```

After making a selection the following text comes up prompting the end user to make a selection:

```
Please select a task from the following list or quit[q]:
        1) Insert
        2) Delete
        3) Browse
Make your selection:
```

Finally, one of three menus come up based on the user's selection. The subsequent menus depend on the choices made in this menu. For the selection corresponding to Insert (1), the menu is as follows:

```
Please select a field to edit:
        1) STATE:
        2) PHONE_NUMBER:
        3) ZIP:
        4) LAST_NAME:
```

```
        5) FIRST_NAME:
        6) MIDDLE_INITIAL:
        7) CITY:
        8) ADDRESS_LINE_1:
        9) CUSTOMER_ID:
       10) ADDRESS_LINE_2:
Make your selection, continue [c], or quit [q]:
```

We have laid the framework for the application, discussed the scope of the application, designed the database, and for demonstration purposes, designed a primitive user interface for the example application. The next section discusses the implementation of the application with the emphasis on building modular, reusable, evolving code. We have kept the application simple enough for novice programmers, yet detailed enough to provide a reasonable discussion of real issues associated with building real-world applications.

Implementation

This section discusses the implementation of the project and the details of the code behind the application. We will choose a language and an API for the project. Then we describe our object-oriented design and show how it is implemented. Finally, we discuss how the application could be further enhanced and analyze how we could have better implemented our application.

Choosing the language/API

Some thought should be given to choosing a programming language because not all languages are created equal. For our example, it is assumed that the end product is needed quickly, but that it should be versatile enough to grow into a large, multi-faceted program (and perhaps even out grow the somewhat arbitrary definition of standalone database application).

Another factor is: what was the language built to do? If it were built to crunch numbers then it is probably a poor choice for this text-based user interface. We will choose Perl, but Python, C++, or perhaps even PHP could just as easily have been chosen. Perl has a dynamic that has made it very popular in the Linux world, as well as very popular in the database world. It is easy enough for shell programmers to grasp quickly and structured in a manner that appeals to the C programmer in us all. In addition, it is an object-oriented language with inheritance (even multiple inheritance) and data protection. Also, a recent poll of Linux users regarding scripting languages ranked Perl as the number one scripting language for programming that is not Web-based.

Object-oriented programming

Object oriented is a particular way of designing and implementing the code. It allows methods (functions) and data to be bundled together. These bundles are known as classes and are the framework for the objects that are created by them. The objects are known as an instance of the class. Object Oriented Programming (OOP) is essentially writing programs that act like real world objects. Real world objects typically have functions and state information about the function.

Take a CD player, for example. The data would be the number of tracks and the name of the album, and the functions would be play, stop, fast-forward, and rewind. The data or state information (which track, for example) is accessed by the functions that are known as methods. All of these methods and data are referred to as public, because the end user can manipulate them. Unfortunately, often problems solved by a program aren't actual objects and we have to make them fit into this model. This is referred to as abstraction. Rather than go into a lengthy discussion of object-oriented programming (OOP), I provide some common terms in OOP and short snippets of how this is accomplished in Perl. Perl hackers are welcome to skip this section and dive right into the code.

Object	Also known as instance of a class. The data and its methods bundled nicely in a neat little package.
`$table;  #`	Has data attributes and methods of our table.
Constructor	Initializes an object (sometimes adds data, usually not).
`$table=customer-> new();  # $table`	Now has the `data` # attributes associated with customer.
Attributes	The data (properties) about the objects. These should not be directly accessed.
`$table->{STATE_CD}  #`	The end user of the object doesn't need to see this.
Method	A task that an object can perform. Often referred to as the object's behavior.
`$query=$table->delete ("customer_xyz");  #`	Writes query to delete customer xyz.
Encapsulation	The hiding of how and where the attributes of an object are stored.

Note   Instead of allowing the program to access `$table->{STATE_CD}` directly, we provide a method to do that instead.

Inheritance	The use of methods in another class.
`$table-> action_menu();  #`	Use the `action_menu` method from menu class.

This essentially sums up all of the aspects of object-oriented code used in our simple example. There are some other advanced features that are not used in our example (such as multiple inheritance and destruction) that I leave to the interested reader to discover.

The customer class

The customer class is somewhat static and hard coded by Perl standards, but it illustrates some practical object-oriented techniques. The Customer table is the object modeled, and the methods or actions that can be performed are assigning values to the table attributes (fields), inserting values into the table, deleting a row from the table based on a primary constraint, or browsing the table based on any of the fields as constraints. This class inherits methods from menu, which inherits methods from the DBI (our chosen API). The Perl package (or class if you prefer) customer.pm is as follows:

```perl
!/usr/bin/perl


package customer;
use menu;

# inherit methods from menu
@ISA = ("menu");


#############################################################################
#
#
#
# Constructor - one row of customer table, initially empty
#
#
#
#############################################################################
sub new {
  my $proto=shift;
  my $class=ref($proto) || $proto;
  my $self={};
  $self->{FIRST_NAME}=undef;
  $self->{MIDDLE_INITIAL}=undef;
  $self->{LAST_NAME}=undef;
  $self->{ADDRESS_LINE_1}=undef;
  $self->{ADDRESS_LINE_2}=undef;
  $self->{CITY}=undef;
  $self->{STATE}=undef;
  $self->{ZIP}=undef;
  $self->{CUSTOMER_ID}=undef;
  $self->{PHONE_NUMBER}=undef;
```

```perl
    bless($self,$class);
    return $self;
  }


  ##############################################################
  #
  #
  #  One method to access each field in table, if called with
  #  value assigns it to field if empty returns value of field.
  #  Note: not yet inserted into table.
  #
  #
  #
  ##############################################################


  sub zip {
    my $self = shift;
    if (@_) { $self->{ZIP} = shift }
    return $self->{ZIP};
  }
  sub phone_number {
    my $self = shift;
    if (@_) { $self->{PHONE_NUMBER} = shift }
    return $self->{PHONE_NUMBER};
  }
  sub customer_id {
    my $self = shift;
    if (@_) { $self->{CUSTOMER_ID} = shift }
    return $self->{CUSTOMER_ID};
  }
  sub first_name {
    my $self = shift;
    if (@_) { $self->{FIRST_NAME} = shift }
    return $self->{FIRST_NAME};
  }
  sub middle_initial{
    my $self = shift;
    if (@_) { $self->{MIDDLE_INITIAL} = shift }
    return $self->{MIDDLE_INITIAL};
  }
  sub last_name {
    my $self = shift;
    if (@_) { $self->{LAST_NAME} = shift }
    return $self->{LAST_NAME};
  }
  sub address_line_1 {
    my $self = shift;
    if (@_) { $self->{ADDRESS_LINE_1} = shift }
    return $self->{ADDRESS_LINE_1};
```

```perl
}
sub address_line_2 {
  my $self = shift;
  if (@_) { $self->{ADDRESS_LINE_2} = shift }
  return $self->{ADDRESS_LINE_2};
}
sub city {
  my $self = shift;
  if (@_) { $self->{CITY} = shift }
  return $self->{CITY};
}

sub state {
  my $self = shift;
  if (@_) { $self->{STATE} = shift }
  return $self->{STATE};
}

##################################################################
#
#
# primary_key - A special case accessor the above assigns the
#
#               appropriate value to the appropriate primary
#
#               key field
#
#
#
##################################################################

sub primary_key {
  my $self = shift;
  if (@_) { $self->{CUSTOMER_ID} = shift }
  return $self->{CUSTOMER_ID};
}


##################################################################
#
#
# insert - writes query that will insert data into database
#
#
#
##################################################################


sub insert {
  my $self = shift;
```

```
# Connect to database
my $dbname='order_entry_db';
my $user='dba';
my $password='dba2pass';
my $dbd='mysql';
my $dbh=DBI->connect($dbname, $user, $password, $dbd);
if (!$dbh) {
  print "ERROR connecting to database; $DBI::errstr\n";
}else {
  print "connecting to database......\n";
}

# create local values to use

my $cust_id=$self->customer_id;
my $first_name=$self->first_name;
my $middle_initial=$self->middle_initial;
my $last_name=$self->last_name;
my $address_line_1=$self->address_line_1;
my $address_line_2=$self->address_line_2;
my $city=$self->city;
my $state=$self->state;
my $zip=$self->zip;
my $phone_number=$self->phone_number;

# create query

my $query="insert into customer values (
'$cust_id','$first_name',
                    '$middle_initial','$last_name',
                    '$address_line_1','$address_line_2',
                    '$city','$state','$zip',
                    '$phone_number','N')";

# execute query
print "preparing and executing sql....\n";

my $sth=$dbh->prepare("$query");
my $error=$sth->execute;
$sth->finish;
$dbh->disconnect();
return $error;


}
```

```perl
#####################################################################
#
#
# browse - writes query that will select data from database
#
#
#
#####################################################################


sub browse{
  my $self = shift;


  # Connect to database

  my $dbname='order_entry_db';
  my $user='dba';
  my $password='dba2pass';
  my $dbd='mysql';
  my $dbh=DBI->connect($dbname, $user, $password, $dbd);
  if (!$dbh) {
    print "ERROR connecting to database; $DBI::errstr\n";
  }else {
    print "connecting to database......\n";
  }

  # create the query
  my $query="select * from customer where 1=1    ";
  foreach $field (keys(%{$self})){
    if($self->{$field}) {

      $query=$query."and $field = $self->{$field}";

    }
    $index[$ii]=$field;
    $ii++;

  }

  # run the query

  my $sth=$dbh->prepare("$query");
  my $error=$sth->execute;
  my @fields=undef;

  # print the rows

  while(@fields=$sth->fetchrow_array) {
    print "@fields\n";
  }

  # clean up
```

```
    $sth->finish;
    $dbh->disconnect();

    return $error;


}


##############################################################################
#
#
# delete - writes query that will delete data from database
#
#
#
##############################################################################
sub delete {
  my $self = shift;

  # Connect to database
  my $dbname='order_entry_db';
  my $user='dba';
  my $password='dba2pass';
  my $dbd='mysql';
  my $dbh=DBI->connect($dbname, $user, $password, $dbd);
  if (!$dbh) {
    print "ERROR connecting to database; $DBI::errstr\n";
  }else {
    print "connecting to database......\n";
  }

  # create query

  my $cust_id=$self->customer_id;
  $query="delete from customer where customer_id='$cust_id'";

  # run the query

  print "preparing sql....\n";
  my $sth=$dbh->prepare("$query");
  my $error=$sth->execute;

  # clean up and return;

  $sth->finish;
  $dbh->disconnect();
  return $error;


}

1;
```

The customer class handles all of the actions that are performed on a table, including inserting rows, deleting rows, and accessing rows. If we wanted to, we could add other methods as well, such as creating the table, or validating the table, listing indices on the table, and on and on. There would be a similar class for product. In the effort to emphasize applications as a life cycle (and programming for that matter), I will point out some improvements that could be made to this class.

First, we see that the variables $dbname, $user, $password, and $dbd are not only hard coded, they are hard coded three times. This doesn't have to be. We could make them arguments for the Constructor or we could make them Class data. In the next section we do this, and consequently have a more versatile class.

 Cross-Reference For further reading, see $man perltootin in the Perl distribution documentation.

Also, as the more experienced Perl object-oriented programmers already realize, this class could have been constructed more dynamically, allowing any table to use one class.

The menu class

The menu class is a superclass of a table class. It is generic enough for any table in the class to use. Any object with hash data types can access the class. Some of the menus are built dynamically, such as fields, and some are built statically, such as the table menu. It is very possible to expand the hard coded menus so that they are more dynamic and versatile with less code. However, for simplicity, they were kept static for our example.

```perl
#!/usr/bin/perl


package menu;
use DBI;
@ISA=("DBI");


############################################################
#
#
# Create a new instance of object, if need be.
#
#   -very flexible constructor used often in
#   object-oriented perl
#
#
############################################################
```

```perl
sub new {
  my $proto=shift;
  my $class=ref($proto) || $proto;
  my $self={};
  bless($self,$class);
}




#################################################################
#
#
# table_menu—displays the tables the user can choose
#
#
#
#################################################################


sub table_menu {
  print ("Welcome.....
          Please select a table from the following list or quit
[q]:
          1) Product
          2) Customer
          3) Order Header
          4) Order Detail
Make your selection: ");
  my $selection=<STDIN>;
  if ($selection == 1) {
    return 1;
  }elsif( $selection == 2) {
    return 2;
  }elsif ( $selection == 3) {
    return 3;
  }elsif( $selection == 3) {
    return 4;
  } elsif ($selection =~ m/[qQ]/) {
    die "Exiting application at users request....\n";
  } else { action();}


}


#################################################################
#
#
# action_menu—displays the tasks user can choose to perform
#
#
#
#################################################################
```

```perl
sub action_menu {
  print("Please select a task from the following list or quit
[q]:
          1) Insert
          2) Delete
          3) Browse
Make your selection: ");
  my $selection=<STDIN>;
  if ($selection == 1) {
    return 1;
  }elsif( $selection == 2) {
    return 2;
  }elsif( $selection == 3) {
    return 3;
  } elsif ($selection =~ m/[qQ]/) {
    die "Exiting program at users request....\n";
  } else { action();}

}


#############################################################
#
#
#   field_menu—displays the keys in the object or in the
#   inheriting object.
#
#
#
#############################################################


sub field {
  my $self = shift;
  my $field="";
  my $ii=1;
  print("\tPlease select a field to edit:\n");
  foreach $field (keys(%{$self})){
    print "\t $ii) $field: $self->{$field}\n";
    $index[$ii]=$field;
    $ii++;
  }
    print("Make your selection, continue [c], or quit [q]: ");
  my $selection=<STDIN>;
  chomp($selection);
  if (($selection > 0) && ($selection < $ii) ) {
    $field=$index[$selection];
    print "$field: ";
    my $input=<STDIN>;
    chomp($input);
    $self->{"$field"}=$input;
    print "$self->{\"$field\"}<<>>$self->{'$field'}<<>>$self-
```

```perl
>{$field}<<>>\n";
    $self->field();
    return $field;

  } elsif ($selection =~ m/[cC]/) {
    return(1);
  } elsif ($selection =~ m/[qQ]/) {
    die "Exiting program at users request....\n";
  } else {
    $self->field();
  }


}


#####################################################################
#
#
# browse_menu—asks user for the constraints;
# calls fields menu
#
#
#####################################################################

sub browse_menu {
  my $self = shift;
  my $field="";
  my $ii=1;

  print("If you would like to constrain on any field please
select:\n");
  foreach $field (keys(%{$self})){
    print "\t $ii) $field: $self->{$field}\n";
    $index[$ii]=$field;
    $ii++;
  }
  print("Make your selection, continue [c], or quit [q]: ");
  my $selection=<STDIN>;
  chomp($selection);
  if (($selection > 0) && ($selection < $ii) ) {
    $field=$index[$selection];
    print "$field: ";
    my $input=<STDIN>;
    chomp($input);
    $self->{"$field"}=$input;
    print "$self->{\"$field\"}<<>>$self->{'$field'}<<>>$self-
>{$field}<<>>\n";
    $self->field();
    return $field;
```

```perl
  } elsif ($selection =~ m/[cC]/) {
    return(1);
  } elsif ($selection =~ m/[qQ]/) {
    die "Exiting program at users request....\n";
  } else {
    $self->field();
  }
}


#############################################################
#
#
# delete_menu—requires user to enter primary key (better if
# implemented like browse_menu
#
#
#
#############################################################

sub delete_menu {
  $self=shift;
  print("Please enter the primary key of the row  you would
like to delete or quit [q]:");
  my $input=<STDIN>;
  chomp($input);

  if($input =~ m/^\s*[qQ]\s*$/){
    die "Exiting upon user request\n";
  } elsif (! $input) {
    $self->delete_menu;
  }else {

    print "Are you sure you want to delete $input? (y or n)[n]:
";
    my $confirm=<STDIN>;
    if ($confirm=~ m/^\s*[yY]\s*$/) {
      print "DM: $input\n";
      return $input;
    } else { $self->delete_menu };

  }
```

Again, we see our menu class doing all the actions associated with menus: namely printing the menus to the screen. Some of the more dynamic methods use the object attributes to drive the menu produced. This is very handy, and if we did the same with our customer class and renamed it table, we could literally supply our constructor with a name of the table or the create statement and instantly have a menu for that table. This is coding for change and has made Perl and OOP very popular. And this leads into our code redesign. On our next cycle of this code, we could make the menus graphical without changing our table classes or driver menus. We simply replace the text-based action_menu method with a graphical action_menu method.

Main

Finally, we use our classes in a program to complete the implementation of our menu-driven user interface. The following code derives instances of customer, product, order_details, and order_headers from their respective classes, which, in turn, derive menus by inheriting methods from the menu class. The menu, in turn, inherits from the DBI API. The only thing that this code needs to know about the classes is what to supply the classes and what is returned. The code is as follows:

```perl
#!/usr/bin/perl


use customer;
use product;
use order_detail;
use order_header;
use strict;


# Strict requires this definition
my $table=undef;

###############################################################
#                                                             #
# Decide which table to use                                   #
#                                                             #
###############################################################


my $table_choice=menu->table_menu();

if($table_choice==1) {
  $table=product->new();
}elsif($table_choice==2) {
  $table=customer->new();
}else { die "ERROR Line 25\n"; }

###############################################################
#                                                             #
# Decide which action to take                                 #
#                                                             #
###############################################################
```

```perl
my $action=$table->action_menu();

if($action==1) {


   ##############################
   #           Insert           #
   ##############################


   my $continue=$table->field();

   if($continue) {

      print "inserting customer into table .....\n";
      my $query=$table->insert();
      my $sth=$dbh->prepare("$query");
      my $error=$sth->execute;

   }

}
elsif($action==2) {



   ##############################
   #           Delete           #
   ##############################

   my $pkey=$table->delete_menu;
   if($pkey) {

      $table->primary_key($pkey);
      my $query=$table->delete();
      print "deleting row where primary key is $pkey. ......\n";
      my $sth=$dbh->prepare("$query\n");
      my $error=$sth->execute;

   }

}
elsif($action==3) {



   ##############################
   #           Browse           #
   ##############################
```

```
my $continue=$table->browse_menu;

if ($continue) {
  my $query=$table->browse();
  my $sth=$dbh->prepare("$query\n");
  my $error=$sth->execute;
  my @fields=undef;
  while(@fields=$sth->fetchrow_array) {
    print "@fields\n";
  }
}

}


##############################
# Close connection          #
##############################

$dbh->disconnect();
```

And finally reviewing the overall interaction of the code, we see a very nice flow of choices, a good deal of control, but a lot of data and code hidden from the user of this code. This is good, but we can always make room for improvement. Our use of number return codes is pretty clumsy, the menu classes could definitely return table names, and with that, coupled with a table class that merely needs a table name to construct itself (hint see the DBI example in previous chapter), we would have a very versatile menu application. It could be applied to new tables without any rewrite. However, we met the requirements of our scope and can therefore claim success for now.

Summary

This chapter illustrates a very basic standalone database application. It demonstrates building a user interface, calling an API, and designing a database for the application. The basic architecture is client server. The API used is DBI. The code is object oriented with the thought of reuse in mind. Most importantly, this chapter demonstrates how to build applications with a life cycle in mind. This flexibility is crucial for success and is a very good argument for going with Linux and UNIX in general. These operating systems were designed with redesign and development in mind.

✦   ✦   ✦

Web Applications

In this chapter, we delve into Web applications by discussing PHP and MySQL.

The New Problem to Solve

The business customer who used the stand-alone application that we constructed in Chapter 15 has a few changes that he'd like to have us make to the application.

For your convenience, the database schema used in Chapter 15 is repeated here.

Because of changes in the economic environment, the customer would like to begin taking orders over the Internet. Using incentives is a good idea, however, the customer should see the benefits of having purchased more than $150 with the next order without having to redeem any certificates.

From these brief requirements, we draw up a quick list of requirements:

1. The customer logs into the Web site, so a login page is needed.

2. The customer's purchase history is looked up in the order database, so the login ID that the customer uses must also be present in the order-entry database, or else linked by some foreign key relationship.

3. A Web page for ordering will be needed, and it needs to be obvious to the customer how to use it.

4. The discount, if any, should be calculated automatically and the savings displayed right on the order form.

After thoughtful consideration of the requirements, we decide to implement the Web pages and the interface to the order-entry database using PHP. There are a couple of advantages to this approach. First, PHP performs server-side execution of the database access as opposed to, say, Java that needs secure applets running on the client. Second, we are still using MySQL as the database and PHP4 has MySQL support included, that is, it doesn't have to be built with MySQL support as the other databases do for PHP. If you use PHP3 and want MySQL support, install PHP3 with the ─with-mysql=DIR option.

Given the data model shown in Figure 16-1, we need to integrate it with our application. The following sections with example PHP code show how you can do this. By extending these examples, you can create more sophisticated applications.

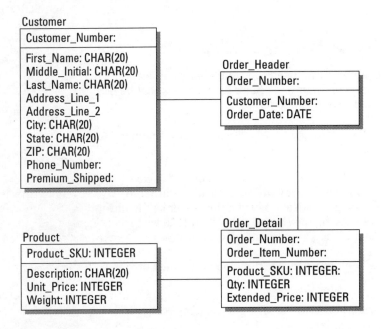

Figure 16-1: Database schema

Security

In our simple data model, there are no fields other than the customer name. By this model we're including the access privileges that the user has through the application (the Web page order-entry system).

Because we are not providing the capability of browsing the order-entry database, which is a capability needed by other groups in a business, we can assume that payment information and security is handled by a separate system, the details of which we'll not get into. Security issues are covered in another chapter.

In our system, the only security requirement that we have is a password in addition to the customer's name so that unauthorized purchases cannot be made. We have simplified the order-entry model so that it doesn't retain customer credit card information, making our security needs minimal for this model.

In our example, we keep security in mind so as not to leave a blatantly obvious hole in our Web site. For instance, we use MySQL's standard password encryption to store the user's password on our site. This prevents an intruder on our server from discovering a user's password, which might be reused by the user. A worst-case scenario would be the customer using the same password as the one they use for online banking. In addition, and more importantly, because this is not an encrypted Web site, we limit the user to only being able to connect to our database. This limits the potential damage or security hole created by hackers who steal our customer's user IDs and passwords before they reach our server. Again, we have kept security to minimum but have tried to keep in step with good Internet practices. At this point the only items necessary to make the site secure are a good firewall to deter an intruder from commandeering our server and an SSL Web site.

Logging in

The customer enters the Web site through the Web URL located at the root of our Web site, known as the index page. A simple log in page is presented in Figure 16-2. The user enters a user ID and password. The user ID uniquely identifies the customer. If the customer has not yet become a member, they are redirected to a new member page that allows them to become a member and then are redirected to the order form page. If the customer is a member and can provide the correct password, then they can make purchases and are redirected to the order form page. PHP code verifies that the username and password are valid. If the username and password combination is invalid, the customer is asked to reenter his or her user ID and password or to create a new user.

The order form is the last page our simple example provides.

 Note   This example assumes that you have some basic knowledge of scripting or some C or C++ programming.

```
// This is a HTML comment line
<<!-- Plain old html embedded in the html script --!>
```

The // tag is the grandmother of all document tags and identifies this document as containing HTML markup tags.

```
<html>
```

The <html> tab signifies the head of the page. It is the top-level element in every HTML document within the HTML tag pair. It encapsulates information and directions that are about the HTML document. There is no actual browseable content inside of this tag.

```
<head>
```

This identifies the text that will appear at the top of the page when it is displayed in a browser—that is, everything between the <head> and the </head> tag pair.

```
<title> Sign in Page </title>
//End of the page heading
</head>
```

The <body> tag identifies the portion of the page that is displayed in the browser. That is, everything between these tag pairs is considered to be either text or images that are to be displayed on a browser, excluding the allowed HTML tag pairs that format the content. The attributes contained in the opening tag are applied globally to the encapsulated text and images and define properties and characteristics. PHP will ignore HTML elements in this file and pass them through unchanged.

```
<BODY
BGCOLOR="#FFFFFF"  //White Background
TEXT="#000000"     //Black Text
LINK="#0000FF"     //Blue for unvisited links
VLINK="#000080"    //Purple for visited links
ALINK="#FF0000"    //Red for Active Links
>
```

The <h1> tag identifies a first-level page heading and is rendered as the most important of the six headings. For this particular heading tag, the heading text is formatted with "align" for the value of the align attribute.

```
<h1 align="align"> Member Log In </h1>
#Another HTML comment line
<!- end html begin php script --!>
#Function Definitions that PHP loads but doesn't execute unless
called
<?
```

This function, customer_pretty_print(), retrieves and "prints" the customer's name and address information on the browser page using the echo "string" function. The name and address are formatted like one would find on any envelope:

First Name Middle Initial Last Name

Mailing Address Line 1

Mailing Address Line 2

City, State ZIP code

The placement on the browser where these lines will appear depends upon the HTML that encapsulates (surrounds) this function when it is called.

```
function customer_pretty_print($userid) {
```

Connect to the database server using the DBA login name and password. It is important that the DBA login remain secure, so don't let the source for this page be displayed on any browser.

```
$link=mysql_pconnect("localhost", "dba", "dba2pass");
```

Once connected to the database server, we must select which database on the server we want. For this application, we want the Order Entry database.

```
$database=mysql_select_db(order_entry);
```

Next, we create a query using the value entered by the customer on their browser (when they see this page) for their ID and pass it to this function when it is called. In this query, the SQL statement has an * for the select list. When it executes, every column (attribute) in the Customer table record will be retrieved (assuming that one exists!).

```
$query="select * from Customer where Customer_id='$userid'";
```

Execute this query (executes on the most recently selected database). If there is some really critical error during the execution of this query, we want to terminate the session. Note that NOT finding a record in the Customer table having this value for Customer_id is NOT a failure. If the query fails for any reason, then the PHP script will end with the message "Unable to display page" displayed in the browser. The value of $result is a positive integer if the query executes successfully. The $result return value is used for fetching the result set rows.

```
$result=mysql_query($query) or die("Unable to display page");
```

Assuming that the query must have been successful (or this script would have died), we pass the $result variable to the mysql_fetch_object() function to get a row result pointer. We'll get specific columns from the result row with a different function. Note that we'll get a valid result row pointer even if there are no rows.

Look at the result set from this query. It may have zero or one row in it. Because we specified the Customer_id attribute as the primary key for the Customer table, there can be AT MOST ONE record having a given value for Customer_id. mysql_fetch_object returns a result row object. Each field of the original select statement's select list is accessed using the object pointer. Note that mysql_fetch_object uses the value returned from mysql_query() execution.

```
$data=mysql_fetch_object($result);
```

Retrieve and test the value for the Customer_id field. If the result set has no rows (which is the case for new customers) the object $data->Customer_id evaluates to FALSE, in which case, this function returns a 0. We wouldn't expect to be using this function unless we were sure that this was an existing customer! Refer to the function check_user() to see how this is accomplished.

```
if($data->Customer_id) {
```

We use the PHP echo "<string>" function to send displayed text to the browser when we want to create text on-the-fly. If we have static text, we will normally encapsulate it in HTML elements only. Except for blank fields as the second mailing address line may be, the echoed text shows up like:

> First Name Middle Initial Last Name
>
> Mailing Address Line 1
>
> Mailing Address Line 2
>
> City, State ZIP code

Display the customer's first name, middle initial and last name followed by a carriage return (new line). The
 HTML element is handled by the browser and causes a new line to begin.

```
echo "$data->First_Name $data->Middle_Initial $data-
>Last_Name<br>";
```

Display the first address line for the customer followed by a new line.

```
echo "$data->Address_Line_1<br>";
```

Display the second address line for the customer followed by a new line.

```
echo "$data->Address_Line_2<br>";
```

Display the customer's City, State and ZIP code followed by a new line.

```
echo "$data->City,$data->State $data->ZIP<br>";
```

Return a 1 to signify that the customer information was found, and that their address was displayed, and then exit this function.

```
return 1;
}
```

If the customer doesn't exist, no records are returned from the SQL Select... statement and the Boolean condition ($data->Customer_id) evaluates to FALSE. Exit this function and return a value of 0.

```
else { return 0; }
}
```

This element signals to PHP to stop processing the contents of this file.

```
?>
```

The following function prints the core login page. It can be used without arguments to create a clean login page, or with arguments to remember a previous state of the login form. The function definition is surrounded by PHP start (<?) and stop (?>) processing elements because we have static HTML immediately at the beginning of the function. As a matter of fact, this function is almost entirely implemented by static HTML. But, this HTML is not displayed unless this function is called! So, we have static HTML that may or may not be sent to the browser.

```
<?
function login($userid="", $userpassword="") {
?>
```

Embedded, static HTML begins here. Nothing from here on (until the next <? element) will be interpreted by PHP. PHP will just pass it along unchanged and it will be displayed on the user's browser as if it came directly from an HTML file.

The <hr> tag, below, causes a horizontal line (with the default width) to be displayed on the page because there are no attributes specified that would override the defaults.

```
<hr>
If you do not have a user id and would like one, please click
```

This is a hyperlink tag that begins with <a href — > and ends with </a>. The word "here" is the highlighted text (it is what the user will click on). This hyperlink invokes the registration form (the file registration.php).

```
<a href="registration.php"> here </a>
```

The <form...> element is an important element for us! It delimits that range of data fields for a form. It also contains the information on how to process the information that is collected from the form when it is displayed. FORM elements cannot be nested. The attributes for the FORM element are:

accept Identifies the acceptable characters sets (can be more than one)

action Identifies the action URL that will process the form contents

method Specifies a method or protocol for accessing the action URL

A method value of "get" will gather all form name and value pairs in a query URL that looks like: URL?name=value&name=value&name=value.

For the element below the method value is "post." This will cause the name/value pairs to be gathered exactly as for "get" but they will be made accessible to the processing script (at the action URL) as environment variables.

```
<form action="index.php" method=post>
```

This element specifies the typeface as monospace using the default point size. Two possible additional attributes are color and size, which do not appear here.

```
<font face="Monospace">
```

This element signifies the beginning of a new paragraph. It puts some spacing between the line of text and the first text-entry box (the text-entry box for the user to enter their own login name).

```
<p> User ID:
```

The HTML input element has no end tag, that is, there is no /input tag.

The type for this element is text. This specifies that a user–editable text-entry box is to appear on the browser for the end-user to enter a string. In this case, we're expecting the username value that we'll use in a subsequent query. The default value to appear in the box is whatever is the current value of $userid, as signified by value="<?echo $userid?>". If this function (login) has been called with arguments, then the value of the $userid argument would appear in the text input box on the browser.

Note the Embedded PHP in the embedded html: the echo function is PHP code! When PHP reaches the <? element, it will begin interpreting the text. In this case, it echoes the value of $userid to the browser and then reaches the end-of-processing element (?>) where it passes the text unchanged to the browser.

```
<input type=text name=userid value="<?echo $userid?>">
```

This signifies the end of the current paragraph.

```
</p>
```

This element signifies the beginning of another new paragraph. It puts some space between the two text-entry boxes that appear on the browser.

Note the single space between the <p> element and the visible text "Password"; the browser will put a single space on the page, too.

```
<p> Password:
```

The next HTML element, the input element, has no end tag, that is, there is no '/input' tag. The input type is password, which is a text-entry field with the data being obscured as it is entered. The name attribute gives a variable name (symbol) for the field when it is submitted for processing for the environment variable that will hold the text that is typed into this field by the user via their browser. Note the Embedded PHP in the embedded html: the echo function is PHP code! When PHP reaches the <? element it will begin interpreting the text. In this case, it echoes the value of $userpassword to the browser and then reaches the end-of-processing element (?>) where it just passes the text unchanged to the browser.

```
<input type=password name=userpassword "<?echo $userpassword?>"
size=12
maxlength=12></p>
```

This is the input element for forms with the type submit. This specifies a button to appear on the form that when activated submits the information on the form to the processing script. The label for the button is specified by the value attribute, in this case Submit.

```
<input type=submit value="Submit">
```

This is the end of the customer login form that is displayed whenever this login function is called.

```
</form>
```

PHP processes the } as the end of the function definition for login().

```
<? } // end block ?>
```

This is the real start of the program. PHP begins processing the contents of the file here.

If $userid is not set (not defined as a variable), then it follows that NOTHING has been set. This implies that the login page has not been sent to the user's browser — yet ($userid is initially defined by calling login.) So, call the login function with all blank fields and no special message in the header.

```
if(!isset($userid)){
    login(); // display blank page
}
```

If $userid is a defined variable, this implies that the login form has been sent to the user's browser. In this case, we presume that the user has filled in the user ID and password fields and clicked the Submit button. However, we need to make sure that both fields are NOT blank. The PHP empty() function returns a TRUE if the string is blank.

```
elseif(empty($userid) || empty($userpassword)) {
```

If either user ID or password is still blank, display a message on the user's browser.

```
    //redisplay the login page.
    echo "<p> you did not fill in all the fields, please try
again<P>\n";
```

Next, redisplay the form with filled-in fields.

```
    login($userid,$userpassword
}
else
{
```

Now, establish a connection to a MySQL server. This server is on the computer localhost (a string constant), and the connection is made using the customer's user identifier that was stored in the variable $userid and the password that was stored in the variable $userpassword.

The at (@) sign prefixed to a PHP function disables error reporting for that function only. By using this technique, we can avoid having esoteric error messages displayed.

```
    @$link=mysql_connect("localhost",$userid,$userpassword);
```

If the mysql_connect call was successful, the value in $link is a positive integer. If the value of $link is 0, it signifies that the call to mysql_connect (with the parameters) was unable to connect to the database server (NOT a particular database) for some reason.if(!$link) {

We assume that the customer made a mistake typing in their username ($userid) or password ($userpassword), so we display a message on their browser to this effect and redisplay the page. <H2><B> starts a level 2 heading on the Web page with any displayed text being bold.

```
    <H2><B>echo "User ID or password incorrect, please try
again."<?B><H>;
```

This is a hyperlink tag that begins with <a href — > and ends with </a>. The word "here" is the highlighted text (it is what the user will click on). This hyperlink invokes the registration form (the file registration.php). Note the end PHP processing tag (?>) just before the link HTML, and the begin PHP processing (<?) tag just at the end of the link HTML. NOBR means No Break and tells the browser that all elements within its boundaries will have no line breaks.

```
    ?><NOBR><A HREF="registration.php"> here </A></NOBR><?
```

When the preceding link has returned here (the contents of registration.php have completed executing) the login function will be called with the current values for $userid and $password. These two variables will have been passed back from registration.php through environment variables.

```
      login($userid,$userpassword);
```

```
  }
  else
  {
```

After the user has successfully logged in, there is no need to keep the connection open to the server, so we'll close the connection

```
    mysql_close($link); //we close because user has no ability to
    do anything
```

If the condition ($link]) evaluates to TRUE, then display a Welcome message on the browser with directions to click on a link.

```
        echo "Welcome $userid<p>\n";
        echo "Is the following billing information correct?";
```

Next, we create a button that will call the next forms — either an order or an update account form.

```
        echo "<form action=orderform.php>
              <input type=hidden name=userid value=$userid>";
```

Call the customer_pretty_print function and display the customer's address for verification.

```
        customer_pretty_print($userid);
```

These PHP echo functions send HTML to the browser to create two buttons. The first button invokes the orderform.php file by virtue of the form action directive several lines above, and the second button recalls this form. (Note the form action directive inside of the second echo() function.)

```
        echo "<input type=submit name=form value=\"Yes,
    continue\">";
        echo "<form action=index.php><input type=submit
    name=start_over
              value=\"No, update my account\">";
```

```
  }
```

```
  }
```

This tag (the ?>) signals the end of PHP processing for this document.

```
    ?>
```

This is the end of the program (the set of .php files). By the time this executes, the user may have done one or more of the following:

1. Logged into the database

2. Updated their profile (name and address)

3. Registered for the first time

4. Placed an order

This is the closing tag for the body of the HTML document.

```
</body>
```

This is the closing tag for the entire HTML document.

```
</html>
```

Listing 16-1 shows the HTML that the preceding PHP code sends to the Web browser. If you copy this code into a file and open it with your Web browser, you'll see the page as displayed (Figure 16-2).

Listing 16-1: **Generated HTML**

```
<!-- Plain old html embedded in the html script --!>
<html>
<head>
<title> Sign in Page </title>
</head>

<BODY
  BGCOLOR="#FFFFFF"
  TEXT="#000000"
  LINK="#0000FF"
  VLINK="#000080"
  ALINK="#FF0000"
 >
<h1 align="align"> Member Log In </h1>

<hr>
 If you do not have a user id and would like one, please click
<a href="registration.php"> here </a>
<form action="index.php" method=post>
<font face="Monospace">


<p> User ID:
<input type=text name=userid value=""> </p>

<p> Password:
```

```
<input type=password name=userpassword "" size=12
maxlength=12></p>
<input type=submit value="Submit">


</form>
</body>
</html>
```

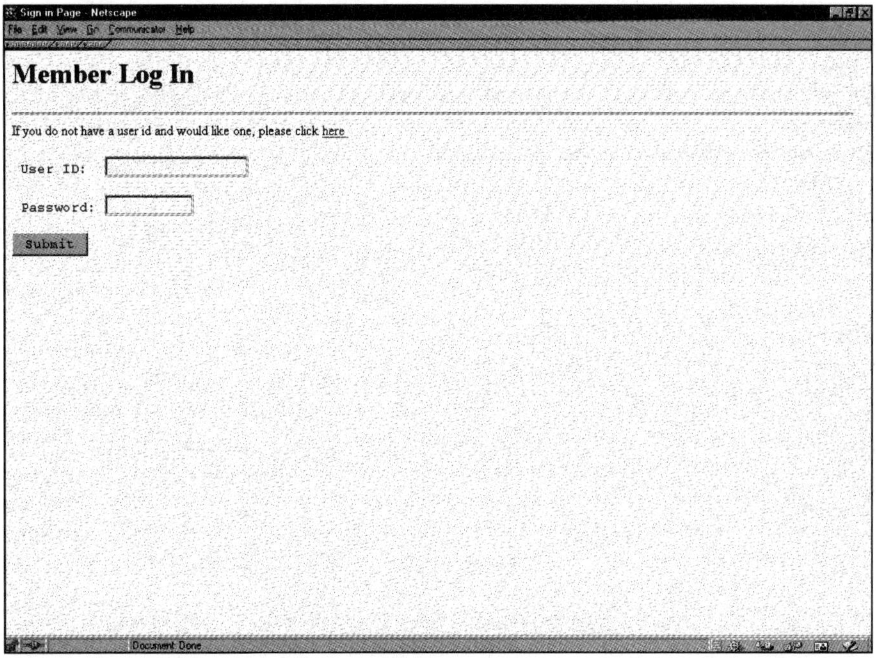

Figure 16-2: The Login Page as displayed on a browser

Figure 16-2 demonstrates several things. First, comments can be one of three forms; second, the ability to build different forms using the same program (dynamic html coding); and third, the ability to interface directly with our database using the built-in mysql functions. The three styles of comments are scripting style (#), C style (/* ... */) and C++ style (//). In practice, it is much more readable to pick one style and stay with it.

The second thing demonstrated is in the main function the first time login() is called. At that point, login() is called without the variables being passed to it; if it is called with certain variables filled in, it displays different pages. This is extremely useful in creating Web pages that interact with the client. This technique guides the end users through filling out our login form correctly. If users only fill in the username, then we prompt them to completely fill out the form and repost their username. A similar approach could also be used to ensure that a roboot is not used to crack the passwords of our valued customers. For brevity, this exercise is left to the reader.

Third, we see that our program is interfacing directly with the MySQL database through built-in database calls. Again, note the dynamic nature of PHP when the database call fails. In this event, we repost the data asking the user to reenter the information.

Fourth, this example shows how to retrieve data from the database using a `select` statement in the customer_pretty_print() function. In the next example, we will explore some other features of PHP as well as learn to insert data into the database.

The following registration form (Listing 16-2 as shown in Figure 16-3) enables new customers to fill in their address information. It reiterates the techniques used earlier and provides several new techniques to make the program more readable and more reusable. The program `registration.php` requires that the user enter their billing information. If any of the fields are left blank, then the page is reloaded with all of the originally entered information and the user is asked to fill out the form entirely. The only exception is Address Line 2, which can be left blank. If the user picks a user ID that is already in use, the program clears the user ID information and reloads the page with a message indicating that the user ID is already in use. If the user does not properly fill in the password confirmation, the program notifies the user that the passwords did not match and asks the user to reenter a password and confirmation. If the user fills in the information correctly, the user is prompted with the same page as seen in Listing 16-1, when the existing user logged in correctly. The new user is asked to verify their billing information and if it is correct, is allowed to begin shopping. If it is incorrect, the user is directed to a page to update his or her billing information. This page is left as an exercise for the reader on his or her own.

Listing 16-2: **PHP code**

```
<html>

The <! and !> tags encapsulate comments.
<!-- Demonstrating use of a include file--!>

#The <? and ?> tags encapsulate code to be executed by PHP
<?include header.inc?>
```

The title for the page as displayed on the browser. The <h2> element is the second largest level of header formatting available.

```
<h2>NEW MEMBER REGISTRATION </h2>
```

The <? and ?> tags encapsulate code to be executed by PHP. The following two functions are related to a customer:

check_user($user_id)	Verifies that a user id exists in the database. Returns Customer_id if it does exist, returns 0 if it does not.
customer_pretty_print($user_id)	Displays customer name and address in a readable form; returns 0 if user id does not exist.

Recall also that function definitions are not executed by PHP until called.

This next function, check_user(), tests for the presence of a customer in the order entry database. This is done by using a simple SQL select statement as an implicit test. If there is a record in the Customer table having a value for the Customer_id attribute that exactly matches the value entered by the customer in the log in name field (on the log in page), then we infer that the user is an existing customer (has ordered from us at least once before).

```
function check_user($userid)
{
```

First, connect to the database server using the DBA login name and password. It is important that the DBA login remain secure, so don't let the source for this page be displayed on any browser.

```
$link=mysql_pconnect("localhost", "dba", "dba2pass");
```

Once we are connected to the database server, we must select which database on the server we want to access. For this application, we want to access the Order Entry database.

```
$database=mysql_select_db(order_entry);
```

Next, create a query using the value entered by the customer for their ID and pass the ID to this function when it is called. In this query, the SQL statement select list only has one field: Customer_id.

```
$query="select Customer_id from Customer where
Customer_id='$userid'";
```

Execute this query (executes on the most recently selected database). If a critical error occurs during the execution of this query, we want to terminate the session. Note that NOT finding a record in the Customer table having this value for Customer_id is NOT a failure. The $result return value is used for fetching the result set rows.

```
$result=mysql_query($query) or die("Unable to find user");
```

Look at the result set from this query. It may have zero or one row in it. Because we specified the Customer_id attribute as the primary key for the Customer table, there can be AT MOST one record having a given value for Customer_id. mysql_fetch_object returns a result row object. Each field of the original select statement's select list is accessed using the object pointer. Note that mysql_fetch_object uses the value returned from mysql_query() execution, above.

```
$data=mysql_fetch_object($result);
```

Retrieve and test the value for the Customer_id field. If the result set as no rows (which is the case for new customers) the object $data->Customer_id valuates to FALSE, in which case, this function returns a 0. Otherwise, check_user() eturns the value of Customer_id (which will match the value passed into this function hen it was called).

```
if($data->Customer_id) {
return $data->Customer_id;
}else { return 0;}
}
```

This function, customer_pretty_print(), retrieves and "prints" the customer's name and address information on the browser page using the echo "string" function. The name and address are formatted like one would find on any envelope:

First Name Middle Initial Last Name

Mailing Address Line 1

Mailing Address Line 2

City, State ZIP code

The placement on the browser where these lines will appear depends upon the HTML that encapsulates (surrounds) this function when it is called.

```
function customer_pretty_print($userid) {
```

Connect to the database server using the DBA login name and password. It is important that the DBA login remain secure, so don't let the source for this page be displayed on any browser.

```
$link=mysql_pconnect("localhost", "dba", "dba2pass");
```

Once connected to the database server, we must select which database on the server we want to access. For this application, we want to access the Order Entry database.

```
$database=mysql_select_db(order_entry);
```

Create a query using the value entered by the customer for the customer's ID and pass it to this function when it is called. In this query, the SQL statement has a * for the select list. When it executes, every column (attribute) in the Customer table record will be retrieved (assuming that one exists!).

```
$query="select * from Customer where Customer_id='$userid'";
```

Execute this query (executes on the most recently selected database). If a critical error occurs during the execution of this query, we want to terminate the session. Note that NOT finding a record in the Customer table having this value for Customer_id is NOT a failure. The $result return value is used for fetching the result set rows.

```
$result=mysql_query($query) or die("Unable to display page");
```

Look at the result set from this query. It may have zero or one row in it. Because we specified the Customer_id attribute as the primary key for the Customer table, there can be AT MOST one record having a given value for Customer_id. mysql_fetch_object returns a result row object. Each field of the original select statement's select list is accessed using the object pointer. Note that mysql_fetch_object uses the value returned from mysql_query() execution, above.

```
$data=mysql_fetch_object($result);
```

Retrieve and test the value for the Customer_id field. If the result set has no rows (which is the case for new customers) the object $data->Customer_id evaluates to FALSE, in which case, this function returns a 0. We wouldn't use this function unless we were sure that this was an existing customer! Refer to the function check_user() to see how this is accomplished.

```
if($data->Customer_id) {
```

We use the PHP echo "<string>" function to send displayed text to the browser when we want to create text on-the-fly. If we have static text, we normally encapsulate it in HTML elements only. Except for blank fields, like the second mailing address line may be, the echoed text shows up like this:

First Name Middle Initial Last Name

Mailing Address Line 1

Mailing Address Line 2

City, State ZIP code

The
 HTML element is handled by the browser and causes a new line to begin.

```
echo "$data->First_Name $data->Middle_Initial $data-
>Last_Name<br>";
echo "$data->Address_Line_1<br>";
echo "$data->Address_Line_2<br>";
echo "$data->City,$data->State $data->ZIP<br>";
```

Return a 1 to signify that the customer information was found, and that the customer's address was displayed. Then exit this function.

```
return 1;
}
```

If the customer's address wasn't found, return a zero and exit this function.

```
else { return 0; }
}
```

This function takes numerous customer parameters and displays them in the fields of a registration page displayed on the user's browser. If this function is called without these parameters, for example, register(), the parameters are displayed as blank fields on the registration page.

```
function register($userid="", $userpassword="",
$reuserpassword="",
$firstname="", $middleinit="", $lastname="",
$address_1="",$address_2="",$city="",$state="",
$zip="",$phonenumber="" )
{
if(!$state) { $state="default"; }
```

This next tag (the ?> tag, below) seems to indicate that PHP processing will end right in the middle of a function definition. However, because we want to include the contents of a file right here, we do it this way.

```
?>
```

The <? and ?> tags encapsulate code to be executed by PHP. In this case, we want the text in the file named registration.inc to be included inside of this file by the PHP interpreter.

```
<?include registration.inc?>
```

The <? and ?> tags encapsulate code to be executed by PHP. The element below signals the beginning of code that will be executed by PHP. The definition of the register() function continues where it left off (there's not much left), except for the included file.

```
<?
```

This is the end of the function definition for register(), but the PHP code continues.

```
}
```

This is where PHP begins to execute the code in this file (registration.php). Note how the <? element just before the end of the register() function encapsulates the following code. This is just fine with PHP.

If $userid is not set (not defined as a variable), then it follows that NOTHING has been set. This implies that the registration page has not yet been sent to the user's browser. ($userid is initially defined by calling register.) So, call the register function with all blank fields and no special message in the header.

```
if(! (isset($userid) ){
```

Call the register function, which will display the Registration Web page on the user's browser. All of the fields will be blank when this page is displayed for the first time, that is, when register() is called without parameters.

```
register();

{
```

Setting the $userid (defined as a variable to PHP, even though it may be a null string) implies that the registration page has been sent to the user's browser. So, test all of the required fields to make sure that they are not blank. Blank fields may occur if the user clicks on the Submit button without completing the required fields.

```
elseif(empty($userid) || empty($userpassword)
  || empty($reuserpassword)
  || empty($firstname) || empty($lastname)
  || empty($address_1) || empty($city)
  || $state=="default" || empty($zip)
  || empty($phonenumber) )
{
```

If any of the required fields are blank at this point, print the special message in the header and call the register function with the field variables as entered by the user previously, including any that are still blank.

The PHP function echo <string> causes the entire string to be sent to the browser, including any HTML elements that may be in the string.

```
echo "All the required fields must be filled in to
continue:\n";
```

This time, register() is called with all the possible parameters. register() was defined earlier.

```
register($userid,$userpassword
,$reuserpassword
,$firstname,$middleinit
,$lastname,$address_1
,$address_2,$city
,$state,$zip
,$phonenumber);
}
```

Another possibility that needs testing is that the user entered their password one way and then reentered it in the password confirmation field another way (an unintentional typo?). If they don't match, call registration() again.

```
elseif ( $userpassword != $reuserpassword )
{
```

The <P> HTML element causes a new paragraph to be inserted into the Web page prior to the messages.

```
echo "<P> Password confirmation password did not match
password.\n";
echo "Please try again. Thank you.";
```

Redisplay the registration page with all of the fields as originally filled in by the user except for the password and the password confirmation fields, which will be blank (note the empty quotes!).

```
register($userid,$userpassword=""
,$reuserpassword=""
,$firstname,$middleinit
,$lastname,$address_1
,$address_2,$city
,$state,$zip
,$phonenumber);
}
```

Test the value of the login name (stored as $userid) to make sure that it is not already in use by another customer. If it is not already in use, the condition (!result=check_user($user_id)) will evaluate to TRUE.

```
elseif(!$result=check_user($userid))
{
```

So, if it's true that the login name (stored as $userid) is not already in use, we can add this customer to the administration database. We use the administration database as our security; we add the user's choices for login name and password. But, first we have to connect to the server as the DBA in order to add this user.

```
$link = mysql_pconnect ("localhost", "dba", "dba2pass") or die
("Could not connect");
```

Connect to Admin database and add the new user. The following SQL query will allow this user to have restricted access to the databases on this server. In our case, there is only the Order Entry database.

```
$query = "GRANT usage on *.* to $userid@localhost identified by
'$userpassword'";
```

If this action fails, we must quit because this is a fatal error!

```
$result =mysql_query($query)
or die("Unable to add user\n");
```

Before we can connect to the Order database and add (SQL insert) the customer's full name and address to the Customer table, we need to select the Order Entry database, which we have named order_entry (case sensitive). If this action fails, we must quit because this is a fatal error! In the event of a fatal error, display the message string in the die() function on the user's browser and quit completely if a fatal error occurs.

```
mysql_select_db(order_entry) or die("Web page unavailable");
```

Next, (assuming the above query was successful) we need to add the customer's full name and address to the Customer table. We use the values as entered by the user on the registration page.

```
$query = "insert into Customer values
('$userid','$firstname','$middleinit','$lastname','$address_1',
'$address_2','$ci
ty','$state','$zip','$phonenumber','N')";
```

Execute the query to add (SQL insert) this customer. Save the return value from the query to test it for errors (but not for fatal errors). If the query was unsuccessful, it is considered a fatal error, so display the message string in the die() function on the user's browser and quit completely.

```
$result=mysql_query($query) or die("Unable to update
profile\n");
if($result) {
```

If adding the customer profile to the Customer table was successful, we give the customer the opportunity to edit this information (using the updatecustomer.php form), or to proceed to the order form.

```
echo "If the following information is correct click";
echo "<input type=hidden name=userid value=$userid>";
echo "echo $userid\n<br>";
```

The following text is displayed as a link, with the word "here" as the link to the order form. The <a> </a> HTML elements encapsulate the link. The three <br> elements insert three line breaks on the Web page prior to displaying the customer's name and address using the customer_pretty_print() function defined earlier.

```
echo "<a href=/orderform.php> here</a> to
continue.<br><br><br>";
customer_pretty_print($userid);
```

The following text is displayed as a link, with the word "here" as the link to the update customer form. The <a> </a> HTML elements encapsulate the link. The two <br> elements insert two line breaks on the Web page prior to displaying the link text. The link text is the word "here."

```
echo "<br><br>If the preceding information is not correct
click";
echo "<a href=/updatecustomer.php> here</a>.<br>";
    }
}
```

The final possibility that we check for is that there is an existing customer having the same login name, for example, there's already a johnsmith. The check_user() function was defined earlier. If a customer already exists with the same value for $userid, we need to inform the user and request that the user choose a different login name.

```
elseif($result=check_user($userid))
    {
```

The <b> HTML element causes all of the following text on the Web page to be displayed in BOLD, until the </b> element is reached.

```
echo "<b> Sorry, username $userid is already in use. Please
select another
username </b>";
```

Repost the registration page with all but $userid set as previously entered by the user. Note that the password and confirmation password are retained because only the login name is required to be unique in the Customer table of our Order Entry database.

```
register($userid="",$userpassword
,$reuserpassword
,$firstname,$middleinit
,$lastname,$address_1
,$address_2,$city
,$state,$zip
,$phonenumber);
    }
```

This ?> element ends the processing by PHP. Anything appearing after it is passed along directly to the browser by PHP.

```
?>
```

```
</html>
```

Listing 16-3 shows the HTML that the above PHP code sends to the Web browser. If you copy this code into a file and open the file with your Web browser, you'll see the page as displayed in Figure 16-3.

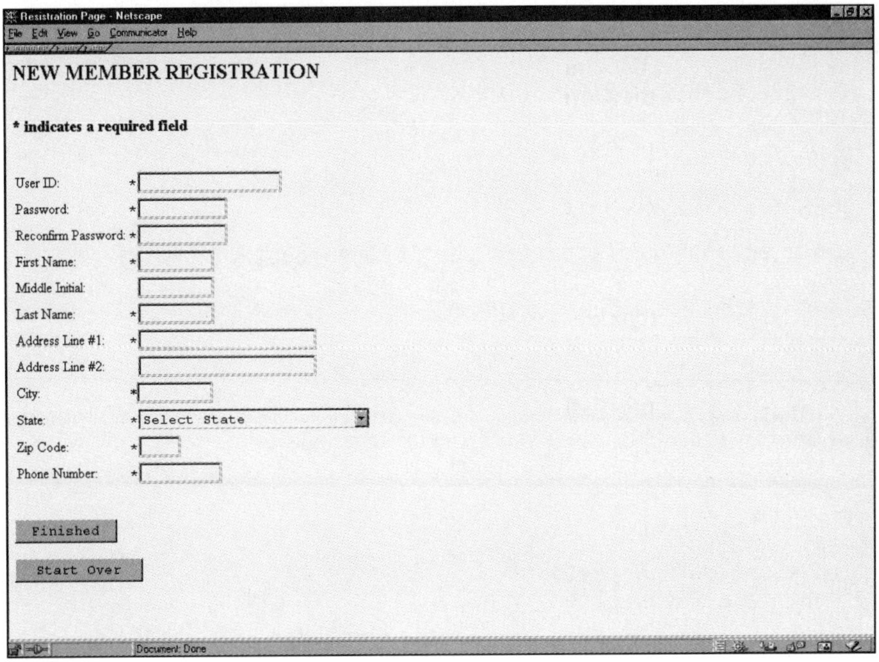

Figure 16-3: New registration form

Listing 16-3: **Generated HTML**

```
<html>

<!-- Demonstrating use of a include file--!>
<!-- a file named header.inc
(actually headerinc but I don't think that should be the case)
now contain html
common to all our Web pages. --!>

  <html>
    <head>
      <title> Registration Page </title>

    </head>
    <BODY
          BGCOLOR="#FFFFFF"
          TEXT="#000000"
          LINK="#0000FF"
          VLINK="#000080"
          ALINK="#FF0000"
          >
```

Continued

Listing 16-3 *(continued)*

```
<h2>NEW MEMBER REGISTRATION </h2>


<br><h3> *  indicates a required field </h3><br>
<table border=0>

<form action="registration.php" method=post>

<tr>
<td>User ID: </td>
<td>
<font face="Monospace">
*<input type=text name=userid size=20 maxlength=22 tabindex=1
value= ></td>
</tr>

<tr>
<td>Password:</td>
<td><form method=post>
<font face="Monospace">
*<input  type=password name=userpassword size=12 maxlength=12
tabindex=2 value=></td>
</tr>


<tr>
<td>Reconfirm Password:</td>
<td><form method=post>
<font face="Monospace">
*<input type=password name=reuserpassword size=12 maxlength=12
tabindex=3 value=></td>
</tr>


<tr>
<td>First Name:</td>
<td><form method=post>
<font face="Monospace">
*<input type=text name=firstname size=10 maxlength=10
tabindex=4 value=></td>
</tr>


<tr>
<td>Middle Initial:</td>
<td><form method=post>
<font face="Monospace">
 <input type=text name=middleinit size=10 maxlength=2
tabindex=5 value=></td>
</tr>
```

```
<tr>
<td>Last Name:</td>
<td><form method=post>
<font face="Monospace">
*<input type=text name=lastname size=10 maxlenth=15 tabindex=6
value=></td>
</tr>

<tr>
<td>Address Line #1:
<td><form method=post>
<font face="Monospace">
*<input type=text name=address_1 size=25 maxlength=25
tabindex=7 value=></td>
</tr>

<tr>
<td>Address Line #2:</td>
<td><form method=post>
<font face="Monospace">
 <input type=text name=address_2 size=25 maxlength=25
tabindex=8 value=></td>
</tr>

<tr>
<td>City:</td>
<font face="Monospace">
<td><form method=post>
*<input type=text name=city size=10 maxlength=15 tabindex=9
value=></td>
</tr>

<tr>
<td>State:</td>
<td><form method=post>
 <font face="Monospace">
*<select name=state size=1 tabindex=10 value=defalt>
<OPTION VALUE="default">Select State</OPTION>
        <OPTION VALUE="AL">Alabama</OPTION>
        <OPTION VALUE="AK">Alaska</OPTION>
        <OPTION VALUE="AZ">Arizona</OPTION>
        <OPTION VALUE="AR">Arkansas</OPTION>
        <OPTION VALUE="CA">California</OPTION>
        <OPTION VALUE="CO">Colorado</OPTION>
        <OPTION VALUE="CT">Connecticut</OPTION>
        <OPTION VALUE="DE">Delaware</OPTION>
        <OPTION VALUE="DC">District of Columbia</OPTION>
        <OPTION VALUE="FL">Florida</OPTION>
        <OPTION VALUE="GA">Georgia</OPTION>
        <OPTION VALUE="HI">Hawaii</OPTION>
        <OPTION VALUE="ID">Idaho</OPTION>
```

Continued

Listing 16-3 *(continued)*

```
        <OPTION VALUE="IL">Illinois</OPTION>
        <OPTION VALUE="IN">Indiana</OPTION>
        <OPTION VALUE="IA">Iowa</OPTION>
        <OPTION VALUE="KS">Kansas</OPTION>
        <OPTION VALUE="KY">Kentucky</OPTION>
        <OPTION VALUE="LA">Louisiana</OPTION>
        <OPTION VALUE="ME">Maine</OPTION>
        <OPTION VALUE="MD">Maryland</OPTION>
        <OPTION VALUE="MA">Massachusetts</OPTION>
        <OPTION VALUE="MI">Michigan</OPTION>
        <OPTION VALUE="MN">Minnesota</OPTION>
        <OPTION VALUE="MS">Mississippi</OPTION>
        <OPTION VALUE="MO">Missouri</OPTION>
        <OPTION VALUE="MT">Montana</OPTION>
        <OPTION VALUE="NE">Nebraska</OPTION>
        <OPTION VALUE="NV">Nevada</OPTION>
        <OPTION VALUE="NH">New Hampshire</OPTION>
        <OPTION VALUE="NJ">New Jersey</OPTION>
        <OPTION VALUE="NM">New Mexico</OPTION>
        <OPTION VALUE="NY">New York</OPTION>
        <OPTION VALUE="NC">North Carolina</OPTION>
        <OPTION VALUE="ND">North Dakota</OPTION>
        <OPTION VALUE="OH">Ohio</OPTION>
        <OPTION VALUE="OK">Oklahoma</OPTION>
        <OPTION VALUE="OR">Oregon</OPTION>
        <OPTION VALUE="PA">Pennsylvania</OPTION>
        <OPTION VALUE="RI">Rhode Island</OPTION>
        <OPTION VALUE="SC">South Carolina</OPTION>
        <OPTION VALUE="SD">South Dakota</OPTION>
        <OPTION VALUE="TN">Tennessee</OPTION>
        <OPTION VALUE="TX">Texas</OPTION>
        <OPTION VALUE="UT">Utah</OPTION>
        <OPTION VALUE="VT">Vermont</OPTION>
        <OPTION VALUE="VA">Virginia</OPTION>
        <OPTION VALUE="WA">Washington</OPTION>
        <OPTION VALUE="WV">West Virginia</OPTION>
        <OPTION VALUE="WI">Wisconsin</OPTION>
        <OPTION VALUE="WY">Wyoming</OPTION>
        <OPTION VALUE="PR">Puerto Rico</OPTION>
        <OPTION VALUE="VI">Virgin Island</OPTION>
        <OPTION VALUE="MP">Northern Mariana Islands</OPTION>
</select></td>
</tr>


<tr>
<td>Zip Code:</td>
<td><form method=post>
<font face="Monospace">
*<input name=zip size=5 maxlenth=6 tabindex=11 value=></td>
</tr>
```

```
<tr>
<td>Phone Number:</td>
<td><form method=post>
<font face="Monospace">
*<input name=phonenumber size=11 maxlength=10  tabindex=12
 value=></td>
</tr>

</table> <br>
<br>
<input type=submit value="Finished" tabindex=13>
<br>
<br>
<input type=reset value-"Start Over" tabindex=14>
</form>

</html>
```

Anything common among all or most of your Web pages could be kept in such files — usually referred to as include files. Also PHP functions that are common to more than one file could easily be included in your HTML source code in this way. In addition to saving retyping, it also increases the readability of the code by hiding unnecessary details. In the previous example, we also see the use of `mysql_fetch_object`, which essentially converts the rows that `mysql_query` might return into data attributes of an object. This allows us to easily use the data from a row without knowing the relative field order, or the format of the fields. This is very intuitive.

The next example illustrates how to build a class that will enable us to better use the object-oriented techniques by creating reusable PHP scripts. Converting our customer functions into a customer class is left as an exercise for the reader. Again, the example uses a simple insert statement that allows the user information to be populated. Users do not actually populate their own fields, rather the DBA populates the fields on their behalf. This is far safer than giving users the ability to manipulate the database. If the users database is stolen, then the thief can only perform very limited services on the database — restricted to the same operations as the original customer, for example, updating the customer's billing address or making purchases on that customer's account. This is far better than a thief being able to discover the database's structure or discovering customer IDs, facilitating the ability to steal passwords as well. The thief is limited to using the Web site as if the thief were a customer.

Our final page is the `orderentry.php` page. This page lets customers buy our products. We added a twist, however: If the customer has been targeted as eligible for your customer appreciation promotion, the customer will receive 25 percent discount.

Looking up prior purchase history

After the customer has been confirmed (or just accepted if we don't want to confirm them), we need to look up their prior purchase history. We can do that with a SQL statement as follows:

```
$query="select First_Name,
        sum(Order_Detail.extended_price) as Previous_Purchases
        from Customer, Order_Header, Order_Detail
        where Customer.Customer_id='$userid'
        and Customer.Customer_id=Order_Header.Customer_id
        and not Customer.Premium_Shipped='Y'
        group by First_Name";
```

The PHP code that does this follows. First, we connect to the database:

```
$link=mysql_pconnect("localhost", "dba", "dba2pass");  //first
connect to
        $database=mysql_select_db(order_entry);?>      // to
the correct database
```

Then we run our query and store the result rows in our variable $result:

```
$result=mysql_query($query) or die("Unable to display page");
```

Then we store the result as an object using the following command:

```
$data=mysql_fetch_object($result);
```

If the value of $result is positive, the query has been successful and $result is used for subsequent retrieving of a result set. If the value of $result is false, an error occurred. Note that a result set of zero rows is *not* an error, so we have to check row count.

Next, this customer's purchase history total dollar amount needs to be compared to the dollar threshold required to qualify for the one-time discount that has been established in the specifications. This purchase threshold has been fixed at $150 to qualify for the discount of 25 percent. We create a variable called $discount and set it to TRUE if the customer has previously purchased $150 or more from us. The following code demonstrates this.

```
if($data->Previous_Purchases > 150) {
        echo "<br><H1> Welcome $data->First_Name you qualify
for
                a 25% discount when you purchase $150 or
more</h1><br>";
        $discount=1;
    }else {
        echo "<br><H1> Welcome $data->First_Name </H1><br>\n";
        $discount=0;
    }
```

Checking for prior discount

Referring to the database schema illustrated earlier in Figure 16-1, we have an attribute called `Premium_Shipped` in the customer record. We use the `Premium_Shipped` attribute to indicate that the customer has already received the incentive. We can reuse the same schema by merely reinterpreting the meaning of the incentive attribute. As an aside, in a more sophisticated marketing application the kind of incentive would likely be tied to a particular promotion and be different for each promotion. In this case, the incentive is the discount. We'll give the discount if the customer has previously ordered at least $150 *and* has not already gotten the discount (that is, the incentive). The population of this attribute — Premium_Shipped — will be assumed to occur through another process after hours (that is, outside of this application).

Displaying the welcome page banner

If the customer is eligible for the 25 percent discount, we want to inform the customer of that by displaying a special message at the top of the page.

The order-entry form

Shoppers typically make several changes to their choice of product, product style, and quantity before committing to purchase. If we were naïve, we would write to the Order Entry database Order Detail table every time the customer made, changed, or removed an item from the order form page. Considering the potential number of simultaneous customers who could be purchasing from our Web site, we would be wasteful of the database's response time if we were to do so.

Instead, we will wait until the shopper commits to their purchase by clicking on the Purchase button to submit the purchase to our Order Detail table. Because we need to use a buffer for the order-entry items, we can initially set up a single-row array for the order form having an array element for each item that is displayed on the form (product description, unit price, quantity ordered, extended price). We'll also have hidden array elements that the user does not see, such as the SKU from the product table. As an alternative to the array concept, we could create objects for each item and have a linked list of objects for the entire order form. The following code shows the array approach:

```
$query="select * from Product";
$result=mysql_query($query) or die("Unable to display page");

$ii=0;
$entry_row[$ii] = new order_form;
        $entry_row[$ii]->init();

        while($data=mysql_fetch_object($result)) {
        $entry_row[$ii]->add_row($data->Description,$data-
```

```
>Unit_Price/100,${$ii},$ii);
        $total=$total+$class[$ii]->subtotal;
        $ii++;
        $class[$ii] = new order_form;

    }
```

The simple class, order_form, wraps each row from product in HTML tags, as well as creates a series of data input fields for the quantity that the customer chooses to purchase of each item. This merits special notice and is the item ${$ii} in our add_row input. It creates the variable $N where $N is 1 through the total number of products. This has no value the first time the page is created; however, every time the person inputs a value into the form and subtotals the form, the variable $N inserts the correct value in the page. A page that determines its own outcome is very valuable but can result in unreadable code, so it is important to use such techniques judiciously.

Using a buffer for the products table

We may also choose to create a local buffer that holds the contents of the Products table. That way, the response time when the customer initially chooses an item (or changes their choice) will be small. The unit price and SKU can be retrieved quickly from the local buffer rather than by querying the Product table each time a change is made to the purchased item field. However, if the number of products is large, the memory requirements of this approach may become too large to be able to support numerous simultaneous customers. In this event, we'd have to resort to other performance enhancement methods.

Processing each line

When the order-entry form is initially displayed, there will be a single line for each product in our product table. Each line is populated with product description and unit price, but the quantity, extended price, Discount and Order Total fields will be empty.

The customer chooses products by filling in the initially blank quantity field. If the total quantity reaches $150 dollars the discount will be taken off of the subtotal.

If the customer changes the ordered quantity, the new Extended Price is calculated and displayed.

When the customer clicks on the Subtotal button, the extended price is recalculated for the current line.

Finally, the Order Total and Discount Amount are updated after each line is updated.

Accepting and Posting the Customer Order

The following sections describe the process of accepting and posting customer orders.

Posting a new order header record

The customer indicates that he or she is ready to purchase by clicking on the Purchase button at the bottom of the page. At this time, the same form processes all of the customer's order detail.

Our first action is to create a new record in the Order Header table. Referring to the Order Entry schema, we see that the Order Header record requires the customer ID, today's date, and a unique order number.

The data for this record comes from the customer's login (the customer ID from the customer's own record in the Customer table, not the customer's name). The order date we'll just take from today's date using a built-in MySQL function. The order number is used as both the primary key for the records in the Order Header table and as part of the primary key for the records in the Order Detail table, so we have to generate the value for it ourselves to make sure that it is unique.

Posting new order detail records

After the Order Header has been inserted into the Order Header table, we can insert one record in the Order Detail table for each item that has been ordered. The reason we create the Order Header record first is that the Order Detail table references the Order Header table by virtue of the Order Number value being part of the Order Detail table's primary key.

The attributes for each Order Detail record are Order Number and Order Item number making up the primary key; the ordered item SKU; the ordered item quantity; and the extended price.

The Order Number matches the same attribute in the Order Header record for the order, so we can just use a copy of the value. The value for Order Item Number is not really important; it just must be unique for the same value of Order Number. This value is simply the ordinal position in the list of ordered items on the Web page.

The ordered item SKU is a foreign-key reference to the Products table. We don't replicate the product attributes in the Order Detail records because that would be violating one of Codd's Rules — that an attribute appear in only one entity. You may notice that we do calculate the extended price and copy it into the Order Detail record for the item. This is because the Unit_Price attribute in the Product table represents the list price. The value in the Ordered Item table will reflect the purchase price, which can be different, because we're offering discounts. We choose to apply any discounts here because it's the best place to record the actual sale price (every item is given the same discount). You may recall that we used the actual price when we determined the customer's purchase history in order to determine whether or not to offer the discount.

Posting "discount given" in the customer's record

Finally, if the customer has accepted the order and has been given the discount, we need to update the `Premium_Shipped` attribute of the Customer table to TRUE for this customer.

Posting new customer data

If this were an entirely new order, prior to inserting a new Order Header record we would have to generate a new Customer record. The data for this new record would normally come from an additional data entry page on the Web site. This page would be triggered by the absence of any Customer record when we searched the Customer table at login time.

Finally, when the customer's order is inserted into the database, we need to display a message on the Web page thanking them for their patronage and encouraging them to come again, as shown in the HTML that follows. This example PHP (and HTML) code shows how accepting and posting a customer order can be accomplished for this application.

```
<html>
```

Include the contents of these two files and process them with PHP as needed.

```
<?include header.inc?>
<?include customer.inc?>
```

Header (visible title) on the page is displayed in the customer's browser.

```
<h2> Order form </h2>

<!- Print table columns-!>
```

Begin PHP processing of the contents of this file.

```
<?

/////////////////////////////////////////////////////////////////
// Class: order_form                                           //
//      members: item,price,quantity, subtotal                 //
//      methods: add_row (adds row to table)                   //
/////////////////////////////////////////////////////////////////
```

Class definitions, like function definitions, don't act until called!

```
class order_form {
```

These class variables are set when an order entry row is placed on the Web page on the order form.

```
    var $item;
    var $price;
    var $quantity;
    var $subtotal;
```

init() creates the Order Form column labels, and sets the form action target.

```
    function init($query=""){   //print table columns
```

This class has embedded HTML to create a column label row when init() is called. Note that PHP stops processing at the ?> and the static HTML is sent to the browser. At the <? at the end of the last line, PHP restarts its processing.

The embedded HTML also sets this form as the target of the form action. The "method=post" property means that variable values on this form are passed using environment variables

```
        ?><table border=0>
        <form action="orderform.php" method=post>
        <th Align=left>Item</th>
        <th Align=left>Price</th>
        <th Align=left>Quantity</th>
        <th Align=left>Subtotal</th><?
    }
```

add_row() inserts another row on the Order Entry form with values as supplied by the function parameters (initially blank).

```
    function
  add_row($sku="",$item="",$price="",$quantity="",$row="") {
```

Each instance of the *this* class holds the values for one order row, set to the values as passed to this add_row member function.

```
        $this->sku=$sku;
        $this->item=$item;
        $this->price=$price;
        $this->quantity=$quantity;
        $subtotal= (real) $price*$quantity;
        $this->subtotal=$subtotal;
```

Use the PHP echo() function to create HTML on-the-fly and to send it to the browser. This HTML creates the visible order item rows that users sees in their browser. The HTML element   is a nonbreaking space. Of special note is the method used to give a name to each element in each row, that is:

```
sku_$row - sku_1, sku_2, ...,sku_N
quantity_$row - quantity_1, quantity_2, ...,quantity_N
price_$row - price_1, price_2, ..., price_N
```

The value for $row is used to uniquely name each input element for easier retrieval later, row by row. $row is a parameter to this method.

```
        echo  "<tr><td> $item </td>
        <td> $price </td>
        <td><input type=text name=$row size=4 maxlength=6
            tabindex=$row value=$quantity> </td>
        <td>    $subtotal</td></tr>
        <input type=hidden name=sku_$row value=$sku>
        <input type=hidden name=quantity_$row value=$quantity>
        <input type=hidden name=price_$row value=$price>";
    }
}  //End of the class definition for order_form


//////////////////////////////////////////////////////////
// Main: build orderform, subtotal orderform or purchase //
//                                                       //
//////////////////////////////////////////////////////////

if($userid){  //Must have the user_id to proceed; we use it
several times!

   if( ! $purchase){  // if not ready to purchase
```

Connect to the database server using the DBA login name and password. It is important that the DBA login remain secure, so don't let the source for this page be displayed by any browser.

```
    $link=mysql_connect("localhost", "dba", "dba2pass");
```

Once connected to the database server, we must select which database on the server we want to access. For this application, we want to access the Order Entry database.

```
    $database=mysql_select_db(order_entry);
```

Create a query using the value entered by the customer for their ID and pass the query to this function when it is called. In this query, the SQL statement select sums the extended_price column for ALL orders. The query has a constraint, the where clause, that constrains the rows to be summed by specifying that only rows in which the value of the Customer_id column in every row matches the value of

$userid for this session (the user who has logged in) should be summed. We also get this customer's real first name by joining the Order Detail table to the Order Header table, which, in turn, joins to the corresponding record in the customer table (there better be only one!). We also only care if this customer has NOT gotten a premium, that is, a discount, previously.

```
$query="select First_Name,
        sum(Order_Detail.extended_price)
        as Previous_Purchases
        from Customer natural join Order_Header
        natural join Order_Detail
        where Customer.Customer_id='$userid'
        and Customer.Premium_Shipped !- 'Y'
        group by First_Name";
```

Execute this query (executes on the most recently selected database). If a critical error occurs during the execution of this query, we want to terminate the session. Note that NOT finding a records in the Customer or Order Detail table having this value for Customer_id is NOT a failure. The $result return value is used for fetching the result set rows.

```
    $result=mysql_query($query) or die("Unable to display page
1");
```

Create a premium_customer object (fancy premium flag) from the result set, if any. It may have zero or one row in it. We don't need to examine any detail; the constraints in the query took care of that for us.

Because we specified the Customer_id attribute as the primary key for the Customer table, there can be AT MOST one record having a given value for Customer_id. The Premium_Shipped attribute may have been true (Y), too, resulting in an empty result set.

The mysql_fetch_object() function returns a result row object. Each field of the original select statement's select list is accessed using the object pointer. Note that mysql_fetch_object uses the value returned from the earlier mysql_query() execution.

```
    $premium_customer=mysql_fetch_object($result);
```

Create a query using the value entered by the customer for their ID and pass the query to this function when it is called. In this query, the SQL statement select list has the customer's name fields from the Customer table. Gather needed customer information.

```
$query="select Customer_id,
        First_Name, Middle_initial,
        Last_name
        from Customer
        where  Customer.Customer_id='$userid' ";
```

Next, execute this query (executes on the most recently selected database). If critical error occurs during the execution of this query, we want to terminate the session. Note that NOT finding a record in the Customer table having this value for Customer_id is NOT a failure. The $result return value is used for fetching the result set rows.

```
$result=mysql_query($query) or die("Unable to display page 2");
```

Now, examine the result set from this query. It may have zero or one row in it. Because we specified the Customer_id attribute as the primary key for the Customer table, there can be AT MOST one record having a given value for Customer_id. The mysql_fetch_object() function returns a result row object. Each field of the original select statement's select list is accessed using the object pointer. Note that mysql_fetch_object uses the value returned from the earlier mysql_query() execution to create a customer object.

```
$customer_info =mysql_fetch_object($result);
```

If the customer qualifies for the discount, then let the customer know. The $150 threshold is a design requirement from the specifications. It means that prior purchases must total more than $150 in order to qualify for the 25 percent discount on this order.

```
if($premium_customer->Previous_Purchases > 150) {
```

Send a special, personalized message to the browser in the largest typeface available (<H1>).
 is the HTML element for a line break.

```
echo "<br><H1> Welcome $customer_info->First_Name <BR>
      you qualify for a 25% discount
      when you purchase $150 or more.
      </H1><br>";

$discount_flag=1; // flag used for later

}else {  //Print standard greeting using the customers
first name.

    echo "<br><H1> Welcome $customer_info->First_Name
</H1><br>\n";
    $discount_flag=0;

}
```

In this query, the SQL statement select list only has one field: *. This selects every column (attribute) from each record. Because there are no constraints (no where clause), this query selects every record from the Product table.

Select all products for building order form lines.

```
$query="select * from Product";
```

Execute this query (executes on the most recently selected database). If critical error occurs during the execution of this query, we want to terminate the session. Note that NOT finding a record in the Product table is NOT a failure, but it would sure be unexpected! The $result return value is used for fetching the result set rows.

```
$result=mysql_query($query) or die("Unable to display page
3");
```

Build the table one row at a time.

```
$ii=0;
```

Here's where each new order form line is built.

```
$object = new order_form;
$object->init();
```

Examine the result set from this query. It may have zero or more rows in it. The ($product=mysql_fetch_object($result)) condition evaluates to TRUE for each row in the result set. The mysql_fetch_object() function returns a result row object. Each field of the original select statement's select list is accessed using the object pointer. Note that mysql_fetch_object uses the value returned from the earlier mysql_query() execution.

```
while($product=mysql_fetch_object($result)) {
```

As long as there are more products, create row objects. Here's where each new order form line is built, by the add_row method of the order_form class (referred to by $object).

```
$object->add_row($product->Product_SKU,
        $product->Description,
        $product->Unit_Price/100,
                                    ${$ii},$ii);

 // keep a running total.
 $total=$total+$object->subtotal;
 $ii++;
 $class[$ii] = new order_form;

}

// Print the total line.
```

```
echo "<tr><td> Total </td>";
if($discount && ($total > 150)) {   // if customer eligible
   echo "<td>\$$total</td>";
   echo "<td>@25% off = </td>";
   $total=$total - $total*0.25;      // give discount
   echo "<input type=hidden name=discount value=0.75>";  //
pass discount to next page

}  else {
   echo "<td>  </td><td>  </td>";
   echo "<input type=hidden name=discount value=1>";  //
else don't pass to next page
}
```

Now, print the total using the PHP *echo* command.

```
echo "<td> $total</td></tr>";

?>  <!- exit php -!>
```

Create a hidden table so that we can pass values from one iteration of this order form to the next; for example, for the Subtotal button to pass the user_id to the browser.

```
</table><input type=hidden name=userid value=<? echo
$userid?>>
```

Pass the number of products to the browser.

```
<input type=hidden name=num_products value=<?echo $ii?>>
```

Create Subtotal and Purchase buttons. The Subtotal button will only calculate a new total for the row and display it on the browser.

```
<br><input type=submit name=subtotal value="Subtotal"
          tableindex=<?echo $ii?>>
<input type=submit name=purchase value="Purchase"
       tableindex=<?echo $ii++?>>
</form>
```

Begin PHP processing here:

```
<?
}
//The user has clicked on the Purchase button!
elseif($purchase)
{
```

Connect to the database server using the DBA login name and password. It is important that the DBA login remain secure, so don't let the source for this page be displayed by any browser.

First, establish a link to database.

```
$link = mysql_connect("localhost", "dba", "dba2pass") or
die("Failure connecting to database");
```

Once we have connected to the database server, we must select which database on the server we want to access. For this application, we want to access the Order Entry database.

```
$database=mysql_select_db(order_entry);
```

Insert record into order header. Create a unique key for the order number by using the current largest value for order number and adding 1 to it.

The prior order number is determined by using a SQL function that returns the maximum value of a column. To prevent the possibility of two nearly simultaneous queries of this sort, which can happen if multiple orders are being inserted at the same time, we lock the table for our exclusive use while we:

Query for the current maximum order number followed by

Insert a record into the Order Header table using 1+max(Order_Number) as the next value of Order_Number.

After we're through, we have to unlock the table so that other orders can be processed.

Create the SQL query string to lock the Order_Header table for our exclusive use. Note that this is a write lock because we'll need to both read and write.

```
$lock="lock tables Order_Header write";
```

Now, execute the SQL statment to lock the table.

```
$result=mysql_query($lock);
```

Create the SQL query string to retrieve the current maximum value in the Order_Number field of the Order_Header table in the Order Entry database.

```
$order_number=" select max(Order_Number) from
Order_Header";
```

The next thing to do is to get the maximum order number. Execute this query (executes on the most recently selected database). If a critical error occurs during the execution of this query, we want to terminate the session. Note that NOT finding a record in the Customer table having this value for Customer_id is NOT a failure. The $result return value is used for fetching the result set rows.

```
$result=mysql_query($order_number,$link)
    or die("Unable execute 1 \n");
```

Look at the result set from this query. It may have zero or one row in it. mysql_fetch_object returns a result row object. Each field of the original select statement's select list is accessed using the object pointer. Note that mysql_fetch_object uses the value returned from the earlier mysql_query() execution.

```
$order_number=mysql_fetch_row($result);
```

Add 1 to the value of $order_number to get the next unique value for Order_Number.

```
$order_number[0]++;  // add one to max order number.
```

Now, we need to generate the SQL query to insert a new record into the Order_Header table using our new Order_Number; the value of $userid for this customer; and the date of the order by way of the CURDATE() function in MySQL.

```
$header="insert into Order_Header
        (Order_Number,Customer_id,Order_Date)
        values ($order_number[0],'$userid',CURDATE())";
```

Execute this query on the database referred to by the value of $link ($link was the return value from the earlier mysql_connect() function). If a critical error occurs during the execution of this query, we want to terminate the session. The $result return value is used for fetching the result set rows.

```
$result=mysql_query($header,$link)    // execute statement
    or die("Unable execute 2 \n");
```

After we're through, we have to unlock the table so that other orders can be processed. We need to use the value of Order_Number that we generated when we insert records into the Order_Detail table.

```
$unlock="unlock tables";                // unlock table
```

Execute the UNLOCK statement. Now, the Order_Header table can be read and written to by others.

```
$result=mysql_query($unlock);
```

Initialize the variables that we'll use for reiterating the list of ordered items.

```
$ii=0;$jj=0;
```

Before we have reached this last line on the Order Form, $num_products was determined in some PHP code when the Order Form was initially displayed. It is the number of products that are displayed, and therefore the number of products that might have been ordered.

```
while($ii < $num_products) {
```

Reference variables are from the previous HTML page (this same page before the user clicked on the Purchase button).

Next, we'll actually make a variable using string concatenation. We need to do this because we named each order entry line field using an index number when this page's HTML was generated by PHP. So, we need to do a similar thing to get to the values after the user has entered them.

```
$qref='quantity_'.$ii;
```

Get the quantity by dereferencing this variable.

```
$quantity=${$qref};
```

Again, make a variable name using string concatenation. We need to do this because we named each order entry line field, in this case the sku attribute, using an index number when this page's HTML was generated by PHP. So, we need to do a similar thing to get to the values after the user has entered them.

```
$sref='sku_'.$ii;
```

Get the part number by dereferencing the variable name that we have created using string concatentation.

```
$sku=${$sref};
```

Once again, we'll make a variable name using string concatenation. We need to do this because we named each order entry line field, in this case the price attribute, using an index number when this page's HTML was generated by PHP. So, we need to do a similar thing to get to the values after the user has entered them.

```
$pref='price_'.$ii;
```

Get the price by dereferencing this variable.

```
$price=${$pref};
```

Determine extended price.

```
$ext_price=$price*$quantity*$discount;

if($quantity > 0) {        // if you want at least one
```

For each item where the ordered quantity is greater than zero (we exclude negative ordered quantities this way) insert into our detail table: the Order Number (generated uniquely for this order); the order item number ($jj), a sequentially generated number incremented for each new item that we insert for the same Order Number; the product SKU ($sku); and the extended price ($ext_price). Note that we don't enter the unit price because we are able to implicitly track discounts this way, even on an item-by–item basis. There is no need to lock the Order_Detail table because the Order_Number is unique.

```
$insert_detail="insert into Order_Detail
               (Order_Number,Order_Item_Number,
                Product_SKU,Qty,Extended_Price)
                values
               ($order_number[0],$jj,$sku,
                $quantity,$ext_price)"; // statement
```

Execute this query on the database referred to by the value of $link ($link was the return value from the earlier mysql_connect() function). If a critical error occurs during the execution of this query, we want to terminate the session. The $result return value is used for fetching the result set rows.

```
$result=mysql_query($insert_detail,$link)
or die("Unable execute $jj+2 \n")  ;

//Increment the variable that we use for Ordered Item Number
$jj++;

    }
```

Increment the variable that we use to get to the next line on the order form so that we can get the SKU, price, and quantity.

```
    $ii++;
}
```

When we're all done inserting the order detail records we close our connection to the database that was opened earlier. The value of $link is our pointer to this database.

```
mysql_close($link); // close link
```

Print a sign-off message on the Order Form. At this point the order form doesn't have the rows of items on it anymore, just the title Order Form. Look at the beginning of this example for the HTML line: <h2> Order From </h2>.

Print the Thank you message in the largest default typeface available.

```
print "<H1>Thank you, come again</H1>\n";

    }
}
```

This is the end of the PHP processing.

```
?>
```

This is the end of the HTML content.

```
</html>
```

Listing 16-4 shows HTML that the above PHP code sends to the Web browser. If you copy this code into a file and open with your Web browser, you'll see the page as displayed (Figure 16-4).

Listing 16-4: **Generated HTML from the Order Form**

```
<html>
  <html>
    <head>
      <title> Registration Page </title>

    </head>
    <BODY

          BGCOLOR="#FFFFFF"
          TEXT="#000000"
          LINK="#0000FF"
          VLINK="#000080"
          ALINK="#FF0000"
          ><h2> Order form </h2>

<!- Print table columns-!>

<br><H1> Welcome Steve <BR>
                    you qualify for a 25% discount
                    when you purchase $150 or more
              </H1><br><table border=0>
          <form action="orderform.php" method=post>
          <th Align=left>Item</th>
          <th Align=left>Price</th>
          <th Align=left>Quantity</th>
```

Continued

Listing 16-4 *(continued)*

```
        <th Align=left>Subtotal</th><tr><td> Widget 1 </td>
            <td> 1.99 </td>
            <td><input type=text name=0
                    size=4 maxlength=6
                    tabindex=0
                    value=> </td>

            <td>    0</td></tr>
                <input type=hidden name=sku_0 value=1>
                <input type=hidden name=quantity_0 value=>
                <input type=hidden name=price_0
value=1.99><tr><td> Widget 2 </td>
            <td> 45.95 </td>
            <td><input type=text name=1

                    size=4 maxlength=6
                    tabindex=1
                    value=> </td>

            <td>    0</td></tr>
                <input type=hidden name=sku_1 value=2>
                <input type=hidden name=quantity_1 value=>
                <input type=hidden name=price_1
value=45.95><tr><td> Widget 3 </td>
            <td> 99.95 </td>
            <td><input type=text name=2

                    size=4 maxlength=6
                    tabindex=2
                    value=> </td>

            <td>    0</td></tr>
                <input type=hidden name=sku_2 value=3>
                <input type=hidden name=quantity_2 value=>
                <input type=hidden name=price_2
value=99.95><tr><td> Widget 4 </td>
            <td> 89.95 </td>
            <td><input type=text name=3

                    size=4 maxlength=6
                    tabindex=3
                    value=> </td>

            <td>    0</td></tr>
                <input type=hidden name=sku_3 value=4>
                <input type=hidden name=quantity_3 value=>
                <input type=hidden name=price_3
value=89.95><tr><td> Widget 5 </td>
```

```
                          <td> 4.95 </td>
                          <td><input type=text name=4

                                  size=4 maxlength=6
                                  tabindex=4
                                  value=> </td>

                          <td>    0</td></tr>
                              <input type=hidden name=sku_4 value=5>
                              <input type=hidden name=quantity_4 value=>
                              <input type=hidden name=price_4
value=4.95><tr><td> Widget 6 </td>
                          <td> 5.95 </td>
                          <td><input type=text name=5

                                  size=4 maxlength=6
                                  tabindex=5
                                  value=> </td>

                          <td>    0</td></tr>
                              <input type=hidden name=sku_5 value=6>
                              <input type=hidden name=quantity_5 value=>
                              <input type=hidden name=price_5
value=5.95><tr><td> Widget 7 </td>
                          <td> 9.95 </td>
                          <td><input type=text name=6

                                  size=4 maxlength=6
                                  tabindex=6
                                  value=> </td>

                          <td>    0</td></tr>
                              <input type=hidden name=sku_6 value=7>
                              <input type=hidden name=quantity_6 value=>
                              <input type=hidden name=price_6
value=9.95><tr><td> Widget 8 </td>
                          <td> 8.95 </td>
                          <td><input type=text name=7

                                  size=4 maxlength=6
                                  tabindex=7
                                  value=> </td>

                          <td>    0</td></tr>
                              <input type=hidden name=sku_7 value=8>
                              <input type=hidden name=quantity_7 value=>
                              <input type=hidden name=price_7
value=8.95><tr><td> Widget 9 </td>
                          <td> 145.95 </td>
                          <td><input type=text name=8
```

Continued

Listing 16-4 *(continued)*

```
                                        size=4 maxlength=6
                                        tabindex=8
                                        value=2> </td>

                <td>    291.9</td></tr>
                    <input type=hidden name=sku_8 value=9>
                    <input type=hidden name=quantity_8 value=2>
                    <input type=hidden name=price_8

value=145.95><tr><td> Widget 10 </td>
                <td> 3.95 </td>
                <td><input type=text name=9

                                        size=4 maxlength=6
                                        tabindex=9
                                        value=> </td>

                <td>    0</td></tr>
                    <input type=hidden name=sku_9 value=10>
                    <input type=hidden name=quantity_9 value=>
                    <input type=hidden name=price_9
value=3.95><tr><td> Total </td><td>$291.9</td><td>@25% off =
</td><input type=hidden name=discount value=0.75><td>
218.925</td></tr>
        </table><input type=hidden name=userid value=swysham>
                <input type=hidden name=num_products value=10>
        <br><input type=submit name=subtotal value="Subtotal"
tableindex=10>
        <input type=submit name=purchase value="Purchase"
tableindex=10>
        </form>


    </html>
```

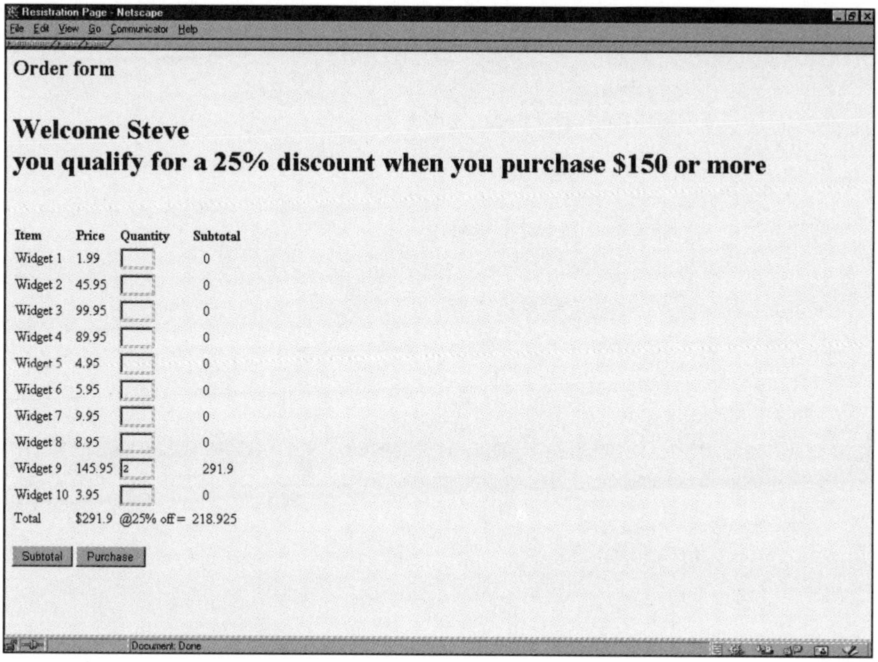

Figure 16-4: The Order Form

When the Order Form has posted the order to the database, the HTML that the PHP code in Listing 16-4 sends to the Web browser is different in that it lacks the lines that make up the order form. If you copy this code into a file and open it with your Web browser, you'll see the page as displayed in Figure 16-5. The HTML is shown in Listing 16-5.

Listing 16-5: **Generated HTML Showing the Order Form after Posting the Order**

```
<html>
  <html>
    <head>
      <title> Registration Page </title>

    </head>
    <BODY

         BGCOLOR="#FFFFFF"
         TEXT="#000000"
         LINK="#0000FF"
         VLINK="#000080"
```

Continued

Listing 16-5 *(continued)*

```
            ALINK="#FF0000"
            ><h2> Order form </h2>

<!- Print table columns-!>

<H1>Thank you, come again</H1>


    </html>
```

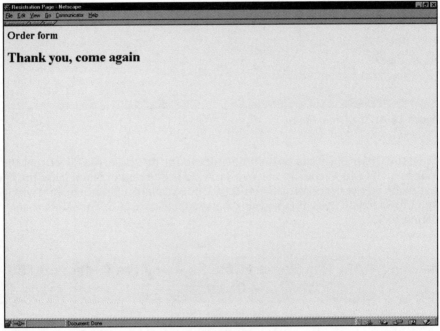

Figure 16-5: The Order Form after processing the order

Summary

In this chapter, we've expanded on the business customer example from Chapter 15 and demonstrated the process by which you can adapt and make changes to Web applications using PHP and MySQL.

✦   ✦   ✦

Administrivia

Administration

This chapter discusses the basic and most important aspects of administering a Linux DBMS.

System Administration

Managing Linux databases often translates as "managing Linux." This section discusses six categories of OS administration:

+ Backing up
+ Managing performance
+ Managing processes
+ Managing users
+ Managing the file system
+ Miscellaneous or intermittent tasks

Backing up

This section examines two tried-and-true Linux archiving commands: `tar` and `cpio`. In addition, the section examines automating the execution of these commands.

tar

tar, short for *t*ape *ar*chive, is the granddaddy of Linux and UNIX backup commands. tar can create archives not only on tape, but on any storage medium. Generalized tar syntax looks like this.

```
tar task mode file/device file-names
```

Table 17-1 outlines tar's syntax.

	Table 17-1	
	tar Parameters and Syntax	
Argument	**Effect**	
task (any of c, r, t, x)	Creates, appends to, gives a table of contents of, or extracts from, an archive	
mode (any of v, w, u)	Operates in, respectively:	
	Verbose mode, displaying the name of every file processed	
	Confirmation mode, that is, waits for your confirmation of every action it intends to take	
	Assigns the user and group IDs of the person issuing the tar command to the files extracted from archives	
file/device, or f	Specifies the file or device on which or from which tar should create or extract	
Filenames	Identifies files to be placed in or extracted from an archive	

Creating an archive with tar

To place all files in the current directory into an archive called tar_fil in the directory /backup, type this command:

```
ls | tar c > /backup/tar_lib
```

After ls generates a file list for tar, tar places those files in the indicated archive.

Extracting files from a tar archive

To restore into the current directory all files from the archive tar_fil whose names end in .hal, use this command:

```
tar xf /backup/tar_fil *.hal
```

Listing the contents of a tar archive

To have tar display the name of every file in an archive, use a command similar to this:

```
tar t /backup/tar_fil
```

Listing items appended to a tar archive

You can ask tar to display the name of every file it processes. For instance, this command would add all files whose names end in .ncc to the end of the archive /backup/tar_fil, and report as it appends:

```
tar rvf /backup/big_lib *.log
```

cpio

The command `cpio`, like the command `tar`, can create and administer archives. But differences do exist. For one, the internal format used by cpio isn't compatible with that of tar. Nor does cpio adhere to tar's method of blocking out space on a storage medium. tar would, for example, allocate an entire 512- or 1024-byte storage unit or block to even a 5-byte file. cpio, on the other hand, manages media in more miserly fashion. For our 5-byte file, cpio would use only 5 bytes of storage. As a result of such differences, tar cannot recognize archives created by cpio.

Table 17-2 describes cpio's syntax.

Table 17-2 cpio Syntax	
Argument	**Effect**
either -o (out) or -I (in)	Copies a list of files to, or extracts files from, an archive
Pass	Copies files from one directory to another, without creating an archive
with out, a	Resets access times for files being copied out
with out or in, B	Uses the nondefault block size 5,120 bytes when copying either in or out
with out or in, v	Uses verbose mode, that is, displays the name of every file processed, whether copying in or out
with in, d	Creates directories when needed
with in, m	Keeps original file modification times
with out or in, c	Uses an older, but more portable, archive format
with in, u	Copies unconditionally, that is, replaces newer versions of files with older ones from an archive, without requesting confirmation

Creating an archive with cpio

To place all files in the current directory whose names end in .txt into an archive called txt_stuf in the directory /backup, type this command:

```
ls *.txt | cpio -o > /backup/txt_stuf
```

After `ls` creates a files list for cpio, the latter places them in the indicated library.

Rename files in a cpio archive

To rename all files in the archive txt_stuf in the directory /backup, use this command:

```
cpio -ir < /backup/txt_stuf
```

With this command, cpio prompts you, one file at a time, for the new name you want to assign to the file being processed.

Extract files from a cpio archive

To restore all files from the archive /backup/txt_stuf to the current directory, type this command:

```
cpio -i < /backup/txt_stuf
```

Archive a directory

To place all of a directory tree, including subdirectories and files, into an archive called big_lib in the directory /backup, type this command:

```
find . -print | cpio -o > /backup/big_lib
```

The `find . -print` section of this command creates a list of all file and directory names in the current path. cpio then receives those names, and understands that the files and directories that they represent can be placed in the indicated archive.

Create a table of contents of a cpio archive

This command lists the names of all directories, subdirectories, and files in the archive big_lib:

```
cpio -it < /backup/big_lib
```

Automating tar

One cannot overstate the value to an administrator of automating common tasks through cron, the Linux batch job scheduler. Certainly backups fall into the category common tasks. This section:

✦ Offers an example of automating a database backup using tar and cron

✦ Explains that automation in detail

The following, a regularly run real-world example, creates a tar archive of all files from the directory /backup whose names end in .txt on the local tape drive. The command assumes, of course, that a tape has been loaded into the drive and that the drive has been made accessible by means of the mount command or automatically at bootup.

```
0 1 * * 2-0 tar cvf /dev/rt/0m /backup/*.txt
```

Table 17-3 dissects this command.

Command Section	Effect
Table 17-3	
tar and cron	
0 1 * * 2-0	Tells cron to run the tar command at:
	no minutes after (0)
	1 AM (1) on
	every date of the month (*) of
	every month of the year (*) on
	every Tuesday through Sunday (2-0) inclusive, in that order
tar cvf	Creates (c) a tar archive, working in verbose mode (v), on the device whose designation (f) is ?
/dev/rt/0m	The indicated file in the directory /dev, from the files ?
/backup/*.txt	In the directory /backup whose names end in .txt

Automating cpio

The following three-line sample shellscript, based on one used at Bell Labs under UNIX, works just as well under Linux to relocate files within a network. The script assumes:

✦ A directory on both source and destination machine, represented by the environment variable $DB, in which all database files reside

✦ All such file names end in .db

✦ The version of Linux in question makes available the rsh command

✦ The name of the remote machine is elsewhere

```
cd $DB
find . -name *.db -print | cpio -ocB | rsh elsewhere `cd $DB
cpio -icB`
```

Table 17-4 scrutinizes this script.

Table 17-4 Automating cpio	
Command Section	**Effect**
cd $DB	Changes to the directory indicated by the value of the environment variable DB, and then ?
find . -name *.db -print	Finds all files in that directory whose names end in .db, and then ?
| cpio -ocB	Pipes that list of file names to cpio, which proceeds to:
	copy out the indicated files to an archive
	use the more portable copy format
	use the nonstandard 5,120-byte block size
	and then ...
'cd $DB ; cpio -icB'	Changes to the database directory on that remote machine and copies in the piped cpio output

Managing Performance

This section examines:

✦ The command top, with which you can observe demands on a Linux CPU in real time

✦ The command netstat, with which you can monitor a Linux server's networking nature

top

The OS command top provides a real-time snapshot of CPU activity. For example, you could use a command similar to the following to take ten such snapshots and then return to the shell prompt.

```
top -d 10
```

Table 17-5 summarizes top's syntax.

Table 17-5	
top's Syntax	

top Argument	Effect
-s some integer	Sets top's display to refresh in the number of seconds indicated
-d some integer	Provides only the number of displays indicated, and then quits
-u	Presents user ID numbers, rather than user names, in top's output
-n some integer	Displays per screen only the number of processes you specify

top shows second-by-second information on performance parameters including:

✦ Averages of loads on the CPU in the most recent time intervals

✦ The number of processes currently being handled by the CPU, and the number of processes in any of several conditions including sleeping, waiting, running, starting, or stopped

✦ The percentage of its time, since top's last report, that the CPU has spent in any of the several conditions, such as idle, interrupt, and swapper, it can be in. On multiprocessor systems, top supplies this information for every CPU.

You need only use the keystroke sequence Ctrl+C, or even more simply type the lowercase letter q, to terminate top and return to the operating system prompt.

netstat

You can use any Linux machine connected to a network to gather basic statistics on network interfaces and protocols, with the command netstat. Structure that command's syntax like the example below, which Table 17-6 outlines.

```
netstat some_argument
```

Table 17-6	
netstat's Syntax	

Argument	Effect
-I	Shows information about a specific network interface only
interface	Specifies the network name of the network interface for which you want statistics
-M	Shows multicast routing tables only

Continued

Table 17-6 *(continued)*

Argument	Effect
-n	Shows network addresses as numbers
-r	Shows all routing tables
-s	Shows statistics for all protocols
-p	Shows statistics for a specific protocol

netstat's interface-oriented output presents cumulative statistics on factors such as packets transferred and packet collisions (tcp protocol). The command's protocol-oriented output offers extensive information on tcp.

Tip netstat recognizes all important protocols, such as arp, ip, tcp, and udp.

Managing processes

By their nature, databases are disk-intensive applications. Running in a distributed processing environment, they also can generate heavy traffic on a net. Monitoring database-related processes is therefore central to managing those processes in order to provide as efficient a use of server resources as possible.

This section investigates three Linux commands that can be invaluable in such monitoring and management:

✦ ps
✦ nice
✦ kill

ps

ps, short for *process status*, provides information on the status of individual jobs currently running. ps tracks those processes by their PID or *process ID number*, a sequential numeric identifier assigned to every task Linux executes.

ps parameters are legion. The examples below illustrate three common uses of such parameters, and Table 17-7 summarizes the most significant parameters.

```
ps -e   (get statistics on all processes)

ps -u root   (get statistics on all processes initiated by a
specific user - in this case, the superuser, root)

ps -tp7   (get statistics on all processes initiated from a
specific station, in this case, the "terminal" designated p7)
```

Understanding the Output of ps

ps -l output is quite extensive, and includes such information as:

✦ Address in memory where a task resides

✦ Amount of memory (in blocks) a task uses

✦ Cumulative time a task has been running

✦ Name of the command the PID parameter represents

✦ Percentage of CPU resources the task needs

✦ Priority at which the job runs; expressed as integers, with lower numbers indicating higher priorities

✦ Process ID number

✦ Process ID number of the current task's parent process

✦ Process status, expressed as an initial, such as S (sleeping), W (waiting), T (terminated), and R (running)

✦ Terminal from which the task runs

✦ User ID of the individual who launched the task

This copious reporting provides many ways for the savvy DBMS administrator to control database-related processes.

Table 17-7
ps Parameters

Parameter	Effect
-a	Displays information about all processes, whether system- or user-initiated
-e	Displays information on all processes, run from whatever terminal
-l	Displays a long listing of process information
-t	Displays information on all processes run from the indicated terminal
-u	Displays a listing of processes initiated by the user you specify by user name

Tracking a user's processes

Assume that one of your Linux DBMS users likes to run every query under the sun at frequent intervals, unnecessarily tying up system resources. To monitor this user's activities more closely, with an eye toward finding patterns in that usage that might allow you to suggest more efficient work habits, use a command like this:

```
ps -u zealot
```

You should see results something like the hypothetical ps output below, which confirms that:

✦ The user in question has run seven database-related processes

✦ The user has exacerbated the load on the server that these processes present, by carrying them out via a telnet session

```
PID     TTY     TIME    COMMAND
15654 ttyp1    0:00    telnet
15977 ttyp1    0:00    sh
15994 ttyp1    0:00    ps
16203 ttyp1    0:57    /usr/local/mysql/bin/mysql
16391 ttyp1    0:32    /usr/local/mysql/bin/mysql employee_db
< address_script.sql > employee_address.tab
16422 ttyp1    0:29    /usr/local/mysql/bin/mysql employee_db
< evaluation_script.sql > employee_evaluation.tab
16534 ttyp1    0:19    /usr/local/mysql/bin/mysql employee_db
< education_script.sql > employee_education.tab
16606 ttyp1    0:15    /usr/local/mysql/bin/mysql employee_db
< vacation_script.sql > employee_vacation.tab
16824 ttyp1    0:11    /usr/local/mysql/bin/mysql employee_db
< training_script.sql > employee_training.tab
16929 ttyp1    0:07    /usr/local/mysql/bin/mysql employee_db
< overtime_script.sql > employee_overtime.tab
```

Respectively, this display's columns indicate:

✦ A process's ID number

✦ The terminal that controls the process

✦ The cumulative execution time for the process

✦ The process's command name

Tracking a Specific Station's Processes

To learn what processes the current shell session at a given station runs, use a command like this:

```
ps -t p0
```

Substitute the appropriate device designation from the /dev directory for our generic p0.

nice

To understand how to use the command nice to manipulate process priorities effectively under Linux, one must first understand how the OS assigns such priorities.

Linux processes run in two modes. If executing its own code, a task runs in user mode, which precludes activities such as:

✦ I/O operations

✦ Interprocess communication

✦ Network communication

Only the OS kernel can launch such activities. However, that kernel itself exists as a RAM-resident process. What connects user to kernel? The OS system call interface acts as this bridge.

The life cycle of any process, therefore, begins when a fork system call gives birth to that process from an existing, parent process. At birth, the new process or some part of it takes up residence in memory, and begins to execute. Should sufficient free RAM be unavailable and a process need wait for completion of some I/O operation, it may spend significant time waiting in memory, or even temporarily be relegated to disk, in swap space, which usually lies outside what most of us think of as a Linux file system.

Even after overcoming such delays, a process must wait for the CPU scheduler to assign it CPU time. Clearly, the efficiency of switching the CPU between processes can critically affect overall server performance.

Left to itself, a Linux CPU lets every process run for a preset interval called a *quantum* or *time slice*. Under this default scheme, a task runs until it completes or until it is preempted by another process that the OS considers more important or immediate.

Tip   Most versions of Linux use 100 milliseconds as the default time slice, but this parameter can be modified by reconfiguring and recompiling the OS kernel.

Such a default method, involving as it does a significant amount of what's called context switching, can also involve appreciable overhead. Recompiling a kernel to decrease the time slice parameter can actually induce greater overhead. Recompiling to increase the size of the time slice can, on the other hand, block CPU access for many users and applications. Furthermore, by default, every Linux process:

✦ Has a priority associated with it at its creation

✦ Has its priority dynamically adjusted during execution, roughly every 40 milliseconds

✦ Usually occupies one of the three priority classes: real-time, system, or user

✦ Will receive the highest priority only if it falls into the real-time category

✦ Can block all other processes access to the CPU if it falls into the real-time category

It becomes clear that using the `nice` command to modify process priority can be critical to keeping a Linux DBMS server's allocation of CPU time even-handed.

Tip   Under Linux as under UNIX, a parameter called the `nice value` or `nice number` indicates a process's priority. Usually, the default `nice value` is 20. To cause a process run at a lower priority, it must be given a higher `nice value`. To cause it to run at a higher priority, it must receive a lower `nice number`.

Caution   Only the superuser can decrease `nice` values, that is, use the nice command to raise a process's priority.

`nice`'s syntax can be summarized as follows:

```
nice some_integer
PID_for_command_whose_priority_will_be_altered
```

So, for example, the following command would raise the priority of a Linux DBMS query from 10, the common default, to 1.

```
nice 1 3572
```

Tip   You must first, of course, identify the process ID of the task whose priority you wish to manipulate before you can change its `nice number`.

Tip   Typically, the range of integers which can be supplied to nice under Linux runs from −20, which assigns the highest possible priority, to 19, which provides the lowest.

kill

`kill` terminates running processes, using the parameters outlined in Table 17-8.

	Table 17-8 kill's Parameters	
Parameter	**Effect**
`signal number`	Sends the indicated numeric signal to terminate a process. 9 ensures that a process dies, but does not necessarily kill it gracefully. 15, while not as quick a kill, offers a process the opportunity to do such housekeeping as closing files.
`process ID number`	Specifies, by PID, the job to kill.

Possible non-default values for the signal parameter include:

✦ 1, known as SIGHUP, short for Signal to Hang Up. SIGHUP simply tells a task to terminate.

✦ 3, known as SIGQUIT, short for Signal to Quit. SIGQUIT tells a task to terminate after doing a core dump.

✦ 9, known as SIGKILL, short for Signal to Kill. As mentioned, SIGKILL cannot be ignored.

✦ 24, known as SIGSTOP, short for Signal to Stop. SIGSTOP doesn't actually terminate a task, but rather pauses it.

Imagine, for example, that you've used the ps command and discovered that a small SQL script you're testing uses an inordinate amount of CPU time, even when running in the background. You can begin to correct this problem by killing your script with a command like this:

```
kill -9 9753
```

Tip To kill a process, you must either own the process — that is, have initiated it — or be the superuser, who can kill any process.

Managing users

Three Linux commands that I believe are particularly valuable in managing user DBMS and OS sessions are:

✦ who

✦ finger

✦ write

who

Depending on your Linux flavor, the command who can supply information regarding logged-in users such as:

✦ Elapsed time since the user's session was last active

✦ The process ID of the user's shell

✦ The user's name

To do no more than learn which users currently have connected to your server, type this command:

```
who
```

Using who with its -q option produces only the names and a total count of currently logged-in users.

finger

The `finger` command monitors the activity of users on a Linux system. By default, for every logged-in user, finger displays information including:

✦ Login name

✦ Terminal write status, that is, whether the ability to write to the machine through which the user logged in has been granted or denied

✦ Idle time, the amount of time the user's current session has executed nothing

✦ Login time, the date and time at which the user established the current session

✦ User's home directory and login shell

You can also finger individual users by supplying their login names to finger.

To discover everyone currently logged into your server, as well as the activities in which they're engaged, use this command:

```
finger
```

Your results should resemble those in Figure 17-1.

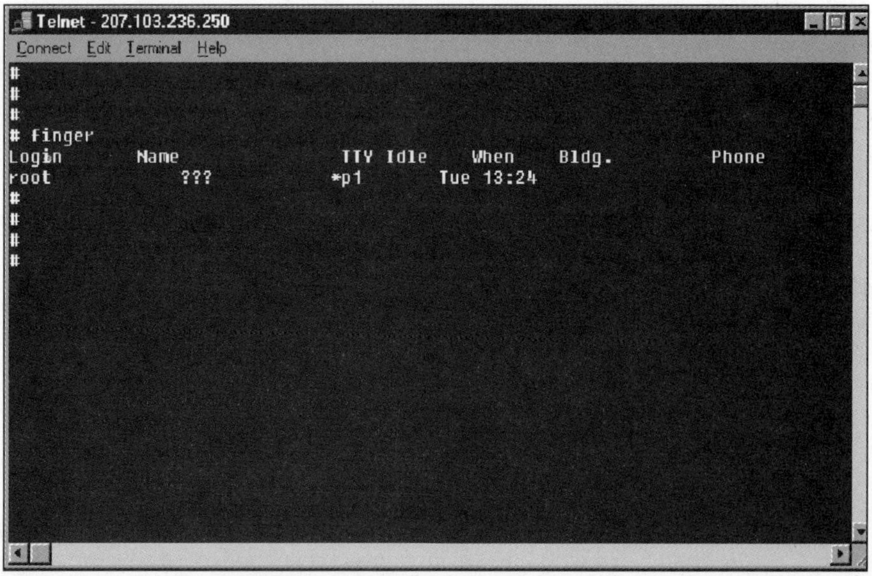

Figure 17-1: finger tells us here that the superuser logged into this machine at 1:23 PM, but hasn't done much more since then.

write

Should a particular user's DBMS-related processes use an inordinate amount of system resources, you can, of course, kill those processes. But to do so without first notifying the user in question of what you're about to do risks, and rightfully so, that user's wrath. Inform the user of what's about to go down (groans accepted and appreciated) with the `write` command.

If you know either the username under which an individual logged in or the terminal to which the user is connected, you can send that user a message with `write`.

For example, to send a message to the system administrator of your Linux server, you could take these steps.

1. At the shell prompt, type:

   `write root`

   and then press Enter.

2. On the next line, type your message; use as many lines as needed, separating them by pressing the Enter key.

3. When you've completed your missive, press Enter one more time.

4. On the resulting blank line, press the keystroke combination **<CTRL>D** to end the write session and return to the shell prompt.

Figure 17-2 illustrates such a sequence of steps.

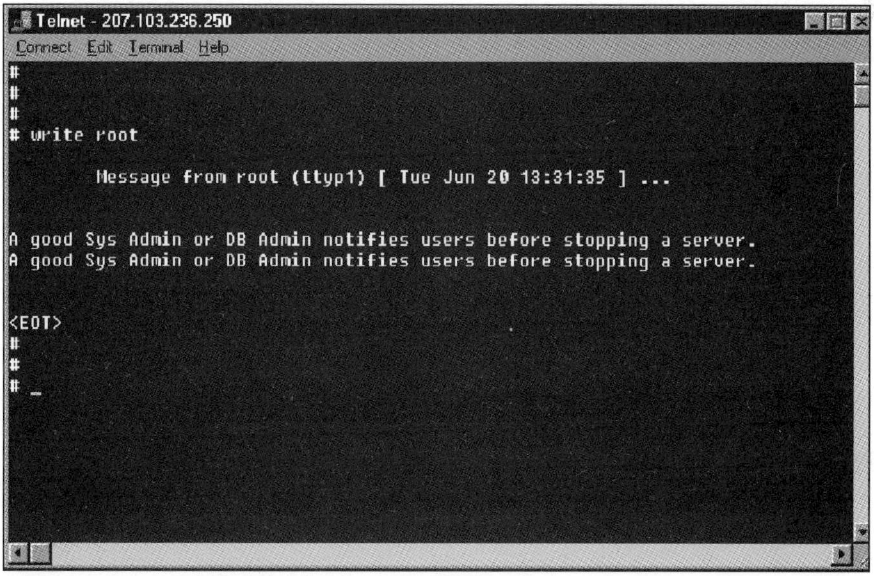

Figure 17-2: I was logged in as root. That's why I saw each line of this write message twice — once as I typed it, and again as I received it.

Managing the file system

The efficient functioning of any DBMS depends perhaps even more heavily than that of other applications on well-managed file storage and I/O. This section reviews these Linux file system management commands:

- ✦ fsck
- ✦ df
- ✦ mount
- ✦ umount

fsck

fsck monitors and repairs Linux file systems on any storage device identified to the OS as containing either character- or block-special files. This means that fsck can help any file systems associated with any storage medium listed in the /dev directory stay healthy.

If fsck finds a file system to be sound, it simply reports:

- ✦ The number of files the file system contains
- ✦ The number of used and free blocks the file system includes

If, on the other hand, fsck detects problems with a file system, it provides the means of repairing the file system.

Tip   On most Linux systems, fsck runs automatically when the machine boots, and at predefined intervals thereafter as long as the machine remains booted. fsck can only be run from the command line by the user root. Under some Linux flavors, however, fsck cannot be run from the command line, even by root, unless the machine is in single-user mode.

You can identify file systems that you wish fsck to check in several ways:

- ✦ By specifying a device name such as /dev/hda1
- ✦ By specifying a mount point such as /home
- ✦ By providing an ext2 volume label, such as LABEL=root

Assuming you're in single-user mode, use a command similar to the following to check all file systems in an interactive fashion, that is, with the opportunity to confirm or forgo each check:

```
fsck -V
```

More Detail on fsck

fsck returns an exit code that represents the sum of any of the following conditions that might exist at the time of the check:

0	no errors
1	file system errors corrected
2	system should be rebooted
4	file system errors not corrected
8	operator error
16	syntax error
128	library error

Naturally, a return code of 0 would be the most desirable.

Or you can use this command to check suitability for mounting:

```
fsck -m
```

Other useful fsck options are:

✦ -A—Causes fsck to try to check all file systems in one pass

✦ -N—Causes fsck simply to display what it would do, but not actually to carry out those actions

✦ -R—Causes fsck to forgo checking the root file system when checking all file systems because the -A option has been supplied

df

df displays the number of free disk blocks and free inodes available for file systems. df gets its statistics from counts kept in the superblock or superblocks. If you specify no argument to df, the command simply reports free space on all mounted file systems.

To report and categorize free disk space across an entire Linux machine, use this command:

```
df
```

Doing so produces output with one line similar to that below for every file system configured on the platform:

```
/home (/dev/vg00/lvol4): 359278 blocks 78969 i-nodes
```

Of course, numbers and file system names vary from machine to machine.

To report on free disk space within a specific file system, use a command similar to this:

```
df /var
```

Tip

If you give pathnames as arguments to df, it reports on the file systems containing the paths, not on those paths.

If you give df the name of an unmounted file system as an argument, it reports the last known amount of free space in the unmounted file system.

mount and umount

When a Linux system boots, it makes all basic file systems accessible. But to Linux, "basic" ordinarily only includes file systems on a hard drive. To make file systems on devices such as a CD-ROM or a diskette available, those drives must be associated with an area of the overall file system; in Linux parlance, they must be mounted.

mount

Imagine you must use vi to edit a text file on a diskette. Imagine further that the diskette was formatted, and the text file created, under a Microsoft operating system. Neither circumstance flusters Linux. A command similar to the following can make your diskette and the files it holds ready for use:

```
mount /dev/fd0 /mnt/floppy
```

This syntax assumes:

✦ The correct designation for the 3.5-inch, 1.44-MB disk drive is /dev/fd0

✦ There is a mount point within the Linux file system called /mnt

✦ There is a subdirectory of /mnt called /floppy

umount

Now let's suppose you've completed your edits, and no longer wish to have the diskette or disk drive accessible. To prevent the drive from being used, type a command similar to this:

```
umount /dev/fd0
```

Tip

To use umount to preclude access to a drive, you must ensure that the medium, whether diskette or CD-ROM, remains in the drive and that your current directory is not the directory under which you accessed the drive. In other words, you may have to use cd to change your current directory before you can use umount.

Miscellaneous or intermittent tasks

This section examines OS maintenance that need only be performed at random or fluctuating intervals.

Reviewing and trimming logs

Linux and Linux DBMS log files can grow at rates approaching the exponential. Allowing such logs to remain unweeded can, over time, choke a server. Several of the OS's simplest commands, however, can help preclude that happening.

ls

With its -1 option, ls can report the size of individual files or of groups of files. For example, if you need to determine the size of a DBMS log file called somedb.log, you could use this command (if the file lies outside the current directory, you need to supply the full pathname):

```
ls -l somedb.log
```

Or, should you need to know the sizes of all log files, you might use this syntax:

```
ls -l *.log
```

wc

As another means of monitoring the growth of DBMS or any other log files, you might use the command wc, or word count. To determine the number of individual bytes in a given file, use syntax similar to this:

```
wc -c some_file
```

To find out how many words a file contains, use a command similar to this:

```
wc -w a_file
```

To learn the number of lines a file contains, use a command similar to this:

```
wc -l another_file
```

To see simultaneously all the information wc provides, use this syntax:

```
wc onemore_file
```

Tip   wc can report on more than just text files; for instance, it will deal with executables without complaint. But in most cases, it makes little sense to use wc in this way.

head

Imagine you wish to retain the first 50 lines of a database log file, and then want to delete that file. In such circumstances, you can use the command head to transfer those lines to another filename. You can tell head how many lines, or even characters, you'd like to see or to transfer. Table 17-9 summarizes head.

<table>
<tr><th colspan="2">Table 17-9
head's Syntax</th></tr>
<tr><th>Parameter</th><th>Effect</th></tr>
<tr><td>-c</td><td>Specifies number of bytes to display</td></tr>
<tr><td>-l</td><td>Specifies number of lines to display</td></tr>
<tr><td>-n x</td><td>Specifies number of characters or lines to display</td></tr>
</table>

Tip If you provide no number to it, head assumes ten characters or lines.

A command similar to that below would preserve 50 lines of our imaginary database log file, preparatory to removing that file.

```
head -l -n50 db_log > db_log_new
```

Tip The formats head -l -n some_integer **and** head -some_integer **produce identical results.**

tail

head's mirror image, so to speak, is the command tail, which reproduces from a file's end, or, with appropriate syntax, from any area of a file, as Table 17-10 outlines.

<table>
<tr><th colspan="2">Table 17-10
tail's Syntax</th></tr>
<tr><th>Parameter</th><th>Effect</th></tr>
<tr><td>-b number</td><td>Specifies number of blocks to be reproduced reproduce from the bottom of a file</td></tr>
<tr><td>-c number</td><td>Specifies number of bytes to be reproduced from the bottom of a file</td></tr>
<tr><td>number</td><td>Specifies the actual number of characters or lines tail must reproduce</td></tr>
</table>

Tip Like head, tail reproduces what it finds. Nothing in its input file is altered from the original.

A command similar to this gives a look at the last 13 lines of a file:

```
tail -13 bakersdozen
```

This command displays the last 100 characters in a file:

```
tail -c 100 century
```

Finally, a command similar to this reproduces the final nine blocks of a file:

```
tail -b 9 innings
```

Notifying users before rebooting the system

Before bringing a Linux database server down, users should be made aware of what's about to happen. Perhaps the most efficient way of doing this involves using the OS command wall.

wall resembles write, but wall sends *individual copies* of the same message to *all* currently logged-in users. As a result, it's the ideal tool for informing them of things such as imminent shutdowns.

For example, you could notify users in advance that a system was about to be brought down with a command such as that illustrated in Figure 17-3.

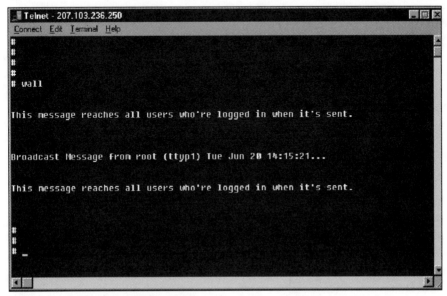

Figure 17-3: The message says it all.

Shutting down and rebooting

The following advice on shutting down a Linux server comes from something of an authority in software development — CERN (the birthplace of such things as HTTP and HTML).

To shut down a machine from its own console, follow these steps:

1. Press the Ctrl, Alt, and F6 keys simultaneously.

2. As a result, you should see a login prompt. Log in as root, and then issue this command:

   `/sbin/halt`

You can also perform this sequence via telnet.

Caution   As the folks at CERN and so many others caution, never power down a Linux machine without first halting it.

Or, you can gracefully halt a Linux system with any of the syntax for the `shutdown` command outlined in Table 17-11.

Table 17-11 shutdown's Syntax	
Syntax	**Effect**
`shutdown -h +6 Server coming down in 6 minutes; log off. please.`	Shuts system down in the specified number of minutes. Displays the indicated message before shutting down.
`shutdown -r now`	Shuts down and reboots immediately.
`shutdown now`	Shuts down, that is, goes to single-user mode or runlevel 1, immediately.

Adding user accounts

The simplest way to add a new user to a Linux system involves using the command `adduser`. To do so, however, you must be logged in as the superuser. Assuming that's the case, just use a command similar to this:

`adduser user_name`

Linux responds by prompting for all information needed to set up an account for the specified individual.

Requirements for Linux Passwords

Under most Linux implementations, passwords must fulfill these criteria:

Length of at least six characters

Characters are from the ASCII character set, with letters being from the English alphabet only

Character mix must be at least two letters (either upper- or lowercase), and at least one numeric or special character (such as % or .) interval before changing password; this is system-specific

Life of password, which is system-specific, must be set

On those Linux systems on which password life has been enabled, a password dies after a predefined period of time, and an account whose password has died is locked until the system administrator re-enables it and must have a new password defined for it even after being reactivated.

Modifying user accounts (passwords)

Usually, modifying a user account means changing that user's password. Do so with a command similar to this:

```
passwd user_name
```

Linux responds by prompting for the existing password, the new password, and confirmation of the new password.

User profiles

Linux systems provide two means of defining user profiles:

✦ Systemwide profiles, stored in the file /etc/profile

✦ User-specific profiles, stored in each user's home directory in a file called, simply and logically, .profile

Whether they're global, that is, systemwide, or user-specific, the contents of a profile execute when you first log in to Linux, and only then. In addition, session traits specified by systemwide profiles can be overridden by those defined in user-specific profiles.

To make any changes in the systemwide profile, you must:

✦ Log in as the superuser

✦ Have write permission on /etc/profile

If both these are true, then follow these steps to make changes in the systemwide profile:

1. Open /etc/profile in any text editor.

2. Navigate to the record that controls the characteristics that you wish to change, and make your changes.

3. Save your changes and exit the editor.

Tip   Linux offers another, similar type of file, called an rc file, which defines the initial functional characteristics, not of user sessions, but of programs. The most significant of these, .bashrc, gives the Bourne shell, the default text-based interface for many of the most important Linux implementations, its startup personality.

To change any of the information in a user-specific profile, you must:

✦ Log in either as the superuser or as the user whose profile will be modified

✦ Have write permission to the file whose contents will change

If both these are true, you can do the following:

1. Open the appropriate .profile file in any text editor.

2. Navigate to the record, which controls the characteristics that you wish to change, and make your changes.

3. Save your changes and exit the editor.

Scheduling with cron

While Linux offers several ways to schedule jobs, the most flexible and powerful relies on the utility cron.

Understanding cron means understanding its scheduling file, called crontab, which usually resides in the /etc directory.

An excerpt from a typical, albeit hypothetical, crontab file looks similar to this:

```
0 12 * * 1-4 /usr/flash/new_script
0 14 * * 2-6 /usr/kg/another_script
0 23 * * 3-5 /home/dbase/sql some_query
```

Table 17-12 outlines the significance of the six colon-separated fields in every record in a crontab file.

	Table 17-12 crontab File Field Meanings	

Field	Meaning
first	Minute at which a job will be scheduled; must be specified as an integer in the range 0 to 59
second	Hour at which a job will be scheduled; must be specified as an integer in the range 0 to 23, with 0 representing midnight
third	Date of the month at which a job will be scheduled; must be specified as an integer in the range 1 to 31
fourth	Month at which a job will be scheduled; must be specified as an integer in the range 1 to 12
fifth	Day of the week at which a job will be scheduled; must be specified as an integer in the range 0 to 6, with 0 indicating Sunday
sixth	Command to run at the indicated schedule indicated in the first five fields

Given these meanings, the line:

```
0 12 * * 1-4 /usr/flash/new_script
```

will run the specified shell script exactly at noon every date of every month, as long as the day of the week in question is any of Monday through Thursday.

Tip   Like many significant Linux system files, the crontab file contains only ASCII text, and can therefore be edited with any Linux text editor, if you have the appropriate access privileges. When you edit crontab, in effect you schedule a job, because the cron utility runs as a daemon in background under most Linux implementations. As a result, there's no need and no way to launch cron from the command line.

Scheduling with at

To run a batch job only once, use the Linux command `at`. For instance, you could use a command sequence similar to the following to monitor early morning login attempts at random.

```
at 12:45 tomorrow
who -u > next_day_log
<CTRL> D
at 12:57 next week
who -u > next_week_log
<CTRL> D
```

This series of commands tells Linux:

✦ To schedule a job for 12:45 a.m. tomorrow, whatever date or day of the week that might be

✦ That it should run the `who` command at that time, placing output in the indicated file in the current directory

✦ To schedule a job for 12:57 a.m. one week from today, whatever date or day of the week that happens to be

✦ That it should run the `who` command at that time, placing output in the indicated file in the current directory

Scheduling with batch

The Linux command `batch` instructs the OS to run something as its workload permits, that is, in background, even if the user who launched batch logs out. Imagine, for example, that you're given a very large file to sort, only minutes before you're due to leave the workplace for the day. You can turn to batch to resolve this potentially sticky situation, with a group of commands similar to this:

```
batch
sort wotta_big_file > sorted
<CTRL> D
```

This sequence instructs Linux to:

✦ Sort, in ascending ASCII order and line by line, the file wotta_big_file, placing the sorted output in a file called sorted in the current directory

✦ Work on this job as available CPU time permits

Database Administration

While managing a Linux DBMS often means interacting with the OS rather than the application suite, some database-specific administration tools do exist. This section discusses several categories of such tools, covering common DBMS management tasks such as:

✦ Creating, dropping, or dumping databases

✦ Importing and exporting

I examine each of these categories for the Open Source Linux DBMSs featured in this book:

✦ MySQL

✦ PostgreSQL

✦ MySQL: Dumping a database

The utility mysqldump dumps the contents of one or more MySQL databases in preparation for backing up and transferring to another MySQL server.

Three personalities exist for mysqldump:

```
# mysqldump [OPTIONS] database [tables]
# mysqldump [OPTIONS] --databases [OPTIONS] DB1 [DB2 DB3...]
# mysqldump [OPTIONS] --all-databases [OPTIONS]
```

Table 17-13 summarizes these variants.

Table 17-13 mysqldump Syntax	
Syntax	**Effect**
`# mysqldump [OPTIONS] database [tables]`	Dumps the contents of the indicated database or tables, with option-defined behavior if desired
`# mysqldump [OPTIONS] --databases [OPTIONS] DB1 [DB2 DB3...]`	Dumps the contents of the indicated databases, with option-defined behavior if desired
`# mysqldump [OPTIONS] --all-databases [OPTIONS]`	Dumps the contents of all databases, with option-defined behavior if desired

mysqldump's most significant options are:

✦ `--add-locks` — Locks tables before and unlocks tables after each table dump; provides faster inserts

✦ `--all-databases` — Dumps all databases

✦ `--allow-keywords` — Creates column names that include keywords; functions by causing mysqldump to begin each column name with the appropriate table name

✦ `--compress` — Compresses all information that passes between client and server; assumes both client and server support compression

✦ `--databases` — Dumps specific databases; does not require table names (all arguments function as database names)

✦ `--flush-logs` — Flushes all MySQL log files before starting the dump

✦ `--force` — Completes the dump even if SQL errors occur during it

✦ `--host=` *named host* — Dumps from the active MySQL server to the named host

✦ `--lock-tables` — Locks all tables before beginning the dump

✦ `--no-data`—Writes no row information; useful when seeking only a schema dump

✦ `--password=`*`password`*—Connects to the mysql server with the permissions associated with the supplied password before beginning the dump

✦ `--quick`—Carries out dump without buffering; dumps directly to standard output

✦ `--user=`*<u>username</u>*—Connects to the MySQL server as the indicated user before doing the dump; default for username: operating system login name of current user

✦ `--where='`*`condition`*`'`—Dumps only those records specified by the condition stated in the where clause, whose single quotes are required

Tip

You can use the `where` option of mysqldump to do an off-the-cuff query, while at the same time you transfer retrieved records to another MySQL database, by using syntax similar to this:

```
mysqldump --database_of_gardening --
where=plant_name='zinnia' | mysql
--host=far_away_machine -C db_of_gardening
```

MySQL: Importing text files

mysqlimport, the command-line interface to MySQL's LOAD DATA statement, accepts options one might expect to use with that statement. mysqlimport uses this general syntax:

```
# mysqlimport [options] database ASCII file 1 [ASCII file 2]
[ASCII file 3]
```

Tip

Because mysqlimport strips off any extension from the name of a file to be imported, and uses the result to decide which table in the indicated database will receive the text file's contents, you must exercise caution in naming files to the utility. For example, if you want to import data from a file called cookies.txt into a table called comestibles, you must first rename the text file to comestibles.txt.

mysqlimport's most significant options are:

✦ `-C` or `--compress`—Compresses all information as it moves between client and server; assumes that both support compression.

✦ `-d` or `--delete`—Deletes all existing data from a table before importing text file.

✦ `-f` or `--force`—Ignores errors such as those generated by a text file not having a corresponding, preexisting table in a database. When used with `-f` or `--force`, mysqlimport attempts to continue the import with the next available text file. Without `-f` or `--force`, mysqlimport exits if a table doesn't exist to receive the contents of a text file.

✦ -h host_name or --host=*host name*—Imports to the MySQL server on the host indicated by the *host name* parameter

✦ -i or --ignore—Does not import input records whose key fields' values duplicate those of existing records

✦ -L or --local—Uses only local input files, that is, files residing on the active MySQL client. Use this option to override mysqlimport's default behavior of obtaining text files from the MySQL server on the default host (the machine specified by the OS parameter localhost).

✦ -l or --lock-tables—Disables write operations to tables before importing text files. Ensures that all tables on the server are synchronized (that is, contain identical data).

✦ -r or --replace—Replaces existing rows whose key fields values are duplicated in those input records with the corresponding input records.

The following code sample:

✦ Uses mysql to create an empty database called pets and a table in that database into which the contents of a text file can be placed

✦ Uses mysqlimport to populate that table and database with five records from the ASCII file felines.txt

```
$ mysql -e 'CREATE TABLE felines (id INT, name VARCHAR(20))'
pets
$ mysqlimport-local pets felines.txt
pets.felines: Records: 5  Deleted: 0  Skipped: 0  Warnings: 0
```

Assume that felines.txt contains these records:

```
001     Sy
002     Cuddles
003     Fuzzbucket
004     Harry
005     WheeleyBoy
```

An inquiry of the newly created and loaded table would produce the following results. In this example, MySQL output is distinguished from the command you enter by italicizing the former.

```
$ mysql -e 'SELECT * FROM trek_good_guys' trek_trivia
+------+---------------+
| id   | name          |
+------+---------------+
| 001  | Sy |
| 002  | Cuddles |
| 003  | Fuzzbucket |
| 004  | Harry |
| 005  | WheeleyBoy |
+------+---------------+
```

Delving Deeper into mysqlshow

Be aware that, if you supply:

✦ No database name to mysqlshow, information on all matching databases will be displayed

✦ No table name to mysqlshow, information on all matching tables in the indicated or in all databases will be displayed

✦ No column name to mysqlshow, information on all matching columns and column types in the indicated or in all tables will be displayed

Note also that in the most recent versions of MySQL, mysqlshow will display information only on databases, tables, and columns for which you have the necessary read privilege.

MySQL: Database summary information

MySQL's command-line utility mysqlshow presents a précis of existing databases and their tables, and of those tables' columns or fields.

Launch mysqlshow with generalized syntax similar to this:

```
$ mysqlshow [OPTIONS] [database [table [column]]]
```

PostgreSQL: Dumping a database

PostgreSQL provides two utilities that dump database contents. The first of these, pg_dump, places the contents of a PostgreSQL database into a script file, that is, an ASCII file that contains query commands and can therefore be used to reconstruct a database, on the local or some other host. The second, pg_dumpall, outputs the contents of all PostgreSQL databases.

pg_dump

pg_dump generates queries that, in turn, recreate all user-defined types, functions, tables, indices, aggregates, and operators. pg_dump then copies out all data as text so that it can be copied in again easily, or even dumped into a text editor for further massaging.

pg_dump's generic syntax has two forms:

```
pg_dump [ dbname ]
pg_dump [ -h host ] [ -p port ] [ -t table ] [ -a ] [ -s ] [
-u ] [ -x ] [ dbname ]
```

Table 17-14 illustrates these forms.

Table 17-14
pg_dump Syntax

Example	Effect
`pg_dump martial_arts`	Dumps both contents and schema of the database martial_arts to standard output
`pg_dump -a jackie_chan`	Dumps only the contents, and not the schema, of the database jackie_chan to standard output
`pg_dump -s jet_li`	Dumps only the schema, and not the data, of the database jet_li to standard output
`pg_dump -t postures tai_chi`	Dumps only the schema and data of the table postures in the database tai_chi to standard output
`pg_dump -t postures -u tai_chi`	Dumps only the schema and data of the table postures in the database tai_chi to standard output, after prompting for a PostgreSQL user name and password
`pg_dump -t postures -x tai_chi`	Dumps only the schema and data of the table postures in the database tai_chi to standard output, but withholds any user- or permission-related information from the dump

Tip   However you structure its command line, pg_dump can write either to an ASCII file or to standard output, as these examples demonstrate:

```
% pg_dump
% pg_dump > dump_out
```

pg_dumpall
pg_dumpall does just what its name suggests — it dumps all existing PostgreSQL databases into a single script file. As a result, it does not recognize the arguments `dbname` or `-t table`. However, its remaining syntax and behavior duplicate those of pg_dump. Also as a result, it should be used with caution.

PostgreSQL: Importing text files
In the same way that it uses the Linux concept of redirecting output to place the results of a dump in an ASCII file, PostgreSQL uses the OS technique of redirecting input to import previously dumped information.

Assume that you've created a text file called native_tribes by using this command:

```
% pg_dump > native_tribes
```

To import this data into another, new database, you can use a command similar to this:

```
% psql -e indigenous < native_tribes
```

PostgreSQL: Displaying database summary information

PostgreSQL provides the utility vacuumdb to clean or to analyze a PostgreSQL database. vacuumdb's generalized syntax in its most usable form, and as it pertains to such analysis, looks similar to this:

```
vacuumdb [ --analyze | -z ] [ --alldb | -a ] [ --table 'table [
( column [,...] ) ]' ] [dbname ]
```

Table 17-15 elaborates on this syntax.

Table 17-15 vacuumdb Database Analysis Syntax	
Example	**Effect**
$ vacuumdb ---analyze pgh_pirates	Gathers statistics on the database pgh_pirates; those statistics can then be used by the PostgreSQL optimizer
$ vacuumdb --analyze -alldb	Gathers statistics on all databases on the local host
$ vacuumdb --analyze -table "infielders(position)" pgh_pirates	Gathers statistics only for the column position in the table infielders of the database pgh_pirates
$ vacuumdb -h mit -analyze doctoral_candidates	Gathers statistics for the database doctoral_candidates running on the remote machine whose host name is mit

Tip   If vacuumdb displays the message VACUUM, it encountered no problems during its analysis. If, on the other hand, it displays vacuumdb: Vacuum failed., something clearly did not compute. To debug such situations, check and if necessary adjust database, table, and column permissions.

As the table above suggests, vacuumdb can be very useful to a Linux DBMS administrator.

Summary

Managing any Linux DBMS requires you to be proficient with:

✦ The operating system commands find, ls, tar, and cpio for backups

✦ The operating system commands kill, netstat, nice, ps, and top for monitoring and managing server status and performance

✦ The operating system commands `finger`, `wall`, `who`, and `write` for monitoring user activities

✦ The operating system commands `df`, `fsck`, `mount`, and `umount` for managing the Linux DBMS's file system

✦ The operating system commands `head`, `tail`, and `wc` for monitoring and managing DBMS logs

✦ DBMS commands such as `mysqlimport`, `mysqlshow`, `pg_dump`, and `vacuumdb` for carrying out DBMS-specific tasks such as importing text files or viewing summary information about a database

✦   ✦   ✦

Security and Disaster Recovery

This chapter discusses the most significant aspects of security and disaster prevention and recovery techniques for Linux-based databases.

Security Tools

Ensuring the security of data requires a concerted, coordinated effort by both management and IT staff. This section outlines the major components of such an effort.

Corporate policy statements

In implementing a corporate security policy, these issues must be addressed:

✦ Determining requirements for policies

✦ Achieving consensus on security objectives

✦ Involving all levels of staff in creating and implementing the policy

✦ Policy format

✦ Policy components

✦ Ensuring proper accountability for security

✦ Policy review, approval, and implementation

✦ Techniques to streamline policy implementation and to ensure acceptance

✦ Techniques for policy enforcement

An example of a corporate security policy statement follows. While this statement addresses only electronic messaging, it can serve as a template for a more broad-based security policy.

This example addresses several of the points noted above, in that it:

✦ Uses clear and readily understandable language

✦ Specifies policy components

✦ Helps to ensure accountability by requiring employees to read, sign, and date the policy statement

✦ Helps to streamline implementation and acceptance by the same means

✦ Helps to ensure policy enforcement by the same means

A Sample Real-World Usage Policy

Computer systems and other technical resources are provided by the Company for the use of the Company and are to be reviewed, monitored, and used in the pursuit of the Company's business. As a result, computer data is readily available to numerous persons. If, during the course of your employment, you perform or transmit work on the Company's computers or other technical resources, your work may be subject to the view of others.

The use of the Company's electronic communication or e-mail in any manner that may be disruptive, offensive to others, or harmful to morale is specifically prohibited. This includes, but is not limited to, the display or transmission of sexually explicit images, messages, and cartoons, as well as the use of any ethnic slurs or communication that may be construed as harassment or disparagement of others. The use of e-mail to solicit or proselytize others for commercial ventures, religious or political causes, outside organizations or other non-job-related solicitations is strictly forbidden. Searches of e-mail may be conducted without advance notice in order to ensure that the purpose of e-mail — to facilitate transmittal of business-related information — is being used exclusively for such purpose.

Rules of ethical conduct and nondiscriminatory behavior also apply to Internet usage. Use of the Internet to send offensive or improper messages (such as racial or sexual slurs) or to solicit outside business ventures, to leak confidential information to outsiders or for personal, political, or religious causes is prohibited. Because all possible actions cannot be contemplated, the list is necessarily incomplete. Thus, disciplinary action may occur after other actions when the circumstances warrant it.

I have read and understand the Corporate Policy Statement set forth above and agree to abide by such Corporate Policy Statement. I further understand that a violation of this policy may be grounds for disciplinary action, up to and including termination of employment.

[Name of employee, signature, department, and date.]

Database auditing procedures

This section sketches database auditing procedures pertaining to

+ Oracle8*i*
+ MySQL

Note The word *sketches* is apt. Covering these topics extensively for even one of these DBMSs requires a book in itself. Only the most important overview-level information is presented here. For further detail, consult your DBMS documentation.

Oracle8*i* auditing

This section outlines Oracle Corporation's

+ General guidelines for database auditing
+ Suggestions regarding deciding upon what goes into an audit
+ Suggested techniques for creating and deleting database audit trails
+ Suggestions for managing audit information
+ General information regarding audit options
+ Managing the size of the audit trail

General auditing guidelines

In the data dictionary of every Oracle8*i* database, is a table called SYS.AUD$. It's this table to which Oracle8*i* documentation refers when it talks about a database audit trail. While either Oracle8*i* itself or its operating system platform can act as the repository for database-auditing information, not all operating systems support database auditing directed to an operating system audit trail. Therefore, this section considers only DBMS-housed auditing.

Using a database audit trail has several advantages, including:

+ It provides the ability to view selected portions of an audit trail with predefined views made available in an Oracle8*i* data dictionary.
+ Oracle tools such as Oracle Reports can be used to generate audit reports.

Deciding what to audit

In deciding what to audit, be conservative. Auditing doesn't unduly stress server resources, but some overhead does exist. To minimize the impact of this overhead on more normal, end-user-initiated DBMS processes and to limit the size of the audit trail created, limit the number of audited events.

For example, suppose you want to investigate suspicious database activity. An effective approach might be to audit unauthorized deletions from specific tables in a database, rather than to perform a blanket audit of all deletions, or, more demanding still, of all database activity.

Oracle Corporation also recommends auditing only the minimum number of statements, users, or objects required to get desired information. In other words, as Oracle8*i* documentation so succinctly and aptly phrases it, *balance your need to gather sufficient security information with your ability to store and process it.*

When auditing for suspicious database activity, protect the audit trail so that audit information cannot be added, changed, or deleted without being audited. On the other hand, if you audit for historical purposes only, after collecting the required information, archive the audit records of interest and purge the audit trail of this information.

Creating and deleting database audit trail views

SYS.AUD$, the single table in every Oracle database's data dictionary to which auditing information flows, requires that several predefined views be activated in order for auditing to proceed. You can create these auditing views by:

1. Connecting to the Oracle8*i* server and to the database to be audited as the user SYS

2. Running the script CATAUDIT.SQL, which creates these views:

```
ALL_DEF_AUDIT_OPTS
AUDIT_ACTIONS
DBA_AUDIT_EXISTS
DBA_STMT_AUDIT_OPTS
STMT_AUDIT_OPTION_MAP
USER_AUDIT_OBJECT, DBA_AUDIT_OBJECT
USER_AUDIT_SESSION, DBA_AUDIT_SESSION
USER_AUDIT_SESSION, DBA_AUDIT_SESSION
USER_AUDIT_STATEMENT, DBA_AUDIT_STATEMENT
USER_AUDIT_TRAIL, DBA_AUDIT_TRAIL
USER_OBJ_AUDIT_OPTS, DBA_OBJ_AUDIT_OPTS
USER_TAB_AUDIT_OPTS
```

Similarly, you can disable auditing and delete audit trail views by

1. Connecting to the Oracle8*i* server and to the database to be audited as the user SYS

2. Running the script file CATNOAUD.SQL

Tip   The full pathname of CATNOAUD.SQL depends upon the OS platform on which you loaded Oracle8*i*.

Managing audit trail information

Depending on events audited and auditing options chosen, SYS.AUD$ records can contain various types of information. But these records always include certain types of information, such as:

✦ Username

✦ Session identifier

✦ Terminal identifier

✦ Name of the object accessed

✦ Operation performed or attempted

✦ Completion code of the operation

✦ Date and time stamp

What's more, and regardless of whether database auditing has been enabled, an Oracle8*i* server always audits certain database-related actions into the operating system audit trail, that is, into the process status information monitored and reported by the OS command ps. These actions include:

Instance startup	Details the OS user starting the instance, the user's terminal identifier, the date and time stamp at which the instance was started, and whether database auditing was enabled or disabled
Instance shutdown	Details the OS user shutting down the instance, the user's terminal identifier, and the date and time stamp at which the instance was shut down
Connections to the database with administrator privileges	Details the OS user connecting to Oracle8*i* as either of the DBMS users SYSOPER or SYSDBA; that is, it monitors users connecting with administrator privileges

Auditing options

Oracle8*i* enables you to set audit options at three levels:

Statement	Defines audits based on the type of an SQL statement. That is, it offers the capability to audit such actions as removing a table by auditing the DROP TABLE statement
Privilege	Defines audits that monitor specific privileges, such as the CREATE TABLE privilege
Object	Defines audits that focus on specific actions applied to specific objects, such as an attempt to run the ALTER TABLE statement on a table called trek_trivia

Enabling audit options

The SQL command AUDIT activates all three categories of Oracle8*i* audit options: statement, privilege, and object. Furthermore, when run to set statement or privilege audit options, the AUDIT command can include a clause, BY USER, which allows you to specify a list of users to whose activities the scope of the auditing will be confined.

To use the AUDIT command to set statement and privilege auditing options, you must have the Oracle8*i* AUDIT SYSTEM privilege. To use AUDIT to set object audit options, you must either own the object to be audited or have the AUDIT ANY privilege.

Caution   The AUDIT command defines and activates auditing options, but it does not enable auditing as a whole. To do that, one must set the parameter AUDIT_TRAIL in the database's parameter file, or run the script CATAUDIT.SQL.

Table 18-1 outlines and gives examples of setting common auditing options under Oracle8*i*.

Table 18-1 Setting Oracle8*i* Auditing Options	
Purpose	*Syntax*
To audit all successful and unsuccessful connections to and disconnections from the database, regardless of user, by session	AUDIT SESSION;
To audit all successful and unsuccessful connections to and disconnections from the database, by user as well as by session	AUDIT SESSION BY wheeley, goobie;
To audit all successful and unsuccessful uses of the DELETE ANY TABLE system privilege	AUDIT DELETE ANY TABLE;
To audit all unsuccessful SELECT, INSERT, and DELETE statements on all tables by all database users as well as by access	AUDIT SELECT TABLE, INSERT TABLE, DELETE TABLE BY ACCESS WHENEVER NOT SUCCESSFUL;
To audit all successful and unsuccessful DELETE statements run against the table feline_breeds, by session	AUDIT DELETE ON feline_breeds;
To audit all successful SELECT, INSERT, and DELETE statements on the table LIFEMAKER owned by the user JHOGAN	AUDIT SELECT, INSERT, DELETE ON jhogan.lifemaker WHENEVER SUCCESSFUL;
To audit all unsuccessful SELECT statements	AUDIT SELECT ON DEFAULT WHENEVER NOT SUCCESSFUL;

Disabling audit options

The simple command NOAUDIT disables Oracle8*i* audit options. The following examples illustrate using NOAUDIT in a variety of circumstances:

```
NOAUDIT session;
NOAUDIT session BY clemente, stargell;
NOAUDIT DELETE ANY TABLE;
NOAUDIT SELECT TABLE, INSERT TABLE, DELETE TABLE
```

```
NOAUDIT DELETE ON bucs;
NOAUDIT SELECT, INSERT, DELETE ON hanh.peace;
NOAUDIT ALL ON emp;
```

Managing the size of the audit trail

Table 18-2 summarizes the Oracle8*i* commands needed to keep an audit trail's size manageable and reasonable.

Table 18-2
Managing Audit Trail Size

Purpose	Syntax
To delete all audit records from the audit trail	`DELETE FROM sys.aud$;`
To delete all audit records generated as a result of auditing the table SCI_FI from the audit trail	`DELETE FROM sys.aud$ WHERE obj$name='SCI_FI';`

Tip

To archive audit trail records for historical purposes, an Oracle8*i* administrator or user with administrator privileges can copy the records in question to another table, with a command sequence similar to

```
INSERT INTO some_table SELECT * FROM sys.aud$
```

and export the audit trail table to an operating system file.

Caution

Only the database user SYS, a database user who has the DELETE ANY TABLE privilege, a database user to whom the Oracle8*i* administrator SYS has granted DELETE privilege on SYS.AUD$, and can delete records from the database audit trail.

An auditing example

Assume you must audit an Oracle8*i* database for

✦ Unauthorized changes in passwords, tablespace settings, and quotas for some database users only

✦ Inordinately high numbers of deadlocks

✦ Unexplained deletions of records from a specific table in a specific user's schema

You, that is the Oracle8*i* administrator SYS, can accomplish your task with these commands, executed in the order shown:

```
AUDIT ALTER, INDEX, RENAME ON DEFAULT BY SESSION;
CREATE TABLE tommy.lbr;
CREATE VIEW tommy.books AS SELECT * FROM tommy.lbr;
AUDIT ALTER USER;
AUDIT LOCK TABLE BY ACCESS WHENEVER SUCCESSFUL;
AUDIT DELETE ON tommy.lbr BY ACCESS WHENEVER SUCCESSFUL;
```

MySQL

MySQL's auditing capabilities enable you to derive detailed information regarding tables and to monitor the efficiency of queries.

Getting information on a table

Use the command `myisamchk` and some of its options to create table descriptions or statistics. Table 18-3 summarizes `myisamchk` syntax.

<table>
<tr><td colspan="3" align="center">Table 18-3
myisamchk Syntax</td></tr>
<tr><td>Syntax</td><td>Function</td><td>Example Output</td></tr>
<tr>
<td><code>myisamchk -d some table</code></td>
<td>Describe mode: produces a description of the named table</td>
<td>

MyISAM file: companv.MYI

Record format: Fixed length

Data records: 1403698 Deleted blocks: 0

Recordlength: 226

table description:

Key Start Len Index Type

1 2 8 unique double

2 15 10 multip. text packed stripped

3 219 8 multip. double

4 63 10 multip. text packed stripped

5 167 2 multip. unsigned short

6 177 4 multip. unsigned long

7 155 4 multip. text

8 138 4 multip. unsigned long

9 177 4 multip. unsigned long

193 1 text

</td>
</tr>
<tr>
<td><code>myisamchk -d -v some_ table</code></td>
<td>Produces a verbose description; that is, a description of the named table that identifies each item as it is displayed</td>
<td></td>
</tr>
</table>

Syntax	Function	Example Output
`myisamchk -eis some_table`	Shows only the most important information about the named table. Slow; it reads the whole table	Checking MyISAM file: company
		Key: 1: Keyblocks used: 97% Packed: 0% Max levels: 4
		Kev: 2: Kevblocks used: 98% Packed: 50% Max levels: 4
		Key: 3: Keyblocks used: 97% Packed: 0% Max levels: 4
		Key: 4: Keyblocks used: 99% Packed: 60% Max levels: 3
		Key: 5: Keyblocks used: 99% Packed: 0% Max levels: 3
		Key: 6: Keyblocks used: 99% Packed: 0% Max levels: 3
		Key: 7: Keyblocks used: 99% Packed: 0% Max levels: 3
		Key: 8: Keyblocks used: 99% Packed: 0% Max levels: 3
		Key: 9: Keyblocks used: 98% Packed: 0% Max levels: 4
		Total: Keyblocks used: 98% Packed: 17%
		Records: 1403698 M.recordlength: 226 Packed: 0%
		Recordspace used: 100% Empty space: 0% Blocks/Record: 1.00
		Record blocks: 1403698 Delete blocks: 0
		Recorddata: 317235748 Deleted data: 0
		Lost space: 0 Linkdata: 0
		User time 1626.51, System time 232.36
		Maximum resident set size 0, Integral resident set size 0
		Non physical pagefaults 0, Physical pagefaults 627, Swaps 0
		Blocks in 0 out 0, Messages in 0 out 0, Signals 0
		Voluntary context switches 639, Involuntary context switches 28966

Continued

Table 18-3 *(continued)*

Syntax	Function	Example Output
`myisamchk -eiv some_table`	Shows only the most important information about the named table and identifies each item as it is displayed	

Table 18-4 elaborates on the most significant of the information `myisamchk` produces.

Table 18-4
Understanding myisamchk Output

Parameter	Significance
Keyfile	index file
ISAM file	Name of the ISAM (index) file
Isam-version	Version of ISAM format
Creation time	When the data file was created
Recover time	When the index/data file was last reconstructed
Data records	How many data records the table contains
Deleted blocks	How many deleted blocks retain reserved space
Datafile: Parts	Indicates total number of data blocks. In an optimized table without fragmented records, equals the number of data records
Deleted data	Total bytes of non-reclaimed deleted data
Datafile pointer	Size of the data file pointer, in bytes; usually 2, 3, 4, or 5. For fixed tables, serves as a record address; for dynamic tables, is a byte address
Keyfile pointer	Size of the index file pointer, in bytes; always a block address
Max datafile length	How long the table's data file, that is, the .MYD file, can become, in bytes
Max keyfile length	How long the table's key file, that is, the .MYI file, can become, in bytes
Recordlength	Actual space each record takes, in bytes
Record format	Format used to store table rows. Can be any of Fixed, Compressed, or Packed

Parameter	Significance
Key	A given key's unique number
Start	Where in the record an index part starts
Len	How long an index part is
Index	Whether or not a value can be duplicated for an index. Possible values: unique or multiple
Type	Data-type of index. An ISAM data-type with the possible values packed, stripped or empty
Root	Address of the root index block
Blocksize	Size of each index block; default 1024 bytes
Rec/key	A statistical value used by the optimizer; indicates how many records there are per value for this key
Keyblocks used	Percentage of the keyblocks used
Packed	Whether or not MySQL has been successful in its default practice of packing keys of CHAR, VARCHAR, or DECIMAL fields, which keys have a common suffix
Max levels	Depth of B-tree for a key. Large tables with long keys have high values here
Records	Number of rows in the table
M.recordlength	Average record length
Packed	Percentage space saved due to MySQL's default practice of stripping blanks from the end of string fields
Recordspace used	Percentage of the space allocated to the data file that it has used
Empty space	Percentage of the space allocated to the data file that remains empty
Blocks/Record	Average number of blocks per record. A reflection of how many links a fragmented record contains. Should stay as close to 1.0 as possible
Recordblocks	Blocks, that is, links in use
Deleteblocks	Blocks (links) deleted
Recorddata	Bytes in the data file in use
Deleted data	Bytes in the data file deleted or otherwise unused
Lost space	The sum in bytes of space lost due to updating records to shorter lengths
Linkdata	The sum of the amount of storage used by pointers that link record fragments in a dynamic format table

Speed of queries

MySQL's creators cite two factors that significantly affect the speed of queries.

1. The more complex the configuration of MySQL access permissions, the more overhead exists, and the greater the possibility of queries executing more slowly.

2. In the absence of GRANT statements, MySQL optimizes permission checking. Therefore, in very-high-volume query scenarios, foregoing grants may expedite query execution.

To estimate average query execution time, you can use this command, whose output appears immediately afterward:

```
mysql> select benchmark(1000000,1+1);
+------------------------+
| benchmark(1000000,1+1) |
+------------------------+
|                      0 |
+------------------------+
1 row in set (0.32 sec)
```

This output indicates that MySQL can execute 1,000,000+ expressions in 0.32 seconds. (The command and output above were produced on a Pentium II 400 MHz PC.)

Operating system auditing procedures

Auditing activity under Linux is simplicity itself. Run the ps command regularly and often — run it as a cron job that automatically reports processes that might indicate suspicious activities.

For example, the following script looks for attempts to connect to a Linux box by means of a telnet session as the superuser root. Upon finding any such connection, the script logs it to a history file, which, in turn, is sent as a broadcast message to the system administrator. In addition, all such attempts are logged to a cumulative history.

```
while :
do
if test -n `ps -uroot | grep telnetd | cut -c3-12`
then
echo > hack_log
echo `date` >> hack_log
echo "Hack-in attempt as root detected - PID and TTY are: \c"
>> hack_log
echo `ps -uroot | grep telnetd | cut -c3-12` >> hack_log
echo ^D >> hack_log
write root < hack_log
cat hack_log >> hack_hist
fi
sleep 60
done
```

Incident reporting procedures

To have an effective basis for instituting security protection tools — such as the script in the previous section — a system administrator needs an effective system for reporting suspect activities. This section outlines steps that can be taken to establish a security policy and incident reporting.

Establishing a security policy

A security policy begins with accurate risk assessment; that is, with an evaluation of the value of your data and the impact upon your organization of the loss or compromise of that data or of the systems that create it. Factors to consider in such an evaluation include:

✦ Defining general guidelines that specify such parameters as how long a system under attack can be allowed to remain active on a network; when to shut down a compromised host; when to revert to backup copies of data

✦ Documenting and inventorying tools needed for intrusion response; for example, ID software, backups, file system recovery tools

✦ Documenting suspicious incidents to capture as much information as possible

✦ Documenting contact information for the individuals who discover suspicious incidents

✦ Documenting all important administrative information about a system that appears to be under attack; for example, OS versions, IP addresses

✦ Documenting the primary purpose of a system that appears to be under attack; e.g., payroll, R&D

✦ Documenting evidence of intrusion, including apparent method of attack, source IP address of attack, and so on

Responding to intrusions

Several steps should be taken in response to suspected system intrusions.

1. Document the characteristics of an attack; that is, note such factors as:

   • Whether it was a denial of service or root compromise attack

   • Whether the attack destroyed data or compromised systems

   • Whether the attack is ongoing

2. Inform users immediately upon detecting an attack. Because you may have to shut down the system being assaulted, users should be prepared to close files and log off temporarily.

3. Prevent the intrusion from spreading. If the attack is a denial of service, but the security and data of a host system is intact, filtering countermeasures should be employed to prevent the attacker's source address from connecting. If the attack involves the compromise of local security, shut the system down, disconnect it from its network, and then restart it in single-user mode in order to analyze its file system and log files.

4. Attempt to identify the source of the attack. You should at least be able to identify the attack's source IP addresses. You can then use this information to determine the origin site as well as contact information at that site, and to get in touch with the administrator in question. This individual may be able to aid you in finding the user on the remote system who initiated the attack.

5. Notify all relevant levels of management. They must make the decision as to whether law officers must be involved in any further investigations of the attack.

6. Create a report on the attack that is as detailed as possible. Use this document as the basis for improving network and system security. That is, learn from history, so that it does not repeat itself.

Physical security

Monitoring the physical security of a system means monitoring direct physical access to a machine. Tools for controlling such access include:

✦ Locked doors

✦ Locked cabinets

✦ Video surveillance

✦ PC locks

✦ BIOS security

✦ Boot loader security

✦ The commands `xclock` and `vclock`

✦ The syslog daemon

This section briefly discusses the last five of these.

PC locks

PC case locks function in various ways, depending upon the nature of the motherboard and the construction of the PC's case.

Some such locks require breaking a case in order to break the lock. Others simply prevent plugging in new or mice. Regardless of the technique involved, however, an attacker who has some small amount of skill in locksmithing can easily defeat most PC locks.

BIOS security

A PC's Basic Input/Output Services or *BIOS*, the lowest level of its software that can configure or manipulate x86-based hardware, communicates with the Linux Boot Loader or *LILO*, and with other Linux boot methods, to determine how to boot up a Linux machine.

> **Tip**   Other hardware on which Linux can run, such as Macs and Sun workstations, present their own analogs to an x86 machine's BIOS. On a Mac, you'll find OpenFirmware; on some Sun machines, you'll see the Sun boot PROM.

A machine's BIOS can be a significant tool in preventing attackers from rebooting the machine and manipulating Linux to their purposes.

Many x86 BIOSs enable you to set a boot password and to specify other security settings. While such passwords aren't inviolable, because they can be reset, they do offer some first level of defense against attack.

> **Tip**   Under S/Linux, that is, Linux for SPARC processor machines, the EEPROM can be set to require a boot password.

Check your BIOS or EEPROM documentation to determine whether such security measures can be put in place on your machine.

Boot loader security

All Linux boot loaders enable you to set a boot password. For instance, LILO offers password and restricted settings. Enabling the password parameter causes LILO to require a password at boot time. Enabling the restricted parameter causes LILO to require a boot-time password only if you specify other options, such as single to indicate booting to single-user mode, at the LILO prompt.

> **Tip**   Neither BIOS- nor LILO-defined boot passwords prevent an attacker from booting from a floppy, and then mounting a root partition. Therefore, if security measures controlled by bootup passwords are to be fully effective, they must be accompanied by disabling, in a PC's BIOS, the capability to boot from a floppy and password-protecting the BIOS.

> **Caution**   Any server protected by a boot password cannot be booted unattended. Remember that when deciding whether to establish bootup passwords.

xlock and vlock

Two utilities exist that enable you to lock a Linux console so that no one can tamper with, or even look at, your work. These are *xlock* and *vlock*.

xlock simply locks an X-based display. xlock usually is included in any Linux distribution that supports X. Ordinarily, you run xlock from any xterm window; xlock then locks the display, requiring a password to unlock it.

vlock enables you to lock some or all of the virtual consoles on a Linux machine. You can, therefore, lock just the one you happen to be working in at the moment, or lock all of them. vlock ships with Red Hat Linux.

syslog

A Linux syslog daemon can be configured to send log data to a central syslog server. Unfortunately, such logging data typically travels unencrypted, which means that a skilled hacker might view log data as it is being transferred, thereby gaining access to sensitive information about a network.

Check the documentation for your syslog daemon. If it functions in the way just described, substitute a version of syslog that encrypts logging data as it transmits it.

In monitoring the logs created by this daemon, pay particular attention to

✦ Short or incomplete logs

✦ Logs containing atypical or unusual timestamps

✦ Logs which carry incorrect permissions or ownership

✦ Records of reboots or restarting of services

✦ su entries

✦ Logins from atypical or unexpected sources

Logical security

In most cases, implementing logical security means implementing a firewall. This section outlines that task.

Selecting a firewall

It is important to understand the most common security techniques used by firewalls so that you can choose the package and technique most appropriate to your environment. The most significant firewall methodologies are:

Packet filtering   Works by distinguishing destinations based on IP addresses or specific bit patterns. May not be suitable for security policies that require a finer degree of control, because packet filters cannot protect against application-level attacks and may be susceptible to IP fragmentation or IP source-routing attacks. On the plus side, many routers employ packet filtering, so implementing this security technique may be effectively free.

Application-layer filtering, also known as gateways or circuit-level proxies	Concentrates on the application layer of the OSI reference model, enabling it to use dedicated security proxies to examine an entire data stream at every connection attempt. Circuit-level proxies function as agents for internal and external users, and are specific to OSI application-level utilities such as FTP and telnet, or to protocols such as Oracle's SQL*Net. Under application-layer filtering, no outside packets traverse the firewall, making this method a good choice in environments that require a high degree of detail of security control.
Multilayer inspection firewalls, also called dynamic filtering	Analyze all packet communication layers and extract any relevant communication and application state information by parsing IP packets, retaining state information about the connections involved in the operating system kernel. Multilayer inspection can be faster than application layer firewalls, but multilayer methods also carry more overhead.

Configuring a firewall: Questions to consider

Often an administrator configures a firewall to allow specific traffic such as OSI application-level services in both incoming and outgoing directions. However, a few factors exist which may make such a configuration problematic:

✦ A firewall at a remote site may deny traffic of the type you've permitted.

✦ The maximum number of concurrent connections that a firewall has been configured to permit may be insufficient at either end of a connection, or may simply not match between the end points of the conversation.

✦ The maximum data throughput supported may be insufficient at either end of a connection, or may simply not match between the end points of the conversation.

 Most frequently, firewalls perform better under Linux than under 32-bit Windows operating systems because Linux can better exploit the underlying hardware. However, using slower NICs at the Linux end can even out this performance imbalance.

 Fully exploiting the capabilities of a feature-rich firewall requires 100 Mbps Ethernet connections. Even with such connections, encryption can significantly lessen data throughput.

A firewall's performance benefits significantly from increased RAM and CPU resources. Adding memory can increase throughput, but only when connections to the firewall expand to fill previously existing RAM. Similarly, the faster a CPU, in general, the faster the processing of firewall software.

Caution Running a firewall on a machine that employs symmetric multiprocessing (SMP) machine may or may not improve firewall performance. Some firewall vendors report that their products simply don't run on such machines, or that the firewall in question doesn't benefit from SMP-augmented processing horsepower.

Firewall logging

Firewalls typically use four basic types of logging: SNMP traps, the operating system syslog daemon, logging to a text file, and logging to the system console.

Caution While enterprise-scale firewalls have excellent logging facilities, simpler firewalls tend to lack fully featured security logging and reporting.

The Simple Network Management Protocol (SNMP) and syslog usually direct their output to a network host, thereby offering centralized reporting and the capability to perform historical analyses. Many firewalls, while they also use SNMP traps, typically log only basic security events such as user authentications, ignoring more sophisticated security questions such as:

✦ Denial of Service (DoS) attacks

✦ IP spoofing; that is, mimicking a legitimate IP address

Logging through syslog provides firewalls easy integration of the information they produce into an existing network. Local logs, that is, those stored on the firewall appliance itself, wrap around, or replace older entries as needed as a log fills up. While useful for realtime troubleshooting, local logging may not be well suited for historical analysis.

In selecting a firewall and configuring its logging, one point is paramount: Security must be capable of easy redirection to an external operating system text file. Without this capability, an administrator loses much by way of security management, because no amount of automated filtering can replace log analysis by administrators knowledgeable in the needs and nature of a system or network.

Disaster Prevention and Recovery

This section examines two categories of tools and techniques for disaster prevention and recovery: environmental protection (that is, protecting and ensuring a PC's power supply) and backups.

Environmental protection

Ensuring sufficient, and sufficiently clean, power to a Linux (or any) computer means using either or both of two types of power conditioning equipment: surge suppressers and uninterruptable power supplies.

Surge suppressers

Surge suppressers attempt to preclude excess energy — power spikes — from damaging a computer. Suppressers function by placing a Metal Oxide Varistor, or *MOV,* between the energy source and the computer, in a method analogous to that used by a fuse.

However, surge suppressers have two very significant shortcomings:

✦ Most surge suppressers don't inform you when their MOV ceases to function.

✦ Most surge suppressers provide no power to permit you to carry out a clean shutdown of a system.

Because ungraceful shutdowns, also sometimes called *harshing a system*, can seriously damage it, surge suppressers cannot be your only line of power defense. You must also consider uninterruptible power supplies or *UPSs*.

Uninterruptable power supplies

A UPS provides surge protection for a computer's power cord, and, in some models, for a phone line as well. Furthermore, a UPS contains a battery that can supply the power needed in emergencies for clean shutdowns. Many UPSs can be configured to shut down a machine without operator intervention.

Many good Linux-compatible UPSs exist. Among the best are products from Tripp-Lite and APS. These vendors each produce a number of UPSs that wear like iron, and that are backed by lifetime warranties that are invariably quickly honored.

Backups

Regardless of the media to which you plan to archive your data, a written backup plan and a hardcopy backup log form the core of any effective archiving. These components help to ensure that backups execute as scheduled, that they have been verified, and that they have been labeled and properly stored.

Scheduling backups

Perhaps the most important consideration in scheduling backups involves deciding how often to back up. Experts usually recommend that anything — whether data or software — critical to operations should be backed up daily. In addition, full-system backups should be performed once weekly. For incremental daily backups, five tapes per week should be used for no more than two weeks, requiring a total of ten tapes for these daily backups. For full-system weekly backups, two tapes per week should be used for no more than three weeks, therefore requiring a total of six tapes total for full system backups.

Physical diversity

Another important characteristic of backups is that of physical diversity, that is, storing the same data on more than one physical device. Most common implementations of this form of backup involve some use of the combination of hardware and software solutions known generically as RAID (redundant array of inexpensive disks).

Tip   Most flavors of Linux provide RAID utilities; these tools have been expanded in the most recent stable kernel release, 2.3.

Geographical diversity

Multiple copies of backup media, typically tapes, help ensure swift recovery from disasters, whatever the circumstances. Keep only one copy on site; distribute other copies to offsite locations.

If a backup houses sensitive or proprietary data, place one copy in a safety deposit box. In any case, send a copy of your backup to a secure storage facility outside your immediate geographical area, but still readily accessible.

Disaster recovery plan

A serviceable disaster recovery plan, one of the most important tools a system or network administrator can have, should include information on:

✦ The operating system itself, particularly information on its configuration

✦ Operating system maintenance tasks

✦ The database itself, particularly information on its configuration

✦ Database maintenance tasks

✦ Operating system and database backup procedures

✦ Operating system and database statistics, and the procedures by which those were gleaned

✦ Any applications that interact closely with the database

✦ Any specialized files such as SQL or OS scripts that contribute to operating system, database, or statistical information

Furthermore, such a plan should consider these requirements:

✦ You must choose those databases and supporting files most critical to your organization, and note these as the material to be recovered first, leaving less crucial data to be recovered at a later time.

✦ You must perform the recovery of critical data with relationships between that data in mind. That is, if Table B contains information that will make sense or be usable only if Table A exists, recover Table A first.

✦ Ensure that backups are stored both onsite and offsite.

✦ However cumbersome it might seem, back up both software and data daily. This technique enables you to avoid time-consuming selective backups.

✦ Educate staff in the importance of disaster recovery and in the plan you've developed, as well as their role in it.

✦ At regular intervals, simulate a disaster and recovery from it.

This section presents an example disaster plan. This plan, only slightly reworked from one used in a community college setting, can serve as a template for such a plan in any number of environments.

Caution   While this disaster plan is a more-than-reliable example and template, it must be tailored to specific implementations. It will not function out of the box, so to speak, in all situations.

What follows makes up the Disaster Recovery Plan for the student-computing lab at Some County Community College. This document includes:

✦ Outlines of the configuration of the lab's operating system and database platforms

✦ Outlines and brief descriptions of maintenance for each of these platforms

✦ Copies of the shell scripts and other batch files most important to this maintenance

✦ Contact information for all internal and external personnel who might be required to participate in disaster recovery

Operating system and its configuration

We currently run Caldera OpenLinux 2.2. The operating system is backed up weekly and can be recovered from these tapes. In addition, the original distribution media, kept in the Lab's office safe, can be used to re-create the system to some degree. Note, however, that this method would not incorporate such features as symbolic links that have been established since the system was originally loaded.

Operating system maintenance tasks

We use the following operating system commands on a daily basis to assist in troubleshooting the OS.

```
bdf
df
diskinfo
fstab
mntab
ps
swapinfo
```

We run some of these at on an as needed basis and others by means of the shell script eyeball_os, which not only carries out the commands in question, but also sends a broadcast message of their output to the superuser. In addition to these daily notifications, the script creates and maintains a cumulative history of:

✦ Free disk space by using the command df

✦ General disk configuration information by using the command diskinfo

✦ Swap space usage information by using the command swapinfo

✦ Process information relating to connections to the Lab by means of either the Web or the College's Library server by using the command ps

eyeball_os has been implemented as a cron task which runs at 8 a.m. each day the Lab is open. The complete text of the script is

```
df > 2eyeball
echo > 2eyeball
diskinfo > 2eyeball
echo > 2eyeball
swapinfo > 2eyeball
echo > 2eyeball
ps -e | grep httpd > 2eyeball
ps -e | grep zdaemon >> 2eyeball
echo > 2write
echo `date` >> 2write
echo "The following system information, including httpd and
zdaemon PIDs, were detected\c" >> 2write
cat 2eyeball >> 2write
echo ^D >> 2write
write root < 2write
rm 2write
```

In addition to running eyeball_os, we trim operating system and related application log files as required. For example, the Apache log files are trimmed weekly.

Database

We run Oracle8*i* for Linux. The DBMS is backed up daily and can be recovered from these tapes. In addition, the original distribution media, kept in the Lab's office safe, can be used to recreate software only.

Database maintenance tasks

On a weekly basis, we trim all logs with a command like this:

```
tail -100 some_log_file > some_log_file_today's_date
```

Operating system backup procedures

We back up the entire file system daily and the operating system weekly. Thus, both system and data can be recovered from the appropriate tapes fairly efficiently.

We use a tar from root, similar to the generic example below, but with the appropriate file subsystems specified when needed, to carry out these backups. Note that this command must be run by root from root.

```
# tar cvf /dev/hda1 /dev/rtp1
```

Database backup procedures

We back up Oracle daily, using the procedure outlined below.

 Tip   Updated versions of this procedure, as well as a number of other Linux and Linux DB backup and maintenance scripts, can be found at:

> www.backupcentral.com/mytools.html

The script oraback.sh, which carries out cold or hot backups of Oracle, relies on the Bourne shell. oraback.sh further assumes that the oratab file is properly configured and that it should automatically back up every instance listed in the oratab file.

oraback.sh supports

- ✦ Backing up to either disk or tape
- ✦ Backups of either ext2 file systems or raw devices
- ✦ Multitasked backups, thereby offering the ability to reduce backup time by as much as 75 percent
- ✦ Automated notification by e-mail of backup success or errors

To backup all Oracle instances, run oraback.sh from the OS prompt with this syntax:

```
$ oraback.sh
```

To back up specific instances, run oraback.sh with the SIDs of the instances you wish to back up supplied as arguments at the command line like this, but substituting actual SIDs for the generic parameters shown here:

```
$ oraback.sh SID1 SID2 ? SIDn
```

To run a backup at a time specified in the Oracle configuration file oraback.conf, use syntax similar to this:

```
$ oraback.sh at
```

To back up specific instances at a time specified in oracle.conf, combine these syntaxes in this way:

```
$ oraback.sh at SID1 SID2 ? SIDn
```

Installing oraback.sh

Installing oraback.sh means taking these steps:

1. Put the files oraback.sh, config.guess, and localpath.sh in the directory of your choice, but ensure that all three files reside in the same directory.

2. Check, and if need be adjust, appropriate to your environment, these values in the site-specific section at the beginning of oraback.sh:

   - BINDIR — Set to the directory where oraback.sh resides
   - ORATAB — Set to the full path name of Oracle's oratab file
   - ORACONF — Set to the full pathname of the oraback.conf file; note that this name must indicate a directory to which Oracle can write

3. Review, and if necessary adjust, all other variables in the site-specific section of oraback.sh. Those variables include, but are not necessarily limited to:

```
ORADIR
TMP
LOG
PATH
```

Customizing oraback.sh

Oraback.conf serves as the configuration file for oraback.sh. Ordinarily, oraback.conf contains a hostname.master line that specifies options such as:

✦ Which users are authorized to perform a backup

✦ What backup device will be used

✦ On what days and at what times cold or hot backups will be performed

Running oraback.sh with the `at` argument invokes this hostname.master line, which is described in more detail below:

```
hostname.master:[skip]:Cold Day:Cold Time:Hot Time:[tape
device]:users:Parallelism:Backup Dir:Y::user ids:
```

These fields signify:

`hostname.master`	system's hostname; generated by `uname -n` or by host-name, minus its domain name; for example, kg.domain.com becomes simply kg.
`[skip]`	If you want all backups skipped on this host tonight, put `skip` here.
`Cold Day`	The day on which oraback.sh should do cold backups. This can be a day of the week (Fri) or month (03). If there is a blank in this field, cold backups will never be performed.

Cold Time	The time of the day (using a 24-hour clock) to do cold backups.
Hot Time	The time of the day (using a 24-hour clock) to do hot backups.
[Tape Device]	No-rewind tape device, to back up to tape. (Blank for disk-only backup.)
[Users]	A "|" separated list of usernames permitted to run svr-mgr and this script, such as oracle|dba (Blank allows only Oracle.)
[Parallelism]	The number of simultaneous data file copies to run. (Blank=1.)
Backup dir	Must be set to a directory or file system that has enough room for a compressed copy of all database files
[Y]	A Y means to compress files before they are written to tape or disk.
mail ids	Set this to a comma-delimited list of mail IDs to mail success or failure to (for example, dba@herworkstation.com, root).

In addition, there are four predefined functions, unused by default, which are listed in the site-specific section of oraback.sh. These are described here, with their respective usage times.

Preback	Runs before entire backup starts
Preshut	Runs before shutdown of each instance
Poststart	Runs after startup of each instance
Postback	Runs after entire backup finishes

As an example of using these functions, I offer this. To restart orasrv after an instance is restarted, using a script called rc.orasrv.sh, change Poststart as follows.

```
Poststart(){
rc.orasrv.sh
}
```

How oraback.sh functions
Before actually running the backup, oraback.sh checks oraback.conf to determine

✦ Whether the user running the backup is Oracle, or is a valid user. If the user attempting to run the backup is not a valid user, the script will not continue.

✦ If a valid user has started oraback.sh, the script then determines whether the word skip is in field 2. If so, it skips the backup once, and removes the word skip from oraback.conf. (This enables a DBA to manually skip tonight's backup, but does not enable the DBA to accidentally disable backups forever.)

oraback.sh then does one of the following, depending on which arguments it receives:

✦ If given no arguments, it performs a backup of all instances listed in Oracle's oratab file.

✦ If given one or more instance names as SIDs, the script performs a backup of each of them.

✦ If called with `at` as an argument, the script checks oraback.conf to determine whether the day in field 3 (the cold backup day field) is today. If so, it sets the variable `$TIME` to the time in field 4. If not, it sets `$TIME` to the time in field 5. The script then schedules an `at` job that will run oraback.sh at the time specified by `$TIME`.

oraback.sh then checks the hostname.master line in oraback.conf to determine whether there is a tape device in field 6. If so, it labels the tape, making sure that the device will be treated as no-rewind. Then the script checks field 8 for an integer value. If it finds one, the script makes the number of simultaneous copies of database files specified by that value.

Next, oraback.sh asks Oracle questions that will determine how (or if) the SID will be backed up. It asks if the instance is online. If so, oraback.sh makes a set of configuration files needed later. If archiving is running, however, the instance in question is excluded from hot backup.

If an instance is online, logs are on, and the instance is not excluded from hot backups, then the script:

✦ Puts each tablespace into backup mode by using the svrmgrl command `begin backup`

✦ Copies that tablespace's files to the backup device

✦ Takes the tablespace out of backup mode with the svrmgrl command `end backup`

After backup

Upon completing a backup, oraback.sh forces a checkpoint and archive log switch, which causes the online redo log to be sent to an archived redo log.

The script then backs up control files to disk using both svrmgr and a manual copy. Finally, the script makes copies of the essential redo logs and compresses them. (Essential logs are those that span the time of the backup.) If the backup device is a tape, it then backs up all files that were sent to disk to the tape device.

If an instance is offline, oraback.sh only copies data files to the backup device. The script then backs up the control files and redo logs.

Special circumstances

If an instance is online, but archiving is off, oraback.sh checks oraback.conf for a line that reads:

```
HOST:ORACLE_SID:NOARCHIVELOG:[offline|nohotbackups]
```

If it fails to find such a line, oraback.sh notifies you by mail. If it finds this line, the script then looks for the word offline in that same line. Such a parameter tells oraback.sh that the instance in question has no archive logs running, and that the script should always do an offline, or cold, backup of this instance. Therefore, finding the parameter offline causes oraback.sh to:

- ✦ Shut down the instance
- ✦ Carry out a cold backup
- ✦ Restart the instance

If an instance is online, oraback.sh looks for a line in oraback.conf that reads:

```
HOST:ORACLE_SID:::nohotbackup
```

Such a line tells oraback.sh that although ORACLE_SID qualifies for a hot backup, because it has archiving active, oraback.sh should not do hot backups of this instance. Finding such a line causes the script to skip the instance in question when executing a hot backup.

Testing oraback.sh

For testing, select a small instance and run the following command as the user Oracle:

```
$ /usr/local/bin/oraback.sh <instance>
```

Caution Be aware that if the word offline appears in oraback.conf, or if the day that is specified for cold backups is today, the instance will be shut down.

If this test functions properly, install the script as a cron job in Oracle's crontab file, adding a cron entry that contains the command:

```
/usr/local/bin/oraback.sh at
```

Schedule this job to run at 11 p.m. and again at 6:30 a.m.

Using oraback.sh

Ideally, running oraback.sh, as well as backing up Oracle8*i* by other means, should rely on a single oraback.conf file that is NFS-mounted or otherwise shared. Such a shared configuration file enables you to modify administrative parameters simply by editing one document.

As regards oraback.sh's capability to notify you by e-mail, set the SUCCESSMAIL flag in oraback.conf to Y, to be mailed every time an oraback.sh-driven backup runs, successful or otherwise.

Summary

The most critical security and disaster prevention and recovery tools that should be present to support Linux DBMSs are

✦ Computer usage policy statements

✦ Database auditing procedures

✦ Operating system auditing procedures

✦ Physical security

✦ Backups

✦ Disaster recovery plan

✦   ✦   ✦

Modern Database Deployment

Choosing, installing, and developing schemata for the chosen Linux database is an involved enough task, but it is hardly all there is to developing a complete application. There is a lot of theory and industry practice concerning the development and maintenance of applications, and a lot of discussion has gone into the proper role of the database in the overall system architecture. Databases provide transactional integrity to systems. This ensures that system data shows some consistency even in the face of application and hardware failures.

This chapter examines the various ways in which databases can be integrated into applications, especially in light of the many changes brought on by Internet usage and technology.

System Architecture

For a long time the standard architecture of applications was client/server. In this configuration a back-end database is connected to a customized module that contains all the business rules and the user interface. Figure 19-1 shows just how simple the client server architecture can be.

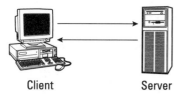

Client　　　　Server

Figure 19-1: A simplified client
server diagram

The key advance to this approach was the machine-independence of the data storage and in-memory application. This allowed IT managers to manage a highly controlled database server while distributing many of the resources involved in executing an application to remote users who might even be on different machine platforms, or running different application software. This made a lot of sense as the personal computer revolution progressed and Local Area Networks (LANs) became cheaper and more ubiquitous.

During the client/server era, databases gained improved connectivity, and "fourth-generation" languages (4GLs) emerged with a combination of database connection, query, and form and report capabilities.

The primary problem with client/server is the tight coupling between the user interface and business logic on the client (often called a *fat client*). This increases maintenance costs because any change to the display and input code affects the business logic, and any change to the business logic affects the display and input code, an unnecessary dependency.

To address this problem and others, the three-tier architecture was developed and has quickly become one of the industry standard architectures. The three-tier architecture separates the business logic from the user-interface code, which is still considered the client. Figure 19-2 illustrates a basic three-tier architecture.

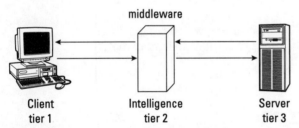

Figure 19-2: A simple three-tier architecture

The database tier has largely the same role as in client/server architectures. The middle tier is the "intelligence" of the application, and can take many forms. Many technologies have emerged that are designed to improve middle-tier applications, including many of the popular distributed-object technologies, such as CORBA and DCOM, and messaging technologies, such as IBM's MQSeries and various XML-messaging protocols. There is actually a vast variety of such technologies from numerous vendors, and they are collectively known as middleware. Any Linux Web server, such as Apache, can act as middleware. Application servers fall into this rather broad category. Some current application servers that run on Linux are BEA Weblogic Server, Blue Stone Total-e-Server (now part of Hewlett-Packard), Oracle Application Server, and IBM's WebSphere. Don't expect to have these servers run on the least expensive hardware, though.

The client in the three-tier architecture is strictly concerned with providing the user a display and gathering input.

On top of this basic three-tier frame, many architectural variations are possible, and are increasingly common. Some developers tend to split the middle tier into multiple tiers depending on particular needs of their applications. For instance, if the application has a specialized localization (l10n) and internationalization (i18n) layer through which all database requests must be channeled in order to accommodate users from different countries, this layer could be deployed as its own tier.

A very common variation on the three-tier architecture occurs in Web-based applications in which the client tier is often effectively divided into two parts: the Web browser on one hand and Web server and server-side scripts on the other. Some developers consider the Web-server actually part of the middle tier, but a well-designed Web server environment in a complex system should probably not contain any elements of business logic and should rather be more concerned with turning middleware requests into HTML, JavaScript, and so forth for browser display. One possible architecture for an n-tier application is shown in Figure 19-3.

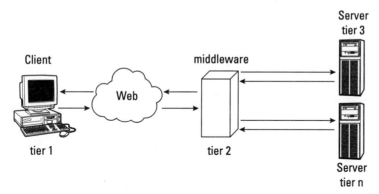

Figure 19-3: An example n-tier Web application

Because of such common variations on the three-tier architecture, it is frequently known as the n-tier architecture.

The above discussion might appear to indicate that any modular division of the system warrants its own tier. Indeed some books on the topic draw example n-tier systems with some of the "tiers" being no more than the logical divisions of the application core. This is a great oversimplification, and developers who seize on the n-tier hype, designing their tiers in the same way they design any system module, end up forfeiting many of the advantages of n-tier systems.

A simple example of overpartitioning is when an application tier is divided among several inexpensive hardware platforms in order to achieve performance goals on the cheap, yet the output of these pieces must be synchronized and assimilated on the neighboring tiers. The real problem here is that the choice of hardware was based solely on price at the expense of other considerations, such as software modularity. The correct decision would have also considered all of the costs of the appropriately sized hardware with the costs of implementation and maintainability over the life of the application.

Designing for n-tier success

The key to determining how to divide systems into tiers lies in understanding how change and dependencies evolve through the system life cycle. Each properly designed tier provides a degree of freedom, which means that it can be changed, even radically, independently of the other tiers. However, adding a tier can reduce the efficiency of development and sometimes runtime performance. Architectural decisions in n-tier systems thus involve a trade-off between degrees of freedom and efficiency of implementation.

Designing systems at the top-level architectural level requires as much careful analysis and design as the other parts of software design, but it is sometimes treated as a mere formality before concentrating on proper design of the detailed application objects. However, the top-level design is probably even more important than the detailed design, and there are several key principles that should serve to guide it. Many of these principles are well-known interpolations of more general structural and object design principles. In practical terms, though, one of the pitfalls of design at the high level is that it is necessary to make assumptions about the availability of functions or capabilities at the lower levels (otherwise, one would be designing at the lower level). When these assumptions don't prove out, the effort necessary to emulate the missing functions can be catastrophic. A common enough mistake that we're all prone to making is to depend on the well intentioned promises of a vendor, say about the availability of a middleware product, only to find out too late that promises are unfulfilled.

Getting back to theory, the most important principle is that of dependency organization. Dependencies between tiers should be organized so that they only go one way; as a directed acyclic graph (DAG) in engineering jargon. This prevents the design from having an inherent chicken-and-egg flaw. For instance, the client tier depends on the middle tier that in turn depends on the database tier, but the database tier does not depend on any other system, and there is no path along the dependencies back to the middle or client tier. A system partitioned in this way does not have any tiers that have requirements that depend on any other tier *other than those to which it is directly connected*. An interdependency graph for a hypothetical architecture is shown below, in Figure 19-4.

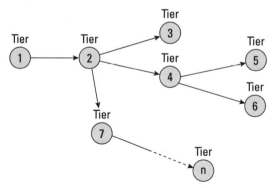

Figure 19-4: A hypothetical Inter-tier dependency graph

What do these dependencies actually entail? A dependency is established when the design of one tier relies on a certain format, behavior, or protocol within another tier.

In an n-tier system that follows this principle, a maintenance change to the middle tier, for instance, does not affect the database tier, and any compatibility layer to minimize the effect of such change also remains within the middle tier, the most cohesive arrangement. This organized approach to dependency is a powerful tool for managing system change, without which maintenance costs can be excessive as multiple tiers need to be updated, redeployed, and tested simultaneously.

The second main principle is an adaptation of the *open/closed principle* put forward by Bertrand Meyer, object development expert and designer of the Eiffel language. It holds that the interfaces between tiers should be *open* to extension but *closed* to modification.

For example, say the client requests a list of employees using a function called `GetEmployees()` defined in the middle-tier interface. If the middle tier is later updated to add the idea of Departments, the developers may be tempted to replace the `GetEmployees()` function with a `GetEmployees(string dept)` which takes a department name. If the new interface completely replaced the old one, it would violate the open/closed principle. Any clients that did not know to add the `department` parameter would cease working and return an error. The problem is that the interface was modified. The open/closed principle would have permitted the developers to add the new function to the interface without replacing the old one. In interfaces that allow function polymorphism, this could be done just by adding a new "signature" to the `GetEmployees()` function that accepts the department string. Where no polymorphism is permitted, a function called `GetEmployeesByDept(string dept)` could be added to the same purpose. This enables the developers to modify the clients gradually and carefully, because the old interfaces are still available and work.

Another important principle is to design tiers to be independent. This means that they have the ability to be located on separate, though connected hardware. Multiple tiers may be initially deployed on the same hardware, and staging or back-up systems might be set up on monolithic hardware. The ability to move some tiers to other hardware is an important reason for ensuring scalability at the hardware level. Achieving scalability by redesigning the application code can be prohibitively expensive and is frequently unsuccessful, contrasted with the sometimes economical alternative of more capable hardware.

There are many other factors that drive n-tier success, such as consistent transaction-propagation and well-planned security infrastructure, including all the numerous general application-design methods that are outside the scope of this book.

Internet Databases

The main technology that turned the Web into the phenomenon it has become was the Common Gateway Interface (CGI), which enabled servers to respond to clients with content dynamically generated by server programs. From those times to the present, and into the foreseeable future, the majority of CGI and other dynamic Web technologies involve database access.

Originally, programmers would write specialized scripts to read and update databases, performing some basic processing of the results. In such cases, there was nothing special about the DBMS to address the fact that the eventual client was somewhere in the Internet cloud. This model of Internet application is still very common, and is a great strength of Linux and open-source because amateur, small business, and small department Web administrators can cobble together a quick PHP-to-MySQL application or the like.

No one can miss, however, that such dynamic Web applications continue to under-lie the growth of the Internet, and are becoming far more ambitious than their humble roots. Increasingly, DBMS vendors are working to seize this entire space by supporting direct Web publishing and querying of databases, or by bundling Web application development tools.

The first challenge for DBMS vendors facing the Internet revolution was scalability. Suddenly, far from the relatively predictable usage patterns of the client/server and even early n-tier architectures, database systems began needing to scale to a barrage of access from all over the world. Licensing under such a situation also became a concern.

 Caution Licensing can sometimes get complicated when a database is exposed to Internet connectivity. Licensing terms from the client/server days were often governed by number of "seats," or distinct users. Of course, when the potential user base is the entire Internet population, this approach can be ludicrous. Many DBMS vendors offer per-CPU licenses to address this issue or limit the number of licensed simultaneous connections. In any case, be sure your license is compatible with your usage patterns. This is also an easy trap to fall into with so many "personal" versions of popular databases downloadable from Linux FTP sites, or tossed about as "conference coaster" CDs.

Database vendors have quite convincingly proven their scalability under Internet loads: new online concerns in areas ranging from financial services to e-commerce have thrived using modern application architecture and the very databases discussed in this book.

For the more modest needs to which this book is targeted, modern DBMS still provides powerful tools for Internet integration.

Universal Databases

The major promise of Object-Relational DBMS is that it allows the development of databases that can store different sorts of objects than the ANSI SQL-92 primitive types (numbers, dates, characters) as first-class content, perhaps even with intelligent search and index capabilities. SQL-99 (formerly SQL-3) was recently finalized, providing a standard for storing heterogeneous objects in SQL databases, but many vendors have been ahead of the standard. Databases that can store such rich types, and that can allow the developer to define stored procedures for manipulating such objects are known as Universal Databases. Universal Databases offer many of the amenities of object-oriented databases such as inheritance of types.

With this capability, Databases can store entire HTML pages, or perhaps just HTML templates, in a manner that enables Web applications to integrate the dynamic content directly into the target Web page. Some DBMSs have full Web server capability, obviating the need for even good-old Apache, although most applications using significant runtime logic will probably such throwbacks to the mainframe era (although a vocal few would just call it a restoration of sanity).

Advanced Applications

Database applications are getting ever more sophisticated, and theory and industry practices are ever in motion to develop proven approaches and solutions for developers. Here are a couple of advanced DBMS application technologies that have been charted by pioneers complete with arrows in back. Several organizations work on standards, benchmarks, and other enabling data, including The Open Group, the Transaction-Processing Council (TPC), and the Object Management Group (OMG).

Transaction monitors

Transaction Monitors and Object Transaction Monitors, often known as TP systems or TP Monitors (for "transaction processing"), are specialized middleware systems that can coordinate transactions among multiple participants, including multiple databases, each of which is managed as a separate transactional resource, with the transaction integrity and boundaries nevertheless being defined across all the resources in tandem. The major example available for Linux is BEA's Tuxedo. TP Monitors extend basic transactions with a model known as the two-phase commit.

For the purpose of this chapter, let's define a transaction as *one or more database operations that must either complete successfully as a group or not at all*. That is, all of the operations must be treated as if they were a single, indivisible operation. *Atomic* is the term that is used frequently, meaning *cannot be divided*. The typical outcome of an unsuccessful transaction is that any completed operations of the transaction are undone, referred to as rolling back the transaction. Transactions are an important part of day-to-day operations in just about every enterprise. Consider a simple order-entry operation and ask yourself, "What are the consequences if this order is only partially posted?"

In a single-phase commit, as we have discussed, the transaction manager signals to all resources simultaneously that they should commit and rollback, and the resources do so without further ado. This is the transaction boundary. Figure 19-5 shows the principal elements of a single-phase commit transaction.

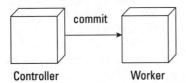

Figure 19-5: A simplified sequence diagram of 1-phase commit transaction

Distributed Transaction Processing (DTP) systems manage multiple transactional resources, such as multiple databases, transactional file-systems, or even legacy components that can be wrapped by a customized transactional resource manager. DTP is a much more complex task than managing a single transactional resource because interprocess communication, multiple levels of concurrency, and possibly very different resources must be herded into a coherent system that does not violate any of the ACID constraints.

In a two-phase commit, the transaction manager first tells all the resources to prepare to commit. Each resource votes either to commit or to rollback. If all resources vote to commit, the transaction coordinator confirms the commit order. If any of the resources vote to rollback, the transaction coordinator instructs them all to rollback. The second commit or rollback instruction is the transaction boundary.

This ensures that all resources are consistent with respect to each other and all clients. An elementary two-phase commit is shown in Figure 19-6.

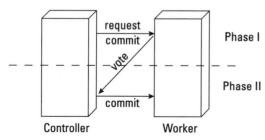

Figure 19-6: A sequence diagram for a simple 2-phase commit

Object Transaction Monitors perform a task similar to that performed by regular transaction monitors, wrapping the various roles in object-oriented interfaces. The major OTM standard is the OMG's Object Transaction Service, or CosTransactions, which is part of the CORBA standard. The placement of an OTM in an n-tier architecture is shown in Figure 19-7.

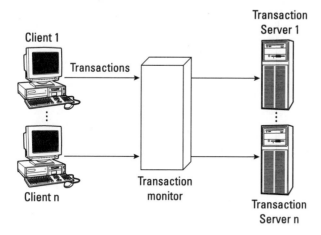

Figure 19-7: The placement of an OTM

The new Enterprise JavaBeans specification, part of the new Java 2 Enterprise Edition, which, according to Sun's indications, may soon be sped on its way to a Linux port, defines a very easy to use OTM system for native objects. Otherwise, unfortunately, there are no OTM implementations available for Linux at the time of this writing.

Summary

This chapter examined the various considerations for integrating DBMS into applications, both traditional and Internet-based:

✦ Applications have migrated from client/server to the n-tier architecture, which supports maximum flexibility and scalability.

✦ Dependencies between tiers should be organized as a directed acyclic (no loops) graph and interfaces between tiers should be extended (augmented with other functions) but not modified (no existing function will change) during maintenance.

✦ Internet database applications have grown from basic scripts to build response pages from query results, and now DBMS vendors are providing a broad set of tools for Internet support.

✦ Distributed Transaction Processing systems allow advanced applications through which multiple databases can be managed in a unified manner.

Hopefully all of the information in this book has been enough to get you up to speed with your Linux DBMS of choice, and to begin thinking carefully about the design of the application you plan to build around it. The next step is to begin experimenting with the system on your own — if you haven't already. Build a prototype of your desired application, and take notes of what works and what doesn't. You will find that Linux can be a very productive environment for the development of database applications.

✦   ✦   ✦

Frequently Used Linux Commands

The following list is a brief description of frequently used Linux commands:

cal	Prints a calendar of the current month, or specified month or year
cat	Concatenates files and sends the result to standard output
cd	Changes the current working directory
chgrp	Changes just the group ownership bits of a file
chmod	Changes the settings of the permission bits for files and directories, for example, read, write, or execute
chown	Changes the ownership (owner, group , public) of files and directories
cp	Copies files and directories
date	Prints the current date in various formats
df	Displays free space on one or more mounted file systems
ftp	Utility for transferring files between host computers using the File Transfer Protocol developed for ARPANet (later, DARPANet)
grep	Finds and prints the lines in one or more files containing a matching text pattern
gunzip	Decompresses file(s) having previously compressed with, for example, gzip
gzip	A file compression utility (see gunzip)
head	Lists the beginning lines of a file (see tail)

ipcs	Displays information on interprocess communication facilities
ispell	Checks the spelling of a file
kill	Terminates a running process
ln	Creates a link for a file, directory, or device
lpr	Sends one or more files to a (predefined) printer queue; prints a file
lprm	Removes a print job from a print queue
ls	Lists the contents of a directory
man	Prints the help, that is, user manual, page for a command
mkdir	Creates a directory
more	Prints (lists) the contents of a file on the screen one page at a time
mount	Mounts a device to the file system at a specified point in the file system tree; mounts a new file system
nslookup	Queries a domain name server for a specified domain name
passwd	Changes the user's password
ping	Looks for the presence of a host (computer) on a connected network
ps	Displays information about currently running processes
pwd	Prints the absolute pathname of the current working directory
rm	Removes one or more files and directories
rmdir	Removes empty directories
rsh	Opens a shell on a remote system
su	Runs a shell as a substitute user; changing user without logging out
tail	Lists the ending lines of a file
tar	Creates, reads, or extracts an archive of one or more files, directories, or tape backup devices
top	Displays information about top CPU processes; shows busiest current processes
zcat	Concatenates a compressed file to standard output

✦   ✦   ✦

Index

Numbers & Symbols

& (ampersand), 303
: (colon), 306
$ (dollar sign), 303
= (equals), 39
/ (forward-slash character), 303
!= (not equals), 39
| (pipe), 304
; (semicolon), 306
? (wildcard character), 302

A

access control, PostgreSQL, 382
access permissions
   account, group and user, creating, 308
   default file, setting, 308
accounts payable/receivable (database evaluation), 203–204
ADABAS/D, 243–244
Adaptive Server Enterprise (ASE), 252
adding user accounts, 642
additions, database integrity and, 45–46
add_row() function, 603
adduser command, 642
ALL keyword, 74, 118–119
American National Standards Institute (ANSI), 70
AND keyword, 74
AND operator, 106–108
ANSI. *See* America National Standards Institute
ANSI SQL-92, 15
ANY keyword, 74
API. *See* application programming interface
application constraints, defining, 215
application development, project planning, 155
application-layer filtering, 671

application programming interface (API), 237
   column binding, 455
   connectivity concepts, 420–423
   MySQL database for PHP, 453–454
   ODBC functions, list of, 422–436
   overview, 419–420
applications
   database. *See* database applications
   standalone. *See* standalone applications
arithmetic operators, 97–98
ASC keyword, 74
ASE. *See* Adaptive Server Enterprise
AS keyword, 74
at command, scheduling with, 645–646
atomic values, 30
attribute object, 55
attributes, 27–28
   PRECISION, 544
AUDIT command, 660
auditing procedures, MySQL
   myiasmchk output, 664–665
   myiasmchk syntax, 662–663
   query speeds, 666
auditing procedures, Oracle8*i*
   audit options, disabling, 661
   audit options, enabling, 660
   audit trail, managing size of, 661
   audit trail information, managing, 659
   audit trail views, 658
   example code, 662
   guidelines, 657
   instance shutdown, 659
   instance startup, 659
   Object option, 659
   Privilege option, 659
   Statement option, 659
   what to audit, 657–658

Continued